RADCLIFFE - ON - TRENT

1837 TO 1920

A study of a village during an era of change

edited by

Pamela Priestland

Cover picture: Radcliffe-on-Trent main street in 1877 painted by Edward Price (1801-1889) from a reproduction of the 1930s. The present location of the picture is not known.

Edward Price was the son of a Staffordshire clergyman who initially trained with landscape artists in Wales and the Lake District. While travelling to Iceland, he was shipwrecked off the Isle of Man (after being trapped hanging over the side of the ship for eight hours), and then spent several months on the island. Time spent sketching in Norway and Sweden led to the publication of two books on his return. He set up four painting academies in the midlands, including one in Nottingham, witnessed the burning of Nottingham castle in 1831, and was in charge of a voluntary constabulary at Newcastle during riots in the Potteries. For a while he was employed by the Duke of Sutherland at Trentham Hall. After living near Ashbourne, and in Sheffield 'where circumstances did not prove favourable', he arrived in Radcliffe about 1868 and lived in Rose Cottage, probably in Water Lane. It was partly thanks to his efforts in collecting the necessary funds that the peal of bells was completed after the rebuilding of St Mary's church. Noted for his vigour well into his eighties, he would think nothing of walking from Bottesford to Belvoir to sketch, and then back to Radcliffe.

© Pamela Priestland and contributors 1989

ISBN 1 872356 00 1

Published by ASHBRACKEN Radcliffe-on-Trent Nottingham

Processing of half-tone pictures by
Reprographic Services of Trent Polytechnic Nottingham

Printed by Derry and Sons Limited Nottingham

CONTENTS

ACKNOWLEDGEMENTS

For the last five years the University of Nottingham and the local branch of the W.E.A. have jointly sponsored a second research project on the history of Radcliffe-on-Trent, this time covering the Victorian period and the early twentieth century. The scale of this volume is a reflection of the amount of source material available, and of the diligent efforts of the research team in grappling with it.

The main contributors are:

    Geoff Alder

    Marjorie Bacon

    Denis Berry

    Elwyn Berry

    Marion Caunt

    Beryl Cobbing

    Sue Drury

    Joan Epton

    Ross Gilks

    Jean Greenwood

    Jean Lowe

    Janet Mossman

    Pamela Priestland

    Anne Wilkinson

    David Wood

Valuable background contributions have also come from Jenny Collins, Pat Dent and John Staton.

Without the goodwill, generosity and support of numerous local people, the project could never have been completed. Thanks are due to all those who have shared their knowledge, provided or processed photographs, and lent documents. The group is also grateful to the staff of the Nottinghamshire Archives Office, and to the staff of the Department of Manuscripts and Special Collections of the University of Nottingham for their unfailing help with manuscripts and newspapers. The Local Studies Library of the Nottinghamshire County Library has generously assisted with photographic material, and the staff have patiently coped with innumerable requests for information. Radcliffe-on-Trent Parish Council and the local library have also put documents and photographs at the disposal of the group. Finally, thanks are due to the local W.E.A. committee and organisers, and to the staff of the Adult Education Department of the University who have given their long-term support to the project.

Pamela Priestland

August 1989

View up the Shelford Road in the early 1900s

FIRST IMPRESSIONS

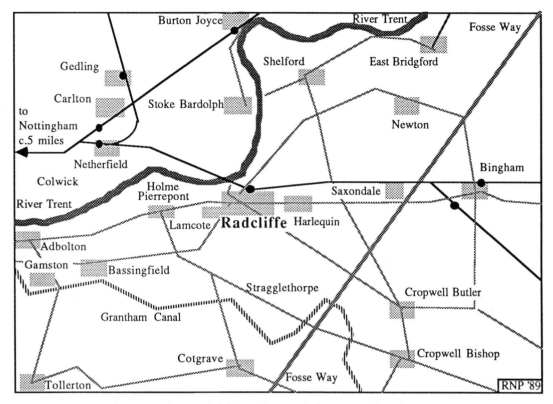

Sketch map to show Radcliffe-on-Trent and the surrounding district in
mid-Victorian times

A previous study of Radcliffe-on-Trent, Nottinghamshire, between 1710 and 1837 has already shown how an apparently tranquil rural community could be affected by change and local controversy. The fuller records of the period from 1837 to 1920 reinforce the impression that Radcliffe was caught up in changing times as a result of both national and local circumstances. Still a fundamentally agricultural community at the start of Queen Victoria's reign, only the older inhabitants would have remembered the lifestyle before 1790 when the great open fields had been worked in strips as they had for generations. The patchwork of hedged fields created by the enclosure process would already have become a familiar landscape. While the individual changes of the nineteenth century may have been less revolutionary, their collective impact nevertheless transformed the village.

Changes in communications

Radcliffe had benefited from good road and river links with Nottingham some five miles away. Between 1758 and 1876 the main road route through the village was under the control of the Nottingham to Grantham turnpike trust, responsibility then passing to the Bingham District Highways Board. In the 1830s coaches to Nottingham, Newark or Lincoln called at the Manvers Arms daily, while carriers delivered goods to and from Nottingham and Newark twice a week, leaving at 5 or 7 o'clock in the morning. As elsewhere, changes in transport were to have a considerable impact. After the opening of the railway in 1850 coach travel declined, but despite some fluctuations in business during the nineteenth century, daily carrier services to Nottingham and twice-weekly services to Newark were still available in the 1920s.

The nostalgic assumption that the slower days of horse traffic meant greater safety on the roads is not borne out by newspaper reports. For example, between April and August of 1844 alone six incidents in the village or involving local people were considered sufficiently significant to be recorded in the *Nottingham Journal.*

While only one involved a fatality - to William Wood, a Radcliffe labourer with three others in a cart which got out of control near Owthorpe - the impression is gained of discomfort and the unpredictability of horses. Single riders could be thrown, as was Mr Marriott who suffered lacerations to the face, as well as back and head injuries, and Mr Nicholl, the local excise officer, who had his shoulder dislocated. (Three years later the latter was again severely injured in the village when thrown head first out of his gig.) More spectacular were the incidents involving public vehicles. When the iron pins of the fore axletree of the *Perseverance*, a horse-drawn van carrying thirty passengers from Stathern, broke about a quarter of a mile from Radcliffe in May, eggs and butter were scattered in all directions and only three or four passengers escaped injury. A month later, a gallant passenger on the *Prince Albert*, the Nottingham to Lincoln coach, was knocked down and run over when he tried to stop the horses speeding up the Shelford Road after the reins had broken. When earlier in the same year a boy had bowled a hoop at a horse, causing it to kick-in the front of a cart and endanger three female passengers, the *Journal* produced a censorious comment on road safety:

> *The bowling of hoops on the public highway has long been a subject of complaint, and we have more than once recorded accidents that could have been caused by this practice. We are happy, however, to state that the authorities of Radcliffe have put a stop to it in the streets of that village.*

Drunken, negligent or 'furious' drivers also added to the problems of road travel in pre-mechanised times, as indicated by frequent cases before the local magistrates. In June 1871 Thomas Carlisle provided a new hazard. He was not only drunk but asleep in charge of a horse and cart which was carrying gunpowder through the village. (He was taking it to Orston plaster pits for blasting, and was fined £1 with 12s costs.)

New technology on the road may have improved communications, but produced different problems. In 1877 Henry Hind, a Nottingham iron founder, was fined for not having a person with a red flag in front of his locomotive traction engine on the turnpike. From the 1880s bicycles became common, but their speeding was soon the cause of complaint in the village. The enforcement of a little known law - that all cyclists should sound bells, blow whistles or make some other noise when overtaking persons or vehicles - produced a deliberate over-reaction in September 1895 when cyclists created 'pandemonium' in the village with their bells, whistles and tin cans, 'almost stopping the services at church and chapel by the unnecessary din they made'. By June 1897 it was reported that the sight of a bicycle around Radcliffe and Bingham was like a red rag to a bull, and residents were retaliating with thorns and nails on the road. Two years later the dangers of the bicycle were emphasised when Dr Percy Truman, a well-known Radcliffe barrister and registrar of Bingham County Court, died from his injuries after colliding with another cyclist on the corner of Cropwell Road.

Motor transport appeared after the turn of the century, although to begin with local car users were few. Mr Wright of Englewood House (now demolished and the site occupied by the Midland Bank) is said to have been the first owner in the village and to have later begun a taxi service. William Reynolds was another early car owner, while Thomas Mercer of Lorne Grove owned a red 2 h.p. de Dion Bouton cycle in 1903. A sign of the future came as early as 1905 when the Parish Council approved the erection of a 'motor car shed' for Mr E.M. Green on Bingham Road. The parish, however, was soon concerned about the speed of vehicles through the village, and in 1909 they failed to get a limit of 8 m.p.h. enforced by the County Council. Accidents were occasionally reported. In January 1910, for example, John Nowell and his son were both injured when a motor car owned by a Nottingham gentleman collided with their pony and cart.

While increased and faster traffic was appearing on the roads, the reverse was true of the river. At the beginning of the period, coal, Crich lime and other goods were brought via the Trent to Radcliffe wharf, but this traffic declined after the opening of the railway. A ferry service was maintained, however, by Edward Parr, the long-standing wharfinger, and then by the Upton family after his death in 1876. A single crossing cost 1d. Although the obligation to maintain the ferry was still

Scene at the ferry early this century

laid down as recently as the 1940s, the service has long since lapsed. By then, with the construction of the weir in the 1890s the character of the river had changed. Throughout the period studied, the Trent could be an asset for trade, recreation and for fishing, often illegally, but it was also notoriously treacherous and village records show that drownings were frequent. Many victims came from elsewhere and were washed down to Radcliffe, but local people, especially children, were also drowned. The *Nottingham Journal* reported the agonised grief of William Upton and his wife in July 1863 when their son got out of his depth with fatal results. Francis Wright aged 7 drowned while bathing with his friends in July 1870, as did 5-year-old Robert Clarke, a bricklayer's son who went into Island Dyke after his cap in June 1879. More cheerfully, John Hainsworth Barry of Radcliffe was awarded the Royal Humane Society's Certificate after saving the life of Oswald Bolton in the Trent in June 1910.

While in the long-run changes in road transport were to have a profound effect on the village, it was the coming of the railway in 1850 that was to have an immediate impact. River trade declined, the carriage of goods to and from Nottingham was affected, and the outside world was opened up to villagers for work and recreation. Even more significantly as it turned out, the railway made Radcliffe accessible to outsiders. Weekend and bank holiday visitors arrived in such numbers that by 1894 the village was being referred to as 'New Scarborough' in the local press. A boom in the licensed trade was one result. Other consequences were problems with law and order and public health.

More permanently, the railway brought Radcliffe within speedy reach of Nottingham for lace market businessmen who built new villas, so beginning the evolution of Radcliffe from working to dormitory village. Speculation in land and house building flourished, and village brickmaking increased. William Hill's brickworks near Saxondale were joined in the 1880s by the Radcliffe Brick Company at the Harlequin, under the management of John George Willey, a newcomer who owned a considerable amount of property in the Bingham Road area. The company was still in operation as late as 1928, although under different management. (One of their stamped bricks has been inserted in a garage at 55 Bingham Road.)

11

Local employment

The railway only gradually provided employment for local people, but the needs of the Nottingham businessmen who used it increased the number of servants in the village. Other occupations included the traditional crafts of the innkeeper, baker, butcher, shoemaker, tailor, blacksmith or wheelwright. In addition there were general shopkeeping outlets. For example, there were nine unspecified shopkeepers in 1832. By the time of Wright's *Directory* in 1915 twelve shopkeepers were listed, and the range of specialised services had widened to include a fishmonger (John Gore), a druggist (Edward Kyte, whose shop was said to be where all the flies went in the winter time), three stationers and newsagents (Frank Barratt, Arthur Rowe and Miss Turner), and a tobacconist (John Bates). From the 1880s, too, a combination of the number of visitors and a campaign for abstinence encouraged the opening of tea and

One of Radcliffe's small shops near the corner of Shelford Road early this century. The two shoemakers are Donald Barratt and Jack Cragg

coffee rooms including those run by Mary Arnold, Luke Lee on Station Street (Shelford Road), Richard Barratt in 1900, and Thomas Roulston on Vicarage Lane by 1908. (Fuller analysis of occupations appears in the chapter entitled A Changing Village.)

The community, however, was predominantly dependent on agriculture. By mid-Victorian times most land was still owned and rented out by a small elite headed by Lord Manvers, the lord of the manor. Two other main landowning families were the Taylors of Radcliffe Hall and the Burnsides of Lamcote House. Some advantage had been taken of the new stock breeding ideas which had coincided with enclosure. The Sanday family, formerly at Holme House, but at Cliff House from about 1860, had a famous flock of Leicester sheep. The Taylors bred horses for stud purposes, while Miss Burnside's huge 'porker' was one of the features of the Christmas meat show in Nottingham in 1878. (Only 11 months old, it weighed 40 stones.) The exchange of ideas was being encouraged too. Robert Butler of Radcliffe was one of a number of Nottinghamshire farmers who met together in

UNRESERVED SALE of a WINDMILL for REMOVAL
TO be SOLD by AUCTION, by JAMES CARTER and SON, on Monday, the 3rd day of May, 1869, at Three o'clock in the Afternoon precisely, upon the Premises, and in one lot,
All that WINDMILL situate at Lamcote Leys, at Ratcliffe, near Nottingham, as now in the occupation of Mr. Robert Green, together with the Brick Mound-House, French Grey Stones, Dressing Machines, Shafting, Gearing, and Millwright's Work, massive Oak Timbers, One Pair of Good Patent Sails, and other Corn Mill requisites. Three months will be allowed for removal.
The Mill stands within a short distance of a Great Northern Railway Station.
For particulars apply to the Auctioneers, Clumber Street, Nottingham.   4923

Newspaper advertisement for the sale of the windmill at Lamcote Leys in 1869

December 1869 to form a local Chamber of Agriculture. The use of improved agricultural technology was also on the increase. One of Radcliffe's blacksmiths was Thomas Allcock, a well-known implement maker, born at Clipston about 1814. His 3-knife chaff cutter was on display at the county Agricultural Show in October 1848. Three years later several of his implements were on display at the Great Exhibition at the Crystal Palace: two iron ploughs on the most improved principle', and a straw cutter 'with every movement that leads to power and speed'.

12

THOMAS ALLCOCK,
AGRICULTURAL IMPLEMENT
MAKER.

Patentee and Manufacturer of the
PATENT SAFETY CHAFF CUTTER,
Fixed and Portable, &c.

IMPROVED DRAGS AND HARROWS.

PATENT SOLID AXLE HORSE RAKES,
Improved Horse Power.

PORTABLE CHAFF CUTTER

With Apparatus for Riddling and Blowing the Dust out.   Price List on application.

The Works: RATCLIFFE-ON-TRENT.

Thomas Allcock's advertisement for a portable chaff cutter
from Wright's *Directory* of 1881

While steam threshing machines were soon common sights, an older form of technology was disappearing. At the start of the period Radcliffe had two windmills, one at Lamcote Leys and the other on Cropwell Road. In November 1844, a Mr Wilson offered for sale a wind post mill in thorough repair, driving two pairs of excellent stones. Mr Kenny owned the one on Cropwell Road in August 1846 when a storm broke two of its sails. The date of its removal is uncertain, but a close of land on Cropwell Road, including the site of the old windmill, was offered for sale in January 1883. Robert Green was the owner of the Lamcote Leys mill by 1850. It was sold and removed in 1869.

Despite improvements, for much of the period studied farming was on the defensive, hit by cattle plague and a lengthy depression. Farmers were also particularly vulnerable to fire hazards. In 1851 Mr J.S. Burgess lost three stacks and Thomas Butler nine before the fire brigade could arrive from Nottingham - a slow process when the request travelled at the speed of a horse. Fortunately both men were insured with the County Fire Office, although Thomas Butler's loss was put at £1000 while his policy was only for £700. (Fire insurance plates can still be seen on the side of 25-27 Main Road.) By 1872, when lightning caused a fire in Robert Brewster's yard, the fire engine could be summoned more speedily by telegraph.

Such large-scale farmers, tenant or otherwise, were in the minority and for most villagers work on the land was through some form of labouring. From the 1870s, however, there was increased emphasis on horticulture and market gardening. Prominent among the winners in the class for professionals at the

Gardening Society's shows from 1875 were Samuel and Thomas Barratt who ran nurseries on the Bingham and Cropwell roads. Famous for their flowers, they were also noted for cucumbers, grapes and tomatoes. Thomas Richmond, Thomas Scrimshaw, Elizabeth Parr, Frank Walker and Thomas Butler were other market gardeners of the 1880s, and the ordnance survey map of 1884 testifies to the large number of greenhouses in the village. Radcliffe's confidence in this sphere is perhaps epitomised by the potato show of 1897, advertised as 'open to all England'. Whether the first prize of £2 attracted entrants from far afield has not been discovered. Another rural enterprise which flourished from 1884 was beekeeping. The county association

Newspaper advertisement for George Turner's bee hives and honey April 1887

of beekeepers had Lord Newark (the son of Earl Manvers) as its president for a time, and the village had several prominent members. The *Nottingham Daily Express* in August 1887 reported that it was not uncommon for a working man in Radcliffe to possess half a dozen hives. Thomas Rose, one of the village's keenest beekeepers, had in his house an observatory hive of the sort designed by George Turner, the local postmaster and wheelwright, whose new hives were widely advertised.

Improving amenities

George Turner's arrival in the village, probably in the late 1850s, heralded the start of improved services. His post office was in operation by the 1860s near the corner of Water Lane and the main street. (He perhaps replaced Joseph Mosley, identified in the baptism register as a postmaster in 1858.) White's *Directory* for 1864 records that letters arrived at 6 a.m. and were despatched at 7.10 p.m. to Nottingham. Some twenty years later money order, savings bank and telegraph facilities were also offered. By then letters arrived twice a day and the last of three despatches was at 8.45 p.m. (Radcliffe objectors to Sunday postal services unsuccessfully petitioned Parliament for their abolition in 1887.) A peculiarity of the shop at the turn of the century was that customers had to wait for a safety catch over the latch to be released from the sitting room. George Turner lived until the age of 86 in 1917, but the post office had moved by 1900 to Frank Barratt's provisions shop, its present site, on the main road near the corner of Shelford Road. At that date there were three postal deliveries a day, the last at 6.55 p.m., and four collections.

Gas was the next service to reach the village, although not without some contention. In 1864 a Nottingham gas bill was introduced into Parliament to bring gas to twenty-six new places, including Radcliffe. Lord Manvers, through his agent George Beaumont, objected to the extension of the service as unnecessary, liable to cause a nuisance, and injurious to vegetable life. Existing works north of the Trent were thought to be affecting the value of his property. James Gorse, a Nottingham businessman renting the Manor House from the earl, spoke at the House of Commons enquiry in support of gas coming to the village. The bill was carried and gas was introduced about 1867, although gas street lamps were only approved by the vestry (the parish's governing body) from 1876. They were replaced by electric lights in 1927. Other improvements included the first causeway or pavement, provided by subscription in 1875. Reading rooms came and went, and a library was recorded in 1877. Piped water arrived from 1898, and after a long struggle improved sanitation came with a sewage farm in 1902. The village's first telephone was installed at Edward Wright & Sons, a printing firm in Bailey Lane. The first exchange belonging to the National Telephone Company was at 20 Bingham Road in 1907, and was taken over by the Post Office in 1913. The number of subscribers grew slowly. In 1908 there were twenty-one, and eighty-four by 1925.

Rich and poor

Judging by sale advertisements from the 1880s, the large new villas built for Nottingham businessmen contained fine furniture, china and paintings, and the lot of the servants who maintained them was beginning to be eased by domestic appliances. Lawn mowers became common, and in November 1893 the sale of lace merchant Louis Collier's furniture on Shelford Road included 'Taylor's new washer and wringer'. For the seemingly well-to-do, however, there could be the public humiliation of the bankruptcy court and the newspaper column when things went wrong. Louis Collier himself had had to struggle out of bankruptcy in the 1870s, and at least seven residents went bankrupt in the 1890s alone. For one well-established contractor living in Walnut Grove it was too much. He was found with his throat cut on his parents' grave in Wales. For the really poor there was the more anonymous threat of the workhouse in Bingham.The poor also suffered most in the cholera and scarlet fever epidemics of the 1840s and 1880s, and they or their children seemed more vulnerable to accidents. Excluding road, rail and river incidents, there were inquests on at least eight children between 1837 and 1902. Four died from burns, three from 'medicine' - laudanum, anodyne cordial, and squil mixture - and one was smothered as it lay in bed with its mother. While occasionally poisoned, their elders were more likely to suffer some form of agricultural injury. In the same period three elderly men fell from hay or straw stacks, breaking limbs or ribs. Two were injured falling from scaffolding or ladders. One was killed by a falling ladder and another by a fall of clay. A horse-powered hay cutter chopped the hand of the feeder up to the wrist in 1888. Others were kicked by horses or run over by waggons. One died in hospital sixteen weeks after being tossed by a cow. The picture, largely dependent on newspaper reporting, is inevitably incomplete.

Mortality and morality

Despite eventual improvements in the sanitary conditions of the village, little overall change in the mortality rate can be deduced from the parish registers and cemetery records. Until the 1880s there was a particularly high death rate among children under the age of 10, and after 1900 the figures are distorted by the inclusion of burials from Saxondale Hospital.

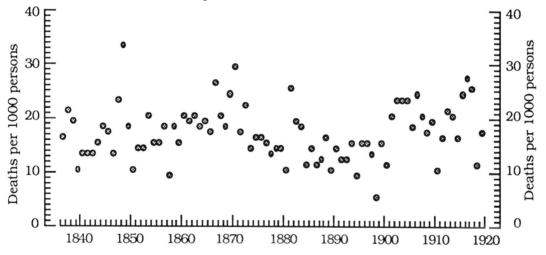

The death rate per thousand of population between 1837 and 1920 based on the parish and cemetery registers

The health of the community was in the hands of a series of village doctors, identifiable from early in the period, and there was some supervisory care from Bingham. By 1874 the village had its own dentist, a Mr Young, who may also have been the veterinary surgeon of the same name, and a nursing association was formed in 1900.

The spiritual welfare of the community was supervised by St Mary's church, enlarged and mainly rebuilt in 1879, the Independent and Primitive Methodists from time to time, and by the Wesleyan Methodists. (Catholics had no outlet in the village, although from 1897 the mission of the Sacred Heart was constituted at West

Bridgford to include Radcliffe, Bingham, Ruddington and Wilford. The pavilion of the Castle Cricket Club, West Bridgford, served as a temporary church.) Morality was no longer controlled by church courts, as it had been as recently as the eighteenth century, but there is little evidence to suggest that this had encouraged any major break with conventional behaviour. A look at the baptism and vaccination registers sheds some light on the situation.

Considerable fluctuations in the birthrate are found between 1837 and 1920, the average being 41 per year. Peak years were 1846 (47), 1860 (51), 1881 (61), and 1904 (67). The lowest year was 1840 (21), followed by 1917 (22), the result of absentee fathers during the First World War. Illegitimate births in these registers average less than two children per year. Between 1854 and 1921, however, a further thirty-eight illegitimate Radcliffe children were born in the workhouse at Bingham. Unlike the parish registers or the workhouse records, the vaccination registers, which were started about 1872, frequently record the occupations of the mothers of illegitimate children. Out of the eighty-four cases in which occupations were given, fifty-six were domestic servants, two were housekeepers and one a domestic help. The next most vulnerable employees were in the lace industry, another ten illegitimate children being born to lace hands, runners, beaders or spotters.

In a rare breach of promise case in 1889 maintenance was awarded to the female plaintiff (a housekeeper) and her expected child. Deserted husbands and wives can occasionally be identified from court cases or poor law records, but divorce was a rarity and confined to the well-to-do. The only Radcliffe divorce case so far found involved Robert Butler, an auctioneer and former cricketer. Although a *decree nisi* was at first granted, this was withdrawn on the grounds of collusion between husband and wife, and despite repeated appeals which dragged on between 1888 and 1893 the unhappy couple were never granted their freedom. Villagers expressed views on what they regarded as impropriety in their own way. A lady in this case was subjected to 'rough music' (i.e. the cacophonous banging of tins, pans etc.), and the words of a song 'appropriate to the occasion' were chalked up on a number of walls. Domestic disputes occasionally ended up in the local courts at Bingham, but serious violence was rare. John Shepherd, a Radcliffe fishmonger, had clearly been influenced by the drama of the times when he threatened to 'Jack the Ripper' his wife of three months. He was bound over to keep the peace for six months. Not until 1901 was there a case of attempted murder. In general, Radcliffe's morality was conventional and her crime petty. The building of a police station in 1875 was not a reflection of the behaviour of the residents.

The outside world

While most lived uneventful lives, scarcely troubling the record writers, there were those who ventured far or who were acknowledged by the world outside their village. The privilege of education helped the son of William Sanday of Cliff House to become a professor of divinity at Oxford from 1895 to 1919. The army was another outlet. Some died in the service, such as 34-year-old Staff Sergeant Robert Butler Brice in Bombay in 1856. Some survived to relate their experiences in the village. Thomas Hinds had served in the 3rd Dragoons during the Peninsular War, dying in 1867 at the age of 75. Another lucky survivor was William Roberts who had lived through the charge of the Light Brigade at Balaclava in 1854. He died in the village in 1885 aged 55. Even more rare was Samuel Morley's Victoria Cross, earned during the Indian Mutiny of 1858. Later residents distinguished themselves in the Boer and First World Wars.

Other individuals known outside the village included Edward Price, the artist, who settled in Radcliffe in the 1870s after an adventurous career. (See page 2.) Thomas Marriott was a record-breaking tricyclist in the 1880s, while Mr Stubbs, a local tenor, made a successful appearance at the Covent Garden promenade concerts in 1889. Charles Ferneley, an artist's son, was a noted photographer who lived on Bingham Road at the turn of the century. By far the most famous of Radcliffe's residents in the period studied, however, were the two Nottinghamshire and England cricketers, George Parr and Richard Daft.

Celebrations

Whatever the divisions of education, wealth or outlook, records suggest that villagers came together to enjoy annual treats or national occasions. There were regular tea parties in the schoolroom for church workers. Plum cake, tea, dance and songs were provided for Edward Brewster's osier peelers in the 1840s. (Basket-making was a local craft.) Celebrations punctuated the building of the railway, and the annual feast in September lasted a week. By 1881 swings, roundabouts, coconut shies, shooting saloons, and a photographer offering 'likenesses' were amongst the attractions in the feast field between the Shelford and Bingham roads now occupied by New Road. Above all, there were the unpredictable royal occasions. Queen Victoria's coronation was celebrated in June 1838 with bands, buns for the children, and an excellent dinner for all males over 13. Four sheep had been donated, and there were three pints of ale each, followed by pipes and tobacco. The females were regaled to their hearts' content with tea, and dancing followed until 11 o'clock at night. The organisers were John Taylor of Radcliffe Hall and Samuel Parr of the Manor House, and the whole affair was paid for by public subscription. A second celebration was restricted to the ladies and gentlemen of the village, and was held on Samuel Parr's lawn when music, tea and punch were provided. When the Queen and Prince Albert passed through the village on their way to Belvoir Castle in December 1843, they drove under five triumphal arches to the sounds of the church bells and the Arnold band, while waggons of flag-waving school children presented 'a lively and interesting *coup d'oeil* with which Her Majesty and Prince Albert appeared much pleased'. Buns, tea for two hundred at the Manvers Arms, and dancing completed the day. The Jubilee of 1887 was celebrated with sports on the cricket ground after a filling tea. A race on penny-farthing bicycles, which ended in a horrifying collision, made the day more than usually memorable. For the Diamond Jubilee of 1897 the streets were decorated with bunting, and the children of Radcliffe and Holme Pierrepont processed, headed by Radcliffe's band. This time there were tableaux on carts, one representing Rule Britannia, and another Queen Victoria herself surrounded by courtiers. Tea and sports on the new recreation ground followed. While the postponement of Edward VII's coronation in 1902 meant that celebrations were restricted, the village was again in good form for that of George V in 1911 with decorated carts, processions and maypole dancing.

* * * * * * * *

In these general impressions of a changing village, and in the narrative of events and analysis of records that follow, familiar names recur such as Caunt, Carnell, Hallam, Marriott, Nowell, Parr, Vickerstaff and many others. It should be borne in mind that such names were frequently found in the locality, and movement between villages was common. In the 1851 census, for example, nineteen separate Parr families appear, with several individuals having identical forenames. It consequently becomes impossible at times to be certain which individual is meant in contemporary records, and any links with families of the 1980s cannot be assumed without conclusive research.

Main sources

Primary
Nottinghamshire Archives Office: Parish registers; DC/BI 4/4/1-18; PUD 4/1/1; PUD 4/5/1-6; PUD 4/6/4-21.
Nottinghamshire County Library (Local Studies Library): *Memories of a villager* DD 121/1/49; the late Fred Cutler's photographs.
Radcliffe-on-Trent: Parish Council minute books; cemetery records.

Secondary
Chamberlain, Colet. *Memories of the Past.* 1960.
Directories of Nottingham and Nottinghamshire 1832-1928.
Radcliffe-on-Trent local history research group: extracts from Nottingham newspapers 1837-1920.
Radcliffe-on-Trent Parochial Magazine 1877.
Trans. Thoroton Soc. *Nottinghamshire Register of Motor Cars and Cycles.* 1903.

A simplified genealogy of the Pierrepont family

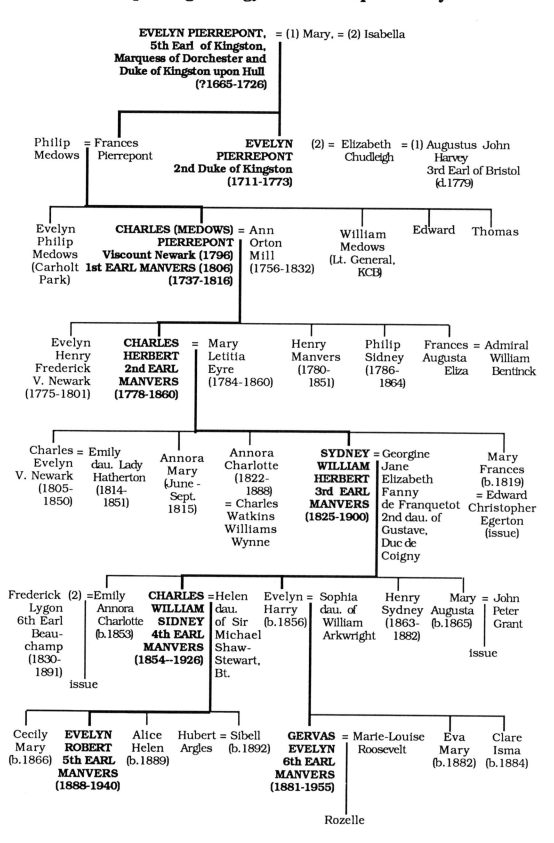

EVELYN PIERREPONT, = (1) Mary, = (2) Isabella
5th Earl of Kingston,
Marquess of Dorchester and
Duke of Kingston upon Hull
(?1665-1726)

Philip = Frances   **EVELYN**   (2) = Elizabeth = (1) Augustus John
Medows Pierrepont   **PIERREPONT**   Chudleigh   Harvey
                     2nd Duke of Kingston   3rd Earl of Bristol
                        (1711-1773)   (d.1779)

Evelyn   **CHARLES (MEDOWS)** = Ann   William   Edward   Thomas
Philip   **PIERREPONT**   Orton   Medows
Medows   **Viscount Newark (1796)** Mill   (Lt. General,
(Carholt **1st EARL MANVERS (1806)** (1756-1832) KCB)
Park)   **(1737-1816)**

Evelyn   **CHARLES** = Mary   Henry   Philip   Frances = Admiral
Henry   **HERBERT**   Letitia   Manvers   Sidney   Augusta   William
Frederick **2nd EARL** Eyre   (1780-   (1786-   Eliza   Bentinck
V. Newark **MANVERS**   (1784-1860) 1851)   1864)
(1775-1801) **(1778-1860)**

Charles = Emily   Annora   Annora   **SYDNEY** = Georgine   Mary
Evelyn   dau. Lady   Mary   Charlotte   **WILLIAM** Jane   Frances
V. Newark Hatherton   (June -   (1822-   **HERBERT** Elizabeth   (b.1819)
(1805-   (1814-   Sept.   1888)   **3rd EARL** Fanny   = Edward
1850)   1851)   1815)   = Charles   **MANVERS** de Franquetot   Christopher
                                   Watkins   **(1825-1900)** 2nd dau. of   Egerton
                                   Williams   Gustave,   (issue)
                                   Wynne   Duc de
                                                                Coigny

Frederick (2) =Emily   **CHARLES** =Helen   Evelyn = Sophia   Henry   Mary = John
Lygon   Annora   **WILLIAM** dau.   Harry   dau. of   Sydney   Augusta Peter
6th Earl   Charlotte   **SIDNEY** of Sir   (b.1856) William   (1863-   (b.1865) Grant
Beau-   (b.1853)   **4th EARL** Michael   Arkwright 1882)
champ   **MANVERS** Shaw-   issue
(1830-   **(1854--1926)** Stewart,
1891)   Bt.
          issue

Cecily   **EVELYN**   Alice   Hubert = Sibell   **GERVAS** = Marie-Louise   Eva   Clare
Mary   **ROBERT**   Helen   Argles   (b.1892)   **EVELYN**   Roosevelt   Mary   Isma
(b.1866) **5th EARL** (b.1889)   **6th EARL**   (b.1882) (b.1884)
          MANVERS   **MANVERS**
          (1888-1940)   **(1881-1955)**

                                                        Rozelle

THE MANVERS ESTATE

In 1837 the estates owned by the second Earl Manvers were extensive. Besides the main property around Thoresby Hall, there were holdings in other parts of Nottinghamshire (including the Holme Pierrepont estate of which Radcliffe -on-Trent was a part), in Derbyshire, Lincolnshire and Yorkshire. There was also some land near Bradford-on-Avon in Wiltshire, property in Bath and a house in Portman Square (later in Tilney Street off Park Lane) where the family stayed when in London. These holdings fluctuated, but a total of some 38,000 acres would provide an 1880s guideline, of which the Holme Pierrepont estate amounted to 9,226 acres at its peak in the 1860s. Land held in Radcliffe and Lamcote made up one-seventh of this last figure.

The family

The second earl's father had been Charles Medows, the Duke of Kingston's nephew, who inherited the estates when the duke died in 1773, but did not take control until the death of the 'bigamous Duchess' in 1788. He then changed his name to Pierrepont (his mother's maiden name) 'by Licence under his Majesty's sign manual', becoming Viscount Newark in 1796 and Earl Manvers in 1806. The eldest son of each Earl Manvers took the courtesy title of Viscount Newark. Compared to their eighteenth century ancestors, the nineteenth century Pierreponts were less concerned with life at court and more with their Nottinghamshire estates. The third and fourth earls in particular had close links with Holme Pierrepont, the latter living at the hall when Viscount Newark and becoming the first chairman of Radcliffe's Parish Council. He lived until 1926, bringing the long-standing control of the village by his family to an end in 1920 when much of the estate was sold.

The agents

The day-to-day running of the various estates was in the hands of agents who reported to a main agent at Thoresby. Henry Horncastle appears to have been the Thoresby agent in 1837, but in 1851 it was William Pickin and by 1883 R.W. Wordsworth. In April 1914 Wordsworth became ill and the job passed to Hubert D. Argles. At the beginning of 1916 the latter joined the army, and Mr Spink took over. When Argles returned from the war he married the fourth earl's youngest daughter, Sibell.

The sub-agent for the Holme Pierrepont estate in 1837 was Robert Burgess who lived at Cotgrave Place, just outside the Radcliffe parish boundary. His death in 1846 was the occasion of a voluminous correspondence between the second earl and Mr Innes Pocock in London in which the honesty of Burgess came to be more and more doubted. (This is discussed below.) His successor was George Beaumont from East Bridgford who died in 1882. His son, another George, followed until in 1885 W.H.P. Norris took over. His correspondence was always sent from the Holme Pierrepont estate office.

Trustees of the estates

As various marriage settlements were made during the nineteenth century, trusts were set up to administer them and trustees appointed. In particular, during the later years of the century, most of the land belonging to the estates was administered by a Trust set up under the Settled Land Acts 1882 to 1890. The first known trustees of the Settled Estates were Thomas Bradshaw (a solicitor of Hull, later referred to as Judge Bradshaw) and the Reverend Henry Seymour (the rector of Holme Pierrepont) in 1885. Bradshaw was soon replaced by H.E. Egerton, a barrister and nephew of the third earl. The Rev Seymour was replaced by Mr Harcourt Vernon in 1907, and he was in turn replaced by Lord Algernon Percy in 1914.

Consequently, although the third and fourth earls behaved as if they owned the whole of their estates outright, they were in fact 'tenants for life'. In addition, much of their holdings had earlier been mortgaged to find dowries for daughters. Thus, to find £400 pin-money and £6,500 a year jointure for Fanny de Coigny when she married Lord Newark in 1852, part of the estates were mortgaged to raise £59,000, of which £10,000 was from Holme Pierrepont. Similarly, in 1880 the trustees of their marriage settlement were directed to raise and pay £2,000 out of the trust funds for the advancement of their second son, the Hon. Evelyn H. Pierrepont (father of the sixth earl). After the death of the third earl in 1900, the dowager countess signed a 'Release of her life interest' in the trust fund. In general, funds in the Settled Estates were subject to severe limitations which the third earl tried to overcome as he sold land at a greater price for building. It seems that it could only be invested in more land or in government funds. He took legal advice and found that he could also invest in railway debenture stock and in ground rents.

I. The estate 1832-1860

The second earl

As a younger son, Charles Herbert Pierrepont had not been expected to inherit the estates, and like his father had embarked on a naval career. In 1801, however, the

2nd EARL MANVERS died 1860

The second Earl Manvers (1778-1860)
from a watercolour.
(By courtesy of the Earl Manvers Will Trust)

year of his elder brother's death, he began following a more conventional training for landowners-in-waiting as an M.P., sitting for Nottinghamshire until 1816, when he inherited the earldom at the age of 38. He had been married to Mary Eyre of Grove in Nottinghamshire for twelve years by then and had three children. Three more were to follow. By the time of Queen Victoria's reign, he was a stocky, white-haired figure with a strong sense of public duty. In particular, medical and educational institutions benefited from his patronage, which included a governorship of the Lunatic Asylum at Sneinton, presidency of the Nottingham Dispensary, membership of Nottingham's General Hospital Board, support for the Mechanics' Institution at Mansfield, and presidency of Nottingham's Ragged School, to which he donated 50 guineas in 1852. He was perhaps influenced in these matters by his mother, who lived on until 1832 and who is credited with acts of benevolence including support of a school at Radcliffe. The earl's forceful personality is revealed in correspondence in the Manvers papers. His bold idiosyncratic handwriting on small paper with vigorous underlinings must often have startled recipients into action.

Financial matters to 1846

Since Radcliffe was part of the Holme Pierrepont estate it is not always easy to separate its fortunes from the rest of the estate. A convenient place to start in trying to make sense of this complex history is with an undated manuscript setting out charges in 1811 and in 1832. There is some ambiguity but they amount in 1832, at the time of the second earl, to at least £120,000, ranging from £10,000 for 'Part of the purchase money for the Cotgrave Place Estate' to £60,000 for 'portions for younger children of present Earl Manvers'. There was also a 'Jointure to Dowager Countess Manvers' (she died in the August of 1832) for £6,500, and an 'Allowance to present Lord Newark' for £2,000, presumably annually. It has not been possible to assess accurately the total value of the estates: the probate of the will of the second Earl Manvers gave his assets as less than £80,000 in 1860. However, the Thoresby accounts indicate a gross income from the property of more than £41,000 (net: £34,000 at least) in 1830, and a gross income in 1837 of more than £44,000 (net: £30,000 at least). This would indicate a value of at least £100,000 for the estates in the 1830s, which would probably have increased by the time of the second earl's death. The considerable difference between the gross and net income is largely accounted for by tithes, taxation (on land, property and payment of poor rates), as well as outgoings on repairs and on the wages of servants. At Thoresby there were twenty-nine indoor servants, two coachmen, a postilion, three grooms, a sailor (presumably to look after boats on the lake), a clerk of works and a large farm staff. There were also permanent staff elsewhere, notably at Holme Pierrepont. A letter of 1837 suggests that the Viscount Newark who died in 1850 without inheriting the earldom was then living at Holme Pierrepont, and, as already indicated, his nephew was based there until his inheritance of the title in 1900.

In 1837 something like a third of the total acreage of Radcliffe belonged to the Holme Pierrepont estate. The earliest known subsequent acquisition was of the dwelling house and school house with garden (used as a playground) and outbuildings in 1844 from Samuel Parr, farmer, and the Reverend J. Smith. The document is a draft, and no price is mentioned. Around the same time Jonas Bettison sold Cliff Hill Close and Holywell Close - just under thirty-five acres - for £4,500 to Earl Manvers. (There were doubtless other purchases for which the evidence has not been found, since by the early 1860s the estate owned about half the village.) The known sale of estate land in Radcliffe around 1845 was that required for the new Ambergate, Nottingham and Boston and Eastern Junction Railway. (An account of the development of the railway is given in a separate chapter.) Some evidence of routine outgoings comes from property and income tax lists for the 1840s. Payments for Radcliffe were in the region of £60 per year. Nearly double was paid on Cotgrave and Holme Pierrepont.

The death of Robert Burgess

Events revealed by the death of the agent for the Holme Pierrepont estate are best related through the surviving correspondence between Earl Manvers and his auditor, John Innes Pocock of Lincoln's Inn Fields, London, and two or three other individuals. Mr Burgess died on November 5th 1846. Lord Manvers, in a letter to Mr Pocock on the 9th mentions

> .... poor Burgess's unforeseen death, which melancholy event took place at Cotgrave Place, on Thursday last after a week's illness, indeed we met at Nottingham on public business last Wednesday se'nnight and were both of us taken ill on the day following.

Pocock then wrote, expressing his sympathy to Mrs Burgess in the warmest terms, indicating

> how much I valued and esteemed my deceased friend for by that title I may surely remember him.

Condolences over, Pocock then had the problem of rent collection to sort out at long-distance, and he needed to know from Mrs Burgess the names of her husband's executors. They were John Hassall of Shelford Manor (agent for the Earl of Chesterfield) and a J.S. Burgess. Rent days were then fixed for the week of November 14th 1846, and three receipts from Smith's bank which follow were presumably for the rent money.

As far as Lord Manvers at Thoresby was concerned the whole matter should have been speedily sorted out. In his typically formidable style he wrote to Pocock on 17th November 'chastising' him for not setting out for Holme Pierrepont at once. Moreover, he expected Burgess's executors simply to

> ....lodge in Smith's Bank at Nottingham the entire sum received on my account and which money I conceive will be only payable to my Order and not liable to any Disbursement (however necessary) connected with the Agency until a successor to that office is appointed.

There was, however, a considerable list of routine unpaid accounts to be dealt with, which a Mr Booker of Nottingham forwarded to Pocock on 23rd November:

I have the honour to transmit herewith an estimate of the liabilities incurred upon the Estate of the Earl Manvers which according to usage would require to be discharged between the present date and March 1847 .... but as I have not had the opportunity yet of examining Mr Burgess's books, I cannot speak satisfactory [sic]thereon.

The list included income tax due, totalling £260.18s.7d, for places as far afield from Holme Pierrepont as Cropwell, Gedling and Lowdham, with an item for Radcliffe of £30.0s.4d for half a year's tax. Sixteen items for tradesmen, ranging from 'Wm. Haynes (Carpenter) suppose £340' to "Carr & Co for Iron castings £2', came to £619.9s.3d. The grand total outstanding was £1,441. 1s.11d.

By early December Lord Manvers had settled on George Beaumont of East Bridgford as his new agent from January 1st, although not without wondering whether some security should be required of him. On December 19th he instructed Pocock to hand over all documents regarding his property in Burgess's archive to Beaumont. There was, however, to be an audit of Burgess's books and Pocock should meet the auditors in Nottingham when that happened. The Earl's one concession to the outstanding payments was seasonable: "The 'Charitable Donations' at Christmas I will undertake myself to liquidate ....'

From this point on, good will was in short supply and the correspondence shows Lord Manvers' progressive disillusionment with the work of the deceased agent. Pocock came up to Nottinghamshire and on December 23rd collected the Holme Pierrepont account and rental books, but left behind the vouchers. Lord Manvers sent the vouchers after him with a letter, the tone of which suggests that Pocock must already have endured a gruelling confrontation:

.... if upon due search being made you are able to explain the lumping charge of £35.1s I shall be glad of it, if not I can only hope that we are about to turn over quite a new leaf with the new agent.

Clearly the long-distance friendship which had developed over the years between Pocock and Burgess had led to some very loose accounting. The letter continues with another criticism concerning a list of subscriptions which Pocock had supplied. The earl was endeavouring with a Mr Peach's assistance to find out when they were actually due '...as in your extract from the Accounts, no mention whatever is made in any one instance of the time when the last payment was made.'

Pocock must have had a miserable Christmas. In his reply on December 24th he had to admit his negligence. Having received the vouchers he had 'searched them for particulars of the items making up the sum of £35.1s charged in the late Mr Burgess's account for 1845, but in vain.' He continued:

I must admit the presumption to be that I have passed the aggregate amount without it upon the faith of his honesty and accuracy. Your Lordship's admonition to me as to turning over the 'New Leaf' will assuredly render me more particular hereafter.

His letter would have crossed with one from Lord Manvers written on the same day instructing Pocock that no payments were to be made until after the audit of Burgess's accounts to guard against the possibility of any being paid twice. After Christmas the earl relented slightly, allowing on December 28th 'just remuneration' to be paid to parties entitled to it for services rendered since Burgess's death. His 'admonition' to Pocock was justified, he said. The laxity was caused because of 'old established intimacy between Agent and Auditor which is an evil that cannot be too much deprecated at all times.' He hoped it would never recur.

Worse revelations were to come. Outraged, Lord Manvers wrote to Pocock on January 11th of his findings when he went to Smith's Bank:

I went to Nottm. on this day se'nnight to meet Mr Beaumont by appointment, & on going with him to Smith's Bank, to arrange the mode of his transacting business with them on my account, as he also banks with that firm; the head Clerk volunteered pointing out to me a great irregularity in the late Agent's mode of doing business with them on my account, to wit that the name of 'Earl Manvers' had never appeared on their Books up to the moment of Mr Burgess's death, a Floating capital of £16,000 per annum, only recognised by them (Smith & Co) as the property of 'Robert Burgess'!! & of course I feel bound to believe that you were not cognizant of the fact, however extraordinary it may appear ....

Pocock's reaction to these revelations has not been found. For the time being he kept his post as London auditor, visiting Nottingham for an audit in April 1847, although with Lord Manvers keeping a careful check on procedures:

I desire you will ascertain at the Nottm. Bank tomorrow that the mode of drawing money adopted by the present Agent [i.e. Beaumont] is in strict accordance with the form of which I sent you a copy some time ago.

By May, Burgess's affairs had been sufficiently investigated for the extent of his negligence to be obvious. On the 2nd the earl wrote:

I am sorry to say that hardly a day passes without affording fresh proof that my late agent at Holme Pierrepont was one of the worst if not the worst of his tribe; for altho' I am still willing to hope that he was not particeps criminis, by taking his share of the Plunder, I have abundant evidence that he allowed me to be robbed wholesale by others, without making the slightest effort to prevent it ....

In an undated letter, presumably to Pocock, he noted further lapses by his agent:

.... the Tenants that came to Nottm. to pay their rents were indulged without stint in Hock & Champagne! All details of a like nature would fill a sheet of Foolscap.

Lord Manvers' response was to penalise those whom he felt had benefited:

... ere many days have elapsed I shall have discharged from my employment every Tradesman and other person in whom Mr Burgess placed unlimited confidence.

That was written on May 2nd 1847. In a letter written in February 1848 it is clear that, in the case of at least some workers employed by the estate, Lord Manvers carried out his threat and was prepared to investigate all their claims rigorously:

Without entering at all into the motives which have induced me since the decease of my late agent to wash my hands in toto of his Satellites Haynes Senior & Junior Carpenters at Radcliffe I wish to know whether you have any recollection, as to the circumstances under which Haynes senior built the house he now occupies at Bassingfield as he says without assistance from his Landlord; whereas I am confident that the materials were all found by me, & I very believe that the labour was also paid for out of my pocket, but the former point I can speak to more positively.

The new agent, George Beaumont of East Bridgford, was also regarded with suspicion by Lord Manvers, who wrote to Pocock on 19th January 1849 that he had

...concluded a lengthened correspondence with Mr Beaumont the result of which I trust will be to induce him to go straight in all transactions of business for the future, which I fear he would very rarely do were he to follow his own bent ....

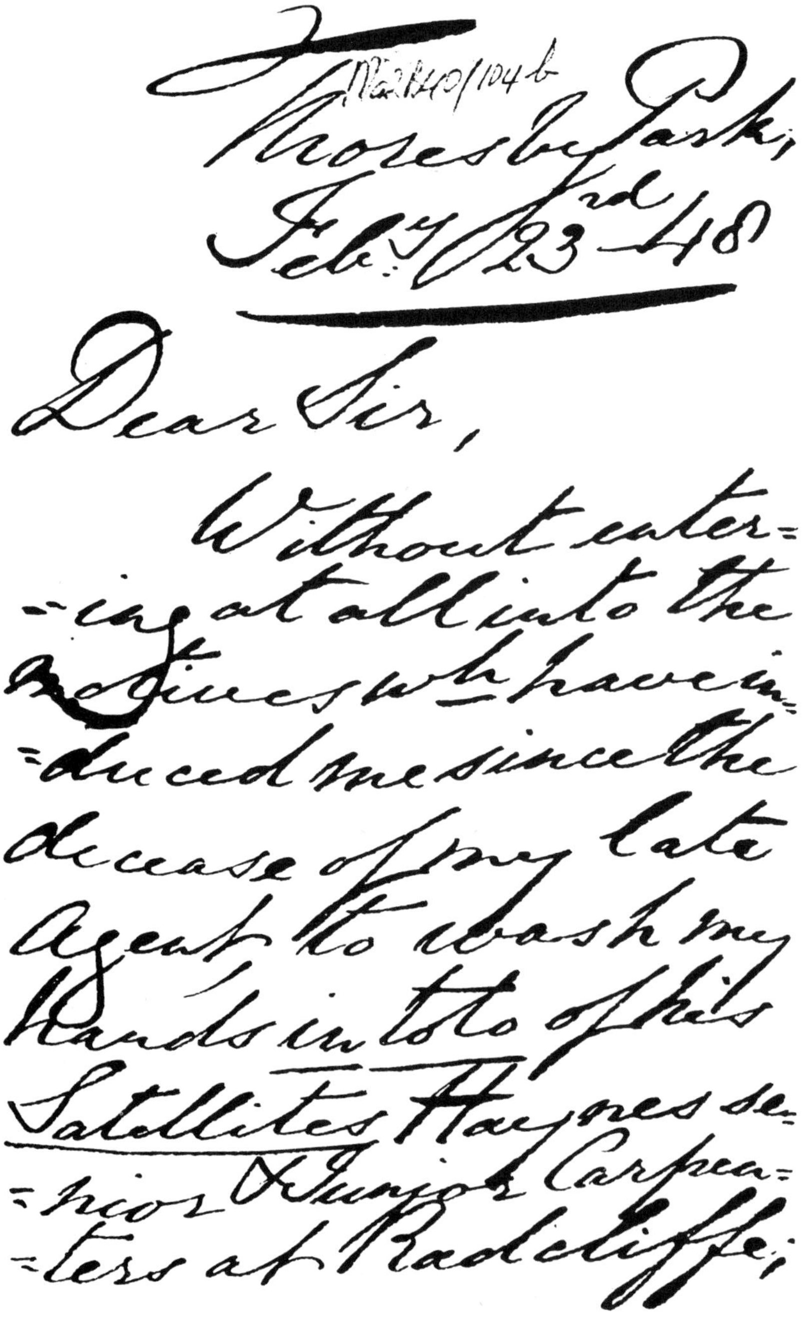

Ma240/104b

Thoresby Park,
Feb.y 23rd 48

Dear Sir,

Without enter=
=ing at all into the
motives w.h have in
=duced me since the
decease of my late
Agent, to wash my
Hands in toto of his
Satellites Haynes se=
=nior & Junior Carpen=
=ters at Radcliffe;

A page from a letter written by the second Earl Manvers to Mr J.I. Pocock in 1848.
His characteristically bold signature appears below
(University of Nottingham Department of Manuscripts
by courtesy of the Earl Manvers Will Trust)

Manvers

24

The earl was evidently not going to have another Burgess affair! Pocock resigned his stressful auditorship on the grounds of ill health in August 1851, but his firm continued the solicitorship in which he retained an interest.

A claimant to the estate

On 26th September 1851 Pocock wrote to Lord Manvers concerning a claimant specifically to the Holme Pierrepont part of the estates:

> .... the Claimant is, or assumes to be, issue of some collateral member of the Pierrepont family, <u>anterior to the late Duke of Kingston in the male line,</u> and supposes that on his Grace's death the Estate would revert to the nearest heir male, leaving out all considerations of females .... But how came it that, one may ask, no claimant started up for any of the Titles held by his Grace, if not the Dukedom, one or more of the other Titles, which were I believe of earlier creation. So great a prize would hardly have wanted Claimants had there been any with well-founded pretensions, and ignorance is not probable on the part of any such person, considering the notoriety of the Duke's death and will, accompanied by the subsequent trial of the Duchess .... [She had been found guilty of bigamy in 1776.]

The claimant is identified in Pocock's letter of 7th November 1851 as Hezekiah B[eers] Pierrepont who had already begun 'an Action of Ejectment'. He was an American Protestant clergyman from Avon, Livingston County, New York State. Although Mr Twopenny, a counsel employed in the Manvers interest, pronounced that he could see no grounds for the claim, Mr Pickin, the Thoresby agent, recalled that fifteen or twenty years previously a Mr Beers Pierrepont had written stating that he had grounds for believing he was the rightful heir, but at this stage they were 'still in the dark as to the real background of the claim.' Nevertheless, the estate was sufficiently uncertain of its ground for Pickin to look up an Act of Parliament of 1759, mark the relevant passages for Lord Manvers, and refer to the Duke of Kingston's will of 1725. In his letter of 29th November 1851 he felt sure that these legal proceedings had given the late duke the indisputable right to dispose of his estates as he did. '...It is thought that the claimant derives his Title from Mr Francis Pierrepont who resided in Nottingham in the reign of Charles I.' Although the claim came to court, Pickin could write to Pocock in February 1852 congratulating him on its termination, at least for the current assizes if not for ever.

The death of the second earl

Throughout these years, routine management of the estate continued. The Manvers papers give details about repair work on tenants' property in Radcliffe, the rebuilding of the houses on the Green, payments for repairs to the chancel of the parish church as well as donations and maintenance work at the school. In July 1859, towards the end of the second earl's life, the Manvers trustees bought Radcliffe Lodge for £2,000 but in October of the same year it was sold to Ichabod Charles Wright for £3,000 of which Lord Manvers received 10%. He seems to have let the manorial rights 'for '£4,000 and £2,000.'

It is difficult to judge whether or not his tenants found him a good landlord. Certainly rents went up after the Green had been rebuilt, but this was to be expected, while land rents rose nationally from the early 1830s to the late 1860s. If there were complaints, they are not to be found in the Manvers papers. The only hint of discontent is found in the election campaign of 1850-1 when his son, Lord Newark, in favour of the corn laws, had unsuccessfully contested South Nottinghamshire. The *Nottingham Review*, supporting the opposition, quoted the views of the *Daily News* of December 11th on the electorate who saw Lord Manvers as:

> ...a bad Protectionist and a worse landlord; greedy of his rents and careless whence they are paid, whether out of produce or capital; so they reject the heir ....

In contrast, the more conservative *Nottingham Journal* was happy to endorse Lord Newark's candidature, and on the earl's eightieth birthday noted that 'this fine old English gentleman lives in the affection of his friends and tenantry and indeed all who have the honour of his lordship's acquaintance'. His countess died in September 1860, and he in the October. His simple funeral at Holme Pierrepont attracted a 'goodly assemblage of persons residing at Radcliffe and the neighbourhood'. The *Journal* approvingly added that 'nearly all were clad in decent mourning and conducted themselves in a most orderly manner'.

II. The estate 1860-1900

The third earl

Sidney William Herbert Pierrepont, like his father, had not expected to inherit the title but in 1850 his brother, Charles Evelyn, twenty years his senior, had died. (An account for eight sets of mourning clothes provided by Jacob Gee of Radcliffe is amongst the Manvers papers.) Educated at Eton and Oxford, the new Lord Newark had immediately shouldered the burden of public service. Although defeated in 1851, he had represented South Nottinghamshire in the House of Commons from 1852, and had become a deputy-lieutenant for the county in 1854. Also in 1852 he had married Georgine de Franquetot, second daughter of the Duc de Coigny, by whom he was to have five children.

The third Earl emerges from the records as a gentler figure than his father, and with even greater dedication to public causes and good works. Donations of money, game and clothing went to deserving causes. He continued his father's work for Nottingham's General Hospital, and made the Royal Midland Hospital to the Blind a second major concern. He also found time to support the newly

The third Earl Manvers (1825-1900)
from a soft point print drawn in 1861.
(By courtesy of the Earl Manvers Will Trust)

formed R.S.P.C.A. from 1871, the Lunatic Hospital, the Nottinghamshire Nursing Association, and the Midland Orphanage and Industrial Training Institution. Like his father he was concerned with educational causes, ranging from the transfer of church schools to board schools, the rebuilding of many local schools as at Radcliffe, the founding of Trent College in 1868, and the founding of University College, Nottingham, in 1877. Nor did he forget the Nottingham Ragged School, supporting its bazaar in 1883 with his wife, who over the years did her share of committee work, stall holding and church decoration. The Earl was also active in religious affairs, presiding at a meeting of the Society for the Propagation of the Gospel in Foreign Parts in 1865, signing a circular against the Romanising practices of the clergy in 1874, supporting the creation of the new diocese of Southwell, and, at the other end of the scale, serving as vicar's warden at St. Mary's in Nottingham in 1880, where he was patron of the living. (The Pierreponts were patrons of fourteen livings.)

County affairs and legal matters also occupied a great deal of his time. He served as magistrate at Shire Hall, at Bingham and at Worksop, regularly attending the Quarter Sessions when the administration of the county was discussed. His

Georgine de Coigny, wife of the third Earl Manvers,
from an engraving of a picture at Bargany

activities ranged from serving as chairman of the Ollerton District Highways Board in 1864, heading a committee to report on a new police station at Trent Bridge in 1870, or laying the foundation stone of Gunthorpe Bridge in 1873, to taking part in arrangements for the new County Council in 1888. (He was anxious that portraits and a bust given by his ancestors should stay in Shire Hall and not go to the county.) He was elected unopposed to the new body, representing Ollerton.

Lord Manvers was nevertheless interested in the more traditional occupations of his class. Estate balls were regularly held at Thoresby, he and his countess attended functions at Buckingham Palace, and the family was regularly in London for the 'season'. Military links were also retained. He served for three years in the Sherwood Rangers and twenty-eight in the South Nottinghamshire Cavalry, which included a troop drawn from Holme Pierrepont, Radcliffe and Bingham. Ten of these years had been spent as commanding officer. After stoically turning out year after year for annual training days, he acknowledged in 1877, 'I do not pretend to be a great soldier myself, or to know much about it but ....' (This disarming approach was to carry him through educational and agricultural meetings too.) By 1879 government expectations of amateur soldiers became higher and Lord Manvers resigned, commenting, 'I feel disinclined to go to school again and learn new duties.' Sporting matters also concerned him. He preserved his fishing rights on the Trent, used Holme Pierrepont as a 'shooting box' for house parties in the autumn, and regularly hunted with the Rufford hounds. He was thrown in 1861, but was still with them in 1886. Two years later he was lucky to recover from a serious accident while out riding at Thoresby.

It was he who was responsible for the present house at Thoresby, the third on the site. Around 1864 the house designed by John Carr was pulled down because, according the *Nottingham Journal* at the time, it was damp as it was on low ground and was close to water. Perhaps there was also some element of keeping up with the other magnates of the Dukeries. With hindsight in 1891 he admitted that he had been wrongly advised about spending so much money on the house because of the agricultural depression to come.

Valuation of the estate 1861

Whatever other interests the third earl had, his main preoccupation was with the efficient running of his lands, and in 1861, the year after he succeeded to the title, a valuation for rental of the Holme Pierrepont estate was made. It included villages from Gamston to Orston and Gedling, and covered 9,226 acres valued at £18,682. Cotgrave was the most valuable, consisting 2,614 acres worth £5,041. Radcliffe was next with 1,036 acres valued at £2,270, and there were a further 282 acres in Lamcote valued at £617.10s.0d. It is this valuation which makes clear that over half the land in the village was now under the earl's control. It gives in detail not only the buildings and acreage held by the estate but also the crops in each field.

Extracts from the Radcliffe Rental of 1861

Bell, Samuel

			a.	r.	p.	£.	s.	d.
76	Cottage Close	Pasture	1	1	33	2	16	9
75	"	Meadow	4	1	30	8	4	3
95	Black Mould	"	3	2	35	6	10	3
96	Dewberry Bush	"	5	-	22	9	10	0
27	Homestead and Building	Manvers Arms Inn Brick and slate stuccoed. 5 rooms on ground floor, 6 chambers. Lean to Dairy & 1 chamber over and attic, stables with clubroom over. Cow hovel. Brewhouse, etc.	-	1	14	28	0	0

Butler, Thomas
[His total holdings came to 275 acres.]

			a.	r.	p.	£.	s.	d.
Pt.112 part Foul Syke } pt.107 part Wet Furlong }	Pt. clover stubbles; pt. cabbages		11	2	33	22	16	6
Pt.112 part Foul Syke	Mangolds		9	3	3	15	4	9
Pt.108 part Raven Acres	Red clover		10	-	-	17	10	0
Pt.108 part " "	Second seeds		6	3	7	11	4	3
109 Upper Dog Hillocks	Farm buildings. Cottage. Yard, etc.. About 4 acres. Pea stubbles, remainder seeded down		13	-	15	18	6	6
111 Far Dog Hillocks	Beans		13	2	20	19	15	0

Although Lamcote was a separate manor from Radcliffe, and as such had a separate rental, for present purposes they are considered together. The principal usage of the fields in acres was as follows:

Pasture	312	Stubble		Meadow	157
Barley stubble	216	(not differentiated)	79	Peas and beans	120
Wheat stubble	180	Oat stubble	61	Fallow	60
Roots (swedes, mangolds, potatoes)	148	Osier	5		

We can infer from this that the harvest had been gathered when the survey was made. The proportion under barley (16%) and the acreage devoted to osiers reflect the comparatively large number of malthouses and the trade of basket making in the village.

Extracts from a report on the valuation given by Hamish Woolley, the valuer, shed some light on the way things were:

The ...Valuation .... is made with reference to the average prices of Farm Produce in the District for the last 7 years. .... It is assumed that the Parish and County Rates will be paid by the Tenants, the Tithe Rent Charge, Land Tax, Drainage Rates and other like outgoings by the Landlord. ....The calculations include an allowance for occasional unfavourable Seasons and the scale of the Estimate is throughout sufficiently low to enable Tenants to do justice to themselves as well as the land. .... In those cases .... in which the rent hitherto paid has been much lower than the general average of the Estate, it is obvious that the Landlord has a right to expect some equivalent for the sacrifice heretofore made, and I do not consider that any special allowance is called for in such cases, except in respect to outlay for improvements of a permanent character, such as Building, or underdraining incurred with the sanction of the Landlord or his agent, and completed to their satisfaction within a very short interval - say 2 years from the commencement of the increased Rental. .... In the matter of draining .... large sums have been expended by the Tenants from time to time, yet only a very small part of what has been done is really effectual - partly because the majority of Tenant Farmers have been until very recently, as many are now, really ignorant of the true principles of draining. ....The same remarks apply with equal force to the system heretofore common of giving Tenants Drain Tiles on condition they pay the labour of putting them in. .... Much of the Estate is well found. It would not indeed be easy to find farms in better condition than those of .... Mr Burgess at Lamcote; those of Mr Sanday and Mr Samuel Brewster, Mr Richard Butler, Mr Thomas Butler at Radcliffe. .... The cottages are valued on a scale somewhat short of their Radcliffe value, as seems proper in the case of a Nobleman's Estate, and those built on the Waste by the Parish Officers or by the predecessors of the present Tenants are valued on the same scale, ceteris paribus, as the others.

(House rents are covered more fully in the chapter on the Expanding Village.)

Sales, exchanges and purchases 1862-1881

Lord Manvers' holdings in Radcliffe were now at their maximum. As the century progressed, economic circumstances adversely affected great landowners, so despite various sales, releases and acquisitions the earl's control of the village was gradually reduced. In 1862 a total of nearly 151 acres of land which were part of the Settled Estates were released, presumably allowing him greater freedom of usage. They included The Manvers Arms and the Manor House. About 480 square yards of land along the Bingham Road was sold to Mrs Mary Eastwood for £40 in 1863. (Her family of stonemasons had already been occupying land there.) In 1864 land was sold for £609 to the Great Northern Railway Company for the construction of a viaduct, and in 1869 land for the cemetery was sold to the Burial Board for £199. In 1869, also, there was an exchange of land with Miss Adelaide Burnside, the Earl getting several closes up Cropwell Road (where the present golf club is on Dewberry Lane and Cropwell Road) and Miss Burnside receiving three closes and a house near to Lamcote House, which she owned. In 1872 two triangular pieces of land totalling 6 roods, and 30 perches near to Radcliffe Lodge were sold to the occupant, Frederick Wright, for £650.

From 1870 the estate tried to join in the building boom in the village by attempting to sell or lease for building purposes some land between Shelford Road and the river. A paper exists listing the conditions under which it was to be sold: the minimum cost of a house was to be £800; not more than one house was to be erected on a plot (apart from an entrance lodge or gardener's cottage); only foreign seasoned timber could be used and so forth. It appears that the estate mistimed its offer for no plots were sold. More successful was a sale in 1879 of several plots alongside Cropwell Road and in Cropwell Butler, the former again with an eye to the housing market. The relevant document starts with the information that John Parr borrowed £8,000 from Miss A.A. Burnside in 1876 to pay off two mortgages of £4,000 each on Ratcliffe Barn Close and New Barn Hill Field on what is now Cropwell Road. Ratcliffe Barn Close was advertised as being a 'tempting site for a gentleman's residence' with extensive views, and only ten minutes drive from Radcliffe railway station. New Barn was '15 minutes drive from Radcliffe' with stabling for six horses. Some at least of this property is noted as having been sold - to George Beaumont, Lord Manvers' own agent, for £3,517. 12s.3d. In 1881 there was some reshuffling when Beaumont exchanged Ratcliffe Barn Close plus a pasture and buildings, nearly 31 acres in all, with Earl Manvers for 19,357 square yards (4 acres, all but 1 square yard) in the village, a small piece roughly where the Black Lion is now and the rest on each side of the present New Road, all prime building land. The exchange highlighted the value of land close to the centre of the village and drew some queries from the Inclosure Office:

(1) *Why cannot Earl Manvers deal with his own land for building sites?*

(2) *The valuer is requested to show on the plan the adjacent land to which he refers, and to state the price realized for it. Has Mr Beaumont land adjacent?*

(3) *What are the circumstances which have given so high a value to land in Radcliffe?*

The answers, presumably by Beaumont as principal in the exchange and as Earl Manvers' agent, show that he was still acting in the earl's interests and not his own. The whole manoeuvre was to circumvent the restrictions on the use of Settled Estate Land.

(1) *The Land is in strict settlements and the money received would have to be reinvested in other land and again settled. The proposed exchange effects the object and increases the quantity of Settled Estates and increases the rental.*

(2) *Before the present demand for building land, he sold three acres at 9s.6d per yard. Mr Beaumont has no land adjacent.*

(3) *Radcliffe is within ten minutes of Nottingham by rail and is the only place within the same radius from Nottingham beyond the new borough boundaries and is exempt from the high rates within them.*

On November 4th 1881 Leonard Lindley, lace dresser, bought about 3,200 square yards of this land from George Beaumont at 6s per square yard, an area lying at the south-eastern end of the main plot (roughly where Rose's garage is now). George Beaumont appears to have sold the remainder of the land back to Earl Manvers for £2,936 in 1885. Some of it was finally sold to Frank Whitby of Nottingham for £221.14s in 1901, but it was not fully developed for another twenty or thirty years.

The agricultural depression

Radcliffe's building boom was temporarily halted in the 1880s by a sewerage crisis (see chapter on Public Health), while the prosperity of the earl's tenants was affected by a long agricultural depression. As early as December 1877 the *Nottingham Journal* was reporting that portions of rent were being returned, particularly around Kneesall and Laxton on the north Nottinghamshire estates. By March 1881 the earl was returning 15% to his tenants. (Lord Carrington near Brigg and Grimsby was having to return 20%). Feelings of resentment against the landed classes grew at this time, and Lord Manvers was fortunate to find a champion in a Mr Frank Huntson at a Conservative meeting. The latter was doubtless overstating the case when he assured his listeners that every penny Earl Manvers drew from his landed property was put back into the land, thus enabling the tenant farmer to carry on his farm under the present depression, and the labourer to find employment.

It was at this time that annual rent reductions became permanent. A letter received by John Green from R.W. Wordsworth of the Thoresby estate office on April 9th 1885 was of the standard form received by all tenants:

In consequence of the present unfavourable condition of Agriculture, Lord Manvers has decided that the time has arrived when some permanent reduction of his Rental must be considered, and I am requested by his Lordship to say that he is prepared to give effect to this to the extent of the abatement of Rent which he has made annually during the last seven years on account of the depression which has existed.

Unfortunately, it is impossible to know in detail how this situation affected the Radcliffe tenants since at the time of writing the Holme Pierrepont estate rental books from 1860 onwards cannot be located.

The Earl made one other contribution to ease the situation for the hard-pressed around this time when he added to Radcliffe's existing allotment system. In

February 1886 he made available to labourers about eighty gardens of some 600 square yards each 'of excellent land' at 5s per year, probably on Shelford Road.

More land transactions 1885-1900

The effect of falling rents must have contributed to the earl's financial problems. In 1885 the mortgages on all the Manvers' estates totalled £151,100 of which £10,000 was mortgaged on the Holme Pierrepont estate to Lady Manvers' trustees. At that time he was discussing with the trustees the advantages of freeing the estates from mortgages, particularly on land which he could sell for building. His trustees at this time were Mr H.E. Egerton, his nephew, and the Reverend Henry Seymour, rector of Holme Pierrepont. The agent was Mr R.W. Wordsworth, his own agent at Thoresby. Two profitable transactions came in 1887 when he sold land for £5,750 to the Nottingham Suburban Railway and another plot for £21,000 to the London and North Western Railway.

The trend of selling to public institutions continued. Land on Shelford Road for the Primitive Methodist chapel was originally offered on December 17th 1890 at 3s per square yard or £120 for the 800 square yards. On 26th May 1891, however, the sum of £168 for 960 square yards was mentioned, i.e. 3s.6d per square yard, the price for which the land was finally conveyed. Whether the Methodists assented to the increase or whether they were duped by Lord Manvers' agent is not clear. The estate was still selling below the market price.

On 20th June 1894 the surveyor, John Wigram, reported to Earl Manvers' trustees on the 'proposed sale to the Nottinghamshire County Council of a site for a Lunatic Asylum' known as Radcliffe Lings farm comprising more than 130 acres near Saxondale:

The present surface agricultural rental amounts to about £140 per annum, and having regard to the character of the soil and present prices of wheat etc. for which this class of land is specially adapted, it must be regarded as quite a full 'times rental'. There is an annual charge of £8.10s.0d for Land Tax showing a net annual rental of £131.10s.0d subject to calls for Building repair, Drainage or other outlay, and expenses of collection, Insurance and management.

I recommend that the sum of £5,200 be accepted as the surface value of the farm as a whole. .... This would shew a certain income at 3% of £156 per annum, and I regard it as quite the maximum current value. The minerals to be reserved and the Timber - the value of which is nominal - to be included in the above purchase money.

With regard to the Minerals however, coal has recently been reported as probably existing under this land, but I understand the County Council will not purchase except with all Minerals.

Mr Wigram then attempted to put a value on the coal, but with limited success. He next listed the attractions of the site for a lunatic asylum, among them the proximity of Radcliffe station, and Saxondale siding for coal deliveries, the availability of building bricks at Lord Caernarvon's (Hill's) Brickyard within 300 yards of the farmhouse, gas and a sewer within 500 yards, and a well.

Mr Wordsworth wrote to the trustees on June 29th 1894 saying that Lord Manvers was prepared to offer the County Council G. Alcock's farm at Radcliffe as a site for the new county asylum in terms of Mr Wigram's valuation and report, and asked for their sanction in a subsequent letter (July 3rd) to sell at £5,500 without minerals or £8,500 with. He could not, however, proceed with the sale of minerals if Lord Newark objected. The upshot of this is not known, but a compromise price of £6,800 was finally paid for the land.

The Court Leet

All this while, the Court Leet of the Manor of Radcliffe, probably dating back to medieval times, had been meeting annually and continued to do so until the First World War. Amongst the Manvers papers there are three surviving rolls for the period studied (i.e. registers listing all those liable to attend the Manorial court). The first runs from 1891 to 1899, and initially contains 361 names but has additions and crossings out over the years. The second runs from 1900 to 1909 with 350 names originally, and the third from 1910 to 1919. Only those occupying land belonging to the original manor were liable to attend the Leet and very few actually did so. The last roll is unfinished, attendances only being marked up to and including 1914. The form of summons to the Court Leet was printed with gaps for names and dates, and that for 1895 reads as follows:

Manor of Radcliffe in the County of Nottingham.

These are to will and require you to give notice that the Court Leet of our Sovereign Lady the Queen, with the Great Court Baron of the Right Honourable Sidney William Herbert, Earl Manvers, Lord of the said Manor, will be held at the House of Mrs Catherine Bell in Radcliffe aforesaid in and for the said Manor, on Monday the Fourteenth day of October next at the hour of Twelve o'clock at noon, and to summon all Persons who owe Suit and Service to the same Court, and then and there to do their Suit and Service. And you are also to summon at least Twelve good and lawful Men of the said Manor, then and there to serve upon the Jury of Homage: and have you then and there this precept.

Given under my Hand and seal this Twenty-fifth day of September in the year of our Lord One Thousand Eight Hundred and Ninety Five.

Henry Wing, Steward.

*To Mr George Turner
Bailiff of the said Manor of Radcliffe.*

Henry Wing was a Nottingham solicitor and George Turner was Radcliffe's post master and wheelwright. The Court Leet for this year was held before Henry W. Tonks, Deputy Steward. The names of the jury at Homage were:

M r	*John Foster (foreman)*		
"	*Simon Thomas Eastwood*		
"	*George Foster*	M r	*Thomas Scrimshaw*
"	*Walter Williamson*	"	*Richard Joseph Turner*
"	*George Upton*	"	*Thomas Bell*
"	*Thomas Foster*	"	*George Whyler*
"	*Philip Richmond*	"	*Edward Foster*

The Inspectors of ditches and drains said that there was nothing to report and that all was well. Thomas Foster, Tom Armstrong, Philip Richmond, John Foster and George Upton were reappointed Inspectors of hedges, ditches and drains for the year ensuing and 'shall from time to time go out and make such Inspection on complaint made and notice thereof from the Bailiff of the Court'. In addition it was 'ordered that the Resolution passed at the Court held in the Manor in 1846 for mowing thistles on or before 31st July in each year be confirmed and adhered to until altered.'

George Bemrose was appointed Pinder (having the job of rounding up stray cattle and shutting them in the pinfold near the site of the present Black Lion). The same Inspectors and Pinder tended to be appointed year after year and usually had nothing to report. In 1890, though, it was maintained that the 'Clap Gate leading from Ogle Lane to Water Lane required painting white so that people can see it at night', and also that the 'hedge of Mr John Green, Farmer, Radcliffe, wants cutting on the north side of the Turnpike Road'. The duties of this nearly obsolete body had been largely taken over by
parish government and were understandably carried out in a perfunctory manner, but the attendance of the Jury was assured by the prospect of hospitality at the Manvers Arms where Mrs Bell lived. (The estate had spent £1.4s.0d on Radcliffe manorial court dinners in 1850 and £2.2s.0d in 1880.)

Death of the third earl

The third earl died on January 30th 1900 in his seventy-fifth year after a bout of influenza. From the 1880s he had shared his public duties with two of his sons. (The third and youngest son had tragically died of typhoid fever while in Rome with his tutor, the Reverend Henry Seymour, rector of Holme Pierrepont.) Although less active in these later years he was nevertheless a Nottinghamshire institution after holding the title for forty years, and the expressions of regret at his passing seem genuine. The *Nottingham Journal* emphasised his philanthropic work, his interest in religion and his devotion to duty. In Radcliffe church the Reverend John Cullen spoke at length of his 'gentle, faithful and kind' character. A peal of muffled bells and the *Dead March in Saul* completed the service. Like his predecessors the third earl was buried at Holme Pierrepont.

An engraving of the third Earl Manvers (1825-1900) from a portrait presented by his tenantry in 1891 (By courtesy of the Earl Manvers Will Trust)

III. The estate 1900-1920

The fourth earl

Charles William Sydney Pierrepont was no stranger to Radcliffe. Born in 1854 and educated at Eton, as Lord Newark he had made Holme Pierrepont Hall his adult home. He had served regularly on the Bingham bench of magistrates, joined in his father's duties around the county, and had been actively involved in Radcliffe's affairs, becoming the first chairman of the Parish Council in 1894. Politically he had also followed in his father's Conservative footsteps, representing the Newark division of Nottinghamshire between 1885 and 1895, and again from 1898 until the time of his father's death. Since 1880 he had been married to Helen, the third daughter of Sir Michael Shaw-Stewart of Greenock by whom he had a son and three daughters.

The inheritance

In fact the new earl had already come into some of his own while still Lord Newark. A year before his death the third earl had given his son a number of properties in Holme Pierrepont, Radcliffe and Cotgrave amongst other places which were 'to go to the use of the said Charles William Sidney Pierrepont during his life without impediment.' This may have been an attempt to avoid the full impact of death duties which had been introduced in 1894. At this time the estate's holding in Radcliffe was 959 acres, with 292 acres in Lamcote, 35 cottages and 11 acres on the Cliff. (This compares with 1,036 and 282 acres in 1861.)

At the time of the third earl's death there were mortgages amounting to £30,000 on the Holme Pierrepont estate, three times the amount in 1885, but by the time his trustees presented their accounts in November they had been reduced to £15,000. The sales to Nottingham Corporation included the land for the county asylum (at Saxondale) and for a sewage farm at Stoke Bardolph.

The accounts were as follows (with shillings and pence rounded off):

Income		£	Expenditure	£
Balance, March 1885		11,362	Mortgages paid off	121,000
Sales	to Sneinton (to May '99)	61,044	Land purchased	13,081
"	to Railways,		Improvements	67,183
	Nottingham Corpn.	135,577	Legal surveyors	4,393
Enfranchisements			Interest to	
	of Copyholders	1,983	Ld. Manvers	313
Interest		1,424	Management	1,386
			Balance at Bank	3,934
		-------		-------
		211,391		211,391

It appears that the duty payable by the fourth earl was £23,697. 2s.10d of which £4,500 was repaid to him by the Trust and in October 1911 a further cheque for £4,197. 2s.10d was sent to him by the trustees, thus reducing the charge on the estate to £15,000. Due to various sales of land, mostly for building, the Trust account was usually in a healthy state from this time. The Reverend Henry Seymour resigned as trustee in 1907 after 23 years and was succeeded by Mr Harcourt Vernon.

Leases and sales 1901-1911

Until September 1900 tenancy agreements were made with Lord Newark, but thereafter with Earl Manvers. An early sale of land was to the Radcliffe Co-operative Society for £150 in 1901. The site measured 160 square yards at the corner of Shelford Road and Main Road, and it had been occupied by John Green, William Dyson and Richard Barratt. The shop subsequently erected was symptomatic of changes in the centre of the village which were gradually to eradicate the old farms and cottages. Estate land was also rented from 1902 for Radcliffe's sewage farm. Another change came after the provision of a new school on Bingham Road by the County Council in 1908. The old schoolrooms on the main road became empty and the earl leased them for a pepper corn rent of one shilling annually to nine trustees including Mr Norris, his agent. The other trustees were listed as eight Unionists and one Radical; four Churchmen, four Non-conformists and one Roman Catholic (although on the final document they were described as 'Gentlemen'). The building was to be used for the parish church Sunday School and on weekdays as a reading room, or for lectures, concerts, public meetings, dramatic performances etc. The premises became known as the Pierrepont Institute.

Two other transactions of interest to the village occurred about this time. For £100 yearly the earl leased 23½ acres on Dewberry Hill to Radcliffe Golf Club in 1909, and in 1911 the estate trustees sold four strips of land amounting to 871 square yards for £50, mostly in front of The Chestnuts, for the purpose of widening the highway. The vicar had already been approached concerning church land on the opposite side of the road for the same purpose without success. It seems that a number of chestnut trees were felled in the process of road making at this time. (The last of the old trees went in 1988.)

Restrictions on the estate

At this time Earl Manvers was becoming impatient at the limitations on his powers of investment of proceeds from sales of land under the trust. It seemed that the money could be invested only in more land or government securities although Mr Wordsworth, the agent, quoted a Mr Johnson of Lincoln's Inn as saying that an enlargement clause of the Trust Deed might be allowable 'so that ordinary Trust Investments may be possible'. However, the idea seems to have been abandoned. One way out was to invest in ground rents - in Walthamstow! In 1911 the sum realised on sales of land in south Nottinghamshire was more than £161,000. Mr Johnson was asked to prepare a scheme for the investment of about £150,000 in funds pointed out by counsel as being permissible. A further drain on the estate came in 1912 when Lloyd-George's Insurance Act began to make an impact. Lord Manvers agreed to give 1s a day sick pay to all employees until they got the Insurance Act payment.

Around 1914 Mr Harcourt Vernon resigned as trustee and Lord Algernon Percy of Guy's Cliffe, Warwick replaced him. A look at the assets of the Settled Estates at

Helen Shaw-Stewart, Lady Manvers and the fourth Earl Manvers (1854-1926) in 1907
from pastel drawings of by Frederick Beaumont
(By courtesy of the Earl Manvers Will Trust)

this time reveals that nearly £150,000 was invested in various ways: £469,000 in railway debenture stocks including Great Western Railway at 4% and Midland Railway at 2.5%; £4,002 in consols; and the rest, nearly £40,000, in mortgages on land and in ground rents.

Cottage improvements and sales in 1914

At the end of 1913 Lord Manvers had two concerns with regard to Radcliffe. One was the state of his existing cottages and, it would seem, the building of two new properties. On New Year's Eve in 1913 Mr Wordsworth (as agent for the trustees) wrote to the surveyor, Mr Wigram, that Lord Manvers had 'made up his mind to deal thoroughly with the conditions of his cottage property' and, since this would not be possible out of trust funds without selling out some of the money already invested, they would have to borrow from the Land Investment Company. The new cottages would be similar to a pair built at Laxton and to one at Edwinstowe.

More significantly, at the same time, Lord Manvers was beginning to make up his mind to sell much of his land in Radcliffe. A reserve price was considered to be that which would produce 3.5% and which would be equivalent to the current rent. Mr Wordsworth at first thought that 'on such a sum no Undeveloped Land Duty can be charged'. The date fixed for the sale was February 18th 1914. By this time, in a letter to the trustee, Mr Egerton, Mr Wordsworth was forced to change his mind about the possibility of tax as all the land had road frontages and would be considered liable for Undeveloped Land Duty. He calculated that

> it would be well to part with it if we could get 40% above the Capital Value which would be necessary to return the present net rent of 3.5%. It will not be possible to get this on all the lots but on some I hope to get more. I shall have to ask the Trustees to let me exercise my judgement.

Mr Hallam, of Wheeler gate, had enquired whether Lord Manvers would sell to holders at agricultural value, but Mr Wordsworth replied that Lord Manvers had no power, under his settlement, to sell except at full market price, but that it would be

35

worth while for holders to consider whether a syndicate might be formed to purchase land. The land was put up for sale in fourteen lots, of which only five seem to have been sold immediately. Several were sold privately later. A Mr Tyler paid £1,300 for two lots consisting of about 17 acres lying between what is now Cliff Way and Hamilton Drive. Lots on each side of this were withdrawn from the sale as also were two other lots on the southern side of Shelford Road and several lots on Cropwell Road. Mr Foster, the auctioneer, paid £1,230 for two pieces of land comprising 21 acres on the southern side of Bingham Road (near where Golf Road is now), and Mr Wright paid £340 for nearly 3 acres near what was then the Golf Club entrance. Four other lots were sold privately, and only the largest, 96 acres and well over half the total, was left unsold. This included a great deal of land to the north-east of Cliff Way stretching to the parish boundary (roughly where the houses now end going out of Radcliffe along Shelford Road). Three lots on the south-western side of Cropwell Road, stretching from the present site of the Black Lion, were sold for £2,000 to John Ashworth, a timber importer of Ruddington Hall, and the land was subsequently fenced by the purchaser for almost £100. A total of £5,395 was realised. These initial speculators often had sub-purchasers, and the sites were eventually used for housing.

Mr Wordsworth retired because of ill-health at this time and Mr H.D. Argles took over as agent. A document which must be dated as post-1914 (since the accompanying plan is based on the 1914 Ordnance Survey map) shows that the estate still owned 571 acres of Radcliffe land, about half the 1861 total, but this was soon to be further reduced. An agreement to sell 38 acres of land, including 3 acres on the north side of the River Trent, was entered into between the Great Northern Railway and Lord Manvers' Trustees in July 1914, but was delayed (presumably because of the war) and not completed until 1919. One other purchaser at this time was Mr A.J. Rowe, then a cycle agent, who paid £650 for a Main Road site of 1,307 square yards. This land adjoining the police station and the Co-operative site, and stretching back to the Methodist chapel, had become available on the death of a long-standing tenant farmer, Miss Elvira Bowring. In due course Mr Rowe progressed from cycles to cars and a garage occupied the site. The old farm house survived until the 1960s. Now the whole area has made way for shops and the town houses of Kingston Court (a reminder of the Manvers family since the Pierreponts held the Dukedom of Kingston-upon-Hull in the eighteenth century).

A significant letting of land occurred during the war itself. There were 72.5 acres within the parish of Radcliffe and belonging to the Holme Pierrepont estate but which lay across the river and to the west of the wharf. In 1916 this was let to the City of Nottingham for £150 per annum. The land seems to have been required in conjunction with the sewage farm at Stoke Bardolph and eventually became part of Stoke Bardolph parish.

Council housing and smallholdings

After the war pressure was put on local councils to buy land for the erection of council houses, and Bingham R.D.C. was no exception. On January 24th 1919, James Haslam, the Chairman of Bingham R.D.C. Housing Committee wrote to Mr Norris at Holme Pierrepont to enquire about the possibility of acquiring one or both of two pieces of land belonging to the estate. The first was on the north side of Shelford Road 'forming the frontage of the two fields occupied by Mr George Bell and adjoining the allotment gardens', and the other 'between Station Terrace and the Lorne Grove property and extending from Station Road to Main Road'. George A. Bell, farmer and innkeeper, and representative of the executors of the late Mr Samuel Bell, was obviously soon approached by the estate and on 2nd April 1919 gave written notice that he would 'quit and deliver up Possession of the Farm known as Cliffe or Shelford Farm on or before the 6th day of April 1920'. On the following day, 3rd April 1919, the estate gave him his formal notice to quit and Bingham Housing Committee adopted a proposal to purchase 21 acres of Radcliffe land, available for £1,500, subsequently reduced to £1,400. (Five acres at Cotgrave was bought for £500 at the same time.) Little time had been wasted, and the committee expressed their appreciation of the way in which the earl had co-operated.

At some time in 1919, too, the County Council took a hand in accelerating the break-up of the Manvers estate in Radcliffe by requiring land from the earl for the

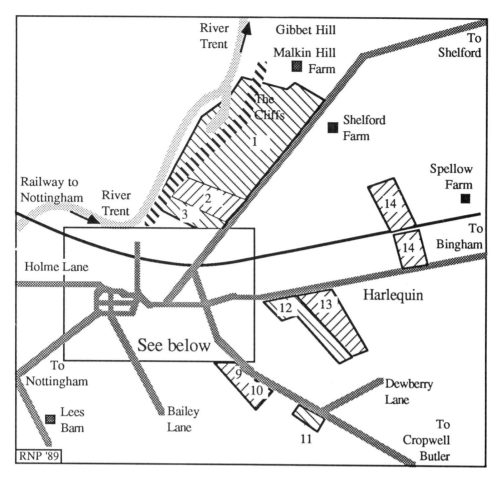

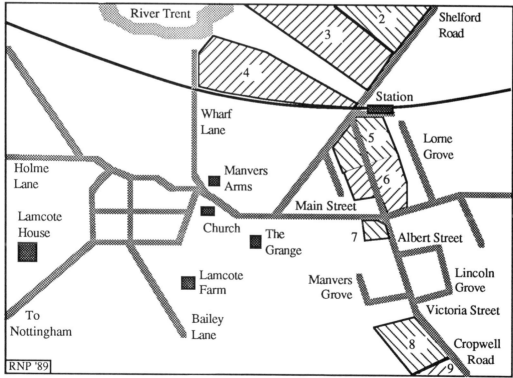

Sketch maps of Manvers estate holdings offered for sale in February 1914
(Numbers relate to lots in sale)

use of ex-servicemen. Estate tenants were understandably anxious about this, and in September it was reported in the *Nottingham Evening Post* that the secretary of the South Notts. Farmers' Union had written to Earl Manvers 'urging that the sitting tenants might have the first option of purchasing their holdings at a fair reserved price'. Lord Manvers replied that the tenants should have every consideration but that the County Council had precedence under the Acquisition of Land Bill.

All this may have merely confirmed the earl's conclusion that the main part of his Radcliffe property would have to go. In February 1920 the tenants on the Holme Pierrepont estate were sent letters explaining the economic problems and giving notice of rent rises. A blank draft reads as follows:

Dear Sir,

Holme Pierrepont Estate

As you have doubtless seen from the Public Press certain portions of my above mentioned Estate are in process of changing hands, the major portion having been scheduled by the Notts. County Council for the use of ex-soldiers, and I regret in certain cases my desire that my agricultural tenants should be able to acquire their own holdings, as some were desirous of doing, cannot therefore be carried into effect.

The result of recent legislation, the large increase of encumbrances charged on Estates, the increase of taxation and tithe (though a temporary limit has been set to the latter) - the rise in wages and the price of materials, the heavy fall of income derived from mineral workings which was devoted in no small degree to the upkeep of my Estate, have caused me to study very seriously and carefully the increased obligations thrown upon me with regard to my Estates, and the question of the necessary re-adjustment of present rentals owing to the increased benefits which have accrued to my Tenants from their holdings. I have looked into the question from all points of view, and as I should deplore the further breaking up of this Estate which has belonged to my family for centuries, I must ask you to be good enough to sign a new agreement as from Lady Day (6th. April) next agreeing that your rent shall from that date be £   per annum.

I much hope that you will forward an acceptance to my Agent Mr Norris by the 12th of March next and failing your acceptance I shall be compelled to give a formal notice to quit at Lady day.

Should you have any good complaint to make, I shall have pleasure in personally giving it every consideration, with the result, I trust, of enabling us to carry on the cordial mutual relationship which has hitherto existed between Landlord and Tenant on my Estates.

Yours faithfully,

Manvers.

The sales of 1920

However reluctant in theory Lord Manvers was for his estates to break up, in practice massive sales of land took place in Radcliffe and elsewhere in 1920. Altogether the County Council purchased 1,346 acres for the provision of small-holdings for ex-servicemen, land in Adbolton, Gamston, Cropwell Butler, Holme Pierrepont and Radcliffe fetching £87,250. It was sold subject to land tax which amounted to £13.3s.3d for Radcliffe. All minerals were reserved to the vendors and the flood bank on the property was to be maintained by the County Council.

Another 348 acres in Radcliffe were auctioned in twenty-nine lots on March 3rd 1920, along with two lots in Lambley. The sale included substantial properties such as the Grange, with some 34 acres of land stretching well beyond the present by-pass, occupied by Messrs W.B. Haynes and Henry Walker. It was bought for £4,550 by Mr Haynes. The Chestnuts was another major property included in the sale, purchased by the occupier, W.P. Green, for £2,800. A look at the list of purchasers

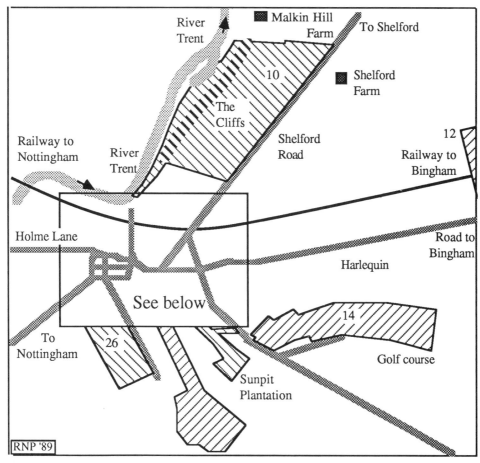

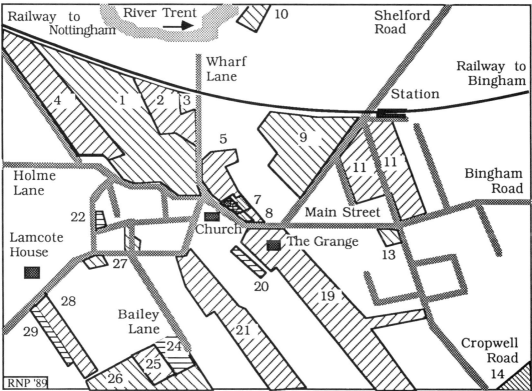

Sketch maps of Manvers estate holdings sold in 1920
(Numbers relate to lots in the sale)

Property from the Manvers estate in Radcliffe-on-Trent sold in 1920.

Lot	Description & position	Tenant	Price £	Acres	Sq yds	Purchaser
1	Small Pleasure Farm [The Chestnuts]	W.P. Green	2,800	14.3		W.P. Green
2	Recreation ground	Parish Council	450	4.9		B. Parr
3	Pasture [beyond Recreation ground]	Mrs Vickerstaff	125	1.2		D. Parr
4	Pasture [off the Green]	W.P. Green	610	5.6		W.P. Green
5	Country residence [Manor House]	G.S. Dawson	2,850	2.5		Mr Kelly
6	Licensed hostelry [Manvers Arms]	G.A. Bell	5,550		1,430	Shipstone
7	Dwelling house [next to Manvers Arms]	P. Richmond	430		1,450	P. Richmond
8	Substantial building [Institute & cottage]	Caretaker	1,150		1,270	S.D. Parr
9	Manor Farm [Shelford Road]	G.A. Bell	1,850	3.4		F. Barratt
10	Arable & pasture [includes cliff & half river]	G.A. Bell	4,000	85.2		A. Ball
11	Pasture [Station Road, i.e. New Road kerbed & sewered]	S.D. Parr	700	3.3		Elwin
12	Pasture & arable [each side of railway, beyond Harlequin]		600	11.4		Betts
13	House, buildings & pinfold [now Black Lion site]	G. Buxton and G.A. Bell	725		4,520	Walker
14	Golf course	Golf Club	3,000	42.2		Elwin
15-18	Pasture and road [Cropwell Road]	Barratt, Roulston, Bell & Buxton	1,725	18.4		---
19	Residence [The Grange]	W.B. Haynes	4,550	34.2		Haynes
20	House [Vicarage Lane]	Mr T. Roulston	500	0.8		Miss Roulston
21	Lamcote Farm [covered by the Canadian estate]	T.J. Elnor	3,500	77.2		Hind
22	Cottage & orchard [near Lamcote corner]	F. Whitworth	450		2,800	Hind
23	Small-holding & house [Water Lane, off Bailey Lane]	Col C. Birkin	850		2,240	Hind
24	Pasture [Bailey Lane]	J. Gore	2,000	3.3		Hind
25	Pasture [between lots 24 & 26]	F. Whitworth	not sold	26.6		---
26	Pasture [east of Lees barn]	P. Richmond	not sold	26.6		---
27	Cottage & pasture [Lamcote corner]	T. & W. Levi	500	1.4		Hind
28	Arable [south of Nottingham Road]	Col C. Birkin	400	4.8		Hind
29	Pasture [next to lot 28]	T. & W. Levi	270	2.0		Hind
	Total on list		38,985	348.4		

at this sale shows that they were by no means the only tenants to buy the property they occupied.

The Book of Sales says that all the lots were sold, fetching (with the two Lambley plots) £41,985, although there is no indication in the 'Particulars of Sale' that lots 25 and 26 were sold. The prices for the other plots noted in the 'Particulars' amount to £39,835 (excluding Lambley). Lord Manvers was selling all except lot 11 as 'Tenant for Life' under the Settled Land Acts. Lot 11 he was selling as absolute owner. All minerals lying below 100 feet from the surface were reserved to the vendor. Way-leave was to be granted for access to underground workings, and whoever mined was to be responsible for damage at the surface. The land sold was still subject to orders of the War Agriculture Committee, under the Defence of the Realm Act (popularly known as DORA) as to ploughing up grass or otherwise. What was referred to as Station Street in fact became New Road. No building was to be erected closer than 15 feet to the road, and the footpaths were to be paved, flagged or asphalted and 'until the same shall be adopted by the Local Authority maintained in proper repair'. No public house was to be built on this lot or offensive trade carried on. Why this lot should be singled out for such restrictions is not clear, unless Earl Manvers could not place such restrictions on land of which he was only 'Tenant for Life'.

The end of the Manvers connection

The long-term effects of the agricultural depression, taxation and the First World War led to the 1920 sale which broke the hold of the Manvers family on Radcliffe. Some lesser property was retained, however, notably around the Green and the wharf. Holme Pierrepont itself also remained in estate hands, although in 1921 the Hall was let to Marshall Owen Roberts of Eastern Hall, Grantham. The fourth earl survived until 1926, but his son Evelyn Robert suffered from mental illness and was unable to hold the title actively. On his death in 1940 the title passed to a cousin, Gervas Evelyn, who decided that death duties prevented him from retaining what was left of the estate. It was sold in 1941.

Main sources

Primary

University of Nottingham: Manvers papers M 3533, 3534, 3535, 3539, 3543, 3555, 3561, 3575, 3587, 3588; M 4889 (1861 valuation); Ma B 529/17, 30, 31, 32, 36; Ma B 539 (for repairs to property); Ma 2B 40 passim (for correspondence re Robert Burgess and claimant to estate); Ma 2B 45/16/106/119/121/169; Ma 2B 49/62/63-5; Ma 2B 50/1/106; Ma 2B 51/102; Ma 2D 16; Ma 2D 18; Ma 2D 21; Ma 2D 24; Ma 2D 25; Ma 2D 39; Ma 2D 46/3/4; Ma 2D 54; Ma 2D 55; Ma 2D 60; Ma 2 M 4 (for manorial court).

Secondary

Bateman, J. *Great Landowners of Great Britain and Ireland.* 1883.

Beckett, J.V. *The Aristocracy in England 1660-1914.* 1986.

Briscoe, J.P. *Contemporary Biographies in Nottinghamshire and Derbyshire at the opening of the Twentieth Century.* 1901.

Phillimore, W.P.W. *County Pedigrees. Nottinghamshire Vol . I.* 1910.

Radcliffe-on-Trent local history research group: extracts from Nottingham newspapers 1837-1920.

ST MARY'S CHURCH AND THE CLERGY

The established church of the Victorian era was broadly based. While challenged from without by Methodism and other nonconformist groups, and to some extent from within by the Oxford movement with its emphasis on ritual, it also developed its own evangelical character as the century progressed, and its activities were marked by a strong social conscience. Although away from the mainstream of events, Radcliffe was not totally untouched by these trends.

St Mary's had undergone many changes since the eighteenth century. The oldest parishioners in 1837 would have recognised the basic structure of the medieval Gothic church. The steeple which had fallen so catastrophically in 1792 had been replaced by a small battlemented tower, 46 feet high and mainly cased, adorned with a sundial (the gift of Charles Pierrepont, subsequently first Earl Manvers, the lord of the manor and patron of the living.) The leaded roof had gone to help pay for the repairs, and a more practical alternative, slate, now covered the church. In the renovations, the Gothic windows had at first given way to smaller ones with a mullion in the centre and later to sash windows. The interior of the nave which, according to a report of 1879, measured 46 by 47 feet, had also been much altered. The old stone pillars and capitals had been replaced by cast iron, and a gallery had been built at the west end which seated 100 and was used by the singers. (The total seating capacity of the church was given as 320 in 1851 but this may have excluded the gallery.) Lighting and heating had been improved by the addition of stone lamps and by a 'flew', presumably for a stove in 1829. At the same time 195 free seats had been provided, although some still remained the 'property' of the occupants. Other changes may be deduced from the churchwardens' accounts. Probably early in the century a wall was built around the churchyard, and repairs to a 'bridge' indicate that the uncovered Syke drain ran nearby. In 1808 trees had been planted, and

St Mary's church from the vicarage garden in 1845
signed by S. G.

42

further entries about mowing the churchyard and clearing away rubbish suggest care was taken to keep it clean and tidy. Without any major rebuilding, therefore, the appearance and character of the church and its surroundings had already been transformed. More dramatic changes were to come.

In contrast to industrial areas where the church of England was losing its appeal, St Mary's in Radcliffe continued to be a focal point of the community. Nevertheless, its overall power had decreased with the decline of church courts, and since the

The vicarage built in 1827.
This photograph was taken in 1973

enclosure of the village in 1790 tithes were no longer paid to the vicar. As compensation the living had been granted about 40 acres of land, much of it on Cropwell Road, so the church now appeared as a landowner at a time when many parishioners had lost their rights in the open fields. As well as the income from this land, the vicar had the income from 32 acres away from local scrutiny in Leicestershire, bought in the eighteenth century with money from Queen Anne's Bounty and from the Pierrepont family. The value of the living was estimated at £100 a year by Throsby in the 1790s. By 1851 this had risen to £170 from land and £3 from fees. (Clerical incomes varied considerably at this period. While a vicar in Halifax earned £1,500, the average annual income of a curate was only £81.) Despite the increase it is clear that the Radcliffe living was far from comfortable. Incumbents frequently had to resort to alternative sources of income to make ends meet, particularly as pluralism (the holding of more than one living) was becoming less acceptable. One improvement, however, had been the building of an elegant vicarage in 1827 to replace the cramped timber and brick house of 1777. (By the 1970s this house was too large for twentieth century purposes and the present house was built to replace it - at least the parish's fourth vicarage. The site is now occupied by Church Close.)

Any study of St Mary's church must be linked to the careers of its vicars, at least two of whom made a considerable impact on the village. After the long occupation of the living by the Davenport family - from 1771 to 1827 - a brief period of short tenures followed before long-term stability returned. Thomas Trevenen Penrose succeeded John Davenport, but he stayed only three years, as did Edward Denison, who left in 1833. The latter is credited with laying out the gardens of the new vicarage, and was said to have 'won the affectionate respect of all' in Radcliffe. As patron of the living, Lord Manvers commented 'that he feared his good friend at Ratcliffe gave more in charity than he received in income'. Radcliffe, however, was merely a staging post on the way to preferment for Edward Denison. The second of nine sons of John Denison, speaker of the House of Commons, from Ossington near Newark, Edward Denison had taken the highest honours at Oxford and by 1837 when aged only 36 he became Bishop of Salisbury. He died in 1854.

William Bury 1833-1845

Lord Manvers next presented William Bury to the Radcliffe living. Born in Doncaster about 1800, he was the eldest son of William Bury of the Minster House, Ripon, a Captain of the 11th Regiment of Foot. He had been a student at Magdalen College, Oxford, ordained priest in 1824, and appointed rector of Longstowe in Cambridgeshire in the following year. When he came to Radcliffe he was aged 33 and brought with him his wife, Julia (Marshall), and three children. By the time of the 1841 census he was credited with nine sons answering to the names of Maxwell, Thomas, Percival, Charles, James, Frederick, Algernon, William and Reginald, ranging from 15 years down to three months. (Two-year old William was to follow in his father's footsteps and become vicar of Attenborough with Bramcote from 1861 to 1875.) There had also been a twin to James, christened Marshall, and a daughter, Marianne, who had not survived. Alice, born in 1843, also died as a baby and was replaced by another Alice in the following year.

As if the house were not already sufficiently filled with children, William Bury supplemented his income by running a small boarding school. Ten male pupils aged from 8 to 15, only three of them born in Nottinghamshire, lived with him in 1841. To help run this household, the Burys employed one male and five female servants, and one foreign governess, making a total of twenty-eight occupants. The large new vicarage must have seemed every bit as cramped as the old one did in the days of Thomas Davenport. Despite this secondary employment William Bury's income must have remained small. His tax assessment in 1843 was for only 3s.6d, whereas that for a wealthy parishioner, farmer Thomas Butler, amounted to £8.19s.2d. In addition to his Radcliffe appointment he held the living of Lowdham from 1839 to 1842.

Church expenses and a new clock

The churchwardens' accounts, although far less explicit than for the eighteenth century, give some impression of routine church concerns. Up to 1837 the expenses of the new gallery of 1829 were still being paid off, but the main period for maintenance and improvement during William Bury's ministry was 1844-5, just before he left. After Queen Victoria and Prince Albert had driven through the village in December 1843 there was some surplus from the money raised by the village to pay for decorations. A flag was therefore purchased 'to be hoisted on the anniversary of any memorable event', and it was also decided 'that a church clock would be a great advantage to the town, and a lasting memorial to her majesty's visit'. (The previous clock had been removed at the time of the steeple's fall in 1792, and although it was replaced there are no references to it after 1802.) More money was now needed for this and a subscription list was opened. William Taylor of Radcliffe Hall and the vicar himself headed the list of contributors with £15 and £10 respectively. The new clock was bought in April 1844 from William Pearce of Nottingham, and the churchwardens, William Taylor and John Green, itemised the purchase in bold lettering in their book. Its two dials were each 6 feet in diameter and the works weighed a ton. The clock alone cost £85, but boxing up the works came to another £5.13s.6d. The purchase proved a good investment for, although it no longer chimes, the clock survives today (1989), its construction date still just discernible. A payment at the same time of £2.5s to a Mr Jennings for 'gilding' could be for the clock, the weathercock, or the sundial - shown with the clock in the drawing of 1845. The parish clerk was routinely paid £1a year for the clock's maintenance.

Just after its arrival there were also substantial payments for repairs. George Bell, the bricklayer from the Manvers Arms across the road, was paid £7.3s.1d, Thomas Haynes, the joiner, £8.7s.2d, Edward Brewster £11.4s.10½d (perhaps for bricks), and John Price, the plumber and glazier, the vast sum of £28.15s.2d - all in

December 1844. In the following June, John Foster, the joiner, and Thomas Allcock, the blacksmith, were paid totals of £21.7s.7d and £9.2s.3d respectively. Although clear comparisons cannot be made with other years as the accounts are partially run together, such sums were unusually large and suggest that some major, but unspecified, work was being undertaken. More routine outgoings included expenses at the time of the archdeacon's 'visitations' in Nottingham, as well as payments for coal, bell ropes, and communion bread and wine. This last item usually cost a standardised 7s.4d by the 1840s and was purchased by the parish clerk - Levi Duke until 1844, and then John Hemsley until 1902. Communion services were held only three or four times a year in William Bury's time, and records are not sufficiently detailed for any assessment of attendance to be made. Two new surplices were bought in 1843 for £2.7s.8d, plus 9s to Mrs Richmond for making them. The clerk was paid for their washing, although later a series of village ladies supplemented their incomes by carrying out this task. New books, probably hymn books, were bought in 1844 for £1.16s.

William Bury's attack on Methodism and his later career

Whether William Bury was well-liked by his flock is not recorded, but he was certainly disliked for a while by the local Methodists for an ill-advised attack from the pulpit, compounded by the publication of a pamphlet in 1837 condemning religious divisions in the parish:

> ...The divisions appear more numerous, and attachment to the Church is certainly not stronger in my Parish now than when I first received the charge of it. For although the attendance at Church may be greater than it was a few years ago, still the majority of the congregation are not in full communion with the Church, but seek instruction through other channels, and attend the ordinances of various dissenting bodies.

(For the reaction to this see chapter on Methodism.) Perhaps his outburst did not please his patron, for a document dated 1839 in the Manvers papers suggests that he was to be paid £1,000 to resign the vicarage of Lowdham in favour of a son of the Venerable J.H. Browne, rector of Cotgrave. He did not do so for three years.

In 1840 his garden was invaded by fruit stealers. As a result four men ended up in the House of Correction at Southwell for two months with hard labour. Perhaps because he was no longer running two parishes, from 1843 he seems to have taken a greater part in local affairs, chairing the village vestry (forerunner of the parish council) in that year. The flurry of church expenditure also began about that time. In 1845, along with fifty other local clergy, he showed that he was as intolerant of Catholics as he had been of Methodists, supporting a petition to the Queen against increasing the grant to Maynooth College for the training of priests in Ireland. In the same year he moved on to be chaplain of Scofton chapel in the parish of Worksop, remaining there until 1863. Whether or not such an appointment was a promotion, the connection with Osberton

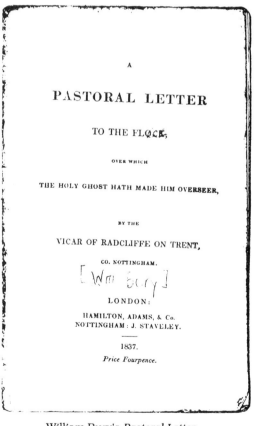

A

PASTORAL LETTER

TO THE FLOCK,

OVER WHICH

THE HOLY GHOST HATH MADE HIM OVERSEER,

BY THE

VICAR OF RADCLIFFE ON TRENT,

CO. NOTTINGHAM.

[Wm Bury]

LONDON:

HAMILTON, ADAMS, & Co.
NOTTINGHAM: J. STAVELEY.

1837.

Price Fourpence.

William Bury's *Pastoral Letter*
published in 1837

Hall and the Foljambe family must have placed him in a privileged position. He was subsequently rector of Pimperne in Dorset until his death in 1886.

Robert Burgess 1845-1873

On William Bury's resignation a young local man took his place. Robert Burgess M.A. was born at Holme Pierrepont in 1819, the son of Joseph Stubbins Burgess, a well-known farmer, and his wife Mary Ann. Surprisingly, he was baptised in the Unitarian High Pavement chapel in Nottingham. After ordination he seems to have been at Sandiacre. (A confidence trickster claiming to be one of his parishioners there was reported to have acquired from him a pair of trousers and 3s.6d in travelling expenses in May 1844.) At the time of the 1851 census he was still unmarried, running the vicarage with the help of a middle-aged housekeeper and a 12-year-old servant boy. It must have seemed a mausoleum after the bursting activity of the Bury household. Ten years later he is listed with a wife, Mary Anne, some four years his junior. By then the domestic help had expanded to two housemaids and a footman, but no children are recorded. In 1871 his wife is not mentioned in the census, but his 78-year-old mother was living with him, as well as two servants and a gardener, Samuel Barratt, later well-known for his horticultural business. He was perhaps encouraged by Robert Burgess, for according to the latter's successor, the vicar supplemented his modest clerical income by taking a market garden, and 'as he had all the trade to himself, thus made a living, poor fellow.' He certainly had greenhouses and kept hens, acted as judge at Bingham horticultural show in 1866, and was noted as a visitor to poultry shows. At his death, his horticultural stock still included 15,000 bedding plants, ferns and camellias, even though much had been sold off earlier. Some glimpses of the day-to-day life of his household appear through the account book kept by John Brice, the plumber and glazier, who recorded numerous glazing and plumbing jobs, paperhanging, and the soldering of kettles, tea and coffee pots. Such routine tasks contributed to a comfortable life-style suggested by an advertisement for the sale of the vicarage's contents after his death. These included elegant glasses in gilt frames, a handsome chiffonier with marble top, a rosewood drawing room suite, as well as a pianoforte, a harmonium, paintings, articles of 'virtu', a small wine cellar and books.

Like his predecessor, Robert Burgess chaired meetings of the parish vestry from time to time. In 1849 he came to the fore when there was concern over the open brook which ran close to the church, and he was one of the sub-committee appointed to see to its being covered over. (The committee's failure is demonstrated by the repeated and growing concern over the matter throughout the nineteenth century.) He also chaired a sub-committee under the 'Nuisance and Removal Act' in 1853, proposed there should be a new bridge over the brook in 1856, and urged the collecting of the church rate at 2½d in the £ be collected 'forthwith'. As the churchyard became full he supported the creation of a burial ground, suffering bricks through his greenhouses during the bitter controversy which followed. (See chapter on Local Government.) Around the same time he enjoyed the distinction of being chaplain to the High Sheriff when John Taylor of Radcliffe Hall was appointed to that office in 1868. For the most part, however, Robert Burgess's days were less colourful, revolving around Bible and Sunday School meetings, choir festivals at Southwell, or ministering to the sick, notably in the cholera epidemic of 1849. For giving free weekday services in Shelford, Newton and Saxondale in the same year he was presented with six handsome silver salts and a butter knife by the grateful inhabitants.

Evidence of other routine church work comes mainly from the churchwardens' books. There were expenses when children were taken to be confirmed in 1847, 1856, 1859 and 1862. Various purchases for services included a crimson cloth for £1.10s.3d in 1847, five cushions round the communion table for £1.6s.8d in 1849, a new bible and prayer book on the instructions of the rural dean for £1.2s in 1852, and a white cloth and a carpet round the communion table in 1855. New wrought iron gates came to £2.1s.3d in 1852. The church was regularly cleaned, the walls being swept and the windows washed by John Hemsley, the parish clerk, who also saw to the cleaning of candlesticks and the stove, to the cleaning of churchyard walks, and to the pruning of ivy. Apart from his own routine attention, the clock needed repairing three times by a Mr Bosworth between 1860 and 1863. It also had both faces painted by John Brice for 12s in 1854. With a curate, William Fox, installed between 1859 and 1862, the overall impression is that St Mary's was kept in very good order during Robert Burgess's ministry.

The effect of the Oxford Movement

The Oxford Movement, led by John Keble, J.H. Newman and E.B. Pusey, favoured a return of the Church of England to High Church ideals and ceremony, and during the 1840s there were some conversions to Roman Catholicism. Perhaps encouraged by this, Pope Pius IX in 1850 anticipated a reconciliation of England with the Church of Rome and issued a bull re-establishing a hierarchy of Catholic bishops in England. The prime minister, Lord John Russell, condemned the 'aggressions of the Papacy', and his views were widely supported. In December 1850 a village meeting was called to discuss the matter, 'no household of note being absent'. According to the *Nottingham Review*, Robert Burgess himself moved an address to his bishop for the suppression of 'all the Puseyite teachers and their practices', and expressed his indignation that some clergymen had allowed the Pope to make 'so insolent an aggression on Her Majesty's rights'. He was supported by the leading residents including William Taylor of Radcliffe Hall, Dr Martin and John Marriott, the local Wesleyan preacher. In the following year a Parliamentary bill was passed to prevent Catholic bishops from assuming ecclesiastical titles, but it soon became a dead letter and was repealed in 1871. Disquiet lingered on, however, and as late as 1874, just after Robert Burgess's death, the county establishment led by Lord Manvers and William Taylor of Radcliffe were still putting pressure on church authorities 'to restrain the Romanising practices of their clergy'. A bill passed in that year to allow the prosecution of clergymen for ritualistic practices was never rigidly enforced.

Despite his apparent opposition to the Oxford Movement, Robert Burgess seems to have come partially under its influence. After an altercation with local Methodists in the churchyard during a burial service in 1858 (see chapter on Methodism), the *Nottingham Review* commented on both his deficiency in Christian feeling and on his 'recently acquired Puseyistical tendencies'. Some confirmation can be found in the churchwardens' book which shows that he increased the number of communion services from the three or four per year under William Bury to as many as twenty-six in 1867-8. From the amount spent on bread and wine it is clear that attendances dropped as the frequency rose, and by 1869 communion services were reduced to one a month.

Religious census 1851

Although church leaders had occasionally tried to gauge the loyalty of their flocks, the only national religious census was taken on Sunday March 30th, 1851. On that day Robert Burgess held a morning service attended by 116 adults and 168 scholars, totalling 284. His evening service was attended by 247, and he pointed out that the Sunday scholars did not attend evening services. Unfortunately he did not fill in the section for the average number of attenders during the previous months, so it is not possible to say how typical this Sunday was. The total attendance at the two Methodist chapels on that Sunday evening was 195. When the total Radcliffe figures were adjusted for duplicate attendance it was claimed that about half the village's population of 1,273 was at some form of public worship on that day. Nationally the census showed that the Church of England could no longer claim to be the church of the majority, although it was in urban rather than rural areas that nonconformity was making most headway. Recent research on the figures suggests that Church of England attendance was only between 25 and 33%, whereas non-conformist attendance was between 30 and 40%.

New pews and furniture 1851

Perhaps coincidentally, but within days of the census being taken, the first of two major changes in the church was set in motion. On April 2nd 1851 Robert Burgess chaired and wrote up the minutes of a village - not church - vestry meeting which was held in the church to discuss the need to repair the church 'stalls'. The Vestry approved his request as long as 'the Vicar engage to provid the money for that purpose without a Rate been levid upon the Parish'. (For a nineteenth century clergyman Robert Burgess's spelling was unusually erratic.) A faculty or licence was granted by the bishop in October which allowed the clearing away of not only all the existing pews but also the pulpit and reading desk - perhaps dating from 1770 in Gabriel Wayne's time - and the clerk's desk. All wall and floor monuments or graves were to be taken up, re-set or covered over. In addition, the door leading out of the tower was to be stopped-up so that the re-seating and alterations could be carried out. The old material was to be re-used or sold. The cost of the re-pewing and the provision of a stone pulpit and reading desk according to Bailey's *Annals* for 1852 came to £300. As this was raised by subscription, the vestry got its way about the alterations not being charged to the rates.

The new chancel 1858

A more permanent change came in 1858 when the present chancel and side chapel were completed. Responsibility for the chancel traditionally lay with the patron of the living, Earl Manvers. In 1850, the second earl had arranged for minor repairs to be carried out. Thomas Eastwood supplied stone and did repair work around the south doorway costing £1.7s.9d, while George Bell repaired and pointed the walls, and did some slating which came to £5.2s.10d. The Manvers papers record costs in great detail foɹ this period, including John Brice's shilling for repairs to leading, and Thomas Allcock's 7d for sharpening four hammers and three chisels. Minor repairs were not enough, however, and in July 1857 a faculty was sought for a new chancel in the early English style, with a vestry and organ gallery on the north, and a south aisle chapel. A stone screen with clustered shafts and open tracery was added to separate the chancel from the south aisle, and two parclose screens were added on the north side near the new organ gallery. (The organ was formerly in the west gallery). A stained glass triplet window by Hardman was inserted above the altar, and the floors were paved with the best Staffordshire tiles. Externally, Bulwell stone was relieved with bluestone bands round the building and over the arches. The architect was Charles Bailey of Newark-on-Trent, and the builders were Messrs Denvelt of Nottingham.

The chancel area was also reseated at this time in pitch pine. In the front of one of the parish registers Robert Burgess drew up a plan to show who was entitled to the new seats. Behind himself came 'C. Wright Esqr' of the banking family then living at Lamcote House. Less prestigious names followed, with four or five families in a row, and one, two or three seats reserved for each of a total of forty families. (Perhaps Robert Burgess was not particularly happy about the allocation of seats, for in January 1866 he was listed as an attender at a meeting in favour of abolishing the pew system.) According to White's *Directory* for 1864 the new chancel area had added 120 seats to the church. Altogether 427 could now be seated on the ground floor and 100 in the gallery.

On April 20th 1858 the church reopened with a dignified clerical procession and a communion service supported with 'hearty' choral accompaniments. The total cost amounted to £1,200, of which £300 had been provided by Lord Manvers. (Presumably the building of the side chapel was not part of his responsibility.) The *Nottingham Journal* reported that the rest had been 'munificently provided by the Reverend Robert Burgess, whose labours and liberality' were 'right nobly appreciated'. It is little wonder that the bishop, at the end of a lengthy sermon, urged the congregation at the opening to contribute generously to relieve the vicar of his financial burden. There was a remarkable response: £617.18s.1d was collected that morning and over £100 at the evening service. Perhaps it had all proved too much, for 'it was the subject of universal regret that severe indisposition prevented the excellent vicar from taking any prominent part in the celebration'.

The church faculty also allowed for the enclosure of part of the churchyard and the removal of headstones and monuments where necessary. A bill for the levelling of church walks and 'sod' came to £2.8s.6d in 1858, and Mr Blatherwick was paid 1s.6d for watering. Other items in the churchwardens' accounts for 1857 suggest that windows and stonework in the main part of the church, and the churchyard wall, were also given some attention as if to make the whole worthy of the new chancel. All such alterations and rebuilding were typical of a period when the church of England was being revitalised. Locally, All Saints, Bingham, was completely restored by Sir Giles Gilbert Scott in 1845, while St Mary's at Bleasby was restored in 1845, 1852 and extensively in 1869 by Ewan Christian. One other cause was taken up by Robert Burgess - the organ. Although it had already been improved by Groves of London, a sermon was preached in aid of the organ fund in November 1861. In November 1871 it was enlarged and improved by Lloyd and Dudgeon of Nottingham.

A critical parishioner

Despite all these improvements not everyone was satisfied with the quality of services held in St Mary's. Mr N.H. Pownall, a professional gardener and campaigner in the abstinence movement, was sufficiently roused to express his views in the *Nottingham Journal* in March 1872. He gives an interesting insight into the Sunday morning routine. After complaining of the tediousness of church services, he felt that even the clergy must dread such a morning's work. His letter continues:

> *And how the poor Sunday school children in the gallery manage, or can be expected to manage to behave decently, is a wonder to me, seeing that they have been at school an hour or an hour and a half at scripture lesson before they come to church. Surely, surely something can be done to make our church services what they ought and were originally intended to be - short, hearty, earnest exercises of prayer, worship and praise.*

The death of Robert Burgess

Nevertheless, Robert Burgess seems to have been remembered with affection by his parishioners. The ill-health which marred his attendance at the opening of the chancel continued. In August 1862 the *Nottingham Journal* reported that on medical advice he and his wife were setting off on a three months' holiday. His death at 2 a.m. on December 18th 1873 was recorded by the schoolmaster who described him as 'much beloved and respected'. He was buried in the cemetery which he had helped to create, and in due course £200 was raised by public subscription for a stained glass west window to his memory in the church. He had been vicar for twenty-eight years and was aged only 54 when he died.

The church photographed before 1878

John Cullen 1874-1914

It was John Cullen, an Irishman claiming descent from one of the great families of Cullens of the fifth century, who was to change the face of Radcliffe. Born in 1838, he was the son of a country gentleman of Newport, County Tipperary. After studying at St. Aiden's and Trinity College, Dublin, he became curate in 1865 at St. George's, Wigan, in Lancashire, and was then at Knipton in Leicestershire (where he married in 1869) from 1867 to 1869. For the next five years he held a curacy at Bottesford in Leicestershire, and then took up his post in Radcliffe on February 2nd 1874, when the school was closed so that a welcoming tea party could be arranged in his honour. He arrived with a German wife, Leontine (Dorndinger), who was the daughter of a barrister, and two children - a three-year old daughter, Evelyn, and a baby son, Cecil, who was also to become a clergyman. A third child, Frederick Adolph, who died at the age of six months, is commemorated on a diamond-shaped brass plate in the former baptistry of the church. By 1881 the vicarage household was completed by a young German governess, Agneta Roether, a housemaid and a cook.

The Rev. Dr. Cullen.

The Reverend John Cullen

The new broom

Something of a scholar and minor poet - in 1869 he had published *Horae Poeticae*, a collection of poems mainly written in his youth - John Cullen was also 'a man of very strong and pronounced views' who, according to a newspaper article, delivered 'his conviction without any hesitation'. However adequately the parish had been run by Robert Burgess, it was now to be energetically organised. From the first, the church records were put in order. A Preacher's Book was provided to record the names of visiting preachers and readers, as well as notes about collections. His inscription at the front mildly reproved his predecessors:

> *This book was bought by the Churchwardens in order that a record of all preachers may be kept, to comply with the law as laid down in the 52 canons. No book had been kept previously; or if so, it cannot be found.*

In 1868 compulsory payment of church rates had been abolished and perhaps because of this Robert Burgess's churchwardens do not appear to have kept up their accounts from the end of 1869. John Cullen made sure they were reintroduced from April 1875. (The day-to-day expenses of the church were now funded out of offertories.) Early in 1876 he helped inaugurate a local branch of the Church of England Temperance Society, and he began a parochial magazine in 1877. He also encouraged the Young Men's Christian Association, as well as coal and clothing clubs in the village. There was some early criticism, however, of the lack of church decoration for the harvest festival compared to the time of his predecessor when it 'was hardly to be excelled in the county'. In contrast, complained a writer to the *Nottingham Journal* in September 1874, there were only 'two wreaths of corn (very clumsily put together) hung across the stone pulpit', a few cut flowers and some plants in pots. There seems to have been less music too, for the Radcliffe choir was no longer listed as participating in choral festivals.

The influence of Frances Burnside

John Cullen's interests were to lie in a more evangelising direction, and in November 1875 his parishioners were shaken out of any religious complacency by the organisation of a 'mission' in the village. The zeal needed for this was partially provided by a prestigious resident, Frances Burnside of Lamcote House. The third of four daughters of the Rev John Burnside, rector of Plumtree until 1865, and sister of the current rector, Frances was recorded in 1871 as living with two of her sisters, Mary and Julia, and waited on by eleven servants. (Julia was married to a Burnside cousin, and the absent eldest sister, Adelaide Ann, seems to have been the owner of Lamcote House.) In a memoir written at the time of Frances's death, the Rev W.H. Aitken explained that at the beginning of 1875 she had gone with her sisters to the seaside where they had attended a mission which had had a profound effect on her. After some hesitation she had plucked up enough courage to return to the mission church and acknowledge her conversion, and when she and her sisters had returned home 'all the country-side was astonished at the change'. Her own household was 'revolutionised' and all its members soon professed 'to have accepted the salvation of God'. Frances at once 'took counsel with the vicar' about the furtherance of parish work. As a result, a weekly prayer meeting was established in preparation for the forthcoming Radcliffe mission, and each Monday morning John Cullen held a brief service of prayer, reading and exposition at Lamcote House. Frances herself led a bible class for young women on Sunday afternoons and a meeting for mothers on Mondays. She and her sisters attended all church services and went round the parish house by house testifying to the salvation she had experienced.

Radcliffe's first mission 1875

The first mission began with an address to communicants in the schoolroom on Saturday, November 6th 1875, and from the Sunday to the following Friday special services were conducted by the Rev William Aitken, with John Cullen in support as reader. In a circular to parishioners he urged attendance, describing the mission as

> *...an aggressive movement - a special effort on the part of the Church of Christ to increase and extend the knowledge of God, and to convert men... Come quickly... Come frequently... Come as you are... Let me also entreat you to use your influence with your friends; ask them to come. Encourage those who are timid, or ashamed, or unwilling, to come. If you know of any persons who live in sin, or who are careless and indifferent, ask them to come...*

Such missions had become a feature of the established church in response to the dynamic tactics of both nonconformists and Roman Catholics. Moreover, Radcliffe's mission followed the arrival in England of American revivalists I. Sankey and D.L. Moody in 1873. Altogether seven autumn missions were recorded in the Radcliffe *Preacher's Book.* (The others were in 1880, 1883, 1890, 1898, 1904 and 1907. There may have been more, for in 1912 John Cullen claimed there had been nine.) He was well satisfied with the outcome of the first, noting that 'many souls were added to the church,' and that the number of communicants had doubled. As regular attendance figures are not available it is impossible to judge how long-term the effects were.

The death of Frances Burnside

Soon after the Radcliffe mission another was held 'in a neighbouring large town'. Frances Burnside threw herself into the work for this with the same energy that she had shown in Radcliffe. Within weeks she lay dying. A few hours before her death she remembered to send a religious book to a sick child, and then with her voice failing

> *she managed to express what her wishes were; and her last act on earth was to grasp the pen with her poor trembling, dying hands, in order to sign a paper which was to give a considerable sum to the cause of God.*

It was probably the mission and not Radcliffe which benefited from this. (Probate records show that her sisters declared that the value of her effects did not exceed £80,000.)

She was aged 46 when she died. Her funeral on January 1st 1876 was an impressive affair. The cortege left Radcliffe in the rain, and bells tolled in both Radcliffe and Cotgrave as she was taken to the Burnside vault at Plumtree. By the time John Cullen conducted the service there the weather was fair. On the following day Radcliffe church was draped in black for services to her memory, and he subsequently published the two sermons he preached: *The Watcher on the Shore* and *The Work of Life's Day and the Night of Death.* Her work for the church in Radcliffe was eventually commemorated by a brass eagle lectern given by her sister Adelaide Ann, by a window inscribed to her memory in the south aisle, and by an inscribed silver chalice decorated with jewels. (She was commemorated in Plumtree church by an organ presented by her nephew, and by stained glass windows on the south side of the chancel.) Her surviving sisters, particularly Adelaide Ann, continued to work for the church and to carry out benevolent acts in the village.

The decision to rebuild the church

When the idea of enlarging St Mary's church first came to John Cullen is not clear, but the Church of England was still encouraging rebuilding work, and it may be significant that Plumtree church had been restored in 1873-4, while Holme Pierrepont, Cotgrave and Shelford churches all re-opened in 1878 after restoration. On Sunday November 4th 1877 the following notice was posted on the church door:

> *A church Vestry Meeting will be held at the Church Schools, Radcliffe-on-Trent, at 4 o'clock p.m. on Thursday Nov. 8th 1877 to consider as to the advisability of enlarging the Parish church, and of deciding upon the best means of carrying it out.*

It was signed by the churchwardens, J.B. Taylor and Frederick Wright.

On the following Thursday John Cullen chaired a meeting of fourteen prominent male parishioners headed by the two churchwardens. (Frederick Wright was a banker whose family had formerly occupied Lamcote House and who now lived at Radcliffe Lodge, and John Taylor was a magistrate from Radcliffe Hall.) The others were William Sanday, the builder of Cliff House and now a retired farmer; James Gorse, a hosiery yarn agent living at the Manor House; Richard Daft, the former cricketer and currently a cricket outfitter and brewer living in what is now Walker's Yard; Simon Eastwood, a stonemason on Bingham Road; George Turner, the postmaster, carriage-builder and general jack-of-all-trades from the corner of Water Lane and the main street; John Green, the farmer occupying The Chestnuts; Thomas Stone, an 'agricultural horseman' living on Vicarage Lane; brothers Samuel and Thomas Barratt, nurserymen of Bingham Road and Cropwell Road respectively; Henry Parr, owner of the Black Lion and a joiner living on Bingham Road; Robert Millington, a sack and canvas manufacturer living on Shelford Road near Chestnut Grove; and Henry Palin, a farmer from the corner of Cropwell Road and the main street.

It was this socially mixed but affluent group who took the decision not merely to extend, but to sweep away what remained of the medieval church and to replace it with a fundamentally new building. With the exception of John Taylor of the Hall who was 65 and William Sanday of Cliff House who was aged 60, they were very much of John Cullen's own generation. The youngest of the rest was Samuel Barratt at 30, and the oldest was 49-year-old James Gorse. The vicar himself was 39. They gave the following reasons for their decision:

> *In consequence of the now rapidly increasing number of houses and inhabitants in Radcliffe and of the Congregations at the Parish Church having lately very materially been augmented, and also taking into consideration that there is every prospect of the village becoming much larger than it is now, it is considered advisable that the Parish Church should be enlarged as speedily as possible, so as to provide sufficient Church accommodation for the people.*

The effect of the recent mission may have partially accounted for the increase in attendance mentioned in the statement.

A committee was instantly set up consisting of the vicar, churchwardens and seven from the first meeting: Messrs Sanday, Daft, Gorse, Green, Samuel Barratt, Millington and Parr. They were joined by four more: Samuel Bell, the builder and landlord of the Manvers Arms; John George Willey, a former provisions merchant living on Bingham Road; Samuel Cave Tomlinson, headmaster of a small boarding school; and William Rockley, a retired builder from Bailey Lane. Charles Buckland, a hosier living at Northcote House on Bingham Road, and his neighbour John Goodwin, a bank manager from Salisbury Cottages, were later added to the committee. John Cullen was its secretary, Richard Daft assistant secretary, and Frederick Wright, the banker, was appropriately made treasurer. A record of their meetings was kept in a book now deposited in the County Archives Office. At first sight it appears to be intact, but on closer inspection it is clear that certain pages are missing, perhaps only coincidentally at times of controversy.

Early pledges of money

The first consideration was money. By the meeting on November 8th pledges amounting to £1,800 had already been made. Mary Burnside, the late Frances's sister, headed the list with £800. Her sister Adelaide promised £500, Frederick Wright £400, and John Cullen himself £100. By November 28th these substantial sums had been boosted by £500 from Lord Manvers. There was also the promise of a new organ from William Burnside, the nephew of the Lamcote sisters. On March 19th 1878 still more pledges were announced: Adelaide Burnside was increasing her donation to £800 to match her sister's, and Frederick Wright was raising his to £600. The meeting received the news with 'thanks and acclamation'. As it was not intended that the new building should cost more than £3,000, and as grants were often made for church work, it must have seemed that the target was within easy reach. In order to raise the rest of the money, the village was divided into three areas, with two canvassers calling on each house. Richard Daft and Thomas Stone were to cover the area from Palin Row to Shelford Road, including Station Terrace and Shelford Road itself; James Gorse and John Willey were to go from Shelford Road to Lamcote House and back by Water Lane; William Sanday and Samuel Barratt were to visit Hogg Lane, Mount Pleasant and all the central block of the village. There was no doubting the committee's energy.

Dispute over free seats

One other issue was thrashed out at this preliminary stage. The sums promised at the first meeting were all on condition that a considerable number of church sittings would be free. At first, on Frederick Wright's suggestion, it was agreed that empty seats should be considered free after the organ had ceased playing before each service. (When Radcliffe Lodge, Wright's home, had been sold earlier in the century, a seat in the church was advertised as part of the sale.) This did not go far enough for the more radical on the committee, including John Cullen himself. On November 18th 1877 the matter was again 'discussed in an earnest and animated manner'. There was a clear division between those who thought that nobody should have the right to a particular seat and those led by John Taylor, the churchwarden from Radcliffe Hall, who wanted some privilege retained. He suggested that one-third of the seats could be appropriated, and the rest free. At this point, he had to leave the meeting 'on some urgent and pressing business'. Richard Daft went with him. In their absence, the rest of the committee looked at the matter 'from every point of view' and resolved that all seats in the enlarged church should be considered free. At the meeting on February 13th 1878 John Cullen drove home his victory by reading extracts from a volume on the law of church seats lent him by Mr Harford, a Manchester coroner who was secretary of the Free and Open Church Society. He offered to lend the book to anyone who was interested. No takers are recorded.

Competition to find an architect

It was agreed that the enlarged church should hold 700 people, all on the ground floor, as opposed to the 527 of the existing church, including 100 in the gallery. No galleries were to be allowed. (A pamphlet published in 1841 giving advice to churchwardens had categorically stated, 'Galleries are altogether bad.') More light was needed in the church, and a larger organ chamber for the promised new organ. The advertisement announcing a competition for an architect was to be placed three times in three Nottingham papers and in the *Architect*. Designs, in accordance with the Church Building Societies' regulations, were to be submitted 'under a motto or mark' with the name of the architect in a sealed envelope to the vicar by February 1st 1878, and a premium of £10 was to be given to the architect whose plans were adopted.

Twelve designs were received. The committee examined them on Wednesday February 13th, and for the next three days they were available for the parishioners to see. Three designs came nearest to the committee's requirements, and an outside architect, E.W. Godwin of London, was called in to make the final choice. He selected the design labelled *Spes*. Although some modifications would be needed, he was optimistic that these could be carried out within the £3,000 limit. 'The Envelope containing the name of the design so marked was then opened by the vicar when it was found to be Messrs Goddard and Paget of Leicester.'

Three building stages planned

The amendments suggested by the London architect were basically agreed by Goddard and the committee on March 19th. In May the tender of Barlow Brothers of Oakham, building contractors, was approved provided they could find two acceptable sureties. In fact the proposed bondsmen were not entirely to the committee's satisfaction, but after assurances from Goddard and Paget it was agreed that Barlow Brothers should be hired. (As it turned out, the Radcliffe committee's misgivings were justified.) On June 28th the faculty from the bishop was granted which allowed the work to be carried out in three stages.

Stage 1 entailed taking down the existing north and west walls of the church and tower, restoring the south walls, and forming an entirely new nave, aisles, porch and baptistry. In this stage the tower was only to be rebuilt to the height of the north aisle. Re-flooring and re-seating were to be included. When the faculty had been applied for, the anticipated cost of this stage had already been as much as £2,940. This figure was instantly out of date. Goddard and Paget's new estimate was £3,290 - well over the original limit for the whole scheme.

Stage 2, at an estimated cost of £800, involved the extension of the new north wall to form vestries for choir and clergy, an organ loft and chamber, and a heating chamber beneath. Despite the new chancel of 1858, the triplet east window was to be changed to let in more light, two new windows put in the south chapel, a row of seats removed to make room for a nave entrance, and the altar space improved and enlarged. A new pulpit, lectern and reading desk were to be provided. (The existing pulpit and desk dated from 1852.) The work on this stage was not to start until the greater part of the money had been raised. It was this stage, with some suggested additions, that was going to prove particularly controversial.

Stage 3 dealt with the completion of the tower (how was not specified), the general restoration of defective masonry, iron and woodwork, and other alterations and improvements. A total of £741 was estimated for this work.

Escalating costs

Goddard and Paget's 'whole' tender now stood at £4,831. This was £350 more than the estimate in the faculty, and about £1,800 more than the top limit they had originally been given by the committee. And they had not done yet. While they would deduct £350 for the old material and a further £25 if the work was done in one contract, there would inevitably be extra costs. For example, they recommended that the seating should be in pitch pine instead of deal - for another £100. Ancaster instead of Bath stone would be another £25. If items such as heating, gas fittings, and the pulpit were to be covered, then £5,000 would be needed. That was on May 13th. On July 31st they submitted some additional estimates to include a new widened chancel arch and extra tombs. Depending on how many stages were eventually carried out, the extra cost could be as little as £85 or as much as £600. The committee's financial optimism of the previous March must have been badly shaken. On August 8th they decided to abandon the chancel part of the scheme because of 'insufficiency of funds', deciding 'it wd not be prudent to anticipate an increase to them to the extent that wd have been required'. Despite some further hesitation about this, the chancel of today's church therefore remains essentially the work of Robert Burgess.

Goddard and Paget's design for the chancel in 1879 (reduced).
The window shown never replaced the existing lancet windows
(Nottinghamshire Archives Office, RT1/1-4S.
Reproduced by permission of the Principal Archivist)

Dispute over the chancel window

Another reason for modifying the chancel scheme concerned the triplet east window. It appears from the minutes that the 'restoration' of this would have meant its removal to the west end of the church and its replacement by a larger one. When doubts had been first expressed about the chancel stage in May, it had been suggested that the larger window might be used at the west end of the church instead, and by leaving the chancel window where it was the architects would knock £10 off their estimate.

While the committee was still hesitating about what to do, William Sanday received a letter from Robert Burgess's widow and her two sisters strongly objecting to any plan which involved the removal of the east window. Although evidence from the minutes and from newspapers is incomplete, it can be deduced that Mrs Burgess was one of three Marriott sisters whose father had at one time lived at Lamcote House and who had committed suicide while in Leicestershire in 1857. The chancel window may have been provided by or been dedicated to him, hence the family's objection to its removal. (Alternatively, they may have simply been objecting to the alteration to Robert Burgess's work.) The committee, feeling that their intentions had been misunderstood, wrote to the sisters and explained that it was the architects who had recommended the window's removal in order to let in more light. This was to no avail, and on August 7th the committee had to acknowledge that the scheme was 'extremely repugnant' to the feelings of the three women. At the same time they hastened to add that they had never actually come to any conclusion about the window's removal. When the Marriott family's solicitor formally confirmed their opposition, the committee abandoned any thoughts of the scheme, recognising that the faculty did not give them powers to go ahead against objectors. This change from the original plan complicated matters, however, since it would have to be approved by the Incorporated Society of Architects in order not to jeopardise a grant. It was perhaps as a way of placating Mrs Burgess that the committee decided in October that there should be a collection for a west window dedicated to her husband, costing between £100 and £120. (The sum of £200 was reputedly raised.) Goddard and Paget sent in an estimate for £56, presumably for a more modest version than the one they had originally intended for the chancel. This west window survives today as Robert Burgess's memorial.

Indecision about the chancel

Although the committee had apparently abandoned the main part of the chancel alterations on August 6th, they constantly wavered over the matter. On August 26th they had a long discussion with Mr Goddard about whether some aspects of this stage could after all be incorporated into stages 1 and 3. In particular, they wanted to retain the heating and organ chambers, and even the raising of the chancel arch. The latter was not only structurally difficult but expensive. After the architect had left, the committee discussed finances and 'found them to be so much more serious than contemplated' that it was unanimously decided that it would 'not be wise' to undertake any additional work beyond what was absolutely necessary. The heating chamber might qualify for this, but not the alteration to the arch which was rejected for the second time on September 5th. The committee, however, was not noted for its firmness of purpose. The matter should have been discussed again early in February 1879 but was 'postponed!' At a special meeting on February 17th it was decided to go ahead at an estimated cost of £190. Lord Manvers had come to the rescue with a donation of £160, and he was given a vote of thanks for 'so kindly meeting the wishes of the committee respecting the chancel arch'. (He also contributed £70 in 1883 for further work in the chancel.)

Appointment of a clerk of works

On June 4th 1878 John Cullen was asked to write to Goddard and Paget to ask if the £2 a week which they would charge for providing a clerk of works would include all expenses and sufficient attendance to see that the work was properly done. The figure clearly seemed high to a committee faced with mounting costs. One of their number, Henry Parr the joiner, made a verbal application for the post on June 13th at the bargain rate of 25s a week. He left the room and the committee agreed in his absence that he would be competent to do the job, 'it being understood that Mr Parr be not paid should anything occur to render....' At this point the page ends and there is a gap in the minutes. In the light of controversy to come, the suspicion must arise that some pages were deliberately removed.

Quarrel over the organ

In July the committee heard that William Burnside of Gedling House was having second thoughts about giving the organ he had offered. Almost certainly it had been intended as a memorial to his aunt Frances, but Radcliffe, it seemed, had received his offer ungraciously (perhaps because the existing organ had been improved as recently as 1871), and word had reached him that the committee 'would prefer a gift of money'. Hastily the committee passed a vote 'that the original offer of an Organ was not to be deviated from'. Optimistically they wrote to William Burnside in August asking him to come over with the organ builder to meet the committee and discuss arrangements for adapting the existing chamber. Mr Burnside, however, was not to be placated. He sent a curt note to Frederick Wright:

> The Organ question must remain till my aunts come home. It is a very sore subject of no pleasure now. I am very much annoyed indeed & did not [think] I should be so treated.

The committee's humble response is recorded in the minute book on August 29:

The committee beg to acknowledge the receipt of Mr William Burnside's letter in reply to the resolution passed by the committee in reference to the Organ & exceedingly regret that any doubt shd have been expressed to Mr Burnside that the Organ would not be acceptable, the committee wish Mr Burnside distinctly to understand that they have never entertained any idea but one of full appreciation of such a noble offer & look forward with hope to its realisation.

Their hopes were not to be fulfilled. On August 31st William Burnside settled the question, laying the blame for the dispute at the door of the churchwarden, John Taylor of Radcliffe Hall:

I have decided not to give the Organ or any money after Mr Taylor's remarks. I may put a small window in the south aisle if my aunts have no objection.

The matter was raised at the committee meeting on September 5th, but as John Taylor was absent it was decided to postpone the discussion until the next meeting, called by special circular. The page is missing on which any minutes from this meeting would have been recorded. Radcliffe did get the memorial window to Frances Burnside, but Plumtree seems to have got the organ. The committee must have regretted John Taylor's expensive lack of tact, for a new organ had to be bought in 1880 from Lloyd & Co. for £53.16s.

Interim arrangements

The problem of how to cope with a congregation while the church was out of commission was solved by Frederick Wright's purchase of twelve dozen chairs at £1 a dozen from a firm in Birmingham for use in the schoolroom. The two guineas which it cost to licence the room for services came out of the church restoration fund. John Taylor was to approach Mr Bosworth about the care and cleaning of the clock and ask if the addition of chimes for the quarters was possible. James Gorse was to contact Taylor's of Loughborough about arrangements for the bells. Estimates for several sizes were received by the end of July.

Building problems

With plans mainly decided, a clerk of works appointed and arrangements made for services, the actual building work began some time in the autumn of 1878. The project then faced the uncontrollable hazard of the climate. Cold weather set in early and brought the building work to a standstill. On December 26th the committee agreed that because of the delay caused by the long frost the builders should be given an extension of three months beyond the time originally stipulated. They felt less charitable in the new year. By February 28th they had inspected the site and found 'the damage done by the weather much more serious than was expected'. Their immediate reaction was to cancel a payment of £400 to the contractors, although they soon thought better of this, and to send a telegram to the architects urging them to come over from Leicester and examine the state of the stone.

In the meantime, this reaction had prompted the contractors to get Pictor and Sons, Bath stone merchants, to comment on the quality of stone they had supplied. They claimed that although the Corsham stone, damaged in the recent severe frosts, was more suited to internal than to external work, it was extensively used all over England and they had supplied thousands of feet in Nottingham. Newly produced stone was especially vulnerable, and the preceding winter had been the worst for twenty-five years. Nevertheless, now the worst was over, they felt sure that the stone would ultimately give the committee satisfaction.

The architects first sent a clerk of works to inspect the site. He immediately advised that all work should stop until further inspection had taken place. Mr Clifton, their senior clerk of works, then came, and a report was submitted before the committee meeting of March 13th exonerating the workmanship and materials:

We have made a careful examination of the dilapidations at the church now being rebuilt at Radcliffe-on-Trent and find that the damage has been caused entirely by the very severe frost acting upon the wet stonework, and is not in any way due to bad workmanship or material. The perished portion must be carefully and judiciously cut out and new stone reinserted.

However, the report had to acknowledge that there had been some malpractice:

> *It is to be regretted that the foreman of the Masons thought it proper to attempt to hide the defective work by plastering it up after the work was stopped by our Clerk; but with this exception we have no fault to find with the work.*
>
> *We apprehend no difficulty in properly restoring and making the masonry in every way strong and substantial but careful supervision will be necessary.*

This last point touched on one of the committee's own weaknesses.

Disagreement about site supervision

Their decision to appoint their own man, Henry Parr the joiner, as clerk of works at a lower fee than would have been required by Goddard and Paget's clerk was now questioned. The architects implied that this supervision had been inadequate:

> *We strongly advise that a thoroughly competent person be employed to examine the work and give instructions once or twice a week whilst the stonework is in hand and we beg to suggest that Mr Clifton our Senior Clerk of the Works be appointed to this office.*

His charges would be £1 a day and 3rd class travelling expenses - a considerable increase on the 25s a week that Henry Parr was charging, even if visits were kept to a minimum. With Henry Parr at the meeting, the committee discussed the suggestion and turned it down. Goddard and Paget's response was chilly in the extreme:

> *We ..... regret that you have not thought proper to take our advice as regards the employment of a competent Clerk of Works to superintend the necessary repairs to the church through the stone-work being damaged by frost. This being the case we must decline any responsibility as regards the repairs. It is important that you should instruct your Clerk of Works to be there the whole of the time the men are at work, & see that he perfectly understands <u>our</u> orders & properly carries them out.*

The committee's response was equally icy. They could not 'relieve Messrs Goddard & Paget from the responsibility of the execution of the repairs .....' and suggested 'a frequent personal supervision on the part of the architects'. This slur on the conduct of the architects was not allowed to pass unanswered. They wrote to Richard Daft on March 25th, instructing the committee about the role of an architect, pointing out that he could not be held responsible for defective work, nor could he be in frequent attendance on the site.

> *It is therefore important that a competent overlooker should be employed to carry out the instructions of the Architect in his absence, and thus insure the work being properly done. We consider that the Clerk of Works you have employed is not sufficiently acquainted with stone work to undertake the supervision of the repairs required by damage done by the frost.*

While blaming the frost rather than the clerk himself for the situation, the architect pointed out that the delay caused by the correspondence could be 'seriously imperilling the stability of the building'. In the face of this the committee's resolve crumbled and they agreed to employ the architects' clerk once a week, but in conjunction with their own Henry Parr.

Leicester
March 25th 1879

To Mr Richard Daft.

Radcliffe Church.

Dear Sir,

It is evident that the Committee's ideas do not agree with ours as to the duties of an Architect

The small percentage that an Architect receives is for drawings and general superintendance, but certainly he cannot be held responsible in any way for defective work. It is of course impossible he should be always on the building, neither can he be expected to visit himself, or send any competent person to examine the works, even should he consider it necessary, more than once a fortnight.

If more than this attention on the part of the Architect is required, in consequence of the non employment or incompetency of the Clerk of Works, then the Architect is allowed to charge for his visits according to the time expended, extra and above the usual commissions.

It is therefore important that a competent overlooker should be employed to carry out the instruction of the Architect in his absence, and thus ensure the work being properly done.

we consider that the Clerk of Works you have employed is not sufficiently acquainted with stone work to undertake the supervision of the repairs required by damage done by the frost.

This we have before explained to you, and we suggested to you in our report, what appeared to us the best way of getting rid of the difficulty.

We do not now, nor have we at any time imputed blame to the Clerk of Works, and should not have considered extra supervision necessary had not such serious damage been done by the frost, and extra care been required to see that the masons properly make good the defects

In the meantime we must remind you that the works are being proceeded with, and the delay caused by this correspondence may be seriously imperilling the stability of the building.

We remain
Yours faithfully
Goddard & Paget.

Goddard & Paget
Leicester
March 25

A letter from the architects Goddard and Paget, March 25th 1879, disagreeing with the restoration committee about the supervision of building work (reduced)

(Nottinghamshire Archives Office, PR 2898.
Reproduced by permission of the Principal Archivist)

New heating system

In addition to the alteration to the chancel arch, a new heating chamber and system was to be retained from the original stage 2 of the rebuilding scheme. Even this was not plain sailing. Goddard and Paget favoured a system using a small boiler and hot water pipes about 4 inches in diameter. The committee, however, were impressed with the so-called 'hot air' system in use in Bingham church. When the architects looked into this they felt that it was probably unsuitable for Radcliffe because the height of the chancel would not allow a sufficient height of flue, unlike the tower of Bingham church. The controversy over the supervision of the building was then at its height and it seems that the committee was determined to get its way over something. A Mr Peach prepared a hot air scheme similar to that in use in Bingham and on March 20th this was compared with Goddard and Paget's hot water plan. Mr Peach's scheme was chosen.

Final financing and the reopening of the church

From April 1879 financial matters became more pressing. The contractors asked for a further payment so the treasurer, Frederick Wright, was asked 'to get in some more of the promised subscriptions'. This hand-to-mouth financing could not cope when in October Barlow Brothers requested another £500. The committee protested that this was unjustified 'considering the amount of work yet to be done'. Even if the work were completed and handed over they were at a loss to know how such a sum would be justified. At first they were prepared to offer £300. When nothing was heard from the contractors they declared they were not prepared to make any further payment until additional work specified by the architects was done. On Goddard and Paget's intervention, however, they offered £200, less £50 to the architects for some iron work.

At this point, October 22nd 1879, the committee assessed the financial situation. After the £200 had been paid they would be left with a mere £16.17s.11d in hand but with £800-worth of work still to be done. There was nothing for it but to take out a bond which would allow them to overdraw their bank account to that amount. This meant that members of the committee were personally responsible for the debt. Frederick Wright, as a bank partner, could not sign the bond, but in the following January he added to his existing donations by giving £20 per year for three years to help cover this.

Although the documents are by no means complete, the explanation for Barlow Brothers' silence and erratic charging becomes clear. By the middle of 1880 they had gone bankrupt, with Goddard and Paget handling their affairs. An account of August 6th indicates that they were in liquidation. Presumably the severe winter of 1878-9 had hampered their business, and the Radcliffe committee's initial hesitation in accepting them as contractors had proved justified.

As early as November 1879 services could again be held in the church and the chairs specially purchased for use in the schoolroom sold off. A special service was conducted by the Bishop of Nottingham on Thursday November 6th 1879 at 2.30 p.m. In the evening, the Hon W. Byron M.A., now married to Mary Burnside, was due to preach, but being ill the service was conducted by the Rector of St Nicholas in Nottingham instead. A notice for these services and those on the following Sunday ends with the following message:

Liberal offerings are earnestly requested from all who attend the Service as a large debt remains on the Church.

Fundraising and the settling of bills were to continue to dominate church activities for the next few years. The chancel work still had to be completed. As the original east window had been retained, it still seemed dark, so the earlier scheme for additional windows in the north wall and in the side chapel was carried out. These were donated by Lord Manvers. According to the *Nottingham Journal* the whole chancel and chapel was painted a light blush buff with Morse's new invention 'Calcarium', described as something between oils and water colours. There was also new flooring, new clergy seats and desks for £30, and a reredos from Jones and Willis of Birmingham for £60. Bills were carefully scrutinised. Overcharging on the west window and on the chancel arch was instantly spotted. From December 1878 the 'ladies' had organised bazaars and sales of work, raising a total of £747.9s.9d. Concerts raised £31.10s, offertories another £262.7s.6d. On June 6th 1882 the *Nottingham Journal* announced that a lady from India had given a piece of Cashmere needlework, valued at 30 guineas, to Mrs Cullen to be sold for the restoration fund. When John Cullen's biblical poem in five cantos, *The Captivity*, was published in 1883, it too was sold in aid of the rebuilding at 1s a copy.

On January 8th 1883, the committee met in the schoolroom for the last time. Goddard and Paget's final bill had been paid in the previous October, and although the chancel was not reopened until November 8th 1883, and bills for internal fittings continued throughout 1884, the committee's work was basically accomplished. The final balance sheet for the structural work, including two new bells, showed an expenditure of £5,094. 15s.2d. The greatest part of the income came from donations totalling £3,507. 5s.6d, headed by Adelaide Burnside's final sum of £955. The Church Building Society gave a grant of £120. Altogether £5,106. 18s.8d was raised.

Design of the tower

At no point in the documents is the controversial 'saddle-back' tower of the completed building mentioned. Goddard and Paget's surviving plan and sectional drawings leave the design of the tower vague. Their 'Abstracted Specification' of April 1878 mentions the existing tower as one of the parts of the church to be carefully taken down and stacked on the ground ready for re-use. It seems unlikely that so unusual a design would have been passed without comment by a village committee used to a castellated tower or to traditional spires. Perhaps such discussion was recorded on pages missing from the minute book. The story accepted in Radcliffe is that the German-French character of the rebuilt tower was due to the influence of John Cullen's German wife, Leontine, who wished to be reminded of home. Certainly it does not seem to have been part of the original design.

Reaction to the striking new landmark was not wholly favourable. On September 1st 1887 the *Nottingham Daily Express* published an article which referred to St. Mary's church as a monument to the 'energy, zeal and determination' of the vicar, while describing the previous building as 'very poor, inconvenient and unsightly'. A correspondent signing himself M.R. vehemently disagreed:

Now, whatever the moderns may think of it, the inhabitants in general have more respect for the old church, as it had been greatly improved in its interior, as well as enlarged, during the incumbency of the late vicar, Mr Burgess. Its tower was more to be admired than the saddle-backed one of the present church.

The completed church about 1905

Towards the end of his life even John Cullen had doubts about the saddle-back tower. In the back of the church vestry minute book he recorded his ideas in 1910 for the further improvement of the church. These included the following:

> A spire should be erected on the Tower, which would be a splendid landmark for miles around, and would look fine. The Tower would not support a stone spire, so it should be of oak, covered with lead shingles. The stones of the gables of the present Tower should be used as buttresses to the lower part of the Tower .....

A less dramatic idea was put to the parish council on March 28th 1911:

> Mr Godber suggested that a suitable thing to do in commemoration of the coronation of King George V would be to improve the Church Tower by taking off the saddletop and finishing the tower with a parapet instead.

The resolution was passed. If it had been carried out the removal of the saddle-back would doubtless have provoked as much controversy as its retention.

Radcliffe's religious census 1882

On January 1st 1882 Radcliffe held its own religious census. (The total population in 1881 had been 1704.) Worshippers at St. Mary's totalled 267 in the morning and 293 in the evening. The old church would easily have accommodated either congregation. Worse still from the Anglican point of view, the Primitive and Wesleyan Methodists jointly attracted more attenders - 280 in the morning and 338 in the evening. The *Nottingham Journal* in reporting these figures drew comfort from the fact that after all adjustments had been made for duplicate attendance and for those unable to attend, then 779 people had attended a church service on that Sunday - 45% of the population - and only 7% of potential attenders were absent.

On January 6th the paper published a letter from *Dubitans*, a former Radcliffe resident, who expressed doubts about the piety of his old neighbours:

> I know that they are the best people on earth, except, perhaps Binghamers; but I very much doubt indeed if 547 adults of Radcliffe went to church and chapel in the morning of last Sunday, and 631 adults in the evening. I doubt that very much - very much indeed.

In questioning the make-up of the congregations he gives us a glimpse of Victorian church-going habits:

> It would be interesting to know (and in my opinion the census is not worth a deal unless we do know it) how many of these attenders at devotion were adults - 16 and upwards; and then, again, how many were male and how many were female. If all the children were counted the census does not go for a deal, because they are obliged to go, made to go by their parents ..... When one looks over a congregation in either church or chapel nowadays one is struck with the disproportion there is between the bare heads, masculine, and the feminine hats and bonnets .....

(It is clear from the rebuilding documents that church power nevertheless lay with the men, except in the rare cases of women with considerable financial independence such as the Burnside sisters.) *Dubitans* concluded his subjective appraisal of Radcliffe's religion with a final blast of scepticism:

> My friends, I'm afraid you are not so good as you are made out to be, I wish you were. I know there's nobody like you, generally, but 779 of you at church and chapel last Sunday? Oh! get out, you're joking!

His view can be contrasted with a decorous account of villagers flocking to the four services held on a Feast Sunday, in the parochial magazine in 1877.

Bells and bellringing

However doubtful the religious commitment of his flock, John Cullen continued his forceful ministry by improving the church bells. The work was only partially completed at the time of the rebuilding. In 1878 the restoration committee had written to Taylor and Co. of Loughborough requesting estimates for the removal, storage and subsequent re-hanging of the four bells. There was some recasting work, and the committee also wanted to purchase two additional bells. Taylor and Co. recommended that Radcliffe should not 'have less than an 11 cwt tenor as they have a very poor and light sound, not such as people expect to hear from Church bells'. Mottoes were also to be inscribed:

Ad Gloriam Dei 1886
Ring in the thousand years of peace 1886
Laudo Deum Verum 1882
Come when the music calleth of the Church Bells silvery sound
Jesus be our speed 1879
All men that hear my mournful sound repent before you lie in ground 1879

The last two inscriptions were taken from earlier bells. (See *Radcliffe-on-Trent 1710-1837*. p. 57.) A bill for £138.14s.6d was paid in January 1880, but a bell committee led by James Gorse of the Manor House and the artist Edward Price was at work raising funds until 1886 when the last two bells and their fittings, costing £56.3s and £44.19s respectively, were hung. The completed peal was first rung on Easter day 1886, and a plaque commemorating the efforts of the fundraisers was put up in the church baptistry. Provision was also made at this time for the hanging of two further bells, and these were added in 1946.

From 1882 the 'Bellringers Rules and Attendance Book' provided a record of the men who rang the bells. It was doubtless John Cullen who encouraged them to start the book and he took the chair at the first annual meeting. The first captain of bellringers was A.R. Goodwin, and the normal number in what seems to have been a very tightly-knit group was between eight and ten. At first attendances at services were marked in a register by ticks, but in 1885 the following symbols were adopted:

morning service	/
early morning service	—
afternoon service	|
evening service	\
all services	✳

The book was kept by the captain, and each member of the group received 'remuneration' according to his attendance. Until 1900 the bellringers themselves 'solicited once a year from house to house for the remuneration of the Band'. In 1888 Arthur Rushton had 5s stopped from the account due to him for not doing his share of collecting. The vicar also made a contribution and in 1890 he redistributed amongst the other bellringers 3s.7d and 2s.10d that he should have paid to W. Bradley and W. Levi for their 'not ringing on Christmas Eve'. In March 1900 the vicar and churchwardens resolved that the ringers' money should be collected for them and that they should be guaranteed the sum of £12 per annum. Such payments were later abolished.

Routine matters

All this while John Cullen was taking numerous other matters in hand and documenting his activities. He pasted notices and newspaper cuttings about the rebuilding in the parish register. An additional note records that the churchyard, no longer being used for burials, was laid out, laid flat and grassed, while he personally planted evergreens in the autumn of 1880. A stone tablet, provided by subscription in 1885, was set up in the church to commemorate early contributors to the Jeffrey Dole, the parish's oldest charity. Communion services were now held weekly, rather than fortnightly or monthly, and there were prayer meetings in the schoolroom on Friday evenings. His churchwardens' accounts, although less detailed than those of a century before, do give an impression of the everyday running of the church. Communion wine cost 2s a bottle in 1875-6. A year later it was bought in bulk, a dozen bottles on two occasions costing £1.8s a time. Surplice washing was continued by a long line of parish ladies - Mesdames Smalley, Whitehead, Pike, Marshall and Carnell. Payments for church cleaning appear regularly, but problems of cost arose later. John Cullen found donors in the 1900s to contribute to a church cleaning fund - Colonel Cantrell-Hubbersty regularly gave £5 and the vicar himself was often amongst those who contributed the rest. The clock was still routinely looked after by the parish clerk - John Hemsley until 1902. After so much refurbishing at the time of the rebuilding few major purchases are recorded. New kneelers in January and March 1890 at a total cost of £13.15s were one of the few substantial items. According to the vestry book, leakages were stopped in the tower and vestry by April 1897 and there was expenditure on church gates before April 1899. Two special items in 1901 record the death of Queen Victoria. Bell mufflers cost 3s.6d, and decorations for the church at her memorial service came to 11s.8d. Other routine payments were for gas and coal bills and for fire insurance, the latter paid for the first time in 1876 at £2.9s. A note at the back of the churchwardens' book indicates that the church was relit with incandescent gas lamps from February 28th 1913. Although the accounts were frequently overspent, by no means all the offertories went to St Mary's. Christmas day collections were often for the poor fund, and at the vestry meeting in April 1897 John Cullen summed up a typical year's donations to hospitals, the Indian famine fund, home and foreign missions, as well as the choir and Sunday School. In April 1912, £2.6s was contributed to the fund to help the victims of the *Titanic* disaster.

The interior of the church decorated for Queen Victoria's funeral

Concern for children

He took a particular interest in the children of the parish, visiting the school, teaching regularly and summarising the inspectors' reports in the log book. Probably the first confirmation service ever held in Radcliffe took place in March 1877 with 35 of the 83 candidates coming from the village. He introduced the singing of hymns by children on the Feast Sunday in 1877, and he encouraged the Sunday School, arranging special services on its centenary in the summer of 1880. On that occasion 215 Sunday school children were each presented with a bound bible, with the name of the school and the centenary stamped on the cover in gold, surrounded with a wreath of flowers. (The services of Robert Millington, his Sunday School superintendent who died in 1886 at the age of 48 are remembered on a brass in the church.) Towards the end of his life the churchwardens' accounts record Sunday School treats and prizes, respectively costing £8.14s.9d and £7 in 1912. (A choir treat in the same year cost £6.10s.) In 1960 an elderly resident remembered scrambling for sweets which he provided at the village feast. The effect of his distress at performing the burial service for a number of young children in 1882 is referred to in the chapter on Public Health. On the twenty-fifth anniversary of his ministry in 1899 a stained-glass window by Evans of West Bromwich was dedicated to him in the baptistry by those he had baptised. Above the main images of Christ, John the Baptist and the Holy Ghost appear eight cherub heads to symbolise children who had died since baptism.

Sunday school teachers 1903
Back row: Mr P. Todd, Miss Barratt, Miss Foster, Mr S. Loach, Miss Rawson
Miss Daft, Miss Packwood, Mr Dougall
Front row: Miss Hallam, Miss E. Parr, Rev J. Cullen, Miss Clifton, Miss Howard

The churchwardens' election 1888

Amidst this tranquil routine came the occasional flurry of excitement. In April 1888 the church vestry at which churchwardens were sleepily appointed erupted into controversy which reached the newspapers. While Samuel Cave Tomlinson was smoothly appointed vicar's churchwarden, there was unprecedented opposition to the re-election of John Green of The Chestnuts as people's churchwarden, with George Bell of the Manvers Arms standing against him. John Green received 18 votes and George Bell only 14, but the latter's friends considered the outcome sufficiently close to justify a poll. This took place in the schoolroom on 6th April, and the result was still close: 165 for John Green and 148 for George Bell. A large crowd gathered to hear the result which was greeted with cheers and loud hooting. The cause of the dispute is unclear, but the *Nottingham Daily Express* hinted at defections in the parish:

> *Like a number of other church people at Radcliffe, Mr Bell, we are informed, has been in the habit of attending a neighbouring church rather than the church of his parish, and this is stated to be the cause of his defeat.*

Despite his victory, John Green refused to stand in the following year and his place was taken by Thomas Barratt.

The organ of 1893

The saga of the organ, after the offence taken by Mr Burnside, continued even after a replacement was purchased in 1880. This new instrument was soon found to be 'much too small for the requirements of the church', and as early as February 1887 a concert was held in aid of the organ fund. In 1892 fund raising was launched in earnest with a donation of £100 from Mrs Noel, the former Adelaide Burnside, supplemented by the harvest festival offertory. Soon a suitable second-hand 3-manual organ, built by Messrs Brindley and Foster of Sheffield, was located in the possession of a Mr Samuel Meggit. It was purchased for what was considered the bargain price of £250, although at the opening concert in October 1893 £100 had still to be raised. The satisfaction at this new purchase was then marred by some undignified wrangling in a court case.

Dr Percy Truman, the well known barrister who was to lose his life in a cycling accident, was also an accomplished organist who had undertaken to negotiate the sale of the organ for Samuel Meggit to Radcliffe 's churchwardens. Dr Truman was to have £50 of the £250 for himself as commission, but on being introduced to the churchwardens Samuel Meggit had gone over the solicitor's head so ruining his chance of making his profit. In March 1894 Dr Truman sued Meggit for breach of contract. James Haslam, the Radcliffe churchwarden, was particularly vague in court about the price paid and could not produce a receipt. Judgement was given against Dr Truman, who lost a subsequent appeal in June 1894.

Despite the soured atmosphere, music at St Mary's seems to have been well catered for during the later part of John Cullen's ministry. Robert Buxton, the organ blower, was given a rise from £1 to £1.10s in January 1895, but the job does not appear to have been popular since the names change with more than usual rapidity around 1900. The new organ was regularly tuned and cleaned, the ladies of the parish raising £10 for this at a garden party and sale of work in April 1903. The names of organists occasionally appear in the records - Mr Clarke in 1882; Mr Robinson by 1902. Not until September 1913 does a specific item refer to payment for the organist - £20 at that time and £9.4s.6d in the following February. Purchases of music books for the choir appear in 1876, and with greater frequency between 1895 and 1898 when James Browne, the schoolmaster, was responsible for providing them.

John Cullen's writings

Throughout his ministry, and particularly in his later years, John Cullen continued his writing of religious tracts and verse. In 1881 he produced a small book on confirmation. Chapter 2, on the obligation of the Christian covenant, he introduced with a pointing hand and an admonition: 'READ THE WHOLE CHAPTER.' All those confirmed were presented with a copy. Some poems and idylls were published in 1882, and in March 1886 he received Queen Victoria's thanks for the tribute of respect paid to her in his work *Queens Regnant*. This had been originally written for recitation at Baltimore Female College in that year and was dedicated 'To all good women in every land', earning for him the reputation of a supporter of women's suffrage. Perhaps it was the general appreciation which he received from American reviewers which led to his being given an honorary Doctorate of Divinity by Illinois Wesleyan University in 1893. In August 1892 it was announced that he had been instrumental in obtaining a grant for a working poet, Mr W.H. Ecritt of Guildford. *Songs of Consolation* appeared in 1893 (which included a poem to a brother who died in 1849), while in 1899 came *The River Trent: an idyll*, produced after twenty-five years in the village. The eleven poems in this were illustrated by photographs depicting the course of the river. The eighth and ninth poems were entitled *Radcliffe-on-Trent* and *The Radcliffe Bells*. As a result of frequent travelling he published *Sunny Scenes in Europe* and *Sunny Scenes in the British Isles*. In 1906 Leontine Cullen died and he dedicated *In Memoriam* to her. Many of his poems (including *Ian and Edric*, a blank verse discussion on theological themes with Edric posing suitable questions for Ian to answer) were collected together in a 359-page volume called *Poems and Idylls* and republished or published in 1913. It was presumably in connection with this that Mr Wordsworth, Lord Manvers' agent at Thoresby, wrote to him in June 1913, 'I am afraid that I do not see my way to subscribe to the book you mention...'

RADCLIFFE-ON-TRENT

FROM this red cliff I look around,
The winding Trent runs clear below,
And, like its onward, affluent flow,
May peace in all those homes abound!

For here the seventh Henry slept
Ere he to Stoke his legions led,
And there o'er friends untimely dead
Surviving mourners sorely wept.

From hence I view the meads and
fields,
Where browse the flocks, where grows
the corn
And where each day, and night, and
morn,
All bounteous nature blessing yields.

Here Spring her crown of verdure
weaves,
While songs in break, and bush, and
dell,
Of secrets and of gladness tell,
Behind the hedge, beneath the leaves.

Here Summer pours her glory down.
And every path is bright with flowers;
And here, to pass the sunny hours,
Come wan, thin faces from the town.

To them we give a welcome sweet,
For rural sights must glad their eyes,
And silence, here, contrast with cries,
And roaring brawling of the street.

Here Autumn in her afterglow,
Doth touch with gold the stately trees,
Which shower it down with every
breeze
Upon the fruitful land below.

Here Winter clothes the earth in
white,
While on our hearths the crackling
fires
Awaken in our hearts, desires,
And in our homes create delight.

Two poems by John Cullen published in
The River Trent: an Idyll 1899

THE RADCLIFFE BELLS

HARK to the Radcliffe bells,
Their music sweet outwells
O'er hill and dale, and river, at this
evening hour.
Majestic the sound they fling,
Welcome the news they bring,
Of peace, and joy, and love; of glory
and of power!

On holy Sabbath days
They call us forth to praise
Our God who made, and loves, and
keeps us day by day.
To Him our prayers ascend, -
Our patient God, and Friend;
Who offers all His heaven, and points
Himself the way.

At Christmas and Eastertide
Their sound floats far and wide,
To tell of Jesus' birth, and triumph
o'er the grave;
Glory, and peace, and mirth,
He sendeth down to earth,
For He has conquered death, and
liveth now to save!

The cheerful marriage bells!
Of joy their music tells,
Which sounds so loud and sweet o'er
Trent's clear water now;
And on the village green,
On birthday of our Queen,
We hear their loyal sound, and bared
is every brow.

Each happy, glad New Year,
Their pealing sound we hear,
Which tells of hope and joy, o'er
sorrow past and gone.
Forward our glance is cast,
For tho' our years sped fast,
Yet they can never fail who with the
Lord march on.

The sad funereal chime,
Tell life's allotted time,
And grief and sorrow sore do fill our
aching breast;
For soon, alas! we go
To join the house of woe,
And follow to the grave where weary
pilgrims rest.

John Cullen's last years

John Cullen retained his forth right personality until almost the end of his long ministry. In 1885 he showed his Tory commitment by trying to prevent the use of the schoolroom by the Liberals (see chapter on National Politics), and again in 1908 when he warned the Manvers estate against a radical who was behind an application to use the now redundant schoolroom for the Territorial Army and the Boys' Brigade. In 1890 he used Goddard and Paget again to build a room on to the vicarage for church meetings and functions. As the money was raised by public subscription, there were those, such as a correspondent to the *Nottingham Guardian* in February 1892, who complained that the parishioners had received little benefit. Nor was he particularly popular with the Manvers estate about his finances. Despite the sale of glebe land on Cropwell Road for building purposes, which had increased the value of the living from £173 in 1874 to £250 in 1881, he felt obliged to approach Thoresby about his income early in 1899. Mr Wordsworth wrote to a Nottingham solicitor about the Radcliffe living as the 'Vicar has been making one of his 'appeals' to Lady Manvers and Lord Newark.' It was felt that 'he might have looked a little nearer home first!' It seems unlikely that any assistance was forthcoming since Kelly's and Wright's *Directories* for 1908 and 1915 respectively give the yearly value of the living as £260, only £10 more than in 1881. (Wright's figure of £280 in 1900 was presumably an error.)

There were opportunities for celebrations and stock-taking along the way. After fifteen years in the parish he was given an umbrella. A later presentation was a walking-stick. In 1910 he was 72-years-old and still had urgent plans for the parish

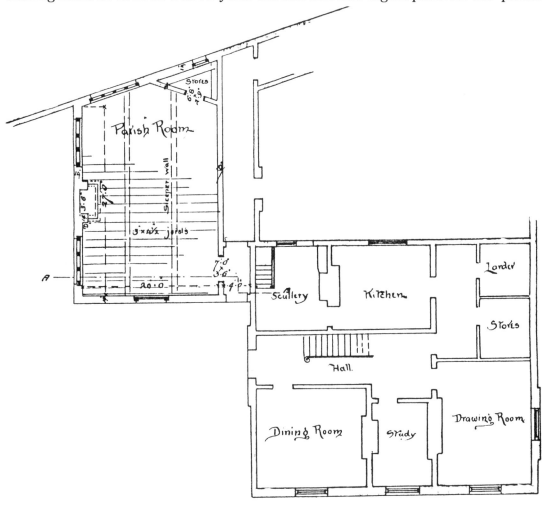

Ground floor plan of the vicarage and new church room 1890 (reduced)
(Nottinghamshire Archives Office, PR 20,182.
Reproduced by permission of the Principal Archivist)

which he put to the church vestry meeting on March 23rd, and then placed in the back of the minute book. Realising that his time was running out, these were 'things for the new Vicar to see to, and to accomplish'. Including his idea about removing the saddle-back roof on the church tower and replacing it with a spire, he listed nine points. Amongst these were the 'finishing' of the church with a new organ chamber and new vestries on the north side as originally intended in Goddard and Paget's scheme of 1878. He wanted two more bells added (this was done in 1946), and alterations to the chancel chapel, including the pews moved to face east, the door moved, a porch added, and a large spire of oak and lead shingles erected outside containing a bell to summon weekday worshippers. Further improvements would be a lych gate, a new churchyard wall, new Sunday schools built in the grounds of the old vicarage (on the site occupied by the present vicarage) in a mock Tudor style, an 'ashpit' for the vestries, and a place for ladies' cloaks and wrappers and for men's hats and umbrellas. In addition, he felt that a mission room was much needed 'at Mile end road, commonly called The Harlequin'. He added a note that many of the furnishings in the old schools, as well as flags and banners and trestle tables at the vicarage, and furniture and cutlery in the recently-built church room, all belonged to the church. 'The new Vicar may be very thankful to find all these things here. When I came there was nothing.'

In 1912 he published *Life through Death*, a sermon preached on the third Sunday in Lent in 1912 when he had spent thirty-eight years in Radcliffe. At the end he added a summary of the state of the church. There had been 210 communicants at Easter. He recalled the Radcliffe missions, the rebuilding of the church, the religious meetings and societies, and recorded how since 1897 the Sunday Schools had supported the expense (£65) of a missionary school in China in memory of the Ku-Cheng Martyrs. Apart from the Radcliffe missions (of which he was personally in charge of two), he had held missions in other parts of the country including London, Northampton, Huddersfield, Bath and Edinburgh. He had visited many other places and had been to the continent twenty times to preach the gospel.

To mark his thirty-eight years in the parish a concert was held to help swell a fund being raised. *The Trader* for October 5th 1912 recorded the occasion. Prestigious patrons on the programme included Lord Manvers, Colonel Cantrell-Hubbersty and Colonel and Mrs Birkin, the current occupants of Lamcote House. The vicar and his daughter received a number of guests at the vicarage before the concert began, and the entertainment was organised by Mrs W.H. Redgate. It consisted of a mixed programme, divided between local performers and outsiders including Ernest Hastings, the well-known 'London entertainer'. The programme was opened by the Radcliffe hand-bell ringers. Miss Dorothy Truman, a 'charming little dancer' performed a *pas seul*, and Miss Dorothy Redgate sang 'Eyes that used to gaze into mine' and 'I know a lovely garden', both rendered with 'much feeling'. Mrs Gordon Hardy was at her best in recitative pieces such as 'Ruddles Christmas Dinner', and Madame Wilson Moulds sang two songs of bygone London. After an interval the same artistes performed again, and were joined by Mr W. Downing, who sang 'Because' and 'The Lute Player', and by Mr R.W. Soresby, who played a piano solo. (The latter was now the church organist.) It was a happy occasion, with the churchwarden, Thomas Rose, expressing on behalf of the people their gratitude for the vicar's work, and hoping that he would live long among them.

By the beginning of 1914 John Cullen was ill and the Reverend A.R. Johnson was curate in charge. Messages of sympathy were sent from the bellringers and the church vestry meeting. His patron, Earl Manvers, was less sympathetic. On January 3rd 1914 Mr Wordsworth wrote to the solicitor D'Oyley Ransom of Nottingham indicating that Lord Manvers felt that if the Bishop could persuade John Cullen to resign, 'this would be immensely to the benefit of the Parish of Radcliffe'. There had been some suggestion of a pension of £150, but Lord Manvers would not give more than £25 per year. In the event he was not called upon to give even that, for John Cullen died on May 6th 1914. After a funeral service in Radcliffe, he was buried beside his wife and infant son at Bottesford where he had been curate 40 years before. He is still remembered by elderly residents as a white-bearded figure in a flat clerical hat, travelling in a wicker-sided trap. Many would have agreed with Colet Chamberlain's retrospective verdict in 1960: 'A benevolent personality, greatly beloved, revealing a real patriarchal influence throughout the village.'

Robert Cecil Smith 1914-1931

John Cullen must have been a formidable figure to follow. The young man who took on this daunting task was 29-year-old Robert Cecil Smith. Although born at Woolston in Buckinghamshire, he had spent his boyhood at Coddington, near Newark, where his father was vicar. After being educated at the Magnus Grammar School, Newark and St Edmund Hall, Oxford, he was ordained priest in 1910, and came to Radcliffe in 1914 from four years as curate at St Thomas church, Longford, in Coventry.

As was customary on the arrival of a new incumbent, a terrier (list of property) of the living was drawn up in May 1915, which is now deposited in the Nottinghamshire Archives Office. Unfortunately a full picture cannot be obtained from this since it has suffered damage from mice over the years. Nevertheless, the details relating to the vicarage house are clear, and show that it then consisted basically of ten rooms: drawing room, dining room, study, kitchen, pantry, scullery, two cellars, six bedrooms, bathroom, lavatory and dressing room. Two of the bedrooms were built over the church room which had been added by John Cullen. This measured 28 feet by 19 feet. Inside was the paraphernalia needed for church meetings - piano, two hanging book cases containing bibles and hymn books, two tables, a prayer desk, twenty-two bent-wood chairs, eight wood chairs, six forms, and an iron hat and umbrella stand. The room was lit by gas and contained a fireplace. In a cupboard was kept the crockery and cutlery for which John Cullen had considered his successor should be grateful.

A damaged section of the terrier records the church windows, seven memorial tablets and plates (all of which survive today), vessels, the bible, prayer books, psalters and hymn books for choir and clergy, as well as about 150 hymn and prayer books for general church use. The three-manual organ was now supplemented by an American organ. The land assets of the living are also listed, but on a damaged portion of the document. Since the sale of some land for building purposes in John Cullen's time, the glebe land on Cropwell Road now totalled just under 36 acres. (About another seven acres were to be sold at the end of 1921 on the eastern side of the road including the present bowling club and land for housing nearly up to the former golf club.) A half acre of land facing Lincoln Grove was noted as being up for sale in the terrier, but was not in fact sold until 1935. Apart from the vicarage garden and just over an acre of land in Ogle Lane, the living's main land assets were still the 18th century purchases in Hose and Wymondham, Leicestershire, amounting to 32 acres. There was some interest from £119.15s.11d from lands sold, a crown pension of £1.3s.10d a year, and interest from investment stock, the details of which have been destroyed.

Church maintenance and war-time work

Apart from the introduction of Ancient and Modern hymn books in place of Church Hymns in 1915, the early part of the Reverend Cecil Smith's ministry suggests that the routine of the church continued undisturbed. Something, however, had to be done about the heating system. The offertories on September 20th 1915 totalled £5.7s.5d and went towards new heating apparatus. In December of that year an Arden Hill gas steam radiator costing £9.13s.9d was put in on the north side of the church. It was still not good enough, and it seems that the decision was taken to replace the heating system put in against Goddard and Paget's advice at the time of the rebuilding. Any assets in the churchwardens' accounts in 1919 were put towards 'Heating the Church' account. In the following April the church vestry hoped that outstanding money for the reheating might be raised at a garden fete, and that the new equipment could be in before the winter. The total cost, listed at the back of the churchwardens' book, was £456.16s. Of this £105 was for bricklayers and joiners, and the rest for a low pressure hot water system. By March 1922 the reheating debt was paid off, but in order for the churchwardens' accounts to remain solvent a voluntary additional collection of £51.7s had to be made.

Other work carried out in Cecil Smith's time included repairs to the spouting on the tower, cleaning and regilding the weather vane, and testing the lightning conductor, all in 1920. In 1923 there were repairs and alterations to the chapel, and the organ was rebuilt in a new organ chamber at last. A chancel screen was given in

1924 by Mrs Lloyd Dexter of Radcliffe Hall in memory of her first husband, Samuel Smith, and his son, and the choir vestry was put at the west end of the church. A chapel screen was provided in 1929.

Cecil Smith's ministry coincided with the First World War. There is little of drama that emerges from the records, but the church undoubtedly played its part with offertories going to military, Red Cross and prisoners' funds. The church readily gave permission for the erection of a stone tablet to the memory of Charles Wightman Pike, mortally wounded near Ypres in 1917. The bell-ringers paid their tribute to the many killed, and a war memorial was unveiled in 1921.

Conclusion

The siting of the war memorial inside the churchyard symbolised the close link that still existed between the parish church and the community. Throughout the period studied its presence is unmistakable, whether through the quiet benevolence of a Robert Burgess or the missionary zeal of a John Cullen. How far it inspired spiritual commitment in the ordinary parishioner is difficult to assess, but the national religious census of 1851, and Radcliffe's own census of 1882, both suggest that although many still took part in Sunday worship, it was almost as likely to be at a nonconformist chapel as at the Anglican church. In this respect Radcliffe conformed to the national trend. Nevertheless, the nineteenth century was a dynamic period for St Mary's church: a new clock, new bells, new organs, a new chancel in 1858, and the rest almost totally rebuilt in 1879, providing an unmistakable landmark on the village skyline.

Main Road and church about 1903

Main sources

Primary

Nottinghamshire Archives Office: Radcliffe churchwardens' accounts PR 1510; church restoration minute book and accounts PR 1508, 2897-8; rebuilding specifications and secretary's notebook PR 20185-187; preachers' book PR 2879; vestry minute book PR 2900; terrier PR 2887; faculties PR 2888-2896; Radcliffe parish registers and Mormon records (I.G.I); plan and elevation of church RT1/1-4S; school log books SL 135 1/1-7.

Nottinghamshire County Library (Local Studies Library): census returns on microfilm for 1841-1881; religious census of 1851 on microfilm; *Weekly Express* 1 April 1921 in Doubleday Scrapbook III 167; *Nottingham Trader* 5 Oct 1912;

Nottingham Evening Post 20 March 1972; villagers' reminiscences DD 121/1/48 and 49.

Radcliffe-on-Trent Parish Council: vestry minute book 1839-1875; parish council minute books.

Radcliffe-on-Trent Bellringers: rules and attendance books.

University of Nottingham: archdeaconry mss A 82a, Ex 199 Ex 200; Manvers papers Ma 245/106c, Ma B 529/6, Ma B 529/17, Ma 2C 18, Ma 2C 18a, Ma 2C 166.

Secondary

Aitken, W.H.M.H. *Memoir of Miss F.E.B.*, published in Cullen, *The Life after Death* (see below).

Assoc. Arch. Socs. IV (1858) XIV.

Best, Geoffrey. *Mid-Victorian Britain 1851-1875*. 1971.

Bury, Wm. *Pastoral letter* 1837. R.o.T. L.22 in Local Studies Library.

Chamberlain, Colet. *Memories of the past*. 1960.

Cullen, John. *Horae Poeticae*. 1869.

Cullen, John. *Poems and Idylls*. 1913. (Includes works published in 1899).

Cullen, John. *The Life after Death and the Things to Come*. 1876.

Cullen, John. *Two sermons*, preached Jan. 2nd 1876.

Doubleday catalogue, Local Studies Library.

Gay, John D. *The geography of religion in England*. 1971.

Godfrey, J.T. *Churches of Nottinghamshire. Hundred of Bingham*. 1907.

Nottingham and Nottinghamshire *Directories* 1832-1928.

Pevsner, N. , revised Williamson E. *Buildings of England: Nottinghamshire*. 1979.

Priestland, P.(ed.). *Radcliffe-on-Trent 1710-1837*. 1984.

Radcliffe-on-Trent local history research group: extracts from Nottingham newspapers 1837-1920.

METHODISM

Methodism had taken root early in Radcliffe. It is probable that meetings were held in the village from about 1789; more certain evidence exists of a meeting house in 1794 and of a chapel in 1796. Later evidence suggests that this must have been on Hogg Lane. The society was soon regarded as one of the most stalwart in Nottinghamshire. Its name appeared on the first circuit plan published in 1802 and in the following year a list of membership shows that 153 people belonged to it. In this early period Methodism was already being split by controversy and the original movement was therefore distinguished from splinter groups by being called Wesleyan. Radcliffe, which belonged to the south circuit, remained loyal to this branch of Methodism and during the 1820s shared in its revival in Nottinghamshire. The momentum, however, could not be sustained and by 1839 membership had dropped to 80 with 160 Sunday scholars. For these figures and much of the early history of Methodism in Radcliffe we are indebted to 'Anonymous', writing in 1889, Radcliffe's centenary year. As the minute books of the south circuit have not survived, his history is all the more valuable.

A clash with the established church

There is no evidence that Methodism in Radcliffe ever suffered from organised opposition as occurred in some places, but its progress aroused much antipathy among members of the established church, as two incidents during the next fifty years showed. The first of these occurred in 1838 when the vicar, William Bury, mounted a much publicised attack on Radcliffe Methodists from his pulpit. In addition, he had written a pamphlet addressed to the parish, whom he designated 'The Flock over whom the Holy Ghost had made him overseer'. This was bound to provoke a reaction from nonconformists and with some glee the *Nottingham Review* reported on it on May 25th and published extracts from the reply written by a Wesleyan minister, the Rev Stephen Kay of Nottingham, entitled *The Clerical Fiction of Apostolic Succession and Episcopal Supremacy*. The lines were now drawn for a theological debate which soon developed into a more personal one. Mr Kay described William Bury's writings as:

> *a wanton, insidious and unprovoked attack upon a Christian society to which your beautifully rural village was for many a long year almost exclusively indebted for a Gospel ministry....*

He may have been referring to the years when, the steeple of the parish church having fallen on the main nave, services of the Church of England must have been disrupted, rather than merely attacking the quality of St. Mary's vicars. Mr Kay, said the *Review*, had 'given the Vicar such a flagellation as will make him recollect his pastoral letter as long as he lives,' and had demolished his arguments on the apostolic succession (at any rate to the editor's satisfaction). He had maintained, moreover, that the dissenters of Radcliffe owed nothing to the Church of England:

> *Take them all by house row, and point out the man, if you can, who was ever savingly converted to God in the church... It is indeed quite possible that such an one may exist; but we have yet to learn his name.*

The next week on June 1st the *Review* scathingly continued with:

> *...a little epistolary correspondence at the end of the pamphlet, showing some of the amiable peculiarities of the Reverend Vicar; his Christian love to his flock, his opposition to exclusive dealings, and his ardent desire to work in charity with all men. Such ever be the Vicars of Radcliffe, and then the Dissenters will have no occasion to shut up their chapels, or to fear the Church will run away with their congregation.*

The letters written by the Rev Bury, which the *Review* then printed, were addressed to a Mr M. This could possibly have been John Morley, a Sunday school teacher and a member of the chapel choir whose occupation was either a maltster or a bootmaker. More probably, however, it was John Marriott, a tailor and draper originating from Bingham, who at the age of 27 was already a leading member of the Wesleyan Society. He became a local preacher, a post he held up to his death in 1865 and he was also probably an assistant overseer to the parish. The vicar, in an attempt to excuse his hostile behaviour, explained what had particularly irked him and he threatened to withdraw his custom from any tradesman, including Mr M., who, as far as he was able to discover, was a party to it:

> *Almost every Sunday afternoon, in the very middle of Divine Service a number of children from the Methodist chapel, come running down past the Church in a most tumultuous, disorderly and noisy manner, to the disturbance of the congregation. The children are thus systematically taught to neglect Church and to pay no regard to God's ordinances or to His ministers. They hear the bells ringing for Church, but they are prevented from paying any attention to the summons. ....in very few villages is the Sabbath so openly and constantly profaned as in Radcliffe.*

Mr M. was admirably temperate in his reply. He defended the Society, but promised that:

> *If the children have behaved improperly in returning from [Sunday] school, they shall be severely reprimanded, and we shall endeavour to prevent similar occurrences in future.*

This was not good enough for the vicar who spelt out the reply he was expecting. Mr M. should have promised to try to persuade the teachers to close the school in time to conduct the children to church in an orderly manner, though even this was less than ideal as it left the young to be instructed by 'unauthorised and incompetent teachers'. Mr M. then wondered 'how a disregard of the Church's bells' (which still bothered William Bury) 'constitutes a neglect of God's worship'. But the last word was given to the vicar, who returned to the theological argument and claimed that ' in almost every large place many of the Wesleyans are turning to the Church'. ('What a nutshell circle some men seem to move in,' jibed the editor of the *Review*.)

The sequel to this acrimonious debate was a happy one according to the Methodist historian, George Harwood, albeit at the expense of the vicar who made 'a most honourable and ample expression of regret... to a full congregation in his own church'. An anonymous foreword in a posthumous reprint of Mr Harwood's book said that William Bury 'left behind him in Ratcliffe a name held in higher esteem by none than by the Wesleyan Methodists of that village'. (For further information on the Rev William Bury see chapter on St Mary's Church.)

The chapel of 1839

Mr Harwood also claimed that as a result of this incident, the chapel at Radcliffe was so crowded that a new one was planned, but the decision to build had already been taken by May 22nd 1838 when permission had been obtained from the Nottingham District Committee, 'the debt remaining not to be more than £700'. The need for a larger chapel probably had more to do with a thriving Sunday school, the Wesleyan emphasis on teaching the young being at this time well ahead of their Anglican rivals. On June 14th a meeting was held in Mr Brewster's malt rooms and, with upwards of 300 people attending, nearly £200 was raised. After tea, 'suitable addresses were delivered to an attentive audience' including one by the Rev Stephen Kay. This time a report was made by the *Nottingham Journal* which described the room as being:

> *tastefully decorated with flowers; the motto in the centre of the room, which was ingeniously composed of flowers was ' Peace and goodwill to all'.*

An apt choice in the circumstances.

The minutes of the Nottingham District Committee record that work had begun by May 14th 1839 and the opening services were held on August 9th of that year. A well-known preacher from Yorkshire, Mr Dawson, opened a series of services with a sermon on 'Through this man is preached unto you the forgiveness of sins'. The Rev Stephen Kay was amongst those who officiated, no doubt with particular satisfaction, and the celebrations were rounded off on August 15th with a public tea meeting in the schoolroom. (Tickets at 1s each were on sale in Nottingham at Mr F. Ward's, bookseller, Parliament Street.)

The splendid new chapel with which Radcliffe Wesleyans embarked on the Victorian age and which was intended 'to be a lasting ornament to the village' was built on a site adjacent to the Cliffe Inn on a plot of land bought from a Mr Ogle in the previous year. The total cost of building, including the chapel-keeper's house, came to £1,360 of which £505 was contributed and £855 remained as debt. The design of the chapel was to be much criticised later for its awkwardness; two vestries behind the pulpit resulted in the latter being pushed rather far forward into the centre. A gallery extended round the building and a number of forms were placed on each side of the first floor as free seats for the poor and scholars. Altogether there was room for 400 with 300 below in the schoolroom. Anonymous concluded his description:

The Wesleyan Methodist chapel on the main street opened in 1839. It was demolished in 1967. The figure in the gateway is said to be Bill Nowell, chapel keeper

No attempt was made at decoration, the whole of the interior remaining precisely as it was finished by the builders, except the pulpit, which was painted in imitation mahogany.

The old chapel on Hogg Lane, whose gallery was sold to the Methodists at Cotgrave, was bought by Robert Brewster, a member of the Society, who converted it into a malthouse. It was used as such for some forty years and in 1887 it was reported as being occupied by Thomas Barratt as a currier's (leather dresser's) shop. Subsequently Walter Harrison & Sons Ltd used the building for storing agricultural supplies until at least the 1950s. The whole area has since been redeveloped.

Sermons, songs and tea

Radcliffe's links with Wesleyans in Nottingham had always been close and its pleasant situation on the river, along with its new chapel, attracted many visitors. In pre-railway days there would be 'great boat loads of friends from Nottingham' arriving to join in the Society's anniversary celebrations, such as one described by the *Nottingham Review* on 30th July 1847:

Mr Shelton's large boat arrived from Nottingham about two o'clock with nearly 400 people. Mr Waddy from Sheffield preached a very interesting sermon and nearly 500 took tea in Mr John Brewster's orchard.

Music had always been an important feature of the branch's services. At one time there was a small orchestra of 'clarionette', violoncello and flute and in 1845 a special tea meeting was held to raise £12 for a bass instrument. It was the choir which particularly attracted visitors to the Nottinghamshire Sunday School anniversaries which were held in turn in all the villages near Nottingham. Sometimes, according to Anonymous, as many as 750 people crowded through the doors of the chapel and these were social as well as religious occasions. In 1840 the last surviving minister ordained by John Wesley, the Rev John Hicklin of Newark, delivered the sermon.

These events, with their collections, brought much needed revenue to the Society which otherwise depended on its pew rents for income. After the opening of the new chapel, they averaged £40 a year, a membership of 82 being recorded in 1847, but Anonymous tells us that by 1856 membership had dropped to less than 60 and annual pew rents to £13 a year. The charming rural scenes described by the *Review* in the 1840s belied the troubles which were about to afflict Wesleyanism.

The Reform Movement of 1849

The drop in membership and consequent loss of income was attributed directly by Anonymous to the controversies of 1849, controversies which took place on a much wider stage than that of Radcliffe, but which involved the village Society and threatened its unity. In all denominations this was a period of debate about clerical authority and in Wesleyanism it surrounded the autocratic style of leadership of the Rev Jabez Bunting, who refused to concede even minor reforms in the constitution which governed Methodism. Three leaders of the reforming party were expelled in the summer of 1849. One of them was the Superintendent of the North Circuit, the Rev Samuel Dunn, and another the Rev James Everett who had made a great impression in Nottingham as a preacher. When it was realised that the latter had a long standing engagement to preach at Radcliffe a few weeks later on August 28th, the village Society suddenly found itself at the centre of the storm.

The *Review*, which supported the reformers, threw itself into the fray and on the 17th reported attempts by Conference 'blockbusters' to prevent Mr Everett from fulfilling his engagement:

> ..... *it is hoped the friends* [at Radcliffe] *will be firm and that Mr Everett will go and preach out of doors if the people cannot have their own chapel for him.*

The same edition of the paper reported a meeting held by the reformers to argue their case at the Mechanics' Hall during which a handbill announcing the coming event at Radcliffe was provocatively read out to the assembly. On August 24th the *Review* enlarged on the crisis:

> *The spirit of disaffection is spread far and wide. Great fears are entertained lest the South Circuit as well as the North should catch the fire and every exertion has been made, and we learn with success, to prevent the Rev James Everett from preaching at Radcliffe ..... deputation has followed deputation to that place, till at length the last, consisting of four travelling preachers, the Rev John Lambert at their head, succeeded in warding off for a time, the 'great evil' of Radcliffe having a sermon from their old, tried and beloved friend the Rev James Everett.*

Then the *Review* went a little too far:

> *We fear the information we have heard respecting the* <u>mild</u> *and* <u>friendly</u> *spirit manifested by this deputation is true and that the* <u>sleek</u> *and* <u>smooth</u> *tongued John Lambert did designate the Rev James Everett as a fire brand.*

It subsequently withdrew this statement. But Mr Everett still had friends in Radcliffe, as a tea party held in the following October at the Mechanics' Hall demonstrated. A motion in support of the reformers was seconded by John Marriott who stated:

> ..... his decided conviction that the Conference was not able to properly manage its own affairs and expressed a determination to use all the abilities God had given him in storming the Citadel until the walls should be demolished and all its internal arrangements and movements were exposed to public view.

As in all Methodist conflicts, strong passions springing from deep felt convictions were aroused and when in the following year a booklet was published in Nottingham in support of the Rev Bunting, the author lashed out at the 'Three Most Noble Martyrs' and their friends:

> Some there are in this towne and neighbourhoode who are especiallie delighted at theire owne conducte and doinges, whether it be laughinge and sneeringe at ye preacher duringe publick worshippe, like one narrowe-minded, snivellinge, do-nothinge, conceited upstarte at ye village of Radcliffe-on-Trent is saide to do .....

Could he have been referring to John Marriott? But, although chapels in the north circuit were torn apart, expulsions continued (including leading members of the Society at Cotgrave), and a new branch of Wesleyan Methodism called the Reformed was founded, 'no actual division of the Radcliffe Society occurred' according to Anonymous. Everett's opponents seem to have been successful in keeping him away.

John Marriott himself may well have averted the crisis by his submission to the authority of Conference. This is confirmed by his presence as a speaker at the first annual tea party meeting of the Nottingham Branch of the Wesleyan Methodist Local Preachers Mutual Aid Association on November 24th 1852, held in the tea rooms of the Arboretum. Tensions between clerical and lay elements in Wesleyanism were still apparent in the speeches of some delegates, but whatever his private reservations may have been, John Marriott continued as a loyal member of the Wesleyan Connexion. Five years before his death in 1860 he spoke movingly of his life at one of the Local Preachers' Meetings:

> He was happy to stand there as a Local Preacher which he had been for more than 50 years. He thanked God that he had not spent his strength for nought and he trusted that every heart would bound with thanksgiving for the benefits of the Society .....

Local preachers and trustees

Anonymous suggests that the decline in the fortunes of the Society was not just due to the Reform Movement. 'Strong pillars of the church were taken away by deaths and removals and their places in many instances were not occupied by their successors.' He may have been referring to John Morley who died in 1841 and to Edward Barker, among others. The latter was a blacksmith and local preacher of many years, who died shortly before the opening of the chapel and who must have been a member of the branch from its very inception. But the local preachers listed on a circuit plan of 1844 and the trustees of the chapel in 1856 show many who came from families with a long tradition of support for Wesleyanism in Radcliffe. The Brewsters, in particular, had always played an important part in the Society. John, a brickmaker and farmer who died in 1824, was probably a founder member and he used his considerable influence and economic resources to good effect, acting as a generous benefactor and giving support to other local societies, such as Cotgrave, in defiance of landlord opposition. His close friendship with Thomas Tatham linked Radcliffe not just with Methodism in Nottingham but with John Wesley himself. His two sons, John and Robert, carried on the tradition. John junior, a farmer of 105 acres employing three labourers and a boy, probably occupied what is now known as Old Manor Farm on the Shelford Road. It was in his orchards that so many visitors attending anniversaries took their tea and it was his brother Robert who lent his malt rooms for meetings. His son, also John, became a minister working in Newfoundland as well as nearer home and he regularly returned to officiate at functions in the village.

Among the trustees were John Foster and Jacob Gee. The Fosters were an extensive family, all butchers and later some of them cattle dealers, and associated from the beginning with Wesleyanism. Jacob Gee, originally from Holme Pierrepont, was a journeyman tailor and cottager with a fine family endowed with resounding biblical names - Jacob, Samuel, Kerram (or Jessom), Rebecca and Abigail.

The funeral of William Roulstone

The Roulstones were another old Radcliffe family. In 1841 there were at least four branches, including William's, working as basket makers. This was unlikely to have been a very lucrative trade and William's background was one of poverty. He did not learn to read until after his conversion when he was 23 years old, but he became a local preacher. He died in 1858 at the age of 85 and after sixty-four years as a member of Radcliffe's Society. His funeral was the scene of the second incident which revealed the resentment which the continued success of Methodism still aroused in some members of the established church. It was still customary for the Anglican minister to officiate at Methodist funerals and in 1858 the incumbent was the Rev Burgess. No doubt he was unaware, as he presided over the burial of William Roulstone in St. Mary's churchyard, that his every word would be reported in the *Review*:

This usually quiet village has been thrown into a state of some excitement by the conduct of the vicar. After the burial service was concluded and the vicar had retired, the time-honoured practice of singing a verse over the remains of the departed was observed. There were thirty or forty good singers present, and they commenced the doxology 'Praise God from whom all blessings flow' - a verse as unsectarian and free from objection as any that could have been selected.

The vicar, however, did object as the *Review* reported with relish:

Before the first two lines were ended, the Rev R. Burgess, the vicar, came back in breathless haste, evidently much excited, and exclaimed in a loud voice, 'I will not have this brawling here.' The singers persisted, and in spite of angry expostulation concluded the verse. Mr Burgess told them at the close that they were not Christians in their behaviour, or they would have desisted from their purpose. He had 'prejudices', he added, and 'they ought to have respected them'. The singers retired peacefully, with the conviction, however, that the deficiency in Christian feeling was certainly not exhibited by them.

A final comment put the affair into a much wider perspective:

This simple occurrence, viewed in connection with the recently acquired Puseyistical [high church] tendencies of the vicar, has been the general topic of conversation, and much surprise has been expressed by all parties at the vicar's procedure.

Primitive Methodism

Despite the evident strength of the Wesleyan party in Radcliffe, it had not gone unchallenged during these years. Two other groups, the Primitive Methodists, followed and replaced by the Independent Primitive Methodists who broke away from them, had established societies in the village. The latter subsequently in their turn disappeared and the Primitive Methodists returned.

Primitive Methodism had originated in Staffordshire. Its basic principles were no different from those of the Wesleyans, but its supporters felt that Methodism had lost touch with the spirit of its founder, and so they put greater emphasis on holding large open-air meetings, on exhortation and on 'singing and hallelujahs'. Its members soon earned themselves the name of 'Ranters' and its leaders were expelled on disciplinary grounds. The poorest and least literate responded to its missionary work which Harwood, in his private journal (quoted by Swift in his book *The Lively People*), described as 'a rough style of Christianity ..... but ..... suitable for the people'. Neither the historians of Wesleyanism in Nottingham nor Anonymous in Radcliffe mention the Primitive Methodists in their published work; evidence perhaps of feelings of disapproval and grievance at their missionary success. The Wesleyan Society in Radcliffe may have unwittingly provided a fertile ground for their cause, for despite the presence of humble families such as that of William Roulstone, they had always been proud to number more substantial artisans and tradesmen among their converts and they may thus have appeared a little exclusive.

The Primitives first preached in Radcliffe in 1817 and enthusiastic reports were made of the success of these early efforts, especially after a great Camp Meeting was held in June of that year on Priest Hill to the east of the parish. But their societies were less tightly organised than those of the Wesleyans and it is difficult to be sure just how successful they were. The first indications of a meeting house in the village could have been the registration of 'A certain Dwelling House' by Francis Green on May 6th 1818 and later of 'A certain Workshop' by John Mabbott on March 30th 1819 as places of worship in returns made to the diocese, although no denomination is specified. An account of the first meeting house, perhaps referring to this period, was sent in by a correspondent of the *Nottingham Daily Express* in 1887:

> *They commenced preaching first in a cottage, I remember a weaver's shop, built by Thomas Dent, was altered and made into their first chapel near to where there had been a Dame school, taught by one 'Old Sally Morley' which stood next Mr Daft's present house. The chapel has now become a shop occupied by Mrs. Snowden.*

The names mentioned in this account appear in deeds connected with the Royal Oak and Walker's Yard area of the village. (Sarah Morley's will was proved in 1819. She bequeathed property to Ann Mellors, who had lived with her, and who married a Thomas Dent. They sold their property in 1827. Mr Daft's 'present house' of 1887 is now the Scout Hall in Walker's Yard.) In 1829 the Return made to the Chief Constable of Worksop in connection with the repeal of the Corporation and Test Acts confirms that there was a Primitive Methodist chapel in Radcliffe as well as a Wesleyan one. It was to have a short history as the Leaders' Quarter Day Minute Book of the South Circuit shows.

In 1830 a new room was opened in the village and a Brother Hodgkin was requested to preach at the ceremony. In the following January Brother Mabbott of Radcliffe was recognised as having 'a credential to preach amongst us'. The society was now fully fledged, appearing in the Preachers' Plan of 1831 and holding services twice on Sundays at 2 and 6 o'clock. The preachers who served the society included Castledine, Baxter and Shepperson from Bingham, Hodgkinson and two others from Ruddington, John Parrott from East Bridgford, George Mabbott from Redmile and one from Hyson Green. In addition Radcliffe was allowed to hold a Love Feast and Missionary Meeting, and a Sacrament, and in September of the same year Brother Mabbott (presumably John) was judged to have proved himself and was raised to be an accredited Local Preacher. Not all was going smoothly, however, and the Leaders' Minutes give ample evidence of much dissension among the various Local Preachers, particularly concerning the Circuit Steward of the time, J. Whitby. The causes of this dissension may have lain in the personality of the Steward, but in the area surrounding Radcliffe there were also matters of principle at stake.

At the same time as Primitive Methodism was developing in Radcliffe, so too it was in Bingham and in some of the surrounding villages, many of the members sharing the same surname and perhaps being related. The communities of some of the village societies were thus closely linked and were soon to fall from grace together. The first sign of trouble came at the end of 1831 when it was ordered that George Mabbott of Redmile 'sink two figures' as a preacher on the Plan, usually a punishment for having neglected preaching appointments. The next year Radcliffe's services were reduced to the evening one only and it was noted that the society did

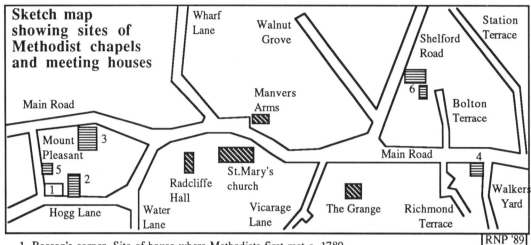

Sketch map showing sites of Methodist chapels and meeting houses

Wharf Lane
Walnut Grove
Station Terrace
Shelford Road
Manvers Arms
6
Bolton Terrace
Main Road
Mount Pleasant 3
5
2
1
Main Road 4
Radcliffe Hall
St.Mary's church
Hogg Lane
Water Lane
Vicarage Lane
The Grange
Richmond Terrace
Walkers Yard

RNP '89

1. Beeson's corner. Site of house where Methodists first met c. 1789.

2. Site of first Wesleyan chapel 1796.

3. Site of second Wesleyan chapel opened 1839.

4. Approximate site of building used by Primitive Methodists in early nineteenth century.

5. Probable site of Primitive Methodist chapel from 1865,
    perhaps using building created earlier by Independent Primitive Methodists.

6. Site of existing Primitive Methodist chapel opened 1893.

not have a Sunday School. Then in June 1832 a solemn resolution was passed:

> *That Henery Castledine, Geo Baxter, Geo Mabbott, Saml Shepperson and John Mabbott be considered no longer as members of our Connexion for base immorality and attempting to make a division and bad conduct to Mr Whitby .....*

A split between the main body of Primitive Methodists and a small group led by those named in the resolution (mainly from Bingham) had developed and the latter now formed themselves into the Independent Primitive Methodist Connexion. [Henceforth they are referred to as Independents, but are not to be confused with the Independent Methodists who were a separate organisation operating elsewhere.]

Their 'base immorality' referred to their objection on principle to the paying of wages to itinerant preachers. This, they felt, created a priestly caste which was unscriptural. Such views were not new. As long ago as 1817 when one of the founders of Primitive Methodism, William Clowes, had visited Radcliffe he had remarked:

> *At this place I experienced a little trouble from a certain person who had broached some unsound sentiments. One of the principal was that the society ought not to support the regular travelling preachers, but only those who were missionaries.*

On that occasion Clowes had persuaded 'the certain person' (perhaps John Mabbott in his younger days) to his point of view, but now, in 1832, the rift was final for in December of the following year Brothers Hallam and Hodgkin were informed that the Leaders' Meeting highly disapproved of their conduct in 'allowing John Mabbott to Preach in our Pulpits'. There were further efforts to limit the influence of the rebel group and it was resolved that 'an affectionate letter be sent to Barkeston advising them not to allow the Bingham Preachers to Preach in our Pulpits'.

For a number of years the Primitive Methodists struggled to maintain their position in Radcliffe. Preaching twice on a Sunday was resumed and in June 1833 Edward Spencer was appointed Class Leader. A year later he came on the plan as an exhorter, and arrangements were made for a Travelling Preacher to visit the community once in a quarter. But Edward Spencer seems to have retired because of ill health and by 1838 Radcliffe no longer appeared on the Circuit Plan. A few references in the Minutes to 'Radcliffe' between 1842 and 1845 almost certainly belong to Ratcliffe-on-Soar and although classes were formed nearby at Newton, Saxondale and Shelford the Primitive cause was temporarily lost in Radcliffe.

The only evidence that a society might still have existed in the village at this time is a notice which appeared in the *Nottingham Journal* on 20th December 1844 of a Temperance Meeting held in the 'Primitive Methodist Meeting House'. One of the main speakers, however, was an Independent preacher and this, together with the fact that the Independents had registered first a house as a place of worship in 1839 and then a chapel in 1843, suggests that the reporter had made an error and that the meeting was held in the new Independent chapel.

It is clear that the Independents had stepped in where the Primitives had failed. They had already published a Preachers' Plan in 1839 and Radcliffe is included along with Tithby, Hoveringham, Gunthorpe, Elston, Shelford and Scarrington. Each of these village societies was autonomous, but a loose form of federation was organised between them to provide mutual support. The historian James Vickers describes their early days:

> *For fifty years these societies might be called home churches, as they met in cottages or rented rooms. These churches have had their own peculiar field of labour chiefly among agricultural labourers in small villages and hamlets and amid, until recent years, hostile surroundings.*

The Independent Primitive Methodists' chapel

The chapel registered by Thomas Smith, labourer, on May 27th 1843 is described in a conveyance of January 6th of that year as a freehold estate of three cottages in Mount Pleasant, sold for £180 by Mr Robert Butler Price, baker. Thomas Smith was one of the trustees and others from Radcliffe were William Howard, a farmer, later to be a maltster, Thomas Whitworth, baker, Robert Johnson, labourer, John Glew, wheelwright and William Rockley, joiner. John Mabbott appears to have moved away from the village because he is included among trustees from Bingham along with other founders of the movement there.

The religious census of 1851

These events are confirmed by the Religious Census in which only two religious bodies, apart from the Church of England, are reported as being in the village. The figures returned show that the Wesleyans had 114 free sittings, 120 'other sittings' and free space or standing room for 100. The number estimated to have attended Divine Service at their chapel on Sunday 30th March 1851 was:

Wesleyan	Morning	Afternoon	Evening
General Congregation	66		90
Sunday Scholars	49		30
	115		120
Average number of attendants during 12 months:			
General Congregation	180		30 (sic)
Sunday Scholars	70		30
	250		330

The Independents, in a chapel erected in 1843 and described as a separate and entire building used exclusively as a place of worship, had 70 free sittings and 50 'other sittings', with 'Free space or standing room for 100 including the free sittings and standing room'. The estimated attendance on 30th March was:

	Afternoon	Evening
General Congregation	60	75
Sunday Scholars	-	-
Average number of attendants during 12 months:		
General Congregation	55	70
Sunday Scholars	-	-

A remark was added to the return:

The meaning of Independent is this. They are a separate Denomination from the Primitive Methodist. Independent of any Paid Ministry, those officiating in this place are men who like St. Paul can say 'these Hands adminster to my own necessities' working with their hands the six days and reason with the people and exhort the Sabbath.

Signature: Thomas Smith, Steward and Leader, Radcliffe-on-Trent.

The baptismal register of the Independent Primitive Methodists

The new society settled down to a regular routine of its own, apparently ignored by the Wesleyans. The *Nottingham Journal* reported its annual tea meeting on 8th February 1856, a businesslike affair with the secretary presenting his report and a number of visiting speakers. Between 13th October 1844 and 19th January 1862 a baptismal register was kept. A closer look at the families registered there and at the list of trustees confirms their humble origins. Thomas Smith himself was 63 years old in 1851, an agricultural labourer born in Wakesford, Derbyshire while his wife, Sarah, was then aged 60, a lace runner born in Burton, Nottinghamshire. Only two among the trustees were certainly Radcliffe born. All, however, except Thomas Smith himself and possibly John Glew were family men with children. Thomas Smith's name does not appear in the register, a large proportion of those officiating at the baptisms being from Bingham, and on one occasion in 1859 a Wesleyan minister was employed.

The register contains fifty-eight separate baptisms, between one and six every year except 1846 when there was none, representing thirty-three different families. Of these, twenty-three can be identified in the census returns and half their number have an agricultural labourer as head of the household, some later changing to other occupations such as land drainer or boatman. One was a brazier and tinplate worker, one a beerhouse keeper, one a maltster and there was a joiner, a couple of shoemakers and a couple of cottagers. It is impossible to know from these labels how affluent these people were, but there is a complete absence of members of those families known to be among the more substantial in the village. Of those whose place of birth is known, more than half came from Radcliffe, but a sizable minority was born outside the village. Fourteen of the twenty-three families appear to have moved to the village after the 1841 census even though eight of their heads of household stated later that they had been born in Radcliffe. It could be that they had left to serve their apprenticeships or to work as hired agricultural labourers elsewhere, returning when they started their families. They and the newcomers who moved in during the next twenty years looked for support to the Independents rather than to the more prosperous Wesleyans.

The abrupt end to the register in January 1862 comes as a surprise. Perhaps the ageing leader, Thomas Smith, found it difficult to hold the group together; three years later he died at the age of 77. The dependence of such small groups on strong leadership made them particularly vulnerable when any member was lost. Many of the families found in the censuses who had made up his congregation moved away from Radcliffe in the ensuing years; of those identified in the register nearly two thirds had left by 1871 and over 80% by 1881. Even allowing for the deficiency of the 1871 census and the fact that the baptismal register would only represent a portion of the total society, this is a very considerable loss of those in their prime of life. No doubt some of the community joined the Wesleyans and the Primitive Methodists when they returned to Radcliffe and three couples were buried many years later in unconsecrated ground, evidence that they had not joined the Church of England.

The reinstatement of the Primitive Methodists

Not much is known about the return to Radcliffe of the Primitives. Mr Arthur Rose, who was born about 1876 has left us his reminiscences in which he states that he had once read a record that Radcliffe was first missioned from Bingham; but this may, of course, have referred to the Independents. A local tradition suggests that they first met in the house of his father, 37 Water Lane, but it seems fairly certain that before long they had taken over the Independents' chapel. Along with it they

Date of Baptism	Childs Name	Parents Christian Name	Name		Age When Baptised	Preachers Name
1844 Oct 13	Ellen Daughter of	Wm & Edeth	France	Ratcliff on Trent County of Nottingham		Thos Simmons
1844 Nov 10	Wm Son of	Geo & Ann	Kirkham	Do		Thos Simmons
1844 Dec 1	Elizabeth Daughter of	Henry & Frances	Breedon	Do		Geo Berry
1844 Dec 1	Rebecca Daughter of	James & Harriott	Caunt	Do		Geo Berry
1845 Jany 26	Jane Daughter of	Wm & Sarah	Richmond	Do		J Doncaster
1845 March 30	Wm Son of	Michael & Elizabeth	Kitchin	Do		Thos Simmons
1845 June 1	Sarah Daughter of	Geo & Martha	Exon	Do		Thos Simmons

The first page of the Independent Primitive Methodists' baptism register
beginning in 1844 (reduced)
(Nottinghamshire Archives Office, MR 15/36(K)
Reproduced by permission of the Principal Archivist)

inherited the Independents' old 1844 baptismal register, for on the front cover, beneath the heading is a bracketed note: 'This is the chapel that now belongs to us - J. Barfoot.' This gentleman was a minister of the Primitive Connexion whose name appears on their stations in 1877. Mr Rose described the chapel he remembered from his boyhood:

...an old square building where Miss Edie Walker lived on Knight's Hill which Mr Barnes bought for £65 and turned into a house and shop. [This presumably refers to its subsequent fate.] There was a double door in the centre, gallery on the left hand side and the singing seat on the right hand side and the pulpit in the centre, facing the gallery; three forms with backs

facing the singing seat, small forms for the children in the centre.

The move into the chapel was perhaps a quiet affair for no newspaper report of the occasion has been found and the minute books have been lost, but the date of April 14th 1865 is recorded in a pamphlet for a re-opening service in 1931. Extracts quoted there from the minute books show that the first trustees of the chapel were Messrs G. Caunt, R. Clarke, T. Burrell, W. Flower, G. Rockley from Radcliffe, G. Swannick from Shelford and G. Wisher from Cropwell. The Reverends W. Cutts and T. Fletcher were the ministers.

From February 6th 1872 the names of children from Radcliffe appear in the Nottinghamshire Primitives' baptismal register, and J. Barfoot's signature can be found there from time to time. The local religious census of January 1882 also shows the Primitive Methodists firmly back in the saddle, with no sign of the Independents. The census, whose accuracy had been much disputed, made the following return:-

	Morning	Evening	Total
Church of England	267	293	560
Wesleyan	232	247	479
Primitive Methodist	48	91	139

Though the Society was now fully established, missionary zeal continued unabated as Mr Rose described with some exhilaration:

We used to have revivals and mission services ..... we used to mission the street mornings, bottom of the village quarter to five, start Palin Row and sing down street. The greatest favourite march tune was 'Grace is flowing like a river' and at night there used to be short speeches or exhortation, then they turned it into a Love-feast ..... It used to create a great influence - hymn singing and many giving their experience.

One mission in particular, which came from Ruddington, made a deep impression on the young Arthur Rose:

Some came in a carrier waggon to mission the village, and they used to go to Mr Rockley's up Bailey Lane, where Mr Loach lives now and turn their horse out in Mr Rockley's field. He used to keep a few cows ..... As soon as they came out, got in a circle and started singing, an old jackdaw used to come to a tree and shout 'Amen, Hallelujah'.

With such support they could hardly fail!

Their old square chapel on Knight's Hill was soon outgrown and by 1890 there were plans to build a more ambitious one. Negotiations were opened with the trustees of the Manvers estate to buy a plot of land called 'Bowrings' orchard' on the Shelford road. The Primitive Methodists' initial offer was, according to Mr Wing, the estate's solicitor, in a letter to the Reverend Seymour, another of the trustees:

.... about one half of the market value i.e. were we to choose our time for selling, but I daresay we should not get a great deal more than they offer were we forced to sell now. Full market value is legally the only basis on which Trustees ought to act, but there are peculiar elements in the present case (which will at once suggest themselves to you) and it may be very politic to meet them to some extent.

Mr Wing then suggested a price of 3s a yard or £120 for 800 square yards which 'though not market value would be a substantial sum and bring in, of course, a good deal more than the present rental'. Methodism had come a long way since the 1790s when the estate steward of the time had bridled at the very mention of a Methodist chapel. The trustees of the estate, although one of them was a minister of the Church of England, now showed a good deal of sympathy. One of the 'peculiar elements' Mr Wing referred to may have been the fact that the 'close proximity of Radcliffe to

Holme Pierrepont makes it important that any leniency which can be shown should be'.

The Primitive Methodists, for their part, were profusely grateful, and through their minister acting for them, Benjamin Fell of Nottingham, they agreed to raise their offer to the required amount. This was accepted on condition that the plot in question did not deprive the estate of frontage needed for access to land at the back. In the end 960 square yards for £168 were bought (i.e. at 3s.6d per square yard) so the Manvers estate trustees may have felt that they had not done too badly out of the transaction. The Primitive Methodists, however, had certainly obtained a bargain judging by the fact that only four years later a Mr Knight offered 5s.6d a square yard for land adjoining the chapel. This offer may have been in connection with a plan mentioned by Arthur Rose to build a caretaker's house for the chapel and two shops (which were intended to cover the costs of the transaction). Mr Rose, however, remarked darkly that 'some detrimental talk' scotched the plan.

Mr Arthur Rose, his wife and three sons (Cyril, Sam and Teddy) in the early 1900s

The chapel on the Shelford road

A draft conveyance of 28th July 1891 with a sketch outline of the land concerned shows an irregular plot bounded by the Shelford road on the north, land retained by Earl Manvers on the west and south, and land occupied by Miss Morley and Miss Robotham on the east. It was described as 'being a portion of a certain croft or orchard heretofore held with a messuage of the earl in the occupation of Edith Bowren'. The chapel trustees agreed to build and keep in good order walls on all sides. Thirteen of these trustees came from Radcliffe, headed by William Clay, evangelist, George Henry Barnes, joiner and wheelwright, and Richard Rose, cordwainer and father of Arthur to whom we owe the reminiscences. Among the others were a tailor, several labourers and a cottager, a coal merchant, a railway watchman, a fitter and a plate layer. They do not appear to have been in any hurry to build because in a letter of September 1891, Benjamin Fell wrote to Mr Wing:

> ..... it is reported that the tenant occupying the land we have bought at Radcliffe is consulting a lawyer with a view to causing us trouble and if possible preventing our building or taking possession of the land. May I ask you to instruct me please what notice she will require ..... I called to see the people and said we had no wish to disturb them for the present and they were quite welcome to the fruit, etc. I further said we would not hurt them with the rent if they wished to keep it until we wished to build and if they so desired we would take the land after the fruit was gathered and relieve them from any rent at all.

Arthur Rose confirmed that there was a delay: 'We had a marquee on the land and a great bazaar before any building was on ....' According to the 1931 pamphlet the turf was sold from the site for £3, and some of the members volunteered to dig the foundations. £5 was allowed for this in the bill of costs.

The date engraved on the foundation stone is 10th June 1893. The ceremony was timed to coincide with a Primitive Methodist Conference in Nottingham, so it was well-attended by ministers from all over the country. The occasion was partially marred, however, by an accident to the President of the Conference as he was walking from Radcliffe station. A cyclist, 'approaching very rapidly from behind', knocked him down, causing him to be 'much hurt for some considerable time afterwards'. Fortunately he recovered sufficiently to be able to address a public meeting after tea in the Wesleyan Chapel, and the ceremony took place as planned. Several stones commemorated leading members of the Society. Prominent amongst them was the name of 'Master Arthur Rose' and he explained how it came about that he, a mere stripling of 17 years, was so honoured. Every Saturday night he had had the task of collecting a penny a week from sixty homes. In four years he had raised £52. In addition, money was raised by six or seven ladies with sewing meetings and

The Primitive Methodist chapel on Shelford Road
photographed about 1920

bazaars. The architect was W. Sutton and the contractor John Lewin of Netherfield. The latter's charges were £815, and the total, with other incidental expenses, came to £1,435. 4s.0d. Donations raised £232.2s, special efforts (Mr Rose and the sewing ladies?) £272.2s.10½d, the foundation and opening services brought in £251.4s.10d, and £70.13s.6d was brought over from the old chapel account; £575 was borrowed.

Again according to the 1931 pamphlet, the first sermon was preached in the new chapel in October 1893 by the Rev J. Stevenson, followed in the afternoon, by the Rev M. Potts, Radcliffe's Wesleyan minister. The trustees' troubles were not yet over, however, for the new chapel was deficient in many ways. Mr Rose described how:

> *After the opening ceremony, people complained of draught to legs and feet so all the pews had to be boarded in. There were complaints about the noise over the grates, so we had to get coconut matting down the aisles ..... there had to be extra money found for fencing and a wall.*

Later £47 had to be spent on heating and in 1895 a schoolroom was added. Floods in the boiler house forced the congregation into the schoolroom for services on occasions and involved hours of pumping out water on Saturday and Sunday mornings. With sacrifice and toil these problems were overcome and the chapel remains as a witness to these endeavours to this day.

Interior of the Primitive Methodist chapel showing the original pews
before their removal in 1975

The Wesleyans from 1851

The Wesleyans were still the predominant nonconformist group in Radcliffe, as the two religious censuses of 1851 and 1882 showed. They had survived the traumas of the crisis of 1849 relatively intact and were able to concentrate on the struggle to pay off the debt on the chapel. By 1872 this was £480 and was finally cleared by a concerted effort through donations from the trustees and congregation and a gift of £50 with a loan of £50 without interest from the Chapel Fund Committee. This left them free to improve the interior of the chapel by repainting and revarnishing the woodwork, the cost of £170 being almost completely realised by collections at the opening service in the newly decorated chapel, at which one of the preachers was the Rev J. Brewster.

Modernisation had already begun in 1863 when the old colza lamps were replaced by petroleum lamps, they in their turn being superseded by gas lighting in 1873. The old chapel had had no heating at all, but coal stoves were used in the present one and these were replaced by a method of heating hot water in 1875. More significant in its reflection of changing attitudes was the decision to replace the forms, which had been free seats, with pews. This was at 'the considerate suggestion of a member of the congregation who offered to defray half the expense' and, said Anonymous, was 'for the greater comfort of the occupants and to obliterate a somewhat invidious distinction'. Finally in 1878 the design of the interior of the chapel, always considered to be unsatisfactory, was completely altered, thus adding 100 new seats as well as room for a new orchestra and a new American organ.

These improvements would hardly have been possible if there had not been something of a revival in the fortunes of the Society and the appointment for the first time in 1875 of a resident minister, the Rev Walter Scott Page, greatly assisted this. Pew rents increased by £12 and the contribution of the Society to circuit funds was brought up to £60 a year from £40. With a division of the Halifax Place circuit and the inclusion of Radcliffe in the Arkwright Street circuit in 1876, the Rev Page had to leave and it was not until 1882 that he was replaced by the Rev J. Knight on condition that the branch brought their contributions to circuit funds up to £135 a year. In the interim students from Headingley College had been brought in to help the itinerant ministers and local preachers. The confidence and optimism of this period reached a peak in 1884, when the Society was again deprived of its resident minister.

The Jubilee of 1889

The improvements of the 1870s left the chapel estate still in debt although Anonymous informs us that during the ten years 1879-1889 the revenue account annually yielded a small surplus. Writing just before the Jubilee celebrations he anticipated that the debt would be much reduced by collections, enabling the Society 'to enter upon its future with a very light financial burden, leaving its resources more available for the aggressive work of the church'. His optimism was justified for the two days of services, Sunday November 3rd and the following Thursday brought in, according to the *Express*, £121 'considerably more than was hoped for'. The occasion, which celebrated the founding of the local society a hundred years before, was also one of great rejoicing:

> *The large building was packed with enthusiastic and devotional congregations at each of the three services. The choir was largely augmented for the occasion and additional instrumentalists assisted. Mr Ed. Stone presided at the organ and at the morning service the anthem 'How beauteous are their feet' was sung, solos taken by Mrs W. Haynes.*

Visiting preachers on the two days came from as far afield as Belfast (the Rev Wesley Guard) as well as locally, Mr John Cripwell and the Rev John Hind. The *Express* gave a brief history of the branch up to 1889 and added that it

> *now boasts something like 500 worshippers ..... much good work continues in connection with the chapel by means of a mission band, which conducts open-air services and cottage prayer meetings.*

The congregation

The Wesleyan Society which celebrated its centenary in 1889 was a close knit one, in many respects like an extended family. Its members would have found in the the various offices and activities of the branch a focus, not just for their spiritual life, but for their social needs as well. There were more opportunities for involvement for both sexes than were offered by the Church of England, but there is no doubt that it was still a male dominated organisation. From the local preacher Mr Henry Richards down, all the offices - the Society Stewards, the Stewards of the Poor Fund, the Chapel Stewards, the Mission Band and the Trustees - were held by men. Not surprisingly the Sewing Meeting was run by women with its own Treasurer and Secretary, and two out of the five Leaders were women, but the Sunday School was led by two male superintendents and a male secretary and there were seventeen male teachers as against fifteen female ones. Women predominated in the choir, although all but one of the instrumentalists was a man; but no doubt aesthetic considerations played their part here.

By 1889 many of the well known names of the past had disappeared altogether among the families gathered in the chapel. There were no Marriotts and no Roulstones, and the Rev Daniel Tatham (the son of Thomas Tatham of Nottingham, the friend of John Brewster) who had chosen to retire at Cedar House in Radcliffe, had died in 1871, although his locally born wife lived for some years after him. The name of Brewster had also disappeared, although the Stones and Greens were linked with it by marriage, and the mantle of that family, as representing the most prosperous in the community, seems to have fallen on the Haynes family. Two of them, Samuel and his nephew Thomas, had married two of John Brewster's daughters, Elizabeth in 1846 and Sarah in 1844. Thomas's sons and their wives were among the trustees; they were leaders, stewards, teachers and above all, members of the choir and orchestra, where Mrs W. Haynes was the soloist who elicited much praise from the press. The Haynes family were also related by marriage to the Morleys, as were the Beestons; in the same way, the Fosters were linked with the Uptons, joiners originally from Saxondale. All these families played an active part in the Society, but the less affluent, such as the Nowells and the Richmonds, both labouring families, also variously served on the Mission Band, as a Steward of the Poor or as teachers and in the orchestra. Other modest members were the Eastwoods. Mary Althea and Priscilla (a dressmaker) lived with their widowed mother, a cottager with just two acres. They were Sunday School teachers, aged 32 and 27 years respectively in 1871 but only admitted to being five years older at the next census! John Vickerstaff, the chapel keeper for more than thirty years, who lived in the chapel house with his wife, a lace worker, and their seven children, was a farm labourer.

New families had joined the Society on moving to Radcliffe, some clearly the product of the new railway age. Matthew East was a railway carpenter and John Marshall a plate layer from Lincolnshire. The railway had brought others, commuting from Radcliffe to work in Nottingham, such as the lace manufacturers Edwin Green and W.F. Green, a trustee, and Jabez Underwood living in Lorne Grove, who was an instrumentalist whilst his wife, Harriet, was treasurer of the Sewing Meeting.

A story about a Nottinghamshire hymn writer William Matthews (born 1750) which was sent in to the *Nottinghamshire Weekly Guardian* in 1935 neatly encapsulates the strong sense of tradition which characterised this period of the Society's history, as well as the emphasis given by it to music. Under the direction of the organist, Mr Edward Stone, Matthews' hymns were still popular in Radcliffe in the 1880s. A visiting minister who tried to introduce something new met some opposition:

..... one of the congregation rose and exclaimed 'Mr Minister you started a tune noan of us knowed; now we'll hae one as yer doan't know', and another of Matthews' pieces 'Foundling' was sung with a gusto which nearly raised the roof.

The Wesleyans and the village

The Society was not, however, insulated from local affairs and many of the men among its members aspired to public life. Of these the most prominent were again from the Haynes family who, sometime towards the end of the century, moved into the imposing Grange on the Main Road. Thomas senior was on the Board of Guardians from 1852-1858. So too was his son, who was also at various times an overseer, a Jeffrey Dole charity trustee, a J.P. (1907) and a parish councillor between 1896 and 1916. At his death in that year he was a Rural District Councillor and his place on the parish council was taken by his son William Brewster Haynes. Others who were parish councillors were James Upton, (who was also a Rural District Councillor), Thomas Foster, and Richard Barratt, a shoemaker, the two latter being Jeffrey Dole trustees as well. The Wesleyans who, a hundred years and more before, had founded their society in defiance of the establishment, both ecclesiastical and lay, had now become part of the establishment themselves.

December 1905.

Vol. I. Nº 9.

Wesleyan Methodist Church,
Radcliffe-on-Trent

MONTHLY MAGAZINE.

Sunday School: Morning, 10, Afternoon, 2.

WEEK NIGHT MEETINGS

Prayer Meeting,
Monday, 7.30.
Preaching Service,
Thursday Evening, 7.30

SOCIETY CLASSES:

Monday (Juniors only)
Boys 7.15.
Tuesday (Juniors only)
Girls 6.30.

Tuesday,	7.30.
Wednesday,	7.30.
Friday	7.30.
Sunday Morning,	9.30.

Y.P.C.A.

Tuesday, 8.0.

BAND OF HOPE.

Thursday, 7.0.

MINISTER'S BIBLE CLASS.

Friday, at 8.0.

Public Worship : Sunday Morning, 10 30.   Evening, 6.30.

Minister :   REV. THOS. MILLER, Bingham Road, Radcliffe-on-Trent.

All literary matter for publication to be sent to the Minister.
All matters and enquiries respecting this Magazine and its distribution must be sent to the Secretary, MR. SADLER,
Lorne Grove, Radcliffe-on-Trent.

The cover of the Wesleyan Methodist magazine December 1905 (reduced)

The last organ in the Wesleyan chapel photographed about 1948

The Band of Hope

In its account of the Jubilee of 1889, the *Express* reported that there was a Band of Hope with 100 members attached to the chapel. Although the temperance movement and Methodism were closely linked and Methodist pulpits had long been used to preach the temperance cause, the relationship was not always an easy one. This must have been particularly true in Radcliffe where so many of the leading Wesleyans were maltsters or publicans. From Robert Brewster onwards there were always a few in every generation. The Haynes family, although also involved in farming and joinery, included maltsters and licensed victuallers from Thomas in 1841 through to William Brewster Haynes in the early 1900s. Other Methodists engaged in the trade were the Howards and the Chamberlains and even the Independent Primitive Methodists, more closely associated with the temperance movement than the Wesleyans, included publicans and maltsters among their members.

Many Methodist branches at this time sought to provide their localities with alternatives to the public house and heavy drinking. The Reading Room referred to in Wright's *Directory* of 1879, Thomas Foster being secretary, and Richard Barratt's Coffee and Tea Rooms were perhaps opened with this object in mind. Swift, in his book *The Lively People* quotes the *Methodist Magazine* which reported that a library was opened in 1897 by the Wesleyans. Arrangements were made with the Mechanics Institute 'for a liberal supply of papers, periodicals and books' and a 'very bright and warm room' was provided. An added attraction was the fact that the room was open to both sexes.

The resident minister

Anonymous quite clearly linked the success of the branch with having a resident minister, but it is not certain when one was permanently acquired. Wright's *Directory* of 1889 does not mention one, but in 1894 and 1895 two are named as living at Hollyhurst (31 Bingham Road) - the Rev James H. and the Rev James R. Clementson. They were immediately succeeded by the Rev Jabez Edward Creasy and in 1897 by the Rev J.S. Lewis. From 1900 onwards resident ministers are regularly named. The frontispiece of a monthly magazine dated December 1905 (Vol. 1 No. 9) has survived with the name of the Rev Thos. Miller, Bingham Road printed at the bottom. Two others, the Rev Ellis in 1908 and the Rev Snowden Walsh from 1910 to 1913 also lived at Hollyhurst, while in 1920 the Rev W. Jones, M.Sc., who was also chaplain to Saxondale hospital, was in residence. There are no signs, however, that the Primitive Methodists had acquired a resident minister by this date, and in 1893 their chapel was still not licensed to perform marriages.

A social gathering at Hollyhurst in 1912.
The Rev Snowden Walsh and his wife are on the right

The two communities, the Wesleyans and the Primitive Methodists, continued on their separate ways throughout this later period. Moves towards unity among the various branches of Methodism were afoot elsewhere and culminated in 1932 when Conference decided on Union. But practical amalgamation took very much longer, especially in villages such as Radcliffe. Not until July 1953 were the last services held in the old chapel of 1839 (it was pulled down in 1967), after which all the Methodists of the village joined to worship together in the chapel built for the Primitives on Shelford Road.

Main sources

Primary

John Rylands' Library, Manchester: Nottingham District Meeting Minutes.

Nottinghamshire Archives Office: Radcliffe parish registers; Canaan Street Leaders Meeting Minute Book MR 15/20; Quarter Day Minute Book MR 15/19; Nottingham South Circuit MR 15/18; Nottingham Circuit Report MR 15/17; Primitive Methodist Leaders Meeting Minute Books MR 15/17 - 20; Conveyance: 6th January 1843 DD 27/1; Return of Chief Constable of Worksop QDR 2/5; Independent Prim. Baptism register MR 15/36 (K); Wesleyan register 15/11-13.

Nottinghamshire County Library (Local Studies Library): census returns; religious census.

Public Record Office: Places of Religious Worship RG 31/3.

Radcliffe-on-Trent Parish Council: cemetery records.

University of Nottingham: Manvers Papers Ma 2 C & D.

Secondary

Anon. *A century of Wesleyan Methodism in Radcliffe-on-Trent.* 1789-1889 1889.

Anon. *A pleasing and interesting historie of three most noble martyrs* 1850.

Chamberlain, Colet. *Memories of the past* . 1960.

Clowes, Wm. *Journal*. 1844.

Harwood, G. *A history of Wesleyan Methodism in Nottingham*. 1872.

Primitive Methodist Chapel, Radcliffe-on-Trent. Pamphlet. 1931.

Radcliffe-on-Trent local history research group: extracts from Nottingham newspapers 1837-1920.

Rose, A. Typescript of unpublished reminiscences.

Swift, R. *The lively people*. 1982.

Vickers, J. *History of Independent Methodism*. 1920.

THE COMING OF THE RAILWAY

The first recorded railway line in England was at Wollaton near Nottingham where horse traction was used from 1604 to take coal to the river Trent. Some 200 years were to pass before the steam railway age dawned, reaching a climax in the 1840s when there was intense railway investment and speculation throughout England. In the first place railways were developed for freight and the idea of using them for passenger traffic was an afterthought. They therefore posed an instant commercial threat to existing canal companies which often had to be bought up to silence them. As railways also required land, thus interfering with property rights, every enterprise had to be authorised by Act of Parliament. When all expenses were taken into account, it is not surprising that promoters were more likely to lose money by railway investment than make a fortune.

The railway reached Nottingham in 1839 from Derby, the terminus station being built in the Meadows just outside the town. The company concerned, the Midland Counties Railway, amalgamated with two other lines to form the Midland Railway under the leadership of George Hudson the so-called 'railway king'. At about this time Nottingham Corporation formed a railway committee which examined thirty-five projects. One scheme which interested them was for a line from Ambergate via Ripley, Alfreton and Bulwell to Nottingham proposed by the Nottingham, Erewash, Ambergate and Manchester Railway Company. Another was for a Nottingham, Vale of Belvoir and Grantham Railway, and a third was for a Nottingham to Boston Railway without a connection to Grantham. In September 1845 these three projects were amalgamated to form the Ambergate, Nottingham and Boston and Eastern Junction Railway. (A local provisional director was William Taylor of Radcliffe Hall.) An alternative project was the Grand Union Railway, a parallel scheme running east to King's Lynn with a branch line to Boston. In 1846 the first scheme was authorised, and the promoters of the second merged their interests with it.

At the same time, Grantham had been trying to get the main line from London to York to pass through the town as part of the Great Northern Railway route. George Hudson of the Midland Railway saw this as a threat to his monopoly of transport in the east midlands and he promoted and obtained the right to build a railway from Carrington Street station in Nottingham to Lincoln. This was intended as a counter-argument in Parliament against the Great Northern's bill, on the grounds that the area was adequately provided for. Hudson failed to stop the bill, however, and 1846 saw the authorisation of lines from London to York via Grantham and from Ambergate to Boston in June and July respectively.

Early difficulties

Locally, the original route west of Saxondale deviated from the line eventually built, passing south of Radcliffe, more or less on the line of the present by-pass and continuing towards West Bridgford some 200 yards south of the A52 (Nottingham to Grantham) road. By December 1846 this scheme was in difficulties, presumably financial, or through opposition from the Nottingham and Grantham canal. Some unspecified problem caused Lord Manvers, through whose land much of the proposed line was to run, to write to Mr Pocock, his London solicitor:

> *I am on the eve of a regular <u>stand up fight</u> with the Boston and Ambergate Railway Co. who are attempting an outrageous breach of faith with me on the Holme Pierrepont estate, but matters are not yet sufficiently ripe to enter further upon the subject.*

It was subsequently decided to cross the river at Radcliffe and join the Midland's Nottingham to Lincoln line at Colwick. Hudson and the Midland readily agreed to this, and gave the Ambergate (as it became known) running powers into the Midland station. By 1849 the proposals for the lines west of Nottingham and east of Grantham had been abandoned and these areas were served by other companies.

The Midland tried to buy the Ambergate in 1846 and again in 1847. However Graham Hutchinson, who owned a considerable number of Great Northern shares, bought up Ambergate shares and thwarted the Midland's attempts. Not everyone agreed with Hutchinson's initial actions, some shareholders favouring a merger with the Midland as an established company. Mr Mitchell, a critic at the shareholders' meeting in February 1848, spoke of the transfer of shares to 'men of straw'. He proposed that a committee of five directors and five substantial shareholders should look into the running of the company and suggest economies. 'If people thought this was crying stinking fish, their property was already so stinking that 999 men out of 1,000 would not give anything for it,' he claimed.

Such a committee was set up and reported back in May 1848. The new estimate for the cost of land was £320,000 (£100,000 more than originally quoted) while the cost of plant, rolling stock, buildings and machinery for maintenance and repair was expected to be £260,000. The total cost of the whole line from Ambergate to Boston was estimated at £2,600,000, excluding £232,500 for the purchase of canals.

Arguments with Lord Manvers

The principal landowner with whom the Ambergate had to deal in the Radcliffe area was the forthright second Earl Manvers. A Mr Mason was his principal negotiator with the company, but to a large extent he was instructed by George Beaumont, the earl's local agent. By October 1847 Mason and Beaumont had provisionally agreed with the company a figure for the sale of land which may have been as much as £340 per acre, but at this point the company brought in their own valuation officer, a Mr Wilmot. The sum he recommended is not recorded, but it was clearly a much lower figure, for it caused the following explosion of wrath from Lord Manvers in a letter to Beaumont:

With respect to any overture on the part of the Ambergate Co. or their agents, I need hardly tell you that when I listen to it the impression uppermost in my mind must be, that it is based in treachery and falsehood, as I cannot believe them capable of becoming honest in any transaction whatever unless by accident.

The railway's figure is made clear in December when Wilmot wrote to Mason:

I think the sum of £280 per acre a high price under all the circumstances. This sum I am willing to give but cannot exceed it.

Two days later Mason wrote to Beaumont expressing surprise that the earlier figure should have been retracted, continuing:

Perhaps it may be advisable to prevent any further trouble or annoyance to Lord Manvers for me to offer to take £300 per acre and so settle the affair...

Beaumont was not prepared to go as far as that. In the draft of a no-nonsense letter to the railway's board on 18th December 1847 he wrote:

My opinion is that the sum of £340 per acre ought to be given for the land and severance of Lord Manvers ..... Offer at £310 per acre and this 'without prejudice as to any future proceedings'; if not accepted go to a jury - in that case the whole of the line must be paid for on touching a part and I fear Lord Manvers will feel himself justified on the score of reciprocal retraction in not considering in the least the accommodation, the interest or the wishes of the Company.

The same day as his letter to the company, Beaumont wrote to Mr Percy more in sorrow than in anger:

I had hopes negotiations for Lord Manvers' land was progressing with some pleasing indication of being terminated in a speedy way, and possibly in a manner to give material satisfaction - but I fear I calculated too soon - I am compelled to learn today that the movements are retrograde on your behalf than which nothing is more calculated to vex or annoy ......

His lordship seemed more satisfied than I expected with the engineering accommodations and the progress towards us settling the case without a jury which under my care the matter had been brought to. Is it wise, then, to disturb this harmony by retraction? We know what we shall be obliged to do - and rely upon it, the stoutest resistance possible will be made. You must see our difficulty and obviate if possible.

It would seem that these letters bore fruit for further negotiations followed but on January 11th 1848 Beaumont wrote to Mason expressing further dissatisfaction:

A mistake occurred, I find, on getting out the quantities from the faint ink the Engineer has used and the hurry of doing the business ..... Society is now sadly constituted and the collective body of Railway proprietors are not over scrupulous as to the means they use to get property cheap ..... In fact an umpire or jury would annoy Lord Manvers very much, and we should not gain a great deal if any.

Beaumont still had reservations:

The only thing I fear is we do not know the end of the Company's requirements, their damage by severance or their limit of requisite land, it not being staked out.

On 22nd January 1848 Wilmot wrote to Mason that 'it now appears to be arranged' that the sum should be £300 per acre making a total of £3,637 for 12 acres, 0 chains, 24 perches. Two days later Mason wrote to the company's solicitor, Percy, to ask for two extra clauses to be inserted: that further land would be paid for at £310 per acre, and that all and every expense should be met by the company.

The Reverend Henry Bolton
The matter was hardly settled when another letter from Beaumont to Mason showed that further trouble was on the way, this time concerning the Rev Bolton, the owner of Radcliffe Lodge who also rented some additional land from Lord Manvers. By this date he was living in the Park, Nottingham, and was about to let the Lodge to the railway contractors for their headquarters while construction work took place locally. George Beaumont was incensed when he heard that Bolton had asked such an outrageous price for his land that the railway line had been diverted, without consultation, through the osier beds of John Brewster, the earl's tenant at The Chestnuts:

They have deviated the line about 20 yards to avoid Bolton's few perches of land, for which I hear he asked £700!! This deviation throws the line further into the osier bed, and I think after a valuation had taken place notice of such alteration ought to have been given us and moreover the line ought most certainly to have been staked out before our valuation.

Despite this deviation, the railway still had to cut through the grounds of Radcliffe Lodge, leaving some part isolated. This affected the land rented by the Rev Bolton from Lord Manvers. The clergyman was anxious to obtain his full rights and on 27th January 1848 wrote to Beaumont:

The railway company, in giving me notice as occupier of land under Lord Manvers have partly offered to build a bridge. Under the circumstances, in order that I may know how to treat with them, may I request you kindly to inform me whether his Lordship has <u>stipulated</u> with the railway to build bridges for his tenants where requisite? And if not, whether you think in this case his Lordship would assist me in requiring one?
You, no doubt, know also whether his Lordship has reserved the timber on the land required by the railway, or whether it belongs to the railway. It is a small matter and as such I must apologise for naming it at all and only do so indeed because I am writing. The owners of Radcliffe Lodge have always

planted, reared and cut down and used as they pleased, the ornamental trees on the land rented from Lord Manvers, and I have in like manner done the same, with Mr Burgess's [the former agent] full knowledge. There is only one tree standing on the land about to be taken by the railway - a Horse Chestnut - worth (it may be) perhaps (I should guess) about forty shillings top and all together. If you think well and that you can with propriety give leave, I shall be glad to make use of this tree as I shall have some expenses of fencing (besides what the railway will do). But under present circumstances I would on no account do so without leave. You will, I hope, excuse my naming it and also do me the favor [sic] to reply to my first enquiries by the earliest post you conveniently can as our days of negotiating are limited.

In reply Beaumont indicated that Lord Manvers' generosity was limited:

I shall not require from the Railway company any bridge to connect the land you hold with any other property of Earl Manvers and this arrangement has been made with the concurrence of Earl Manvers.
     The Horse Chestnut tree his Lordship gives up to you for your use to be appropriated to any purpose you may think fit.

On 31st January 1848 Bolton again wrote to Beaumont:

In answer to the railway notice, I beg to say ..... by a special arrangement and exchange of land the Compensation I require under the circumstances is £40.

On the reverse Beaumont has written, 'H.B.'s claim for tenant's right on the Ambergate railway: £40!'. The clergyman's claim was obviously considered extortionate. Something must have been agreed between Lord Manvers and the railway company, however, about a bridge over the cutting, for in March 1851, Beaumont acknowledged to Welby & Wood, solicitors for the railway:

£250 was received by Earl Manvers to supercede the need of a bridge across the deep cutting at Radcliffe near Mr Bolton's house.

Despite evident satisfaction with arrangements in January, the Rev Bolton dug in his heels about quitting the land he rented, for on 4th February 1848 Mr Percy wrote to Beaumont on behalf of the railway company:

On attempting to treat with the Rev Henry Bolton he most distinctly states that he has not received any notice from Lord Manvers or his agent to quit at Lady Day <u>next</u> and that he is entitled to hold until Lady Day 1849. Having understood from you yesterday that Mr Bolton's tenancy will expire legally at Lady Day <u>next,</u> I shall be glad to know what his legal position is and of the other tenants of Lord Manvers who occupy any part or parts of the land contracted to be sold by his Lordship.

There is no record of Beaumont's reply, but the contractors were certainly in possession by the following Lady day.

John Brewster
     John Brewster, whose osier beds had been further encroached upon as a result of the Rev Henry Bolton's demands, wrote to Beaumont asking for guidance as to the value of the land in connection with his own application for loss of tenant rights. Beaumont's reply of 27th February 1848 reads thus:

The land sold by Lord Manvers to the Ambergate Co. at Radcliffe is valued according to its locality and the damage caused by severance. The severance of Radcliffe Wharf, and the land near Radcliffe Lodge, is also a considerable item. The Company have claimed from Lord Manvers a <u>detailed valuation</u> - that precedent in the price of land in Radcliffe might not be established - which they expect would act unfairly towards them.

The tenants of Lord Manvers will be expected to give possession to the Railway Company, on receiving a fair and equitable compensation for Tenants' right and all legal and accustomed demands.

Presumably such a detailed valuation was made, but there is no trace of it in the documents relating to the railway business in the Manvers papers.

The effect on the wharf

Throughout the railway correspondence there are fragments of information about the wharf, the manager of which was Edward Parr. Half the wharf was owned by the estate, the tenancy being in the gift of the Radcliffe agent, and Parr had obtained his tenancy, at £30 per annum, from Mr Burgess, Beaumont's predecessor. In October 1847 it had occurred to Beaumont that the value of the wharf was well in excess of £30 rent and should not be assessed at that figure by the valuers. He wrote to Lord Manvers:

It has always been considered an adjunct to the agency of the late Mr Burgess for which the nominal sum of £30 per annum was realised. The agent, superintendent or manager (E.Parr) having as his most ample remuneration or wages the house, Warehouse buildings and land, five acres, the Ferry and some perquisites at least together making upwards of £100 per annum, by which he has become rich and independent - now the Railway want not only to take part of the Wharf land, but in some measure, and that considerable, infringe upon or nullify these privileges and emoluments, and it must not be accepted in argument from the Railway Company that £30 p.a. was the value of this portion of the estate ..... I caused Parr at the Wharf to be put under notice to quit by the Executors of Mr Burgess for safety and to ensure full powers to contend with the Railway Company. I, also, gave him notice.

While Mr Mason thought that the wharf would not be affected by the railway construction, Beaumont, in addressing the company on the subject, was distinctly uncomplimentary:

There is not the slightest doubt the wharf should be a consideration for I do not see upon what principle of common sense or honesty any company of adventurers can infringe upon settled rights or forcibly take them away without any remuneration.

In a post-script to a letter to Mason on January 11th 1848 Beaumont mentions that he had been made 'an offer of the sum of £100 per annum for Radcliffe Wharf and buildings without the field'. As Edward Parr was to remain at the wharf for a further twenty-eight years, we must assume it was he who made the offer. Perhaps he did not yet envisage the loss of river trade that the railway was to cause.

In April Beaumont wrote to the contractors demanding compensation for any injury done to the close of land at the wharf, to be decided by mutually agreed persons. Friction was still continuing in January 1849 when Beaumont wrote directly to the Ambergate Railway Company telling them that if they needed an extension of privileges or any temporary occupation of land for railway purposes they should give the requisite notice and not permit

any parties ..... to tamper with the Tenants and lead them from their duty. Such irregularities give me infinite trouble and anxiety and can but tend to weaken that confidence I am desirous to maintain.

Some months later the problem over the wharf land was sorted out, at any rate to the railway company's satisfaction, John Hall for the contractors having paid 'Mr Parr of Radcliffe £13.0s.0d for his tenant rights on 11th Nov. last'.

Lord Manvers' final account

Meanwhile, negotiations with the Manvers estate and the railway were nearing completion. On the last day of January 1848, Wilmot, the railway's valuer, wrote again to Mason indicating that the directors would deposit the first instalment of £1,000 so that the contractors could begin work. This suggestion caused the following outburst from Lord Manvers to the unlucky Beaumont:

....as I do not at all comprehend with what view the advance of £1000 has been made instanter, I desire most distinctly to explain that I will not allow a spade to be struck into the ground until the entire sum of £3,700 has been lodged in the bank at Nottingham .....

However the company's solicitor, a Mr Percy, had already pointed out:

...The Company shall only be required to invest or otherwise deposit the purchase money in pursuance of the provisions of the Land Clauses Act ...from time to time as they may take possession of any part of the land.

Consequently, his lordship did not get his way and records show that he was in fact paid in three instalments: £1,000 on 2nd February and on 9th May, and a final instalment of only £1,400 on 9th June 1849. (The agreed sum never seems to have been the same for many weeks together.)

A document signed on 18th November 1850 by W. Booker on behalf of Lord Manvers sets out the totals of the lands taken for the railway from the estate in Radcliffe:

		a	r	p	£	s	d
Lands	N of R.Trent	3	1	04	786	0	0
"	S to the Wharf Road	4	3	06	1,360	10	0
In severance with the Wharf and its appurtenances					300	0	0
Land late in occupation of H. Bolton		1	0	15	416	10	0
" from	J. Brewster's homestead						
" "	Richard Stone		1	1	35	612	10	0
" "	J. Brewster (Brick Kiln Close)			1	30	69	0	0
	Total	11	0	18	3,544	10	0
Deduct for wall as agreed					12	0	0
					3,532	10	0

It may have been in connection with his experience over the railway in Radcliffe that, according to a correspondent to the *Nottingham Journal* in 1871, about this time Lord Manvers declared before Parliament, 'If possessed of sufficient power I would consign the whole of the railways of this kingdom to that place which the presence of your lordships forbids me to mention.'

Construction work started

Well before these financial matters had been resolved, work on the line actually began. There were at least two contractors overall, Messrs Greaves, Adams & Smart being responsible for the eleven mile section from Colwick to Bottesford, which included a viaduct across the Trent. The first sod for the railway was cut at Bottesford in February 1847 by Mrs Norton of Elton Manor, the wife of the chairman of the railway company, but because of the protracted negotiations with the Manvers estate it was a year later before work started at the western end of the line. In March 1848 the Ambergate Railway Company was able to report to its shareholders that the 6¾ miles from Bottesford to Grantham was well under way, with 404 men and sixty-three horses being used, whereas near Radcliffe materials had only been assembled the previous month ready to begin work on the timber viaduct as soon as the weather permitted.

The bridge erected over the river Trent consisted of three brick arches of 32 feet 6 inches span and one cast iron arch of 107 feet span by Clayton, Shuttleworth & Co. of Lincoln. During the construction of the line it was found that there was a deficiency of earthworks from cuttings to form embankments so it was decided to build a viaduct from the bridge to the wharf at Radcliffe, a distance of 45 chains.

Although there was scarcely a dry day for the first two months, sufficient progress was made for the *Nottingham Journal* to report on 26th May 1848 that the viaduct over the Wharf Road and Mr Brewster's osier holt was about to be completed. There were thirty bays in the viaduct, measuring 30 feet from centre to centre, and a similar height from the ground to the top of the rails. The pile timbers averaged 45 feet in length, a total of 100,000 feet of timber being used for 250 piles. The weight of screws and bolts was estimated at about 45 tons, while the four cast iron girders across Wharf Road weighed about 18 tons. The joints were capped with iron plates to combine elegance with strength. The first waggons with earth were taken across from the cliff cutting that week: each waggon held 2½ cubic yards, weighing about 2½ tons. Altogether the viaduct was termed 'a very stupendous affair'.

A train crossing Radcliffe's original wooden viaduct

A celebration

At this point Messrs Greaves, Adams & Smart decided to give their workmen - more than 300 of them - a treat to celebrate the completion of this section of the enterprise. A banner bearing the words 'Success to the Ambergate Company' decorated the head of the viaduct, while the grounds of Radcliffe Lodge, let to the contractors as their headquarters, were used for the main part of the celebration. The lawns were decked with flowers and evergreens, several marquees were erected from the friends of the contractors, and in front of each floated a banner with 'Welcome' on it. A figure of Britannia in appropriate costume 'towered majestically in the centre of the greensward', and it was reported that the long tables bent beneath the weight of goodly viands. At 2 p.m. a brass band, having already paraded through the village, went onto the viaduct from which three waggon loads of soil were tipped 'amidst the shouts of the assembled people'. The spread, which was voted first-rate, was provided by Mr George Starkey and Mr Oliver Beckitt. Sadly the weather, which had dogged the early days of the enterprise, struck again. At about 2.45 p.m. when the dinner was only part finished, dark clouds came over, and there followed one of the heaviest storms in memory. In the words of the *Journal* reporter:

> The workmen, who were seated at the tables, had no covering to shield them from the pelting rain, which deluged dishes and spoilt pie crusts. A very laughable scene occurred. They rose en masse, and each selecting an article from the table, one a pie, another a joint of meat, some the liquor and others the bread and cheese, they rushed helter-skelter beneath the trees, or into any place which afforded shelter. The visitors beneath the booths sat it well until the rain made progress through the awning when most of them rose, not appreciating a flooded seat; and not a few of them resorted to the expedient of creeping under the tables where they remained until they were driven out by the water streaming upon the floor.

The weather must have improved, for later in the afternoon the workmen, preceded by the brass band, chaired Mr Greaves and his partners round the lawn. The cloths and visitors booths were removed and Mr Greaves took the chair for the rest of the proceedings. The entertainment started with the glee singers. Then followed toasts in bumpers to each member of the royal family, followed by a song, and a toast to the Duke of Wellington. Another glee was followed by a speech on improvements brought about by British inventions. This was followed by a toast to the directors and to the solicitor. To steady themselves, soup was served next, but the spirit of the occasion had truly settled on the crowd, as yet another toast followed - this time to the engineer - and another glee. A Mr Cox then rose to his feet, and declared that when they saw such a man as Mr Sanday of Holme Lane giving assistance to the undertaking, they should feel grateful to him. The men rose to the challenge and toasted him in bumpers - three times three, and one more. This swept the proceedings along, for there then followed toasts to the acting engineers, to Butler Parr, and the resident villagers of Radcliffe; then a toast to Mr Cox who replied, praising Mr Greaves who gave a fair day's wages for a fair day's work; more toasts to the company's inspector, to Earl Manvers, the county noblemen, Captain Taylor and the county magistrates, John Oldknow, Mr Bowley and the visitors. The *Journal* summed up the characteristics of the day:

> *A good dinner, good appetites, a good storm, a good run and good-humoured countenances.*

Further progress in 1848

On 1st September 1848 the railway board reported to the half-yearly meeting. By this time the western abutment of the bridge crossing the Trent was 7 feet above the foundation course. A coffer-dam had been laid, the centre pier was in the course of construction and the eastern abutment begun. More bad weather led to flooding which hindered the workmen, but the contractors had a good stock of stone and were pushing ahead. In October the company expected that the bridge for the Shelford road would soon be completed.

Accidents to workmen

Even at this early stage the construction of the railway through Radcliffe was not without its human tragedy - which did not get reported to the shareholders, although it found its way into the *Nottingham Journal*. On 30th June 1848 the county coroner held an inquest at the Manvers Arms on Samuel Henson, a single man aged 20. He had been at work on the cutting for the railway when he was buried by a sudden fall of earth. He was immediately extricated and was conscious, but suffered internal injuries from which he died the same day.

A double accident occurred in the following month. On 28th July the *Journal* reported an inquest held on an Irish labourer named James Sheridan, aged 22, employed at Radcliffe by the railway contractors. On the previous Monday afternoon, he had been working on a travelling crane used to lower heavy blocks of stone and other materials. With a man named Boot he was on the top platform holding the windlass. Other men were adjusting the stone, which had been suspended for about two minutes, when one of the teeth of the ratchet broke, the jerk causing three other teeth to shatter. Instantly the windlass spun round, striking Sheridan on the forehead and knocking him off the upper platform on to that below. His head was severely crushed and blood flowed from his mouth and nose. He was taken to the office but died a short time after a surgeon arrived. Boot was also knocked down and fell into the foundations, a distance of 26 feet. He was taken unconscious to the General Hospital in Nottingham where he was believed to be recovering slowly. The inquest jury attached no blame to any of the men and brought in a verdict of accidental death on Sheridan, but added:

> *The jury is of the opinion that the upper platform is too small for the safety of the workmen, and that the ratchet wheel of the crane is too weak, and ought to be made much stronger, or an additional ratchet should be affixed to the crane.*

There is no indication whether these recommendations were implemented, nor if any compensation was paid to either victim. A few weeks later a Cropwell Butler labourer fell 14 feet while working on the railway, the nails and flesh of his two middle fingers being torn up to the second joint. In June 1849 Richard Clarke, aged 20, was caught between two waggons and the lower part of his body was badly crushed. Such accidents were a local reflection of the great loss of human life associated with the creation of the national railway network.

Drownings

The river, notoriously treacherous at Radcliffe, took its toll of unwary workmen too. The *Journal* of 11th July 1848 carried a report of three tramps searching for employment (presumably as labourers on the railway). They came to Radcliffe ferry and on asking the fare were told it was a penny each. As the three had only two pence between them one volunteered to swim across. He undressed and gave his companions his clothes to take in the boat. He started off swimming well, but the current was very strong and carried him to a 'levy hole', where he called out twice for assistance. The boat was too far off to get to him before he was drowned. His companions unsuccessfully dragged for him for the remainder of the day.

In the following winter, flooding caused the laying off of a number of men. In mid-December when the floods had subsided, one of the men, William Pepper, approached the sub-contractor asking for work without success. He then asked for wages due to him and was told to come back that evening. This occurred on the north bank of the Trent. He used the ferry to cross to his lodgings in Radcliffe, and went to another boat to fetch his shovel. To reach the place where it was lying he had to walk on the gunwale of the boat, and while doing so fell into the water. He tried to save himself by catching hold of one of the piles, but owing to the rapidity of the current he was swept away. The ferry boat immediately shoved off and drags were used, but not until four weeks later was the body found, partly buried in sand 300 yards below the spot where he had fallen in.

More problems

Apart from accidents to their workers, the contractors also had to cope with a potential strike, disease and thefts. In June 1849 Robert Ward and Richard Chance were each sent by the Bingham magistrates to the House of Correction at Southwell for a month for 'endeavouring by intimidation' to compel workmen on the Ambergate line to cease working. The newspaper report does not state why the men wanted a stoppage.

In 1849 Asiatic cholera arrived in Nottingham and wrought havoc in Radcliffe in September of that year. (See section on Public Health). Inquest reports indicate that navvies were living in one of the houses badly affected in Mount Pleasant, and a Radcliffe tradition associates the outbreak with railway workers on shifts successively occupying the same beds. It is not possible to tell from the parish register if any of the navvies died in the epidemic, but the railway contractors, together with the gentlemen of the vicinity, opened a subscription to assist the families of the victims. By October 5th the fund stood at £30.

Theft by employees as well as by outsiders was also a problem. The *Nottingham Journal* for 3rd November 1848 recorded the following case at Shire Hall:

> *John Lee was charged with stealing a belly-band and a pick-axe, the property of Messrs Greaves, Adams & Smart of Ratcliffe. Mr Joseph Adams said the prisoner had been in their employ for the last nine months and left them on Saturday night last. He was employed at Ratcliffe as store-keeper and had of course free access to the store room. He had no right to take any of the things off the premises. The witness could swear to the axe by the maker's name on it.* [The police searched Lee's house at Radford] *and found the belly-band and the pick-axe in a chamber, with a great number of other things of a like nature, but which the complainants could not swear to. John Andrews, saddler of London Road, Nottingham, said that as he made the belly-band for Messrs Greaves, Adams & Smart he would swear to it by the workmanship. The prisoner's defence was that his masters had four dozen pick-axes from Leicester, and that as there was one over, he took it as his right.*

Lee also claimed that he had bought the belly-band in the market place in Nottingham, but the magistrates thought there was a sufficient case against him to commit him for trial at the Quarter Sessions. There in the January he was found guilty but recommended to mercy. He was sentenced to one month's imprisonment, two weeks of which were to be spent in solitary confinement.

At the mid-summer sessions of 1849 Thomas Chapman of East Bridgford, a boatman aged 27, was also found guilty of stealing from the railway contractors at Radcliffe. This time two iron bars had been taken. Thomas Straw, a Radcliffe blacksmith, bought them from him for five shillings. Chapman was sentenced to three months' imprisonment, of which three weeks were to be in solitary confinement.

Alleged thefts also occurred between workmen. In January 1851 Edward Turner, a labourer aged 40, was charged at Bingham with stealing a fustian coat belonging to John Wilkinson. The latter, who was also a labourer working on the railway at Bingham but living in Radcliffe, left his coat one afternoon by the weighing machine house in the charge of another workman named Reedman. It was there overnight, but had been moved the next morning. Shortly afterwards Reedman found it concealed between a crane and the wall of the loading shed, and left it there. Later it was found to have been removed again. P.C. Gillman, however, found it the following day in Turner's house. Turner said he found the coat in the yard, and not knowing whose it was he took it home with him. A very good character was given to the prisoner by several persons and he was found not guilty.

Another workman employed by Mr Greaves on the railway in January 1851 benefited by not trying the 'finders keepers' principle. William Allcock found a gold watch 'between the field where they get gravel for ballast and the bridge over the Trent at Radcliffe'. It was described as a 'splendid gold watch with a gold chain and seals'. It would have been of considerable value and was soon claimed by a gentleman who 'liberally gave him all the silver he had with him, which amounted to half a crown'.These two last incidents show that work continued on the railway even after its opening in July 1850.

The grand opening

The grand opening of the section from Colwick to Grantham had been scheduled for June 4th 1850, but part of the embankment at Grantham was not consolidated, and it was another five weeks before the government inspector passed it as satisfactory. Running powers had already been obtained for Ambergate trains to go into the Midland station at Nottingham. At this stage the Ambergate line was seen as no threat to the Midland and was actually being eyed as a possible take-over option. Indeed there was a subsequent bid to this effect. A few days before the opening, however, the railway company was still without locomotives and two had to be borrowed from E.B. Wilson's locomotive works at Leeds. At last, on Monday 15th July all the endeavour came to fruition.

In Radcliffe Mr Greaves and his partners rose to the occasion again, giving their workmen and friends a grand treat. On the Monday and Tuesday three sheep were roasted whole. The women of the community had tea and a dance on the Green in the evening. Similar rejoicings took place at the other end of the line in Grantham where the shops closed at 1 p.m. and a large crowd gathered at Grantham station to witness the departure of an express train to Nottingham and its return at 3.30 p.m. carrying the mayor of Nottingham, the directors of the railway company and a full load of passengers. The mayor of Grantham then led them in procession to the Guildhall where a lavish meal was served to 105 guests. Even so, these celebrations were considered to be rather low key, greater splendour being required at the opening of the Great Northern line two years later rather than 'the narrow meanness displayed on the opening of the Ambergate line'.

Reporters who travelled on the line at its opening were generally impressed. The *Nottingham Journal* commented:

> *This entrance to Nottingham will unquestionably afford one of the most picturesque prospects in the county. From this elevation the passengers will see below them the River Trent rolling onwards like a silver stream meandering through meadows, tinged with emerald and gold.*

Other writers praised the viaduct at Radcliffe as 'very fine' and of 'great strength and magnitude', noted the line's pleasant course through Radcliffe and Bingham, and the high cultivation but 'flat aspect' of the surroundings. The track was described as 'one of the smoothest ever built, without the least oscillation or rocking'. The station architecture came in for scant praise, however. One writer commented: 'The station houses are, with the exception of that at Bingham, small and of rather mean appearance.' Another described the buildings at Radcliffe as 'neat', but everywhere was 'built with due regard to economy' and 'all the necessary offices, warehouses, etc. are built for use, not ornament'. (The architect of the final station buildings along the line was T.C. Hine, whose later work in the Lace Market and the Park came to epitomise Victorian Nottingham.)

The impact of the growing railway network can be appreciated by the euphoria with which the *Nottingham Review* for 19th July 1850 greeted the new line:

The opening of the railway from this town to Grantham supplies another link in the great chain of inter communication which will yet, doubtless, embrace every considerable part of the country. The rapidity with which this great iron revolution is extending over space is wonderful and unparalleled, except by the strangeness and speed of transit which has itself been achieved by the iron road (chemin de fer) and the Vulcanian Pegasus - that most wonderful of the adaptations of steam power ....

The leader writer then contrasted the speed of the clumsy stage coach 'cleaving the wind at a velocity of some six miles an hour' with that of the steam propelled locomotive of the present era:

Instead of a transit three times a week, occupying six hours, the journey is now accomplished more than as many times a day, in about an hour each journey.

Contractors' sale and final celebration

Almost immediately after the opening, Greaves, Adams & Smart prepared to leave Radcliffe and sell off their entire stock and equipment in the village. The following notice appeared in the *Nottingham Journal* of 19th July 1850:

Ambergate Railway: to be sold by auction
July 23, 24, 25 at Radcliffe.

The whole of the valuable plant of Messrs Greaves & Co. consisting of several thousand feet of Memel and oak timber in baulks and trees; deals and battens, Yorkshire stone landings, 14 carts, one light spring cart, 3 timber drugs, one dray, water cart, 7 stone drays, one pair 10 ft. wheels, 14 capital draught horses, 30 sets of horse tackle, 150 x 2½ yard earth waggons, 2 beam mills, 3 hay cutters and knives, 12 portable mangers, 4 corn bins, 2 weighing machines, and large quantity of weights, several round stave and step ladders, wheelbarrows, quantity of foreign poles, old sleepers, wheelwrights' wood, joiners' benches, 6 sets of smiths' tools, anvil and bellows, turning lathe, screw tackle, large quantity of screw bolts, scrap iron, rails, etc; 12 temporary boxing crossings and 20 x 6 feet ditto; 11 pile engines, nippers and monkeys, 3 sets of gauntree tackle 3 powerful cranes, and 3 portable travelling ditto, complete; large quantity of strong chains and pulley blocks, 2 screw jacks; capital clay mill, 24 inch rollers, a one horsepower Engine, suitable for thrashing etc.; 2 Archimedes pumps, 4 powerful crabs, 1 six horse portable steam engine, circular saws, shaft, drum and straps, 2 locomotive steam engines, temporary buildings, doors, frames, ovens and boilers, and a great quantity of other effects.

A year later in July 1851 the railway contractors celebrated the completion of all work on the line by giving their workmen 'a most excellent dinner' at the Royal Oak in Radcliffe. After the loyal toasts, the health of the founder of the feast was drunk. This toast was responded to by the foreman of the works, who eulogised the character of their employer for his straightforward conduct manifested towards all in his employ, and for his readiness at all times to help those who were willing to help themselves. At the end, the speaker was pressed to offer the workers' united thanks for this and several other treats that Mr Greaves had given his workforce, and they expressed the hope that he might live long to enjoy the fruits of his honesty and industry. Perhaps only workmen resident in Radcliffe attended this dinner because there is no evidence of the presence of large numbers of navvies in the village when the census was taken in April 1851.

Early services

Once under way, the Ambergate Railway soon had nine engines. The first three came from E.B. Wilson's works in Leeds where the 25-year-old David Joy, who was the first locomotive superintendent for the Ambergate, had previously been chief draughtsman and from where he had borrowed the engines for the opening. The new trio were 4-wheeled tank engines which weighed only 16 tons but were capable of 30 miles per hour when hauling a train of twelve coaches and which were able to cover the 21 miles between Nottingham and Grantham in less than 1 hour. They were soon joined by two Hawthorn 2-2-2 engines and three 0-6-0 goods engines, but the pride of the line must have been the 2-2-2 Jenny Lind designed by Joy in 1847 and which was considered the finest engine of its day. A little later the line used a number of 18 ton 2-2-2 'Little Sharpie' tender engines made by Sharp Brothers of Manchester.

When the railway opened in July 1850 there were four passenger trains in each direction on Monday to Saturday with two on Sunday. (See timetable opposite.) There were four classes of travel and the fares from Nottingham to Radcliffe were: first class 1s.6d; second class 1s.0d; third class 6d; Parliamentary or government class 5¼d. (This was a cheap stopping train provided under an 1844 statute.) The luggage allowances were 100 lbs, 60 lbs and 40 lbs for the first three classes respectively. In addition, a warning was issued:

The Company do not guarantee the arrival of trains at the respective stations at the times stated, but will use their best endeavours to ensure punctuality.

Even at the cheapest rate the cost of a trip from Radcliffe to Nottingham and back (10½d) would have been prohibitive for labourers and their families. At this very time agricultural labourers in Cotgrave were on strike to keep their wage at 10s per week. From 1st August 1850 a revised and curtailed timetable was in use, with the abandonment of both the 1.15 from Nottingham and the 2.20 from Grantham, as well as the re-timing of the 11.00 from Grantham to 12.35 p.m.

Excursions stopping at Radcliffe became a notable feature of the period and as early as 23rd August 1850 the *Nottingham Journal* carried an advertisement for an excursion to Belvoir Castle every Tuesday and Thursday leaving Nottingham at 10.20 a.m. and returning from Bottesford at 7.12 p.m. The fares were 4s.6d first class and 3s second class including admission to the castle grounds, but a return ride by carriage or omnibus between Bottesford and Belvoir cost an extra 1s. On Monday 9th September 1850 an excursion train left Nottingham at 10.20 a.m. for Grantham and a visit to Belton House. First and second class fares were 5s and 3s.6d respectively including admission to the grounds. Carriages between Grantham and Belton were extra, and the return train left at 6.50 p.m.

During the 1860s such excursions from Radcliffe proliferated, some requiring considerable stamina. One example is a cheap day excursion to London leaving Radcliffe at 3.40 a.m. and arriving in London at 8.10 a.m. at a cost of 6s. A four day return trip cost 20s for first class or 10s in covered carriages. Local events included a flower show and gala in Nottingham and a temperance gala in Grantham at a cost of 6d and 1s respectively from Radcliffe. Trips were arranged to race meetings in Nottingham, Huntingdon, Doncaster and York. Velocipede races at Grantham and the opening of the new dock at Hull by the Prince of Wales were both given excursion facilities in 1869, as was the Humber rowing regatta in the following year. Numerous events at the Crystal Palace including international exhibitions and music festivals were also regularly served by excursion trains calling at Radcliffe. It was not until July 1873 that trains were running to the little fishing village of Skegness. The Great Northern is considered to be responsible for its development as

Amber Gate, Nottingham and Boston, and Eastern Junction Railway.

NOTTINGHAM AND GRANTHAM.

TIME-TABLE FOR JULY, 1850.

GREENWICH TIME IS KEPT AT ALL THE STATIONS.

STATIONS.	DOWN. Nottingham to Grantham.					Sundays.		FARES from Nottingham			
		1	2	3	4	1	2				
	Miles	1st 2nd and 3rd Class	1st 2nd & Gov.	Express	1st 2nd and 3rd Class	1st 2nd & Gov.	1st 2nd and 3rd Class	1st Class s. d.	2nd Class s. d.	3rd Class s. d.	4th Class s. d.
Departure from		a. m.	p. m.	p. m.	p. m.	a. m.	p. m.				
Nottingham	...	10 10	1 15	3 45	9 5	9 0	8 0	...	...	...	...
Ratcliffe	5¼	10 25	1 39	3 58	9 20	9 16	8 16	1 6	1 0	0 6	0 5½
Bingham	9	10 37	1 56	4 8	9 33	9 30	8 30	2 3	1 6	0 9	0 9
Aslockton	10¾	10 42	2 4	4 13	9 39	9 36	8 36	2 7	1 9	0 11	0 10½
Elton	13	10 49	2 14	4 20	9 47	9 44	8 44	3 3	2 1	1 1	1 1
Bottesford	15½	10 58	2 28	4 29	9 56	9 54	8 54	3 11	2 7	1 4	1 3½
Sedgebrook	18¼	11 6	2 43	4 36	10 5	10 4	9 4	4 7	3 1	1 7	1 6¼
Grantham	22½	11 15	3 0	4 45	10 15	10 15	9 15	5 0	3 9	1 11	1 10½

STATIONS.	UP. Grantham to Nottingham.					Sundays.		FARES from Grantham.			
		1	2	3	4	1	2				
	Miles	1st 2nd and 3rd Class	1st 2nd & Gov.	Express	1st 2nd and 3rd Class	1st 2nd & Gov.	1st 2nd and 3rd Class	1st Class s. d.	2nd Class s. d.	3rd Class s. d.	4th Class s. d.
Departure from		a. m.	a. m.	p. m.	p. m.	a. m.	p. m.				
Grantham	...	8 40	11 0	2 20	7 0	7 30	6 30	...	...	...	...
Sedgebrook	4¼	8 53	11 18	2 30	7 12	7 43	6 43	1 3	1 0	0 6	0 4½
Bottesford	7	9 3	11 34	2 38	7 22	7 53	6 53	1 9	1 2	0 7	0 7
Elton	9½	9 12	11 46	2 45	7 30	8 2	7 2	2 5	1 7	0 10	0 9½
Aslockton	12½	9 20	11 56	2 51	7 38	8 10	7 10	3 0	2 0	1 1	1 0¼
Bingham	13¼	9 28	12 6	2 57	7 46	8 18	7 18	3 5	2 3	1 2	1 1½
Ratcliffe	17¼	9 42	12 24	3 8	7 58	8 32	7 32	4 8	2 11	1 6	1 6¼
Nottingham	22½	9 55	12 46	3 20	8 10	8 46	7 45	5 0	3 9	1 11	1 10½

PASSENGERS LUGGAGE.—The Company do not hold themselves responsible for Luggage, unless Booked and paid for according to its value.—100 lbs. weight of Luggage is allowed to First Class, 60 lbs. weight to Second Class, and 40 lbs. weight to Third Class Passengers, not being Merchandise, or any other Articles carried for hire or profit; any excess above that weight will be charged.

The Company do not GUARANTEE the arrival of the Trains at the respective Stations at the times stated, but will use their best endeavours TO ENSURE PUNCTUALITY.

JOHN GOUGH, Secretary.

The timetable for July 1850
(Nottinghamshire Archives Office, DD539 3-4.
Reproduced by permission of the Principal Archivist)

Four types of engine used in the early days of the Ambergate line.

Top left: built by R.B. Longridge & Co (cylinders 11" x 15"; wheels 5' diameter)
Top right: built by R. & W. Hawthorn & Co (cylinders 16" x 22"; wheels 6'6" diameter)
Bottom left: built by E.B. Wilson & Co (cylinders 15" x 20"; wheels 6'3" diameter)
Bottom right: built by E.B. Wilson & Co (cylinders 16" x 24"; wheels 5' diameter)

(Based on drawings in the Nottinghamshire Archives Office, DD539 3-4.
By permission of the Principal Archivist)

a resort and soon visitors from Radcliffe were among the thousands arriving by excursion train.

While these excursions were opening up the country to local people, trains were also bringing visitors to Radcliffe. Occasionally they were attracted by a special event such as a cricket match in 1869 between Radcliffe and the Eleven of All England with tickets available at Boston, Lincoln, Nottingham and intermediate stations. The railway staff must have shown a certain amount of expertise in the management of these events. In June 1872 the *Nottingham Journal* reported on the visit of 500 Good Templars on a picnic to the village. Not all the company was tee-total and some became 'market merry' if not 'tight'.

Notice of an excursion train to a pantomime in 1866

Thanks to the excellent arrangements of the Railway Officials who ran a special train from Nottingham, the excursionists, both sober and tipsy, reached home in safety about half past nine.

More typical were the numerous visitors 'with slender purses' who arrived at weekends and each bank holiday, Radcliffe being the first stop out of Nottingham on the Grantham line. For example as many as 2,000 came by train on Whit Monday 1881. While the resulting trade was welcomed by some, numerous problems resulted. (See section on Law and Order.)

Amalgamation with the Great Northern

Soon after the opening of the railway the shareholders were demanding a profit from the venture. In August 1851 the London & North Western and the Midland companies were negotiating for the Nottingham to Grantham line at a 3.5% premium on the paid up capital whilst taking all the liabilities. In December 1851 an extraordinary meeting called by the Ambergate considered and rejected the proposition for a working agreement and eventual lease of the line. The Great Northern company was to be more successful. In February 1852 some 25,000 Ambergate shares, forfeited through non-completion of payment, were sold off in 350 lots in two hours at between £4.13s.9d and £5 per share, realising £120,000. Consequently the *Manchester Guardian* in early April 1852 could state that the Ambergate had come to a definite agreement with the Great Northern who would work the line, pay all expenses and hand over 70% of the gross receipts from July. For two years from 1st July 1853 the Ambergate would receive the same dividend as the Great Northern and after that 4% on the capital, with the Great Northern having the option to take the line at par at any time. By August 1852 the Great Northern was therefore working the line while still using the Midland's track from Colwick into Nottingham.

Disputes with the Midland

At that time the Midland's route to London ran via Derby with all passengers inconveniently having to travel twice along the track between Derby and Trent Junction. The Great Northern's line between Peterborough and Retford was soon to be completed and they recognised the advantages of a more straightforward run from London to Nottingham via Grantham and through Radcliffe. This offered a shorter journey time than the Midland's route. However the Midland obtained an injunction to prevent this. The Great Northern ignored the injunction and was soon advertising through-trains from London to Nottingham via Grantham at a saving of 15 minutes. The Midland decided to take action. When the Great Northern's first train from London reached the Midland's station in Nottingham, Midland locomotives from Colwick both preceded and followed it. Whilst the Great Northern

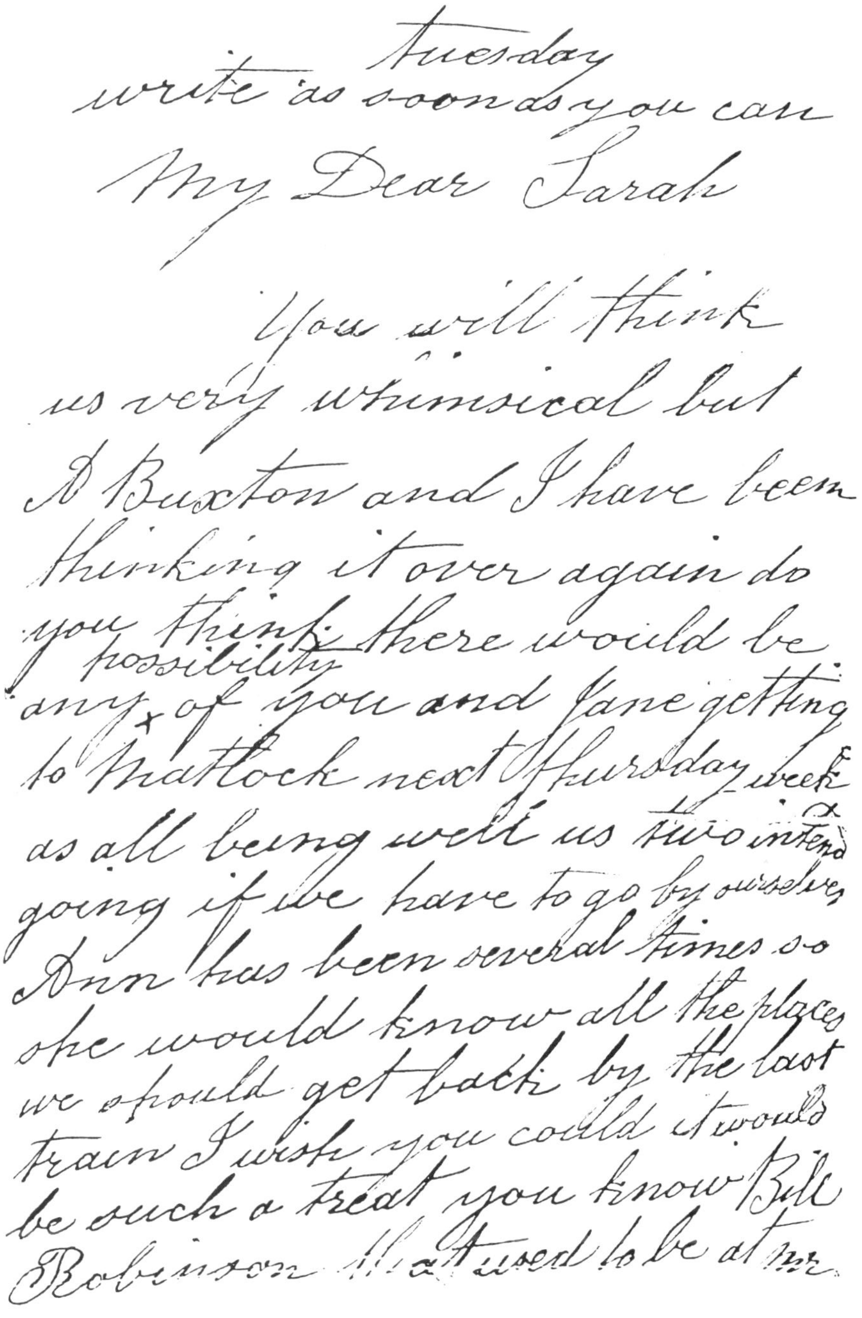

Tuesday
write as soon as you can
My Dear Sarah

You will think
us very whimsical but
D Buxton and I have been
thinking it over again do
you think there would be
any possibility of you and Jane getting
to Matlock next Thursday week
as all being well us two intend
going if we have to go by ourselves
Ann has been several times so
she would know all the places
we should get back by the last
train I wish you could it would
be such a treat you know Bill
Robinson that used to be at m

The railway brought the possibility of recreational travel to Radcliffe people.
In this extract from a letter written about 1874,
Annie Stone suggests to her daughter, Sarah Taylor,
that they make a visit to Matlock by train

engine was changing ends ready for the return journey it was forced into a shed by the Midland's engines. The rails were taken up and there it stayed for seven months.

Legal arguments and further harassment followed. Great Northern goods had to be taken by cart between Nottingham and Colwick and their booking clerk at Nottingham was repeatedly threatened with eviction. Thus in February 1853 a bill was presented to Parliament for the laying of parallel track from Colwick to a new station (Nottingham London Road Low Level) in what is now Great Northern Street. In 1854 it was authorised that the Ambergate be leased by the Great Northern for 999 years from April 1855. The new parallel line opened in 1857 and Radcliffe's connection with the Midland line at Colwick was removed, to be re-instated in 1967 when Radcliffe's trains once more used the Midland station. London Road station, opened on 3rd October 1857, served as the headquarters for the line until 1923 when it became part of the London & North Eastern Railway.

Further developments 1854-1876

From the very beginning it had been felt that the railway would have to acquire the Grantham Canal. Negotiations had begun as early as 1845, and the Ambergate finally concluded the purchase on December 29th 1854. Over the years, shareholders expressed their disquiet from time to time about the management of their affairs. In March 1857, for example, they felt they were losing coal trade to the Midland who were believed to have plans to annihilate the Ambergate line. They also suspected that the Great Northern was benefiting more from the 1854 agreement than they were.

In May 1860, the name of the Ambergate company was changed to the Nottingham & Grantham Railway & Canal Company. The new body considered the expenditure involved in introducing an electric telegraph on the line as well as the erection of a waiting room at Radcliffe in March 1861. The telegraph was essential for the proper working of the line and the cost of £900 would be met by the sale of surplus land. The chairman admitted to the loss of money when the canal was closed by frost, but claimed that the working of the line was first class and that they had an excellent young man as manager who was second to none outside London.

In November 1865, the first chairman of the board, Mr W.F.N. Norton of Elton Manor, died at the age of 84. His obituary in the *Nottingham Journal* noted that

..... by his agreeable manners [he] won the good opinion of the rival sections of his brother directors, and often poured oil on the troubled waters when discussion on the canal question threatened to interfere with the harmony of the board.

Two months later the Great Northern announced that they were to introduce an improved third class carriage on the Nottingham to Grantham line, and that the first of twenty coaches was due to leave the building depot in Doncaster. These carriages were 25 feet long and were divided into two sections; one of three and the other of two inter-connected compartments. The announcement in the *Journal* goes on to say:

It will be remarkable for the excellent accommodation afforded; not only will the seats be of greater width than in the ordinary carriages now in use, but the space between each will be increased. There will be abundant light, and not the least advantage is that a person of ordinary stature can stand upright in any part without coming into contact with the top - a desideratum all railway travellers will fully appreciate ..... The contrast between the new carriage and some of the trucks - for they deserve no better name - elsewhere in use for the conveyance of third class passengers is very great and other railway companies would do well to follow the example of the Great Northern.

Further improvements came in 1872 when the Great Northern announced that they were extending to their second and third class traffic 'comforts and advantages almost exclusively reserved hitherto for the first class passengers'. This applied particularly to the provision of foot warmers during cold weather.

A new extension from Colwick to Pye Bridge in the Erewash valley was announced by the Great Northern on 17th October 1874 which would enable trains from Radcliffe to reach the Derbyshire coalfields. This line would leave the existing line north of the river Trent at Rectory Junction in Colwick, which at that time did not yet have a station. About half a mile north of Colwick the proposed line would cross the Midland's line from Nottingham to Lincoln on a bridge. The line near Gedling was considerably above road level. It was expected that Gedling station would be used by Carlton people wanting to go into Nottingham as the Midland's trains were described as 'few and far between'. The operations would then

> .... proceed through a moderately deep but hard cutting across the valley over the Lambley road and penetrate the Mapperley hills by reason of a long cutting and a tunnel.

This line, which terminated at Pinxton, opened in August 1876. Its benefits were noted by a writer in the *Nottingham Journal* in April 1881:

> A year or two ago the short cut which they have made from Radcliffe to the Erewash valley proved to be an incalculable advantage, for while the Company's main object was to get to the coal fields of the Erewash and Leen valleys, the inhabitants of Eastwood, Newthorpe, Kimberley and Basford have profited by the facilities for passenger traffic which have come as a necessary consequence.

Another change came in the 1890s when Saxondale junction was widened.

Incidents along the line

In the early days of the line neither signals nor points, which were worked alongside the track, were considered the responsibility of anybody in particular. Signalling was on a time-lapsed basis using semaphore arms by day and lights by night. At first the same signals were used to control the trains in both directions.

Goods waggons might be attached to passenger trains and this not only delayed the trains but put extra strain on the not very robust engines resulting in breakdowns and slow running. The last train frequently did not get to Grantham until after midnight, some two hours late.

Straying animals also caused problems. As early as August 2nd 1850 a sheep belonging to a Bingham farmer had strayed onto the track and was killed by a 'luggage' train. No damage was done to the train. A similar accident was reported on October 4th when a flock of sheep belonging to Edward Brewster of Radcliffe wandered onto the line and five were killed.

In 1852 it was reported that the guard on a train to Nottingham realised that the speed was slackening. He tried to attract the driver's attention by pelting him with small bits of coal which he could reach from the front carriage. Eventually the train stopped altogether and the guard went forward, only to find the crew asleep.

In 1852, also, traffic was increased with extra trains taking materials to the Great Northern 'Towns Line' which was being extended from Peterborough northwards through Grantham to Newark and Retford. When this line opened in August the Ambergate trains were diverted from the original station at Wharf Road, Grantham, to the main line station. The staff of twenty-two at Grantham included William Skinner, an engine cleaner aged 23, whose wife Fanny and baby son William had been born in Radcliffe. At the end of the same year the line was used to speed 64 men of Prince Albert's Own Regiment from Nottingham to Grantham to arrest the leaders of striking workers employed in the consolidation of parts of the main line.

The *Journal* of 13th January 1854 reported that owing to a heavy fall of snow the railway had ceased operating for two or three days but it is not clear if this was because the engines were not equal to the task or because the points were frozen. In the same year three young men were convicted of netting fish in Radcliffe on the private property of the Ambergate Railway Company. They were discharged on payment of a fine of 6d and costs of 6s.6d.

Good things happened too, however unintentionally, for in February 1866 a young married couple left Nottingham for Bingham on the Saturday night at 10.15

p.m. Before the train reached Bingham the woman had given birth and it was reported that mother and child were well.

Sparks from passing engines could set light to grassland in dry weather, and in July 1868 the danger was of sufficient interest for the *Nottingham Journal* to publish a report from a Bingham correspondent that nine fires had been seen in fields adjoining the track.

More serious accidents

There were more serious incidents too. An old man named John Wreck of Radcliffe was knocked down by a train while trespassing on the railway on his way to Whatton wakes. The *Journal* for June 16th 1865 reported that he was overtaken by a luggage train whose engine struck him, and he fell violently on his face. He was attended to immediately and was found to have sustained only a few bruises. The railway authorities conveyed him back home.

William Frisby was laying some fresh sleepers on the viaduct near the river Trent in February 1876 when he slipped through and fell 24 feet, smashing several ribs. He was taken home and received medical attention but remained in a precarious state for some time.

The Black Lion Inn at Radcliffe was the scene of the inquest on Henry Wright Morley in July 1880. Morley had been found by Henry Wilkes, a shunter from Colwick, lying about three feet from the down line at Radcliffe near the viaduct. The night foreman at Colwick sidings had met the deceased on the line on the far (northern) side of the river late on Saturday night. He had told the foreman, 'I'm not afraid of being knocked down, I'm used to this part.' It transpired that Morley, a cordwainer by trade, had gone into Nottingham on the Saturday. He was seen by the stationmaster at Gedling at 9.44 p.m. and appeared to be perfectly sober. Just as the train was starting Morley jumped down, saying he was for Radcliffe. The station master told him he would have to walk as there

John Carrington, a Radcliffe platelayer, killed at Nottingham London Road (High Level) station in 1901

was no train that night, and told him how to reach the ferry. His body was found about half an hour's walk from Gedling station. Two different drivers had seen him on the line. The following morning some hairs and flesh were found on the side buffer of the 11.10 train from Grantham. The verdict was accidental death while trespassing on the railway.

Two gravestones in Radcliffe cemetery bear reminders of later accidents. In December 1893 John Tinkler, a 42-year-old platelayer with four children, was between the tracks on the wharf bridge greeting the driver of a slow moving coal train, when he was decapitated by an express passenger train on the up line. John Carrington, aged 28, was killed on the line in December 1901 at the Great Northern's High Level station in Nottingham. He had been screwing up rails on the down line when hit by a train from Grantham. His parents lived at a farm on Shelford Road. Recently married, he left a wife and young baby.

Deliberate obstruction of the line

A potentially serious episode occurred in 1880. Henry Whyld or Wilde, a former employee of the Great Northern but subsequently employed by the London & Great Western at Colwick, was charged with putting an obstruction on the line with intent to endanger life. After being dismissed by the Great Northern, Whyld had continued to lodge in Radcliffe, and had been stopped on occasions from crossing the Trent by the viaduct and bridge as a short cut to work instead of using the ferry at a cost of a shilling a week. On being questioned about the incident on the line, Whyld denied that he was any longer living in Radcliffe, claiming that he now lived in Derby although he could not remember the name of the street. However, a number of railway employees had continued to see him in the Radcliffe locality, and he had been specifically observed on the night in question. The driver of the 8.42 p.m. train from Nottingham gave evidence that the line had been clear when he passed, but the driver of a coal train thought that he had seen an obstruction on the line by the viaduct at 9.10 p.m. He had stopped the train and found nothing, but at Grantham that evening he had discovered two cuts in a right-hand wheel of his engine. In daylight pieces of iron chair (the fastenings which hold the rail to the sleeper) were found on the up line.

William Rose, the local foreman platelayer, said one chair had been missing from the store on the night of 12th-13th February 1880. Footprints had been traced by Police Sergeant Allwood to Highland [Island] Lane and up the side of a ladder on to the embankment by the viaduct. A cast of the imprints exactly matched boots belonging to Whyld. George Upton, the Radcliffe ferryman, gave evidence that he knew the prisoner well, although he had not crossed for a week and owed him a week's fare. Whyld had told him, 'I should like to see the bridge blown up and swimming down the Trent.' The Bingham magistrates committed him for trial at the Assizes, and in the following April he pleaded guilty. After offering on his knees 'a rambling petition which was utterly unintelligible' he was sentenced to 5 years' penal servitude.

Services in 1887

With the exception of the Great Central Railway from London Marylebone to Nottingham Victoria, opened in 1899, and the Nottingham Suburban Railway through the St Ann's district, opened in 1889, all passenger lines in the locality were in use in 1887 and an examination of the Radcliffe timetables for that year gives a clear picture of activity at the village station in the last quarter of the century.

Eastbound trains at Radcliffe originated in Pinxton, Nottingham, and as far west as Stafford. Their destinations might be Newark North Gate, Grantham, Skegness, Leicester Belgrave Road or Market Harborough. The Radcliffe traveller had a choice of direct routes to London. He might, for example, catch the 8.40 a.m. and travel via Grantham to arrive at London King's Cross at 11.45 a.m. and then perhaps return in a coach which formed part of the 8.30 p.m. London King's Cross to Edinburgh 'Pullman and East Coast Sleeping Car Express' as far as Grantham. He could then make a connection and arrive home at 11.15 p.m. after giving the guard special warning of his wish to alight at Radcliffe before the train continued to Nottingham. Alternatively he could have reached London by catching the 9.36 a.m. which only stopped when required to take up passengers, and which proceeded via Melton Mowbray and Market Harborough and offered connections to Northampton Castle and London Euston, arriving at 1.00 p.m. Although westbound trains might take a traveller to Nottingham London Road or to Derby Friargate, the use of the Midland's services from those towns to London would have involved a change of station.

Radcliffe had a spacious goods yard with the usual facilities for handling coal, builders' materials and cattle along with a small goods shed to deal with the agricultural traffic. The signal box was in the centre of the goods yard opposite mile post 123 from London King's Cross, and it commanded a good view in both directions from the outside of the curve on which the station is built. The main station buildings were on the Nottingham platform. The small waiting room on the Grantham platform had a large canopy and an ornate valance and was reached by a gracefully arched iron footbridge, which was removed in 1977.

Amongst all this activity one class of passenger - the ordinary worker - had not really been considered. It was not until the last decade of the century that special concessions were introduced. By 1896 Radcliffe Parish Council was raising the question of workmen's early trains to Colwick and Nottingham, and in September of that year tickets could be bought by the day from Radcliffe at a workman's rate to reach Nottingham by 8 a.m. and to return after 4 p.m. on weekdays, or after 12 noon

Rail services from Radcliffe-on-Trent in August 1887

Weekday services

Eastbound trains			Westbound trains		
From		**To**	**From**		**To**
London Road	5.41	Grantham	Grantham	7.39	L.Road & Stafford
London Road	7.11	Newark North Gate	Grantham	8.46	L.Road & Pinxton
London Road	7.41	Grantham	Mel.Mowbray WO	8.52	London Road
London Road	8.11	Mar.Harborough	Mar.Harborough	9.18	London Road
Stafford &			Newark North Gate	9.33	London Road
Pinxton & L.Road	8.53	Grantham	Grantham	9.46	L.Road & Stafford
London Road	9.03	Skegness	Grantham	10.25	London Road
London Road	9.31	Mar.Harborough	Mar.Harborough	11.35	London Road
Burton-on-Trent	9.36	Grantham	Grantham	12.26	L.Road & Pinxton
Burton-on-Trent	10.21	Grantham	Radcliffe	1.43	London Road
London Road	10.50	Mar.Harborough	Grantham	2.06	Eggington Junction
London Road	11.11	Newark North Gate	Newark North Gate	2.25	London Road
London Road	12.04	Grantham	Mar.Harborough	3.09	London Road
London Road	12.41	Newark North Gate	Grantham	3.18	L.Road & Stafford
London Road	1.15	Radcliffe	Grantham	4.10	L.Road & Pinxton
London Road	2.04	Mar.Harborough	Grantham (Wed)	5.03	London Road
London Road	2.10	Newark North Gate	Mar.Harborough &		
London Road	SO 2.45	Radcliffe	Leicester Bel.Rd	5.28	London Road
Pinxton	3.11	Grantham	Bingham	6.20	L.Road & Pinxton
London Road	3.16	Mar.Harborough	Newark North Gate	6.20	London Road
		& Leicester Bel.Rd	Grantham	7.14	London Road
London Road	4.56	Newark North Gate	Mar.Harborough &		
Stafford	5.09	Grantham	Leicester Bel.Rd	7.54	London Road
Pinxton	6.26	Grantham	Grantham	8.00	L.Road &
					Burton-on-Trent
Derby Friargate	7.34	Grantham	Skegness	8.23	London Road
London Road	8.40	Radcliffe	Newark North Gate	8.45	London Road
Derby Friargate	10.07	Grantham	Radcliffe	9.00	London Road
			Grantham	9.16	L.Road & Pinxton
			Grantham	10.35	London Road
			Grantham	11.15	London Road
			Grantham	11.25	London Road

Sunday services

Eastbound trains			Westbound trains		
From		**To**	**From**		**To**
Burton-on-Trent			Grantham	1.44	L.Road & Pinxton
& London Road	8.49	Grantham			& Burton-on-Trent
London Road	9.11	Skegness	Grantham	4.47	London Road
Burton-on-Trent			Skegness	8.15	London Road
& London Road	12.06	Grantham	Grantham	8.32	London Road
Derby Friargate					& Burton-on-Trent
L.Road & Pinxton	3.11	Grantham			
Burton-on-Trent					
& London Road	6.36	Grantham			
London Road	9.16	Radcliffe			
Burton-on-Trent					
& London Road	10.14	Grantham			

Notes: L.Road = Nottingham London Road (Low Level);
Mar.Harborough = Market Harborough;
Leicester Bel.Rd = Leicester Belgrave Road;
WO = Wednesdays only; SO = Saturdays only.

on Saturdays. Two years later the Parish Council was asking for workmen's weekly tickets to be issued.

Complaints to the railway

In 1898 and 1899 there were disputes between the parish and the Great Northern over the responsibility for asphalting the footpaths between Shelford Road and the station. The Parish Council complained in November 1898 that the state of the path was affecting 'the convenience and comfort to a very considerable extent' of Radcliffe people. By the following March the company agreed to do the work but warned that their 'asphalters were very busy at the moment'. Responsibility for an unpaved strip near the station was denied by the county surveyor in July 1899 who claimed 'our boundary is at the end of the cottages'. Eventually this too was surfaced by the railway company.

A formed Radcliffe resident, J.D. Gorse, who until 1889 had lived at the Manor House, travelled from the village by train in December 1899 and found conditions far from satisfactory. His letter of complaint appeared in the *Nottingham Daily Guardian*:

> *Sir, I left Radcliffe yesterday (Sunday) evening. There was not a fire in either the ladies' or general waiting room. The 'booking hall', arranged out of the old goods shed, had a stove, and a lot of people around it were smoking. The train due at 9.25 left at 9.45. Twenty minutes on the cold and semi-dark platform was not pleasant. A Radcliffe resident said to me.'There is but little care for passengers at this station at any time; and the trains on Sunday evenings are often very late.' I gave a feeling echo to his words. Such a comfortless state of things will perhaps be improved upon if you kindly insert this.*

A few days later Mr Gorse found a supporter, signing himself W:

> *Sir, The thanks of all passengers on the G.N. Railway using Radcliffe station are due to Mr Gorse for drawing attention to the very wretched accommodation provided by the company. May I also point out that if we were furnished with a few foot warmers during the cold weather, and cleaner carriages, it would conduce greatly to our comfort. The state of the first class carriages at times is a disgrace to any company.*

Another frequent cause of complaint was the low level of the platform compared to the height of a carriage entrance. It was partially responsible for the death of 78-year-old William Draper, a printer from Walnut Grove, in December 1902. After falling asleep, he had been suddenly awakened as the train was pulling out of Radcliffe, and the drop had caused him to fall and be dragged by the train. Despite the inquest jury's rider, it was not until May 1904 that the platform level was raised.

A prosecution

Whatever the conditions, one Radcliffe passenger in 1901 clearly preferred first class travel. As he held a third class season ticket at the time, what the *Nottingham Daily Guardian* described as an 'interesting railway prosecution' followed in January 1902. Joseph Middleton, a commercial traveller living at Albert Villa on Cropwell Road, had been regularly observed at Nottingham London Road (High Level) station arriving in plenty of time for the 10 o'clock train but waiting until the last moment before boarding, and then entering a first class compartment. Followed by a ticket collector to Radcliffe one night, he was observed to pass the barrier without tendering an excess fare, and was only then challenged. Middleton offered the ticket collector 2d, but this was not accepted. He next sent what was described as a 'very impudent letter' to the railway company. In this he complained of the 'very gross neglect of duty' on the part of officials who had not come to him for the excess fare on the train, particularly the collector who instead of asking for the fare travelled from Nottingham to Radcliffe 'thus leaving his post and duty at Nottingham when he need not have done so', and then refused to take the money when tendered. He continued:

When I get into a first class compartment I expect your employees to come and ask for the difference, and I am very willing to pay. I had no thought or intent to defraud the railway company, but I do not think it is the duty of the public to run after your employees and tender the money ..... When I ride first class it is because the third class smoking compartments at the latter end of the train are full. I think there are not sufficient smoking compartments on the trains, that is, third class. In these days of keen competition I do not think it good policy to annoy passengers or offend customers, and this can be avoided if your staff will do their duty. I enclose two stamps in payment of the fare.

The stamps were returned. The railway company's solicitor denied that the letter had encouraged their decision to prosecute. When evidence was given that there had been plenty of room in the third class compartments on the night in question, the Bingham magistrates found for the railway. Mr Middleton was not only fined £1, but had to pay costs amounting to £3.15s.4d.

Rebuilding the Radcliffe viaduct

As early as 1864 it was clear that because of increased freight traffic the original wooden viaduct across the meadows to the Trent at Radcliffe was in need of replacement by something much stouter, and plans were drawn up to infill most of the structure with an earth embankment and to replace the rest with brick arches. The extra width of this new structure required the purchase of more land from the Manvers estate. It was agreed that

..... the existing cattle arches under the embankment of the present line should be lengthened throughout the widening; a good and sufficient supply of water should be provided in the field in lieu of the pond shown on the map and a proper brick culvert should be erected.

On the northern side of the river the railway company was to be at liberty to abolish the 'flood' access to the land at Radcliffe (the Hesgang pasture to the north of the river was still part of the parish of Radcliffe-on-Trent) over the level crossing at Netherfield, but they were to provide another access in lieu thereof by constructing a proper siding to a cattle dock at some place to be agreed later, and to convey cattle to and from such a dock at all reasonable times or at the request of the vendor's tenants in time of flood. Plans show the height of the embankment well above the levels of the floods of 1852 and 1864. However due to local opposition the plans were much modified and most of the timber construction remained in place.

Perhaps with the Tay Bridge disaster of 1879 in mind a correspondent to the *Nottingham Journal* of February 17th 1881 again raised the matter of the timber viaduct:

Sir ..... I wish to know what provision has been made to render thoroughly secure the apparently insecure wooden structure known as Radcliffe Bridge? I have often been nearly under it when trains have been crossing it and I want to confess, I have wondered how such a structure could safely stand the enormous weight, especially as I have seen the bridge really sway and bend under it.

*   As we all have at times occasion to cross it, I think it quite time that public opinion should strongly speak out and compel the company to substitute a really substantial one with strong girders, before some dreadful accident - some accident must generally occur in these matters - before companies take the matter in hand. All gentlemen to whom I have spoken who have crossed it are of the opinion that they consider it 'the most unsafe part of the journey to London or anywhere else on the Great Northern main line'. The past and present floods must seriously increase the danger, as it is an old bridge.*

(signed) *Prevention is better than cure.*

The editor re-assuringly added: '... no doubt the railway authorities take care this bridge is surveyed from time to time to satisfy them of its security.' A second correspondent, however, voiced his fears the next day. 'There is no bridge I fear to go over so much as Radcliffe Bridge.' He pointed out that trains were ordered to go over it slowly. 'If there is no danger, why should this be the case?' Perhaps the company was waiting for a crash and deaths before taking action.

It was another twenty-eight years before work began on a new viaduct in January 1909 under the supervision of the chief engineer, Mr A. Rose. Work was interrupted during the winter for several weeks because of floods, but it was finished on 5th September 1910. The new portion consisted of twenty-eight spans, eighteen of 24 feet 11 inches and ten of 25 feet 7 inches, with a double abutment between them. The foundations of the piers averaged 10 feet in depth, going through a bed of gravel into a bed of marl. Local bricks were used, faced with Staffordshire brindled bricks, the whole work being done in cement. There were cutwaters in the brickwork at each end of the piers with coping stones and caps of Derbyshire stone. Throughout all this work the line never closed, although there was only single line working on Sundays and a speed limit of 5 miles per hour.

Rebuilding work on Radcliffe viaduct in 1910

Services in the 1920s

Bradshaw's railway Guide for July 1922 gives a picture of the services through Radcliffe just before the amalgamation of the railways to form the 'big four' companies. With the opening of the Great Central's Nottingham Victoria station in 1899 and the link from Sneinton through London Road (High Level) to Weekday Cross Junction the traveller from Radcliffe had a choice of three routes to London. At 7.21 a.m. a train left Radcliffe for Market Harborough with connections through to Northampton Castle and London Euston arriving at 11.55 a.m. The 7.35 a.m. from Radcliffe to Grantham would allow him to reach London King's Cross in just over 3 hours (arrival 11.15; 10.40 on Mondays and Fridays). However the 7.18 a.m. to Nottingham arrived in Victoria station at 7.34 a.m. just in time perhaps to catch the 7.40 a.m. to arrive in London Marylebone at 10.36 a.m. Local services still served Pinxton, Derby Friargate and beyond with more trains terminating at Burton-on-Trent or Uttoxeter, but fewer covering the whole route through to Stafford. To the east arrangements were almost unchanged from 1887 with services to Grantham (and Skegness), as well as to Newark North Gate via Cotham, and southwards to Melton Mowbray and Market Harborough via Harby & Stathern. The direct service to Leicester Belgrave Road, however, had been withdrawn.

Rail services from Radcliffe-on-Trent in July 1922

Weekday services

Eastbound trains			Westbound trains		
From		To	From		To
Nottingm.Victoria	6.00	Grantham	Grantham	5.31	Derby Friargate
Derby Friargate	6.35	Newark North Gate	Grantham	7.36	Nottingm.Victoria
L.Road (Low Level)	7.21	Mar.Harborough	Radcliffe	8.05	Derby Friargate
Nottingm.Victoria	7.35	Grantham	Grantham	8.28	Pinxton
Burton-on-Trent	8.44	Grantham	Newark North Gate	9.08	Derby Friargate
L.Road (Low Level)	9.00	Mar.Harborough	Mar.Harborough	9.18	L.Road (Low Level)
Uttoxeter	9.57	Grantham	Grantham	9.38	Uttoxeter
L.Road (Low Level)	11.01	Mar.Harborough	Mar.Harborough	11.37	L.Road (Low Level)
Uttoxeter	12.00	Grantham	Grantham	12.13	Stafford
Nottingm.Victoria	1.12	Radcliffe	Radcliffe	1.40	Nottingm.Victoria
Ilkeston	SO 1.40	Skegness	Grantham	2.08	Derby Friargate
Nottingm.Victoria	2.05	Newark North Gate	Skegness	SO 2.43	Nottingm.Victoria
Uttoxeter	2.31	Grantham	Grantham	3.18	Uttoxeter
L.Road (Low Level)	3.01	Mar.Harborough	Newark North Gate	3.58	Nottingm.Victoria
Nottingm.Victoria	3.08	Grantham	Mar.Harborough	3.37	L.Road (Low Level)
Pinxton	4.49	Radcliffe	Grantham	4.53	Burton-on-Trent
Burton-on-Trent	5.15	Grantham	Radcliffe	5.11	Pinxton
Nottingm.Victoria	5.46	Newark North Gate	Mar.Harborough	5.23	L.Road (Low Level)
L.Road (Low Level)	6.01	Mar.Harborough	Grantham	6.23	Nottingm.Victoria
Nottingm.Victoria	6.30	Grantham	Grantham	7.18	Pinxton
Ilkeston	SX 7.25	Radcliffe	Grantham	8.13	Burton-on-Trent
Burton-on-Trent	7.56	Grantham	Newark North Gate	8.38	Nottingm.Victoria
Derby Friargate	9.13	Grantham	Mar.Harborough	9.26	L.Road (Low Level)
Ilkeston	SO 10.21	Radcliffe	Grantham	9.28	Nottingm.Victoria
Burton-on-Trent	SX 10.41	Grantham	Radcliffe	SO 10.30	Nottingm.Victoria
Burton-on-Trent	SO 10.51	Grantham			

Sunday services

Eastbound trains			Westbound trains		
From		To	From		To
Derby Friargate	10.39	Grantham	Grantham	9.34	Derby Friargate
Derby Friargate	12.49	Grantham	Grantham	2.29	Derby Friargate
Derby Friargate	2.39	Grantham	Grantham	3.44	Derby Friargate
Derby Friargate	9.24	Grantham	Grantham	8.46	Derby Friargate

Notes: Mar.Harborough = Market Harborough;
Nottingm.Victoria = Nottingham Victoria (Great Central);
L.Road (Low Level) = Nottingham London Road (Low Level)
SO = Saturdays only; SX = Saturdays excepted.

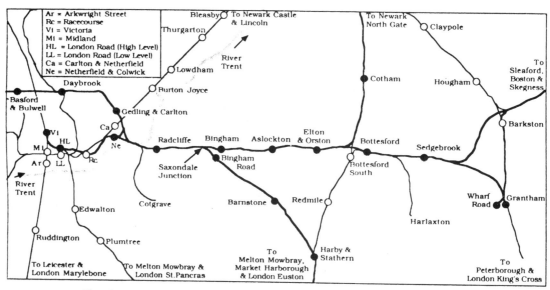

Sketch map of the local railway system around Radcliffe. The heavy lines show routes used by direct services from the village between c.1887 and c.1922

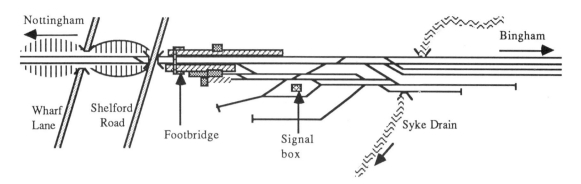

Sketch plan of Radcliffe station based on the 1914 Ordnance Survey

A westbound train at Radcliffe station c.1912

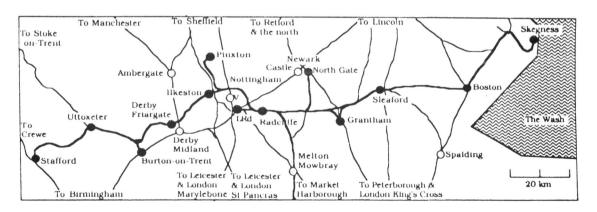

Sketch map of the completed railway system around Radcliffe.
The heavy lines show routes used by direct services from the
village between c.1887 and c.1922

117

Employment and change

The opening of the railway did not initially bring many new jobs to people actually living in Radcliffe. In the 1851 census only seven railway employees are listed: William Harris, railway agent, born in Nottingham, married with eight children; his second son working as a railway labourer; four other labourers (Richard Parker, William Rose, Francis Ward and Thomas Clarke) born respectively in Bingham, Kinoulton, Shropshire and Sussex, the last with a wife from Matlock; and James Booth, the station master, born in Nottingham.

Some station masters appear to have settled in the village, while others regarded Radcliffe as merely a staging post to promotion. James Booth was aged 45 in 1851 and had nine children, born in Grantham, Billingham, Boston and Nottingham. He soon left Radcliffe, his place being taken by John Bird about 1853. In 1864, John Hepworth was in charge, and William Robertson in 1871. Robert Theobald is found by 1877 and was still there in 1886. (At this time the station masters lived on Shelford Road, but in the 1900s they occupied

Station master John Salmon c.1913.
(The London & North Western railway operated trains through Radcliffe, hence the background notice board)

the last house on the right in Lorne Grove.) John Clark was station master about 1900, William Hayward by 1908, and John Salmon from before the 1914-18 war to well beyond. There may have been others in between.

By 1881 the overall number of railway employees in Radcliffe had risen to twenty-eight. Of these, nine were labourers, six - including a foreman - were platelayers, five were clerks. Two signalmen, two porters, two carpenters, one railway collector and the station master made up the rest. Only six were natives of Radcliffe, although a further eight were from neighbouring villages, including Cotgrave, Shelford and Car Colston. These were mostly platelayers or labourers. Lincolnshire provided a signalman, three clerks and a carpenter. The station master was from Berkshire and the railway collector from London. In general, therefore, the more senior the position, the further afield the worker's place of origin was likely to be. There were two exceptions. One labourer was born in Scotland, and one platelayer in Cambridgeshire. Half, however, of those employed on the railway were locally born, and this was as true of older men as of those born since the railway opened in 1850. Only one of the six mentioned in 1851 was still working for the railway and living in Radcliffe in 1881. This was William Rose who had risen from being a labourer to a platelayer. This is the same William Rose who featured the previous year in the case against Henry Whyld. Not until the 1914-18 war was there any challenge to male dominance in the railway industry. Some female labour had then to be used, and Gladys Breedon of Cropwell Road became a familiar sight as porter on Radcliffe station.

If the Methodist and Anglican marriage registers are anything to go by, sons and daughters working or marrying within the Radcliffe railway community were the exception rather than the rule. Frederick Daniels, a signalman at Beeston when he married Alice Barnets (a shoemaker's daughter) in 1881, eventually did settle in Radcliffe, for one of his daughters is shown as marrying Robert Clarke, also of Radcliffe in 1908. John Townsend, engine driver, was the son of the brickyard foreman in Radcliffe, and he married dressmaker Ellen Caunt in 1883. William

118

Upper: Gladys Breedon, Radcliffe's woman
porter during the 1914-1918 war
Lower: William Todd, signalman,
in his later years

Rose appears again in 1885 when his son Samuel, an insurance agent, married Sabina Footit, the daughter of a Radcliffe shepherd. Frederick Huskisson, a platelayer, had three daughters who married a Heanor carter, a Radcliffe plumber and a Manchester French polisher respectively between 1911 and 1915. Exceptions who did continue the railway connection include William Clark, the station master's son who married a Radcliffe girl in 1894. (Her father's occupation is not listed.) In 1881 William Bakewell, a porter of Station Terrace had at least two sons, one of whom followed him into the railway service. (The other married Sarah Rockley, daughter of George Rockley, gentleman.) Even more exceptional was the Todd family. William Todd became a signalman at Radcliffe about 1883, working on the railway for fifty years altogether. Of his thirteen children, three sons - John in the control office, Eddie as guard and Walter as porter - followed their father into the railway service. Walter began work in 1899 and like his father completed fifty years' service, most of it at Radcliffe. His son George, in his turn, became a porter locally.

From the point of view of trade, the effect of the railway was to reduce river traffic to insignificance and to obliterate the wharf. In 1851 there were eight Radcliffe men who earned their living on the river. By 1881 there were none. Even more significantly, the railway opened up the village to the wealthy businessmen of Nottingham and thus contributed to the building boom of the 1870s around the Chestnut Grove, Shelford Road and Lorne Grove areas. Radcliffe's character began to change from agricultural to suburban as a result. The railway also allowed day trippers to come in vast numbers, contributing to the prosperity of the village, while creating specific problems associated with public houses and disorder. For the ordinary villager, however, it brought ease of access to Derbyshire, the Vale of Belvoir and the seaside, as well as convenient travel much further afield for the better-off. Not until the 1950s was the railway seriously challenged by the internal combustion engine.

Main sources

Primary
Letter from Annie Stone by courtesy of Mr A. R. Taylor.
Nottinghamshire County Library (Local Studies Library): census returns.
Nottinghamshire Archives Office: Wesleyan chapel marriage registers; Radcliffe parish registers; parish council minute book Pa C 35/1; DD 234/2; timetables and drawings of locomotives DD 539/3-4; DD PF 145/30.
Radcliffe-on-Trent Parish Council: minute books.
University of Nottingham: Manvers papers Ma B 237 1-76 passim; Ma 2B 40/11c; Ma 2B 40/181; Ma 2B 40/185b; Ma 2D Box no. 39/1-3 bundle 2.

Secondary

Bradshaw's 1887 and 1922 railway guides.

Cossey, Frank. *Grantham and railways.* 1983.

Cowen, Newspaper Cuttings 1894-1917. (University of Nottingham library, local studies section.)

Nottingham and Nottinghamshire *Directories* 1864-1928.

Grinling, C.H. *The history of the Great Northern Railway 1845 to 1895.* 1898.

Leleux, Robin. *Regional history of the railways of Great Britain*, Vol. 9: the east midlands. 1976.

Parker, D. *The railway through Radcliffe.* Radcliffe village guide, 1979.

Radcliffe-on-Trent local history research group: extracts from Nottingham newspapers 1837-1920.

Radcliffe's signal box
with signalman William Todd

Walter Todd by the station cattle
gate during the 1914-1918 war

A CHANGING VILLAGE

The study of how Radcliffe developed during the nineteenth century has been approached in two ways. By using census returns and local *Directories* it has been possible to discover the size of population, the number of households and the range of occupations in the village. An impression of changing village life has also been gained from looking at a selection of mainly domestic buildings and their occupants. Rentals, estate papers, rating lists, newspaper advertisements, maps, house deeds, and sales catalogues, as well as census returns and parish registers have been used to piece together information on this aspect of the subject. The final picture, however, is still far from complete.

I. A social survey

The national census

The first national population census was taken in 1801 and was essentially concerned with discovering whether deserted houses in the countryside indicated a declining population and therefore vulnerability to attack by Napoleon's France, or if spreading slums in the towns indicated a rising population and a coming famine. Censuses have been taken every ten years since (except 1941). About 1837 a national census office was established and it became possible to seek and to analyse more information about households. The head of the household on census night was required to complete the form and the enumerator collected it the next day, if necessary helping with the completion of the return. The national reports to Parliament emphasise caution in interpreting the information collected. Questions could be misunderstood; there was a wide variation in common names for occupations and the meanings attributed to them; there could be a genuine uncertainty about age. The official report on the 1881 census considers that the sex of the population was the only definite set of facts! Full information from census returns is only released one hundred years after being taken.

Population and houses in Radcliffe 1801-1921

Date of census	Population	Occupied houses	Persons per house	Change in population Persons (+ or -)	Change in population %age (+ or -)	Change in houses occupied Houses (+ or -)	Change in houses occupied %age (+ or -)
1801	761	155	4.9				
1811	924	167	5.5	+ 163	+21	+ 12	+ 8
1821	993	181	5.5	+ 69	+ 7	+ 14	+ 8
1831	1125	217	6.2	+ 132	+13	+ 36	+20
1841	1246	243	5.1	+ 121	+11	+ 26	+12
1851	1273	266	4.8	+ 27	+ 2	+ 23	+ 9
1861	1371	295	4.6	+ 98	+ 8	+ 29	+11
1871	1339	300	4.5	- 32	-2	+ 5	+ 2
1881	1704	340	5.0	+ 65	+5	+ 40	+13
1891	1868	407	4.6	+ 164	+10	+ 67	+20
1901	2093	471	4.4	+ 225	+11	+ 64	+16
1911	2735	nk		+ 642	+31		
1921	2849	535	5.3	+ 114	+4		
1981	8215						

(Note: the great increase in population after 1901 can be largely accounted for by the inclusion of Saxondale Hospital in parish figures.)

Migration

A check has been made on the place of birth of heads of household as shown in the 1851 and 1881 censuses. This indicates the movement into Radcliffe from Nottingham and elsewhere during the intervening years.

Birthplace of heads of household

Year of census	1851	1881
Radcliffe	143	137
Nearby rural parishes	41	46
Nottingham	7	28
Nottinghamshire	39	57
Elsewhere	36	72
Totals	266	340

Classification of occupations 1851 to 1881

A most significant innovation in the 1851 census was a 'scientific' attempt to classify occupations and classes. The enumerator was instructed to pay particular attention to the column headed 'Rank, Profession or Occupation.....', and the list of ranks, professions and occupations continues with the following instruction:

> *The Superior Titles of PEERS and other PERSONS of RANK are to be inserted as well as any high office they may hold. Magistrates, Aldermen and other important public officers to state their profession after their official title.*

Those in the army, navy and civil service come next, then clergymen, followed by the legal and medical professions, professors, teachers, writers and scientific men, and artists. It insists that people specify both their occupational role and their field of work. Vague and general terms such as 'merchant' and 'clerk' were considered objectionable. Children over the age of 5 were to be recorded as 'scholar' or, if being taught regularly at home, 'scholar at home'. A woman's role was clearly perceived:

> *...the occupations of women and children regularly employed from home or at home in any but domestic duties to be distinctively recorded [but] the occupations of the mistresses of families and ladies engaged in domestic duties are not expressed - as they are well understood..*

Although the 1851 census had incorporated the first attempt to classify occupations and status, it was not considered to be very successful because the instructions had not been read or were not understood. For the 1861 census a new occupational classification was prepared with a guide for the enumerators. Six broad classes were proposed:

Professional	National or local government; defence; learned professions.
Domestic	Household; children; entertaining & performing.
Commercial	Buying & selling; conveyance (transport).
Agriculture	Working on land or with animals.
Industrial	Art & mechanic production; working with textiles & clothing; food & drink, and animal, vegetable & mineral substances.
Indefinite or non-productive	Labourers - branch of labour not defined; persons of rank & property, not under office or occupation; supported by the community or of no specified occupation.

For the 1881 census another dictionary of occupations was prepared because the old one was obsolete. Leading manufacturers were asked for occupational names and eventually provided a list of 12,000. Many of these names were little more than nick-names and proved to be shortlived. It was in this census that the only definite facts were claimed to be gender!

Persons of rank and the professions

The 1851 census return shows that Radcliffe had two or three 'persons of rank', including William Taylor, magistrate of the county, aged 68 and spending census night at home with three members of his family, three visitors and seven servants. (His house, Radcliffe Hall, is not mentioned.) At Lamcote House, one of the few homes named in the return, were George Bacon aged 45 years, a merchant (the type being unspecified), Mary, his wife, and four servants. In addition, there was the widow of an army lieutenant living and educating her children in a household with three servants.

Next in the enumerators' instructions came five groups which today might be called 'professional' and which include all levels from General in the army to Chelsea Pensioner; from attorney to clerk. A vicar (Robert Burgess) and a doctor (William Martin), both about 30 years of age, were recorded in Radcliffe in 1851 along with two schoolmasters, one schoolmistress, three governesses and a police constable. One officer of the Inland Revenue is recorded as being 28-years-old and living with his wife and step daughter, but where he worked or what he did is not revealed. However, there was one famous 'professional' - George Parr - recorded as being aged 24, the son of a Radcliffe cottager, and giving his occupation as 'cricket player'. Radcliffe was not yet a village of commuting or retired professionals, but for the most part consisted of people who worked and produced in and around their homes, perhaps taking their produce to Nottingham or to other markets.

Although it is not possible to make direct comparisons, some impression is gained of change by 1881. Only one figure would qualify as a 'person of rank' in 1851 terms - John Bagshaw Taylor JP, William's son now aged 69, living with his wife, son and seven servants. Amongst the professionals were two clergymen and a missionary, five schoolmasters, a schools' inspector, a doctor, an accountant, a solicitor, an inland revenue officer and a bank manager. (George Parr still listed himself as a cricketer although he had retired by this date.) Outside these categories, and reflecting new status were the director, manager, four merchants and six manufacturers now living in the village.

Agriculture and gardening

In 1851 there were nine farmers, working a total of 1,133 acres or about two-thirds of the fertile land. Most would have been tenants of the Manvers estate. These farmers employed between them twenty labourers and six boys, and most (seven of the nine) also had domestic servants. One small farmer with only 20 acres also had an income from the shared ownership of two threshing machines. Sixteen cottagers with holdings from 2 to 20 acres farmed a further 134 acres in the parish, but they employed no labour from outside their families. Three were widows and four mention additional occupations - carrier, cordwainer, tailor and land-drainer. There is one entry for a 'grazier of 11 acres'.

Roughly a third, that is eighty-five, of Radcliffe's households were headed by agricultural labourers in 1851. Another twenty agricultural labourers are also listed. The employed youngsters, aged 12 to 23, include seventeen plough drivers, three farm servants, two farmer's boys, a farm boy, a plough boy and an agricultural servant. Farmers were required to state the number of labourers they employed (in addition to detailing those living in their households), but the number of agricultural labourers and other workers elsewhere in the census return greatly exceeds the number of labourers the village farmers admitted employing. The same situation occurs in all the neighbouring parishes. Perhaps those employed casually or seasonally would not have been included. Another possible explanation lies in the instructions given to enumerators which require precision - nobody is to be described just as 'labourer'. Besides agricultural labourers, Radcliffe had three rail labourers, two maltsters' labourers and one bricklayer's labourer.

In the censuses of 1851, 1861 and 1871 the number of farms remained at about ten, but the area farmed declined slightly from 1,133 to 1,075 acres. In 1881 the number of farmers had dropped to five, three of the former farmers having retired. During the same period the number of cottagers declined from sixteen to twelve and their acreage reduced from 134 to 63. As the number of farmers and cottagers declined, so did the number of labourers. Whereas in 1851 eighty-five heads of household (30% of the households in the village) are recorded as agricultural labourers, in 1871 the number had dropped to thirty-four (10%), and in 1881 it was down to twenty-three (6%). Others who called themselves farm labourers or farm boys dropped from forty-five in 1851, to thirty-seven in 1871 and to only eleven in 1881. This overall decline in the numbers earning a living in agriculture may have been partly due to the gradual urbanisation of the village, but it must also have been a reflection of the long agricultural depression of the late nineteenth century.

It is still difficult to make complete sense of the excess of agricultural labourers - five times the number declared to be employed by the village farmers in 1851. It was still three times the number in 1871 and nearly twice the number in 1881. A similar situation is found in all the surrounding parishes.

The reduction in numbers of those engaged in farming by 1881 was partly compensated by a rise in the number of heads of household who were gardeners and nurserymen, from two in 1851 to twelve in 1881, but unfortunately the census did not require them to indicate if they were market gardeners or how much land they worked.

It is not practicable to explain the ups and downs of what may be called 'agricultural support services', except to note that there seem to have been more experts living as heads of household in the years of the 1861 and 1871 census. Four or five blacksmiths, one to four flushers (drainers), and one or two wheelwrights are always present. In addition there are usually one or two cattle dealers, corn-dealers, or pig-dealers, as well as a miller, the horse breaker, the harness maker and several others. There was also a veterinary surgeon and a castrator.

Traditional trades and industries 1851-1871

Some trades and crafts still used the medieval guild titles of master, journeyman and apprentice in 1851, but in most cases there were also men working in these trades who either had no claim to guild titles or preferred not to give them, perhaps because such titles were now ornamental rather than significant. The workers in the following table were all men, although the cordwainers had some women binders to assist them:

Occupation	Masters	Journeymen	Apprentices	Without title	Total
Food and drink					
Butcher	4	2	3	4	13
Maltster	2	1		4	7
Miller & baker		3		1	4
Clothing & footwear					
Cordwainer	3	2	3	7	15
Tailor	4	3	1	3	11
Building					
Carpenter & joiner	2	2	3	4	11
Plumber & glazier	2			4	6
Bricklayer & plasterer	1	1		4	6
Stonemason	1			1	2
Others					
Basketmaker	1	3	1	1	6
Harnessmaker	1			1	2
Blacksmith	2	3	2	1	8
Wheelwright		1			1
Brazier & tinplate worker				1	1
Totals	23	21	13	36	93

An analysis of the 1871 census shows that compared to 1851 a number of these traditional crafts were already in decline in Radcliffe.

Occupation	1851	1871	Occupation	1851	1871
Food & drink			Clothing & footwear		
Butcher	13	5	Cordwainer	15	3
Maltster & Brewer	7	5	Shoemaker		4
Miller & baker	4	1	Tailor	11	5
Flour dealer		1			
Building			Other		
Bricklayer	6	2	Blacksmith	8	5+1a
Stonemason	1	1	Wheelwright	1	3+1a
Plumber & glazier	6	4	Saddler & harness maker	2	4
Carpenter & joiner	11	8	Brazier (& publican)	1	1
Builder		1a	Sawyer		1

Total for 1871 = 50   (Note: 1a = one apprentice.)

In 1851 there had been a total of ninety-two men in these occupations and nearly two-thirds used medieval guild terminology. In 1871 there were no masters, only one journeyman and three apprentices. There is an obvious decline in the butchery trade, suggesting that in 1871 cattle and sheep were less likely to be killed locally than sent alive to the Nottingham market, presumably by way of the railway opened in 1850. Perhaps the prevalence of cattle plague (foot and mouth disease) from the mid-1860s also drove some workers into other occupations. Boot and shoe manufacture, which had been a widespread local industry, declined sharply in all areas of the country except Northamptonshire and parts of Leicestershire in this period and Radcliffe shared the decline. Four new occupations appear in the 1871 census: apothecary, bookbinder, surveyor and watchmaker. Whether these worked in Radcliffe or in Nottingham is not clear. Only the saddlers and wheelwrights seem to have held or increased their numbers over the twenty years, and blacksmiths declined only slightly. The real fall in their numbers would be seen after the turn of the century with the coming of motorised transport.

Transport services

The river in 1851 was still the main means of transport for heavy goods, and it provided the main occupation for eight households. There was a wharfinger (the manager of the wharf), a boat-master, a boat proprietor (a widow) and six men described as watermen or boatmen. All except one were heads of households. A comparison with later years demonstrates the increasing importance of the railway at the expense of the river, and to some extent of road traffic. By 1871 the wharfinger described himself as a coal dealer. There were only two boatmen, both the elderly heads of households, and in 1881 there were none. Nevertheless, from other records it is clear that the Upton family in particular supplemented their income by maintaining the ferry across the river.

William Morley was a cottager with nineteen acres who, according to White's *Directory* for 1844, carried by road to Nottingham on Mondays, Wednesdays and Saturdays leaving at 6 a.m. In 1851 he was assisted by his son and a 26-year-old clerk (the only clerk mentioned in the village in the 1851 census). By the time of publication of the 1853 *Directory* the carrier service had been cut to Saturdays only as in July 1850 the railway had been opened. By the 1871 census William Morley was aged 77 and no longer occupied as a carrier. A Michael Ki(r)tchen, however, was described as a postman and rural messenger and he had an assistant living with him as a lodger. Kitchen was born in Cotgrave in 1815 and probably came to Radcliffe to marry a local girl and to work as a bricklayer's labourer in about 1840. As the village expanded there seems to have been more scope for carrying, despite the railway, for in Morris's 1877 *Directory* John Wright is listed as the village carrier to Nottingham on Mondays, Fridays and Saturdays. In White's *Directory* of 1885-86 John and Edward Wright were working together as carriers and were proprietors of a 'goods removing van'. A William Wright is listed separately as a carrier, and there was sufficient business for both enterprises to send carts to Nottingham daily.

The first road worker in the censuses is William Nowell described in 1871 as a road labourer. In 1851 when he was 47 years of age he considered himself to be an agricultural labourer. In 1881 there was again one 'labourer on roads' aged 54 who lived in Mount Pleasant next door to the carter and the carrier.

While there were only six adults concerned with railway transport in 1851, none of them born in Radcliffe, twenty years later eighteen earned their living on the railway. Of these only four were born in Radcliffe and all but four were heads of households. Apart from the station master, a porter and a railway carpenter they were all employed as labourers. In 1881 the number of railway workers had increased to twenty-eight. Only nine were now listed as labourers, the rest being employed in far more specialised occupations. Six were born in the village. (See chapter on The Coming of the Railway, page 118, for further information on this topic.)

Women's and children's work (domestic industry)

G. Caldwell   NOTTINGHAM.

Judith Buxton (1815-1897) in her later
years. She was a lace-runner in 1851

In 1851 'lace-running' followed agricultural labourer as the most widespread occupation in Radcliffe. It was a domestic industry practised in sixty-five households, that is more than a quarter of the village homes. Thomas Morley, a 43-year-old widower, described himself as 'Lace-Agent and Shopkeeper' and he must have played a significant role in organising the work in the village for the Nottingham lace manufacturers. Altogether there were 110 lace runners and all were female. Twenty-six were girls under 15 years, fifty-two were women aged 16 to 30, twenty-four were aged 31 to 45, seven were aged 46 to 60 and one was over 60 years of age. In five households lace running was the only source of earned income, but usually there was only one lace-runner in a household. This local female labour was providing by hand the needle-run patterns dictated by fashion for a Nottingham industry which, early in the nineteenth century, was employing about 15,000 men, women and children to operate between 1,500 and 1,800 point-net frames. Workers earned perhaps 4s a week for a 12-hour day. By 1851, however, the machine which was to destroy hand-run patterned lace had already been invented and domestic lace-running was doomed.

Altogether nineteen women in 1851 were described as dressmakers or milliners, another six were sempsters, two were straw-bonnet makers, one was a cap-maker and there was a 78-year-old knitter. Mary Whyte, aged 37 years, was a 'Dressmaker Mistress', and living in the same house she had a 17-year-old niece listed as a dressmaker apprentice.

Changes in the lace industry

In the 1861 census the number of women lace workers had fallen to sixteen, aged from 19 to 68 years, and there was still a lace agent in Radcliffe. Ten years later there were forty-one lace-runners, aged between 12 and 76 years and an agent, but in 1881 there were only ten young lace workers and none of them was described as 'runner'. They were lace-clerks, lace-clippers, lace-spotters or just lace-workers and some may have worked in Nottingham travelling in and out on the railway.

At the other end of the production scale there was a lace manufacturer, 50 years old, living at Clyde Villa in 1871. By 1881 there were five lace manufacturers living in the village (one employing thirty hands), two lace merchants and one lace designer. All, except a newcomer to Radcliffe, employed one, two or three servants and with one exception, who lived in Back Lane (now Water Lane), they all probably lived in the Lorne Grove and Shelford Road areas. Between 1851 and 1881 Radcliffe had changed from a village of working homes for female outworkers to a residential park for the wealthier members of the lace industry occupying houses conveniently near the railway station.

Children, work and school

Most children aged between 5 and 11 years were described as 'scholars' in 1851, suggesting that they went to school. (There was a boarding school as well as the main village school at this time.) School log books later indicate that absenteeism was high, particularly at times of harvest, violet-picking or osier-peeling. Work was likely to start earlier for girls, mainly but not exclusively lace-running, than for boys. At the age of 14 one third of the children were still at school. Assuming that the responses are accurate Radcliffe was providing school accommodation for about 235 children with just over twenty-five in each year group between 4 and 9 years old, and less than half that number for the older year groups.

In the 1881 census 293 scholars appear, including those at the local boarding school, 180 of them aged between 5 and 11. (Five 2-year-olds and even a 1-year-old are described as scholars.) There is no significant difference in the numbers for each sex for any age range, although overall seven more girls than boys were in receipt of education. Many children of school age in this census, however, do not appear as scholars. It is hard to believe that at least some of Richard Daft's four listed children or the seven of the coachman William Skinner, for example, were not in receipt of education somewhere. The figures may, therefore, need to be viewed with caution.

Personal and domestic servants

In 1851, apart from the domestic staff in the three large households already mentioned (Radcliffe Hall, Lamcote House and that of the army widow) there were in Radcliffe forty-two women servants with ages from 14 to 42 years, and eight men servants with ages from 7 to 50 years. In addition, living on their own were a butler, a housekeeper, five charwomen (three of them heads of households), four laundresses and a game-keeper. By 1881 there were some sixty-three female servants who lived-in, many employed in the new villas. Of these, thirty-six were between the ages of 11 and 20, and twenty-three between 21 and 30. Twelve male servants lived-in, mainly on the farms. All but two were between the ages of 11 and 20. Also living at their employers' were twelve housekeepers, seven nurses, a cook, a groom and coachman, an under groom and an ostler. Living independently were three coachmen, two grooms, two female domestic servants, a cook, four housekeepers and five charwomen. In general, servants who lived-in had been born outside Radcliffe, and presumably Radcliffe provided servants to households elsewhere.

Commercial and other services

In 1844, White's *Directory* listed seven shopkeepers in Radcliffe specifying that most of them were also bakers. The 1851 census records one shopkeeper only , who was also the lace agent mentioned earlier. Three other shopkeepers are mostly still working, but they are now called grocer. Three persons traded in coal: an agent, a dealer and a higgler. By 1881 the range had widened, and business became multi-purpose. For example, amongst the seven bakers was 57-year-old John Reynolds who was also a miller, a corn, cake and seed merchant, a grocer, and a wine and spirit agent in premises at 27 Main Road subsequently occupied by the Calladine family. He is not included in the census tally of five other grocers (four of them female), four shopkeepers and two assistant shopkeepers. In addition, a co-operative shopman is found in the 1881 census. This reflected the appearance of the Co-operative Stores founded in 1874 in Hogg Lane. It provided the services of butcher, coal dealer, draper, grocer and general provisions merchant. By 1905 it was occupying premises at the corner of Shelford Road. Three smallware dealers also appear in the 1881 census. The latter included the business of Henry Taylor, begun

Advertisement from the Parochial Magazine of 1877

by his wife Sarah about 1878 on the Bingham Road. In the 1880s the Taylors moved to premises formerly used as a bakery next to the then Black Lion on the main street. The business continued there for three generations until 1984.

In 1851 public hospitality was provided by five inns: the Black Lion, the Nag's Head, the Old Red Lion, the Manvers Arms and the Royal Oak although the last is not named. The household at the Manvers Arms was headed by George Bell. He was also a builder employing four men, and had two sons and five young daughters living at home. Despite boasting an ostler there were no resident guests at the inn on census night. Only the Nag's Head had two overnight guests: a 48-year-old machine builder from Scotland and a 29-year-old journeyman carpenter from Maplebeck. By 1881 the Nag's Head no longer appears, but the Cliffe Hotel is named, run by Frederick Summers and his wife, their household completed with a great niece, a servant girl and one boarder.

II. Homes and families

1. The old village

From the time of enclosure of the great open fields in 1790, the pattern of the village had begun to change. New houses had appeared away from the village centre, and by early Victorian times there was already a mingling of old, new and improved buildings. The opening of the railway in 1850 was to lead to large-scale development, particularly from the 1860s, as fields within easy-reach of the station were sold off for building purposes. Although continuity can be detected in a study of some individual households, newcomers from Nottingham, who found Radcliffe an attractive and convenient place in which to live, contributed in the long run to its change from working to dormitory village.

The supply of houses overall kept pace with demand. In the fifty years between 1801 and 1851 over a hundred houses were added to the village. About 200 were added over the next fifty years, by which time there were 471. Over that hundred years the number of houses had risen by just over 300% and the number of people by 275%.

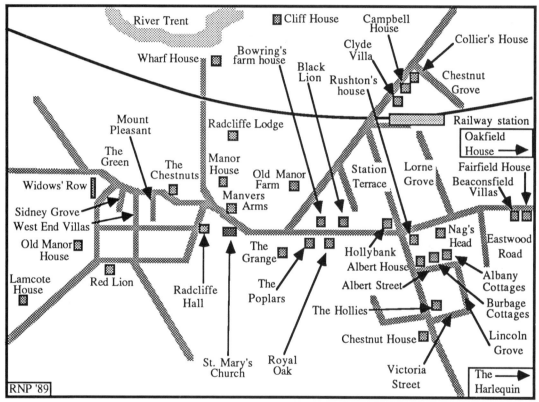

Sketch map showing the main areas and buildings referred to in the text

The Green

Many workers lived in homes clustered around the old village centre on Radcliffe Hill (the lower part of Bingham Road), in Bailey Lane, Back Lane, the Mount Pleasant area, and the Green. This last area is unique in having documented evidence about its history which shows that it was to undergo transformation, not as a result of the railway, but at the instigation of the second Earl Manvers. It has therefore been the subject of particular study.

The village green was formerly wasteland on which many rude dwellings of mud and stone had been erected with thatched roofs, but about 1849 or 1850 .. Earl Manvers ...took down twenty-eight of these humble abodes. He built sixteen or seventeen comfortable homes which he let at a moderate rent.

129

Thus wrote a correspondent in the *Nottingham Daily Express* in September 1887, and his recollections were basically accurate. In the eighteenth century the Pierrepont estate had included property on the Green amongst houses 'on the waste,' for which in 1726 3d a year was paid as chief rent. In 1746 only seven houses are specifically noted on Butt Green of indeterminate ownership. Their numbers grew, however, and parish accounts of the 1820s confirm that they were in constant need of repair, and were inhabited by the poorest of the village. By the 1840s the Manvers estate was charging small rents for these properties. It was around 1850 that Lord Manvers took the first step in converting the Green into a much sought-after residential area.

According to an estate valuation there were thirty-six houses on the waste in 1840. (A comparison with census returns shows a close identification with the Green.) Most were radically repaired from 1850 and five new cottages built. In 1851 only eight cottages could be assessed for rent, a nominal sum being charged for the rest 'not yet pulled down and rebuilt'. After completion of all the work there were twenty-three cottages, rather more than the correspondent recollected. Accounts have survived for the building or major repair of ten of these, and repairs are mentioned in four other cases. Delays in rent collection suggest major refurbishment of six others until as late as 1853.

Demolition, rebuilding and repairs

James Upton's account for 'pulling down the cottages on the Green' shows that work began in April 1850. Thatch and tiles were removed from houses, pig sties and privies. Floors were taken-up, fire grates removed, and foundations and paths dug-up. Those first affected were the Nowell, Spencer, Reek, Flower and Marsh families. Four of the five were headed by agricultural labourers. The exception was Joseph Flower, described as 'schoolmaster' in the published version of the 1851 census. It seems likely that this was a misreading of 'shoemaker', for he appears as a cordwainer in 1861. Beginning in June, the Nowells and Spencers' cottages were rebuilt first. (It would be interesting to know where the occupants were housed during this time.) They were built of brick with 'slate on walls, bedded in cement to prevent damp', and had stone sills and slate roofs. 'Rammel' was wheeled in 'to keep floors dry', which were then laid with brick 'bedded in mortar'. Window frames, doors and porches were oak, painted, or grained and varnished. Inside, the cottages were finished with plastered walls and ceilings, and they were lime-washed throughout. They also had pig sties, a well, a privy and ashpit, a paved path to a pump, and they were fenced all round. The accommodation was still small. An 1861 valuation shows that Joseph Flower's house had two rooms and a pantry on the ground floor, one chamber (bedroom), and a coal house. Joseph Reek's was smaller still with only one room and a pantry on the ground floor. The five houses had a total of twenty-eight occupants in 1851.

At much the same time, substantial alterations were going on at five other cottages, each occupied by an agricultural labourer's family. William Barnard's coal house was demolished, and two more substantial ones erected. This entailed the virtual rebuilding of a chamber. His chimney was repaired and repointed, and the whole house was coloured twice over. He also had a new front door and 'parlour window frame and shutters'. At the time William was aged about 75, his wife 71, and they shared the house with eight children or grandchildren. Similar alterations were carried out at 63-year-old John Vickerstaff's cottage in August 1850, including removing thatch and tiles from his pig sty and privy, repairing and pointing the walls, and the building of a new bedroom. This eventually left him with a two-up and two-down brick and tiled house, plus coalhouse for himself, wife and two adult children. Their neighbours were John Carnell, his blind wife Sarah, and a granddaughter. Next door was their son, another John Carnell with a wife and child. The younger couple had the larger house (two-up and two-down), while John senior managed with one-up and one-down and a coalhouse. The repairs here were all minor - replacing windows, repointing chimneys, repairing tiles, painting walls, and limewashing pig sties. Coping had to be relaid on fence walls that had been 'thrown of[f]', perhaps evidence of vandalism on the building site. The Vickerstaffs' other neighbour, William Walker aged 55, had a new pig sty, privy and ashpit, '21 squares of glass', and repairs carried out similar to those at the Carnell houses.

William, his wife and five children were accommodated in one downstairs room with pantry and a single bedroom above.

Contractors and supplies

The principal contractor for the building or repair of these ten cottages was an estate tenant, George Bell, builder and innkeeper from the Manvers Arms. He drew up the accounts, but it was his 25-year-old son Samuel, a bricklayer by trade, who was chiefly responsible for the day-to-day work. For example, together with other bricklayers, labourers and a boy, Samuel spent forty-six working days on the Nowell and Spencer cottages, and fifty days on the three other new cottages. Pay was standard - 3s.10d a day for bricklayers including Samuel, 2s.2d for labourers and 1s.3d for boys. George Bell died a little more than a year after the work on the Green started. Five months earlier the other main contractor had died. This was James Upton, a master joiner aged about 46 at the time of the work on the Green, and also a tenant of Lord Manvers. His account for 1850 runs to twelve sheets and includes hundreds of miscellaneous items: hanging doors, repairing and altering window frames, putting on roofs and chimneys, putting up shelves and handrails, fixing privy seats and door handles. The total bill came to £47.4s.9d. His rates of pay were comparable with those of George Bell - 3s.8d a day for himself and 2s.2d for his labourers - and his business had to support eight children, including twins. One son was a bricklayer's labourer and another a joiner's apprentice in 1851.

There were fifteen other contractors and suppliers, not all of them local men. Francis Poole, for example, was a maltster in East Bridgford who supplied bricks, and four or five suppliers were in Nottingham. Sand was sent from Gamston and from the 'Trent at Holme'. Lime came from Bulwell and Owthorpe, and floor bricks from Cropwell. Although Radcliffe brick making was established before this date, the nearest supplier in the accounts was Isaac Hill at Saxondale.

Goods were delivered to Radcliffe by the newly-opened railway, by boat to the wharf, or they were sometimes fetched direct from the supplier. George Bell provided men and horses as necessary:

To 2 men and 2 lads 3 days each loading and unloading bricks from wharf	18s
To 5 journeys to Nottingham for slates, plaster and firegrates	£1
To 2 trucks and lime from Radcliffe station	10s

The quantities of materials used are precisely recorded. Building the five new cottages took 61,700 bricks of various kinds, ranging from 10s to 27s per thousand. In addition there were 2,500 flooring bricks at £2.10s per thousand, and 2,500 'best dressed brick' for flooring at £2 a thousand. It took four days and five men to move these from the wharf to the Green. (In addition, 31,000 bricks removed from the original buildings were dressed, presumably for re-use.) Also supplied were 86 tons of sand, gravel and silt, 3 cwt of lead at 25s.8d per cwt, '32 squares 3 feet imperial slating' for about £41, and, for three of the cottages, 15,500 nails at 17s, thirty-two bunches of reeds at 8s, and 330 feet of zinc spouting at 6d a foot. Plain painting was paid for at 6d and 'oak painting ' at 1s.6d a yard. Much of this work was carried out by James Brice, a plumber and glazier from Bailey Lane, who also supplied pumps with new 'buckets and suckers', lead flashing and 57 feet of new glass.

The total cost of the rebuilding and repairs to the ten cottages was around £520. It is difficult to assess the precise amount spent on each cottage since so many different contractors were involved. George Bell charged about £25 each for the Spencer and Nowell cottages, and £20 each for those of the Reek, Flower and Marsh families. On top of this, however, must be added a proportion of glazing, plumbing and painting bills, as well as the cost of buying and transporting materials and fittings such as stoves and boilers. George Bell's bill for repairs to the Barnard and Vickerstaff cottages came to £17.19s.6d, but again sundry work was done by other people, notably James Upton. The estate was in no hurry to settle contractors' accounts. Payment to the Bells and James Upton for work completed in the autumn of 1850 was made on February 24th 1851, while John Smart, who supplied sand and gravel, had to wait a year for his money.

Widows' Row

The accounts have survived only for 1850 and, despite their detail, they are insufficiently descriptive to make identification with surviving buildings possible. In particular, it would seem unjustified to associate even the new cottages described above with what is known as Widows' Row. These five single-storey slate and brick cottages were provided by Lord Manvers around this time traditionally for widows of workers on his estate. In the valuation of 1861 there are four properties which were probably in this row, having identical values of £1.10s per year, each described as having two rooms and a pantry, and with no mention of

A cottage on Widows' Row

upper floors. They were occupied by Sarah Caunt, Betty Roberts, Sarah Richmond and Maria Richmond who in the 1861 census are specifically mentioned as living in 'Almshouses', as is Sarah Ogle, the occupant of a brick and tile cottage valued at only £1 a year. All but Maria (Mary) Richmond were widows aged between 51 and 79. At the time of the census in that year, however, Mary aged 24 was living with her mother Sarah. The fifth house was occupied by John Richmond, an agricultural labourer, and his family, so perhaps the estate was occasionally flexible over the rules of occupancy. Despite being new-built, by the 1880s Widows' Row was one of the areas of the village criticised for its inadequate sanitary arrangements.

Rents

Before the improvements, rents for cottages on the Green were as low as a shilling a year, or even 6d a year in the case of William Nowell, reflecting the poor quality of accommodation. At the most active time of rebuilding, no individual rent was paid for the majority of cottages, but a block charge of 13s appears in the rental books. For most tenants it was a different matter once the work was finished. William Nowell's 6d became £3.10s, and rents for the rest varied from £1 to £3.10s annually. These amounts remained constant up to 1860 at least and the increases did not cause any great exodus of tenants or cases of rent arrears. Only John Carnell senior defaulted for any length of time - five consecutive years - but the amount was not cumulative and must presumably have been paid during the course of each year.

Families on the Green

Although the majority of heads of households on the Green in 1851 were agricultural labourers, they also included a gardener (who served as parish clerk), a former laundress, a charwoman, a coal agent, a bricklayer, and (probably) a shoemaker. While Radcliffe as a whole was in the throes of change, the Green presents a picture of comparative stability, with families resident for many years. For example, of the thirty-six occupants of 'houses on the waste' in the rental assessment of 1840, twenty-two are still listed in 1850 and ten in 1860. Between 1850 and 1860 twenty-three residents were there for at least seven years. The long-term impression of stability is increased by the fact that two names - Richmond (first noted in 1827) and Nowell (first appearing on the 1840 rental) - were still there or had reappeared by 1941 when the Manvers family sold up the remnants of their estate in Radcliffe. Three families have been studied to reflect both life on the Green and the economic pressures of the nineteenth century.

The Nowell family

William Nowell (1802-84), one of the Green's agricultural labourers, was the son of another William who had been in need of financial help from the parish during the difficult times of the 1820s. His brother, presumably also an agricultural worker, had been 'kill'd from a wagon' in 1824, and in those days William himself had been in occasional need of parish relief. By 1841 he was married with five

132

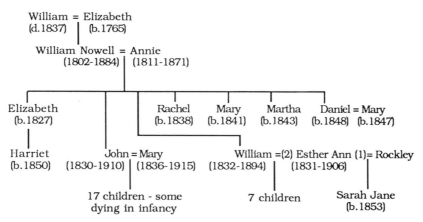

William = Elizabeth
(d.1837) (b.1765)

William Nowell = Annie
(1802-1884) (1811-1871)

Elizabeth
(b.1827)

Rachel
(b.1838)

Mary
(b.1841)

Martha
(b.1843)

Daniel = Mary
(b.1848) (b.1847)

Harriet
(b.1850)

John = Mary
(1830-1910) (1836-1915)

William =(2) Esther Ann (1)= Rockley
(1832-1894) (1831-1906)

17 children - some
dying in infancy

7 children

Sarah Jane
(b.1853)

children, the eldest being fourteen. Two more were born in the next seven years.

The Nowells were one of the families to have their cottage rebuilt in 1850. The increase in their rent from 6d to £3.10s a year suggests a vast improvement in the standard of accommodation which may have compensated for the extra outlay. Even so, the brick and slate cottage was still tiny, with two rooms and a pantry on the ground floor, one chamber (bedroom) and a coalhouse. In the 1850s the pressure on space must have been considerable, even though the eldest son, John, was living at the Manvers Arms where he worked as an ostler. By then there were other wage-earners in the family, too. William was following his father's occupation as an agricultural labourer, and two daughters - Elizabeth and Rachel (or Sarah) aged 23 and 13 - worked at home as lace runners. Ten-year-old Mary, a 'nurse' in the 1851 census, would have spent much of her time looking after her blind baby niece, Harriet, as well as her brother Daniel aged 3. Only 8-year-old Martha seems to have escaped some of the pressures around her by attending school.

Harriet, probably Elizabeth's daughter, was to suffer through her disability. By 1858 she was in Nottingham's blind asylum where she would have received some training. Radcliffe contributed to her upkeep, the cost rising steeply from £1.4s in 1858 to £9.15s in 1861. She must have returned to her grandparents in Radcliffe from time to time, for she was there when the census was taken in 1861. By 1870 she was in the Bingham workhouse, identified as the victim of an assault. She returned to the blind asylum, but in 1874, when she would have been 24, she left to live in Nottingham. She was allowed 3s a week, paid to her through the Nottingham Poor Law Union. As the policy against giving relief outside a workhouse was tightened up, Nottingham decided to discontinue her allowance in 1880 on the grounds that she was unable to earn her living, and it was decided that she should again be admitted to a workhouse. The rest of her story is not yet known.

At the time young Harriet was staying with her grandparents in 1861, the family circumstances had changed considerably. The eldest son, John, was now married and had left ostling for agricultural labouring. He was living with his father-in-law, Francis Hopewell, a cattle dealer, on the Holme Lane end of the Green and already he had three children. (There were to be seventeen altogether, some dying in infancy. In 1907 he and his wife were photographed on the Green at the time of their golden wedding.) Sarah (Rachel), now aged 23, was still living at home, but was married to labourer John Parr and had two young children to look after. Martha and Daniel, at 17 and 13 respectively, were also still at home, and now described as 'servants'. Consequently, William and Anne still had six people as well as themselves sleeping under their roof. By this time William's ability to work might have been affected by a serious accident when employed by Mr Parr of Cropwell five years previously. While threshing with a steam machine, he slid off a straw stack onto a fork stuck in the ground. The shaft ran some eight or ten inches into his groin.

The Nowells had two contacts with the law between 1869 and 1871, one on either side of the penal fence. Daniel was perhaps harshly treated one wet winter's day, when soaked through he took a waterproof coat from Cotgrave Place, the Hon Henley Eden's house. Daniel claimed that he had intended to return the coat, but the Bingham magistrates sentenced him to a month's imprisonment. William Nowell, whether father or son is unclear, saw justice done when his watch was stolen by a

Golden wedding celebrations on the Green in 1907
Back row: Liza, Frank, Sam, George, Sarah
Middle row: Jenny, ?, Mary (Hopewell) 1836-1915, John Nowell 1830-1910, ?
Front row: Anne, Kate

drunken man in West Bridgford. The culprit was imprisoned for four months.

By the time the census was taken in 1871, the Nowell cottage on the Green had only four occupants. William at 67 was working as a road labourer. His wife, aged 63, was to die in the November of that year. An 8-year-old granddaughter, Sarah Ann, was living with them, and there was now room for a lodger, an elderly bachelor described as a saddler.

From this time branches of the Nowell family were associated with Methodism, with bell-ringing at St Mary's, and were found in Hogg Lane and Bailey Lane, as well as in Nottingham as milk suppliers. Nevertheless, continuity on the Green was maintained. William's eldest son, John, remained on the Green, perhaps in the Hopewells' house, dying in 1910 aged 81, three years after his golden wedding celebrations. His son George then appears as tenant. After William himself died in 1884, valuation lists show that his son William took over the tenancy until his own death in 1894 aged 62. (His widow is then listed as tenant until 1906.) Walter Nowell, a son of this William junior, and his widow Annie (married at the Wesleyan chapel in 1885) are remembered by elderly residents of the 1980s as living in the cottage at the corner of Holme Road and Island Lane.

John Hemsley

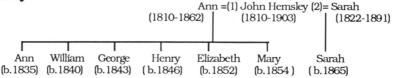

John Hemsley (1810-1903) was another long-standing resident on the Green. He was born in Cotgrave but had settled in Radcliffe with a wife, Ann, and young family by 1841. By 1861 he had six children, three sons and three daughters, although only four were living at home. His brick and tile cottage was larger than most - two rooms, a small back kitchen and a lean-to pantry on the ground floor, three 'chambers' upstairs, and a piggery and coalhouse outside. For this the family paid the modest rent of £2 a year in the 1850s, but at the time of the 1861 valuation, the Hemsleys' cottage was one of the few to have its recommended rental raised - to £4.

John Hemsley's main occupation was as a gardener, but he had a small second income through holding the office of parish clerk, a post he took over from Levi Duke in 1844. The churchwardens' accounts give a glimpse of his fees and duties. For example, he purchased the bread and wine for communion services, and looked after the clock, for which he was paid £1 a year. His dues at Easter and Christmas 1845 were £3.3s.2d and £1.4s.6d respectively. By 1875 the regular fees were standardised at £3 a quarter, rising to £4 quarterly by 1881.

The church connection was reinforced by his second son, George. Aged 18 in 1861, he was employed as a footman by the vicar, Robert Burgess. The two sons still living at home in that year followed their father's occupation as gardeners. Two daughters were still at school. In the following year Ann Hemsley died, but it was not long before John, now in his fifties, remarried. His second wife, Sarah, came from Shepshed in Leicestershire and gave him another daughter, Sarah. Towards the end of his life his son Henry shared the house on the Green with him, renting two furnished rooms.

John Hemsley 1810-1903

John Hemsley served as parish clerk for fifty-eight years, retiring in 1902. He died in the following year aged 93 and was buried in Radcliffe cemetery.

The Carnell family

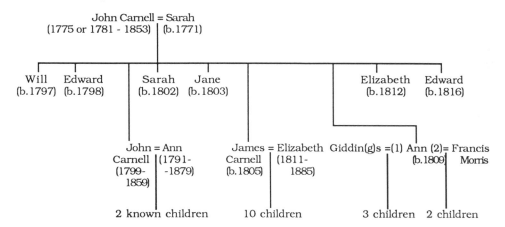

John Carnell (1799-59) was one of many with that surname in Radcliffe and the surrounding villages. He was the son of another John who had originally come from Oxton in Nottinghamshire, and by 1841 they were living next door to each other on the Green, both occupied as agricultural labourers. By 1851, his mother (Sarah) was aged 79 and had gone blind. She was widowed two years later, but she stayed on in her own cottage until at least 1859, being recorded as 'John's widow' and paying 34s a year in rent. No record of her death has been found in the Radcliffe burial register. Perhaps she returned to Bottesford, where she was born, or moved to the workhouse in Bingham. By 1861 her cottage was occupied by the family of her younger son, James, who had previously lived on Radcliffe Hill.

Before that time Sarah had suffered another blow with the death of her son, John, in 1859 at the age of 60. He left a widow, Ann, in their cottage which had been repaired, but not rebuilt, in 1850. John had carried out major work on the cottage himself, and the Manvers estate acknowledged their debt to him in the 1859 rental. Alongside Ann's name is the following note: 'Rent reduced for life in consideration of Buildings done by late Tenant.'

Consequently, she had only to pay 5s a year for the two-up and two-down cottage instead of £3, benefiting from the reduction until her death in 1879.

The main Carnell household on the Green now became that of James (1805-82), Ann's brother-in-law, in the much smaller cottage next door, its rent valued at only £1.10s a year in 1861. Life treated these Carnells harshly. There were ten children to provide for (although the age gap of twenty-three years between oldest and youngest meant that they were never all at home together) out of a labourer's wage, supplemented by the earnings of James' wife as a washerwoman. Their unmarried daughter, Ann, helped her mother with this work, continuing in her own right as washer of surplices and cleaner of St Mary's church from 1876 until 1913. She stayed on in the family home until 1915, the year before she died. By this time the rent was only five shillings a year more than it had been in 1861. The sons were mainly employed in some form of labouring, although George was at one time a brickmaker.

By the late 1870s James was in financial difficulties, and receiving some help from the Bingham Poor Law Union. In 1879 three of his sons were ordered to pay 1s a week each towards their father's upkeep, but they disputed the order on the grounds that he was able to work. He was then aged 73. Not until 1881 did two agree to pay, and even then the payments were soon disputed and discontinued. The wrangle was a reflection of the difficulties experienced by families during a period of agricultural depression, enhanced by the fact that two of the sons were no longer living in Radcliffe. James' death in September 1882 resolved the matter. His widow continued to live on the Green until her death in 1885, when the cottage was occupied by her daughter Ann.

Mount Pleasant

Continuity in other areas of the village predominated by labourers and artisans is less easy to discern. Property was often owned by private landlords rather than the Manvers estate so records are scanty, but census returns suggest that comparatively few families remained in one property for long. An exception was the Raworth (Roworth) family on Mount Pleasant. A newspaper advertisement in the summer of 1844 shows that John Walker, a farmer from a long-established family at Gilmore Nooks in Radcliffe, sold two 'substantial and well-built freehold dwelling houses' on Mount Pleasant in that year. The joint premises were occupied by two tailors, Thomas Raworth senior and junior, and their families. A room on the upper floor was used as a workshop, and the joint household accommodation comprised four rooms and a pantry on the ground floor, five chambers (bedrooms), an excellent cellar, a backyard, and other conveniences including hard and soft water pumps.

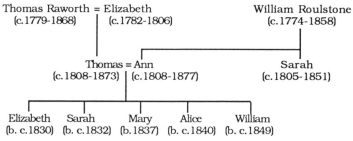

In 1851 Thomas senior, who had been born at Aslockton, was aged 73 and lived with his Radcliffe-born wife, aged 69. Thomas junior's household was far more crowded. As well as himself and his wife, who worked as a dressmaker, (both were aged 43 and had been born in Radcliffe), there were three daughters working as lace runners, one daughter at school, and a 2-year-old son. In addition, Thomas's sister-in-law and father-in-law lived with them. The latter was Thomas Roulstone, a 77-year-old widower who worked as a basket-maker. By 1861 this industrious household was considerably depleted. Thomas junior and his wife had only their

FRYERS OLD-ESTABLISHED
SHOEING FORGE,

Ratcliffe-on-Trent, Notts.

Heading for a notice in 1892 when Fryer's smithy passed to John Henry Hallam

Particulars :- ————————

In Shop :- 15 pro. new cart horse Shoes, 7 pairs templet Shoes, 40 various tools (Swages &c) 58 various tools, Shelf and bracket, Deal cupboard with 3 shelves, pair of circular bellows, 16 Scythe handle irons, 19 lbs. horse nails, 25 pro. fire tongs, Poker and Shovel, 117 lbs new steel, 10 templets (Miss Burnsides) 8 pro. new nag Shoes, 4 ditto Screw heels, Shoe stick, Boy & shoeing tools, Empty tool box, 1 horse rug, 50 lbs. screw nuts various (old & new), 2 new Curry Combes, 20 lbs washers (Various), 11 Chain swivels, 8 lbs. old screw eyes, 4 new plough Clasps, 32 new bucket ears, 4 new Chain T's, 3 hasps, 7 ft. wood bench, 1 pr. 6in Vice, 1 pr. 6½ in. Vice, nail pointer, drilling machine as fixed, Frame drill, pr. Beam Scales, weights 25 lbs, gas bracket & visible gas piping, new scythe blade 5 callipers, 3 pro Compasses, 2 iron Guages, 172 lbs. various nuts & bolts, 18 Coach screws, 2 pro. india rubber Shoe pads, 9 old files, 2 rasps, 5 file handles, 5 new gimlets, 5 old ditto, 17 mole trap springs, oil Can & spot, 6 fork Sockets, 3 Screw drivers, 2 do. handles,

Carried Forwards

Extract from an inventory of blacksmith's stock drawn up for John Henry Hallam 1892

12-year-old son at home, although the senior Raworths were still living next door. In April 1864 the two houses were again sold, and the tenants were given as Thomas Raworth and Marriott Carnell. What had happened to the senior Raworths is not clear as Elizabeth did not die until 1866, and Thomas survived until the age of 90 in 1868. In 1871 Thomas junior was still working on Mount Pleasant as a tailor. He died two years later at the age of 65, his wife dying in 1877. It is possible that the Raworths' tailoring premises were converted into a bakehouse, for from March 1876 advertisements appear for the sale of a dwelling house on Mount Pleasant, formerly occupied as two messuages, together with a bakehouse and outbuildings, currently occupied by Richard Adamson. When the same property came up for sale in February 1882 it was let to Messrs Wright and Barratt. It was then described as a dwellinghouse and bakehouse, 'well and substantially built and let to respectable tenants'. (There is no mention of a Mount Pleasant baker in the 1881 census.)

Other property in the area easily identified from advertisements included Fryer's smithy, a business run originally in conjunction with the Royal Oak Inn, at the corner of Mount Pleasant and the main street. In October 1892 the business, described as 'the oldest established in the village' was up for sale. An inventory of blacksmith's goods totally £34 shows that the business passed to J.H. Hallam from Willoughby and then his son. The Duxburys later occupied the site. On the other corner was a block which also had a frontage to the main street and to Mount Pleasant itself. In April 1889 this contained a butcher's and three houses behind occupied by Messrs Bell, Howard and Tinkler, the whole producing a rental of £62.5s a year. An extension of this corner block in June 1903 included seven freehold dwelling houses, one with sales shop and bakehouse, a detached butcher's shop with slaughterhouse, and outbuildings. The tenants were Messrs John Wright, Williamson, Bell, Harris, Hale, Vincent Wright and Stevenson, the gross rental now producing only £50.2s. The names suggest some continuity of occupancy.

Although these sales details indicate that the area was dominated by small businesses and craftsmen, this impression is misleading. Of the thirty-three households specifically mentioned as being on Mount Pleasant in the 1881 census, seventeen were headed by some type of labourer. By this date Mount Pleasant had suffered cholera, and was about to be stricken by scarlet fever. Its inadequate sanitary arrangements made it the subject of attention during the village's public health crisis of 1882. The area was demolished in the mid-twentieth century.

Inns and malt rooms

Other working households which could provide some employment for villagers were those of the maltsters and inn-keepers. The census returns show that the malt trade was an important aspect of Radcliffe's economy, with an average of five maltsters in the village throughout the nineteenth century. Some farmers who grew barley carried out their own malting, but setting up in business was expensive because of the heavy excise duty involved. When John Green started up in premises opposite the Chestnuts in 1843 he had to provide sureties for the Malt Duty Board of £1,000 from John Alcock of Linby and Robert Green of Radcliffe. Perhaps the best known name in Radcliffe's brewing circles was that of Butler Parr, who occupied a prominent house on the main street. He inherited long-established brewing premises in what is now Walker's Yard from his father, Richard, in 1855. After the cricketer Richard Daft married his daughter Mary, the two men went into partnership, and Richard Daft continued running the business on his own after his father-in-law died in 1872. The Dafts lived in the Rosary, now associated with the Scout Hall. Butler Parr's son, another Butler some seventeen years younger than his sister, became the ale and porter agent for the Home brewery in Nottingham, perhaps symptomatic of the decline of brewing in Radcliffe in competition with largerenterprises. Wright's *Directory* for 1900 records only three maltsters and Kelly's for 1908 only two. Nevertheless, older residents in the 1980s still recall the malting carried on early in the century by the Haynes family near Lamcote corner and in two places on Water Lane, and by the Chamberlains in premises behind shops on the main street near the Water Lane corner. Demolition work in 1988 made them, now modified, more visible. They are currently used as a cold store.

The former Chamberlain's malt rooms on the main street

It is clear that the maltsters were sometimes also retailers through the village's inns and beerhouses. The five in the 1851 census were, with one exception, of long-standing. (A sixth, the Cliffe Inn was to develop from a beerhouse later in the century.) The Nag's Head, run in 1851 by Sarah Buxton, a 'Beerhouse Innkeeper', was probably 6 Bingham Road and is not named in other censuses. The Black Lion, now a butcher's shop at 10 Main Road, can be identified in much earlier records. Edward Lockton, also described as a maltster, was the landlord from at least 1827 and was still there in 1841 when he was fined for serving drink out of hours on a Sunday. Some time in the 1840s John Beeson took over, previously a beerhouse keeper in the village. In the Beesons' time the occupants were in the habit of locking the door from the inside and then climbing out through the window. Mrs Beeson was reported in March 1849 to have suffered a broken arm as a result. In the following June the Black Lion was up for sale. The potential of its site stretching from the main street to Shelford Road near the forthcoming station, was well advertised. George Parr and then Henry Parr subsequently ran the inn, and the latter continued to own it for the rest of the century, putting in landlords as he turned his attention to building. Amongst the best was George Sands, in 1871 a young Nottingham man and former railway employee, who earned the congratulations of the Bingham magistrates in 1875 for having reformed the house. By then he was perhaps tactfully living in Bingham. The problems he had faced were doubtless caused by the influx of visitors from Nottingham, and his successor - Thomas Kell, a 40-year-old Yorkshireman in 1881- clearly came to the village expecting to make his money out of this visiting trade. After brushes with the law over illegal drinking, he was outraged when the *Nottingham Journal* waged a public health campaign, advising visitors against coming to the village. Perhaps the stress was all too much, for he died in October 1883 after a short but painful illness aged only 44. His widow Jane, twelve years his senior and with three daughters - two from

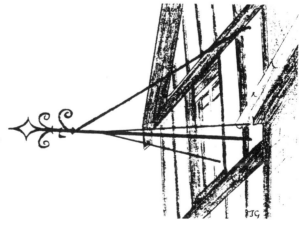
The old Black Lion sign bar on the butcher's shop now occupying the premises

a previous marriage - took on the running of the Black Lion, perhaps bowing to the increasing campaign against alcoholism by combining the inn with a tea garden. On her death in 1892 she was succeeded by her daughter, Fanny Dudley. By 1900 John Fryer was the landlord, and subsequent names up to 1928 include Albert Edwards, Frederick W. Platts and Harold Brownson. In that year new premises across the road were built on the site of Buxton's farm house and the village pinfold.

The Black Lion and garden at the corner of Station Terrace
in the early twentieth century

The Royal Oak in the 1870s when Sarah Fryer was the licensee

140

Across the road, the Royal Oak was situated close to two breweries, tenements and small shops. From deeds going back to 1780 it is clear that the site was repeatedly bought, mortgaged and sub-let by speculators both from Radcliffe and Nottingham. For example, the wharfinger Edward Parr invested money in it, as did William Eastwood, the village stonemason. From further afield the names of Mr Heymann of West Bridgford and Robert James, a Nottingham hosier, appear in the deeds. An elderly correspondent in the *Weekly Express* in 1887 recalled that the inn was once known as the Duke's Arms. From at least 1818 to 1834 it was the Plough, when it was taken over by Thomas Haynes, 'victualler', and became known as the Royal Oak. He died in 1843 after having mortgaged the premises, and in 1848 they were conveyed to Samuel Haynes, who remained until his death at the age of 43 in 1855, combining the work of landlord with that of joiner. Charles Buxton, assisted by his wife Sarah, appears as landlord in 1861, but by 1871 the Buxtons were replaced by the Fryers, who, like the Haynes family, had interests in a second occupation - that of blacksmith. After Paul Fryer's death in Sheffield in 1874 at the age of 37, his widow Sarah, with three young children, continued to run the inn as well as retain control of the blacksmith's business on Mount Pleasant, which was apparently worked by relatives. From 1881 Robert Hallam owned the Royal Oak, combining it with running one of the breweries alongside. (The other was Richard Daft's.) By 1900 Walter Hubbard was landlord, but in 1908 Sarah Fryer's son John was in charge, having had a spell at the Black Lion, and he was still there in 1928. In more recent times the families of Saxton and Redgate have been associated with the Royal Oak prior to its being taken over by Whitbread's Brewery in 1981.

Although all the village inns were used from time to time for meetings, public enquiries, auction sales or inquests, it was the Manvers Arms, formerly the White Hart, which was used most often for these purposes. Owned by the Manvers estate, it was also a regular stopping point for coaches and carriers' carts. One family, the Bells, occupied the inn during the period studied. George Bell, born at Brindley, was the landlord by 1832. Aged 32 at that date, as has been seen he also worked as a builder. By 1841 he and his wife Elizabeth had had nine of their ten children, and their household was completed by an ostler, an apprentice and two female servants. Ten years later his son Samuel was a journeyman bricklayer working on the Green, taking over as landlord when his father died at the end of that year. Samuel and his wife, Catherine, produced six children, and the household of the 1860s and 1870s was swelled by his mother as well as by servants and a few residents. On the whole, however, the Bells catered for large visiting parties rather than residents, and outings of Oddfellows or Manvers estate dinners are regularly recorded at the Manvers Arms. From the 1861 estate survey it is clear that the inn was well equipped for such events, with five rooms on the ground floor and six chambers above. Outside was a lean-to dairy with a chamber over, and an attic. There were also stables, with a club room over the top, a cow hovel and a brewhouse. For this accommodation the Bells paid £28 a year. Occasional excitements are recorded in the local newspapers - a fire in Samuel's haystack in 1871, a fire in the inn in May 1888 when a chambermaid left a lighted gas jet by curtains, and the problems caused by the influx of visitors. From 1861 the range of the family's activities was stretching beyond innkeeping and building to farming. In that year Samuel rented 15 acres of meadow and pasture, and by 1881 he had increased his holding to 168 acres. When he died in December 1883 his widow ran the inn until their son George Alfred, (a fine singer, a trained bricklayer, and with a rented farm on Shelford Road)

The Manvers Arms in the early twentieth century

took over. The family's farming and innkeeping interests continued until 1920 when most of the Manvers estate was sold.

The former Red Lion on Water Lane

The Red Lion on Water Lane with its own malt rooms was another inn under the control of one family for many years. The Hallams had owned it since the eighteenth century and Robert Hallam was in charge by 1851 when he was 37, with a wife some ten years older than himself. From the census returns he seems to have had five sons and a daughter, but the ages are erratic and not all the children can be found in the parish register. A notice in the *Nottingham Journal* in September 1873 advertises the forthcoming sale of the Red Lion, along with two grass fields and gardens comprising just over 3 acres. In the event the Hallams remained, although *Directories* suggest that for a while Robert looked after the malt rooms, while son Samuel took over the inn. It was Samuel in 1889 who suffered the indignity of being charged by an enraged bull which had galloped from Holme Pierrepont and found him standing in the Red Lion doorway. The bull propelled him five or six yards up the inn passage before disappearing to wreak more havoc. At the age of 60 in September 1902 he suddenly died at his work. The shock was so great for his wife Emma that within the hour she too was dead. They were buried at Holme Pierrepont. The Red Lion was sold for £4,450 in the November and a Frederick Spencer took over. Other occupants in the early twentieth century include George Foster and Mrs Emma Bradshaw. Between the two World Wars the future Edward VIII, while visiting Lamcote House as Prince of Wales, is remembered as a visitor there. The Red Lion closed in 1952 when a license was granted to the Trent Hotel on Shelford Road.

Farm houses

While some farms, where the agricultural labourers of Mount Pleasant and similar areas would have been employed, were on the outskirts of the parish - Spellow and Lings farms on the Bingham Road, or Hall farm towards the Cotgrave boundary - a number of farm houses still lay in the centre of the village, often rented from the Manvers estate. Typical of the more modest ones was that in the main street occupied in 1861 by Joseph Bowring (Bowren). While the house and buildings were worth only £8.15s.6d a year in rent, more than 75 acres of land throughout the village brought the total annual valuation close to £126. Joseph and his wife Edith had had at least eight children, five of whom survived to maturity. The sons, however, had all died by 1869, and when Joseph himself died in 1873 at the age of 88 he left three daughters to carry on the farm. All were long-lived, and the last was Elvira, remembered by an elderly resident of the 1960s as dressed in a white apron and print sun bonnet bringing her cows down from the Butts field (now Golf Road) to be milked at the farmhouse. She died in 1912, and although the site was occupied by Lunn's dairy for a while, it was bought by Arthur Joseph Rowe, a cycle agent from Station Road, from Lord Manvers in 1914 for £650. The old farm house was in

Elvira Bowring 1824-1912

142

due course obscured by petrol pumps, and the site is now occupied by shops. Of the other Manvers estate farmhouses, only five were substantial enough to be worth more than £20 a year in the 1861 rental. (This excluded the large acreage of rented land.) One, about which little is known, was occupied by John Parr in the Water Lane area. With its orchard, paddock and garden it was valued at £25.11s.6d a year.

Bowrings' farm house.
The site, next to the former police station, is now occupied by shops

The Grange

Another was Thomas Butler's brick and slate house, with brick and tile outbuildings, worth £21.10s.9d a year. It can probably be identified with the Grange, or at least with a house on that site. (Thomas's brother, Richard, rented Old Manor Farm on Shelford Road, formerly occupied by a branch of the Brewster family, and subsequently by the Bell and Barratt families. It was worth only £12 a year at this time, but its three acre plot was sold for £1,850 in 1920.) A house on the site of the Grange existed at the time of enclosure in 1790, although the current building was doubtless expanded during the nineteenth century. Apart from renting the house, Thomas Butler farmed about three-hundred acres. A married man of 37 in 1861 with eight children, he was to engage in a bitter struggle with the Burial Board when they wished to take one of his rented fields for a new cemetery, but with Lord Manvers on the side of the Board, he lost his fight. He and his wife, a sister of George Parr the cricketer, died in 1870 just before the ground was opened.

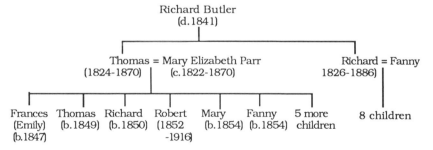

His son, another Thomas, continued at the Grange, looking after his seven younger brothers and sisters, and extending his lands to 420 acres. By the 1880s, Thomas Holmes, a farmer and corn merchant born in Edwalton, was living there. His place was taken by Thomas Haynes by 1900, a J.P. and prominent Methodist. Haynes nevertheless owned three sets of malt rooms in Radcliffe and another in

143

Grantham. When the Manvers estate sold the Grange in 1920 it was bought by the existing tenant, along with some thirty-four acres, for £4,550. The more recent history of the house is associated with Waldo and Rhona Dowson (land and house agents), Dr Allaway in 1923, the County Council, and the Parish Council from 1975.

The Poplars and the Chestnuts

The Poplars, painted in 1848 by Samuel Parrott. The house was then occupied by
John Green and subsequently by Butler Parr

After building the former Cedar House (16 Shelford Road) about 1832, John Green rented from Lord Manvers the brick house and buildings on the main street, part thatched and part tiled, originally known as The Poplars. Picturesque as the house appears in a painting by Samuel Parrott in 1848, the house was prone to flooding as the Syke Drain flowed past its grounds, and access was by a wooden footbridge. The Manvers estate papers show frequent payments in the 1850s for repairs to the drain, fence, walls and bridge outside John Green's house. His descendant reports that ground floor furniture had to be piled onto a table to avoid flood water. Perhaps for this reason the house's annual value was only £20.12s.3d in 1861. The Green family eventually moved to the Chestnuts, a more valuable property opposite the church. Their old house then became known by the name of the next occupant, the maltster and cricketer Butler Parr. After his death in 1872, his son, another Butler Parr, the brewery agent and prominent member of the Parish Council, continued to rent the property until purchasing it in 1901, along with its yard and paddock, for £1,500. There was serious flooding in 1922 and this Butler Parr built Field House behind in 1927. The old house was demolished about 1938 and later replaced by shops and a car park.

In the meantime, the Green family farmed from The Chestnuts, valued at £35.11s a year in 1861 and previously occupied by Samuel Brewster. Before its conversion into a hotel, and latterly into an old people's home (Rushleas), it was a substantial farmhouse - a three-storeyed building is shown on the site on a map of 1710 - with a dining room to the left of the front door, and a drawing room to the right. There was a large kitchen - painted 'Yellow Oaker and Blew' for 6s by John Brice in 1866 - and seven bedrooms. Outside were barns, loose boxes and pig sties on the edge of the road. This house earned its name from the trees which were formerly in its grounds, but which came to line the main street after a road widening scheme in 1911. The last of the old trees were removed in 1988. The Greens remained associated with The Chestnuts, even after their main interests moved to Cropwell. Miss Sally Green bought the house and fourteen acres from Lord Manvers for £2,000 in 1920, but it was soon afterwards sold to Mrs Blew-Jones, the daughter of Colonel Birkin of Lamcote House. Miss Green moved to a house in Wharf Lane converted from a cart hovel belonging to the Chestnuts.

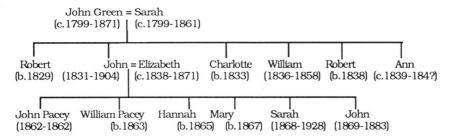

The Manor House

Across Wharf Lane, the Manor House was valued at £40 a year in 1861. Built in the late seventeenth century, this brick and slate house was considerably altered and extended in the nineteenth and twentieth centuries. In the early part of the nineteenth century it was rented with twenty acres by Samuel Parr. His son, George Parr the cricketer, was born there in 1826. Two daughters, another son, and a 3-year-old 'boarder' also lived there with Samuel and his wife Mary in 1851. Three-year-old Samuel Brittle, whose name is to be found in future cricket lists, boarded with them. Samuel Parr died in 1857 at the age of 76, and the Manor House was then occupied by James Dufty Gorse and his family for more than thirty years. He was one of the new breed of Nottingham business men who were to move into Radcliffe until the 1890s. Aged 33 in 1861, he was a hosiery yarn commission agent, born in New Radford and with offices in Fletcher Gate, Nottingham, and at Long Eaton by 1879. Six daughters and two sons are recorded in the census returns, so it is not surprising that his house contained not only five bedrooms in 1861, but a nursery as well. He also employed five servants.

James Gorse was active in his adopted village. He was a successful dog breeder, consistently winning prizes both locally and nationally between 1864 and 1870. He continued to rent land from the Manvers estate as his predecessor had done, using it at least in part for cattle since in 1888 the Inspector of Nuisances approved his premises for the selling of milk. He was particularly involved in organising the recasting and purchase of bells for the rebuilt church. He was also a keen advocate in 1882 of Radcliffe having a Local Board so that it could undertake its own sanitary improvements. When a local labourer, fearful of the increased rates and rents which might follow, opposed the idea, James Gorse advised him to look for work in Nottingham. Ironically, seven years later he was doing exactly that himself, having to leave the Manor House because of financial difficulties.

The reports of his appearance in the bankruptcy court in July 1891 make interesting reading. By then he was living in The Park in Nottingham. Since leaving Radcliffe over two years previously, deeply in debt as a yarn agent, he had set up in business as a coal merchant in Radford Boulevard, and also as a mineral water manufacturer, contracting more debts but expecting to recoup his losses from his two new businesses. The vagaries of the English climate were too much for him, however, as 'the seasons were very disastrous'. As a result, his debts now amounted to £8,796.12s.7d and his assets to a mere £102.2s.6d. While his son Frank was involved in these business arrangements, his second son remained associated with Radcliffe and was a keen member of the local cricket team. One of the latter's sisters - Clara Thompson - is also known to have remained in Radcliffe.

James Gorse was by no means alone in getting into financial difficulties - there were at least three other bankruptcy cases in Radcliffe around this time - and one of his successors at the Manor House in 1904 had similar problems, though on a smaller scale. At that time George Lynes Bates, a brass founder and engineer carrying on business as the Batesmith Injector Company in Crocus Street, Nottingham, owed over £60 in rent and had to leave. The house was then let to Gerrard Septimus Dowson. In 1920 Lord Manvers sold it with two acres of land for £2,850, and it has since become a home for the frail and elderly.

The Manor House c.1910 when the Dowsons were in occupation

The Wharf House

The most valuable house owned by the Manvers estate in 1861 was the Wharf House worth £50 a year, probably because of the landing and trading rights which went with the property. When the open fields had been enclosed and land redistributed in 1790, half the wharf went to small 'shareholders' in the village. (In 1905 such obsolete rights were still occasionally recorded in the Manvers papers at a rental of 9d a year.) The other half of the Wharf belonged to the estate, and for a substantial part of the nineteenth century it was let with the house to Edward Parr, one of Radcliffe's 'characters'. According to the *Nottingham Daily Express* in 1877, the number of nights he spent away from his home could be counted on one hand, and he refused to leave even when the floods were highest. Like most of the estate houses, the Wharf House was brick and tile, with three rooms and a kitchen on the ground floor, four chambers (bedrooms) and two attics. In addition it had a warehouse, a coalhouse, a piggery, a cowhovel, and a garden. It had been built in 1820, replacing an earlier house. Originally substantial profits must have been made through the landing of coal and other heavy goods, but business would have fallen off after the coming of the railway. Edward Parr was well insulated from the declining river trade, however, and had shrewdly invested his money in housing and land. When he died at the age of 92 in January 1876 - eleven days after the death of his 79-year-old wife - he left property in Mount Pleasant, Bailey Lane and Bolton Terrace, as well as a large area of adjacent building land. His property was sold in March 1876 and the proceeds divided amongst his own and his wife's relatives, since he had no children of his own. The Upton family subsequently became associated with the wharf and the ferry, with 'Trot' Upton, so called because of lameness, charging 1d to take people across the river. When the house was finally sold by the estate for

The Wharf House built in 1820,
now demolished

146

£1,475 in 1941, one of the conditions of purchase, as required by law, was the maintenance of 'the Ferry Service as enjoyed by the Public'. The decline of river trade can be gauged by the annual rental of the house and eight acres of land in 1941, which amounted to only £40, that is £10 less than it had been eighty years earlier.

Radcliffe Hall

Three long-established privately owned houses - Lamcote House, Radcliffe Lodge and Radcliffe Hall - qualified as belonging to an upper stratum of Radcliffe society in the mid-nineteenth century. Nevertheless, Radcliffe Hall, a late eighteenth century house with nineteenth century extensions, had its roots firmly in farming. The Taylor family, originally from Lancashire, but acquiring estates in Radcliffe and Woodborough in the eighteenth century, continued until 1873 to farm through tenants 162 acres of land which reached southwards from the Hall. In other respects the Taylors qualified as gentry.

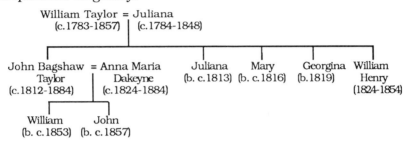

As has been seen, in 1851 William Taylor was a widower aged 55, living at the Hall with his son, John, and two daughters - all unmarried and in their thirties - and with seven servants: butler, coachman, housekeeper, ladies' maid, housemaid, kitchen maid and footman. Another daughter had died in 1844, and a son who was a captain in Her Majesty's Corps of Gentlemen and had served in India was found dead in London with his head in a bath of water in 1854. (After evidence from his brother that he had been subject to epilepsy after returning from India, a verdict of 'Death from natural causes' was recorded at the inquest.) Despite these tragedies, William Taylor remained active in public life, serving as a county magistrate at both Shire Hall in Nottingham and at the Bingham petty sessions. Having a landed interest, he attended the Nottinghamshire Agricultural Protection Society, and as church-warden he chaired a meeting in Radcliffe in 1850 when there was general concern about the influence of the 'Romish' movement. He had also been caught up in the 'railway mania' of the 1840s, being on the provisional committee of the Newark and Sheffield Railway in 1844, as well as being a provisional director of the Ambergate and Nottinghamshire Railway in 1845.

On his death in 1857 his son, John Bagshaw Taylor, became the owner of Radcliffe Hall, a man very much in his father's mould when it came to public service. As churchwarden and participant in parish affairs he was a benevolent figure, lending his land for public occasions, or contributing to the church rebuilding fund. As a local magistrate he was as active as his father had been. In 1868 he was High Sheriff of the county, attending numerous functions including a review of the South Nottinghamshire Yeomanry Cavalry (of which Lord Manvers was colonel), a meeting to organise the visit of the Royal Agricultural Society to Nottingham, and an inspection of the Lunatic Asylum at Sneinton. He also became involved in a controversy with John Denison of Ossington, M.P., who accused him of political bias in his timing of candidates' nomination days. John Taylor declared himself astounded at the accusations, professed to have left the arrangements to the under-sheriff, and demanded an apology for the public insult. There is no evidence that he received one. His interest in local affairs continued after his year as High Sheriff, and he is found at a Conservative Association dinner, and chairing meetings to consider the adoption of the Local Government Act or of a Local Board during the village's public health crisis in 1882.

John Taylor married in 1854 when he was in his early forties. His wife, Anne Marie Dakeyne, was some thirteen years his junior. Having given birth to a stillborn daughter in 1855, she went on to produce two sons, John and William, and she was probably the Mrs Taylor who was presented in November 1876 with a bracelet worth 50 guineas from a London jewellers after serving as church organist for nearly fourteen years. John Taylor gave up farming in 1873, but continued at the Hall for another ten years. He then sold his horses, carriages, implements and remaining animals, and let the house, initially for two years. The death of his wife around this time may have affected his decision. According to White's *Directory* the occupant in 1885-6 was Leonard Foster, a Nottingham contractor. The contents were finally sold in 1890, and the advertisement in the *Nottingham Daily Express* gives the first real glimpse of the house and its contents. As well as its drawing and dining rooms, study, workroom, servants' hall and kitchens, the Hall contained six principal bedrooms, seven maidservants' bedrooms and two manservants' bedrooms. Amongst the contents sold was a small library of books. Outside were a greenhouse, an apple chamber, a coach house and stables.

John Taylor lived until 1893, the electoral register recording him at Westbourne Lodge, Scarborough. He was buried alongside his wife at East Bridgford. The Hall was then vested in William Henry Wood Taylor, his younger son, who sold it in 1905 to Samuel Smith of Elm House, Cropwell Road, a Nottingham lace manufacturer. Smith died in 1912 and the Hall was then occupied by his wife Helena until 1939. During the First World War she opened up the hall as a convalescent home for wounded officers, marrying one of the patients, Captain Lloyd Dexter. The Hall was sold to Mrs Ivy Gianelli of West Bridgford in 1939, and was acquired by the Royal British Legion in 1951.

Radcliffe Hall in 1904

Radcliffe Lodge

This rendered brick house is said to have been built in 1791, just after the enclosure of the open fields, by the banker Colonel Samuel Wright. The land, however, remained part of the Pierrepont, subsequently Manvers, estate. It is difficult to gain a clear picture of ownership and occupation. The Rev Henry Bolton, famed for his vinery and fruit-growing, was an early occupant and probable owner, but the parish register reveals that William Turbutt 'Gentleman' was living there between 1817 and 1819 when three children were born. Wright's *Directory* for 1832 gives the Reverend Edward Bolton's address as the Lodge, but from the late 1830s the house was regularly offered for sale. A newspaper advertisement in July 1837 emphasised the convenience of its situation: close to the turnpike road with coaches and mails passing daily, near to the wharf for coal supplies, and in good hunting country. The building was 'modern, handsome and tasty', on an elevated site, commanding 'much admired' prospects, and surrounded by beautiful scenery and 'pleasure walks'. Its dining, drawing and breakfast rooms, library, housekeeper's and servants' hall, ten excellent bedrooms with others in the outbuildings would have made it a rival to Radcliffe Hall. It also had a brewhouse, cellars, stables for hunters, a dovecote, and fully-stocked gardens with greenhouses and double hot house 90 feet in length, 'clothed throughout with vines in full bearing'.

In the following year there were further inducements to buy: the right to a pew in the parish church, the availability of between 4 and 20 acres of land including the 'Ice-House Close', the payment of very little land tax. In June 1839 the Lodge was either still for sale, or for sale again, this time recommended for 'the family of a gentleman or retired and opulent tradesman'. There was an air of desperation about the further claim that it was now 'at its lowest price by Private contract for if not sold during the present month or early in July it will probably undergo material alteration and be no more offered to the public'. Its fate after this advertisement - still being repeated in August - is not known. In 1848, however, correspondence about the railway makes it clear that the Rev Henry Bolton, then living in the Park, Nottingham, was the owner. For three colourful years the Lodge then became the headquarters of Greaves, Smart and Adams while they built the railway through Radcliffe. The use of its grounds for the celebration when the bridge over Wharf Lane was completed is recorded elsewhere. (See page 99.)

For a short time from 1852 the Manvers estate acquired the Lodge, apparently for Lord Newark, but the occupant from that year was Henry Smythe, reputedly a linen draper from Nottingham who failed in business. By April 1859 an extensive sale of his furniture took place, including his piano, gallery of oil paintings and engravings, plate, china, books, linen, wines, as well as his carriages, harness, horse, saddlery and conservatory of greenhouse plants. The trustees of the Manvers estate, who seem to have foreclosed on his mortgage, now sold the Lodge to Ichabod Charles Wright, the banker and scholar who was in residence at Lamcote House around this time. He in turn passed it to his son Frederick, another banker, who in 1862 was described in the *Nottingham Journal* as of both Mapperley Hall and Radcliffe Lodge.

It was another ten years, however, before Frederick Wright took up permanent residence. In the intervening period two occupants have been identified. A Captain Stewart of the 11th Hussars arrived in 1859 and was still there at the time of the 1861 census with his wife, mother-in-law, two young children and two servants. Charles Henry Smith next appears in the records, described as a manufacturer in 1871, with a wife called Sarah, five children, a governess form Jersey (Mary Sarah Millais, almost certainly related to the artist of that name), and five other servants.

Radcliffe Lodge in 1901

Shortly afterwards Frederick Wright took up personal residence and his son was born at the Lodge in 1872. He was a benefactor to various causes including Nottingham's General Hospital and Shelford church, and he donated £660 to the rebuilding of Radcliffe church, acting as the fund's treasurer. In 1878 he left Radcliffe for Lenton Hall, putting the Lodge up for sale. Its accommodation was essentially similar to that described in 1837, but it now had fourteen bed and dressing rooms, and one of its front halls contained a billiard table.

The Lodge was now bought by Richard Grundy, the auctioneer and estate agent, who divided the house, the two halves being known as North and South Lodge. Perhaps this was because his partner, Charles Morris - from a family of Cotgrave farmers and the first captain of Trent College - had recently married his daughter. (After practising alone for some years after the death of Richard Grundy in 1880, Charles Morris took W.J. Place as his partner.) The Morrises do not seem to have been permanent residents, however, until the late 1880s. In White's *Directory* of 1885-6, Tom Potter, the colliery owner and future county councillor, and a Mrs Skinner are listed as residents. With the Morrises after this time were the Lamberts, in lace manufacture, and both parts of the Lodge appear in newspaper reports as venues for concerts and soirees. Mr George Gregg, a prominent Wesleyan, lived there early this century, but between 1923 and 1930 it became a school for about forty boys, since when it has been subdivided again into several residences. Today, the gardens, so well-cared for in the time of the Rev Thomas Bolton, have now matured and would surely still meet with his approval.

Lamcote House

The early history of the third 'gentry' residence, Lamcote House, is obscure. According to nineteenth century reminiscences it was built by a Nottingham confectioner, Mr Topott, and earned the nickname 'Sugar Plum Hall', either from his profession or from the shape of its trees. (After enclosure in 1790 Mr Topott owned land now occupied by the golf course.) Firm evidence of the date of its building has not been found, but it was occupied in 1807 when Mr Topott wrote to Lord Manvers about the payment of a rate assessment. The Manvers papers also indicate that some rent was paid to the estate, presumably ground rent, and that in 1811 John Burnside had an interest in Lamcote property. It is the latter's family which in the long run came to be associated with Lamcote House, and some information about portraits at Plumtree indicates that Mr Topott married a sister of the Rev John Burnside, rector of Plumtree, and so was perhaps son-in-law of the John of 1811.

Firm information about the occupancy of the house is not found until the 1850s, but it is tempting to assume that in the 1830s Francis Wright, described as 'esquire' of Lamcote, was in residence with his wife Selina. Three children were born to them between 1834 and 1837. As Francis belonged to a junior line of the banking family and was to be high sheriff of the county in 1842, it is difficult to see where in Lamcote, other than at Lamcote House, he could have lived to suit his status.

In 1851 George Bacon, a 'merchant', his wife and four servants were living there, replaced by Thomas Marriott by 1856. A well-known magistrate, and almost certainly the father-in-law of the Rev Robert Burgess, Radcliffe's vicar, he brought his occupation to a dramatic end in December 1857 by committing suicide while on a visit to another son-in-law, the Rev J.M.W. Piercey of Slawston in Leicestershire. Suffering from depression, he drowned himself in a water cistern while looking over a new house being built for the Pierceys at East Langton. He was judged temporarily insane at the inquest and buried at Saddington near Market Harborough. From later correspondence in the church records it seems that he was associated with the new window in Radcliffe's chancel, which was about to be rebuilt at the time of his death. The furniture sale which followed Thomas Marriott's suicide gives a glimpse of the interior of Lamcote House in the mid-nineteenth century. The dining and breakfast rooms were furnished in 'the finest Spanish mahogany ...of the most substantial make.' The elegant drawing room contained items in 'Zebra and Rosewood' and a noble console table and glass (the plate of the glass was 102 inches high). Also included in the sale were rich window draperies, the 'superior' contents of eight bedrooms and dressing rooms, furniture from the hall, staircase and servants' offices, and handsome china services. The house was advertised to let in the following March, along with its hothouse, pleasure grounds and gardens, stabling for six horses and eighteen acres of adjoining land.

The next occupant was Ichabod Charles Wright of Mapperley, already noted in connection with Radcliffe Lodge. In November 1859 the *Nottingham Journal* reported that a valuable hunter from the Wright stables at Lamcote had been killed. At the time of the 1861 census Ichabod Charles, then aged 65, was in residence with his wife Theodosia, the daughter of Lord Denman, and four children whose ages ranged from 31 down to 15. Of these, Frederick at 20 was the third. A butler and four female servants lived in, while a coachman and his family lived in a house at the stables. The presence of so eminent a figure suggests that Radcliffe's prestige was rising. Not only was he a banker and the author of two works on currency, but he had enjoyed a distinguished academic career and was the translator of Dante's *Divine Comedy* and Homer's *Iliad* into English verse. He was also to be M.P. for Nottingham from 1868 to 1870, the year before he died. During their brief residence at Lamcote the Wrights provided some excitement in the village when their second daughter, Frances, was married in May 1861 at Radcliffe church to Mr Edward Cropper of Thorntonfield near Gainsborough. The *Journal* gave a full account of the bridal procession of five carriages, and of the six bridesmaids dressed in white net trimmed with blue ribbon and with white tulle bonnets. The bride's dress, showing 'simplicity and taste', was in a similar style, with a veil of white silk thrown over a fragile coronet of orange blossom.

By July 1862, Henry Hawkes, J.P. of Spalding is noted in newspaper items as being in residence at Lamcote House. He too provided a daughter for a wedding at Radcliffe church, this time to a Sussex clergyman in 1863, but the *Journal* does not seem to have found this worthy of such coverage as the Wright wedding. The next identifiable occupants were the Burnside sisters, the daughters of the Reverend John Burnside of Plumtree. As he is noted as having an estate in Radcliffe in White's *Directory* of 1864 and the name is associated with land earlier in the century, it is perhaps this family who owned the house throughout the intervening years.

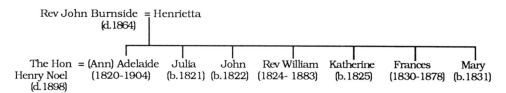

Significantly, Frances Burnside gives Lamcote House as her place of birth in the 1871 census, which, if correct, suggests that the family had been in residence around 1830. It is, however, a newspaper report of a fire at Lamcote House which indicates that the Burnside sisters were there by 1867. The cause of the fire was an overheated flue. A messenger was sent to Nottingham for the fire brigade, but by the time it arrived the fire had been put out, causing damage to no more than a window, which could be repaired for £30 through the Burnsides' policy with the Imperial Fire Office.

The eldest sister was (Anne) Adelaide, born at Plumtree in 1820. Although she herself is not listed as in residence in the 1871 census, her younger sisters Frances, Mary and Julia are, as well as her nephew. The household was staffed by eleven resident servants including a butler. It was Frances who, after visiting a seaside mission with her sisters in 1875, underwent a religious conversion and worked for missions in Radcliffe and Nottingham until her untimely death in 1876. Even without Frances's evangelising spirit, Lamcote House became a focal point for religion and charity in the neighbourhood. In particular, Adelaide's generosity to the church, the children, and the elderly of the village seems to have been well appreciated. After her sisters married or died, the community must have wished her joy on her own marriage in her 70s to the Hon Henry Noel, uncle of the Earl of Gainsborough, who joined her at Lamcote House. He took an equally active part in local affairs as the chairman of the parish council from 1894 to 1898, the year of his death. Adelaide Noel continued her work for the parish until her death in 1904, although incapacitated during her last years after a fall in church.

Lt Colonel Charles Birkin became the next significant owner of Lamcote House, making it a centre for fashionable society, while continuing the Burnside tradition of involvement in the local community. It was his daughter, Mrs Freda Dudley Ward, who, having met the Prince of Wales (the future Edward VIII) in Belgrave Square during an air raid, caused the prince to be a familiar figure in the village after the First World War. On Colonel Birkin's death in 1932, the house was advertised for sale, along with the 200-acre Lamcote farm. Its ground floor accommodation included a main hall 40 feet long, as well as morning and dining rooms, and a very fine drawing room facing west and measuring 36 feet by 21 feet. There were eleven principal bedrooms and dressing rooms, a schoolroom, a service lift, and generous staff accommodation. Comfort was assured at this date by central heating from a boiler in the basement. After the Birkins' time Lamcote House was never so glamorous again. It was later divided into apartments and finally demolished in 1980, leaving only its wall and gateway to suggest former glories.

Lamcote House, demolished in 1980

Other examples of houses in the old village - such as the Vicarage (built in 1827 and now demolished), the Old Manor House near Lamcote corner (dating from the eighteenth century), Barrow House next to Lamcote Motors with its barn containing a beam dated 1604, a modest farm house in Bolton Terrace, Richmond Cottage opposite the churchyard, a timber-framed house now 35-37 Water Lane, and many more - indicate that Radcliffe had its quota of distinguished or idiosyncratic dwellings by mid-Victorian times.

2. The new buildings

The pattern of expansion was to change once the railway brought Radcliffe within easy reach of Nottingham. New houses, many described as middle-class villas, sprang up in the fields close to the station. Joiners or carpenters such as James Upton and Henry Parr, or bricklayers such as William Vickerstaff, became builders. Long standing Radcliffe names - Foster, Butler, Barratt - appear as estate agents and auctioneers. By 1883 the Radcliffe Brick Company, managed by J.G. Willey, was taking advantage of the new developments. Women, too, were owning property - nearly 9% of the village's ratable property in 1879 and almost 10% by 1894. House letting in the new areas became an investment for owners from both Nottingham and Radcliffe.

As early as June 1849, before the railway had even opened, the shrewder residents were recognising the potential of nearby land. One such was Henry Parr who not only acquired the Black Lion advertised as 'most eligibly situated for building purposes', but in due course owned many of the artisan houses and gardens of Station Terrace which were built on much of its original land. The 1861 census records some fourteen households headed by three labourers, a gardener, two boatmen, two bricklayers, a butcher, a washerwoman, a blacksmith, a groom, a coachman and a corn miller.

Cliff House

At the other end of the social scale a new house on Shelford Road challenged the well-established gentry houses of the village. This was Cliff House, built about 1862 overlooking the river, with eight bedrooms, three reception rooms, its own lodge and five acres of grounds. Its creator was William Sanday, the former occupant of Holme House, whose family had been prominent as agents for the Manvers estate, and who had been a noted sheep breeder. From the account book of John Brice, a plumber and glazier in the 1860s, it is possible to date the progress of the building, including the erection of a vinery. William Sanday retired young from farming - he was only 45 when Cliff House was being built - and having moved to Radcliffe with his wife and two daughters he played an active part in local affairs, sitting on numerous committees, and helping with fund-raising for rebuilding the

William Sanday 1817-1897

church. He did not quite leave livestock behind, for geese and poultry were kept in the grounds. A local story tells how one Christmas all the geese were taken, but a gander was left, bearing an envelope with a note inside:

Good morning Mr Sanday
Your geese are very handy.
We've bought them all at a penny a piece
And left the money with the gandy!

Cliff House, now demolished

Mr Sanday's reaction is not recorded. On his death in 1897 Frances Whitty, a lace manufacturer, occupied Cliff House, followed by Henry Roberts in the 1920s. It was demolished to make room for the building of Oak Tree Avenue, with only part of the estate wall and the lodge on Shelford Road surviving.

Clyde Villa and Campbell House

In general, Shelford Road attracted more modest, but still affluent, middle-class housing. Clyde Villa (now The Cedars) advertised as 'adjoining railway station' was an early example built around 1862. When it was sold in February 1868, it was described as 'compact and pretty', with dining room, drawing room, large and small kitchens, a dairy, cellars and four good bedrooms. Its garden was well-stocked, and it had a gig house, a stable and outbuildings. Some of the contents sold in 1868 indicate considerable affluence and comfort. The drawing room contained furniture in 'beautifully figured walnut wood', with rich Brussels carpets, a chiffonier, and chimney and pier glasses. The dining room was furnished in mahogany, and included an extending frame dining table and a 6 ft. sideboard. Chairs, sofas, oil paintings, engravings, silver and plated goods, china and glass also featured in the sale. In the gig house was a nearly new pony phaeton made by Kinder of Derby, and a Norfolk dog cart. In 1871 Clyde Villa was owned by Mr W.F. Green, a Nottingham lace manufacturer, but occupied by Edwin Green, at that time a 50-year-old lace manufacturer with the firm of Berry & Green in Nottingham. He had been born in Orston, but his name is frequently associated with property dealing in Radcliffe. According to an advertisement for the sale of his furniture in September 1878, he then decided to return to the south of England. Shortly afterwards he appears in the electoral register as living in Brighton, but his removal was only temporary, for he was subsequently to live in Radcliffe at a house called the Hollies on Cropwell Road, where he died much respected in 1888 at the age of 68.

In the meantime, William F. Green was living next door to Clyde Villa in Campbell House (now Broadlands Rest Home), the second in a row of three elegant new villas. In 1881 his household consisted of his wife, five children and three female servants. When it was advertised for sale in 1892 it boasted three reception rooms, a library, two kitchens, a dairy, eight bedrooms, bathroom facilities, a coach house, harness room, a tennis lawn and ornamental and kitchen gardens. In the following year it was withdrawn from auction at £2,050. Louis Francois Collier, a French bankrupt lace manufacturer who made good, built the third house (now demolished at the corner of Shelford Road and Chestnut Grove). The opulence of its furniture sold in April 1893 was matched by the practicality of its domestic equipment which included 'Taylor's new washer and wringer'.

Land sales

In the late 1860s and early 1870s more land came onto the market for building purposes: 'abutting upon the highway on one side and the railway on the other' in 1867, or along the cliff for 'first class villas' in 1869. The latter stretch of land was put up for sale by the Manvers estate, and their advertisement gives a eulogistic view of why this site and Radcliffe in particular provided opportunities not to be missed:

> It has been determined to open out this most desirable site for the erection of first class villas standing in their own grounds, where all the delights of the country, coupled with pure air and exquisite scenery can be enjoyed without the expense of keeping horses and carriages.
>
> Advantages are offered in this locality not possessed by any other building sites near Nottingham.
>
> A bed of excellent Brick Clay is close at hand, and arrangements can be made to provide bricks early in spring for those who agree for sites during the coming winter .....

Perhaps the prices asked were too high, for advertisements continued for seven months, and there was little development along the cliff until after the 1914-18 war.

Nevertheless, building land prices in Radcliffe continued to rise, encouraged by increased rates in Nottingham and nearby villages. The situation was summed up on May 20th 1878 by the valuer for one of the other major landowners in Radcliffe, the Humphrey Perkins' School of Barrow-on-Soar:

The demand for building land at Ratcliffe which I foresaw and mentioned in my report of March 28th 1873 as likely to arise within 8 or 10 years ..... has developed more rapidly than I expected ..... This is partly the result of the recent Nottingham Improvement Act which has included most of the other Villages round Nottingham within the Rating area of the Town, when the permanent charges are likely in future to be extremely heavy owing to the enormous outlay in progress or in prospect for Improvement works.

The demand was to come from 'wealthy Tradesmen or Manufacturers having business in Nottingham.'

Chestnut Grove

It was probably from the sale in 1874 of eight lots of freehold building land adjoining Shelford Road, and near the railway station, that Chestnut Grove and nearby houses were to develop. (The deeds of one property record that 1330 square yards of land were purchased from Barrow School Trust by Edwin Green before the end of 1875.) A number of purchasers built on the site, but the owners rarely occupied the houses. Dr Ellam and James Radford were among the first occupants of a pair of semi-detached houses there in 1877. A second pair was being built in 1878, offered for letting by mid-summer by the firm of T. & R. Millington of Canal Street, Nottingham, makers of canvas sail and sacking, and dealers in coal dust and cement. Like Edwin Green, the Millingtons were speculating in housebuilding, and the monogram on numbers 1 and 3 Chestnut grove, dated 1878, probably refers to Thomas Millington who retained ownership until the 1890s. Their original specifications included a larder, wine and other cellars, dining and drawing rooms, kitchen, scullery and china closet on the ground floor, three bedrooms, bathroom and linen closet on the first floor, and four bedrooms, linen closet and store rooms on the second floor. The gardens at front and back commanded extensive views, and there was an abundant supply of hard and soft water. (This would be from wells as piped water did not reach Radcliffe for about another twenty years.)

Decorative head on a house in Chestnut Grove

By 1881 the area was well-established, a much sought-after enclave of middle-class prosperity. In residence was Abraham Pyatt, a widower with two children, his household run by a housekeeper and two female servants. By profession he was a prosperous timber and slate merchant in Nottingham, where in 1899 he was to become mayor. William Thorne was a wine merchant born in London and his household consisted of his wife and four children, as well as a nurse, a housemaid and a page. At the house known as Caernarvon Villa was Charles King, a commercial traveller born at Welbeck, Cambridgeshire. William Burgess, at Grandholme Villa, was the director of a carriage works in Nottingham, living with his wife, seven children and two female servants. George Parr, a maltster born in Cotgrave, had a wife and three children, also supported by two female servants. All five men were in their thirties.

Round the corner on Shelford Road was Robert Millington, with his wife, three children, their governess and two female servants. He was part of the firm of T. & R. Millington who were responsible for two houses in the Grove, He was also a churchwarden, superintendent of St Mary's Sunday School, and on the committee for the rebuilding of the church. He died at the age of 48 in 1886.

Lorne Grove

Another area being developed at about the same time, but in several stages, was Lorne Grove, traditionally named after the Marquess of Lorne (later Duke of Argyll) who married Princess Louise, Queen Victoria's daughter in 1871. In June of that year a substantial five-bedroomed house with walled garden, stables, coach house and other outbuilings was offered for sale. (It seems to have been known as Northfield House and then Montpelier House by 1888, and is probably the currently named Lynton House.) Along with it went a close lying to the south, then used as garden ground, 'well adapted for building purposes', and having the advantages of an elevated site near the station. Mrs Ann Wright was in occupation at the time. How much building went on immediately is not clear, but in June 1878 a Mr Laslett of Lorne Grove was offering seven freehold plots for sale. To the above advantages he could add the pure air, splendid views, proximity to the Trent and, ironically in the light of controversy to come, drainage already laid in the centre of the Grove. A month later an architect named Laurence Bright of the Town Clerk's chambers in Nottingham was asking for tenders to build a pair of semi-detached houses, and from 1879 advertisements offering houses for rent show that Lorne Grove was second only to Chestnut Grove as a haven for middle-class families.

Houses in Lorne Grove about 1910
Lynton House (Montpelier House) is on the left

Rents were variable. Addison Villa was on offer at £30 a year, Hampden Villa at £26 and No. 2 Lorne Villas for £19. The latter was owned by W.F. Green. At the beginning of 1881 semi-detached houses with seven main rooms were advertised at £32 and £35 per year, but the market seems to have been temporarily saturated with middle-class residences, for the advertisements were repeated at regular intervals for a year, and the rents gradually reduced to £25 and £28 per annum. (On average, Chestnut Grove rents were £10 a year more.) Nevertheless, three more plots were offered for sale in 1888.

Of the thirteen households in Lorne Grove in the 1881 census, two did not list any living-in servants or domestic help, and three had more than one servant. The occupations of the householders were, however, similar to those found on Chestnut Grove: an East India merchant at Grosvenor Villas, an accountant at Hampden Villas, two lace manufacturers (one at Claremont Villas), a lace merchant, a lace designer, an elderly clergyman, John Simpson at Northfield House described as 'out of business' but undoubtedly speculating in the Radcliffe property market, an 'annuitant' and a solicitor at Cromwell Villas, a widow with a commercial traveller for a son-in-law at Addison Villas (the other house being unoccupied), a stationer, and - at Granville House at the corner - Dr Ellam, having unwisely moved from Chestnut Grove as events were to turn out during the drainage crisis of 1882. Three further houses were unoccupied. No head of household was born in Radcliffe, and their ages ranged from 30 to 77.

Developments along the Bingham Road

The next area to be developed was Bingham Road. In June 1877, land at the corner of Bingham Road and Cropwell Road came up for sale and the decorator R.J. Rushton, later remembered for his flowing white beard, was advertising his house for renting at £18 a year in October 1879. (His son's advertisement can still be discerned on the Bingham Road side of his house.) In the previous April the Jeffrey Dole commissioners recognised that land let for the poor on Bingham Road could be put to much more profitable use by being let for building purposes, but there is little sign that the new houses were completed by the time of the 1881 census. After Granville House at the corner of Lorne Grove, the first occupied house was Northcote House. A hosier, Charles Buckland, lived there with his wife, two young children, his father and two servants, and the house was filled with 'superior household furniture' according to an advertisement two years later. Salisbury Cottages next door were occupied by the families of John Goodwin and John Adlard, a bank manager and an assistant schools inspector respectively. The artisan dwellings of Palin Row came next and then there were no dwellings until Spellow Farm was reached.

Oakfield House

It was during the next few years that Oakfield House helped to occupy this space. An advertisement for its sale in 1891 by Mr W.H. Burgass, the managing director of the Nottingham Brick Company based at Carlton and probably the original owner, indicated the scale of its opulence. On the ground floor it had an oak-floored entrance hall, a dining room (20 feet by 20 feet) with a square bay window, a drawing room, breakfast room, butler's pantry, large kitchen and second kitchen. There were five principal bedrooms on the first floor, with bathroom, w.c. and store closet, and two bedrooms, two storerooms and a billiard or school-room on the floor above. There were also coal, beer and wine cellars, and outside there were the stable, carriage house, washhouse, gardener's cottage, tennis lawn and a kitchen garden in a high state of cultivation. Today, the house is a Salvation Army home for the elderly, but the decorative 'B' symbols can still be seen as reminders of Mr Burgass's day. Rating lists suggest that it was bought by a Thomas Middleton, while Mr Burgass moved to Chestnut Grove.

Building on the other (southern) side of Bingham Road also took place so that gradually the old tenements of Radcliffe Hill were being overshadowed by Victorian developments. Twin Cottage was there by 1880. Much of the new property came to be owned by J.G. Willey, the retired provisions merchant who took an active part in

38-40 Grantham Road and Fern-lea, 28 Grantham Road
Based on architect's drawings of 1889

local affairs and was responsible for the Radcliffe Brick Company. He lived at Fairfield House until 1897 (later owned by Mr Foster, the auctioneer), and additionally owned Beaconsfield Villas, two other pairs of semi-detached houses, two detached houses and three cottages, all on the Bingham Road. Rentals were less than on Chestnut Grove or Lorne Grove, semi-detached houses on Bingham Road being let for £17 a year in June 1882, and at £18 and £26 in 1887.

It was in November 1882 that Simon Eastwood, the stone mason, sold off land along the Bingham Road which had been held by his family since the time of enclosure. Nine lots were advertised, and the proposed Eastwood Street had already been sewered and kerbed, but the first six pairs of houses were not built until 1912. From the end of the 1880s development also increased on today's Grantham Road (then part of Bingham Road) and at the Harlequin. Fern-lea, 28 Grantham Road, was built for William Upton in 1889. Six houses were planned for the Harlequin in 1899 and another six in 1902, with land sold for a proposed new street in that year.

Cropwell Road

New villas on Cropwell Road were begun around 1880. In that year Thomas Buxton, a 26-year-old builder living on Cropwell Road, purchased a section of church land for £290 from the vicar, John Cullen, with the approval of the ecclesiastical commissioners and Lord Manvers, the patron of the living. At the corner of the newly made Albert Road he built the substantial detached house (now Albert House, 21 Cropwell Road) which he sold in January 1881 to Robert Smith, a cottager of Holme Pierrepont for £590.

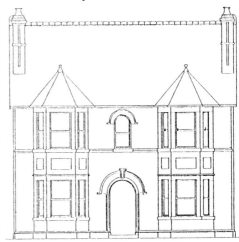

Chestnut House, 16 Cropwell Road, 1892-3
Based on an architect's drawing of 1889

Further developments soon followed. In November 1882 building leases for 99 years came up for sale, and a month later two lots, including the site of the old windmill near the present golf course, realised £1394.15s.7d. The Hollies at the corner of Victoria Street was occupied before 1888. (A Captain Smith sold it in 1893 for £1.200.) Round the corner from Albert House in Albert Street came Albany Cottages built in 1885 and Burbage Cottages built in 1891. Building on Lincoln Grove and Victoria Street occurred in 1891 and 1896 respectively, but most houses were built between 1901 and 1903. Typical of the development on the western side of Cropwell Road was the house built by Henry Parr in 1892-93, now known as Chestnut House.

A temporary halt to the building boom

Nevertheless, despite the *Journal's* confident assertion about the village in December 1882 - 'Certainly land is not decreasing in value' - Radcliffe's building boom had not gone unchecked. Not only had there been the slow take up of rented property in Lorne Grove over the previous year, but in May 1882 the Manvers estate had failed to sell twenty-two plots of land which some forty years later were to become New Road. By waging a campaign against the village's insanitary state in that year, the *Journal* itself had been largely responsible for this temporary decline in the property market. At an enquiry in 1884 it was acknowledged that few houses had been recently built because of newspaper pressure. A further result of the crisis was that any new building had now to have its sanitary arrangements approved by the Bingham Board of Guardians, and this slowed down development.

Confidence recovered, but by the end of the 1880s there was a second distinct decline in the property market reflected in falling rents. In 1887 the rent of an occupied semi-detached house in Chestnut Grove had reached £55 a year, but had fallen to £35 by 1890. From then on advertisements mentioned 'moderate' rents, the 'low' price of, or 'cheap', building land. It can be no coincidence that several bankruptcies occurred in the village around this time. Not only did James Gorse go bankrupt at the Manor House, but so did Thomas Wardle on Bingham Road in 1889, Samuel Barratt, the market gardener living at Hollybank in 1890 (the house became

Hollybank at the corner of the main street and New Road,
demolished 1973

a Social Club about 1925 and was demolished in 1973 to make way for shops at the corner of the main street and New Road), and Mr A. Souter, a stationer in Lorne Grove in 1891. The latter's business partner, Miss L. Carmen of Briar Cottage went bankrupt with him. It was perhaps a reflection of the general economic decline caused by an agricultural depression.

By this date, older, more central parts of the village had also been developed: building land was sold in the Bailey Lane area in 1876, and again in 1878, this time at 3s.9d a square yard. Bailey House (later Brick House), owned by the Rockley family, proved difficult to sell from 1901. From 1881 semi-detached houses in Walnut Grove were advertised for £30 a year. West End villas were occupied by 1894, mainly owned by Mrs Noel of Lamcote House. New houses were built on Ogle Lane in 1889, 1904, 1908 and 1911. Manvers Grove was begun about 1902, and was originally intended to link up with Walker's Yard, where a 'building' was converted into a dwelling house in 1907 for Mr Walker. Bibby Cottages in Sidney Grove were built in 1908. By the time of the First World War, therefore, the village retained its old, now in-filled, centre but was dominated by a fringe of Victorian villas mainly on its eastern side. The next upsurge in development came after the First World War when more building land came onto the market.

Main sources

Primary
Nottinghamshire Archives Office: Radcliffe-on-Trent parish registers; church-wardens' accounts; minute books of the Bingham Union Board of Guardians PUD 5/26/6-15; electoral registers; sale catalogues DD M 60/2, DD MS 90; Radcliffe-on-Trent Sanitary Committee minutes PAC 35/2; Rate books PR 15,628 1-20; Plumtree notes PR 15,623.
Nottinghamshire County Library (Local Studies Library): census returns 1841 - 1881.
Radcliffe-on-Trent Parish Council: cemetery records.
University of Nottingham: Manvers estate rentals, Ma B 104/21/2, Ma B 539 passim for rebuilding on the Green, M 3587, M 3618-20, M 4889, Ma 2D, Ma 2B 45/169a; John Brice's account book (photocopy) Acc 605.

Secondary

Chamberlain, Colet. *Memories of the Past.* 1960.

Cutler, Fred. Photographic collection in the possession of the County Library.

Guide to the Census reports GB 1801-1966, HMSO. Office of Population Census and Survey.

Halls, Zillah. *Machine made lace in Nottingham in the eighteenth and nineteenth century..* City of Nottingham Art galleries and Museum Committee, 1964.

Nottingham and Nottinghamshire *Directories* 1832-1928.

Potter Briscoe, J. *Contemporary Biographies.* 1901.

Radcliffe local history research group: extracts from Nottinghamshire newspapers 1837-1920.

Radcliffe-on-Trent *Parochial Magazine.* 1877.

Information for this section has also been supplied by Mrs M. Blissett, Mr C. Green, Mrs K.F. Holman, Mr J. Nowell, Mr A. Reed, Mrs B. Rutter, Mr A.R. Taylor, Miss P. Walker and Mr C. Wright.

NATIONAL POLITICS

Although Radcliffe was largely preoccupied with local affairs, it was not isolated from national politics, partly because the constituency in which it stood - South Nottinghamshire until 1886 and Newark from that date - was represented by Lord Newark, a son of the village's major landowner and lord of the manor. As the franchise was gradually extended throughout the nineteenth century, Radcliffe also experienced a growth of political activity in the village, particularly in the 1880s.

Queen Victoria's reign opened with the franchise recently extended to the middle classes after the reform bill riots of 1831 when Nottingham Castle had been burned. However only fifty-nine privileged male property owners or occupiers appear in the Radcliffe electoral register of 1839-40 at a time when the population was about 1,240 and there were some 243 households in the village. Twelve of those listed did not even live in Radcliffe. The association of the franchise with property is made clear at the sale of two freehold dwelling houses on Mount Pleasant in July 1844. The advertisement is headed: 'Votes for the South Division.'

Voting lists could be amended as circumstances changed, and anyone claiming or challenging voting rights could have his case heard at annual 'revision' courts. Until 1872 Radcliffe cases were dealt with in September or October at the Chesterfield Arms, Bingham. Between 1872 and 1884, Radcliffe voters had to poll at West Bridgford rather than Bingham, and voting claims were then heard at the Trent Bridge Inn. From 1884 the village had its own polling station and claims were heard at the Manvers Arms. Not until 1872 was there a secret ballot. Until then poll books were open, allowing landlords to exert pressure on politically non-compliant tenants, and voting took place over two days.

The 1846 by-election

Information about Radcliffe's modest political involvement begins with the by-election of 1846 which took place in the midst of a national crisis over the corn laws. While the agricultural interest favoured the retention of the laws, Sir Robert Peel, the Conservative prime minister, realised that famine in Ireland and harvest failure in England necessitated their removal to allow the importation of cheap corn. One of the two South Nottinghamshire M.Ps. was the Earl of Lincoln, appointed chief secretary to the Lord Lieutenant of Ireland and a committed Peelite. Under pressure from the Nottinghamshire Agriculture Protection Society he resigned his seat to test his electorate's feelings. His opponent was T.B.T. Hildyard of Flintham, representing the protectionists.

The election was a lively affair, with Lord Lincoln and Mr Hildyard galloping from one part of the district to another to rally their supporters. Windows were broken at Newark. At Bingham, Mr Foster of Saxondale was pulled from his horse and had to be rescued by friends and police from an angry crowd when he made derogatory remarks about Lord Lincoln. However, Bingham and Newark seemed to be the only areas to favour Lord Lincoln. By the second day of the poll it was clear that the protectionists would win. Lord Lincoln recognised the pressures on tenant farmers and absolved them of their promises to him if it meant going against their landlords, 'the benefit to himself being by no means commensurate to the injury they might bring upon themselves'. Hildyard won by 687 votes.

The poll book for the Bingham district was published and shows that only nineteen out of the fifty-eight or so Radcliffe property holders entitled to vote actually did so. Perhaps most preferred not to commit themselves publicly on so contentious an issue. Of those who did turn out, eleven voted for the protectionist Hildyard and eight for Lord Lincoln. Amongst those listed was John Morley, soon to be involved in a malt tax scandal, who owned freehold property in Radcliffe, but was then resident in Manchester, the headquarters of the Anti-Corn Law League. He came back to vote for Lord Lincoln. Despite the latter's defeat the corn laws were repealed, causing a split in the Conservative party. Peel's government was technically brought down over an Irish 'coercion' bill in 1847. The two South Nottinghamshire seats were then held by Hildyard and Colonel Rolleston, followed by Robert Bromley, all protectionists, until the latter's resignation in 1851.

161

Elections in 1851 and 1852

It was the 1851 by-election which first brought 25-year-old Lord Newark, the future third Earl Manvers, into the political arena. He was opposed by Mr W. Hodgson Barrow of Kelham on personal rather than national issues, for both men were high churchmen and protectionist conservatives. Lord Newark, however, was aristocratic, inexperienced and unknown, having become heir to the Manvers earldom only the previous year on the death of a much older brother. Despite having the support of the *Nottingham Journal* his election campaign proved hard work.

In his main speech he showed his landed interests. While he thought that every good landlord was desirous of assisting his tenants, if not by lowering rents, then by drainage or other improvements, it was the duty of every tenant to co-operate. A listening heckler retorted, 'How can they when the landlords have all the money?' The question of malt tax - currently the cause of a much reported trial stemming from Radcliffe - was also raised. Lord Newark hesitated. Although repeal might be advantageous, many protectionists had not yet made up their minds on the subject. 'He wished to have it fully discussed before giving any positive opinion.' Great uproar followed this pronouncement, and a shout of 'No cheap ale for you!'

If a report in the *Daily News* of December 11th 1850 (printed in the *Nottingham Review* of December 20th) is to be believed, the campaign was being bitterly fought two months before the actual poll, and Lord Manvers' reputation as a landlord was a key issue:

> *The Dukery of all places in England is in rebellion. Mr Bromley having resigned its representation, the tenant farmers are resolved on choosing a member of their own. They'll have none of Lord Newark; not they. They know the worth of Lord Manvers to a penny, so repudiate his son. They see in that great aristocrat a bad Protectionist and a worse landlord; greedy of his rents and careless whence they are paid, whether out of produce or capital; so they reject the heir or his titles or his farms. They have been too often deceived by the dukes and their offspring; so they ignore the well-understood role of the Dukery; that a ducal son or nominee has the first claim to their votes ..... [and] have insisted on an honest plain-speaking squire of their own kidney.*

From Radcliffe's point of view the second Earl Manvers was an active landlord at this time, carrying out repairs and rebuilding on the Green, and elsewhere in the village. No poll book has been found to show how far local voters were influenced by the anti-Manvers campaign, but Lord Newark was defeated by only eleven votes.

In the following year, however, Lord Derby's Conservative government was brought down after a powerful attack by Gladstone on Disraeli's budget. Lord Newark stood again, this time alongside Mr Barrow, and the former adversaries were returned unopposed for the two South Nottinghamshire seats. He remained in the House of Commons during Lord Palmerston's prime ministership, entering the Lords on the death of his father in 1860. Not until the 1880s was there another contested election in South Nottinghamshire, both seats remaining firmly Conservative.

The Liberal challenge

Although in 1867 the franchise was extended to all ratepaying householders in towns, some restrictions remained in county areas. (In 1867-68, before the bill took effect, Radcliffe's electoral register listed seventy-one men with voting rights. There were eighty-four electors after the bill. This figure can be set in the context of the 1871 census when there were three-hundred households and a population of 1,339.) By the 1880s a campaign was launched to extend the vote to rural workers. If the campaign succeeded, particularly now that the secret ballot was in operation, the balance of power in the counties might change. Consequently the Liberal party, normally stronger in towns, became active in the South Nottinghamshire district for which two members were returned.

Mr S.B. Bristowe, standing as Liberal candidate against the Conservatives T.B.T. Hildyard and George Storer in the election of April 1880, came to Radcliffe to address a meeting in a large shed at the Black Lion. He felt that a new start was being

162

made in the south division with the first contested election since 1851- and that had been between two Conservatives. If the Tories (led by Disraeli) stayed in power there would never be an extension of the franchise, so he urged his listeners to vote Liberal. Moreover, the Conservatives had raised the income tax to 5d in the £. 'A man named Butler here misbehaved himself and had to be severely reprimanded by the Chairman (Mr Haynes).' A report on polling day in the constituency suggested that while Wilford had a strong sprinkling of Liberal voters, Radcliffe 'probably counterbalanced this advantage'. Nationally the Liberals, led by Gladstone, swept to power, but locally they were soundly beaten. Mr Bristowe polled only 1,445 votes compared to 2,491 and 2,227 respectively for Storer and Hildyard.

Formation of the Conservative Association

Recognising, however, that Bristowe had posed a real challenge at a time of agricultural distress, the local Conservatives for the first time organised themselves on a formal basis. In September 1880 the first Conservative dinner was held in the schoolroom under the chairmanship of another Viscount Newark (the future fourth Earl Manvers), and was addressed by the two local M.Ps. Already the Radcliffe Conservative Association could boast sixty members. By the time of their annual dinner in November 1881 it was clear than many of the Radcliffe establishment had joined, including the vicar, Dr Campbell, John Taylor from Radcliffe Hall, Richard Daft the former cricketer, Samuel Bell of the Manvers Arms, J.G. Willey, William Sanday, Messrs Green, Butler, Marriott and many more.

At this second dinner the Rev John Cullen, in replying to a toast to the clergy, somewhat strained religious analogy by suggesting that the church was his idea of Conservatism. It had thrown off what was necessary at the Reformation, and it should always be an example of obedience to the law. Each of her ministers must take an oath of allegiance before they could minister and must set an example of obedience to the powers that be. Any church or sect that refused to obey the law must inevitably perish. In his speech, Lord Newark stayed on more practical ground, asserting that when again they were asked to give a verdict in South Nottinghamshire, should strong opposition spring up, they would be well prepared to meet the foe. He added that Conservative landlords had done all they could to mitigate the distress which had come upon them.

Extension of the franchise 1884

The anticipated contest began with an acceleration of the campaign for extending the franchise in 1884. Reform meetings were held in Bingham in April and August. At the latter Gladstone was urged not to dissolve Parliament before the bill was passed by the Lords. The reformers had their way, and the counties were given a similar franchise to that enjoyed by the boroughs since 1867. Radcliffe's electorate on the pre-reform bill register of 1885 was 141. After the bill came into effect 356 voters were listed, including five not on the district lists but registered as voting in Radcliffe. Significantly, twenty-seven out of the sixty-eight ownership voters did not live in the village. (There had been 358 households and a population of 1,704 in 1881.) Radcliffe also became part of the Newark constituency at this time, for which only one M.P. was returned. Earlier in 1884 the Corrupt and Illegal Practices Act prohibited the use of hired vehicles for conveying electors to the polls. Polling stations had therefore to be at a convenient walking distance, and it was for this reason that Radcliffe was given its own for the first time, shared initially with Holme Pierrepont.

Despite the passage of the 1884 reform bill, the Liberal government's problems at home and abroad, including the issue of Irish home rule, greatly weakened its administration. Defeated over an increase in beer and spirit duties, Gladstone resigned, and the minority Conservative caretaker government which took over soon called an election. It was this election which proved the most contentious in Radcliffe during the period studied.

The Liberals and the schoolroom

In March 1885 Lord Newark indicated that he was ready to follow the family tradition and stand for Parliament. The first hint of trouble came in a letter of July 7th to the *Nottingham Journal* from Edwin Green and H. Sharp, respectively chairman and secretary of a Liberal committee in Radcliffe. They complained that although the schoolroom had been twice let for Conservative meetings, its use had been denied to the Liberals. They warned that Lord Newark would soon wish 'to be saved from his friends, who thus publish to the electors their anxiety to prevent his opponents from obtaining a hearing'. They appended a statement sent to papers all over the country justifying their complaint:

> The Liberals of Radcliffe-on-Trent recently applied to the Committee of the National School for the loan of the schoolroom for a meeting of electors of the district. There is no other convenient room in the village available for public meetings, and it is frequently let for them and for concerts, etc. On one of the schoolroom walls is exhibited a notification of the terms upon which the room can be hired. Not long ago it was let for a Ball, and on two recent occasions it has been lent for Conservative meetings. ..... The posters announcing these Conservative meetings still remain on the board placed in the schoolyard, adjacent to the public road, and at the head of it are painted the words, 'Parish Notice Board'. The school is a public elementary one, receiving a Government grant, and it is supported largely by public subscriptions, nonconformists being among the subscribers and being regularly solicited to subscribe. The School Committee, through their chairman, the vicar of the parish, refuse to let the room to the Liberals for a meeting of electors. They decline to give their reply in writing, but the vicar explains that the applicants will clearly see how impossible it is to let the schoolroom to them because the landlord of the premises is Earl Manvers, the father of Lord Newark, the Conservative candidate, and what an insult it would be to these gentlemen to let the schoolroom for such purpose.

The first response came the next day from *An Elector*:

> .... The effect of such conduct really recoils on those who resort to it, and the impression is that the Vicar of Radcliffe is fearful of the enunciation of political truth, and has abandoned that judicial feeling which ought to be pursued by men who are professed teachers of religion to the public .....

His solution was that as it was summer it would be better to hold the meeting 'under the broad canopy of heaven'. In any case, the Radcliffe schoolroom could not hold all the Liberals of the district.

Tom Potter a manager of Digby colliery living at Radcliffe Lodge, soon to be Radcliffe's representative on the new County Council, now came to the defence of the Conservatives. The Liberals, he claimed, had misrepresented the facts:

> ...What the vicar told the gentlemen who called upon him was that the schools were the freehold property of Earl Manvers, that the School Committee were tenants at will, and that Earl Manvers could turn them out the next day and build a factory on the land if he thought well, and that under these exceptional circumstances he could not see his way to grant the use of the schools for the purpose of holding a meeting in opposition to his son's candidature without Earl Manvers' consent. This consent the Liberal Committee appear to have taken no steps whatsoever to obtain ...

Not only had neither the vicar nor the school's committee any personal objection to the Liberal meeting, but the Conservative Association had written to Lord Manvers asking if he had any objection - prior to any knowledge that the Liberals were not satisfied with the vicar's attitude. Lord Manvers had replied that he had not the slightest objection and had given his full consent. Tom Potter continued:

> I can easily understand that the Liberals of Radcliffe were more anxious to have the schoolroom refused than granted, but the Conservatives being anxious to hear their opinions had great pleasure in making the application to Lord Manvers ....

164

Messrs Green and Sharp for the Liberals were not prepared to let the matter rest there and a second letter from them was published on July 12th. They reaffirmed that two of their members had waited on the vicar who would not give a reply in writing:

In the long conversation that took place, the Vicar personally assigned many reasons why the schoolroom could not be let to the Liberals. Some of these were as ridiculous as the ones reproduced here by Mr T. Potter, who appears seriously to believe that a public elementary school, receiving a considerable government grant, and paying their landlord a rent ...... can be turned out of their holding without notice ....

(The correspondence from now on was in danger of degenerating into a wrangle about how much the nonconformists - from whom the Liberals drew much support - actually contributed to the school.) The writers considered that it had been up to the school board to get any consent from Lord Manvers. 'What the Conservative Committee have to do with the matter is not apparent to us.' Moreover:

.... Mr T. Potter's innocent surprise that the Liberal Committee took no steps to obtain Earl Manvers' consent betokens a childlike simplicity for which he has not hitherto been credited.

The vicar now felt compelled to justify his actions. He wrote to Mr Green, and his letter was forwarded to the *Nottingham Journal* with a request for publication:

The Conservatives of Radcliffe have taken the step which you and your party would have taken viz. to ask the use of the schoolroom from the owner.
He gives his consent that it may be used for a Liberal Political Meeting, and, as I told you all before, that it was not possible for me to let the school under the peculiar circumstances by which we are tenants, of course you can now have your meeting.

The Liberals were not prepared to let the vicar have the last word. Mr Sharp's reply was published on July 13th:

... I am desired to say that we are unable to recognise your communication as a bona fide offer of the use of the National Schoolroom, for the following reasons:-
1. We can scarcely suppose that your committee expect us to accept, as a privilege specially granted by the landlord, that which, by invariable usage and in all previous instances, has been accorded as a public right, on the sole responsibility of the tenants, the School Committee. The form and manner in which you have thus chosen to convey your offer must, we venture to think, render it as distasteful to Earl Manvers and Lord Newark as it is unacceptable to us.
2. The offer is not made until after the lapse of a week from the time your committee's refusal to let the room to us, not until several days after it was well known that we had engaged and our arrangements had been completed for another place of meeting.
Your committee while labouring under the strange delusion that they are neutral in politics have evinced their strict impartiality by twice allowing the Conservatives to have the use of the schoolroom, but refusing it to the Liberals until the Conservatives had intervened for the use of it to be granted to us.

The Liberal meeting, July 17th

What started as a possible error of judgment by the politically committed vicar had erupted into a major controversy, and the tone was set for the remaining five months of the campaign. The immediate concern, however, was still that of the Liberal meeting. The belated offer of the schoolroom was not taken up, and on the pleasant evening of July 17th William Wright's nearby field was used as the venue.

The main speaker was Mr Earp, who could not resist referring to the 'churlishness and interference' of the school authorities. He also contrasted the conduct of Radcliffe's vicar with that of the incumbent of Coddington who had presided at both Liberal and Conservative meetings, and who 'taught the fear of the Lord rather than fear of the landlord'. Cheers and laughter greeted this sally. Mr Earp had thought that at Radcliffe, within the shadow of Holme Pierrepont, 'some aristocratic behaviour would have been met with at the hands of the clergyman of the parish'. National issues were then raised, only for Mr Earp to be interrupted when 'the bells in the parish church close at hand were rung', causing him 'some difficulty in making himself heard'. (Baffle boards would not yet have been added to the belfry.) A Mr Calvert, later identified as a Conservative, ran off to get the bells silenced, and Mr Earp, supposing correctly that it was practice night, claimed that they were joy bells ringing him welcome. The meeting passed off without further incident and Mr Earp's selection as Liberal candidate was approved.

The vicar's sermon

As if he had not already been at the centre of enough political controversy, the Rev John Cullen decided to try influencing his flock from the pulpit. On August 1st the *Nottingham Journal* published a letter from A.W.T. (a Mr Thomas of Chestnut Grove) under the heading 'The Vicar of Radcliffe again':

The vicar of Radcliffe appears to consider his parishioners so densely ignorant and incapable of forming their own political opinions, that last Sunday evening he deemed it necessary to give them some political counsel from the pulpit, and advised them as to the sort of candidate for whom they should not vote. With great thoughtfulness he announced at the morning his intention for the evening, kindly giving his flock the opportunity, of which they largely availed themselves, of staying away from a homily for which they had no relish. The vicar's qualifications for advising his parishioners in secular affairs may be estimated from the fact that his newspaper reading is, by his own account, limited to a weekly church paper.

It is greatly to be hoped that the local Conservatives will refrain from trying to curb our worthy vicar but will continue freely to let him 'have his head,' as he bids fair, if permitted to follow his own course without interruption, to prove a most valuable auxiliary to the Liberals in securing a majority in Radcliffe at the next election.

After this the Rev Cullen seems to have kept a low political profile, and the campaign temporarily took on a more conventional tone with reports of Lord Newark's speeches in various parts of the constituency, some comment on his alleged reference to the working men of the Bingham district as the 'lower orders', and another letter from A.W. Thomas urging the *Journal* to report a Liberal meeting in Cropwell Butler at which there was an overwhelming majority in favour of Mr Earp's candidature. This apparent Liberal headway and a rough reception given to Lord Newark at Balderton provoked 'disgraceful scenes' in Radcliffe in October.

The second Liberal meeting, October 22nd

Mr Earp had decided to speak again in Radcliffe and this time the schoolroom had been booked without difficulty, but what followed was a near riot as a number of prominent local Conservatives decided to disrupt the meeting. The *Nottingham Journal* considered that without a doubt Radcliffe was entirely disgraced by the 'ignominious and fanatical conduct' in the schoolroom of 'a band of ignorant ghouls, hired specially for the purpose of upsetting Mr Earp's meeting'.

(They) *entered the schoolroom, the floor of which was thickly strewn with pepper, bearing large sticks in their hands and playing upon two whistles in a most discreditable manner, and at once gave evidence that there was some organised scheme about to be carried to perfection ......*

The group was encouraged by Samuel Barratt, the nurseryman and current overseer of the poor, Henry Parr the joiner, James Upton who was Lord Newark's woodman, Amos Parr, gardener to Lord Newark, three members of the Daft family including

Richard himself, James Browne the schoolmaster, J. G. Willey, Tom Potter and others. Some had come from a funeral, perhaps having drowned their sorrows too lavishly. Mr Earp was greeted with a 'storm of hooting and howling'. Then Samuel Barratt climbed on the reporters' table and called for three cheers for Lord Newark, who would do more for them in a week than Mr Earp would do in a lifetime.

> .... The scene which here ensued was one of the most disgraceful which has ever been witnessed in Radcliffe, and will stand as a lasting condemnation towards Lord Newark and Toryism. On Mr Dawson [the chairman] attempting to open the meeting, he was assailed with cries of 'Give them Dawks in Paris (whatever that may mean) that will settle them.' Henry Parr then mounted the platform and shouted at the top of his voice 'Ladies and gentlemen, Mr Earp says that there is not a gentleman amongst you.' At this stage disorder seemed to reach a climax, for the audience made an ugly rush to the platform, brandishing chairs over their heads, and shouting in a boisterous fashion. The platform was then stormed by a band of young lads, who kept up a stream of whistling and shouting all the time Mr Earp and the chairman, Mr Dawson, were attempting to gain a hearsay.

When the police - an inspector and sergeant - were requested to remove the disorderly members of the audience they, perhaps understandably, refused, but order does seem to have been partially restored, allowing Mr Earp to make some remarks, although not part of his official address. He thanked his audience for their 'cordial reception', albeit slightly mixed with 'pepper'. As a cricketing people he recognised that they had learned to stick to their 'wickets' (a reference to the sticks that had been carried), and he hoped that his friends would rally as firmly to him in the future. Speaking of cricket, however, he had thought it engendered fair play. 'I would have thought that Radcliffe, which has given birth to two such cricketers as Parr and Daft, would have known how to receive one of the opposite team.' Referring to the opposition shown to Lord Newark at Balderton, Mr Earp pointed out that he was not responsible for the ardour of his supporters any more than Lord Newark was of his, though he felt sure that the latter would disapprove of what had happened. He was particularly astonished that the demonstration was organised by those who had just come from the graveside of an old friend of his. He hoped that on the morrow they would not be any the worse for the exercise of their lungs.

On the morrow James Browne, the schoolmaster, noted in his log book:

> School in a very dirty condition this morning after a meeting of the Liberals last night. Desks marked and very dirty as well as several broken. Several maps also found to be injured.

As he had himself attended the meeting, the state of the school must have come as no surprise.

Thomas Earp's fortitude was commended by *One in Earnest* in his letter on 'Radcliffe Rowdyism' which appeared in the *Nottingham Journal* on October 24th:

> Mr Thomas Earp was to have spoken here tonight but an organised opposition consisting of schoolboys, or so-called men, drunken with beer, led on to such disgraceful proceedings, encouraged by men in the village who ought to have known better, that Mr Earp was not permitted to speak a word. If the Conservative party imagine the Liberals are going to lose anything by this disgraceful conduct, they are mistaken. No one with any sense could help expressing admiration for Mr Earp as he sat it out from 7.30 to 10.15 .... Let every working man rally round a candidate they have so much reason to be proud of. We won't be put down by such 'dirty weapons' as the Tory party used tonight ......

Mr Earp gets a hearing

A month later Thomas Earp made his third visit to Radcliffe to try to get the Liberal viewpoint across. The schoolroom was again the venue. On his arrival he was greeted by slight hisses from youths at the back of the hall, but loud and protracted cheering drowned out this opposition. He said that his last visit to Radcliffe did not count, and he wanted the Radcliffe Conservatives to think well of him as he would be their representative. When he claimed the right of free speech, however, the youths at the back of the hall created a disturbance which lasted for some time. Eventually he was able to state his policies - a rein on the proceedings of the House of Commons, better local government, and free grammar school education. Compared to the previous occasion the meeting could be described as 'exceedingly orderly'.

Radcliffe did not feature prominently in the rest of the campaign, although Lord Newark was very active. He had already been accused of exercising undue influence on voters in Cotgrave by going from house to house to get labourers' votes. He was subject to 'an exhibition of the most blackguardly conduct' there by a group of youths 'led by some party not resident in Cotgrave' who showered his brake with stones and bricks. On polling day on December 2nd he covered a great deal of ground. Starting from Holme Pierrepont he drove through Cotgrave, Cropwell Bishop, Cropwell Butler, Radcliffe, Bingham and Newark from where he took the train to Southwell for further visits. Despite Thomas Earp's confidence it was reported that 'Lord Newark polled very strongly in Radcliffe'. Voting took place at the school which was closed for the day. The results were announced the next day and the school had again to close 'owing to a demonstration in the village as soon as the result of the polling of yesterday was made known'. Lord Newark was the comfortable overall winner, polling 5,283 votes to Thomas Earp's 3,529. His total campaign had cost him £1,151. 9s.8d.

Lord Newark as M.P.

Lord Newark represented the Newark division initially for ten years. During that time the impetus of Conservative organisation was maintained. Benjamin Disraeli, Earl of Beaconsfield, had died in 1881 and two years later the Primrose League was founded in his memory for the maintenance of Conservative principles. (Primroses were said to be his favourite flower.) The league was active in Nottinghamshire by 1886, and in May of that year the first meeting of the Pierrepont Habitation took place in the Radcliffe schoolroom. Viscountess Newark was appointed Ruling Councillor and a large committee was elected to include eight members from each polling district. This was followed towards the end of the month by a huge Conservative demonstration at Holme Pierrepont when over 600 sat down to an excellent tea.

Predictably Lord Newark was strongly opposed to Gladstone's Home Rule Bill, and he stood unopposed as a Conservative Unionist in the 1886 election. Throughout 1887 and 1888 he kept up a busy schedule of local speeches in support of Lord Salisbury's government, while running the gauntlet of an opposition campaign waged by the *Nottingham Daily Express*. After a speech in Radcliffe in October 1888 the newspaper's leading article criticised him for inflicting on a small audience 'a repetition of his stale sneers at Mr Gladstone'. His continued opposition to Home Rule for Ireland provoked the following explosion from the *Express* in July 1889:

> *How long will the electors of South Notts. consent to make themselves a laughing stock in the eyes of the country by returning a member so incompetent and so ridiculously ignorant as the noble lord who represents them in Parliament?*

Lord Newark, however, continued to satisfy his constituents, predicting civil war if home rule was granted, presenting petitions to Parliament from local groups, and speaking in the district until his resignation before the 1895 election. His place was taken by the Hon Harold Finch-Hatton, but on the latter's resignation in 1898 Lord Newark returned to the Commons until the death of his father in 1900 when he took his place in the House of Lords as the fourth Earl Manvers.

The Liberals unsuccessfully contested the seat in 1900 and Sir Charles Welby became Conservative and Liberal Unionist M.P. for the Newark division. Conservatives continued to dominate the constituency for the rest of the period, although the Liberals put up a spirited fight over tariff reform in 1906. The Radcliffe schoolroom was again used by both sides. Mr A. Moreton Mandeville, the Liberal candidate, attracted 500 to his meeting, and Mr J.R. Starkey suffered some 'good natured interruptions' to his Conservative speech. It was all very tame compared to the contest of 1885. Although the Liberals won nationally, Mr Starkey was elected by 328 votes. He held onto the seat in the two elections of 1910, by majorities of 879 and 742 over the Liberal Mr R. Burley Wallis, and he was returned unopposed in the election of 1918.

Radcliffe's overt concern with national politics seems to have coincided with the period of franchise extension in rural areas and with representation by the family of the main local landowner. Once the constituency passed out of Pierrepont hands, the village does not seem to have been such a focal point for political meetings. Despite the strong Liberal challenge in the 1880s the description of Radcliffe as a stronghold of Toryism would seem justified in the nineteenth century.

Main sources

Nottinghamshire Archives Office: electoral registers; school log book SL 135/1/2.
Nottinghamshire County Library (Local Studies Library): list of Nottingham and Nottinghamshire candidates at Parliamentary elections.
Radcliffe local history research group: extracts from Nottingham newspapers 1837 to 1920.
University of Nottingham, local studies collection: Poll Book for the South Notts. Election, 1846.

LOCAL GOVERNMENT

The parish was originally the area served by a church to which the parishioners paid tithes, but by the sixteenth century the central government recognised that the parish could also be used as an area for secular administration. In particular the Vestry, a meeting of parishioners which until 1868 was able to levy a church rate, was also empowered to collect money for the relief of the poor. These funds continued to be known as 'poor rates' even when the cash was raised for purposes far removed from poor relief.

By the nineteenth century Radcliffe's Vestry, while still retaining its links with the churchwardens, was increasingly concerned with the recommending of candidates for the offices of constable, overseer of the poor, waywarden or surveyor of the highways who were then approved by the magistrates. These local officials had their duties prescribed by a bewildering array of acts of Parliament, and they were guided and controlled at county level by the magistrates at Quarter Sessions. At national level they were supervised by the Poor Law Commissioners at Whitehall from 1834 until 1847, when a Poor Law Board responsible to a minister of the crown replaced the commissioners, and by the Board of Health established in 1848. In 1871 the Local Government Board was set up to administer the law relating to both poor relief and public health. These concerns, however, were also partially dealt with by an intermediate body, the Poor Law Union organised from Bingham, on whose board Radcliffe had two representatives.

Successive governments during the nineteenth century took steps to establish a more representative system of local administration. Initially this was far from the case. For example, the magistrates who wielded administrative power at the Quarter Sessions were appointed not elected, and the Vestries Act of 1818 had established only a limited voting system based on rates paid on land and property. (Ratepayers assessed at under £50 were entitled to one vote, whereas those assessed at over £150 were allowed six votes.) This system was swept away by two major acts of Parliament: the Local Government Act of 1888 which set up County Councils and transferred virtually all the administrative powers and responsibilities of the magistrates to elected councillors; and the Local Government Act of 1894 which established Urban and Rural District Councils and Parish Councils. This last act was particularly progressive since it not only gave the franchise in local elections to all males entitled to vote in parliamentary elections, but to women too, even allowing them to be elected. (At national level women did not get the vote until 1918.)

Whilst the system was 'fine-tuned' by subsequent legislation, no further basic changes were made until the 1970s. A study of Radcliffe's haphazardly-kept vestry book, rating books, sanitary committee minutes, and the meticulous parish council minutes, supported by newspaper and census material, shows how this system affected the inhabitants of the village.

I. Ruling bodies and their main concerns

The parish Vestry

Meetings of the Radcliffe parish Vestry were held at the Manvers Arms at a cost of £1 per annum (from 1869), although it may be assumed that the landlord, George Bell, made some profit by the sale of refreshments to those present. Numbers attending the meetings were not generally recorded in the minute book, except between 1868 and 1875 when the attendance ranged from a minimum of seven to a maximum of forty-five. Perhaps not surprisingly, purely routine meetings called to appoint officers and set the rates tended to attract less than a dozen, while larger issues such as finding a burial ground and laying out sewers drew attendances of thirty or more. It is difficult to establish the number of ratepayers in the village eligible to attend and vote at the Vestry. In a poll held in 1869, a total of 101 votes were cast, but because of the multiple voting system, the number of actual voters would have been far fewer.

There was no permanent chairman, the first business of each meeting being to

[Proposed ✗ by Samuel Bell and seconded by Richard Adamson that Richard Butler be re-elected Overseer, carried unanimously. Proposed by Richard Butler and seconded by Paul Fryer that Thomas Silcock be re-elected Overseer carried unanimously. Proposed by Thomas Morley & seconded by Samuel Bell that a vote of thanks be given to the Overseers for the very efficient manner in which they have conducted the business of the Parish carried unanimously

Proposed by Thomas Haynes an seconded by Henry Parr that Richard Butler be re elected waywarden carried unanimously. Proposed by ~~Thomas Haynes that~~ Richard Butler and seconded by Thomas Haynes that a vestry meeting be called on the 17th of May 1872 at 7. P. M. to consider the Sewage and drainage through the village and the necessity of making Foot Paths, carried unanimously.]

An extract from the vestry minute book for April 5th 1872 (reduced)

elect one from amongst those present. In March or April each year a meeting was held to appoint officials. It is noticeable that the same names crop up year after year with the offices rotating between them. Originally no payments were made although expenses were met, but by 1836 the constable was being paid £12 a year, and around this date, too, an overseers' allowance of £4.4s was usually paid each March. On instructions from the Poor Law Commissioners such payments lapsed, but in March 1842 it was resolved by a close vote of nineteen to seventeen that a paid officer be appointed as overseer of the poor. As a result, John Marriott, a middle-aged tailor and draper, became assistant overseer at a salary of £13 per annum in March 1843, which became £15 from March 1844 and £17 from March 1846, remaining at that figure until his resignation in 1865. There were two candidates to succeed Marriott and the opportunity was taken to reduce the salary to £15, but in April 1870 it went back up to £17 'on account of the extra work caused by the alterations in the Poor Laws and division of the rates for voting purposes'.

In 1845 it was resolved that ' the Guardian [of the poor] receive for his services in future the sum of twenty shillings'. This officer was Radcliffe's representative on the Bingham Board of Guardians, the body which provided a workhouse and supervised the poor of the whole district. The twenty shillings became 'too Sovrings' (sic) in March 1850 and £3 in March 1856. Another paid officer from the middle of the century was the sanitary inspector, a position held by Mr Stone in July 1868 at a salary of £2 per annum.

The impression from the records is that the village was generally well served by its basically amateur office-holders, or at least there is evidence that their contemporaries thought so. On March 29th 1867 the Vestry unanimously resolved:

that the thanks of this meeting be given to Mr Richard Stone as Guardian and Mr Richard Butler as Overseer for the very efficient manner they have conducted the business of this parish.

This resolution regarding two of Radcliffe's more substantial farmers was not unique, although it is not repeated often enough to be seen as a routine 'vote of thanks'. Inevitably, there were some exceptions to the rule, and penalties were occasionally incurred for neglect of duty. For example, the *Nottingham Journal* recorded in July 1876 that a subsequent overseer, George Turner - village postmaster and wheelwright - was summoned by the district auditor for failing to make up his accounts for the previous year and wilfully neglecting to attend the half yearly audit at Bingham. The 'financial condition' of the parish was said to have been thrown 'into complete chaos' as a result. Turner's excuses - his wife's illness and pressure of business - were not accepted and he was fined the full penalty of 40s for each offence, plus expenses, a total of £10.3s.

Committees of ratepayers

A means often adopted to deal with a specific issue was the appointment of a committee of ratepayers, either to consider and report on a proposal, or to supervise its carrying out on behalf of the full Vestry. A list of such committees indicates the major topics of concern between 1842 and 1887:-

April 1843. Committee of four. *To superintend and pay the expenses for the emigration of such poor persons and their families to the United States of America or to some of the colonies belonging to the British Government as shall appear most proper to such committee with the approbation of a majority of the ratepayers in Vestry assembled.*

October 1843. Committee of five. *To make provision for poor families wishing to emigrate in the free passage ships to Australia.*

November 1845. Committee of churchwardens, overseers and five ratepayers. *To adjust the rate of the Parish.*

Date uncertain. Committee ..... *To see that all nuisances are removed.*
This committee reported in October 1849, although there is no record in the vestry book of its appointment. It was set up after an outbreak of cholera and appears to have been mainly concerned with the condition of the brook running through the village, which was becoming an open sewer. It was decided to wait upon Mr Hood, surveyor of the turnpike, to see whether the commissioners of the road would help with covering the brook.

A further committee of the vicar plus four prominent residents was then formed. *To carry out the covering in of the brook.*

March 1850. Four persons appointed *to form a Board of Highway.* Their appointment was renewed the following year.

April 1851. Committee of five under the chairmanship of the vicar appointed *to re-pew the Parish Church......without a Rate been levid upon the Parish.* [sic.] This seems to have been a rare occasion of church business occupying the time of the parish Vestry, as opposed to their merely collecting church rates.

September 1856. Committee of four. *To inspect and report the nuisances in the Parish, also with power to look to their removal.*

January 1860. Committee of seven. *To improve the sewerage of Radcliffe and cover the drain as soon as possible.*

April 1860. Further committee of five. *To supervise sewerage improvements, costs to be defrayed from the Highway rate.*

June 1860. Above committee to continue in office.

March 1863. Four ratepayers plus surveyor of highways *for the removal of nuisance.*

November 1868. Burial Board of ten appointed with a view *to selecting a site for a cemetery.* In the following year Mr S. C. Tomlinson was appointed clerk to the board at an annual salary of £5.

May 1872. Committee of six. *To supervise culverting the brook from east end of churchyard to Mr Gorse's field.*

May 1872. Committee of five. *To make footpaths through the village, money needed to be borrowed on the security of the Poor Rates.*

April 1875. Further committee of seven. *To examine into and report on the drainage question.*

November 1875. Five 'Lighting inspectors' appointed *to arrange installation of gas lighting, with a sum of £100 voted to meet the outlay in purchasing standards, brackets, lamps etc..*

March 1881. Committee of five ratepayers set up following long discussion on new rating assessments which were considered excessive when compared to other parishes in the Bingham Union.

April 1887. Rating committee of seven gentlemen set up *to assist the overseers.* (To do what is not clear).

Raising money

The meetings called to set rates seem to have attracted the poorest attendances. There was no form of year-on-year budget, and rates were collected at irregular intervals, presumably when the need for money was pressing. It would also seem that local officials met some of the costs from their own resources in the first instance, as a Vestry held on 27th April 1865 indicated (inter alia):

... a church rate of two-pence halfpenny in the pound was granted to defray the debt due to the Churchwarden for the past years expenses and to meet the expenses of the present year.

There is only one piece of evidence in the minute book to show that collection of the rates did not always run smoothly. On April 29th 1851 it was resolved that:

.. notice be given to those ratepayers that are in arrears that unless their arrears of rates are paid up forthwith, legal proceedings will be taken.

The last rate levied prior to April 1851 had been of 2½d in the pound in November 1848, so that the period of grace allowed before pressure was applied could hardly be called unreasonably short, and there is no evidence of any proceedings actually being instituted.

In October 1850 the Radcliffe Vestry adopted an act passed in the August which permitted the rates on tenements assessed at under £6 per annum to be collected from the owners instead of the occupiers. There is unfortunately no way of knowing whether landlords were able to increase their rents accordingly, but rating books from 1878 onwards show that these small occupiers paid only about one third of the rates due on a property.

The following is a table of all rates levied from 1839 to 1870, recorded in the minute book. They indicate the continuing link with the church until 1868, as well as the varying amounts and irregular timing of the precepts for general parish concerns:

Date	Amount in £	Reason given for precept
10th October 1839	10d	£70 to be used to liquidate debt, balance for the poor.
2nd June 1840	5d	Church rate.
16th March 1841	2½d	Church rate.
27th March 1843	2½d	Church rate.
5th March 1844	5d	Church rate.
8th April 1845	10d	Use of the Poor and other purposes of the Parish.
12th September 1845	5d	Church rate.
9th November 1848	2½d	Church rate.
29th April 1851	5d	'A rate'.
20th January 1852	2½d	Church rate.
19th December 1854	2½d	½ a Poor Rate.
19th December 1854	2½d	Church rate.
27th March 1856	2½d	Church rate.
27th March 1856	2½d	Highway rate.
27th March 1856	5d	Poor rate.
23rd March 1858	2½d	Church rate.
24th March 1859	2½d	Church rate.
9th April 1861	2½d	Church rate.
9th April 1861	7½d	For the highways.
9th April 1861	5d	Poor rate.
27th April 1865	2½d	Church rate.
17th April 1868	2½d	'A rate'.
14th April 1870	1s 8d	To meet the expenses of the parish for the coming year.

The precept of 1s.8d in the £ levied in April 1870 is double any known previous one, and something like six or seven times the average over the preceding years. This was presumably to pay for the new burial ground.

An incomplete set of poor rate books deposited in the Nottinghamshire Archives Office covers the period from 1878 to 1894. They show that while the rate in the £ was never so high again, it never fell below 5d (1878), and rates were sometimes collected twice a year. The smallest sum collected at one time during these sixteen years was £157.19s.11d in January 1878, and the largest was £665.10s.8 d in May 1890. (See charts opposite.)

It was on the strength of these poor rates that local officials could could borrow sums to meet larger items of capital expenditure, but the reason for that expenditure had to be sanctioned by a vestry meeting and the decision to fund it by a loan similarly authorised. Then the approval of the magistrates, the Poor Law Commissioners, or latterly the Local Government Board had to be secured, such proposals thus being closely examined and commented upon.

There were only three loans sanctioned by vestry meetings during the period from 1839 to 1875, when the book becomes less informative. These were:

October 1843. An unspecified sum authorised. *To be raised or borrowed as a fund for defraying the expenses of poor persons .... willing to emigrate.*

July 1870. *A Sum not exceeding £800 to defray* the cost of the new cemetery and expenses connected therewith.

May 1872. *A Sum not exceeding £200 for a term of 30 or 50 years to pay for culverting the brook from the east of the Churchyard to its termination in Mr Gorse's field.*

As the range of parish responsibilities increased, however, additional rates were regularly raised for specific amenities. For example, from the 1870s a ratepayer would not only be liable for the traditional poor rate, but for gas lighting and

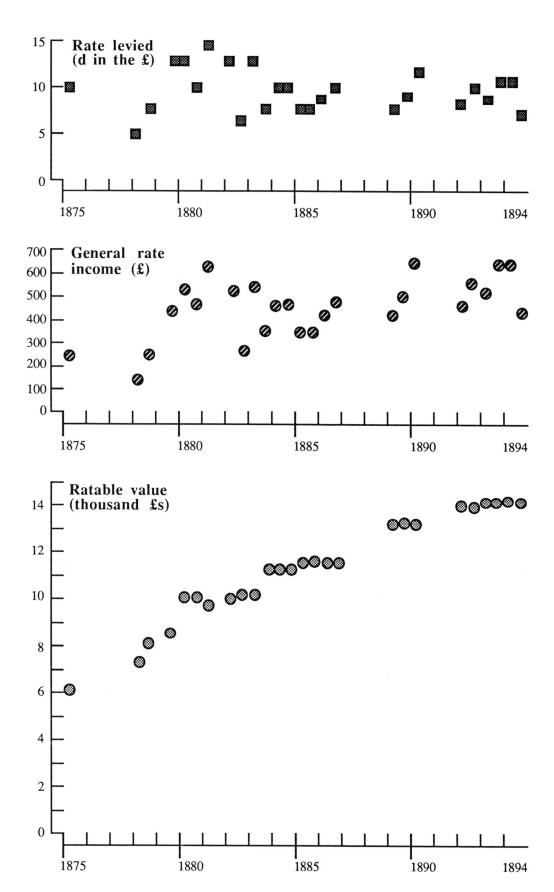

Graphs to show the rate levied, the general rate income and the deduced ratable
value of the parish between 1878 and 1894

sanitary rates too. Alongside this system of parish rating was a regular county and county police rate imposed by the magistrates. By the 1880s the system was cumbersome and confusing.

The County Council
The Local Government Act of 1888 swept away the traditional system of county government by magistrates at Quarter Sessions, replacing it with county councils on which all the councillors and half the aldermen were re-elected every three years.

The main powers conferred on the new councils included: the maintenance of main roads and bridges, and the removal of tolls previously collected by the Turnpike Commissioners; the appointment and supervision of coroners, and medical officers of health, and the operation of the Public Health Acts; responsibility for the police, and for assize courts, court houses, judges' lodgings, police stations and similar buildings; the licensing of theatres and other places of entertainment; the provision of asylums for pauper lunatics, reformatories and industrial schools; the appointment of public analysts, officers to oversee the Explosives Act and responsibility for all acts relating to contagious disease of animals, wild birds, weights and measures.

The new authority was given power to levy a rate to cover its costs (although some income also derived from central government and other sources), but parish overseers and others retained the right of appeal to the justices against the basis or standard of the county rate applied in their district. The Local Government Board in London retained a general power of supervision over the actions of the county councils.

The election
From November 1888 the process was set in motion for electing the first county representative for the local division which covered Clipston, Cotgrave, Edwalton, Holme Pierrepont, Keyworth, Lodge-on-the-Wolds, Normanton, Plumtree, Shelford, Stanton, Tollerton, and Widmerpool as well as Radcliffe. James Gorse of the Manor House chaired the first meeting to discuss the matter, but declined to stand as a candidate because of his advancing years. A letter was read from Thomas Potter, in which he offered his services. He was a manager of Digby Colliery currently living at Daybrook House, but he had been an occupant of Radcliffe Lodge for six years. A committee was set up to look into the matter and it seems that some fourteen individuals were invited to contest the division. Apart from Tom Potter only one was prepared to do so. This was Henry Smith, a wealthy farmer from Cropwell Butler, who, according to the *Nottingham Daily Express* 'through pressure of gentlemen had at last reluctantly agreed to come forward although he did not wish to be elected'. At a meeting in mid-December it was being claimed that Tom Potter's name had been advanced 'in an underhand manner'. This was denied by the chairman, and Potter was then officially proposed and seconded as candidate. An amendment proposing Henry Smith as candidate instead was rejected by sixty votes to five. His supporters now said that he would certainly not withdraw, and that he would act quite independently of the Radcliffe electors. A contested election was therefore inevitable between two Conservative candidates.

In January 1889, Tom Potter was enthusiastically received at a meeting of electors in the Radcliffe schoolroom. He claimed to have heard that pressure was being brought to bear on labourers by some farmers to vote for his opponent. At this there were cries of 'shame.' His reply to the farmers was, 'You are voting by ballot; so am I.' He disapproved of new arrangements for police supervision, favouring the sole control of watch committees. He wanted as many roads as possible to be declared main roads so that their expenses could come out of the county rate. He thought that the village would be £200 to the good under the new system, and he pointed out that he had resisted an invitation to stand for Newthorpe, preferring to 'stand or fall by Radcliffe'.

On election day itself, January 15th, the contest was 'carried on with spirit', although the *Express* noted that Smith's supporters seemed to have woken up only at the eleventh hour. At Radcliffe the walls had been freely placarded with posters by both parties. Tom Potter's invited support as the 'proved working man's friend' who offered 'good wages and regular work'. Henry Smith claimed he would keep the rates down and would also be 'the working man's friend'. Polling was held in the village schoolrooms at Radcliffe, Keyworth and Cotgrave, and supporters lent carriages to take voters to the polls. (James Gorse sent two and Messrs Haynes three for Potter, and there were six others on his behalf.) Counting took place in the Radcliffe schoolroom, and a large crowd gathered outside 'with manifest excitement'. Of the 1,037 electors, 788 polled and there were ten spoiled papers. The result was a victory for Tom Potter by 466 votes to 312. By comparison the 1892 county council election was a tame affair with Potter returned unopposed. He was succeeded in 1898 by C.W. Wright, but was again the local representative in 1907.

The District Councils

Whilst the new county authority obviously affected the actions of the amateur officers of the Radcliffe parish Vestry, a fresh Local Government Act in 1894 had an even more profound influence. By this, district councils were established at an intermediate level between the county and the parish. Locally this meant that the old Board of Guardians of the Bingham Union was replaced by the Bingham Rural District Council.

Each parish within the district elected the same number of councillors as they had previously elected guardians of the poor (two in Radcliffe's case). One third of the councillors were to retire each year, but there was also provision for application to be made to the County Council for an order that all the councillors retire every third year, thus obviating the need for annual elections.

District councils assumed all the powers and responsibilities of the sanitary and highways boards established under previous acts, and they also became responsible for the protection of public rights of way and of common land in their districts. The following rather esoteric powers were also transferred to them from the justices at Quarter Sessions: the licensing of gang masters, dealers in game, passage brokers, emigrant runners, and operators of knackers' yards; the granting of pawnbrokers' certificates; the abolition of fairs and alteration of days for holding fairs; the execution of acts relating to petroleum and to infant life protection. As in the case of the County Council, the new councils were given power to levy a rate to defray their costs and also powers to borrow money.

There were four contestants for the two Radcliffe seats at the first election: Thomas Bell, Henry Parr (joiner and builder), Henry Palin (farmer), and James Haslam (insurance agent). The successful candidates were Henry Palin and Henry Parr with 224 and 181 votes respectively. The first clerk to the new District Council was R.H. Beaumont, who held office until 1914 when he was succeeded by I.W. Mason.

The Parish Council

On the same day that the district councils were created, the 1894 act also set up parish councils in place of vestries. A parish meeting consisting of all the parochial electors had to be convened at least once a year. This was empowered to elect councillors although if five electors, or one third of those present, demanded a full poll, such a poll had to be arranged. That in fact happened in 1894, 1896, 1897 and 1913. A parish meeting also had to give its consent before the Parish Council could (inter alia) incur expenses which would involve levying a rate in excess of 3d in the pound; adopt or abandon the provisions of the Watching and Lighting Act, the Baths and Washhouses Act, the Burial Acts, the Public Improvements Act, and the Libraries Act, or sell or exchange any land or buildings belonging to the parish. (Not all such powers were relevant to Radcliffe-on-Trent in 1894.)

Elections

The act prescribed annual elections in March, and, after 1894, these took place in 1896 and each subsequent March until 1899. In March 1898, however, a resolution was passed that parish elections should be held triennially as the annual elections 'are detrimental to discharge of duties'. The Local Government Board and M.P. were to be informed of this opinion. There is no record of a reaction from the Board at that time, but in January 1900 an order was received that there should be no election in 1900, that one should be held in 1901 and that thereafter they were to take place every three years. This was carried out, with only the 1916 election being omitted in the midst of the Great War.

The number of Radcliffe's councillors was established at thirteen, and thirty-three candidates stood at the first election in December 1894. The *Nottingham Daily Guardian* noted that there was plenty of excitement in the area and that all classes would have representative candidates: churchmen and Conservatives; Liberal churchmen; the Progressives who were running five or six candidates; whilst the two chapel bodies - Wesleyan and Primitive - had amalgamated with the Co-operative Stores to run six or seven candidates. Unfortunately, the paper did not allocate names to each category.

name	No. of Votes	name	No. of Votes
1 Armstrong Tom	50	18 Morris Charles	53
2 Barratt Richard	104	19 Noel Henry	57
3 Barnes George	50	20 Parr Butler	98
4 Bakewell William Jr	65	21 Parr Henry	63
5 Beeson John	70	22 Pike Henry	40
6 Beeson Thomas	29	23 Lord Newark	44
7 Bell George Alfred	92	24 Priestley George	16
8 Bell Thomas	98	25 Richmond Philip	36
9 Dann John William	9	26 Richmond Joseph	6
10 Dyson William	48	27 Rushton Robert James	72
11 Foster Thomas	66	28 Rose Richard	53
12 Fryer Robert James	32	29 Selby Alexander	7
13 Green John	48	30 Scrimshaw Thomas	64
14 Hallam James	9	31 Upton John	25
15 James John	35	32 Willey George John	47
16 Knight Samuel	35	33 Wright Edmund	76
17 Marshall Henry	54		

Candidates and voting figures recorded in the minutes of a meeting on December 4th 1894 to initiate the Parish Council

There was slightly less interest at the second election in 1896 when the number of candidates dropped to twenty-five, and only sixteen stood at the third. The numbers standing thereafter ranged between thirteen in 1901 and eighteen in 1904 and 1922, except for the single year of 1913 when thirty would-be councillors presented themselves to the electors. Perhaps some particular issue causing extreme local controversy during the early months of 1913 gave rise to this sudden increase in interest at the parish elections, but a search of extant records - including the local press - has so far failed to reveal what it might have been.

The first candidates

One of the successful 1894 candidates is listed in the minute book as 'Charles William Sidney Pierrepont, commonly known as Viscount Newark', and his occupation is given as 'nobleman'. He was elected chairman and retained that office until March 1898, when he did not stand for re-election to the council, being returned in that year for a second spell as M.P. for the Newark division. He became the fourth Earl Manvers in January 1900.

Only one man - Butler Parr junior who lived at The Poplars on the main street - was elected to the very first council and remained continually in office into the

(Top left) The fourth Earl Manvers, who, as Lord Newark, was the
first chairman of Radcliffe's Parish Council in 1895
(Top right) George Barratt, the first clerk to the Parish Council
(Lower picture) Butler Parr, chairman of the Parish Council from 1904 to 1928
photographed at Skegness

1920s. Like his father before him, he was associated with the brewing industry and took a major part in local and sporting activities. In addition to his duties on the Parish Council he served as one of Radcliffe's district councillors and was also a trustee of the Jeffrey Dole charity. He was first appointed vice-chairman of the council in 1898 and retained that post until becoming chairman in 1904. He resigned from this office in 1928 and died at the end of 1934.

William Bakewell junior of Station Terrace ran him a close second. Described as a platelayer in 1894 and a railway foreman in 1901, he was elected at each poll from 1896 onwards, except in 1901 when he did not stand. However, when Henry Buxton refused to take the seat to which he had been elected in May 1901, William Bakewell was promptly co-opted to fill the vacancy. With initially fourteen months less service than Butler Parr, he was to remain on the council long after the latter's departure, probably into the 1940s.

Of the twenty unsuccessful candidates at the first election, seven did not stand again, two stood again without success in 1896 and did not reappear, two achieved success at their second attempt, one at his third, and two at their fourth. Four others had mixed fortunes: George Barnes of Mount Pleasant did not stand again until 1899 when he was successful; Samuel Knight of Bingham Road stood again in 1904 but was again unsuccessful; Henry Pike of Albert Street was elected at his second attempt in 1898 but was not re-elected in the following year, and although co-opted to replace John Upton who died in April 1900 he did not stand again: and Joseph Richmond, a labourer of Mount Pleasant, after a second unsuccessful attempt in 1896 waited until 1904 before standing unsuccessfully again.

An unusual case was that of Samuel John Durant, a retired engine driver of Albert Street, who served as a councillor for three years without being endorsed by the electorate. He was first co-opted onto the council in May 1911 to fill the vacancy caused by the resignation of Frederick Wait, but when he offered himself for re-election in 1913 he was rejected. However, when another vacancy arose with the resignation of Arthur Johnson in April 1916 Durant was again co-opted, only to resign himself a year later.

Early meetings

The newly elected council met for the first time on Monday 31st December 1894 in the schoolroom. The meeting had been formally convened by Thomas Haynes Junior, a maltster from The Grange. As former overseer he initially took the chair to supervise the transfer from the old form of government to the new. There was a full turn out of councillors:

Thomas Armstrong	grocer	Bingham Road
Richard Barratt Snr.	shoemaker	Shelford Road
George Alfred Bell	farmer	
Thomas Bell	maltster	
Thomas Foster	butcher	
John James	farmer	Holme Pierrepont
Charles Morris	auctioneer	The Lodge
Viscount Newark	nobleman	Holme Pierrepont Hall
The Hon Henry Noel	gentleman	Lamcote House
Butler Parr	brewer's agent	
Henry Parr	builder and joiner	Bingham Road
Robert James Rushton	decorator	Bingham Road
John George Willey	gentleman	Bingham Road.

It was at this first meeting that Lord Newark was elected chairman, while the Hon Henry Noel became vice-chairman. Henry Parr was elected waywarden. The new council also appointed an external treasurer, Francis Abel Smith, of the Nottingham firm of Messrs Samuel Smith & Co. It seems that George Barratt had already been appointed as clerk at £8 a year. The latter was an estate agent living at that time on Walnut Grove. Two resolutions were then carried - one to collect a precept for the sum of £15 on January 21st 1895 to meet the expenses of the council, and the second that the meetings of the council be open to the public. (The right of public access to district and parish meetings was actually enshrined in the 1894 act unless the council specifically resolved otherwise.)

The second meeting was held on 28th January 1895 and considered a letter from the lighting inspectors, who had been appointed by the parish Vestry in 1875 to establish gas street lighting in the village under the provisions of the 1833 Lighting and Watching Act, suggesting that their powers and responsibilities should be taken over by the council. This was agreed, and a committee of seven was appointed to oversee the street lighting. A second committee of seven was appointed to take over the powers of the Burial Board, set up by the Vestry in 1868. It was also proposed that the council appoint four trustees to supervise the village's Jeffrey Dole charity, two to replace the overseers and two the churchwardens, but an amendment was carried that first an application should be sent to the Charity Commissioners asking that property owned by the charity and the administration of it should be transferred from the current trustees to the council.

An account was then received and considered from Thomas Haynes, the overseer, giving the costs he had incurred during the first parish meeting held on 4th December to initiate the new council procedure:

2		Registers	1s	0d
2	dz	Notice to candidates	1s	6d
1		Minute book	7s	6d
		School managers for lighting and heating room	2s	6d
		Bill posting	1s	0d
		For services of Geo. Barratt (Par. Clerk) & as messenger to Returning Officer	£1 1s	0d
14		Notices of first meeting of Council		6d
		Postage stamps	3s	10d
			£1 18s	10d

The returning officer's account for holding the poll came to a further £11.18s.8d. It was agreed that these accounts should be paid, so the council's first precept of £15 was already well depleted. It was then moved that the clerk, Mr George Barratt, be appointed assistant overseer 'to carry out all duties as appertain to the office of an Overseer of the Poor' at an annual salary of £40, and this was carried after the defeat of an attempt by Henry Parr to reduce the salary to £35.

The third meeting was held on 22nd April 1895 as the annual meeting, and various decisions were made. Francis Abel Smith was reappointed as treasurer subject to him signing a bond. In turn the treasurer asked how many and which councillors were empowered to sign cheques, and it was agreed that any two of Lord Newark, George Bell, Henry Parr and Butler Parr could sign, plus the clerk.

A letter was also received from the Bingham Rural District Council stating that it was intended to delegate to the Radcliffe Parish Council 'the power that can be delegated to a parochial committee under the Public Health Acts'. Such a local committee had been appointed, subject to the authority of the Bingham Union, after a public health crisis in the 1880s. In practice little changed as the Parish Council merely formed itself into a committee consisting of all the councillors to carry out these duties, any five to form a quorum. They continued to be assisted by professional officials.

Other decisions included the creation of a finance committee consisting of all councillors, with seven needed for a quorum, and confirmation of the Lighting and Burial Acts committees, the former reduced to six. With the procedural arrangements for the next twelve months now established, the council decided it need now meet only quarterly, as long as the committees met as required. (In April 1896, however, it was agreed that the full council should meet monthly, which they continued to do into the 1920s.)

Two potentially contentious issues were then raised at this third meeting. Councillor Butler Parr moved that enquiries be made 'as to whether any rights of way that would be of use to the inhabitants of this parish have been stopped', and he joined three others on the committee which was charged with making enquiries and reporting back. Councillor Richard Barratt followed this with a proposal that 'the council take into consideration the question of the boundary between this parish and that of Holme Pierrepont, with a view to having it settled', and a boundary committee of four (including Lord Newark and the Hon Henry Noel) was formed. This matter did not take long to settle, or rather, not settle. Contact was made with the clerk to the County Council who dauntingly advised 'that a Local Government Board enquiry would run the parish to great expense', but if the question were left for a while he would endeavour to settle it by arrangement between the two parishes. Butler Parr's subsequent motion 'that the subject of the boundaries be dropped' was prudently carried.

Finance

Of particular concern to the electors was the scale of the precepts levied on them. The parish council minute books give a clear indication of the general pattern of expenditure, as well as of that relating to lighting and the cemetery. The sums involved between 1894 and 1920 are indicated in the diagrams opposite. It must be emphasised that a special sanitary rate, a poor rate and precepts from the County Council would also have to be taken into account for a complete assessment of local government expenditure in Radcliffe-on-Trent during this period.

Inspection of nuisances

A succession of public health acts in the second half of the nineteenth century laid steadily increasing responsibilities on all the local authorities to improve hygiene generally, and they were assisted by paid officers who were apparently qualified to at least some degree. The inspector of nuisances for Radcliffe was appointed by the sanitary committee of the Bingham union until 1894 when the new Rural District Council took over appointments. The first reference found is to Edward Arnesby, appointed before 1872 and earning £70 a year in April 1882. He died in May 1883 and John Williamson Wright took his place until December 1891. Charles Parnham was then appointed at the reduced salary of £40 per annum and held the job for just six years before resigning, when William Whitworth of Tithby secured the post at the original £70 salary. At his re-appointment in 1904 he was urged to be 'more zealous in future', but in the following year he was asked to resign when accused of forging workmen's signatures on receipts for money they had not in fact been paid. The next inspector was Albert Marston of Newgate Street, Bingham who received £80 per annum, and by 1912 C. Kendrick held the post although the date of his original appointment is not known.

The problems referred to the inspectors were many and varied, and a short selection gives the clearest impression:

> ..... to inspect a leakage from closets on to the footpath adjoining Mr Williamson's butchers shop. (December 1896).
> ..... to make arrangements for disinfectants to be put into gullies belonging to the public drains, where necessary. (February 1898).
> ..... Letter from Mr G.H. Blatherwick referred to the Inspector, complaining of sewage matters and soap suds emptying into the open dyke on each side of the road from drains belonging to houses near his in Cropwell Road. (March 1898).
> ..... complaint from Cllr. Foster that house occupied by J. Woolstencroft in Water Lane used as a dwelling house by five persons and as a warehouse for rags and bones and likely to be injurious to the health of the neighbourhood. (June 1900).
> ..... also a complaint from Cllr. Chamberlain that liquid matter had drained through the wall of ashpits near Mr Williamson's shop, over the footpath and into the road. (also referred to the inspector - June 1900).
> ..... Inspector of Nuisances instructed to make inquiries as to the number of drains not connected to new sewers and see that connections made. (December 1902).
> ..... Inspector's attention to be drawn to a nuisance caused by a traction engine drawing trucks of night soil through the village and leaking into the road. (June 1909). This complaint was regularly raised until 1917.

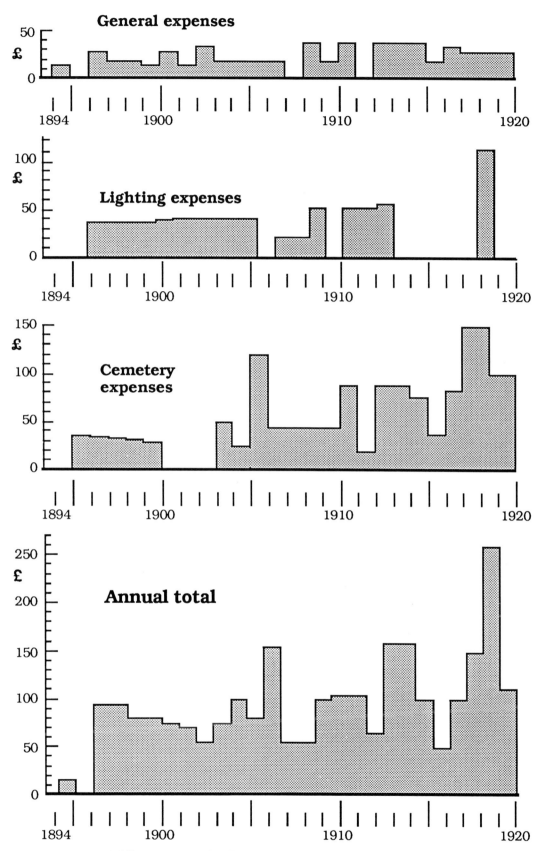

Radcliffe-on-Trent Parish Council general expenses, lighting expenses,
cemetery expenses and annual total expenses for the years 1894 to 1920.
(Gaps may indicate incomplete records)

The inspector of nuisances was also referred to as the sanitary inspector from about 1908, and his duties seem to have widened from about that time. When a local resident wrote to the council and asked for the sewer in Cropwell Road to be extended to Dewberry Lane, it was the inspector who was asked to produce an estimate for the work involved. In 1920, some eighteen years after the opening of the sewage farm at Lees Barn, funded from Bingham, the inspector wrote to the Parish Council concerning many complaints received by him 'of the unsanitary condition of many ashpits and closets in the parish'.

The full question of sanitation in the village during the Victorian period constitutes a veritable saga and has consequently been dealt with in a separate chapter on public health.

Building bye-laws and the surveyor

Another local responsibility which had originated in the days when the Bingham Union had acted as the rural sanitary authority was the approval of all plans of new and extended buildings. This was no form of town planning, but was for the implementation of regulations concerning standards of building, provisions of kitchens and toilets, waste disposal and similar matters laid down in various Public Health Acts. The Parish Council took over these duties from 1894, with the assistance of the District Council's sanitary inspector, Mr Parnham, and their surveyor, Mr A.R. Calvert. Drawings of all proposed work had to be submitted to the Parish Council prior to commencement, and new buildings could not be occupied until they had been inspected and certified to conform with the approved plans. The following list of building work which would have required approval has been compiled from the council minute books:

	1896-1899	1900-1904	1905-1909	1910-1915	1916-1920
New houses	18	39	21	25	10
Extensions & repairs to houses	-	16	12	9 plus *	4
Improved sanitary arrangements	-	3	5	3	4 plus
New commercial premises	2	6	4	-	-
Alterations to commercial premises	-	4	1	-	2
Sundries	1 engine shed	2 new streets	1 motor car shed 1 new school 1 new street 1 golf club	1 cow shed 1 cement store	1 new street 1 pigsty

* Plans were passed in August 1914 for alterations and additions to an unspecified number of houses in Sidney Grove and Hogg Lane for Thomas Stafford.

It should be borne in mind that 'extensions and repairs' to houses may also include 'improved sanitary arrangements'.

Arthur Richard Calvert had originally been appointed by the rural sanitary authority of the Bingham Union to the part-time post of surveyor for Radcliffe in November 1885 at a salary of £5 per annum, but the appointment automatically lapsed with the local government reorganisation of 1894. However, Calvert continued to serve the new Parish Council as their surveyor although he received no pay, but in 1896 was constrained to write to the Local Government Board in Whitehall in an attempt to get matters regularised. The board could offer little in the way of constructive suggestions, only confirming that the 1894 Local Government Act did not empower the Parish Council to appoint or pay a surveyor, nor did it automatically transfer Calvert's appointment to the District Council. Fortunately, Bingham then solved the problem by offering to pay Calvert his £5 per annum to act as Radcliffe's surveyor without a legal appointment, and this arrangement worked satisfactorily (with a doubling of his salary in 1911) until June 1920, when Bingham terminated it on their appointment of a full time surveyor to cover the whole district. Although Calvert owned some property on Cropwell Road, he lived in Nottingham where he was a partner in the firm of Calvert & Gleane which operated from 18 Low Pavement. He certainly earned his £5 a year, as building work was going on apace in the village during his time in office.

In June 1911 the District Council pointed out that Radcliffe were using out-dated bye-laws in regulating the standards of building in the village. After receiving a copy of the Local Government Board's new model bye-laws, Bingham eventually decided in July 1913 to adopt the new bye-laws for the whole of the district, with the addition of a couple drafted by Calvert specifically to cover problems experienced in Radcliffe.

Eastwood Street problems

At about the same time that revision of the bye-laws was under consideration, events following construction of a new street across land adjoining Bingham Road and owned by a Mr Eastwood gave a good idea of the conflicting interests of the developers trying to maximise their profits and the role of the Parish Council in seeing that reasonable standards were maintained. In January 1912 the council received plans for the construction of six pairs of houses for three separate developers in Eastwood's field, and they were approved subject 'to the street sewer being made in accordance with the bye-laws and the requirements of the Public Health Acts'. During the following month the council resolved that '...on no consideration must surface water be allowed to go into a sewer in Eastwood Street', but in March a letter from Calvert caused the councillors to order the sanitary inspector to test the sewer as laid and report on its condition. This report was duly received in April:

> According to the wishes of your council I have examined the drain or sewer in (Eastwood Street) and also tried to trace its outfall.
> At the top end of the street where a connection is proposed to be made from property in course of construction I found 9" drain stoneware pipes laid without any jointing whatsoever. After pouring large quantities of strongly coloured water into the pipes I watched for same to appear in both your main sewer and the old culvert, but no trace of the coloured water could be found in either.
> Before any connections are made to this drain or sewer it should be placed in a sound and water tight condition with necessary manholes, and properly connected to the main sewer at the bottom of the street.

Not surprisingly, Calvert was ordered to give notice to all owners in Eastwood Street (now Road) that the sewer would not be allowed to be connected to the main sewer while in its present state, and Bingham authorised the parish to threaten legal action if the notices were not obeyed. Calvert then seems to have done some investigations of his own and presented another report on July 1st 1912 which put a somewhat different complexion on the whole matter. He had discovered that Eastwood Street and its sewer had been constructed 'very shortly after 1883', while the date of the first bye-law was not until October 1885. The sewer had been connected to the drain laid in the hedge ditch in Bingham Road, but when the main sewer was laid in Bingham Road some years later, the Eastwood Street drain had not been connected to it. The developers of Eastwood Street now contended that they had a right to connect to the 1883 drain as it had been constructed before there were either bye-laws or sanitary committee and so could not be illegal. The matter was ultimately resolved by the Bingham authority's decision that it would be prudent to lay a new sewer down the length of Eastwood Street and connect it to the main one in Bingham Road. The existing pipes were to be used solely as a storm water drain.

The Parish Council's relations with other authorities

The council's relations with the two higher local authorities were generally cordial, although strains appeared at various times, and being the junior authority, the parish invariably had to give way.

The county surveyor (E.P. Hooley during the authority's early years) was one who could be relied upon to stand no nonsense. When Radcliffe councillors requested in August 1897 that footpaths be asphalted between the Nottingham Road entrance to the village and the Manvers Arms they were told that the county would 'within the next two months if possible, kerb and make up with gravel the footpaths on the Nottingham Road .....' - a much shorter distance than the council thought necessary. They then had the temerity to repeat their request and received the following stinging reply from Mr Hooley:

> *My instructions from my Council .... [are] to carry out the work mentioned in my letter to you of August 11th for the public safety, it having been represented to the Committee that the undefined footpath at this point is most dangerous to foot passengers using the same after dark.*
>
> *I have no instructions to carry out any new tar paving work at Radcliffe this year, but I shall be pleased to lay any request of your council before my Improvement Committee, though I fear if I presented your present letter - which to say the least is argumentative - but little good would result. My Council take the line of public safety first and local convenience (may I say luxury) afterwards. If you will approach the Committee, as other Councils do, by petition, I shall as stated be pleased to lay the same before the Committee in due course ....*

Surely the bald minute 'resolved that a petition concerning footpaths be prepared' does less than justice to the feelings of the Radcliffe councillors.

Earlier the same year (May 1897) Radcliffe's clerk had been instructed to write to the county surveyor and call his attention to the fact that a roadman from Radcliffe had been dismissed from his employment after 40 years' service on the roads, although he was still physically able to work, and to ask whether it was possible for him to be re-instated. The reply was both prompt and uncompromising:

> *I cannot, of course, enter into any argument with your council as to the why and wherefore of John Richmond having been discharged; suffice it to say that I take upon myself the whole responsibility in the matter. It is not possible under the circumstances to reinstate him, but may I point out that he has not been employed by this council for the period of years mentioned.*

Disagreements with the Rural District Council at Bingham centred on Radcliffe's sanitary problems and dissatisfaction with the manner in which they were being tackled by the District Council. Attempts to turn Radcliffe into an urban district so that the village would have more control over its own affairs failed in 1900 and 1907. Another method tried by the parish to increase its influence on the deliberations of the District Council was to obtain an increase in the number of representatives on that body. The idea was first mooted in February 1909 when the clerk was asked to make enquiries 'as to the proper course to take to obtain an increase in the number of representatives'. At the March meeting the clerk duly reported that although the 1894 Local Government Act had set the number of each parish's councillors on the district councils to be equal to the number of guardians of the poor formerly elected for that parish, section 60(1) of the act allowed the County Council to vary the number at its discretion. The idea was not pursued at that time, but it was resurrected in 1913 and in June of that year it was resolved to apply to the county to increase the number of Radcliffe's district councillors from two to four on the grounds that 'the proportion the population and assessable value of the parish bear to the total population and assessable value of the district would more than justify ..... such an increase'.

The clerk to the County Council wrote on 12th August 1913 to say that three county councillors had been deputed to hold a local inquiry in conjunction with representatives of the Leicestershire County Council, and this inquiry was held at the Shire Hall in Nottingham on December 5th 1913. Councillors Butler Parr, James Haslam J.P., Thomas Haynes J.P., and James Upton were appointed to represent the parish. The decision of the county's inquiry is not recorded in the parish minutes, but as Radcliffe continued to elect only two district councillors it was obviously negative from the village's point of view. The outbreak of the Great War less than a year later must have presented other pressing problems to absorb local attention. After the war, however, Radcliffe was one of a number of parishes in the county in danger of being absorbed into an enlarged city of Nottingham. After an eleven-day enquiry in 1920 there was considerable county rejoicing when the Ministry of Health turned down the city extension scheme.

II. Village amenities

Both the Vestry and the Parish Council provided or maintained a number of amenities during the period studied. Of those for which the village, rather than the Bingham authority, were responsible, the history of four has been looked at in some detail: the burial ground, street lighting, the playground and the drinking fountain.

The burial ground

The need for a new burial ground became urgent in the 1860s as the village continued to grow and the churchyard was reaching capacity. On 10th November 1868 the parish Vestry met at the Manvers Arms to appoint a Burial Board and to select suitable sites for a burial ground. There were nineteen at this initial meeting - an unusually good turnout. A board of nine was appointed, consisting mainly of local farmers, but headed by the vicar, Robert Burgess. At 48, he was already in far from robust health, but still supplemented his modest clerical income by using his land as a small-holding, specialising in greenhouse plants. Alongside him sat John Taylor, the local magistrate and landowner from Radcliffe Hall, and William Sanday, the retired farmer from Holme Pierrepont and the builder of Cliff House. Samuel Cave Tomlinson, who ran a local private school, was made secretary of the board at a salary of £5 per annum, and it was anticipated that money would be borrowed for all expenses on the security of the poor rates.

Choosing a site

It is clear from surviving burial board papers that initially four sites were seriously considered, each of about an acre: two on land up Cropwell Road and two on Shelford Road. Objections were raised to these four sites, so a fifth was proposed. It was this site, accessible from Vicarage Lane and ultimately the one chosen, which was to engender bitter controversy in the village, and set the Vestry against its own appointed Burial Board. Owned by Lord Manvers, the land was occupied by Thomas Butler, a local farmer, who violently objected to its being taken for use as a burial ground. Although the board was not initially enthusiastic about this site, they soon decided that it had many features in its favour. Of the sites under consideration it was by far the closest to the church, and would therefore avoid the necessity of building a chapel for burial services. It could almost be considered an extension of the churchyard, and it was felt that any problems regarding drainage could be overcome. In March 1869 the board met in Samuel Tomlinson's schoolroom to furnish replies to queries about the site by the government's medical inspector, Dr Holland, and it seems that official approval was subsequently given, subject to certain regulations. Thomas Butler, however, refused to give up so easily and clearly had considerable support in the village, particularly amongst the occupants of neighbouring land and tenements. A 'memorial' was sent to London, and a public inquiry was the result, headed by Dr Holland, who visited Radcliffe for the second time on May 25th 1869.

Demonstrations and a public inquiry

Dr Holland arrived soon after two o'clock and, attended by Thomas Butler's solicitor and numerous parishioners, went immediately to view the site. He was greeted by a somewhat unintelligible demonstrator. According to a reporter from the *Nottingham Journal*, a man who seemed to have been freely imbibing in something stronger than 'the cup that cheers', was arrayed in heavy chains and carried on his breast a board on which were chalked the words, 'I am for the Burial Board'. His message seemed to baffle the onlookers and the *Journal* reporter wondered if his chains signified that he was a lunatic who had escaped from some place of confinement. The party then proceeded to view a five-feet deep hole in the ground, which had presumably been dug by the opposition to show the unsuitability of the site since it was filled with water to within a foot of the top. At this point a second demonstrator appeared, 'a country woman', who in no measured terms protested that they wished to bury the villagers like dogs, and throw them into a wet hole in any fashion. Her passionate outburst only served to amuse the official party.

After inspecting some pumps, the party moved to the Manvers Arms where the inquiry was to be held. Much of the rest of the day was spent in hearing the opposition's case: that the site had not been adopted by a full vestry meeting, that it could never be adequately drained, that the water supply from springs in the field would be cut-off to neighbouring houses or the water in wells polluted, that it would encroach on a private occupation road (Vicarage Lane), that the bishop would not approve the site as being too far from the church, and that it would destroy the value of the land which was intended for building purposes. (Butler's opponents were to say that he would be happy with any site as long as it was not his own.) So long did all this take that the inquiry was adjourned until June 23rd, when Dr Holland returned to the village. This time expert witnesses were called by both sides. On Thomas Butler's side a builder and a contractor from Nottingham testified that they 'had never seen a piece of land so ill adapted for a cemetery'. The board was represented by William Sanday who was well acquainted with land drainage in the district, and had even made a trial hole in Miss Richmond's adjacent plot. As a result he thought the statement that the field could not be drained 'simply ridiculous', and proceeded to outline a basic drainage scheme at 11 feet which would be adequate. It became clear that Dr Holland did not see the drainage problem as grounds for turning down the site, but he was concerned that the site had not been sanctioned by the majority of villagers.

Victory for the Board

In the meantime, Thomas Butler had found an ally in Butler Parr (senior), a leading member of the village Vestry, whose house and land lay near the proposed site. In a strongly worded resolution, which appears amongst loose papers and not in the vestry minute book, the Vestry agreed unanimously under his signature that

> the site selected in the field in Mr Butler's occupation is undesirable and unsuitable and the Vestry rejects and disapproves of such site, and requests the Burial Board to select some other site.

The Vestry also refused to allow the Burial Board to negotiate or borrow money for the purchase of the site.

By now Dr Holland's findings had been accepted by the Secretary of State. The site was approved, subject to support from the parish. The Burial Board and the Vestry were now in opposing camps, and the matter was put to the test at a meeting on September 24th 1869. The heat of the issue, and doubtless some drumming up of supporters, produced an exceptional attendance of forty-five. Thomas Butler's amendment that the site was unsuitable was carried by a show of hands, twenty-seven votes to fifteen. The board, however, was not to be beaten so easily. William Sanday leaped to his feet and demanded that there should be a poll of all ratepayers. This was held on the following Saturday, with even Earl Manvers voting in support of the board's choice of site. The result was a defeat for Thomas Butler with sixty-three votes compared to the board's eighty-eight. Butler's party, however, did not lose with good grace. As the *Nottingham Journal* recorded, there was

> ..... a good deal of bad feeling in the matter, for on Saturday night several advocates of the proposal now carried had brick heads thrown at their windows, and a greenhouse and vinery of the Rev R. Burgess suffered considerable damage. A deal of threatening language was used which put the whole village in fear.

Completion and consecration

Despite this intimidation, matters at last seemed to be progressing smoothly for the victorious board. On November 12th the *Nottingham Journal* carried a notice asking for tenders for the 240-yards-long wall (it was to cost a total of £185), and on December 30th the conveyance of the land for £199 was signed by Lord Manvers. In February the Rev Burgess proposed that up to £800 should be borrowed for the completion of the cemetery on the strength of the poor rates. Altogether, costs for the land, wall, gates, drainage, planting, fees and expenses, including the forthcoming consecration of the ground amounted to £640. Two untimely deaths must, however, have marred the feeling of satisfaction. On March 4th 1870, Thomas Butler's wife Mary died, and on 20th May he too was dead. Both were aged only forty-five. Perhaps the stress of the preceding year had proved too much. At least neither had to suffer the indignity of being buried in the detested new ground, and significantly Thomas's funeral was not conducted by the Rev Burgess.

On 9th June 1870 a dignified consecration service took place, unblemished by demonstrations or violence. The Lord Bishop Suffragen of Nottingham was met from the 1.20 p.m. train from Lincoln by the vicar who acted as the bishop's chaplain for the day. Lunch was provided by John Taylor at Radcliffe Hall. Robing at the vicarage was followed by a 3 o'clock service in the church. During this the vicar, supported by his churchwardens, John Taylor and Samuel Brewster, presented the bishop with the petition for consecration. The choir and clergy, some from adjoining parishes, then filed out by the west door to the eastern gate with the Burial Board leading the way. On arrival at the part of the ground to be consecrated (part was left unconsecrated for non-Anglican burials), psalms were sung as the procession made a circuit of the area. A crowd behaving 'in a most exemplary manner' then surrounded the central figures, a carpet having been spread for the bishop's chair, as legal documents were signed and the consecration service completed. The happy occasion was followed by tea on the vicarage lawn to choral accompaniments, while in the evening John Taylor placed his field at everyone's disposal for various amusements.

Illegalities resolved

A few days later the board must have been appalled to receive legal advice on their application for the loan from Edward Wolstenholme, a Nottingham lawyer:

I am of opinion that the Burial board is not well constituted .... The proceedings must therefore be commenced anew.

The embarrassment of this after the consecration had actually taken place can well be imagined. His grounds for this opinion were that the board had never in the first place put a formal resolution to the Vestry that a new burial ground should be provided. Their whole proceedings had been illegal. A meeting was hastily called for 4th July 1870 when the final resolutions were at last put before the Vestry. As the burial ground was already inaugurated and Thomas Butler was dead, it was too late for any further protests. A legal board, fundamentally the same as had already been serving, was appointed to act under the control of the Vestry. Ten days later the proposed loan was formally approved, and on July 25th the purchase of the land belatedly sanctioned. At last the cemetery was legally in being.

Already on 13th July it had its first occupant - William Martin, the village's well respected surgeon who died in Buxton while hoping to improve the state of his own deteriorating health. In December 1873 the Reverend Burgess joined him. Later notables buried in this original part of the cemetery include the two cricketers, George Parr and Richard Daft in 1891 and 1900 respectively.

Controversy over an extension

After the opening of Saxondale hospital by the County Council in the early years of this century, the Parish Council became concerned at the large number of 'pauper burials' - up to half of all interments - so that space was rapidly being filled. The matter was raised at a county council meeting in January 1903 on Radcliffe's behalf by Mr C.V. Wright who pointed out that at the present rate the cemetery would be filled in another year or eighteen months. He felt that land should either be provided at Saxondale or that Radcliffe should be given funds to purchase new land. The asylum visitors' committee rejected such proposals on the grounds that the asylum had added some £4,000 to the ratable value of the village. By February 1904, the Parish Council felt obliged to take action, and a ratepayers' meeting was called to choose between two sites. What followed was a minor repetition of the controversy aroused at the creation of the original burial ground.

The cheaper of the two sites was on Shelford Road at £320 for four acres. The more convenient site, owned by Lord Manvers, adjoined the original ground but would cost £550 for two acres. At the February meeting eight-five voted in favour of this second site and only four against. The opposition, however, led by Thomas Haynes of the Grange who occupied the land, mustered its support. Some credence was given to their case when two test graves filled with water, and Earl Manvers refused to drop his price. At a meeting in June, called to decide whether or not a loan of £1,300 should be requested from the Local Government Board, Thomas Haynes argued against the selected site on the grounds of cost, size and the impossibility of any future expansion. He dismissed counter-arguments about the distance from the church as 'sentimental reasons'. As only twenty-five ratepayers attended this meeting, he demanded a poll of all ratepayers. In the event they elected to apply for the loan by 168 votes to thirty-seven, a surprisingly light poll considering the population was over two thousand, and the main street was thronged with interested bystanders during the evening of the poll. A government inquiry then took place in November 1904 which sanctioned the loan. By the time Thomas Haynes' tenancy had expired and the land had been drained, it took until 1908 before the extension was consecrated.

Ironically, concern about the size of the site and numbers of burials subsequently became unnecessary. Today, despite a four-fold increase in population, only about sixteen burials take place per year, compared with fifty-three in both 1903 and 1904. Improvements in health and preference for cremation help to explain this reduction.

Street lighting

The Lighting and Watching Act of 1833 gave local authorities the power to light the streets at night if the local ratepayers so wished. Nottingham proposed extending its gas supply to the village in 1864, but it was not until 1875 that Radcliffe's Vestry called a preliminary meeting at the Manvers Arms on Tuesday November 16th at 10 a.m. to discuss the matter of street lighting and how the costs should be met. Actual decisions were taken at a meeting a fortnight later when a resolution put by William Sanday and seconded by William Rockley proposed that

> the Lighting Act of William the Fourth be adopted in this parish and that the Inspectors to be hereafter appointed shall take it as an instruction from this Vestry that the lighting is not to commence at an earlier date than September in the year 1876.

This was carried by seventeen votes to seven. It was also agreed that there should be five lighting inspectors, and £100 was voted to 'meet the outlay in purchasing Standards Brackets Lamps etc'. The first five inspectors were William Sanday, Frederick Wright, James D. Gorse, Edwin Green and William Rockley, but nothing is known of their activities from the vestry book.

When the Parish Council took over from the Vestry early in 1895 the committee numbered seven, and from the minute books it is clear that only the central part of the village was lit - the main road through the village centre from Lamcote to the Cropwell Road junction, plus what is now Water Lane, Hogg Lane and Mount Pleasant. It may also have progressed a certain distance up Cropwell Road, Bingham Road and Shelford Road, which were being built up by then. Various attempts were made over the years to extend the area covered by the street lighting, but they generally failed. For example, a request from the Golf Club in 1909 for lighting to be extended up Cropwell Road as far as the club entrance seems to have come to nothing, while in August 1911 a parish meeting was convened with a view to extending the lighting to the whole village. Two resolutions had to be put: the first to abandon the Lighting act for that area in which it was currently in force, and the second to adopt the act for the whole of the parish. However, the first resolution was defeated by twenty-three votes to four with four abstentions, so matters could progress no further. Councillor Edward Houldgate then put a compromise proposal:

> ...... *that this meeting is of the opinion* [that] *the time has arrived when the village lighting should be carried out in such a manner that every inhabitant or visitor may go about in safety, and that it be an instruction to the Parish Council Lighting Committee to carry out our wishes, (Viz) lamps to be lighted when necessary and not put out before 11.00 p.m. or for the main road and station approach before 11.30 p.m.*

This was rejected by ten votes to four, so the results of this meeting were entirely negative. Whether this was due to general satisfaction with the status quo or whether it indicated a reluctance to meet the costs of improvements is not clear. One way forward was for residents to purchase and erect private lamps to which the council would supply gas, and the lighting inspectors' minutes of November 13th 1913 record seven private lamps being supplied with gas, one in Lorne Grove, two in Walnut Grove, one in Chestnut Grove, two in Lincoln Grove and one in Bailey Lane.

The lamplighter

A seasonal lamplighter was appointed, and lighting was operated during winter months only, normally from the middle of September until early April. The lamplighter was ordered to commence his rounds half-an-hour after sunset and lights were extinguished before midnight, and were not lit at all during a period of full moon if the skies were clear. The earliest known lamplighter is John Bell, who was being paid 9s.6d per week to go out twice each evening throughout the lighting season. He was replaced in September 1900, as he was then working away from Radcliffe, by the one-armed Fred Footit at the same rate of pay. (By then the latter was also being paid 1s.6d per week to oil the swings at the playground and chain them up each Sunday.) The lamplighter's wages were increased to 12s per week in January 1909, but in October 1912 were reduced to 11s.6d and in 1913 raised to 11s.8d. The reasons for these small adjustments are not recorded. The services of a lamplighter were not needed for much of the war, but it was Fred Footit who re-lit seventeen of the more important lamps on Boxing Day 1918, still at a wage of 11s.8d per week. From the 1919-20 season he was paid £1 per week. Due to ill health, he lit 'his' lamps for the last time on Friday January 28th 1921.

Costs

In 1899 there were about fifty street lights in Radcliffe, and an enquiry to the Nottingham gas department as to the amount of gas consumed by a lamp in an hour brought a reply that 'at the price we charge to your Council a lamp would burn for 200 hours for two shillings'. A total of £22.10s.2d was paid for gas consumed in 1903, and this had risen to £23.15s.8d ten years later, perhaps through an increase in both price and the number of lamps. Other regular costs were for items of maintenance. The lamplighter was paid for periodically cleaning the lamps - normally 2d per lamp - and in September 1907 the cheapest tender received to paint thirty standard and fifteen bracket lamps was £5.10s from the local firm of R.J. Rushton & Sons. Each autumn the Nottingham Corporation gas department reconnected the lamps and meters in preparation for the coming lighting season. This work was done free of charge - until 1904, when a bill was received for 13s.9d. In reply to the clerk's request for an explanation, a letter was received from the city gas offices in George Street dated October 18th:

> *..I would inform you that in your case it has been a mistake that you have not been charged before. Other councils, Parish, Urban and District, have paid the charge for years, consequently we are only putting you on the same basis they are on. This explanation will no doubt be quite satisfactory to you and the account is returned herewith.*

A cheque was drawn the following month, and thereafter a regular annual account was received and paid.

Technical progress

In September 1902 the Parish Council had complained to the city gas department about the poor gas pressure in the village and received a reply that the city was laying a new gas main from Trent Bridge to Lady Bay, which would greatly improve the supply to Radcliffe. The technology employed in the street lighting seems to have undergone little improvement for many years. In 1900 the Nottingham city gas department had offered a new type of burner on approval. Within a month of testing the gas department was asked to replace the old burners. Not until 1910 were incandescent burners tried in two lamps, supplied by the Gas Maintenance Co. Ltd. Three years later the inspectors were authorised to convert all the lamps to this new type of burner. (An order for 'two dozen inverted incandescent burners' went to C. Bray & Co. Ltd. in 1919 at a cost of £7.5s.)

Vandalism and accidents

Vandalism was a constant nuisance, the lamps making irresistible targets for stone throwing. In November 1898 a reward of 5s was offered for information leading to conviction of offenders. In 1909 the amount was doubled, in 1911 the same offer was repeated, and in 1920 it was doubled again to £1. However, when in October 1911 two men gave information that 6-year-old Frank Goodband had thrown at and broken a lamp in Narrow Lane, it was resolved not to pay the reward as the information did not lead to a conviction, the boy being too young to prosecute.

The lamps proved as irresistible to horses as to small boys. In November 1903 a lamp was knocked over by a horse and cart belonging to Thomas Barratt senior, a nurseryman, but he refused to pay the repair bill of £4.8s.10d on the grounds that it was an accident. When the councillors put the matter in the hands of their solicitor, Mr Robert Hallam, he advised that for the action to succeed they would have to prove negligence, which would be very difficult. The matter was dropped. The council fared better in a case in July 1912 when a runaway horse and van belonging to Meredith & Gamble, a Nottingham laundry firm, knocked over another lamp. This time the repair costs of just over £4 were met by the National General Insurance Co. Ltd.

Wartime blackout

In 1915, with the start of Zeppelin activity, the council held a special meeting in September and decided that only the lamps along the main road from Lamcote corner to Eastwood Street should be lit, with the tops and sides shaded with green paint to the mantle level. A month later the decision was changed to lighting all the lamps but with glasses shaded (for which work a tender of 15s was accepted), and with the lamplighter extinguishing them from 9.00 p.m. After mid-February 1916 lamps were not re-lit, although it was not until August that a formal resolution was passed 'that the street lights be not lighted for the duration of the war'.

Coincidentally, a meeting of the council was scheduled for Armistice day, November 11th 1918, and immediately the lighting inspectors were instructed to consider how to get the lights back on at the earliest opportunity. The inspectors met three days later, the clerk reporting having visited the fuel and light controller and the city gas department in Nottingham, and giving the welcome news that gas would be available so long as only 50% or fewer of the lamps were recommissioned. It was decided to light seventeen - those mainly on Main Road, plus one each in Cropwell Road, Shelford Road, Lorne Grove and Bailey Lane, and two each in Water Lane and Narrow Lane.

The playground

It was at a council meeting held in October 1895, that Richard Barratt moved a resolution 'that the council shall provide a playground for children', which was passed without dissent. From such quiet beginnings originated a proposal which generated its share of local controversy, but which still provides one of the major amenities of the village nearly a century later.

At a parish meeting a month later the ratepayers approved the basic idea by forty-two votes to nil and agreed that five acres in Palace Field, to include the hillside plus part of the field at the base of the hill, was the most suitable site. The council then appointed a playground committee, who met on the site at 9.30 a.m. on Christmas day to confirm its suitability before approaching the owner, Lord

Manvers. A letter from his agent (R.W. Wordsworth) indicated that the council could have the land on an annual tenancy of £17.10s per year, payable half-yearly, the landlord paying land tax and tithe and the council paying local rates. The council was also required to fence its area securely at its own cost, and also pay any claims of the outgoing tenant (Mr John Green) in waiving his right to twelve months' notice. When it was discovered that John Green's claims for compensation came to £91.3s.9d, it was decided to defer completing any agreement for twelve months so that formal notice could be served and compensation avoided. A lease, rather than a tenancy, was also requested in view of the outlay needed to set up the playground. As a result, Lord Manvers agreed to a ten-year lease.

The jubilee scheme

In January 1897, just after the playground committee had resumed meeting, the Parish Council considered a circular from a committee set up in London to organise a national celebration for Queen Victoria's diamond jubilee which fell later that year. One of its suggestions was the provision of more publicly-owned recreation areas. This coincidence caused the council to decide that the playground could appropriately form the basis of the Radcliffe celebrations. Moreover, the expenses could be met by public subscription rather than by the rates. A subscription list was immediately opened, and the following sums were pledged by those present: £5 from The Hon Henry Noel and £25 on behalf of his wife; £1 each from councillors Barratt, Butler Parr, T. Bell and Henry Marshall; 5s each from councillors Foster and Bakewell. By the end of February the clerk could report further pledges of £20 from Lord Manvers, £5 from Viscount Newark, two guineas from county councillor Tom Potter, £2 from councillor Haynes, and £1 each from councillors Bell and Rushton. Total pledges so far stood at £66.2s. A circular drawn up by the clerk was then approved for printing, which listed the pledges already made and asked for subscriptions from the public.

It was apparently at this point that opposition was provoked. The parish meeting, which had approved the idea of a playground was now eighteen months in the past, and had not been particularly well-attended. There had been no public airing of the intention to fund the playground by subscription and use it as a means of celebrating the diamond jubilee. Readers of the *Nottingham Guardian* of February 12th 1897 were left in no doubt of the feelings of one correspondent signing himself *Sanitas*:

> *...The Radcliffe-on-Trent parish council have decided that the village requires an open space, a recreation ground of about five acres in extent and for that purpose have chosen a portion of a field now under several feet of water, within a few yards of the Trent, the same distance from the railway and likewise from the open drain conveying nearly the whole of the sewage of the village into the river. As the scheme is not of great repute among the ratepayers the council have hit upon a new way of raising the required money instead of making an addition to the rates. They are going round with the hat and saying it would be a nice way of marking the year of the record reign. Setting aside the fact of the space being out of all proportion to the requirements of the village, the danger of its surroundings and its unsalubrity are so glaringly apparent to all but those who will not see ....*

Sanitas continued at some considerable length to advocate that available funds should be channelled into sanitary improvements, which were in fact the responsibility of Bingham Rural District Council. He found, however, a sympathiser in James Haslam, an insurance agency superintendent living in Lorne Grove, who had been defeated in the first two parish council elections. His letter criticising the Parish Council appeared in the *Guardian* on February 23rd 1897:

> *....Appointed to make all necessary arrangements for getting in order the new playground, they are face to face with an outlay of money which if raised would not be raised without a lot of complaint. They therefore have decided that the commemoration horse shall run for them and this without consulting the Parish in any way. I see no reason why a piece of land leased*

only for ten years should have money spent on it to mark for all time such a unique event as that of this year. A gigantic mistake was made here ten years ago in celebration of Her Majesty's Golden Jubilee, and I for one will see that if any money is subscribed it shall be devoted to something more lasting than a meat log and a band of music. Then, however, the committee represented the Parish for the purpose of 'celebration', now the Parish is to have no voice in the matter but simply to subscribe and say nothing. I am much mistaken if the appeal will receive a tittle of the support that would be accorded a well considered scheme and I trust that every ratepayer will refuse to be driven in this way.

Instead, James Haslam recommended that the money should be spent on a village hall or library to improve the social and intellectual status of the village.

Completion of arrangements

Meanwhile, despite such carping, the committee's arrangements were going ahead. The lease from Lord Manvers was signed at a council meeting on 10th May. The fence was ordered, its specifications being:

333 yards or thereabouts (more or less) wrought iron tubular fence, four feet high above the ground, 21 inches below the ground, five tubular horizontal rails all one inch diameter, standards of Girder Iron $1^{3/4}$ inches wide with double-pronged feet and placed three feet apart.

Materials were delivered to Radcliffe station.

A meeting was held on May 13th to discuss final arrangements for the opening. It was agreed to invite the Hon Mrs Noel to perform the opening ceremony, but she declined and that function was eventually performed by Richard Barratt, chairman of the Parish Council, a member of the playground committee and mover of the original resolution. The lack of a gate in the new fence was realised, and the clerk was authorised to obtain tenders from village joiners and arrange for the work to be done. It was also decided to make a recommendation to the Parish Council that there should be a treat for all the children up to the age of fourteen on Jubilee day, with an offer of £20 towards the costs from the playground funds.

Three more committee meetings were held before opening day, on the 10th, 16th and 19th June, and a flurry of decisions were taken: that the new fence be varnished at a cost not to exceed $1^{1/2}$d per yard; that a permanent flagpole be erected; that a stile be erected where the new fence crossed a footpath; that the Great Northern Railway Co. be approached and asked to fence off the base of their embankment for safety reasons; that local tradesmen be allowed to set up stalls on the ground on opening day free of charge; that an application received from a Bingham entrepreneur to erect swing boats and coconut shies be refused; that the clerk be directed to employ a man to mow the nettles and rough grass; and that the Radcliffe brass band be engaged to play 'on the lowest terms that can be arranged, not to exceed six pounds'.

The opening

Although Queen Victoria had actually ascended the throne on June 20th 1837, the officially proclaimed day for the national celebration of her diamond jubilee was June 22nd 1897, and the Radcliffe festivities got under way at 1.00 p.m. when a procession of children and young people formed up and proceeded to the new recreation ground behind the brass band. After Richard Barratt had declared the playground open the procession circled the five acres before returning to parade through the village, stopping at intervals to sing the national anthem, *Rule Britannia* and the jubilee hymn *Oh! Lord of hosts.*

The following day's issue of the *Nottingham Journal* records that at 4.30 p.m. nearly a thousand people sat down at four locations to tuck into a meat tea, while a hundred children from the infants' school went to Radcliffe Lodge to receive a gift from Mr and Mrs Morris. 'The remainder of the day was spent in the recreation ground, where a good programme of sports was gone through'.

A Co-operative Society dray on Wharf Lane at the opening of the playground
for Queen Victoria's diamond jubilee

After the celebrations

The committee met for the first time after the opening celebrations on July 20th
1897 and thereafter monthly during the summer and autumn but only occasionally
during the winter, a pattern which was to be followed in ensuing years. The bill for
the fence, including the varnishing, came to £41.18s.7d, but £1 was withheld, 'one of
the columns not being satisfactory'. Other minor bills were settled, and the clerk
was able to report at the end of August that the total subscription income had
amounted to £93.8s.5d, total expenses were £63.4s.1d, and a healthy cash balance
remained of £30.4s.4d. The committee also produced its own bye-laws, which appear
in the minute book, but the local government board insisted on its own list of model
clauses which have not been recorded. Early attention was given to equipping the
playground, and within a month of the opening two swings, a see-saw and a seat 'to
be fixed round the tree situate furthest from the road' had been arranged. Four more
swings were provided the following year at a cost of £8.17s. Swings were oiled once a
week but chained up to prevent use on Sundays. To keep the five acres of grass under
control, tenders were invited for grazing by sheep, an offer of £1 being accepted. A
number of football teams were permitted to use the ground at a standard charge of 2s
per match, and periodically they were allowed to close the ground to the public and
charge for admission. Local tradesmen who set up stalls were charged 1s per day,
and in July 1901 permission was granted to the Radcliffe brass band to play in the
evenings until 9 p.m. From April 1904 two playground inspectors were appointed to
superintend the maintenance of fences and equipment at the ground, reporting to
the full committee which met less frequently.

In 1920 it became known that large areas of the Manvers estate, including most
of the Radcliffe holdings, were being sold at auction, and the playground was to go
under the hammer. The council decided that the freehold should be purchased by the
parish, and the annual parish meeting gave approval to expenditure for the purpose
not exceeding £500, the money to be raised by a loan repayable over twenty years.
The voting was nine for and five against, which seems to indicate a fair degree of
apathy on the part of the ratepayers. At the subsequent council meeting it was
agreed to apply to the County Council and the Ministry of Health for sanction for
the loan. Butler Parr, then chairman of the Parish Council, attended the auction on
March 3rd 1920 and secured the playground freehold for £450, using £45 of his own
money to put down the necessary deposit. When formal application was sent to the
Public Works Loan Board for the money, a reply stated that treasury policy required

local authorities to obtain their loans from local sources wherever possible. It was consequently decided that the clerk would publish notices at the post office and the Co-operative stores asking for offers of a loan of £500 over twenty years. The result was a letter from William Dyson on behalf of the trustees of the local lodge of the Manchester Union of the Independent Order of Oddfellows offering to lend the money at 6% per annum, repayable within twenty years. The offer was accepted, the mortgage deed being signed at a council meeting on October 11th, and the deed of conveyance of the land from Lord Manvers on 13th December 1920. The playground was thus safeguarded for the parish.

Drinking fountain and horse trough

In the days of horse power the sight of drinking troughs was a normal feature of the urban landscape, but the vast majority of them have now disappeared. The combined drinking fountain and horse trough in Main Road, Radcliffe-on-Trent, although no longer used for its intended purpose, is protected by being listed as a structure of historical and architectural interest. The first move in its provision came in a letter from a Miss Cooper addressed to the Parish Council in July 1895, asking the councillors 'to consider the great need of a drinking trough in the principal thoroughfare'. The council did agree to consider the matter, but nothing further was done at that time. Six years later Miss Katherine de Hersant inquired whether the council would maintain a drinking fountain and horse trough if such an amenity were to be provided by public subscription. Before coming to a decision the council asked the Nottingham city water department about the probable cost of supplying water. They supplied the following information:

> ... if your Parish Council erect a drinking fountain and cattle trough we would supply it through a meter .....as we do those in the City. The consumption varies in different localities, being as low as 2,000 gallons and up to 20,000 gallons per quarter, the average being 12,000 gallons. All work in connection with the supply, putting in service, fixing meter, etc., would have to be borne by your council.

The County Council surveyor was conditionally amenable:

> ... I do not think my council would wilfully place any obstacle in the way of such a proposal as you name in your letter, but I cannot think that they would allow such to take place unless a plan and elevation were made and laid before then showing what you propose .

The Parish Council was sufficiently happy with these replies to pass a resolution on September 9th 1901 that if the fountain and trough were provided by public subscription they would accept it as a gift, maintain it, and supply it with water.

A committee was formed with the Hon Mrs Noel as president, Miss de Hersant as secretary and Mrs G. Lynes Bates as treasurer, and the sum of £100 was raised. (The final cost is not now known.) Mr G.H. Blatherwick produced the design which was approved by both the Parish and County Councils, and the construction was entrusted to Mr J.G. Thomas of Lenton Boulevard, Nottingham. The main part of the finished work was of Pilth stone in the form of a large cupola ornamented with a finial of classic design and supported by similar finials on each side. The trough and bowl were of polished red granite and the whole construction was 11' 6" high, 6' 6" in breadth and 2' through in the narrowest part of the shaft.

Events seem to have progressed smoothly. By June 10th 1902 the council chairman was authorised to sign an order on the city water department making the parish responsible for the water charges, and the Hon Mrs Noel had agreed to perform the unveiling ceremony. By this stage, however, it had been realised that, as with the playground, the new amenity could serve a double purpose. Queen Victoria had died and the coronation of Edward VII was imminent. Consequently the wording of the inscription on a copper plate fixed just above the horse trough read as follows: Erected by public subscription to commemorate the coronation of Edward VII June 26th 1902. Unveiled by the Hon Mrs Noel. Alas for the best laid schemes of the council! In March Mrs Noel tripped over a mat in church and had to be carried back to Lamcote House with a broken hip, never to resume her full activities again. In June the new king was taken ill with appendicitis and his coronation was postponed until August 9th. The original plate, with its double inaccuracy, remains legibly in place (1989) to confound the unwary local historian!

The unveiling ceremony

It was decided that most celebrations scheduled for 26th June should be cancelled in view of the king's illness, but that the unveiling of the new trough and drinking fountain could, with propriety, go ahead. Therefore at 2.30 p.m. the children from both day and Sunday schools were drawn up in a square in front of the fountain. A short prayer was given by the Rev H. Needham, and 'Oh God our help in ages past' was sung by the gathering to the music of a band of local instrumentalists. According to the *Nottingham Daily Express* Mrs Noel's place was taken by Miss Yeomans (her companion) who 'most gracefully carried out the unveiling and declared the foun-

The crowd at the unveiling of the horsetrough and drinking fountain.
Mrs Sarah Scrimshaw (1851-1927) is in the centre

tain open'. The water was turned on with a decorated key which was subsequently presented to Mrs Noel as a souvenir. A second clergyman, the Rev A. Page, then delivered a few appropriate sentences and Mr Richard Barratt, chairman of the Parish Council, proposed a vote of thanks to Miss de Hersant for her kindness in 'officiating' - presumably a reference to her overall organisation of the event.

It would seem that fair use was made of the new facilities, which allowed horses passing along Main Road to quench their thirsts from the trough at the roadside, and villagers to quench theirs from the tap and chained metal cup on the path side of the structure. The cost of water in 1904 was £1.6s.6d, which - making due allowance for meter rent - indicates that about 12,500 gallons was used. Eight years later the cost was up to £1.18s (about 24,000 gallons). From the end of 1916 the quarterly sums paid to the city water department were always 5s.5d, the minimum charge quoted in 1902, so presumably no water was passing through the meter as a war time economy. In May 1919 with peace once more established, councillors Bakewell, Rushton and Upton were asked 'to examine the drinking fountain and cattle trough' and report what should be done'. In August an estimate received from W. Eastwood for £6 for cleaning and repairing was accepted. The subsequent account was paid in November, so it is reasonable to assume that the fountain and trough were once more serving the community from the autumn of 1919.

Main sources

Primary

Nottinghamshire Archives Office: Radcliffe parish registers; parish council minute book 1894-1902 PaC 35/1-2; rating books PR 15,628 1-20.

Nottinghamshire County Library (Local Studies Library): census returns; newspaper cuttings re extension of city boundaries q L32.03.

Radcliffe-on-Trent Parish Council: vestry minute book; parish council and committee minute books; burial board papers.

University of Nottingham: Manvers papers 3 Ma 2D 16

Secondary

Chamberlain, Colet. *Memories of the Past.* 1960.

Radcliffe local history group: extracts from Nottingham newspapers 1837-1920.

PUBLIC HEALTH

I. Drainage and disease 1837-1882

One of the main concerns of Victorian England was the need to improve the nation's health. Epidemics of cholera and typhoid were common, particularly at the beginning of the period, while smallpox, diphtheria, scarlet fever and measles all contributed to a death rate which was high by modern standards. Some health care for the poor was provided by the poor law unions, and medical officers of health were now being appointed. (A Mr Rowland was Bingham Union's medical officer for the district in which Radcliffe lay from 1836 to 1872.) Progressive local authorities also recognised that unpolluted water supplies and effective sewage- disposal were essential if standards were to improve. Nottingham benefited from Thomas Hawksley's scheme for piped water from 1830, and although the effects were not fully felt in the cholera outbreak of 1832, the town escaped comparatively lightly in that of 1849.

Radcliffe was not so fortunate. The village's water supply came mainly from wells, and much of its waste found its way into the streams which eventually reached the Trent. A painting of the main street in 1839 shows the chief of these streams, the Syke Drain, crossed by foot bridges, flowing along the south side of the street towards the church. (See page 144.) This brook began its journey near Saxondale and flowed westwards through fields between the Shelford and Bingham roads. (Today it is visible near Addington Court.) From there it meandered through the main part of the village before crossing the road at the Green, and then turned north-east to run alongside Wharf Lane before reaching the Trent. On canvas it presents a picturesque scene. In reality it often smelt and was frequently blocked. As the population increased, it became totally inadequate as a key part of the drainage system, and the need for its improvement, along with the eradication of 'nuisances', was a major concern of village ratepayers in Victorian times. In this, Radcliffe was merely reflecting national trends. General dilatoriness in finding a solution which did not hurt the pocket may also have been typical. The glare of publicity in which the embarrassed village found itself in 1882 was not.

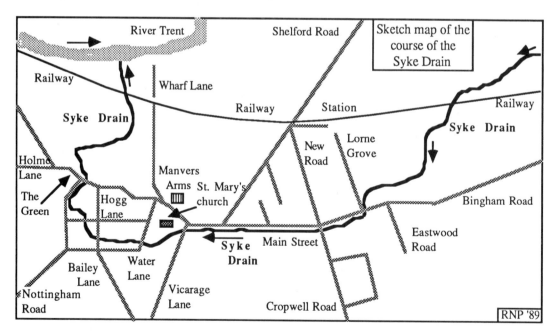

The cholera outbreak of 1849

As the nation was swept by the great cholera epidemic of 1849, precautions were taken locally. The *Nottingham Journal* reported that on September 11th a Dr Gill of Nottingham gave an illustrated lecture in Radcliffe's schoolroom on the cause of the disease. His advice to the 'numerous and respectable audience' came too late. On September 18th the vicar, Robert Burgess, wrote 'Asiatic cholera' in the burial register alongside the name of the first of twelve victims. This was 26-year-old Ann Robinson, 'a stout healthy person', who according to the *Journal* died at 1 a.m. and was buried the same evening. Her baby, Harriet, was buried on October 3rd and the last cholera victim on November 14th. Their ages ranged from infancy to 74 years, and seven of them were female. Four families were particularly badly hit: the Robinsons, the Hemsleys, the Breedons, and the Caunts - of whom four died. There were also a great many other cases that were not fatal according to the *Journal* for September 28th.

From the inquest reports on that day in both the *Journal* and *Review* it is clear that there were poor sanitary conditions in a number of village houses. The misnamed Mount Pleasant was at the centre of the outbreak. At the inquest on 5-year-old Jane Caunt (whose grandmother was buried the same day, and whose mother died while the inquest was taking place) it was revealed that

> *the house is situated in a very unhealthy situation, there being a great number of pigsties, privies etc. in the neighbourhood; part of the house is also situated over a privy, and there has always been an ill smell throughout the house.*

Another factor associated with the Radcliffe cholera outbreak of 1849 was the presence of navvies at work on building the railway. The Caunts' house had been used as lodgings for railway workers, and a village tradition linked the spread of the disease with the over-use of beds by navvies on shifts. As already noted in the chapter on the railway, there is no evidence that navvies died in the outbreak, but the railway contractors clearly felt some responsibility for the victims. Along with other gentlemen of the neighbourhood they organised a subscription which by October 5th had reached more than £30. Services for a special 'day of humiliation' were held in the parish church on Friday September 28th. (Similar services had been held in Nottingham on the previous Tuesday.) The whole day in Radcliffe, despite its occurring in feast week, was 'kept with becoming solemnity'.

Dr William Martin

While it was the vicar who sustained the spirit of the parish during the cholera epidemic, it was Dr William Martin who coped with the practical needs of the victims. The presence of a resident doctor in the village was itself a sign of progress. He appears in the 1841 census and remained until his death in 1870. Born about 1812 at Brickworth Lodge in Huntingdonshire, he was described as a Licentiate of the Hall, London. His wife, Sophia, some two years his senior, had five children by a previous marriage, and was to bear him another four. His devotion to duty during the cholera outbreak was recognised at a dinner in his honour at the Manvers Arms on December 26th 1849. The *Nottingham Journal* reported that after an 'appropriate speech' the vicar presented him with a purse containing nearly £20 collected by the inhabitants of the village 'for his kind and liberal attention to the poor during the late prevalence of cholera and fever'. His work amongst the poor seems to have been a constant feature of his life, and not merely in Radcliffe. In 1864, as honorary secretary of the Nottingham Provident Medical Aid Institute (to which contributions were paid to cover the cost of future treatment), he was presented with a 'timepiece' for his valuable services, notably among the poor of St Peter's parish.

Such gifts were no doubt welcome to a practitioner with a large family to support, and perhaps a number of patients who could not afford fees. Over the years he tried to gain a secure position as medical officer for the west district of the Bingham Poor Law Union at a salary of £30 a year. His appointment in 1857 must have brought some relief, but as he was 'not qualified in one of the Four modes' required by the Poor Law Board he was replaced in 1859 when a fully qualified medical man was found. He was still paid by Bingham for midwifery and vaccination cases, but it was not enough. In May 1863 the *Journal* reported his appearance before the Nottingham bankruptcy court. In 1867 he regained the post of medical officer for Bingham Union, but on the same temporary basis as before. By

1870 his health was deteriorating. The *Journal* noted that he had caught cold while out on a long visit to his patients. Neuralgia followed which gradually affected the spinal cord, causing paralysis. His death occurred in July 1870 at Buxton where he had hoped the baths would relieve his condition. The affection in which he was held was made clear in a newspaper report at the time:

> *He was loved and respected by both the rich and the poor, but it is the poor who will feel his loss the most keenly - to them he was a friend as well as a doctor.*

His body was brought back to Radcliffe, and he was buried in the controversial new village cemetery - its first occupant.

Early measures

At national level some progress was made in the wake of Edwin Chadwick's devastating report on sanitary conditions in 1842. An act for the removal of 'nuisances' was passed in 1846, and in 1848 local boards of health were created, based on the poor law unions, under the supervision of a general Board of Health. The effect on Radcliffe is noticeable in the Bingham minutes from 1848 with the regular reporting of 'nuisances' and referral to the magistrates if they were not removed. Nevertheless, the first positive steps in the village came as a result of the 1849 cholera outbreak. On September 28th the *Journal* reported that 'there had been no sanitary proceedings until Wednesday, when a parish meeting was called, and a Committee appointed'. Early in October Bingham Union could assure the Board of Health in London that, led by the vicar and William Taylor of Radcliffe Hall, a house by house search for nuisances had been undertaken in an effort to check the spread of cholera. Bingham Union itself organised the distribution of three-hundred notices throughout its forty-two parishes concerning the cleansing of houses and removal of nuisances. From October 11th the progress of Radcliffe's committee began to be recorded in the village's vestry book. After the immediate removal of nuisances, the next most obvious area for improvement was the open Syke Drain running through the main street. As this was a turnpike road, the Rev Burgess was dispatched to see if the turnpike commissioners would assist in covering the drain - perhaps to save money on the rates. Whether or not they helped is not known, but the Manvers estate papers show that considerable repair work was done in 1850 on the stretch outside The Poplars, then occupied by John Green but owned by Lord Manvers.

The Syke Drain in 1860

Whatever was done around 1850 had little long-term effect. In 1859 an outbreak of smallpox affected Radcliffe and the nearby villages of Cropwell Butler and Tithby. A report in the *Nottingham Journal* for December 2nd rashly asserted that in Radcliffe's case at least the cause must be neglect of vaccination, for the village's sanitary arrangements were 'in a very proper state'. One week later *A Radcliffeite* expressed contrary views to the editor in no uncertain terms:

> *Your visits to Radcliffe must have been few and far between, or you could not have put anything so foolish in your paper.... You will find an open ditch running through the middle of the village, and to this ditch run the drains of all the water closets of the place. In dry weather, particularly dry <u>warm</u> weather, people put their handkerchiefs to their noses and hurry past.*

Radcliffeite's remedy for this 'stinking evil' was to make a brick arch over the ditch, which could be done 'at a trifling cost'.

It can be no coincidence that at a vestry meeting held on January 26th 1860 it was agreed that 'it is absolutely necessary that the sewerage of Radcliffe be improved and the drain covered over as soon as possible'. This time George Beaumont, Lord Manvers' agent, led a committee to look into the matter. Subscriptions were to be collected and any shortfall made up by a rate. Perhaps it was the suggestion of cost which provoked further correspondence in the *Journal*. On March 2nd came a belated reply to *Radcliffeite* from *Veritas*, pointing out that there was already an inverted arch over the drain for some distance 'which answers admirably when it is attended to', and ridiculing the idea that the cost of covering the drain would be 'trifling'. It would lead to 'a reckless expenditure of public money, incurring a debt which would take a long time to liquidate'. The mortality rate averaged less than fourteen per thousand, he assured his readers, while if a handkerchief, cloak or shawl was held in Radcliffe, it was not to the nose but to the mouth, as a respirator in cold weather.

A week later *Ever-hope* added his views. While everyone agreed with *Veritas* that the drain could not be covered at a trifling cost, he supported *Radcliffeite's* comments about the insanitary state of the village in summer:

> *The whole place was tainted with a huge abomination; an open stagnant sewer receiving the sewerage of all the village and stinking horribly. Tastes are acquired, and many here are so used in summer to these things, they rather like it than otherwise; they have become acclimatised, seasoned as it were, to the nastiness of the place.*

Ever-hope also accepted the mortality figures given in *Veritas's* letter, but felt they had been 'given for a purpose to upset the present movement now in progress to cover up the ditch'. He added:

> *It is simply a matter of pounds, shillings and pence. Where it will fall heavily it is very natural they should suggest expedients, rather than face the expense at once. We have two or three good practical farmers who can drain their own farms on scientific principles, and could as easily have remedied the ditch, had they not feared to drain their own pockets at the same time.*

Despite, or because of, this vigorous correspondence the committee pushed ahead with its proposals. In April 1860 it was agreed that the drain should be 'inverted with a Staffordshire brick channel for the sewage and Bulwell slab stone sides', the channel to be one foot wide and the sides two feet wide. The material was to be purchased 'as cheaply as possible', and Samuel Bell, builder as well as keeper of the Manvers Arms, was to carry out the work. The exact length to be covered was still being decided by the Vestry on June 4th. By then £255.10s had been collected. How much the scheme finally cost is not known. Perhaps the rate in April 1861 'for the highways' - three times the normal figure - contributed to it. Over twenty years later, at the height of a much greater controversy, George Beaumont looked back with satisfaction at the achievements of his committee. 'They had good reason to be proud of their sewer, for it was an enormous improvement on the dirty old brook.' He had felt it would 'render Radcliffe famous for ever'. However proud he felt at the time, Radcliffe's drainage system was still far from adequate for a village with an increasing population and which was attracting vast numbers of visitors from Nottingham.

Smallpox vaccination
The smallpox outbreak which preceded the improvements to the drain in 1860 is not well documented. There is no reference to it in the Bingham Union minute book, but an epidemic affecting children is suggested by entries in the burial register for the second half of 1859. Out of nine burials between July 20th and December 31st only one was of an adult. The suggestion in the *Journal* that the outbreak was encouraged by neglect of vaccination is difficult to substantiate from surviving records. From 1840 Bingham Union had agreed that medical officers should vaccinate 'all who may apply'. Sessions in Radcliffe initially took place monthly, later quarterly, in Mrs Richmond's schoolroom. (In 1876 the vaccination station was in the house of Sarah Gee, a druggist and smallware dealer, who was paid 20s a year. In 1882 it was moved to the house of Sarah Fryer, a widow who ran the Royal Oak.) The vaccinator was paid 1s.6d for each successful case, and significant numbers of villagers availed themselves of the opportunity - fifty-seven out of a total of 241 for the whole of the west district in 1841. (At that time there were 119 from East Bridgford and twelve from Cotgrave.) In 1853 vaccination was made compulsory. Vaccination registers only exist from 1871, but from these it is clear

that by then almost all children, ranging from Lord Newark's son at Holme Pierrepont Hall to labourers' children on Holme Lane or at Spellow Farm, were being vaccinated by the end of their first year. The infants who died in the 1859 outbreak may well have been too young to be vaccinated. No evidence has been found to suggest that children died as a result of vaccination.

Between 1871 and 1898 out of a total of 1,302 Radcliffe vaccinations, 1,113 were recorded as successful. Of the remainder, fifty-two males and thirty-eight females died before being vaccinated. A further nineteen (thirteen males and six females) were issued with 'certificates of insusceptibility'. Fifty-six were not vaccinated locally because parents moved away. The rest possibly objected on principle, although they were not yet legally entitled to do so.

In 1870 such objectors formed an anti-vaccination society in London. Local objectors asked for Lord Newark's support in 1884, but the *Nottingham Journal* reported his rejection of their views and his firm belief in the good that vaccination had done. Not until 1898 did 'conscientious objectors' receive legal exemption. In that year twenty-two exemption certificates were issued for Radcliffe going back to 1885. Although Bingham Union then closed its local vaccination stations, there does not seem to have been an immediate drop in the public's acceptance of vaccination. Only three or four exemption certificates were issued each year until after the act of 1907 which confirmed conscientious objection and withdrew the stamp duty on exemption certificates. Then vaccinations dropped dramatically. In 1920, out of forty-four children listed in the vaccination register, only ten were recorded as having been successfully vaccinated.

Improvements 1860-1872

In the meantime, other routine health and sanitary matters continued to need attention. In 1863 another committee was appointed to see to the removal of nuisances, and as a result of a sanitary act of 1866 Richard Stone was paid £2 a year from 1868 to act as the village's sanitary inspector. After William Martin's death in 1870 the village continued to have resident doctors. (His widow even kept hold of his medical officer's post for a month.) The 1871 census return shows that his son Charles was then a medical student, while lodging in the household was John Adams, a qualified Irish surgeon who was to die in Ireland at the end of 1873. Other medical names briefly associated with Radcliffe around this time include a Dr Aitken in 1871 and Dr Robert Murdock who probably replaced Dr Adams. Robert Murdock left the area to join the ill-fated H.M.S. *Eurydice* in February 1877 which sank in the following year. He was drowned, along with all but two of the crew of four hundred. A plaque in the church commemorates his loss. After this time, John Ellam and Archibald Campbell became the resident practitioners.

Inevitably, the Syke Drain needed attention again by 1872. After protracted discussions at vestry meetings it was agreed that a section of the old culvert starting at the corner of the churchyard, where a trapdoor was to be fitted, and ending in 'Mr Gorse's field' was to be taken up and replaced with a new culvert four feet in diameter. The levels and outfall were also to be improved, and a loan was to be sought of £200 for a term of thirty to fifty years.

Bingham Rural Sanitary Authority

In 1871 the general Board of Health was replaced by the Local Government Board which now supervised both poor law and public health matters. By a public health act in the following year, poor law unions were empowered to act as rural sanitary authorities responsible to the new Local Government Board. The result was that often the same elected parish representatives now sat on two bodies acting in two different capacities. The Bingham guardians of the poor continued to handle poor law matters, including related health problems, while the Bingham Rural Sanitary Authority supervised health matters for the whole community, including sewage, drainage, nuisances, water supplies and epidemics. The two bodies each appointed their own officials and met consecutively once a fortnight in the workhouse board room in Bingham. Inevitably there was some overlap, partly because officials and representatives were often the same, and partly because the health of the poor affected the community as a whole. As separate minute books now had to be kept, however, a much fuller picture can be obtained of the state of public health locally.

Dr James Eaton

Although some existing officials were confirmed by the new sanitary body, Dr James Eaton of Bingham, medical officer of health responsible for the district around Radcliffe, was a fresh appointment. His salary of £100 a year was paid jointly by Bingham and the Local Government Board.

A colourful character, he was born in 1834, probably the son of a prosperous farmer at Saxondale. At the time of his appointment he was married with four young children and was Bingham's resident doctor. In 1875, by an overwhelming vote, he was also appointed medical officer to the workhouse by the poor law guardians. Almost immediately came the first signs of the unorthodox behaviour which was to lead to friction with the Local Government Board in London. The latter received a complaint from Dr Wooton, his predecessor at the workhouse, that he had been signing blank certificates in advance for vaccinations carried out in Radcliffe by Charles Martin (William's son) who was still unqualified. The Board insisted that Dr Eaton provide proof that the vaccinations had indeed been carried out, and issued an official reprimand. By 1876 his negligence in sending in reports to the Local Government Board led to threats that he would not be reappointed. In the following year he was requested to use his journal rather than slips of paper for his reports, and his attendance at meetings was irregular. In June 1878 the master of the workhouse complained about the long visits he made to the nurse's room with the door locked, while patients complained of neglect. A month later he was incapable of attending either the sanitary authority or poor law meetings, the chairman of the latter having seen him in a state of intoxication. He was forced to resign as medical officer to both the workhouse and the sanitary authority in September 1878, the posts being taken by Dr Wright of East Bridgford.

A lesser man would have been finished. It says a great deal for the charm of his personality that his Bingham Union friends soon rallied to his side. In 1879 he was made deputy medical officer to the workhouse, and was overwhelmingly re-elected to the full post when it again became vacant in 1881. The Local Government Board, however, refused to sanction this appointment on more than a temporary basis in 1882 (despite the fact that Bingham offered to pay his expenses themselves), in 1883 (when they refused to see a deputation on his behalf), or in 1884, although he was again appointed deputy in that year. It was a similar story with regard to the post of medical officer to the sanitary authority. In 1881 he and another candidate challenged Dr Wright's reappointment. Eaton and Wright tied on the first vote, but the latter was beaten on the second. Incredulously, the Local Government Board wrote to ask if this was the same Dr Eaton who had been removed for drunkenness and misconduct. On confirmation that it was, the Board refused to approve the appointment. This time Bingham was insistent, but the doctor had to be content with only the £50 half salary paid locally since the Board would not make up the rest. Although his eccentric behaviour continued, he was later to act in an exemplary and self-sacrificing manner in a time of crisis, and he was so respected in the Bingham community that the choir stalls near to the organ in the parish church were dedicated to his memory after his death in 1911.

Increasing problems 1874-1880

For much of the critical time that Radcliffe was about to face, Dr Eaton was the official medical representative of the Bingham authority. From a study of this body's sanitary minutes it does not appear that Radcliffe's sanitary condition or proneness to epidemics was any worse or any better than that of other parishes in the Union. Nor was the sanitary body particularly neglectful of its duties. The village's problems grew as its population increased - from 1,273 in 1851 to 1,704 by 1881, and an already inadequate sewerage system was never more than patched. The sanitary officials did as much as the parish asked of them. The fact that Radcliffe could never convincingly make up its mind what should be done, particularly when it came to paying, was perhaps the crux of the problem.

In November 1874 the Union's inspector of nuisances reported to the sanitary authority on the state, yet again, of Radcliffe's Syke Drain, recommending that it should be covered. The sanitary officials, determined to have the matter remedied, wanted the support of the parish, so a vestry meeting was called. It was then proposed that the whole of the old drain be taken up and the existing 4-foot culvert, presumably the section done in 1872, be extended from the church 'up to the bridge' across the turnpike road (close to where the police station was shortly to be built), provided the money could be borrowed by the Union. When the plans led to an application for a loan of £500 from the Local Government Board, Radcliffe's enthusiasm faded. By April 1875 Mr Green, Radcliffe's representative on the Bingham authority, was asking for the abandonment of the project. Instead, a new sewer should be created which could be paid for without having to raise a loan. The modest scale of this new scheme can be gauged by the fact that it cost £9.16s.4d instead of the original £500.

Throughout the Union,1876 was a bad year for disease. Dr Eaton reported on cases in Radcliffe of scarlet fever, smallpox, and typhoid fever, including one fatal case of the latter. Premises were cleansed and well water was checked. The inspector of nuisances, however, found little on which to report - a filthy privy and ashpit in the Royal Oak Yard, one nuisance on Station Street (the lower end of Shelford Road), and the need for the outfall of the sewer into the Trent to be cleansed. Records for 1877 and 1878 again showed little need for alarm.

By this stage the impact of the Public Health Act of 1875, by which local sanitary authorities were given powers to enforce regulations relating to drainage, sanitation and water supplies, was being felt in Radcliffe. The village had been doing its sums again and decided that it was paying too much in rates for the services supplied by Bingham Union. At a public meeting held in the schoolroom in November 1879, reported by the *Nottingham Journal*, resentment was expressed at having to contribute to the whole district. James Gorse, the prosperous hosiery yarn agent living at the Manor House, felt that 'Radcliffe people had much to gain and nothing to lose by ridding themselves of the present association with other parishes, some of which were very sleepy indeed...' Under the 1875 act Radcliffe should apply to be an independent local government board so that it could run its own affairs efficiently and cheaply. If Arnold and Beeston, he argued, had been able to improve their sanitary arrangements and mortality rate by such means there was no reason why Radcliffe could not benefit similarly.

On paper Bingham sanitary authority adopted a neutral stance to Radcliffe's request to the Local Government Board in London for independence. In practice Bingham could not have been enthusiastic about the prospect of losing one of its main ratepaying parishes. When an inquiry was held before a Local Government Board inspector in February 1880 'several charges of negligence' were made against the Bingham authority, but in the end Radcliffe's request was rejected, mainly because the population was too small. It would, however, be possible for 'urban powers' to be conferred on Bingham respecting Radcliffe, which would mean that Bingham Union would have greater control over the village, particularly through planning applications and building regulations. This was not at all what Radcliffe had had in mind.

More immediately, the combination of criticisms at the local inquiry and the temporary replacement of Dr Eaton by a more zealous medical officer of health led to an inspection of the village in February 1880. It was found that ten properties required additional privy accommodation. Only three of these were owned by residents of the village, perhaps an indication of why it was difficult to enforce improvements. Drains on one other property needed attention, and inevitably a stretch of the Syke Drain needed covering, this time for a distance of about twenty yards on Radcliffe Hill - today's Bingham Road. With further work on open drains on both Bingham and Cropwell roads during 1880, and some other routine improvements up to August 1881, the village should have been put into a sound sanitary state.

The scarlet fever epidemic of 1881-2

There could have been no preparation for what was to come. In October 1881 an outbreak of scarlet fever was to set in motion a train of events which shattered any complacency, aroused intense feelings and had the village in uproar by the middle of 1882. It is impossible to do full justice to the complexities of the story in the space available, but an outline has been put together from the burial register, the 1881 census return, the school log book, the sanitary authority minutes, and, above all, from the pages of the *Nottingham Journal*.

In health matters the year began routinely enough with the usual crop of diseases, including scarlet fever, reported throughout the Union. In February two cases were reported from Thoroton. In March there were eight cases, including three at Radcliffe. Out of twenty cases in May, sixteen were in the Bingham workhouse. Only seven cases were officially reported in September and October. None was in Radcliffe.

The first hint of anything unusual in the village is found in the log book of James Browne, Radcliffe's schoolmaster. On October 31st he noted that several cases of scarlet fever had occurred, though at some distance from the school. Four days later the school was closed for a month because of the outbreak. The need for this is made only partially plain in the sanitary authority minutes:

November 3   *1 case at Bingham, cases at the homes of William Speed*
               and Thomas Bradley - all progressing satisfactorily

November 17   *1 death at Bingham, 32 cases in Radcliffe and 2 deaths*

Although the number of cases cannot be assessed accurately, it is clear that the position was far worse than that indicated in the minute book. The Radcliffe outbreak had begun in a labourer's cottage occupied by the Speed family on Spellow Farm near Saxondale. By the time Dr Eaton, now reinstated as medical officer, was reporting to the meeting on November 3rd that all cases were progressing satisfactorily, 11-year-old Harriet Speed was dead. Her 4-year-old sister Mary was buried on November 6th, and another sister and two brothers were to die in the epidemic. At a farm on the other side of the Bingham road Thomas Bradley's 11-year-old son was dead by November 13th. Altogether in November the names of eight children aged between two and eleven appear in the burial register. The census return indicates that the disease had travelled down the Bingham road to the main part of the village. As early as November 19th a small item appeared in the *Nottingham Journal* making the medically unsound link between the unsatisfactory sanitary state of Radcliffe and the prevalence of scarlet fever.

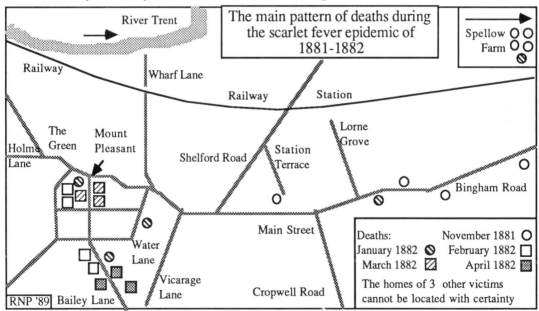

December brought a respite. By then the Bingham sanitary authority had distributed two-hundred leaflets giving advice on how to deal with and prevent the disease. At their meeting on December 1st it was reported that four other families had been affected, but the cases were described as mild and Dr Eaton thought the epidemic was declining. On December 5th the village school reopened, but the attendance was low. Later, this reopening was to be blamed for the spread of a second wave of infection.

The first Radcliffe death of 1882 was that of 6-year-old George Speed on January 4th. In January and February Dr Eaton reported a significant number of cases and deaths throughout the Union, but Radcliffe was the worst affected until March, when both Keyworth and Shelford were hard hit. Between January and early April eighteen Radcliffe children died, aged between four months and nine years. The last isolated case in the village was reported to the sanitary meeting on June 29th. By then a clear pattern to the disease had emerged. The victims lived mainly in the poorer areas of the village and their fathers were mainly labourers. Bailey Lane, Back Lane (now Water Lane), the Green and especially Mount Pleasant were at the centre of the epidemic. Like the Speeds at Spellow Farm, several families suffered more than one bereavement: the Walkers lost four daughters aged between one and four years; the Kirkhams lost three children; the Caunts, and the Richmonds each lost two.

John Cullen's letter

On February 24th the school had been closed for the second time and did not reopen until May 8th. Early in March the vicar, John Cullen, distressed at having to preside over the burials of so many young children, decided to take matters into his own hands. He wrote directly to the Local Government Board in London asking them to take action about the sanitary condition of Radcliffe. Unwittingly he was responsible for turning a tragedy into farce and making Radcliffe the laughing stock of the county. On March 25th the Local Government Board wrote to the Bingham Rural Sanitary Authority, enclosing a copy of the vicar's letter, and asking what means they had taken to stop the spread of the disease in Radcliffe. As a result, Bingham asked Herbert Walker, a civil engineer from Nottingham, to inspect and report on Radcliffe's sewers. He did so in the company of Dr Eaton, Edward Arnesby (the inspector of nuisances), and several residents of the village. The unjustified link between the epidemic and the inadequate sewerage system had been irretrievably forged.

II. The village and the *Journal*

Herbert Walker's report

Herbert Walker presented his report to the Bingham meeting of April 20th 1882. It was a devastating indictment of the sanitary state of Radcliffe. After describing the route and existing culverting of the Syke Drain, and the route of another sewer which drained the Lamcote area, he condemned the artificial dykes by which sewage and storm water were taken from these drains to the Trent as being 'in an offensive condition'. In the other direction, the drain passed under Dr Ellam's house (Granville House at the corner of Lorne Grove and Bingham Road), the covered part ending immediately beyond Lorne Grove. When the wind was in the west, the smell was most offensive. He found that sewers in Cropwell Road, Lorne Grove and Bailey Lane lacked ventilation or means of inspection. In general the contents of drains were allowed to percolate into the adjacent wells. Soil pipes from water closets and waste pipes in newly built houses near the station went straight into drains without ventilation. In Clarke's Yard sewage percolated between paving stones and soaked under house floors. In the rear were middens full of manure and garbage. At Widows' Row there was an objectionable arrangement of two privies and an ashpit used by about thirty persons. The drains in Butt Green, Thraves Yard, Sheppards Row and Mount Pleasant were in most cases nearly choked with filth. The last area came in for particular condemnation:

> At Mount Pleasant I saw the most disgusting closet arrangement it has ever been my lot to witness. It consists of a small place entered direct from the street, taken out of the living room of two cottages. The boarded floor is movable, and forms a dry ashpit or receptacle for the combined garbage of the neighbourhood, while the excreta, instead of being mixed with the ashes is conducted by means of a 'shoot' into a deep panterpit or well in the street, which I am told has not been emptied for years. The condition of this place and the noxious gases which escape therefrom is beyond description. The

room over is occupied by the tenant of the adjoining cottage as a sleeping room, and it has no means of ventilation except the window, which is immediately over the abomination before mentioned.

Houses on Mount Pleasant in the early twentieth century

Herbert Walker's solution to these ills was to use the powers provided by the 1875 Public Health Act to force all defaulting property owners to provide proper privy and ashpit accommodation. The authority should also appoint someone to remove nightsoil regularly and to cleanse privies and ashpits. Owners of private property should be compelled to do away with 'the present apologies for drains' and substitute efficient ones. The main culvert of the Syke Drain should be continued by public authorities, and where it crossed private property the owners should be compelled to conform.

The report was not widely circulated at first, but Bingham had copies printed and sent to each guardian. Consideration was delayed for a fortnight, and then another fortnight, so that Radcliffe could first hold a public meeting to discuss its contents. This meeting was duly reported in the *Journal* on May 20th. The vicar presided, supported by John Taylor of Radcliffe Hall, William Sanday of Cliff House and J.G. Willey, Radcliffe's guardian on the sanitary body. Much of the meeting was spent in a lengthy discussion of the relative merits of Radcliffe becoming a local board (already rejected by the inquiry of 1880), and the exercising of 'urban powers' by Bingham. Most of those present seemed to be against either course, and speakers in favour of the local board idea were frequently interrupted. (Such opposition was undoubtedly caused by the fear that rates and rents would rise.) Eventually a more constructive point was reached when it was decided to ask the Bingham authority to remedy the various defects described in Herbert Walker's report. The meeting was then adjourned for a week until Tuesday May 23rd. The wheels of local reform were turning very slowly - far too slowly as far as the *Nottingham Journal* was concerned.

May 23rd: the first *Journal* leader

On the morning of the meeting Radcliffe awoke to find that its sewage problems had been widely publicised in a long leading article in the *Journal*. (The paper, run by the Bradshaw family, was available in the village from 6.30 a.m. at George Turner's post office.) The article began innocently enough with an extract from Wright's *Directory* drawing attention to the picturesque scenery and 'improving' nature of the village. After (unfairly) blaming the village for its failure to acquire a local government board at the time of the inquiry two years before, and suggesting that there had been an epidemic in that year, the writer then castigated those poorer villagers who 'on fully considering the matter, came to the conclusion that, taking everything into account, it was cheaper, healthier, wiser, better, to have scarlet fever, diphtheria and typhoid.' The *Journal* then made plain its reasons for starting a campaign against Radcliffe:

> *If Radcliffe-on-Trent were completely isolated from the rest of the world, no sensible person could possibly object to the speedy decrease of that portion of the 1,700 intelligent Radcliffe people who do not want to stir into their stinks or make an end to them. But Radcliffe-on-Trent is close to a large town, is a constant resort of pleasure seekers, at holiday times and other times, and while it is a source of dangerous infection it may do harm to its neighbours all round. Added to this 'intelligent Radcliffe people' invite Nottingham persons who love pure air, pure water and romantic scenery to come and settle among them. While the drainage is what it is, how can Nottingham people do so with safety to themselves, or to all belonging to them?*

On these grounds there was undoubtedly some justification for the *Journal* taking Radcliffe to task rather than East Bridgford, Whatton or any number of other villages with sanitary problems. Advertisements in the *Journal's* own columns showed that the village had been enjoying a building boom, while the number of weekend and holiday visitors was enormous - 2,000 by train alone on Whit Monday 1881 - and the next bank holiday was only a week away.

The leader writer, however, was only just getting into his stride. He turned next to the argumentative meeting which had been held a week previously:

> *They used the stale old argument of the folk who always oppose sanitary reform if it means taking a few pence out of their pockets - 'I have lived all my life in the midst of these stinks, **I** am none the worse for them, why should anybody else? They have never harmed **me**, why should they, how can they harm others? There is a beautiful simplicity in such reasoning, but in the teeth of Mr Walker's report to the Bingham Rural Sanitary Authority, how can we attach any importance to it? Radcliffe people do not want to know anything of the dangers they run; but Nottingham pleasure hunters, who do not wish to catch scarlatina, or diphtheria, or typhoid fever, if they take our advice, will find their pleasure elsewhere than at Radcliffe - that is to say, until the drainage is seen to.*

Herbert Walker's report was then dealt with in detail. Extracts were quoted, interspersed with the writer's own ironic comments. It was 'cheering to know' that the main drain passed under the house occupied by Dr Ellam. Another aspect was exhilarating for those unfortunate people who went to Radcliffe 'in search of pure air'. Singled out for special mention were 'Mount Pleasant!!' and Widow's Row - the latter 'so called, we suppose, because all the husbands had been killed off by the stenches.' Readers were spared the details about the most disgusting closet arrangement at Mount Pleasant. 'As some of our readers have a spell at their newspapers at breakfast time, in mercy to them we do not copy it.'

After further condemnation of the attitude of Radcliffe working men the article concluded ominously:

> *We have only one word to say to the 'intelligent' working people of Radcliffe, which is this: that until they attend to their drains as they ought to be*

attended to we promise faithfully, so far as lies in our power, to keep public attention directed to the sanitary condition of an unhealthy village which is a constant danger to the large town which has the ill luck to be near it. Till Radcliffe drainage and Radcliffe water are made better it will be wise if Nottingham pleasure seekers keep clear of Radcliffe. If public opinion and public disgust can work through no other channels, they can work through this channel. Let us remember that this goodly apple is rotten at the core - that there is death lurking in those pleasant rural cottages at Mount Pleasant and Widows' Row, and that Radcliffe-on-Trent unless it improves its drainage will soon get the nickname of Radcliffe-on-Sewer.

The ratepayers' meeting

The village was outraged. That evening the schoolroom was packed for the adjourned meeting. John Taylor of Radcliffe Hall was called on to preside, and he began by announcing that the Bingham authority did not seem willing to agree to a request that they should force Radcliffe owners to remove nuisances from their properties without acquiring urban powers. At this point Thomas Kell got to his feet. As a comparative newcomer to Radcliffe who ran the Black Lion he saw his trade threatened by the tone of the *Journal* leader. He raised a much more burning issue than urban powers. The meeting ought to insist on knowing who the author of this 'wicked and infamous thing' was. He was very much 'grieved' about it. Applause and 'hear hear' greeted these sentiments. John Taylor agreed, but pointed out that this was not the subject of the meeting. Thomas Kell was not to be deterred. 'We must find it out; I call upon this meeting to insist on it.' He was supported by a ratepayer who asserted that the article contained a lot of untruths.

Temporarily the meeting became sufficiently calm to listen to the real business in hand. J. George Willey, the village's representative on the Bingham sanitary body, reported how at their meeting on May 18th, despite Radcliffe's opposition, the proposal to apply for urban powers over Radcliffe had been carried. Thomas Kell was on his feet again. This showed that they had been unfairly treated by Bingham, he claimed. They should go for a local government board. It was doubtless a ratepayer who felt that this was the worse of the two evils who told him to 'Shut up.' A succession of Radcliffe worthies now expressed their views. Mr Wright, the village carrier, was 'somewhat incoherent' but assured the meeting that 'Radcliffe was right enough if the people in it were right'. Samuel Barratt, the younger of two nurserymen brothers, read extracts from the article, describing it as 'a tissue of lies'. He claimed that the worst cases were out of the village, and though he was in favour of a local board under very strict management, he did not believe that the rates would not go up. He alleged that there had been an enormous rise at Beeston. Both he and Richard Daft, the cricketer, agreed that the author of the article should be made known. Both men could point to defective drainage and disease in Nottingham. An unidentified ratepayer observed that he did not think there was better water in England than they had in Radcliffe, and if people would keep dung out of the sewage the supply would be better still. ('Hear hear', and laughter.)

At this point someone noticed the presence of a *Journal* reporter. 'Some confusion ensued.' Thomas Kell 'insisted that the meeting had a right to have from the reporter some explanation of the article in that day's *Journal*'. There was agreement from all parts of the room. The besieged reporter appealed to the chairman against 'this most unusual conduct'. He had no knowledge of, and was not responsible for, what appeared in the editorial columns. Even if he had he would decline to give information to the meeting. At this, there was a mixture of applause and advice that he should leave. George Parr (almost certainly not the cricketer) came to the reporter's aid. While feeling that the paper 'was always rather sharp on public matters' and no one present could agree with the article, the meeting was being unfair to the reporter, and the article was nothing to do with the purpose of the meeting. Although he personally was in favour of a local board he hoped nobody thought he had anything to do with the article. The reporter suggested that Mr Kell, who was on his feet again, should call on the editor of the *Journal* for any information. Dr Ellam and Samuel Barratt supported this idea.

When Dr Ellam asked for an explanation of exactly what urban powers would mean, resentment of the Bingham authority came to the fore. It would mean that all

209

the orders would come from Bingham. Everybody who wanted to build would have to submit all their plans to Bingham before they could lay a brick. One voice called, 'What they ought to have done sooner.' Samuel Bell, a builder as well as keeper of the Manvers Arms, was against urban powers. He wanted yet another meeting to consider whether a local board should be applied for. The attractions of this had already been explained: it would be elected by the parish 'who surely ought to know what was required better than farmers who lived here, there and everywhere'. Costs were then assessed. It was reckoned that average outgoings were £356 per year at present. Under a local board they could be £70 a year less. Not everyone was convinced. Jacob Gee, a tailor, moved an amendment which he said consisted of three words only: 'No local board.' As he could not find a seconder his resolution was withdrawn and Samuel Bell's was carried. The report of the meeting concluded that it had been 'conducted in a most irregular manner'. Immediately afterwards one attender was arrested for drunkenness and fined a guinea at the Bingham sessions two days later.

Reaction in the *Journal*

The report of the meeting appeared in the *Journal* on the Wednesday and was repeated on the Friday and Saturday. The reaction to it, and to the leading article, was swift. Villagers, and others, reached for their pens and filled the paper's correspondence columns with their views, albeit largely anonymously. Dr Ellam was one of the first into print on the Thursday. Aged about 60, and originally from Ashbourne, he was the elder of the two village doctors and had been in Radcliffe for about six years. He had previously lived in Chestnut Grove but was currently occupying Granville House. Arguing that the village had been unfairly attacked in the *Journal*, he denied that there had been an epidemic two years previously. (The only evidence found to substantiate the paper's claim is from the burial register. Five burials took place between August 17th and October 23rd 1880. All were of babies.) The place was on the whole salubrious and healthy, but he acknowledged that there were 'sanitary defects that can easily be remedied.' After outlining the circumstances which had led to Herbert Walker being called in, he corrected the

Granville House at the corner of Lorne Grove and Bingham Road
occupied by Dr Ellam in 1882

error that the main drain passed under his house. The stream, he said, passed through a brick culvert under his garden. (Five months later he was to return home from Birmingham to find his garden walls swept away and the house endangered by flood water from that drain. After protracted court proceedings, the owner of the house was awarded damages from the sanitary authority for negligence in the siting of a grating.) Claiming that there were other statements in the article for which there was not the slightest foundation, Dr Ellam wanted his letter published 'to disabuse the minds of the public on this subject'.

Looker-on was more sympathetic to the *Journal*. After ridiculing the 'idiotic resolution' that a deputation should wait on the editor to find out who was responsible for the leading article - whether they went is not known - he concluded, 'It's time we had a little daylight let into Radcliffe. Keep your eye on it please.' Robert Porter of Beeston, a frequent writer of letters to the editor, felt sure that those who knew Mr Walker would believe his report before random statements at an excited parish meeting. He took great exception to Samuel Barratt's claim that Beeston rates and borrowing had greatly increased because of their improvements. 'In an experience of half a century I do not recall a grosser or more deliberate lie.' He demanded that Samuel Barratt should apologise to Beeston. A pedantic letter from *An Inquirer* laboured the joke about Radcliffe-on-Sewer and its derivation. Far wittier was a poem entitled *Those Radcliffe drains* in which *A Man with a Nose* regretted the ending of his visits to Radcliffe as he was no longer able to endure the smell.

May 25th: the *Journal's* second leader

The *Journal's* own response on the same Thursday was to produce another leading article:

> ...We are surprised to hear that our remarks have not been favourably received by the 'intelligence' of Radcliffe. Indignant Radcliffe ratepayers have so far lost all sense of decency or the fitness of things as to call them a 'tissue of lies' etc. etc.... They do not like any more than others to hear plain truth in plain language. While Mr Walker's observations were entombed in his report to the Bingham Rural Sanitary Authority, no hints were made as to their truthfulness or otherwise; but the moment we, from a sincere but probably foolish, desire to hinder Radcliffe folks from drinking sewage or inhaling sewer gas, draw attention to Mr Walker's statements, then they become untruthful.... Mr Walker, if proved to be in error, will, no doubt go into repentant sackcloth and ashes and sit upon any romantic Radcliffe dunghill (if there **are** such things as dunghills in Radcliffe) the ratepayers may select; and so shall we. But if Radcliffe is in an unsavoury condition - it is as well to be quite frank - the fear of offending the inhabitants of Radcliffe will not hinder us from saying what we please, as we please, and when we please upon sources of public danger to public health.
>
> Our advice to the good folks of Radcliffe, including the very intelligent person who is wise enough to suggest that, all things considered, it is perhaps as well to keep excreta out of your water supply, can be set down in a very few words. If their village is unhealthy, ill-drained, has defective sanitary arrangements, let these matters be seen to at once. There is such a thing as penny-wisdom in the world which objects to what ought to be spent to make sanitary matters perfect.... It is no use Radcliffe people being sensitive to criticism. Excessive sensitiveness will not dig drains for them, or improve their wells. They should remember with all humility the truth of the old scriptural saying that 'He that hateth reproof is brutish.' Let them take that to heart.

This mixture of irony, self-righteousness and authoritarian advice did nothing to soothe public opinion in the village.

May 26th and 27th: more poems and letters

On Friday May 26th three more letters were published, as well as a poem signed by *Screech Owl* narrating the events at the parish meeting of May 23rd. The first correspondent, *A Radcliffe Man*, supported the paper and could not understand why Dr Ellam wrote his letter. 'He does not see, poor man, that he is proving all you said about Radcliffe stinks.' The writer added that the village could be put into a good sanitary state 'if the ratepayers were not such noddle-heads. For Heaven's sake keep pegging away at them...' he urged. *A Native* supported *Looker-on* in condemning the resolution requiring the name of the author of the first leader, and praised George Parr for his courageous defence of the reporter. He then blamed the Bingham authority for Radcliffe's plight:

> What have the gentlemen of Bingham ever done? The reply is that they have distributed a few packets of Condy's fluid through their inspector of nuisances, but as to remedying the grave defects of drainage they have systematically avoided that part of the difficulty. I think it is time the proceedings of the sanitary authority were brought to light, especially with reference to a recent appointment of a medical officer of health.

This was an oblique criticism of the reinstatement of Dr Eaton.

The third letter that day was from an anonymous old resident who had been actively engaged in the 'healthfulness' of Radcliffe. He pointed out that the village had been sufficiently alive to the importance of Herbert Walker's report to call the vestry meeting. He confirmed that urban powers worked by Bingham were not wanted, but he felt that more control of their own affairs was. 'We think their love is not an unselfish one, and that we are old enough to walk without leading strings.' He was the first writer to note that it was not so much the main drainage that had been condemned, but conditions on private property. It had been the sanitary body's responsibility to deal with this. The parishioners had paid their charges, and their village had been neglected, 'causing many a blank on a kitchen hearth, where but a few months ago the merry laughter of loving children was heard'. He was sure that so progressive a place as Radcliffe would soon remedy any defects, and concluded with a short complimentary poem which advocated cautious spending.

On the Saturday came another letter from Dr Ellam, offended at the carping of *A Radcliffe Man* about his original letter. He defied him to prove that Radcliffe people drank nothing but sewage. The village would have been decimated by typhoid if that had been the case. The doctor's aim had only been to point out that the writer of the first leader had been misled. He did not deny that the *Journal* had the right to comment on Radcliffe's doings, and he would not trouble the paper again. His letter was followed by a lively poem summarising events in the mode of *This is the house that Jack built*, in which he was featured. *An Odorous Ode* on the same day began, 'Sing a song of sewage', and dwelt on Radcliffe's 'four and twenty stenches.'

The village's growing notoriety was humorously taken advantage of by the writer of a regular series of articles on 'Some Nottinghamshire Villages'. He explained to the editor the reason for his unexpected coverage of Radcliffe, and recalled a violent incident in the village's past:

> .... at this present moment, sir, when public interest has been diverted from the Irish question and the Egyptian imbroglio, to be concentrated on the course of Radcliffe sewage, your readers will probably devour with some eagerness, anything that may be said regarding this remarkable village. If my description is imperfect; if I have neglected to poke my nose into the drains of Radcliffe, to ascertain to what extent its water supply is contaminated with the refuse of the crew yard and the stable, you, sir, are to blame. ...Are you aware, sir, that the parish is indignant. .....you have mortally offended every interest, but especially that of the publican, and the parish has decided to call at your office, and on the point of the pitchfork, and by all the powers of Bacchus to demand an apology....; it is no use trying to throw oil on such violently agitated waters as these. They are desperate people down there, and it is my duty to put you, sir, on your guard. They once burnt in effigy old Stephen Radcliffe, the founder of the church. ..... Neither the publican nor the churchwarden would tell me in what form vengeance would be taken, but .... I think it would be well to have a manual fire engine on the premises for the next few days....

THOSE RADCLIFFE DRAINS,
THOSE RADCLIFFE DRAINS
(Vide Mr. Herbert Walker's report upon the (?)
sanitary conditions of Radcliffe-upon-Trent)

Those Radcliffe drains, those Radcliffe drains,
How in my nose their scent remains.
Where'er I go, what e'er I see,
Foul Radcliffe sewage follows me.
For health I seek the heathery hills,
Far, far from doctors and from pills;
For health I seek the flowery plains -
No use - I smell the Radcliffe drains;
I dive in woods - in vain, in vain,
E'en there I meet the Radcliffe drain.
                        Those Radcliffe drains.

Whoe'er admires a loathsome smell
Let him at Radcliffe choose to dwell.
Pure water has its praises sung.
Is Radcliffe water mixed with dung?
What Earthly Paradise below
Vies with the charms of Widows' Row?
To beat the 'Jockey Club' is hard -
But, ah! the scents of Bennet's Yard!
Sweet rural airs! one vigour gains
With fragrance from those Radcliffe drains,
                        Those Radcliffe drains.

When e'er on pleasure I am bent,
I often walk the banks of Trent,
When rides the sun in cloudless sky,
For shades of Radcliffe then I sigh.
I've trampled through the daisied lea,
To have at Radcliffe pipe and tea.
Now, now, alas! such pleasure's past.
Last trip to Radcliffe *was* my last;
I love not stinks as pigs love grains.
I cannot face those Radcliffe drains.
                        Those Radcliffe drains.

(To be continued weekly until improvements
are made)

A MAN WITH A NOSE

(Printed in the *Nottingham Journal*
May 25th 1882)

---oooOOOooo---

RADCLIFFE RAMPANT
or
THE PARISH AND THE JOURNAL

Trent siders, Trent siders,
To the eyes of outsiders
Your fury and words are amusing,
Your impotent passion
Will bring but the lash on
More keenly - 'the Press' you're abusing.

Thomas K--l, Thomas K--l,
You go 'at it' pell mell,
Your speech is devoid of all reason.
Yours vision's obscure, man,
You'll fall in the sew'r, man,
And lose yourself, quite for the 'season'.

Mr Chairman, Mr Chairman,
Come let us be fair, man,
And find out this 'infamous thing;'
'Who's done it, who's done it?'
We won't let him shun it,
To justice the rascal we'll bring.

Thomas K--l, Thomas K--l,
Your words how they 'tell'
The 'cause' of your 'temper' we know it,
Your 'craft' is in danger,
Your 'grief' and your anger
And the 'thing' how all of them show it.

Bingham Board, Bingham Board,
Ye are but a 'horde'
Of 'farmers' who keep us on 'worrit',
Our village so charming
Ye are but all harming,
While the stench rises still as we 'stir it'.

George W-l-y, George W-l-y,
You're far from being silly,
And it's well there's some sense left among you,
But the 'article's' up,
And Tom K--l's a bit rough,
His 'bark' may 'annoy' but won't wrong you.

Carrier Wr---t, Carrier Wr---t,
Says that 'Radcliffe's all right'
'Tis the 'people' that's all gone astray -
If 'they'd' mind their soundings
And cleanse their surroundings
They'd soon drive the stenches away.

Mr Bar---t, Mr Bar---t,
You're up in a garret,
When you talk about getting to know
Who wrote all the 'tissue
Of lies' in the issue
Of the *Journal* but three days ago.

Mr. Bar---t, Mr. Bar---t,
Whatever you are at,
Beware of statistical statement,
Friend Porter of Beeston
Today puts no jest on -
He 'nails you' and makes no abatement.

Richard D--t, Richard D--t,
You're a gent, 'fore and aft',
But the 'article' bothers your mind.
Comparing smallpox
Is not orthodox,
For comparisons are odious you'll find.

Ratepayer, ratepayer
Comes out with a 'flayer',
The water's as good as can be,
And 'twould be far better
If out of the 'water'
You'd keep all the dunging', says he.

Reporter, reporter
You got in a 'sorter'
A 'kinder' o' scrape or a 'bustle',
Irrepressible K--l
Would screw you to 'tell'
And was almost inclined for a 'tussle'.

Geordie P--r, Geordie P--r,
Now appears in the war,
And sensibly looks on the matter;
Though the *Journal* was 'sharp'
They must not fret and carp
And reporters not 'assault and batter'.

Irrepressible K--l'
In the fire again fell
In his zeal for his parish adopted,
The 'article' wrote,
How it sticks in his throat,
'Twere better by far he had dropped it.

Trent siders, Trent siders
As mutual confiders,
Hear now Messrs Bar---t and El--m,
Let the parish all go
In processional show,
To the 'office' in street they call Pelham.

SCREECH OWL

(Printed in the *Nottingham Journal*
May 26th 1882)

---oooOOOooo---

213

Radcliffe is:-

> The pride of the country
> Her home by the Trent;
> Unsurpassed her salubriety,
> With her money WELL spent.
> Her fine hills and her river
> Show great beauties around,
> And to all who may seek her
> Good health should be found.
> By 'well' is meant wisely,
> And all will agree,
> That a penny in wisdom
> Stops a pound that may flee.

AN OLD RESIDENT

(printed in the *Nottingham Journal*
May 26th 1882)

- - - oooOOOooo - - -

RADCLIFFE-ON-SEWER

This is the village of Radcliffe.

This is the doctor that cures all the ills
That abound in the village of Radcliffe.

These are the stenches, the vapours and smells
That rise from the drains, that flavour the wells,
That make busy the doctor, that cures all the ills
That abound in the village of Radcliffe.

Here's the Surveyor, precise and exact,
Who the cause, with true science, has carefully
tracked
Of all the vile stenches, the vapours and smells
That rise from the drains, that flavour the wells
That make busy the doctor etc. etc.

And here's the report all written so fair
About 'traps' and 'drains' and smells everywhere,
By the Surveyor, precise and exact,
Who the cause, with true science, has carefully
tracked
Of all the vile stenches, etc. etc.

And this is the *Journal* that never would flag
In 'letting the cat jump out of the bag'
About the report all written so fair
About 'traps' and 'drains' and smells everywhere,
By the Surveyor, etc. etc.

And here's the Reporter, steadfast and true,
Who would not be bullied to tell what he knew
Of what's writ in the *Journal* that never will flag
In 'letting the cat jump out of the bag'
About the report etc. etc.

And here's the 'parochial' meeting they hold
In Radcliffe insisting that they shall be told
Who'd written that 'infamous' horrible article
Which did not contain of truth e'en a particle.

But then the Reporter so steadfast and true
Would not be bullied to tell what he knew
Of what's writ in the *Journal* that never will flag
In 'letting the cat jump out of the bag'
About the report all written so fair
About 'traps' and 'drains' and smells everywhere,
By the Surveyor, precise and exact,
Who the cause with true science has carefully
tracked
Of all the vile stenches, the vapours and smells
That rise from the drains, that flavour the wells,
That make busy the doctor, that cures all the ills
That abound in the village of Radcliffe.

SLOW AND SEWER

(Printed in the *Nottingham Journal*
May 27th 1882)

AN ODOROUS ODE

Sing a song of sewage -
    Radcliffe's filthy drains.
Cause of scarlet fevers
    Easily explains.

Sing a song of sewage -
    Sewage in the wells;
Four and twenty stenches,
    Eight and forty smells.

If the wells were opened,
    Lord! there'd be a stink -
This, say Radcliffe idiots,
    Is the stuff we drink.

True we have the fever
    Up and down the street;
True the vilest odours
    Everywhere you meet.

Don't put down the stinkage
    Meat and drink to us -
Folks don't die o' sewage.
    Dash your pant and fuss.

Scents we most delight in,
    With us night and day,
Oh! delicious fragrance,
    Take it not away.

Sing a song of sewage
    Rates for penance sent -
Stand and fall by stinkage,
    Radcliffe by the Trent.

Sing a song of sewage -
    Eight and forty stinks -
Radcliffe man breathes perfume,
    Dungy water drinks.

ANOTHER MAN WITH A NOSE

(Printed in the *Nottingham Journal*
May 27th 1882)

The rest of the article took a more conventional topographical line.

May 29th to 31st: visitors, doctors and the report

Radcliffe must have been relieved that the *Nottingham Journal* was not produced on a Sunday, but the respite was only temporary. On May 29th - Whit Monday - *Nemo* took up the cudgels on Radcliffe's behalf. As a resident of the village he objected to the 'drivels and lies' published in the paper. He refuted the suggestion of any epidemic two years previously, asked how the start of the scarlet fever epidemic so far outside the centre of the village could be attributed to the 'stinks' of Radcliffe, asserted that the poorer members of the village had not objected to the formation of a local board, and (rightly) pointed out that it was the Local Government Board in London who had decided that Radcliffe did not need a local board. He then posed the question which many a Radcliffe resident must have been asking - why of all the villages around Nottingham had Radcliffe been held up as an example of everything which was foul and unhealthy? The answer, already indicated by the *Journal*, lay in the publication the next day of the number of visitors who had come to Radcliffe by train on that bank holiday Monday. There were 1,500, five-hundred fewer than on the same day the previous year. The effect of the publicity perhaps had had some effect and Thomas Kell's fears about loss of trade were temporarily justified.

Dr Campbell, Radcliffe's second doctor, felt obliged to defend the village on the Tuesday. A keen games player, he like Dr Ellam had been in Radcliffe about six years. He felt that the *Journal* had quoted most unfairly from the least favourable parts of Herbert Walker's report. The epidemic had been imported and the village could compare favourably with any other in the neighbourhood. 'Children coming from Nottingham to this district very soon improve in general health, which, I think, is sufficiently indicative of the salubriousness and healthy condition of the place.' To refute Dr Campbell's charge of bias, the *Journal* printed Herbert Walker's report in full on the next day. Readers throughout the midlands were now able to assess Radcliffe's cause of discomfiture for themselves.

Two further letters appeared in Wednesday's edition. A 'Radcliffe Visitor' took both Dr Campbell and Dr Ellam to task, the latter for claiming that outsiders were wrong to say that Radcliffe people drank sewage, when Herbert Walker's report had specifically said that sewage percolated into the wells. The writer then condemned the 'unasylumned lunatics' who said that other villages were as bad, but their sanitary arrangements were not of such concern. 'Nottingham folk don't flock to those other villages as they flock to Radcliffe; don't lodge there; don't build houses there.' He then berated Dr Campbell for saying that the epidemic was imported. 'How does Dr Campbell know it was imported? Dose he want us to believe that Radcliffe, having sewage in its wells, and stenches in its streets, imports the epidemic as it imports its groceries?'

May 31st to June 2nd: controversy over the school

A new dimension was added to the controversy by the second correspondent of the day - *Nemo Secundus*. He criticised *Nemo* for his accusation of lies and drivel in the original leader. No one could deny there were smells in Radcliffe. The only question was whether they were harmful and what could be done about them. In the writer's opinion the recent epidemic was caused through lack of care:

Shortly after the fever first appeared the National School was for a time closed. After about a month, it was re-opened, and would you believe it, sir, that children who had been recently attacked were allowed to attend and thus spread the disease among the rest.

He pointed out that the infectious desquamating period for scarlet fever could last for eight or ten weeks. Consequently, the second outbreak after Christmas 'was caused entirely through the negligence of the school authorities!' Moreover, the surroundings needed to be improved:

The school itself is situated next to a cow shed, and piggery, from which the smell is most offensive, and forms one of the leading stinks in the village. I am informed that this place is cleaned out when the children are attending school, and that although all doors and windows are closed, the smell is fearful. What can the sanitary authorities be about to allow a piggery to exist (and what stinks worse than a foul piggery?) within three or four yards of a National School?

Not surprisingly, this letter caused James Browne, the schoolmaster, to reach for his pen. His reply appeared in the *Journal* on the following day. Of all the exaggerated statements about the health of Radcliffe, he asserted, those by *Nemo Secundus* were the most outrageous:

A most serious charge is brought against the managers and teachers of the schools. They are made to appear responsible for the spread of the epidemic which has been so fatal, and consequently for the deaths of the children. Sir, in the latter part of November last, the managers passed a resolution that no children should be allowed to attend school who had been attacked by scarlet fever until January 1882, which I think would allow for sufficient time for desquamation, nor any children not having been attacked, but who came from homes which had been. This was rigidly enforced, as far as was known, and several scholars were promptly returned. When the school was reopened after the first outbreak there was not a single case but which was convalescent, and the opinion of both medical men was taken before doing so. Nemo Secundus will, I trust, compare this with his statement, and ponder thereon.

Moreover, *Nemo Secundus's* comments about the school surroundings were a long way from the truth. Although the school master admitted complaining about the smell from the boiling of swede turnips for cattle, 'no offensive smells from cow hovels or piggeries penetrate into the schools to my knowledge.'

A second letter on June 1st, from a *Radcliffe Foreigner* explained the long, and by now well-known, saga of Radcliffe's sanitary struggles, and the attempt to have their own local board from 1880 onwards. This writer confirmed the view that 'the machinery of Bingham Union is totally inadequate to deal with a growing place like Radcliffe.' In conclusion, he added:

..... with many parishioners, I consider your criticisms have been perfectly fair, and deeply regret the absurd proceedings of the last meeting; and if you will only let as much 'daylight' into Bingham Union as you have done into Radcliffe's 'sewage' you will find that we are more to be pitied than blamed.

This correspondent would have been glad to know that at the Bingham sanitary meeting on that day some small progress was reported. Dr Eaton had visited all the premises named in the report and served notices on them, while Herbert Walker had been instructed to prepare a further report on the main culvert, its ventilation, and the probable costs of improvement. In the meantime, the parish had been taking matters into its own hands. Twenty owners and ratepayers had requested a meeting to consider the resolution that the parish should be constituted a local government district. Notification that this meeting would take place appeared in Friday's *Journal*.

Evidence that the issues were becoming more bitter, as well as more trivial, came from the three letters published on that same Friday - June 2nd. *Nemo Tertius* picked his way through James Browne's letter, claiming unconvincingly that the schoolmaster's grammar was in almost as unsatisfactory a state as the famous Radcliffe drains. Robert Porter of Beeston surfaced again, reminding readers that he had been waiting daily for a reply or apology from Samuel Barratt. It was the thundering response of *Nemo Secundus* to James Browne's letter, however, which made clear that it would be a long time before normal neighbourliness could be resumed in the village:

I fail to see that Mr Browne has answered my letter. .... He states that when the school was reopened statements were made by both the doctors of the village that the fever patients were convalescent. Is it true, however, as I stated in my letter, that children who had been attacked were allowed to attend the school when it was reopened after Christmas? Further, is it a fact that the second outbreak was the most virulent and caused the greatest number of deaths? If so, it must be evident that the desquamating period had not elapsed, and that the children attending the school, amongst whom the deaths occurred, caught the infection there, for it had been practically stamped out before the schools were reopened. As to the stinks about the school, they have been there for thirty years past, and can be noticed by any person passing along the road. If Mr Browne cannot notice them it must be because he has been amongst them so long; but that does not alter the injurious effect on the children.

There was some slight softening of attack towards the end of the letter:

I bring no charge against Mr Browne, than whom nobody is more respected in the village. I simply state facts, and the public must judge between us.

June 3rd and 5th: more letters and the third leader

The first defence of the Bingham Rural Sanitary Authority appeared in the only letter of Saturday, June 3rd. *Observer* pointed out that the small property owners on Radcliffe Hill, Richmond's Yard, Station Terrace, Barker's or Clarke's Yard, Ogle's Yard, Beeson's Yard, Sheppard's Row, Thraves' Yard and Stone's property had all had a pretty good share of attention from the authority, as there had been considerable expense in re-building privies and ashpits. As for the main drain, some hundreds of pounds were spent on it some twenty years before, and since then several 'works of sewage' had been carried out - from Mr Willey's (Fairfield House on Bingham Road) down to Cropwell Road, on the road leading to the station, in front of Mr Reynolds' and the Wesleyan Chapel, and down to Smith's farmstead. 'How are these things to be reconciled with *Radcliffe Foreigner's* statement as to things being so shocking?' There had been no proof that the water contained sewage, and rather than Radcliffe being a place to breed fever, it was more likely that the fever was brought to Radcliffe from Nottingham through the large influx of visitors. *Observer* ended on a soothing, if over-optimistic, note. 'I think it's time to sober down and come to a better frame of mind. I expect if we were to have a local board they would have something to suit everybody.'

This conciliatory tone was continued on the following Monday when the *Nottingham Journal* published its third leading article on the subject of Radcliffe sewage. After a mildly facetious beginning on the 'Radcliffe drainage question, which we have done our best to ventilate', the writer concentrated on generalities, recognising that there were persons living in country parishes who would gladly welcome an improved system of sanitation in their midst. Amongst them would be those who had migrated from towns in the hope of finding cleaner, healthier surroundings, discovering too late that the place was badly drained or that there was pestilence in the air. Such people would gladly have paid to have the situation improved. But there were other residents whose views consisted of stolid unreasoning opposition:

These are the small farmers, and some of the large ones too, market gardeners and others, who object to improvement on the grounds of expense. These would rather live over an open sewer than pay an additional penny in the pound towards making their own premises more wholesome, and those of their poorer neighbours fit to live upon. ....It is only when an official report like that presented by Mr Herbert Walker, which we published a day or two ago, sees daylight, that public attention is called to the perils to which the rural population is subjected on account of the neglect of those who are supposed to be responsible for their good management. .....No complaint is made; if it were the parish might be saddled with expense, and what is disease and death to the prospect of an additional copper in the pound?

Strong as this leader might be in most circumstances, after the ridicule and public airing of Radcliffe's sanitary failings over the last fortnight, it was almost benevolent in tone. When the writer pointed out that Radcliffe was only one case among many, and then went on to single out East Bridgford for criticism, it must have seemed that the crisis was over and the village's affairs could return to their usual obscurity. Any such hope was premature. The ordinary villagers, having found their pens, were not yet ready to put them away. Moreover the public at large was now curious to know how the Radcliffe community was going to come to terms with its problems. No journalist was going to let a good story drop in mid-flow.

Three more letters appeared on the same day as the third leader. The first was on the irrelevant issue of James Browne's grammar - this time a defence of the schoolmaster and an attack on *Nemo Tertius* by *An Ass* of Cotgrave. The second was a request by *Inquirer of Radcliffe* to Robert Porter, asking what the Beeston rate would be in two years' time, in the light of considerable borrowing. 'I do not think that Mr Barratt has been much misled,' he concluded.

June 5th; Samuel Barratt's letter

The third letter was the long awaited reply from Samuel Barratt himself, at last goaded into action. His defence against Robert Porter's charges was that he had been misquoted in the report of the vestry meeting:

> *I most emphatically deny that I made any such statement in the way that your readers were led to believe by the report in your columns. This arises from the grossly unfair way in which the few remarks that I made were reported in yours of May 27th.*

He claimed that he had made clear at the time that he was merely quoting what he had been told about Beeston's borrowing. The statement was not his. He had been quoted as saying that the worst cases with regard to drainage were out of the village.

> *This is utterly untrue; I said nothing of the kind. I did say that the fever originated, and that the worst cases occurred, about a mile and a half away from the village, in isolated houses, and what is considered to be the most healthy situation; but I said, 'Do not imagine that because I say this I am an advocate for bad sanitary arrangements - far from it; let us have the evils stamped out at once.' A more one sided and unfair report I never read.*

Having castigated the reporter, Samuel Barratt next turned, rather belatedly, to the first leader of May 23rd. The article was ill-informed. There had not been an epidemic two years before and a decision not to have a local board was made by the government official. The article's reference to the stormy meeting at Radcliffe at which the 'intelligence of Radcliffe resolved not to have anyone to look after their drains' was also utterly opposed to the truth. He himself had stated that Bingham had the power to cure the evils pointed out in Herbert Walker's report, and had proposed that the sanitary body be requested to compel owners to remedy the evils at once. What a false assertion it was for the writer to say that 'we resolved not to have anyone to look after our drains.' The remarks about Widows' Row had shown the writer's utter ignorance - Samuel Barratt was clearly not an admirer of irony - and Radcliffe rarely had cases of typhoid fever or diphtheria. It was surely the case that it was the misfortune of Radcliffe to be near Nottingham, with its infectious diseases, rather than the other way round:

> *The only wonder is, that, with the constant communication kept up between this village and Nottingham, we do not have all the infectious diseases that infest Nottingham. There again, if you lived here you would at times on Sundays see the misfortune of Radcliffe being in such close proximity to a large town, for a great many of your townsmen visiting us on Sundays appear to be smitten with a disease of the tongue, for their language, as a rule, to say the least of it, is very dirty. In conclusion, pitch into the Radcliffe drains and stinks as much as you like, but stick to the truth, and ask your reporter to do the same.*

It had taken the best part of a fortnight for Samuel Barratt to put pen to paper, and at last it seemed as if the *Journal* had met its match. That evening the next parish meeting was to be held in the schoolroom.

June 5th: another parish meeting

According to the long report which appeared in the *Journal* the next morning, this meeting was conducted in a very different atmosphere from its two immediate predecessors. John Taylor again took the chair, but this time he maintained control, and for most of the evening the mood was sober and rational. The speakers were doubtless aware that the eyes of the county were upon them. After re-explaining the advantages of having their own local board, as opposed to being under the control of Bingham's urban powers, John Taylor proposed that Radcliffe should be constituted a local government district.

James Gorse of the Manor House was the first main speaker. He explained how the Local Government Board had turned down Radcliffe's application some two and a half years before, and reminded his audience that it was John Cullen's letter, prompted by his distress, that had led to Herbert Walker's report and Bingham's application for urban powers against Radcliffe's wishes. That night a petition in favour of a local board, signed by eighty-three parishioners, had been sent to London (rather prematurely as things turned out). In answering the objection that paying the officers of a local board would prove very costly, he cited figures for five areas, the average of which at £83 he felt would be a fair estimate. There had been rumours that some landlords would raise rents if a local board was set up. Turning to George Beaumont, Lord Manvers' agent, he asked whether he would raise the rents of the tenants under his control. George Beaumont said he would not. A voice called out, 'They're not all like Mr Beaumont.' James Gorse earned some applause when he said that one result of a local board would be better dwellings for the working man. As an outsider, he then defended the newcomers to Radcliffe who had been attacked in some of the *Journal* correspondence:

> Remarks had been made to the effect that if the Radcliffe people had only been left alone Radcliffe would have been a wonderful place. In his opinion it would have been a hundred years behind the times, and he contended that Nottingham people, by living at Radcliffe, had given employment to the men and children, and that consequently Radcliffe had been peculiarly prosperous during the years of agricultural depression which had been passed through. It was an unfortunate fact that the scarlet fever was chiefly amongst the working classes, and that all the deaths occurred in the families of working men. It was therefore to their interest to adopt measures to stay the spread of such diseases.

However rational James Gorses's arguments were, they came from someone far removed from the problems of Mount Pleasant or Bennet's Yard. Just when it seemed that the meeting was being stage-managed to a predictable conclusion, the working men of the village, fearful of rates or rent rises, found a spokesman in Samuel Kirkham:

> Mr Kirkham, a labouring man, who had interrupted the last speaker towards the close of his remarks, and at the request of Mr Gorse had taken a seat at the front of the meeting, said he would like to know what Mr Gorse would do if he had 2s.9d a day, three children, 3s rent to pay, and not a foot of garden. He thought Mr Gorse would not know which end to begin. He further wished to know what [he] would do if the rent were raised.
>
> Mr Gorse, in reply, advised Kirkham and all who were similarly situated to go to Nottingham where they would find work for themselves and for their children. A voice: We will all go to Nottingham. (Laughter and general conversation.)

Some exchanges with Thomas Butler of Manor Farm also indicated that there were others in the meeting not persuaded by James Gorse's arguments. Not only did Mr Butler want an example of any place where rates were lower after the establishment of a local board - which was unconvincingly provided - but he claimed that Bingham would withdraw its request for urban powers if Radcliffe stopped agitating for a local board. James Gorse considered this idea absurd. Mr Butler claimed that the Bingham authority simply wanted to keep Radcliffe in the district. He then introduced a recriminatory element which embarrassed those on the platform:

> He thought the letter sent by Mr Cullen ought not to have been written without consulting the parish. The letter was a mistake, and it was through that mistake they had got into all this trouble.
> The chairman and Mr Gorse said that was past and over, and there was no use talking about that now.

With the vicar sitting alongside them, they could hardly say anything else.

George Beaumont, Lord Manvers' agent, then rose to bring the discussion back to its intended line. Having pointed out that it was not his habit to interfere in parish matters, he reminded the meeting of the improvements to the drain some twenty years previously with which he had been connected. They should be proud of the name 'Radcliffe-on-Sewer' for it was a very good sewer indeed. That work had been done, not at the expense of those who were responsible for their health, but by people who subscribed, assisted by the rates. No body of people could manage anybody else's business so well as they could manage it themselves. His audience was left in no doubt about his support for a local board. He approved of Herbert Walker's report - they were fellows of the same college - and his view that very little trouble and expense would make Radcliffe one of the nicest places in the county was greeted with applause. Although he did not wish to say anything against the members of the Bingham Board individually, collectively he did not think they did their duty in enforcing proper attention to sanitary matters. He cited an example from East Bridgford, where he lived. The *Journal* had done Radcliffe a good turn in pointing out its defects. He wound up his speech with a strong call for the support of a local board:

> If anybody had an interest in improving the present system it was the poor working man, whose children were dying under his eyes. The rates the working man would pay would be very small, and the expenses would chiefly come out of the pockets of richer men. .....Why should the people who had already neglected their duty with the powers they had, have greater powers given them? They were bound to have a local board sooner or later, and the sooner they got it the more economically would they get it to work.

As George Beaumont sat down, his appeal to both emotion and financial common sense must have seemed unanswerable. John Taylor then put the motion to the meeting that Radcliffe should have its own local board. Forty-nine voted in favour of the resolution but sixty-eight were against. All the reasoning and rhetoric of James Gorse and George Beaumont had counted for little against the fears of the Samuel Kirkhams of the parish. The discomfited platform party, however, was not beaten yet. James Gorse pointed out that there were those who had not wanted to face a vestry meeting, but who would no doubt like to express their views on the subject. He therefore demanded that a poll of the owners and occupiers should be held to settle the matter. The applause that greeted this request was interrupted by an opposition cry: 'You will lose in a canter!' The hope that Radcliffe would now be left to carry out its affairs away from the glare of publicity had faded.

June 6th: the reporter and Samuel Barratt

Whether Samuel Barratt was at this meeting is not recorded. Any satisfaction at the publication of his letter that morning must have rapidly vanished at breakfast time on Tuesday June 6th. Not only did the *Journal* publish its lengthy report of the previous evening's events, it published what can only be described as an hysterical and wounding letter to the editor by its chief reporter, attacking Samuel Barratt:

If Mr Samuel Barratt, who writes to your paper today impugning the accuracy of my report, is the ratepayer who acted with such conspicuous indiscretion at the memorable meeting where you were threatened and I was howled at, I have a distinct recollection of him. Mr Barratt complains of the unfairness of my report, and asks me in future to stick to the truth. If ever it is my privilege to follow Mr Barratt's unintelligible sentences on any future occasion, he shall have the whole truth, and I shall be saved the trouble of putting into readable English the utterances of an excited parishioner.

While Samuel Barratt had clearly touched a raw nerve in the reporter, the ferocity of the response seems out of proportion to the offence:

It was Mr Barratt who, when the meeting had decided to proceed with business, and to abandon the irrelevant matter of the Journal article, insisted on knowing the name of the writer, and who ought to be held responsible for the scene which has made Radcliffe the laughing-stock of the county. ... I claim permission to state, sir, that Mr Barratt is one of that fairly large number of persons who have mistaken their vocation. Mr Barratt was never intended for public life, and when men of his stamp address public assemblies, the spectacle is a melancholy one. ...Mr Barratt's only escape is to dispute the accuracy of the report which has made his blunders public property. ..... Surely I gave the meaning of Mr Barratt's remarks. But he does not see it. When next Mr Barratt appears in public your numerous readers shall be favoured with a verbatim report of his observations. It is really a pity that they should be spoiled by condensation and 'doctoring'.

This shrivelling attack seemed to have diverted Radcliffe concerns a long way from the deaths of children. The doctors and the schoolmaster had got off lightly by comparison. Samuel Barratt could only hope that a rescuer might appear in some future issue of the paper. In the meantime there were two more letters to get through in that morning's *Journal*. The first of these was from the indefatigable Robert Porter of Beeston, fundamentally in indignant response to *Inquirer's* question about the rates there, but also dragging up Samuel Barratt's misleading statements about the excessive increases and borrowing. After airing some of Beeston's problems he claimed that the adoption of a local board had meant only an increase of 5d in the £ with improved services, and a decreased death rate. But why anyone in Radcliffe should ask a question about Beeston, as *Inquirer* had done, he considered 'somewhat droll'. The final letter of the day was from James Browne, the schoolmaster, still smarting from the attack on his school and having had his attention drawn to the attacks on his grammar:

When an individual has the bad taste, conceit and ignorance to criticise the omission of a comma in a letter, it must show that he is very deficient in common sense. This is the more apparent when his own epistle and that of his brother Nemo Secundus bristle with badly constructed sentences and worse punctuation.

As my first letter is a complete answer to the second one of Nemo Secundus, I do not think it necessary to go over that ground again. With this, my part in the controversy ceases.

June 7th: the fourth leader in the *Journal*

Not quite. The last word in the debate over the school was yet to come, and when it came to main issues, the *Journal* still had plenty to say. The defeat of those supporting a local board seemed to the *Journal* further proof of the idiocy of rural ways. The placatory tone of the third leader was abandoned, and a full hue and cry in pursuit of sanitary improvement was resumed in Wednesday morning's paper:

At a meeting of the intelligent and non-intelligent ratepayers of Radcliffe-on-Trent on Monday evening, a proposal that Radcliffe should have a local board was rejected by a vote of 68 against 49; consequently there will have to be a poll to settle this interesting question. .....Local Government is the very essence of all our modern life, yet Radcliffe persons, not yet duly qualified for admittance into the nearest lunatic asylum, set their backs up at the very thought, the very name of local government. Local Government means that a parish or district, if so minded, shall have the power of looking after its own affairs, have absolute control over its expenditure. When this is said, Radcliffe people, of the non-intelligent sort, shrug their shoulders and say - 'All very fine. We don't want Local Government. We prefer staying as we are. We don't want to rule ourselves. We would rather be ruled and controlled by the intelligence of Bingham than by the intelligence of Radcliffe. We have got used to all our smells and nuisances. We rather like scarlet fever, sewage in the wells, diphtheria, typhoid fever. We are supremely happy in thinking we are the laughing stock of the whole country. We don't want any improvements if we have to pay for them etc.'

We cannot for a moment imagine that any sensible Radcliffe ratepayer would ever attach any weight to antediluvian silliness of that stamp. Local Government means self-government, but government by Bingham does not and cannot mean self-government for Radcliffe in the same way that government by Radcliffe means it. Let Radcliffe ratepayers remember that fact in time, and act on it.

The campaign seemed to be back where it was on May 27th, but now specifically aimed at affecting the poll. As many opponents of the local board would neither take the *Journal*, nor have the right to vote, it is difficult to know how much effect the *Journal's* views would have on the outcome. A *Radcliffe Visitor* in the same issue contributed a piece of eavesdropping, purporting to show the problems that faced the reformers:

The following conversation was overheard at a street-corner in the 'improving village' of Radcliffe a few evenings ago:-
First Neighbour: 'What'll a Local Board do for us? Will it raise the rates?'
Second Neighbour: 'Yes, it'll raise the rates; sure to.'
First Neighbour: 'Will it raise the rents?'
Second Neighbour: 'Shouldn't wonder.'
First Neighbour: 'Will it hinder me from keepin' a pig?'
Second Neighbour: 'You moan't keep a pig, mun; you moan't keep a pig.'
First Neighbour: (spitting furiously) 'Then dang me if I vote for un; dang me if I do.'
Second Neighbour: (vehemently) Dang <u>me</u> if I do.'
Exit, intelligent and indignant ratepayers. It is ignorance and prejudice of this kind that the folk in Radcliffe who want a Local Board will have to fight.

If this dialogue was accurately reported, it indicated a misplaced fear that interference from a local board would mean the end of an essential addition to the economy of many poorer households.

June 8th and 9th: correspondents still divided
Whatever Radcliffe thought of the *Journal's* latest leading article, a Cotgrave correspondent on Thursday June 8th found much to admire in it. George Hickling, a well known local poet who wrote agricultural notices as well as letters to the editor, considered it 'capital', and calculated to throw oil on troubled waters! While professing to sympathise with Radcliffe's plight, he had clearly enjoyed the 'considerable of a wiggin' that the village had received, thought it was time the excitement calmed down, and acknowledged that Radcliffe people were 'perhaps not a bit worse than other people'. He rubbed home his point that Cotgrave was now such a healthy place, and advised his Radcliffe friends to 'keep quite calm and 'collected' on the forthcoming election day.' (This was over a month away.)

It was left to *Looker-on*, possibly not the same correspondent who had supported the *Journal* in the early stages of the controversy, on the same day to sum up the current situation with a careful explanation of Radcliffe feelings, and a defence of at least some of her people. (Sanitary matters as such hardly came into it by this stage.) He regretted that the question was descending 'into a war of personalities,' and he affirmed that the title of an 'improving village' was justified when spoken and meant honestly, and not as a 'sarcastic sneer'. No parish officers could have been more anxious to do all that they could within their means to improve conditions. *Looker-on* also confirms some impressions gleaned from the correspondence that the older villagers' resentment was not just against the *Journal* but against newcomers to the village, including the vicar. His analysis of the way in which the community was being torn apart makes interesting reading:

> *...They say, do the old parishioners, that it is shameful to make it out that their village is generally a dirty, unhealthy and objectionable place to live in, simply because one or two portions of private property (and some of it belonging to the lord of the manor, who is out of their reach) have not the best sanitary arrangements about them.... They are also indignant that this bad name is being given them, very much at the instigation of the people of today, the upstart people, who have come lately into the place for a healthy, and a pleasant home, and who, apparently being desirous of being somebody, and not because they care for sanitation so much, have set themselves, often in an underhand way, to stir up strife amongst their neighbours in order to obtain their much desired notoriety. The very beginning of this drainage excitement was, I hear, a source of annoyance to the Radcliffe people. The vicar began it by writing a possibly well-meant but injudicious letter to the Local Government Board in London, setting forth, in pathetic terms, his grief and sorrow at the deaths of so many children from scarlet fever. The parishioners blame the vicar for doing this without first consulting with the parochial authorities. They call it in their indignation 'working behind their backs', and a 'step in the dark', and Englishmen-like, they hate that kind of thing.*

Looker-on then attributed the 'incoherent' nature of the parish meeting on May 23rd to the *Journal's* 'thunderbolt of a leader' that same day. The indignation and excitement in the village was further increased by the way the reporter hid or kept back all that was favourable to Radcliffe, and only gave prominence to that which supported the leader. He then came to the defence of Samuel Barratt:

> *I regret that your reporter should have written so sharp and stinging a personal attack on Mr Barratt, for he is one of the best workers for the public good that Radcliffe has in it. He works whilst others talk, and some allowance might have been made for a Radcliffeian born and bred, who speaks and writes warmly in the defence of his native village. I plead now, therefore, for a greater breadth of view in the matter, and I express my hope that whatever may be written more will be written in a kindlier spirit.*

This plea fell on deaf ears. *Looker-on* had shown his partisanship for the old order in Radcliffe. In Friday's paper *Looker-on, no 2* rose to the defence of the new. He accused *Looker-on* of professing to deprecate personalities, while himself making offensive remarks about newcomers and 'upstart people'. His reflections on the conduct of the vicar were 'in very bad taste'. Seeing 'death and disease stalking amongst his parishioners' he was only doing his duty when the local authorities had neglected their work. The defence of Samuel Barratt and criticism of the reporter, who was so 'grossly and vulgarly' insulted while merely discharging his duty, showed that *Looker-on* was tarred with the same brush as those who offended so greatly against good manners on that occasion.

End of the *Journal* campaign
It is clear that by this time there were two irreconcilably opposed viewpoints in the village, but the steam was beginning to run out of the indignation on both sides. Two items in the *Journal* for Saturday June 10th signalled the winding down of the public campaign. First was the final letter from *Nemo Secundus* still waging his battle against the school in far from conciliatory terms:

My attention has just been called to the last letter of Mr James Browne. He seems to me to have all the self-conceit of the pedagogue, and his letter is no reply whatever to mine. I can only hope that the Medical Officer of Health and the Inspector of Nuisances will give his school a little more attention, as I understand the sanitary condition is in a most shocking state.

The main item that day was a long article in a series called 'Jottings' by *Viator*. After recognising that the opposition to a local board in Radcliffe came largely from the poorer occupiers who had got it into their 'dull heads' that rates and rents would rise, the writer acknowledged that there was some reason for these fears. Some property owners had been spreading rumours to that effect. The main part of the article, however, was concerned with a comparison of the lofty approach of James Gorse's advocacy of a local board and the down-to-earth reality of Samuel Kirkham. The advice that he should migrate to Nottingham was on a par with much wider encouragement of emigration which was encouraging large numbers of the best part of the working population to leave England. The article ended as a defence of the working classes, and in an appeal for the improvement of wages as exemplified by the case of Samuel Kirkham 'whose few hasty words were more powerful than the glib sentences of more cultured speakers'.

Suddenly it was all over. There were no more letters, no more leaders, or facetious articles. Whether the *Journal* called a halt to the campaign, or whether it was no longer newsworthy, or whether Radcliffe became weary of washing its own dirty linen in public is not clear. When the poll was finally taken on Tuesday July 11th it was almost an anti-climax. Those in favour of a local board carried the day by 289 votes to 102. If there were demonstrations or rejoicings they were not recorded. The result merited only the briefest announcement in the *Journal* four days after the event.

On the face of it, the *Journal*, the newcomers, the vicar and the parish elite had won. Bingham authority, local farmers, and the village labourers who had opposed the application for a local board appeared to have lost. In reality the result meant little, for it was not Radcliffe who would have the final say, but the Local Government Board in London through a future inquiry. After all the ink - printer's and private - had been spilled, it was debatable whether anyone came out of the affair with credit, however good their intentions. Nevertheless, the revelations provide a unique insight into a Victorian community during three contentious weeks in 1882.

III. Rejection and reform 1882 - 1920

While Radcliffe's problems were being so publicly aired in the *Nottingham Journal*, the Bingham Rural Sanitary Authority continued to hold its routine fortnightly meetings. It is hard to believe that the representatives sitting round the table in the workhouse board room did not discuss the controversial campaign in which they themselves had been indicted. Their minutes, however, reveal no emotional reaction, only a straightfaced response to the central problem.

The parochial committee
Radcliffe had made it very clear that it did not want Bingham to apply for urban powers, and that a majority of villagers wanted to have their own local board. Although neither side seemed prepared to give way, Bingham initially produced a compromise solution familiar to public bodies in all ages. They set up a committee. This was a special parochial body whose members had to hold property of a ratable value of not less than £25 per year. (Keyworth and East Bridgford were offered similar committees, but the latter declined.) It was to meet monthly, at first in the Manvers Arms and later in the schoolroom, and was to deal solely with sanitary matters in the village through inspection, supervision of any work, and consideration of any complaints. Expenses were not to exceed £5 in any one case, and matters had generally to be referred to Bingham for approval. The names of the members at the first meeting on July 4th 1882 indicate that men of considerable

substance were recruited to tackle so contentious a matter: Henry Smith, John Green, Samuel Parr, and Thomas Holmes were all well-to-do farmers. Samuel Bell combined farming with inn keeping and building. Richard Daft was now both cricket outfitter and brewer, and J. George Willey was a retired provisions merchant. Sanitation, however, was perhaps not the concern of a gentleman. Both John Taylor of Radcliffe Hall and William Sanday of Cliff House declined to serve on the committee. Not surprisingly, the minutes of the first few years are very full, giving a detailed picture of the problem spots or negligent occupiers of the village. As the years went by the memories of 1882 faded and the minutes become far less informative.

Herbert Walker's new scheme

Meanwhile Bingham was in negotiation with the Local Government Board in London about acquiring urban powers over Radcliffe, while a memorial containing a counter-request from some eighty Radcliffe parishioners had also been sent off. As a response to Herbert Walker's condemnation of Radcliffe, Bingham asked him for a further report suggesting how manholes and ventilators could be placed along the notorious culvert, with an estimate of probable cost. This scheme was then forwarded to both Radcliffe and the Local Government Board for approval.

To the consternation of the Bingham authority, the board in London disapproved of the scheme. Not only did it fail to remedy the existing evils of cess pools and the danger to wells, since it only provided for the improvement of existing sewage channels, it would also allow pollution of the river Trent to continue in contravention of the Rivers Pollution Prevention Act of 1876. The authority was therefore requested to arrange plans for a totally new system which would provide for the purification of sewage before it reached the Trent.

Herbert Walker duly obliged with a scheme involving land owned by Lord Manvers on the river side of the Great Northern Railway's viaduct. Sewage would be deposited in tanks which would be cleaned out periodically. He thought the scheme would cost about £2,000. Financial alarm bells immediately rang in Radcliffe. On August 3rd, only a week after the new project was presented to the Bingham meeting, Radcliffe held a vestry meeting to protest. Worse was to come. By the time Herbert Walker had checked his estimates he thought £3,700 would be nearer the mark, and that was without the cost of the land. It would therefore be necessary to borrow £4,000 from the Local Government Board, repayable over thirty years. A totally different issue to that of urban powers versus a local board had now been raised.

The government inquiry of 1883

Sensibly, the Local Government Board decided to kill two birds with one stone. Six months after the Radcliffe poll was taken, one inquiry was held at the Manvers Arms on February 1st 1883 to decide both matters.

Captain Hildyard, the government inspector, dealt first with the new sewerage scheme and the sanitary body's request for a loan. Herbert Walker outlined his plans for iron pipes to the seventeen-acre site beyond the viaduct, the sewage reaching tanks by gravitation. The alternative of putting down pumping engines would cost another £70 or £80 a year. Although the scheme had the backing of the Bingham authority and a number of wealthy ratepayers, there was formidable opposition, represented at the inquiry by a barrister, Mr Weightman. Under his cross-examination, the scheme was made to seem less convincing. Herbert Walker had to admit that a strong wind might convey offensive odours to the nearest houses. Although the site of the proposed sewage farm was actually below river bed level, he thought he could effectually embank it to keep water out. It was the best site available, but not ideal. 'The place would not be more of a swamp than it was now. The sewage would go into the land as it did now.'

> Mr Weightman: Then you are giving the Radcliffe people nothing better than they have now. (Laughter.) They have come here to improve the state of things which are objectionable.
> Walker: The sewage of Radcliffe is a small matter indeed.
> Weightman: Then why this £4,000? (Hear, hear and laughter.) You are here as the gentleman who propounds this scheme, which will make Radcliffe a sort

of Eldorado. (Laughter.) We want you to show the people of Radcliffe how they will be benefited by this scheme...

Herbert Walker was beginning to struggle. He thought it would depend on how the farm was managed as to whether any offensive odour would affect the railway station. He knew of no one who objected, but compensation for owners and occupiers had been estimated at £350. As the inquiry continued it became clear that two of the leading opponents of the scheme were the occupant of Radcliffe Lodge, situated close to the site, and George Beaumont, Lord Manvers' agent. Although the latter had applauded Herbert Walker's original report, he thought the scheme unnecessary. He produced evidence that it would be impossible to drain the site adequately, and his opinion was supported by one of the excavators who had worked on the erection of the railway bridge over the Trent.

The inspector then turned to the question of whether or not Radcliffe should be constituted a local board. On Radcliffe's behalf Mr Weightman said 'he could not imagine why the Bingham authority should have opposed the petition, unless they considered their self-love was hurt. Radcliffe had been left in a state of heathenism'. He would call witnesses to prove that Bingham had neglected Radcliffe. It was a great hardship for Radcliffe to have to go through Bingham when anything needed doing. A number of witnesses then supported Radcliffe's petition. Lord Manvers, through a representative, felt that as Bingham had to look after forty villages it could not give satisfaction to all. John Taylor of Radcliffe Hall said he was unaware of any feeling in Radcliffe to oppose anything that came from Bingham. He did, however, feel that the present system of drainage would do with a few trifling alterations. Other witnesses agreed that a local board would improve matters. As the opposition pointed out, however, no specific charges were actually made against the Bingham authority. The inquiry ended after six hours.

The decision
Even before the Local Government Board issued its report, Radcliffe was out to scotch the new scheme. On February 22nd 1883 the Bingham board was asked to stop proceedings relating to Herbert Walker's scheme as being 'excessive and unnecessary and if carried out would be ruinous to the parish for years to come'. Bingham denied they had the power to do this and advised Radcliffe to forward their request directly to London.

One month later, the Local Government Board's decision was recorded in the Bingham minutes. Radcliffe was not to have its own local board. Bingham would be granted urban powers over Radcliffe. On this issue the village seems to have accepted the inevitable at last. The only consolation for many Radcliffe ratepayers was Whitehall's agreement that the sewerage scheme could be reconsidered. They decided to keep up the pressure to have it abandoned altogether. After another village meeting, the parochial sanitary minutes recorded the resolution that 'the proposed sewerage scheme is unnecessary for some years to come'. A deputation was then sent to London - Bingham agreed that Herbert Walker could go too - with a memorial requesting the abandonment of the scheme. In the event, the Local Government Board refused to see the Radcliffe deputation and suggested that the memorial should be sent by post.

The matter dragged on. Radcliffe became absorbed in sorting out bye-laws with the Local Government Board. Then in November 1883 Herbert Walker produced a new scheme using a different site. Eagerly, Bingham accepted the proposals and applied to the Local Government Board for the necessary loan. When the cost of the land was included, this amounted to a formidable £6,500, making the previous scheme seem economical by comparison.

Another inquiry February 1884
Inevitably there had to be yet another inquiry. This began at the Manvers Arms on February 26th 1884, but was transferred to the schoolroom which was 'well filled'. Once again Captain Hildyard was the government inspector, this time having to decide whether Bingham could borrow the necessary money to purchase the new site. The *Nottingham Journal* noted that amongst the attenders were Doctors Ellam and Campbell from Radcliffe, Dr Eaton, the medical officer for the Bingham

authority, George Beaumont on behalf of Lord Manvers, and a representative for Miss Burnside of Lamcote House.

Herbert Walker's new site lay away from the village across the Nottingham Road. It was stated that the nearest cottages were in Bailey Lane, but it was Miss Burnside who objected most strongly to its location. Despite the distance of about 350 yards, it was claimed that the site would be detrimental to Lamcote House. Herbert Walker had to admit that he did not suppose it would increase its value. His scheme was basically similar to the previous one, but the sewage would be pumped to a higher level instead of adopting the gravitation scheme. There would be ample provision for draining basements 'with the exception of the lowest parts of the town'. Allowance had been made for an increase in population from the current 1,700 to 5,000. (It was felt that it would be another hundred years before such a figure was reached.) Much of the cost would be for the connecting of house property to the new system. Out of the four hundred or so houses in Radcliffe it was estimated that not half a dozen were connected to any system of drainage.

The impact of the scarlet fever epidemic and the subsequent furore about the drains was indicated in some exchanges with Jesse Hind, a solicitor, who opposed the scheme on behalf of the parishioners. He pointed out that the ratable value of Radcliffe was about £11,000, so a debt of £6,000 would be a very large liability. Within the last twelve months only four new houses had been built. Herbert Walker attributed this to the 'scare in the newspapers, which made people afraid to come'. He was sure that when the scheme was carried out they would see 'quite the contrary effect'. George Beaumont, describing himself as an 'unfortunate holder of some building land', agreed that there had been a set-back, but thought that it was fear of rates rather than fear of fever that was the problem.

Evidence was next given by the medical men. Dr Eaton claimed that Radcliffe was now a very healthy place (an opinion confirmed by Dr Campbell), that the parochial committee had immediately remedied any defects, and that Herbert Walker's very first scheme - produced immediately after the scarlet fever epidemic and costing a mere £300 - would be quite adequate were it not for the problem of purifying the sewage before it went into the Trent (to comply with the act of 1876). George Beaumont thought there was now no problem of sewage in the Trent and the scheme would be ruinous to Radcliffe for years to come. Dr Ellam agreed that the original modest scheme would be adequate. He also said he had smelt the sewage at the Stoke farm at a distance of five or six hundred yards, and there seemed to have been much illness close by, although he was not prepared to say it was caused by the smell.

The solicitor, Jesse Hind, had spotted a let-out clause regarding the problem of sewage in the Trent. He pointed out that the Local Government Board could only enforce the anti-pollution regulation when asked to give consent to the borrowing of money. If the present scheme was withdrawn and Herbert Walker's original scheme adopted, there would be no need for a loan and the money could be raised by a general rate. If the scheme went ahead against the wishes of the people, he continued, the outlay might well be £10,000 rather than £6,700. The clerk to the Bingham authority, while not agreeing on every count, also felt that the original scheme would be sufficient. 'Speaking personally he would be very glad to hear that that was the termination of the history of the sewage question at Radcliffe-on-Trent.'

He might well have caught his breath at the sight of a letter in the *Nottingham Journal* on March 5th, but it proved to be an isolated case and not the start of another epistolary epidemic. J.B. Walker, the writer, pointed out that George Beaumont, now apparently so unconcerned about the discharge of sewage into the Trent, had in 1879 supported Lord Manvers and J.C. Musters in preparing to take legal action against Nottingham for doing just that. Now he was again ready to allow the 'Silver Trent' to become a public sewer. Dr Ellam came in for ridicule in the same letter. While at the inquiry he had claimed to be able to smell sewage at a distance of five or six hundred yards, his keen sense of smell had not prevented him from walking into a pool of sewage refuse in the dark, from which he had had to be extricated. (Dr Ellam's stay in Radcliffe was proving uncomfortable. A central figure in the *Journal* campaign of 1882, his wall swept away and garden flooded by inadequate drainage, now immersed in sewage, and shortly to be humiliatingly rejected by seventeen votes to two in a bid to become the workhouse medical officer, he left Granville House and Radcliffe history by April 1885.)

Back to the beginning

In the end, Captain Hildyard informed the Local Government Board that the Bingham authority now wished to withdraw its application for a loan, and this was agreed in April 1884 provided expenses incurred so far should be paid. After some twenty-one months, therefore, Herbert Walker's original make-do-and-mend scheme which had been rejected as inadequate was at last approved. The tender of Foster and Barry of Radcliffe for £190, the middle of the range, was accepted. Even though with some extra work at Mount Pleasant their bills came to £239.4s.3d by October 1884, and there was a further £35.10s for making the connections with the new sewers, it was all on a modest scale compared to the £6,500 of Herbert Walker's final scheme.

Routine years 1884-1895

The care of Radcliffe's health now entered a comparatively quiet decade. As elsewhere there were some minor epidemics. Scarlet fever reappeared at regular intervals - 1884, 1889, 1892 and 1894 when the school was closed. A case of typhoid was reported in 1887. Radcliffe escaped a smallpox outbreak in 1884 when Dr Eaton's devotion to duty was rewarded with £10 by a grateful Bingham authority. Smallpox did occur in Radcliffe in 1893 in the house of Robert Buxton, a saddler and milk dealer. Vaccination stations were reopened as a result. In the following year cases appeared in the Widdowson and Lodge households. One victim was removed to hospital, and a nurse was provided for another at £2.2s a week. The authority's auditor banned this extravagance for the future.

For the main part, the minutes of both the parochial committee and the Bingham sanitary body record routine enforcement of building regulations, the licensing of milk sellers from 1887, the inspection of bakehouses, and the constant repairs and alterations to the patched drainage and sanitary system. Occupiers using the 'tub system' had to have gardens to which the contents could be removed. William Vickerstaff was appointed to cleanse and repair all the old drains in the parish in 1885, and Mr A.R. Calvert was appointed surveyor for the village. Ventilating shafts, pig sties, choked culverts, cesspools and the analysis of well water were other frequent concerns. In 1890 new drains from Harlequin houses came to a costly £206.15s.5d. From the end of 1894, with the changes in local government organisation, the parochial sanitary committee in Radcliffe was absorbed by the new Parish Council, although final approval for decisions had to come from the equally new District Council at Bingham. An era of real reform was almost coincidentally about to begin.

Dr Archibald Campbell

Accidental poisoning

A tragic case in 1893, however, highlighted defects in the existing system of labelling medicines. It concerned two patients of Dr Archibald Campbell, the Scottish born practitioner noted for his sporting interests who had come to Radcliffe as a young man in about 1876. He was now aged 40, had recently married the daughter of George Beaumont of East Bridgford, and was currently occupying the Manor House. (He later moved to Dunmore House at the corner of Walker's Yard and Main Street, now replaced by a supermarket.) In January 1893 Dr Campbell had two patients named

William Wright. One was the village carrier for whom he had prescribed aconite liniment for a sprained hand. The other was a 32-year-old platelayer who had been suffering with a cough. After returning from work the latter sent his son with his medicine bottle to be refilled. Dr Campbell was out, and when he returned the maid told him that William Wright's bottle needed filling. Thinking it was for the carrier, the doctor filled it with aconite liniment instead of cough mixture and the bottle was subsequently collected by the platelayer's sister-in-law. After complaining that the 'medicine' did not taste like the other, and that his teeth felt as if they were dropping out, the bottle was taken back and Dr Campbell realised the mistake. It was too late and the patient died later that night. The doctor handed the bottle in at the police station and, badly shaken, gave evidence at the inquest. The coroner thought he had behaved with perfect honesty, but criticised him for the blunder he had made. The jury's rider was to the effect that poisonous drugs should be distinctly marked. Dr Campbell undertook to provide for the widow and three children.

The new asylum and piped water

For many years the various local health authorities had found that the lunatic asylum in Sneinton was inadequate, and although a new one had been opened on Mapperley Plains in 1880, a further hospital was required by the 1890s. Thirty sites were originally considered, and the choice narrowed down to the 130-acre Lings Farm site near to Saxondale on the Bingham Road. At the heart of the farm was a substantial house which could be incorporated into the hospital. The elevated position, the proximity of the railway for deliveries, sewer connections within 500 yards, and a nearby brickyard all helped to persuade the County Council that the position was ideal. It was purchased from Lord Manvers in 1897 for £6,880.

Although the County Council was assured that there was a well thirty-seven feet deep adjoining the farm house, this would clearly be inadequate for a hospital intended to house some 450 patients. Consequently, for the first time Nottingham corporation offered to supply piped water to Radcliffe, although it would cost a quarter more than the borough rate. Parliament confirmed the extension of supply in 1896 and two years later Lord Manvers agreed that the corporation could lay mains along his Trent Boulevard property to the Radcliffe boundary. The earl tried to have as many Radcliffe premises as possible joined to the new supply, but the town clerk made it clear that the corporation's offer was limited: 'I think you will see that we cannot supply every house en route now built, or that may be built... We will supply the Earl and his farms...' As the final agreement with Nottingham made clear, the real purpose of laying-on piped water was to supply the new asylum. The supply to 'houses and premises' was coincidental. Nevertheless, although clean water for the whole village was still some time off, at least it was now on the way.

Controversy renewed

The piecemeal improvements to the drainage system after the 1884 inquiry had not eradicated all problems. In March 1889 William Holmes had written to the Bingham authority about the still open section of dyke on the Bingham road as a receptacle for rubbish. Dr Percy Truman, a local lawyer, complained in 1894, but any response seems to have been lost in the local government reorganisation. Along with Messrs Wardley, Hooper, Wright and Haynes, he tried again in October 1895:

> ...The drains are most offensive and are not flushed. The effect during the late long drought may be imagined.
> In some places Excrement is allowed to run along an open dyke by the Highway Side and in another part of the town the sewerage is run along another open dyke into the River Trent. Local complaint has produced no amendment... Several cases of blood-poisoning have occurred among us and we believe these may readily be attributed to the bad unprotected state of our sanitary affairs...

To those with long memories it must all have seemed very familiar, but a new generation was now on the scene. Improvement was acceptable, and this time it was not Radcliffe that dragged its feet. In fact, the parish council's committee countered all the charges. Not only had the sewers been inspected and not been found wanting, but the sewer outlet three hundred yards from the Trent formed a settling bed which was regularly cleaned out. The alleged excrement was no more than sink water from a labourer's cottage, and the committee was currently negotiating with the trustees of Barrow-on-Soar school, who owned some of the land through which the offending brook ran, for permission to construct a small reservoir for flushing purposes. (Negotiations with the slothful trustees had begun in 1893 and dragged on until 1896, when they foundered as Radcliffe considered rental at £3 an acre more than adequate, while Barrow would not accept less than £25!) The committee had not heard of any blood poisoning cases, and it was their unanimous opinion that the sanitary condition of the village was very satisfactory.

Despite this confident response to Dr Truman's letter, the drainage still left much to be desired. From May 1896 disinfectant in the drains was one stop-gap solution, but in September 1898 it was still recorded that 'the smells from many of the grates in the village are very bad'. Complaints not only about Bingham Road, but about Cropwell Road and the Harlequin, led to the formation of a special committee to review the situation. They identified the cause of the Bingham Road problem as the ending of the improved sewer part way up. For a further 360 yards the majority of houses still emptied into what used to be the open dyke. Although this was now covered at some points, different-sized pipes had been used at different levels by different owners. A new sewer was therefore ordered for this stretch, linking the sound section at the village end with a section at the road leading to the Harlequin brickyard. William Vickerstaff won the contract for £80.5s.9d in October 1898.

Pollution in the Trent

In the meantime came the first of a number of complaints from the Trent Fishery Board at Derby in a letter of September 1897 to the District Council at Bingham:

> It is reported here that a small brook running into the River Trent is much polluted by sewage from the village of Ratcliffe. Can you tell me if the authority there have any scheme in hand for dealing with the matter?

Not only had Radcliffe no scheme in hand, but Bingham went so far as to deny that the brook in question caused any pollution of the Trent, so that it was unnecessary for any scheme to be prepared. The Trent Fishery Board did not agree. A wall was built to hold back the sewage. By September 1898 the board was complaining about this. If there were a flood thousands of fish would be killed by accumulated filth getting into the river over the wall. Both Bingham's inspector and Radcliffe's councillors considered this wall adequate, but a meeting took place in mid October between village councillors and the Fishery Board's water bailiff. The latter's solution was for another wall to be built, fifty yards above the first, with pipes to the river to drain off surface water.

Whether this measure was carried out is not clear, but the whole sewerage situation at Radcliffe was suddenly altered by an announcement from the County Council that they intended to discharge the sewage from Saxondale asylum, now being built, into Radcliffe's sewers and hence into the Trent. Radcliffe's first thoughts were about the apportionment of costs, and a deputation arranged to see Mr Hooley, the county surveyor. Nottingham Corporation also reacted rapidly to the proposal, pointing out that the county had been pressing them for some time to remedy the polluted state of the Trent, that large sums were being spent on taking refuse out of the river, and yet now they were about to add to the pollution problem. The county, having passed on its intentions to Bingham, trusted that Bingham would now take steps to provide a better system.

By the time Radcliffe councillors met the county surveyor they had decided that an improved system of septic tanks should be adopted and they asked Bingham R.D.C. for the necessary powers to carry out the arrangements. Bingham's response was that the existing arrangements for Radcliffe sewage were sufficient for the present, and they adjourned the matter for twelve months! Radcliffe, however, had a strong ally in Mr Hooley, the county's surveyor. (Relations in the past had not always been so amicable.) He gave his opinion that 'if the Local Government Board are acquainted with the facts that board will not share the opinion or approve of the action of Bingham R.D.C.' Radcliffe's reaction was similar to the cry for a local board in the 1880s. At the Parish Council meeting of December 20th 1899 Messrs Barnes and Bates proposed:

> *that whereas the Parish of Radcliffe-on-Trent has assumed a Suburban character with many and varied interests that improvements in regard to sanitary matters are immediately and urgently necessary, and further that the erection of the County Asylum in the parish will cause a larger increase in population and responsibilities, it is in the opinion of the Council desirable that the Parish should be formed into an Urban District and that application be made to the County Council for that purpose.*

Five-hundred circulars were distributed advertising a parish meeting on January 2nd 1900, and the matter was discussed with Lord Newark and other leading ratepayers. It was to no avail. The application was turned down on the grounds that the population was too small. The county recommended, however, that Radcliffe should make a formal complaint to them against Bingham, and then they could take action. Bingham consequently had to give way and on February 1st 1900 they rescinded their resolution that the question of Radcliffe's sewage should be adjourned for a year. Mr W.H. Radford, a civil engineer from Nottingham, was appointed to take on the mantle worn by Herbert Walker a generation before and devise an improved scheme. At last, prompted by the building of Saxondale hospital, after at least fifty years of patching, complaints, public meetings, and newspaper jibes Radcliffe was to acquire a 'modern' sewerage system.

The sewerage scheme 1902

Mr Radford proposed two possible sites, both off the Nottingham Road and close to Herbert Walker's last scheme. A joint Radcliffe and Bingham committee inspected them on August 9th 1900 and chose the one approached from Lees Barn Road owned by Lord Manvers. He was unwilling to sell, but was prepared to lease the site for fifty years at £4 a year. An attempt to beat him down to £3 a year failed. Negotiations with the existing tenant, Mr G. Huskinson, caused some delay.

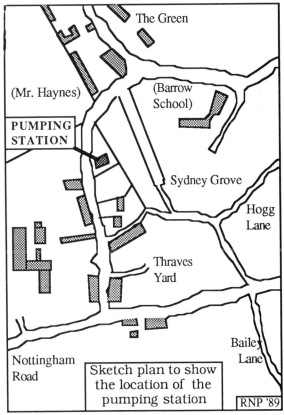

Sketch plan to show the location of the pumping station

RNP '89

Bingham agreed to pay compensation for his crops, but jibbed at paying more than £5 compensation for loss of tenant right in view of 'the unreasonable attitude' he had adopted. They also refused to pay him a further £2 compensation for damage caused by the sinking of four trial holes. The scheme required the purchase of about 400 square yards of land for a pumping station. Lord Manvers was prepared to sell a site near Lamcote corner for £225, but the committee must have thought the price too high, for they instantly approached both the trustees of Barrow School and the vicar about two alternative sites, but in the end Lord Manvers' price was paid.

Mr Radford did his best to keep costs down. His filter beds would merely be pits dug in the loamy soil - 'suitable for a village with limited resources' - although concrete linings would have been better. Two sets of machinery would be needed at the pumping station to raise 6,000 gallons per hour through the 6-inch rising main. By the time he had included the costs of long effluent pipes from the

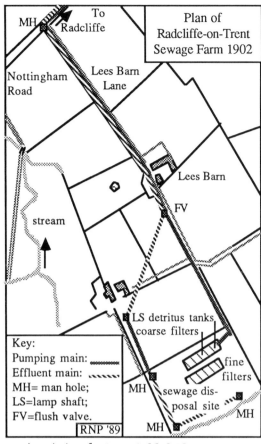

Plan of Radcliffe-on-Trent Sewage Farm 1902

To Radcliffe
MH
Nottingham Road
Lees Barn Lane
Lees Barn
FV
stream
LS detritus tanks
coarse filters
fine filters
MH
sewage disposal site
MH
MH

Key:
Pumping main:
Effluent main:
MH= man hole;
LS=lamp shaft;
FV=flush valve.
RNP '89

farm itself and from the asylum, new sewers to the greater part of the village, the connecting of private drains to the new sewers, the price of land, fees for himself and a clerk of works, his estimate came to £8,050. As a loan was needed, an inquiry would have to be held.

This took place in the schoolroom on June 11th 1901 before Colonel Durnford. He immediately pointed out that the G.N.R.C. would have to give approval to sewers crossing the railway line. The railway asked for £200. Mr Radford discovered he could take his sewer through a culvert under the railway. The railway said this would cost £50. It was then realised that the culvert already belonged to the sanitary authority so the G.N.R.C. was paid nothing. However, the Local Government Board's report did suggest three amendments to the scheme which added to the cost: a change in the level at which the coarse filters discharged to the fine filters; the lining of the filter beds with concrete - as the engineer would have preferred; and additional manholes. Another £650 was added to the scheme so a loan of £8,700 for thirty years at 3.25% was requested. Bower Brothers of West Bridgford won the contract, tendering at £6,948.

Although work on the main site could not begin until after March 25th 1902, to the relief of Mr Hooley, work had begun by February on the asylum sewer. The opening of the hospital was fast approaching with no means of disposing of its sewage. Radcliffe's suggestion that he should organise cess pits could not have been well received. Inevitably, both in the village and at the farm itself, there were problems. An old storm water culvert collapsed in the gardens of two houses as excavations began nearby for the new sewer, and in June the existing sewer along Bingham Road was broken by a traction engine, causing long delays to traffic. A Mr King claimed compensation when construction work dried his well, and the vicar complained that the engineer had refused to connect his drains to the new pipes. There were disputes about payment for metalling the cart track to the sewage farm in order that it could bear the necessary traffic. When the contractors removed trees and a clover crop allegedly without permission there was another lengthy wrangle about compensation. From August 1902 there were complaints about the slow progress of the work and the small number of men employed. It was soon realised that additional surface water drains would be needed to avoid grit getting into the sewers and to keep down the cost of pumping. By November 1902, with a few exceptions, all was complete.

The total cost was less than had been feared - £6,993. 9s.7d with £209.16s.1d left in hand for immediate maintenance purposes. The parish was authorised to superintend the maintenance and management of the sewage farm, but no more than £5 could be spent without Bingham's consent. John Wright of Thraves Yard was appointed to take charge of the pumping station, the filter beds and future house connections for 22s a week, rising to £2.15s a week in 1919. (Initially, owners wishing to be connected had to deposit £2 with the council. Any surplus was returned to the owner when the job was done.) George Vickerstaff was employed to look after the farm at £1 a week, rising to £2.2s in 1919. He was still employed there at the time of his death in 1926. Crops of osiers (willows), potatoes, sprouts, swedes, mangolds, cauliflowers and celery were regularly grown.

A healthier village?

And yet complaints about the state of the drains or about the smells from manholes still abound in the pages of various authorities' minute books. In 1907 a Dr Handford had to be commissioned to assess the situation, and to Radcliffe's dismay the sewerage scheme was found to be defective. Some houses were still unconnected. (A check in August 1906 showed that thirty-eight were not connected, seventeen were doubtful, but 480 were.) Marrow plants were found growing on the filter beds, and an analysis of the effluent as it left the works showed it to be 'weak unpurified sewage'. The Parish Council could not accept Dr Handford's statement that the old parish drain was 'nearly as foul and offensive as before the new purification works were undertaken'. Anyone who had known the previous situation would refute that. Arrangements were made to have the defects remedied.

It would certainly be reassuring to record improvements in health after the introduction of piped water and an effective sewerage scheme. Many diseases were airborne, however, and outbreaks continued much as before, although the high death rate recorded in 1849 and 1881-2 does not seem to have been repeated. (See graph on page 15.) Improved diet may have produced greater resistance to disease. A potentially serious outbreak of smallpox in the Headland family at the Harlequin and in the Flower family 'residing in a row of houses off Cropwell Road' in 1903 was soon controlled. The Flowers were moved into isolation premises at Bingham workhouse and the colleagues of the head of the family, a railway platelayer, were hastily vaccinated. All recovered. A comparison of diseases mentioned in the school log books between 1890 and 1903, and between 1904 and 1920 shows little difference. Measles, mumps, scarlet fever, and scarlatina appear throughout. Whooping cough appears only in the earlier period, but erysipelas and diphtheria appear later, with one death from the latter. During the 1914-18 war two new diseases occurred - infantile paralysis and influenza. Some part of the school was closed three times because of illness between 1890 and 1903. Between 1904 and 1920 it was closed seven times.

Saxondale hospital established

Radcliffe had reason to be grateful to the new asylum as the instigator of clean water and improved sewerage, but resentment arose soon after Lady Elinor Denison had performed the opening ceremony in July 1902. The amount of sewage and quantity of water used alarmed Radcliffe. In November Mr Radford requested the asylum authority to prevent 'rags, cloths and soiled underclothing' from being put in the sewers. There were objections, too, when the number of asylum burials in the village put a strain on existing resources and the parish had to purchase land for an extension to the cemetery. In 1913 and 1914 there was a lengthy wrangle when

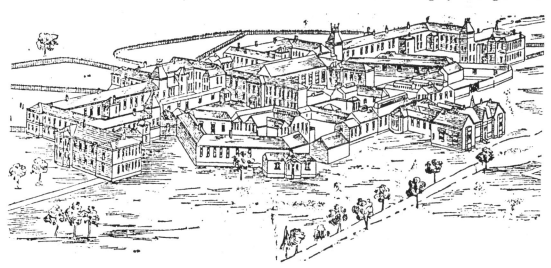

Artist's preliminary drawing of Saxondale Hospital

twelve asylum cottages were built for attendants, to be let at 5s a week. Technically they were just outside the parish boundary and Radcliffe at first refused to accept sewage from them on the grounds that 'there is quite as much sewage in the parish as can be dealt with'. Eventually, Radcliffe accepted responsibility for an annual payment of £1 per cottage, having initially asked for a total of £18. The hospital authorities still considered that Radcliffe was being totally unreasonable.

In 1918 Saxondale became a military hospital, with some staff being given ranks. (For example, Dr Lloyd-Jones, who was in charge, was made a lieutenant-colonel.) Towards the end of 1919 the military left, and the hospital again became the responsibility of the local authority. It was shortly after this that probably the most dramatic incident of its history occurred. In the difficult economic climate of the 1920s, pressure mounted for spending cuts. The Saxondale nursing staff accepted a reduction in wages but refused to work extra hours. Many were now trade union members and they decided to hold out against the management. On March 27th 1922 the management responded by dismissing all the staff, offering to re-employ them only if they agreed to abide by the new conditions. All the female staff refused to sign, as did the majority of the men. On April 11th, having failed to come to terms, the staff went on strike, barricading themselves in by jamming home-made keys in all the locks. When the medical superintendent approached a window, a fire hose was trained on him. One female charge nurse knocked out a policeman, thought she had killed him, and fainted on top of him. The inmates then joined in. According to the *Nottingham Journal* of April 15th:

> *lunatics got out of control and smashed windows, pictures and anything else within reach; hand-to-hand struggles took place between officials and patients, in the course of which Superintendent Smith of the Notts. County Constabulary was bitten on the hand, while others were scratched and buffeted.*

Once the water was turned off at the main, the bailiffs began to make some headway and battered down the doors, causing staff to fight a rearguard battle through the hospital. Eventually the strikers were taken prisoner, and a charabanc was laid on to take them away. A meeting was held in Radcliffe, and the strikers were given much needed financial assistance by the union as they were now blacklisted. A witness of these events recalls how the Rev Cecil Smith was instrumental in recruiting new staff from villages in Lincolnshire. Many were untrained, and a difficult period on the wards followed. After some eighty-seven years in use, the hospital is scheduled for closure (1989), and the old Lings Farm site will be redeveloped.

A village improved

Despite criticisms, continuing illness, and the difficulty of eradicating all sanitary defects, Radcliffe could be well pleased with its improved state of affairs in the early part of this century. Perhaps the *Nottingham Weekly Express*, in attributing Radcliffe's growing popularity to its good sewerage and drainage, was a little premature in stating that both were 'as perfect as science and money can make them'. Those who were to witness the floods of 1922, 1936, 1947, 1967, and of 1977 in the Clumber Drive area, might have concluded that not all problems relating to drainage had been solved. Nevertheless, piped water and a sewerage system did put Radcliffe ahead of many of its rivals, and the snaking Syke Drain, that constant threat to the village's well-being, had at last been (largely) tamed and purified.

Main sources

Primary

Leicestershire County Record Office: records of Humphrey Perkins' School, Barrow-on-Soar ES/23/89-108.

Nottinghamshire Archives Office: Radcliffe parish registers PR 1498-1507; Bingham Union poor law minute books PUD 1/1/1-19; Radcliffe vaccination registers 1871-1920 PUD 4/5/1-6; Bingham Rural Sanitary Authority minute book 1872-1881 DC/BI1/1/1; Bingham Rural Sanitary Authority Radcliffe parochial minutes PAC 35/2; Radcliffe school log books SL 135 1/1-8.

Nottinghamshire County Library (Local Studies Library): census returns.

Radcliffe-on-Trent Parish Council: vestry minute book 1839-1872; parish council minute books 1894 onwards.

Rushcliffe Borough Council: Bingham Rural Sanitary Authority minute books 1882 onwards.

University of Nottingham: Manvers papers Ma 2D 54.

Secondary

Carpenter, Mick. *All for One: Campaigns and pioneers in the making of COHSE.* 1980.

Henstock, Valerie (ed.). *Victorian Bingham.* 1986.

Radcliffe-on-Trent local history research group: extracts from Nottingham newspapers 1837-1920

LAW AND ORDER 1837-1887

It is not possible to present a complete picture of law breaking and law enforcement in Radcliffe as much information has not survived. Few police records involving the village have been found, and only the more serious cases reached courts for which minute books still exist. As detailed information about cases is therefore largely dependent on the vagaries of newspaper reporting, statistical analysis of the subject cannot be undertaken. Nevertheless, there is ample material from which to gain an impression of the main concerns and methods of the period, and a special study has been made of the fifty years from 1837 to 1887.

I. Law enforcement

The parish constable

At the start of Queen Victoria's reign the traditional system of law enforcement was still in operation. This relied on the services of the parish constable, an office dating back to at least the thirteenth century. Over the years the holder was required to perform numerous duties such as arresting felons, maintaining stocks and local lock-ups, summoning juries, collecting the county rate and any national taxes, arranging the apprenticeship of pauper children, seeking-out reluctant fathers in illegitimacy cases, and generally assisting the churchwardens and overseers of the poor in their duties. Radcliffe's constables kept a book recording their activities and expenses from 1772 to 1836, by which time they were paid about £12 a year in addition to their expenses. (Fees were then abolished by the Poor Law Commissioners.) The only indication of the constables' existence in Victorian times comes from the spasmodic lists of names in the parish vestry book from whom the magistrates made their selection. The name of the chosen man is rarely indicated, although it seems possible that William Barratt held the post for five years from 1847 to 1851. With the passing of new legislation, such as the Poor Law Amendment act of 1834 and the County Police Act of 1839, the responsibilities of the parish constable greatly diminished, but on swearing in the new parish constables in April 1851 the magistrates made it clear that the incumbents were not to regard their duties as nominal, and they would be punished if they did not perform them properly. In particular, they were to look 'sharply' after public houses, but only by special warrant could they act outside their own parish. It is difficult from Radcliffe's records to produce specific examples of their work, but it was not until August 1872 that the county magistrates first suggested that parish constables were no longer needed, although a parish vestry could still apply to have one. As the last list of potential constables appears in the Radcliffe vestry book in 1872, it seems that the village did not make a special application, although newspaper reports show that in some places parish constables were being appointed as late as 1886.

Associations for the Prosecutions of Felons

Alongside this official parish system, groups of private individuals had occasionally got together to help enforce law and order for the benefit of their members. A Bingham Association was reported to have had about 100 members at its annual meeting in December 1842, but it seems to have attracted only one Radcliffe man, John Morley. The rewards it offered included £10.10s for the conviction of any person murdering, 'cutting and shooting' or in any other way attempting to murder a member, and £3.3s for the conviction of anyone stealing from members. More widespread was the Association for the Prosecution of Felons and other offenders for Lord Manvers' tenants. Originally founded in 1785 when the 'bigamous' Duchess of Kingston ran the estates, the early minutes show that Radcliffe cases mainly involved a break-in at the wharf, and the theft of cattle and horses. From 1815 the annual meetings became very stereotyped. Dinner, rather than business, seems to have been the main preoccupation, although in 1842 there was a separation of the northern from the southern part of the estates.

On June 1st 1849 the southern organisation was revitalised, and new rules were drawn up at a meeting at the Fox and Crown Inn on the outskirts of Radcliffe.

Rewards.

Burglary, housebreaking highway robbery, foot-pad robbery, setting fire to, or burning any dwelling house, barn, stable, or outhouse, stack of corn, straw, hay, or any other property, or stealing any horse, mare, or gelding. _____ } £ s d | 10 . 0 . 0 .

Stealing any beast, or sheep, or other cattle, or wilfully & maliciously wounding or maiming any description of horse, beast, sheep, or other cattle. ─ } 5 . 0 . 0

Breaking into any mill, barn, stable or other outbuilding, with intent to steal, or stealing any corn, or other description of property thereon, _____ } £ s d | 4 . 0 . 0

Receiving stolen goods knowing them to have been stolen, servants embez= =gling or stealing their employers property, _____ } 3 . 0 . 0

For any other felonious offence. _____ 2 . 0 . 0

Extracts from the rule book of the Manvers Association for the
Prosecution of Felons
(Nottinghamshire Archives Office, DD 54/1
By permission of the Principal Archivist)

Members occupying less than twenty acres of Lord Manvers' lands, and not market gardeners, paid an annual fee of 1s.6d. All other members who were tenants, including market gardeners, paid 2s.6d. Non-tenants could join for an entrance fee of 2s.6d and an annual subscription of 2s.6d. Fifteen rules explained the main benefits and rewards offered. For example, if a felony or misdemeanour was committed on the person or property of a member, his child or servants, all expenses of apprehending and prosecuting the offenders over and above the amount allowed by law would be paid out of the Associations's funds. Section 3 listed rewards to be paid to non-members for the conviction of offenders against members, their children or servants:

> *Burglary, housebreaking, highway robbery, footpad robbery, setting fire to or burning any dwellinghouse, barn, stable or outhouse, stack of corn, straw, hay, or any other property, or stealing horse, mare, or gelding* £10.0s.0d
> *Stealing any beast, or sheep, or other cattle, or wilfully & maliciously wounding or maiming any description of horse, beast, sheep or other cattle* £5.0s.0d
> *Breaking into any mill, barn, stable or other outbuilding with intent to steal, or stealing any corn, or other description of property thereon* £4.0s.0d
> *Receiving stolen goods knowing them to have been stolen, servants embezzling or stealing their employer's property* £3.0s.0d
> *For any other felonious offence* £2.0s.0d
> *For any species of larceny, all convictions under any trespass or other act & every other offence amounting to an indictable misdemeanour* 10s.0d

The total paid-up membership between 1849 and 1855 was eighty-two. A dozen of these came from Radcliffe: Edward Brewster, George Bell of the Manvers Arms, William Taylor, the magistrate from Radcliffe Hall, John Howard, William Morley, George Whitworth, John Palin, Gervas Parr, Thomas Butler, Richard Butler, Richard Foster junior, and one woman - Ann Richmond. The names of the Rev Robert Burgess and Thomas Beeson were crossed through as no payments were recorded. (Over the same period fourteen members came from Cotgrave.)

To begin with, the annual general meeting and dinner was held in rotation at Holme Pierrepont, Cotgrave, Radcliffe (The Manvers Arms), and Nottingham, but from 1858 the venue was always somewhere in Nottingham. There were thirteen on the committee, and at least two in the early days came from Radcliffe - Edward Brewster senior and Thomas Butler. The latter was the injured party in two cases recorded in the annual minutes. In 1851 he claimed £1 for magistrates' and constables' fees when the culprits were convicted for breaking the leg of one of his sheep. (This was probably the case heard at Bingham in 1849 when George and William Dale were each fined 20 shillings for injuring Thomas Butler's sheep.) A year later, after his stacks had been set alight, the association jibbed at paying the reward claimed by one of the witnesses. It was agreed, however, that he could be given £2 'as a present, but not otherwise'.

By this stage the association was £25 in debt and members had to pay out an extra 7s.6d each. By this time, too, a spate of thefts from market gardens was proving expensive, so market gardeners' subscriptions were raised from 2s.6d to 10s, and then to £1. In 1867 an entrance fee of 5s even for tenants was imposed. For non-tenants it was 10s. Perhaps these increased fees were self-defeating, or the work of an official police force was proving effective, for numbers declined. In 1882 John Holmes of Radcliffe was expelled for never having paid even his entrance fee and John Green was four years in arrears with his subscription, while between 1884 and 1888 the total membership was as low as sixteen, with only two members living in the village. In these later years the association seems to have been little more than a gentlemen's annual dining club with the few members treating themselves lavishly. In 1894, for example, eight dinners at the Clarendon Quadrant near Market Street in Nottingham came to £2.4s, but the sherry, champagne, port, spirits, Apollinaris etc. brought the total up to £5.15s.2d. The association eventually extinguished itself in style. On 15th May 1912 four members turned up for the annual dinner at the Albert Hotel. After the meal John Parr, doubtless replete, proposed that 'as the funds of the association are now exhausted it be now dissolved'.

Formation of the county police

For most of the population it was the County Police Act of 1839 which was to point the way for law enforcement. By this act magistrates were allowed to set up a paid county force, and Nottinghamshire took the opportunity of doing so about 1840. These new 'rural police' were by no means always welcome, however, either locally or elsewhere in the country. As early as January 7th 1842 the *Nottingham Journal* reported that a petition against them had been signed 'by every ratepayer in the village of Radcliffe' and given to William Taylor, the local J.P., for presentation to the magistrates at Quarter Sessions. Radcliffe was not alone in holding these views. In May 1843 a number of vestry meetings throughout the county complained of the expense of maintaining such a 'useless body' and wished to be rid of 'so vexatious and unconstitutional a burden'. Radcliffe again subscribed to these views in June, and by the end of the month about 119 out of 261 county parishes had petitioned the magistrates in favour of disbanding the rural police. Even Colonel Rolleston, the chairman who had helped set up the body, agreed that as so many felt it was inefficient and useless it should indeed be disbanded, but the matter was adjourned until the Southwell sessions in October. Despite this apparently overwhelming view, when the magistrates met again they narrowly granted the county police a reprieve by seventeen votes to thirteen.

Village policemen

Criticism still continued from time to time, however. For example, another forty-nine petitions against the continuance of the county force were presented to the Southwell Quarter Sessions in October 1845, and in January 1852 the arrest rate in the county was adversely compared to that in the town. At this date the Bingham district of the county had six policemen. The first identifiable county constable for Radcliffe was John William Parsons who was active from at least the mid 1840s. In the early 1850s constables Blyton, Cooke and Webster were associated with Radcliffe cases. Blyton at least lodged in the village. William Eason (P.C. No. 65) was the main appointment from 1856. He had joined the force at the age of 34 in 1845, and the Nottinghamshire Constabulary's Descriptive Register notes that he was 5' 7¾ tall, with grey eyes, dark brown hair and a sallow complexion. The census returns show that both he and his wife were born at Blidworth, and they had a daughter who was born in Arnold about 1841. Constable Eason had served at Edwinstowe before coming to Radcliffe. He moved to Mansfield in 1861 and then to Warsop, being discharged in 1876 with an allowance of £45 p.a. He died in 1879.

The County and Borough Police Act of 1856 allowed a locality to pay for an additional number of constables from the county force. At the end of the previous December a number of villagers anticipated this clause and agreed to pay for their own police constable at the rate of £60 a year. (This was well above the normal salary, for in 1865 the county was still only paying constables between 17s and 20s a week.) By the time of the next Quarter Sessions in April, however, Radcliffe had changed its mind about the need for this additional constable and he had been withdrawn.

Although a number of police names appear in the newspaper accounts after William Eason's departure, two figures dominate policing in Radcliffe: John Stevenson and George Allwood. The former was born in Radford, worked at first as an agricultural labourer and joined the Nottinghamshire police in 1857 at the age of 23. He was 5' 9" tall, fresh complexioned, with brown hair and grey eyes. His wife, Ann, was two years older than he, and they had a daughter who worked as a lace hand. Before coming to Radcliffe in 1863 he had served at Mansfield and Mansfield Woodhouse, and after ten years in the village he was made up to sergeant. His pay would then be £1.8s per week. (In 1874 the police establishment for the Bingham district was one superintendent, one sergeant and seven constables.) His record shows some of the benefits of his job: a present of £1 from Richard Butler for assisting at a fire in 1869, and the gift of a watch and purse worth £25 from the inhabitants of Radcliffe in 1875. There was, however, another side to the picture. Although crime in the village was comparatively petty, he had to cope with growing problems of drink and violence, particularly in the 1870s. After two cases in 1878 in which he suffered violent assaults he was moved to Burton Joyce. In 1884 at the age of 50 he was discharged as 'incapacitated from infirmity of body' with an allowance of £56 p.a. - two-thirds of his pay.

Sergeant George Allwood, John Stevenson's successor, came in a direct exchange from Burton Joyce. Born at Wellow, he too had begun work as an agricultural labourer, joining the force in 1860 at the age of 25. Described as fresh-complexioned with grey eyes and brown hair, he was 5' 8" tall. After a short spell at Sneinton, he had spent two years in Radcliffe between 1861 and 1863. As a young constable in 1862 he had been struck and abused in a dispute over an ownerless boat. The assailant, a former policeman, complained to the Chief Constable that P.C. Allwood had exceeded his duty, but he was nevertheless fined. Shortly after this unfortunate incident George Allwood's duties took him away from the village, and he served in the Park in Nottingham, Radford, Hyson Green, Bulwell, Sneinton and Burton Joyce before returning to Radcliffe in 1878. By then he had been a sergeant for ten years. He too had to cope with growing disorder during the 1880s, by which time the Bingham district establishment had been increased to thirteen. The 1881 census shows he was married with a 19-year-old son who worked as a warehouseman's apprentice. He could play the piano and was also a member of the local Rifle Volunteers, winning a shooting prize in 1889. The last Radcliffe case with which he has been identified was in January 1891. He was discharged in August of that year with an allowance of £56.15s p.a. and continued to live in the village for some years. He died in Ollerton in October 1913 but was buried in Radcliffe.

The Police Station

When the census was taken in 1881, George Allwood was living in a new police station. Radcliffe's population of 1,340 did not really justify such a deterrent, but the increasing number of drunk and disorderly cases resulting from great numbers of visitors was making it impossible for the police to cope with the situation. Consequently, in October 1874 the Chief Constable had recommended that a police station with attached lock-up, and accommodation for two married constables, be built 'for the accommodation of persons of all descriptions who came from Nottingham, especially on Sundays'. Land on the main street was rented from Lord Manvers for £10 a year and the station was built in 1875 for some £650. Whether more than one officer ever lived there is not clear, but George Allwood seems to have been followed by Sergeants Samuel Herod, George Caunt, and Jason Carlin up to the time of the First World War who all made the police station their home. From September 1891 the station was appointed for use as an occasional court house, but

Radcliffe police station about 1910

240

in the following June the *Nottingham Daily Guardian* reported that the building was in a bad state of repair:

> *The walls were in a bad condition, the cells without any method of heating, and so damp as to be unfit for occupation. The well of drinking water was within 4 yards of the outhouses. There was no scullery and the outhouses were of the old vault principle.*

It was agreed that repairs should be put in hand which would cost £120. Radcliffe kept its police station until 1973. The building has recently been used as office accommodation.

Stocks and whipping post

The police station was a new stage in the execution of justice locally. Much older aids to law and order are only hinted at in the records. The parish constable's accounts for 1800, for example, indicate that there was a rudimentary lock-up in the village at that time. The much-restored whipping post near the church may also have a long history, but it cannot yet be verified from documentary sources. The first reference, so far found, dates only from 1909 when the Thoroton Society reported that the irons had been found and would be refixed on the site where the whipping post had stood. Stocks have an equally shadowy history in Radcliffe. From 1405 they had to be provided in every town and village, but by the 1830s they were generally neglected. The only references that have been found are purely anecdotal. One comes from the reminiscences in 1920 of a John Riley of Radford who had spent his schooldays in the village in the 1840s:

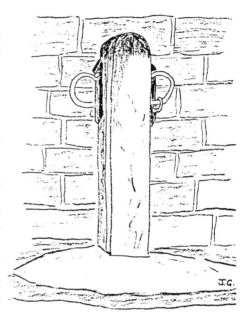

Radcliffe's much restored whipping post, now protected by railings

> *One Saturday, W. Pare, general dealer, had been to market and come home 'market merry' when he met the constable, who took him before the Squire, who gave him two hours in the village stocks. Some children were pelting him with orange peel when I came on the scene and drove them away. He thanked me and did me a good turn in 1846.*

(The good turn was to help the boy run away from school after he had been punished.) According to another reminiscence in the *Newark Advertiser* in August 1889, the stocks had stood at the east end of the churchyard and were pulled down by some mischievous lads. The last occupant was said to be an habitual drunkard named Simpson some forty years earlier.

The local magistrates

The 'Squire' referred to by John Riley was William Taylor of Radcliffe Hall. He and his son, John Bagshaw Taylor, were active in many aspects of Radcliffe life and were the two main magistrates to come from the village during the Victorian period. (See p. 147 for other information.) They belonged to a group of local landowners from whom the magistracy was drawn, and which included Lord Manvers and Lord Newark, particularly when the latter lived at Holme Pierrepont Hall. William Taylor served as magistrate at both the Shire Hall in Nottingham and at Bingham where most of the Radcliffe cases were dealt with. In 1840 and again in 1850 he was on the opposite side of the legal process when lead was stolen off his roof by a workman, and when he was assaulted by drunken companions of one of his employees. (Perhaps his faith in the county legal system was not absolute since he also belonged to the Manvers Association for the Prosecution of Felons.) At his death in 1857 Henry Martin, the chairman of the Bingham bench, testified to his qualities as a magistrate in celestial terms:

> *...It is not more than due to his memory to say he was distinguished by all the social virtues that adorn private life; whilst in the discharge of his public duties as a magistrate, in which I was often associated with him, he was ever actuated by a desire to administer impartial justice. He is now gone to that tribunal whose judgements are faultless, and let us hope that his reward is a blessed immortality.*

His son John also sat on the bench at Bingham and in Nottingham, attended Quarter Sessions in connection with the general administration of the county, and was High Sheriff in 1868. The suggestion in John Riley's account of the incident in the stocks, that justice in minor cases was occasionally summarily executed in the village, is confirmed in a later reminiscence about Radcliffe Hall by Gilbert Elwyn. He recalls that when he came to Radcliffe in 1903 elderly people spoke freely of the time when the Taylors had used the Hall as a court where local offenders were tried for their wrongdoings. Like his father, John Taylor was occasionally the victim of petty crime. He was almost certainly not on the bench when George Vickerstaff, his waggoner for ten years, was convicted of stealing 5 lbs of potatoes from him in October 1870, but he seems to have remained when George Allen was sentenced for damaging twenty-eight gates including Taylor's own.

Newspaper reports of the official cases heard before John Taylor occasionally include some of his comments. In July 1874 two men caught fishing on Lord Manvers' stretch of the Trent claimed that it was clearly understood in Nottingham that they could fish there. 'If you are guided by what they say in Nottingham you may get into a scrape,' he informed them before imposing a fine of 1s with costs. A regular drunkard in May 1879 he described as having been 'on the spree', and he cut short Thomas Kell of the Black Lion, who complained in the August that there had been more lenient treatment in the Retford division with, 'We have nothing to do with Retford.' In fining a man for flogging his stepson in January 1882, John Taylor noted that the fact that the defendant was drunk aggravated the crime, but the bench 'believed the boy was a bad one'. Two cyclists at the same sessions who claimed that they did not know it was wrong to ride on the footpath were assured that their fine 'would be the means of impressing it upon their memories'. In February 1883 he had little sympathy for John Simpson, who brought an action against Bingham sanitary authority for damage to his property after repairs to a drain, because he had contributed to the damage by building over a public sewer. That was one of John Taylor's last hearings. In the previous year, when aged 70, he had sat at Bingham on at least sixteen occasions and had also been telegraphed in May to go to Shire Hall to sit in the place of a missing colleague. (The business had been delayed almost three hours.) The death of his wife in 1883 caused him to move to Scarborough. A newspaper report of his funeral in 1893 claimed that he had served as a magistrate for fifty-one years.

John Taylor's bold signature from the Radcliffe vestry book
in the possession of the Parish Council

The Bingham courts and lock-up

Apart from a rare attendance at a coroner's court held in one of the public houses, a villager's experience of the law in action would normally be in Bingham. Cases of theft, drunkenness, poaching or minor assault were dealt with at the petty sessions there on alternate Thursdays, and civil disputes were heard in a county court held once a month. Each August or September, too, the court turned itself into a brewster sessions for the granting or withdrawal of public house licenses in the division.

Facilities at Bingham were less than adequate, particularly at the start of the period. Until Radcliffe had its own police station from 1875, any prisoners awaiting trial were held at Bingham. A new building was provided in 1852, designed by A.R. Sutton, a Nottingham architect. The original grant of £180 proved insufficient when Lord Chesterfield, who gave the land, insisted on a better quality building than the county had originally envisaged. Up to £225 was finally needed. Even so, in January 1862 the lock-up, by then described as a police station, came in for some criticism from Captain Holden, the chief constable:

> ...the heating of the cells at Bingham police station was very badly arranged ...There was a pipe in one of them which seemed to have been made with no other motive than to afford the prisoners opportunities of hanging themselves.

Repairs were ordered which would cost £10.

Until 1858 the accused faced equally unsuitable conditions once he or she had been brought to court. The sessions were held in a room in a public house for which the authorities were charged £3.8s (£3.12s if the monthly county court was in session), and 1s a week for policemen's lodgings. Although the room itself was good enough, it was inconvenient for the purpose:

> ...witnesses and others were subject to the most improper influences, the place being close to the tap room, and there were other circumstances most prejudicial to the ends of justice.

It was felt that a suitable building could be provided for £200 and would soon be paid for by the savings on rent. R.C. Sutton again drew up the plans, which were approved provided the cost did not exceed £280.

The House of Correction

Most of the accused at Bingham would face a predictable level of fine with costs if found guilty. A few would be sent to the local House of Correction, on Burgage Green at Southwell for a spell of imprisonment which might include hard labour on a treadwheel or solitary confinement. The gaol's origins went back to 1611, but it had been improved and rebuilt about 1806. In 1868 the average number of daily prisoners was ninety-two, and the weekly cost of food per head was 2s.1¾d. (This was 5d more than was spent in Nottingham county gaol, but almost a shilling less than was spent in Stamford.) It was extended and improved in that year and in September 1870 it was reported to have accommodation for 130 males and eighteen females. Its treadwheel, cleanliness and improved diet were all noted at that time. In 1877 it became a government prison, but soon afterwards it was decided to discontinue its use. The last commitment seems to have been on July 7th 1879. The building was subsequently used as a lace factory, and then by a firm of haulage contractors. After a fire it was demolished in 1974, leaving only the gateway standing.

The Nottingham courts

Occasionally, Radcliffe people might find themselves before the Nottingham police court in the town hall or the Shire Hall court if they were involved in petty offences which took place outside Radcliffe, or which involved people from the city or other parts of the county. More serious cases would also be transferred by the Bingham magistrates to the Quarter Sessions held at Shire Hall. Few Radcliffe offences merited trial at this level, and even rarer were cases which went to the Assizes and were heard before judges on circuit. As the century progressed and Radcliffe became a dormitory for Nottingham businessmen, the appearance of residents in civil cases before both the Nottingham bankruptcy court and the Nottingham county court was not uncommon.

II. Law breaking and disputes

Early newspaper reports of crimes and court cases contain little detail compared to those from the 1860s onwards, but a formidable amount of evidence exists for the period as a whole. The years from 1837 to 1887 were selected for particular study, using *Nottingham Journal* reports, supported by other evidence where possible. (In 1887 the *Journal* was absorbed by the *Nottingham Daily Express.*) Unfortunately, the records of the petty sessions at Bingham have not survived, but the Quarter Sessions minutes are extant. Even allowing for the selective coverage of newspaper reporting, and the sparse official coverage of the few Radcliffe cases which reached the Quarter Sessions, some clear impressions emerge.

Some unsolved cases

A number of unsolved incidents give an insight into the customs and concerns of the time. Reports range from the theft of Samuel Parr's three-year old 'bay cart mare', taken from a Bingham Road field one night in 1843, to James Green's manure stolen from his garden in 1844. Radcliffe visitors to Nottingham seemed particularly vulnerable or careless. John Arnold had his black velveteen coat stolen from a cart in Red [Lion] Street in 1854. George Reynolds' overcoat went from a cart standing in St Peter's Square, and Mr Parr's basket containing 20 lbs of butter was stolen from Nottingham market place in 1855. A hamper of meat belonging to Samuel Brewster was taken between Hollowstone and London Road in 1857. Several cases of alleged burglary or theft show the range of valuables kept in local houses. In October 1850 the miller and baker Robert Green locked up his premises to go to a meeting at 6.30 p.m. On his return he found that thieves had taken £5 or £6 in money, one dozen silver teaspoons marked *EG*, four teaspoons and one tablespoon marked *M*, two teaspoons marked *MS*, four teaspoons and four tablespoons marked *G*, as well as a sugar bowl, a silver cream jug, a pair of plated snuffers, an old crown piece marked *EG*, one spade guinea, and two gold rings. It was fortunate that most of his money was in his pocket. The Misses Allsebrook, governess sisters, had their house ransacked while they were at church early in 1851. Their losses were more modest: a silver watch, a few old silver teaspoons, and some money, including the contents of a missionary box. It was a second Samuel Parr, a commission agent, who returned from visiting friends with his wife in February 1852 to find 'some clever Hobbs' had picked the lock of his outside door and gone off with two or three £10 notes of the Stamford and Spalding Bank, two £10 notes of Smith's Bank, Nottingham, £25 in Messrs Hardy and Walkingham's notes, eight sovereigns, seven half sovereigns, two German silver teaspoons marked *A* on the back, and two unmarked German silver salt spoons. 'No suspicion attaches to anyone in the locality,' the *Nottingham Journal* announced. It was less circumspect in March 1860 when it blamed the niece of John Foster, a Radcliffe cattle dealer, for the theft of silver spoons, old coins, a bank note for £500 and a promissory note for £200 from her uncle. The following week the paper had to admit to inaccuracies in names and items stolen, and acknowledge that police suspicions had proved unfounded and that the lady had not been charged. 'We are very sorry to have been instrumental in propagating so injurious a statement respecting an innocent person.'

Cases before the Bingham magistrates

Some examples from the Radcliffe cases will help to indicate the range of minor legislation dealt with in the Bingham courts. Much of it concerned idleness, work and family responsibilities. Two begging cases, nearly forty years apart, show some softening of sentence. In December 1841 Matthew Martin was given a month's hard labour, whereas in December 1880 John Bryan, found with food in his pocket, received only half that sentence. Absconding apprentices could also find themselves before the bench. William Upton's charge against Thomas Parr was dismissed in March 1862 because the boy had not been properly bound by indenture. (Upton then brought a case against the boy's father in the civil court which he also lost.) In the case of Robert Durant, charged in July 1874 with absenting himself from the service of Mr Young, Radcliffe's surgeon-dentist, the verdict went against the boy. He was to pay a week's wages and 10s in costs, but on having no money was given a prison sentence. There was then a dramatic scene with 'a young girl in court advising him amidst much excitement' that 'the fine would be paid'. The enforcement of family responsibilities came within the province of the Bingham court too: 1s.6d a week to be paid by the father of an illegitimate child in June 1847; 1s a week by a labourer towards the maintenance of his father in September 1881; six weeks with hard labour for a man charged with deserting his wife and child, so making them dependent on the workhouse in April 1884. From the 1880s the magistrates also dealt with parents who neglected to send their children to school. Except for repeated cases fines were normally between 1s and 2s.6d.

Numerous other matters reflected the everyday concerns of a busy local community. Infringements of traffic regulations ranged from driving a cart without reins, earning a fine of 2s.6d in September 1841, to obstructing the highway with soil (fined 40s in December 1881), manure (dismissed with a warning in May 1885) or night soil (two fines of 2s.6d in July 1885). Ill-treatment of a horse belonging to Thomas Butler cost Frederick Austin 5s in July 1854. The court, however, thought that Charles Bolton's rough treatment of his neighbour's trespassing bantam was justified and in May 1884 the charge of cruelty was dismissed. Unjust weights, weighing machines or measures brought varying punishments. Edward Parr's two weighing machines at the wharf had not been adjusted, except by himself, in seven years. He was fined 50s in March 1875 with the threat of a full £5 fine if the offence recurred. Six months later Mary Scrimshaw was sent to prison for a month for leaving six lumps of coal weighing 9 lbs on the shaft of her cart when she had delivered half a ton of coal from the wharf to James Upton. Mr Barratt's unjust weighing machine at the Co-operative Stores and Walter Stafford's six faulty weights at his grocer's shop led to £1 fines in July 1879 and September 1885 respectively. Only minor cases of damage to property were dealt with locally. In April 1852 John Parr received the lowest recorded fine of 1d with costs for destroying a fence at Radcliffe. In March 1861 John Walker was fined £1 with costs for damaging Robert Butler's fence, while George Allen of Cropwell preferred to go to prison for fourteen days rather than pay his fine and costs of £4.0s.7d for damaging gates belonging to Thomas Butler, Richard Stone and John Taylor of Radcliffe and Henry Smith of Cropwell. New legislation had also to be taken into account. Cattle 'plague' meant restrictions on the movement of livestock in the 1860s, while failure to have a dog licence meant a fine of 2s.6d for William Barratt in October 1881. In 1887, fear of rabies led to an order that all dogs should be muzzled. Both George Turner and Catherine Bell were fined 5s in that year for failure to comply. All such infringements occurred infrequently. The local magistrates' time was more likely to be taken up with four main types of case: poaching, theft, assault, and illegal or excessive drinking.

Poaching

Perhaps the commonest reason for a court appearance was poaching. A number of men who appeared before the Bingham magistrates for illegal pursuit of game were undoubtedly local, but many came from elsewhere and happened to be caught in Radcliffe. The full penalty was a £5 fine, or imprisonment if it could not be paid, but there were various gradations in the offence. George Beeson was fined only £2 with costs for trespassing in pursuit of game in January 1852. William Parr was discharged for a similar offence in April 1857, but a month later the magistrates fined him £2 with costs for the pursuit of game in Radcliffe and £5 and costs for using snares at Saxondale. The use of nets, traps or snares generally resulted in the maximum fine, and William Parr had already been fined £5 for their use in 1854. William Love was another 'old poacher' who made regular court appearances. In 1855 and 1862 he was unable to pay his £5 fines and on both occasions was sent to the House of Correction in Southwell for two months. In February 1863 he was caught with two other men poaching near the Shepherd houses over the Cotgrave boundary, and all three were imprisoned at Southwell in default of the £5 fines. Perhaps hardship genuinely caused their activities for they said in court that 'if farmers would not find them employment they would commit robbery'.

Poaching gangs in the 1860s led to some violent clashes with authority. In April 1860 one such gang was at work on Lord Chesterfield's land between Bingham and Saxondale and cart loads of game were reported on the road. All but one escaped, including a man thought to be from Radcliffe who got away by shedding his coat.

Perhaps as a result of such activities the heaviest prison sentences imposed for poaching by the Bingham magistrates occurred around this period. In April 1861 William Bemrose and William Longley were sent to Southwell for three months for night poaching on Edward Smith's land at Radcliffe, and they had to find sureties for good behaviour on their release. In December 1864 one man received a similar sentence for shooting a hare on Samuel Brewster's land, his two companions were sentenced to two months each. Although the same maximum fines could still be imposed in the 1870s, sentences were generally lighter than in the earlier part of the period. For example, three men charged with trespassing in pursuit of game on Thomas Butler's lands in August 1870 received fines ranging from only 16s to 20s or imprisonment from 21 days to a month, and in March 1887 Nathan Wilson, a platelayer, was fined 21s for trespass and digging for rabbits on Henry Smith's Radcliffe land.

In the previous December the magistrates had delivered their verdict 'after long consideration' in another case of poaching on Henry Smith's land along the Nottingham to Grantham Road at Radcliffe. (His main interests were in Cropwell Butler where he lived at The Grove.) On this occasion Samuel Barratt senior, Samuel junior and John Martin were seen with a dog and guns. The witness, a man called Rockley, heard the report and saw smoke from Samuel senior's gun, and watched as the dog was sent into a field to find the game, while Samuel junior jumped the hedge, picked up a hare and put it into his pocket. Rockley followed and demanded the hare which was given up. The poachers - probably connected with a respected family of local nurserymen - clearly did not want the matter to go any further and offered money to Rockley who refused it, saying that he was going to report them. The case was then complicated by the fact that the three defendants produced game licences in court, which gave some legitimacy to their activities, even if they had trespassed on Henry Smith's land. The elder Barratt's licence, however, was only dated from November 11th 1886, and the offence had taken place on November 4th. He managed to prove to the court that he had given money for the licence to a man named Parr in October, but that Parr had failed to get it because the Inland Revenue office in Nottingham was closed on the Saturday he went. In the end the magistrates settled on £2 fines for each defendant. Twenty years earlier Samuel senior could have expected a £5 fine or three months' imprisonment for shooting a hare on someone else's land.

While hares and rabbits were the most common game, cases involving partridge eggs occasionally came to court. The most detailed case occurred in 1865 and involved Henry Parr, who at that time ran the Black Lion Inn. He was later to become a joiner and builder of note. The court proceedings were enlivened by a gamewatcher's account of being knocked down in a scuffle which preceded the surrender of seventeen eggs from Henry Parr's pockets. A partridge was also said to fly out from his coat. For the defence George Breedon said that he had been standing on a load of manure some 50 or 60 yards away and he had not seen any bird fly away. Henry Parr's guilt, however, was confirmed by the evidence of a boy who had been offered 5s if he would say that there had been no eggs in the nest. A fine of 5s per egg was appropriately imposed as well as costs. Five years later in June 1870 George Blatherwick was fined at double that rate for stealing two partridge eggs.

Illegal fishing in Lord Manvers' private water on the Trent at Radcliffe seems to have led to more prosecutions in the late 1860s and 1870s than at any other time in the period studied, but no case resulting in the full £5 penalty has been found. There was perhaps particular leniency where there was a suggestion of fishing for sport rather than fishing for gain. In two cases in January 1871 and July 1874 the defendants pleaded ignorance and, apart from the payment of costs, were respectively discharged and fined 1s. In September 1874 two 'respectable looking men' from Nottingham were told in court that Lord Manvers 'had no wish to press the case but only desired to prevent people offending in like manner in future'. They too escaped with only paying costs. In contrast, in November 1869 William, John and Samuel Richmond used spears and a boat to catch eels and were jointly fined £3 with costs, with the alternative of two months in the House of Correction. Ten years later two separate cases of pike fishing led to fines of 30s, the second with the alternative of one month's hard labour. In June 1887 two unemployed Nottingham men were treated a little more leniently. Having been seen on the river bank at night, they aroused the suspicion of Lord Manvers' gamekeeper who lay in wait for them early the next morning. When they appeared, they drew several lines out of the water. Pleading guilty, they said they had been out of work for a number of months and thought they would earn a few shillings by doing what they did. The bench fined them 10s each with the alternative of a week's imprisonment.

Burglary and theft

Burglary was a rare occurrence, and a suspect was likely to be sent for trial at the Quarter Sessions. One case in February 1880 did not get that far. John Swannick, a Radcliffe labourer, was accused of attempting to break into Mr Brewster's house through a kitchen window. In best detective fashion, Sergeant Allwood traced footmarks almost to Swannick's door and claimed that they matched Swannick's boots. Mr Barratt, however, who had made the boots for Swannick was less certain. He thought the impressions he had examined with Sergeant Allwood might have been made by Swannick's or by other boots. Swannick said he had been in a public house until closing time and did not know where he went afterwards. The magistrates gave him the benefit of the doubt, dismissed the case, but warned him that if further evidence was forthcoming he might be apprehended again.

The longest prison sentence for petty theft was for three months with hard labour. William Parr junior earned this sentence in December 1869 for stealing a hop press worth 4s from publican Sarah Buxton's premises and selling it to a blacksmith, William Dickinson, for 1s and a quart of ale - the latter bought from Mrs Buxton. Dickinson had thought the press was sold with her permission and was acquitted. William Parr, however, had been 'convicted on several previous charges' and so received a stiff sentence. (His father was in court on the same day, accusing Samuel Fletcher of stealing two hares from his house. The case was dismissed.) Sentences of one or two months were more common. For example, George Morley was given two months' hard labour in September 1870 for stealing twelve pecks of peas worth 5s from the G.N.R.C. at Radcliffe railway station. He agreed he had moved them from a truck, but not with the intent to steal. Four separate cases of theft from employers led to a month's imprisonment with hard labour in each case. Samuel Walker, a Radcliffe labourer, was found guilty in March 1866 of stealing two pigeons from his employer at Bassingfield. Thirteen had been missed and the two in question were found on his premises. A case in May 1868 involved Richard Cragg who had worked for Thomas Butler for twelve years. Mrs Butler had her suspicions aroused about egg stealing, and placed three eggs in a cowshed. Two were removed, leaving only the nest egg. When Sergeant Stevenson searched Cragg's house he found the two eggs in a cupboard. They were valued at 1½d. In October 1875 Thomas Butler, almost certainly the son of the farmer in the previous case, missed a cutting knife used by Samuel Leverton whom he had employed to cut hay. Leverton had then moved on to cut hay at Parr and Daft's premises, unwisely using the same knife. He admitted it was Butler's before serving his month's sentence. The fourth case concerned a 14-year-old servant girl, Harriet Hallam, sentenced in January 1879 for stealing a gold ring, a shilling in silver and several other articles worth altogether 15s from Thomas Stone.

Opportunist theft was similarly punished. Selina Rowe came to William Rockley's house selling doormats. After he had bought a hassock for 10d he missed a piece of his own carpet which should have been by the kitchen door. It appeared that Selina Rowe had then left a carpet and a hassock with a servant at the Royal Oak before moving on to the Manvers Arms where she was found by P.C. Stevenson. At first she claimed she had received the carpet from a woman selling tapes and cotton, but then pleaded guilty before beginning her month's imprisonment in January 1868. When Joseph Knight left his fishing rods under his seat at the Royal Oak on Whit Monday 1875, they were taken by William Jarvis. On the following Saturday Jarvis returned them, apologising for having taken them in a 'drunken freak'. The magistrates took the view that if he had intended to act honestly he would have brought them back sooner and sentenced him to 21 days' hard labour. George Smith in February 1879 took Henry Buxton's bricklaying trowel while the latter was working on some premises at Radcliffe. He was pursued, captured, and imprisoned for a month.

How much theft was the result of genuine hardship is difficult to judge. Perhaps hunger caused John Magrath and James Ryan to enter Thomas Hallam's house and steal part of a loaf of bread. The latter was unwilling to proceed with the case, so both men were discharged in August 1857. Three Nottingham men who were caught filling bags with turnip tops from a crop in John Green's field were less fortunate. Two who had been convicted before were sentenced to 21 days' imprisonment in January 1869. Fruit trees were an obvious temptation, and cases may not always have reflected need. When four boys were charged with stealing William Sanday's pears in October 1872, the latter said in court that he did not wish to press the charge but merely put a stop to the practice. Three were therefore discharged with a caution and one kept in custody for three days. In October 1874 one boy claimed that he had only been doing what the others did when caught stealing apples from Robert Butler. He was discharged but three others were fined £1 each. The father of one complained that the tree was unguarded. A month later Sergeant Stevenson saw Henry Trant from Sneinton and some other men taking apples from Thomas Stone's garden near Station Terrace. Trant was foolish enough to admit familiarity with the officer: 'You know me; you had me for being in Sanday's garden.' Sergeant Stevenson acknowledged that the young man had 'grown out of his sight' and that he must be locked up. In court full punishment was pressed for as Trant was the sixth man so far that year who had been before the magistrates for similar offences in Radcliffe. He was sent to prison for six weeks without the option of a fine.

In general, however, as with poaching, more lenient sentences seem to have been imposed by the 1880s. Compared to the four men who were given two months' hard labour when found in the Rev Bury's garden in 1840 (only one was actually convicted of stealing fruit), Henry Trant got off quite lightly. Similarly, a month's imprisonment in January 1869 for taking a coat from Cotgrave Place one wet day, allegedly with the intention of returning it, seems harsh compared to the fine of only 5s imposed in December 1886 for the theft of a jacket from Orston Grange.

Few cases of theft by embezzlement have been found, but two examples from the 1880s make an interesting contrast. In December 1881 Joseph Richmond was charged with embezzling threepence from George Blatherwick, a Radcliffe newsagent. The latter had been ill and had asked Richmond to deliver twenty dozens of newspapers in two baskets for 4s. If he sold them all he would be paid more. According to the newsagent, Richmond was not seen again for about a week and then threatened to knock Blatherwick's head off. On going to a public house in Cropwell Butler, Blatherwick found his two baskets and forty-four newspapers. Three witnesses from Cotgrave testified to buying newspapers at 1d each for which he had not received the money. As a result Joseph Richmond was sent to gaol for two calendar months with hard labour. The second case began in April 1882 when a warrant was issued for the arrest of William Henry Bramwell who had been the secretary of a Friendly Society in the village and who had left without handing over funds to the treasurer. The case came to court in the following January when it was clear that the Society was more interested in getting its money back than in the punishment of the accused. While considering the Society negligent, the bench allowed an arrangement whereby the defendant could pay back the money (a total of £49.8s) in instalments of £10 a year.

Assault cases

Until the 1860s reports of assault cases give few details other than names and punishments. One of the most lenient sentences in this period was the mitigated penalty of 6d with costs imposed on William Terry for assaulting John Crampton in February 1843. The heaviest was £5 given to George Parr in December 1855 for assaulting William Foster junior, a butcher. Parr could not pay and was sent to prison for two months. The stiffness of his sentence was probably because this was not his first offence. In August 1851 he had been fined £2 for assaulting William Blyton, a police officer.

As more detailed reports occur, it becomes clear that many of the cases dealt with at Bingham involved domestic matters or disputes between neighbours. Some indication of the tensions in everyday life is found in such cases. When William Roberts, a blacksmith, was accused of assaulting John Wreeke, his elderly father-in-law who was in receipt of parish relief, the latter did not wish to press the charge. The bench, however, insisted on a fine of £2 with costs or twenty-one

Gateway of the house of correction at Southwell

days in Southwell House of Correction. In March 1865 William Richards was sentenced to two months' imprisonment for cruelty and maltreatment of his wife Mary Ann. He had also to find sureties that he would keep the peace for six calendar months on his release. A fine of £3 or two months' imprisonment was imposed on George Holmes in September 1875 after a quarrel with his wife during which his mother-in-law, Elizabeth Hutchinson, had remonstrated. She had suffered an assault for her interference. A well-documented case in July 1887 reveals that despite the Married Women's Property Acts of 1870 and 1882 which gave women independent rights of ownership, financial problems could still occur, perhaps exacerbated by the hardship of the times. Arthur George Parker, a hedge-cutter, expecting his breakfast one morning about 6 a.m. was told by his wife, Elizabeth Alice, that having no money she could not provide him with one. According to her court evidence, he then seized her by the shoulder and violently kicked her with his knee in her back and lower part of the body. He also caught her by the throat and inflicted wounds from which blood flowed. It appeared that the wife and her sister had both had a legacy of £25 from a Mr Oldacre of Gunthorpe. These sums had been handed over to Parker who had banked them in his own name. Since then they had not been able to get at the money or learn anything about it. In reply the defendant protested his innocence, claiming that his wife had occasioned the disturbance. She was very provoking, and he had only shaken her. He was fined 15s, an apparently lenient sentence when compared to some imposed earlier.

Only one court case involving an assault on a child within the household has been found. In this case in January 1882 the compulsory school attendance law introduced in 1880 was partly to blame. When George Brounton, having run away from school, was found in bed by his step-father, Tobias Lambert, he was violently thrashed with a knotted rope. Sergeant Allwood testified that he went to Lambert's house, found the latter drunk and in an agitated state, and 'the little fellow in bed, his arms badly bruised and his head swollen to an unnatural size and bleeding'. In defence, Lambert said, 'The [attendance] officer told me to thrash him but not to break any bones.' The boy, regarded as a bad lot by the bench, was cautioned and promised to attend school regularly. Tobias Lambert, his crime made worse by his drinking, was fined 15s.

In general, few assault cases were reported which concerned children. Two cases of indecent assault on little girls in July 1868 and July 1878 led respectively to a fine of £5, changed to two months' hard labour in default of payment, and a dismissal through lack of corroborative evidence. In May 1880 Jane Osborne was let off with costs after an alleged assault on Ellen Hall, a neighbour's child. Ellen had quarrelled with one of the defendant's daughters, and claimed that the defendant had struck her in the face, knocked her down, knelt on her and placed a hand over her mouth. In defence, Jane Osborne admitted boxing the girl's ears after the child had called her a foul name. She had also struck at the girl with a walking stick.

This last case is indicative that assault charges often arose as a result of a quarrel between neighbours, often female. The liveliest such case to reach the newspapers was dealt with in December 1874 under the headline: 'Model Neighbours at Ratcliffe' and concerned the Bemrose and King households. It appears that on the morning in question Matilda King 'had some words' with Hannah Bemrose. When the latter's husband, William, came home he reacted violently to his wife's being 'so taunted'. According to Matilda King he burst open her door, entered the house, struck her on the breast and pushed her down. He then caught sight of her brother John Henry upstairs, who was allegedly suffering from a fever. While Matilda and her sister Emily tried to restrain him from going upstairs, he caught hold of Emily and tried to strangle her. He then succeeded in reaching John Henry, pulled him off his bed and flung him 'neck and heels' down the stairs. Although 'a good deal injured' John Henry was able to run away and fetch a policeman. Next, Hannah Bemrose appeared and assaulted Matilda King. The Bemrose version of events was rather different, and a counter-charge of assault was laid against Matilda King by Hannah Bemrose. She alleged that after being called foul names she was struck violently across the face with a kind of nettle root that 'grows in gentlemen's gardens'. It also seemed that John Henry had paused in his flight for a policeman to call the Bemroses' son names and strike him on the breast. Moreover, although William Bemrose admitted that he had entered the Kings' house without any right to do so, the door had been open and not broken down by him. He had gone after John Henry King to give him a shaking, and he had not thrown him downstairs. Several witnesses testified as to the general disturbance between the two families, and in the end the bench found the charges proved against only William Bemrose, dismissing all the rest. He was fined 10s.6d, 10s and £1 for assaults on Martha, Emily and John Henry King respectively.

Three other cases involving quarrels between female neighbours are less well documented. In April 1880 Hannah Wright was fined 5s for assaulting Hannah Howard, as was Elizabeth Simpson for assaulting Mary Ann Buckenham with a clothes prop in April 1884. The latter's husband reported that he found his wife bleeding after a dispute as to whether or not she could put her clothes prop on a foot of ground over a wall. In the following February there was 'considerable amusement in court' when Mrs Johnson described how she had heard Elizabeth Walker using very objectionable language about her, and on enquiring the cause had been threatened and struck with a potato masher. Elizabeth Walker shrugged off the 21s fine with the comment that 'they were not to a guinea or two at their house'.

Assaults on women by men also rarely got to court. Two cases in the 1860s resulted in a dismissal and a fine of 5s. Two cases in the 1870s were reported in more detail. Elizabeth Deane, a servant girl at the Manvers Arms, was standing outside the inn when approached by John Pare who had been drinking. According to her evidence he told her to move, threatened to strike her, swore and then struck her in the face. As Pare had gone to work in Hull by the time the case came to court in June 1874, it is doubtful whether the £1 fine was ever extracted from him. More premeditated was the attack by a man from Sneinton Elements on Selina Chamberlain who had recently married a Radcliffe maltster. In September 1875 he was before the Bingham bench for striking her across the face with his walking-stick as she got off the train from Nottingham. He claimed that she was a woman of bad character, having lived with him for seventeen years. When he learned that she was married he thought it his duty to expose her. The magistrates disagreed and imposed a fine of £5, or a sentence of two months' hard labour in default of payment. In a third undetailed case in September 1877 Walter Stafford charged Jane Whitworth with assault and vice versa. His charge was dismissed with him having to pay costs of 8s, while the case against him was proved resulting in a fine of 42s with costs.

Friction at work was another cause of assault cases. In June 1882 John Ashley was charged with assaulting his employee, George Pawlett, at Radcliffe. There had been a dispute over a scythe and Pawlett claimed that he had been threatened with a brandished hoe. John Ashley, however, was ready to take a 'solid' oath that he never threatened Pawlett. Underlying the case was a dispute over the payment of wages, and the matter was settled by Ashley promising to pay George Pawlett. Payment was at the root of another case in April 1885. This time it was the employee, Joseph Roberts, who was alleged to have assaulted the employer, Philip Richmond, for whom he was carting coals. During the whole day he had been asking to be paid, and Richmond said he should have the money when he had completed the work. Richmond claimed that Roberts had knocked him down, blacked his eyes and threatened to kill him. Roberts' version was that Richmond had struck him first and then a free fight had taken place. The magistrates considered that the case against Joseph Roberts was proved and as he was an old offender he was fined £5 with the alternative of one month's imprisonment. His jaunty reply was, 'Thank you: I'll get over that.'

Drink and disorder

Assaults in Radcliffe became linked with other problems in the 1870s. An increase in the number of drinking cases throughout the county had already been noted in a police report of 1865. By then the number of visitors being brought to the village by train at weekends and bank holidays was considerable. In addition to the attractions of scenery along the cliffs was the bonus of good hostelries. Road travellers, too, found Radcliffe a haven, for, apart from the Trent Bridge Inn, West Bridgford had no public houses at this time at which to break the journey from Nottingham. 'Bona fide' travellers at least three miles from home could expect to be served even outside normal hours. While the Radcliffe publicans and beerhouse keepers enjoyed booming business, local law and order problems escalated. At national level there had been some tightening of controls by Gladstone's Licensing Act of 1872 - not enough according to the temperance movement and too much according to the licensed victuallers - and in the August of that year the Bingham magistrates at their brewster sessions laid down the opening hours which were to apply in general to country districts: Sundays from 12.30 to 2.30 p.m. and from 6 p.m. to 9 p.m., and on other days from 6 a.m. to 10 p.m. (Closing time in a town such as Nottingham was 11 p.m. and midnight in London.) Two years later the Bingham bench defined Radcliffe and Bingham as 'populous places' so the main closure time became 11 p.m. On the same occasion they had some advice for village landlords:

> If the publicans in Radcliffe would only shut up their houses on Sunday they would avoid any disturbance on that day and they would not be invaded by Nottingham gentlemen who came there for the purpose of drinking all day, because if they took these six days' licenses they need not supply drink to anyone but a lodger...

The problem of deciding who was a 'bona fide' traveller, who could be served outside licensing hours would not then arise. This advice was too unprofitable to be heeded. A writer in the parochial magazine in November 1877 confirmed that Sundays in Radcliffe were not without draw backs, although, to the credit of the villagers, it was because of a 'strange element':

> We mean the very unlamblike element of the Nottingham pleasure seekers. These persons we have been credibly informed leave Nottingham when the drink selling shops are closed in order that they may get drink in Radcliffe. This they do under the Act of Parliament which allows travellers refreshment. These people crowd the railway carriages, the public houses and the streets. They are a great annoyance to the respectable people of Radcliffe, especially those of the humbler class.

The problems of Sunday drinking, the 'bona fide' traveller and increased drunkenness in Radcliffe were to concern the local magistrates greatly, and it was this situation which had caused the chief constable to propose that Radcliffe should have its own police station, which was duly built in 1875.

Routine drink offences before 1870

A look at the newspaper reports of cases shows the acceleration of the problem. There were occasional infringements of the licensing laws up to the 1870s: Edward Lockton convicted in the mitigated penalty of £2.10s and costs in January 1841 for opening during the hours of divine service; Thomas Ogle fined £2 for selling beer after 10 at night in September of the same year, and perhaps the same man fined £2 again in June 1870 for keeping his house open out of hours on a Sunday; James Rose of the Black Lion fined 10s and costs in July 1853 for allowing gaming to take place in his house; John Walker fined 2s.6d and 10s with costs in 1858 and 1866 for keeping his beerhouse open at illegal hours; Thomas Ogle fined 2s.6d in 1868 for giving a little porter at the time of church service to a woman who had come for some yeast but who had been taken ill. Similarly, Radcliffe had its quota of routine drunkards in the early part of the period, with fines ranging from 1s to 80s with seven days' imprisonment being a regular alternative. Ann Walters was singled out for fourteen days' imprisonment in September 1866, and the steeper fines were reserved for persistent local offenders, notably William Love, John Simpson and William Parr.

Offences in the 1870s

As outsiders contributed to the problem during the 1870s attitudes hardened, and Sergeant Stevenson had to bear the brunt of a deteriorating situation. Twice at least he had to cope with fighting drunks. In the first case, acting on information received, he found James Hayes and Joseph Roberts 'in drink' and with marks on their faces from fighting. Witnesses contradicted each other about whether or not the men 'were fresh', but the bench considered they were, and for drunkenness with disorderly conduct they were fined 20s in April 1874. Roberts failed to appear in court, having also been missing when fined the same amount for a similar offence in the previous August. In April 1875 George Wood and George Wilson were charged with drunkenness and fighting one Sunday night in Radcliffe. Sergeant Stevenson, having found them stripped ready to fight, moved them on, but they merely went further down the street and renewed the disturbance. They had to pay fines of 15s. Drunken visitors also proved a hazard on the road. It was again Sergeant Stevenson who saw two men named Smith and Ward drunk in a cart, galloping down the street in Radcliffe, shouting at each other. They were fined 20s each, with Ward being allowed a week in which to pay as he lacked friends and contributed to the support of his mother.

1877 and 1878 were particularly bad years. At least four drinking cases led to the new standard fine of 12s.6d, and two cases merited fines of 21s. In addition, there were three cases reported in considerable detail indicative of the growing violence and vandalism in the village. (It is not surprising in these circumstances that in 1877 Sergeant Stevenson mistook a slumped figure in Vicarage Lane for yet another drunkard. He had in fact seized hold of the body of a Nottingham man who had shot himself.) In April 1877 a complicated case involved Holme Pierrepont and West Bridgford too. The Radcliffe part of the affair concerned the refusal by nine young Nottingham men on a Sunday to quit the Manvers Arms, their assault of James Bell, and their obstruction of the highway. At least three of the men were also identified in Reuben Clarke's public house between 3 and 4 p.m. as 'worse than drunk'. On being asked to leave they smashed chairs, tables and other furniture, took his licence and tore it up. Mr Clarke did not consider this 'larking', and though they had paid him 8d for one chair it was less than he had asked. They had also stopped the boy who was going for the police, and so left just before the officers arrived. On being cross-examined by the magistrates as to whether he had enquired of each if they were 'bona fide' travellers Reuben Clarke had to admit that he had not, but understood they came from Nottingham. After leaving Radcliffe, the nine men arrived at Holme Pierrepont just after church service. There they stripped for racing, insulted the parish clerk, threw stones, pursued choir boys with a stick, and assaulted both the Rector and Mr Edward Pierrepont, son of the new American ambassador who happened to be visiting with his tutor. (Four were also charged with drunkenness at West Bridgford on the same afternoon.) While recognising the nuisance of 'men from towns', the Bingham bench was obliged to discharge one man and could only fine the rest 'the low sum' of one guinea each.

They took a much stronger line in 1878 when in both cases the victim was Sergeant Stevenson himself. One Sunday evening in March the Sergeant saw Frederick Haylock, a young Nottingham man, drunk and disorderly in the street. As soon as he tried to take him to the new police station, Haylock struck him in the mouth, broke his teeth, kicked him several times and injured his fingers. The policeman's evidence was corroborated and the prisoner was sent to gaol for two months. At the beginning of April Sergeant Stevenson tried to send home George Brewster, a local man, whom he found very drunk near the church. Brewster, who had previously been in trouble for an assault at the railway station, refused to go and suddenly seized the policeman round the neck and struck him a violent blow on the head with his stick. Brewster had to be thrown on to his back before his hold could be loosened. All this took place close to Radcliffe Hall, the home of John Taylor, one of the magistrates trying the case. George Brewster was also charged with assaulting a man named Rolleston on the morning of the same day. After grinning at him and calling him a d--- thief, the accused had stood over him with a stick and threatened to knock his brains out. On asking Brewster his age the bench may have been surprised at the reply: 'Seventy sir.' He was sent to gaol for two months, but was ordered to be examined by a doctor as to his mental condition. It was at this point that Sergeant Stevenson was transferred to Burton Joyce and replaced by Sergeant Allwood.

The police campaign against illegal drinking 1878-9

The authorities clearly decided that there would have to be a clamp-down on drinking in Radcliffe and they began with a campaign against landlords who allowed Sunday drinking outside licensing hours under cover of the law relating to 'bona fide' travellers. Each of the three main public houses was visited by policemen in plain clothes. On May 19th 1878 Detective Pilgrim went to the Manvers Arms and P.C. Wilson to the Royal Oak.

Detective Pilgrim arrived at the Manvers Arms at 5.30 p.m. and found several men in the tap room the worse for drink. He drew Samuel Bell's attention to them who said that the men had arrived in a trap. The policeman went outside to inspect the trap, and on his return found that a quart measure had been filled up again. On enquiry, the men admitted they had come from Nottingham after shutting-up time there. In court there was some dispute about the amount of drink consumed and the degree of drunkenness. Bell's defence was that the men had driven from Nottingham and had gone outside the three-mile limit prescribed by law and so were entitled to refreshment. The magistrates had no option but to dismiss the case on this occasion.

P.C. Wilson had supported Detective Pilgrim's evidence about the men's inebriated state, but his main operation that day had been at the Royal Oak. Having spent the night at Beeston, Wilson reached the inn at about 11 a.m. and found the door closed but not locked. On entering he found fifteen men drinking in the tap room. He was then served with two cans of ale by Sarah Fryer's brother, with no questions asked. He repeated the performance before six o' clock that evening. In court, the defence case was that Wilson was indeed a traveller. This was dismissed as he had not been specifically asked where he had come from before being supplied. Sarah Fryer was fined £5.

In September it was the turn of Thomas Kell at the Black Lion to be investigated. Two police constables again came from Nottingham and were served with drink during prohibited hours on a Sunday without being questioned. It was to no avail that Kell cited his good character in court. His claim that he had indeed asked visitors if they had come by train was not believed, even though a visiting cyclist supported him, and his assistants and daughter said that they had asked the relevant question. The fact that another policeman - having instructions to inspect and report on all the Radcliffe public houses - had found about twelve people being served, with no questions asked, on a separate occasion may well have convinced the bench of his guilt. Because he had no previous conviction and there was no disturbance in his house at the time, he was given the mitigated penalty of £15. (In October he was before the magistrates again, this time for having four earthenware jugs which gave deficient measure. As they were in the bar with the other measures, his claim that they were not used was dismissed and he was fined 25s.)

The clamp-down continued into 1879. In the April Samuel Bell was charged with permitting drunkenness and disorderly conduct at the Manvers Arms. This time it was Sergeant Allwood, the new local man, who had overheard swearing and found eight or ten men in the inn, three of whom were drunk, while one 'smelt as strong as a brewhouse'. Bell denied the charge. The defence claimed that the men were discussing the government's policy regarding South Africa, causing their British blood to be up. They admitted their behaviour was boisterous, and their language not as gentle as would be heard in a drawing room, but they denied they were drunk. The bench was not impressed, fining the men 2s each and Samuel Bell 42s. At the licensing sessions in August 1879 the pressure on landlords was continued. The magistrates took away Kell's licence, although they promised his case would be reconsidered in September. It was at this point that Kell felt he would have had more lenient treatment in the Retford division. Samuel Bell's licence was also suspended until September 18th, and it was not surprising that Samuel Summers' badly-timed application for a licence to sell spirits at the Cliffe Inn was turned down at the same sessions.

Public house incidents 1881-2
Cases related to drink may have been reported with a little less frequency for a year or two - some five cases being found for 1879 and only three for 1880 - but 1881 and 1882 were again bad years with at least thirteen and twelve cases respectively. The increase, however, may well have been because landlords were being particularly careful not to allow trouble on their premises and were sending for the police more often. During 1881 three public houses called for police intervention in four separate incidents. In July Charles Bevin's response to his fine of 15s was: 'It's a very shameful thing.' He claimed he had lost a shilling in the Black Lion and had been refused a light to look for it. He admitted using bad language which continued after the police had arrived who were forced to eject him. Thomas Kell said that the room had been searched, but only a small piece of iron had been found. He had refused to allow Bevin to light some paper to look for the shilling because it would damage the oil cloth on the floor. The Black Lion was at the centre of another incident in which three defendants were charged at Shire Hall early in November and two others at Bingham towards the end of the month. Three Nottingham brickmakers, having been refused drink at the Royal Oak because of their condition, refused to leave the inn. When they eventually went it was to the Black Lion across the road. There they seem to have been joined by a man who recognised them from work. When P.C. Simmonds arrived to eject the men, one of them asked the constable, 'Do you want your head knocking off?' The policeman managed to get one man out but was badly kicked by others. With the help of John Parr and James Upton, who was knocked down and his head injured, Simmons managed to get them to the police station. The Nottingham magistrates said they felt bound to support the police in the execution of their duty and commended P.C. Simmons. Three of the men were each fined 50s or given one month's hard labour for refusing to quit the Royal Oak, two months in gaol for the assault on P.C. Simmons and 30s or 14 days' imprisonment for the assault on James Upton. At Bingham a fourth man was fined £2.2s for assaulting the officer and £2.2s for assaulting Upton. One man was discharged. There were also two lesser incidents at the Manvers Arms in the same year. When George Hallam was drunk and refused to quit in September, he said he had got too much to drink at the village feast and asked to be treated leniently. He was fined 15s. Three men who became noisy and were refused whisky in the December resorted to bad language and were removed by the police. One was fined 25s and the other two £1.1s each.

In August 1882 Sergeant Allwood had been passing the Cliffe Inn when called in to eject Joseph Baxter whose disorderly conduct had been annoying customers. When Baxter had been forced into the road, he turned violent and said, 'You b-----, I'll throw you over this wall.' He had not succeeded. At the brewster sessions towards the end of August the landlord's application for a full licence, supported by a signed memorial from the village, was turned down. Two routine ejections of drunken customers by police from the Black Lion in March and April 1882 were followed by a livelier incident in the December when William Topham and William Thompson let two live rats loose in the tap room. A great disturbance ensued and they were requested to leave but refused, resorting to bad language. Both Thomas Kell and P.C. King were assaulted in the course of their ejection. Topham was fined £3.3s and Thompson £2.2s. As far as the public houses were concerned, these strong arm tactics seem to have worked. In 1883 only one case of drunken behaviour within a public house - leading to an assault on Samuel Bell of the Manvers Arms - was reported. No case has been found for 1884.

Drunkenness in the street

Cases in the street were a different matter, although these too declined after 1882. In 1881 four typical cases involved drunken driving. In the January Thomas Cave and Richard Smith were drunk and disorderly in charge of a horse and cart and tried to drive over a brick wall. They assaulted constables Storer and Asher, attacking the former with a whip and stick, and damaged their cell door in the police station. They were fined £3 each. A fine of 12s.6d was imposed in August for a simple case of being drunk in charge of a horse and cart. In a second case that month George Potter was not only intoxicated in charge of his horse and trap but drove it furiously to the risk of running down children. The 'fashionably dressed young man' who gave evidence in his favour did him no good and he was fined a total of 30s. The message about strong policing in Radcliffe seemed to have got through to John Blackshaw in the September. When charged with drunkenness and furious driving he said it was useless for him to say anything as the police would swear anything. To his fine of 25s from John Taylor he replied, 'Thank you sir.'

Pedestrian drinkers also complained about police tactics in the following month. John Howard and Samuel Smalley, found drunk on the highway, had been asked to go quietly by Sergeant Allwood. They complained that the sergeant had interfered with them unduly, that they had done nothing to justify the interference of the police and called witnesses to prove they were not drunk. The bench was not convinced and they were both fined - Howard 21s as he had a previous conviction and Smalley 12s.6d.

Female drinkers

One other phenomenon is noticeable between 1880 and 1882. Whereas in the rest of the fifty years studied only one case of female drunkenness has been found, six cases involving five women occur in that short period. Mary Ann Smith, 'a wretched looking woman', had been so hopelessly drunk that three men had had to take her to Radcliffe police station in a cart. She was fined 12s.6d in September 1880, as was Phoebe Howard in November, with the alternative of 7 days' hard labour. In March 1881 P.C. Asher had found Mary Small drunk on the road in the middle of the night wearing nothing but a cloth round her neck. She explained that her husband had turned her out, claimed that she had had her night things on, and admitted that she had had something to drink. She was fined 15s. In May Elizabeth Roper was found asleep lying on the causeway by Sergeant Allwood. When he woke her she turned out to be very drunk and became disorderly. She claimed she had been very tired so lay on the path. A constable supported the sergeant's evidence and said he had seen her drunk at Cotgrave, but a defence witness said she was sober. She was nevertheless fined 15s but allowed a week to pay. Anne Durant, an elderly woman, was given a standard fine of 15s in April 1882 for being drunk and disorderly on the highway, but when she repeated the offence her fine in the September was raised to 21s. On the second occasion some men had been wheeling her about in a wheelbarrow to the amusement of a large crowd.

Throughout this period a strong campaign against drink was being waged by local temperance movements. Whether the combined action of the magistrates and the Band of Hope led to improvements is difficult to say, but the total number of reported cases involving drinking in Radcliffe declined significantly from the twelve of 1882 - six in 1883, one in 1884, four in both 1885 and 1886. The decline also coincides with the public health crisis in 1882 when the village was pilloried in the *Nottingham Journal* for the unhealthy state of its drains, and visitors were warned to keep away. For whatever reason, for the third year running in August 1885 the bench could record that in the previous year there had not been a single conviction or complaint against a publican or licensed victualler in the the district. In that year the chairman could also congratulate the public on its excellent conduct. Nevertheless, the problems caused by Radcliffe's influx of visitors were not permanently solved. Indeed, as late as April 1892 there had to be a special sitting of the magistrates at Bingham to investigate an assault on a policeman and riotous behaviour at Radcliffe, much of it associated with drink, on Easter Monday when an estimated 6,000 visitors - surely an exaggeration - 'took possession of the village'.

Persistent offenders

A few Radcliffe names recur in Bingham court cases. As victims or complainants, members of the Butler family probably appear most frequently. As offenders Henry Parr, William Love, John Simpson and William Parr were amongst the most regular court attenders. Of these, Henry Parr was least typical. Born in 1838 he was a prosperous member of the community. By 1863 he was running the Black Lion, being fined 17s.6d for selling ale out of hours in that year. His three other court appearances recorded in the newspapers were all for poaching, and involved the theft of partridge eggs, trespassing in pursuit of game, and shooting a hare on the highway in 1865, 1871 and 1877 respectively. In the last case John Taylor was on the bench with whom he was shortly to sit on the church re-building committee. By then he was a prosperous joiner and builder living on Bingham Road, who also owned a number of house. He would have been well able to afford the fines of £4.5s or £2. He died in Nottingham in 1904 but was buried in Radcliffe.

More typical were William Love and John Simpson, listed as agricultural labourers, and therefore subject to the fluctuations of the rural economy. It was they who, when caught poaching with a third man near the Shepherd houses in 1863, complained about lack of work. William Love had been born in Nottingham about 1826. His wife, Hannah, whom he married in 1850, was some ten years his senior and they had had twins by 1851. Another child was born about 1857. His first recorded poaching offence landed him in Southwell House of Correction for two months in July 1855. His unspecified sentence for stealing two oil skins worth 1s.6d was confirmed at the Quarter Sessions in January 1858. By the time he was imprisoned for two months for using nets in October 1862 he was described as 'an old poacher'. After the episode at the Shepherd houses which led to another spell in Southwell, he seems to have turned to drink. He could only have been free for some three months when he was charged with drunkenness in July 1863 and fined 80s with an alternative of seven days' imprisonment. In the following February, described as 'an old offender', he was back in Southwell for another three weeks for being drunk and riotous. His last recorded appearance was again for drunkenness for which he was given seven days' hard labour in December 1867. Although he has not been found in subsequent records, his wife appears in the 1881 census as a housekeeper.

Between 1863 and 1883 John Simpson's name appears in poaching or drink cases on at least eight occasions. (A well-to-do property owner of the same name appears in the village by the 1880s.) Born in Cotgrave about 1831 he lived on Bailey Lane with his wife, Elizabeth, also from Cotgrave, who in 1881 was working as a laundress. No children are recorded. Whether he was the Simpson who was caught from a gang of poachers on Lord Chesterfield's land in 1860 is not clear. Like William Love, he seems to have turned to drink after the incident at the Shepherd houses for which he was imprisoned at Southwell. In 1864 he was sentenced to two separate weeks' imprisonment with hard labour for being drunk and disorderly and drunk and helpless. He was sentenced again in the following year. It was in 1879 that William Taylor's exasperation with his having been on the spree for some time was expressed in court. 'You have gone too far,' he told him. Simpson pleaded guilty but pointed out that he had not insulted anyone. On that occasion he was fined 12s.6d. The fines increased: 15s in the following March; £1 in February 1883 after being drunk and riotous at 11 at night. He lived on until 1910, eventually dying in Bingham workhouse.

William Parr

It was John Simpson's neighbour, William Parr, who was to have the distinction of making the most frequent number of court appearances. Born in Radcliffe about 1817, he was originally an agricultural labourer, but soon turned to working as a general huckster or dealer. By 1851 he and his wife, Hannah, who came from Fiskerton, had a fifteen-year old son, also called William, who was working as a brickmaker. As a young man, he was probably either the William Parr or William Pare in a group of drunkards who had disrupted a tee-totallers' meeting at the Wesleyan chapel in January 1838. Although brought before the magistrates at Shire Hall, no sentence was passed at the request of the tee-totallers, although costs of 10s had to be paid, and a £10 surety for keeping the peace for a year was required. The 1841 census return spells his name Pears, so he becomes phonetically the most likely candidate to be the W. Pare who was put in the stocks and pelted with orange peel in the 1840s for coming home 'market merry'. The subsequent help he gave to a schoolboy to escape from the authority of his schoolmaster would have been in character. In October 1850 his name appears in the Quarter Sessions minutes as having to give a surety of £10 'to keep the peace generally'. From 1854 the reports of his court appearances at Bingham show a broad range of petty crime including poaching, theft, assault, indecent exposure as well as drunkenness.

The most lenient treatment he received seems to have been for assault cases: two separate shillings for assaulting Mary Ann and John Wright in 1854. When he could not pay the shilling fine for another assault in April 1861 he was sent to the House of Correction for a month. His poaching exploits seem to have been confined to the early part of his career. Fines of £5 were imposed in 1854 and 1857, as well as £2 for trespassing in pursuit of game. In August 1869 he was charged with drunkenness and with assaulting Richard Adamson. He was sent to the House of Correction for seven days. Whether he was the father or the son in two other cases in 1869 concerning the theft of a hop press (resulting in three months' imprisonment) and the theft of two dead hares from the Parr household (case dismissed) is not clear. It was noted on this occasion that the younger of the two had 'been convicted on several previous charges'. In September 1872 Parr was the defendant in a civil case when William Wild claimed £2.10s from him. The latter, having been to Cotgrave and partaken too freely of 'John Barleycorn', had a 'heavy wet' on and was given a ride in Parr's cart. When he reckoned up his expenses the next morning he found himself worse off than expected and claimed the missing money from Parr. Not surprisingly, the judge stopped the case, declaring a non-suit. In one drunk and riotous and two drunk and disorderly cases in 1873, 1875 and 1877 he was fined 10s, £2.12s.6d and 21s respectively. It was in connection with the 1875 case that he notched up his twentieth court appearance. Described as 'an old stager' in August 1878, he was charged with indecent exposure on the public highway at Bingham. He denied the charge (which was covered by the term 'rogue and vagabond' in court) but was sent to the House of Correction for three months with hard labour. In May 1879 he was described as 'an old offender' when fined 10s for allowing his horse to stray on the highway at Holme Pierrepont. For having left his cart obstructing the highway at Radcliffe he was fined 12s.6d in the June.

His next recorded escapade in November of the same year proved to be his last. Sergeant Allwood set events in motion by going to see him about two brushes missing from a sale at Car Colston. Parr said he had bought two brushes and sold them, but one brush was found when the house was searched. A further search later revealed other stolen property. Parr was subsequently seen riding a pony opposite the Co-operative stores [on Hogg Lane] by Thomas Osborne, a stonemason. On learning that policemen had again been around his house he said to Osborne, 'Just take the pony down to our missis, and tell her I'm going to Nottingham to see a lawyer.' He did not get far. Superintendent Somerset had arrived in Radcliffe after receiving 'a communication' and went to the church. On coming out he saw 'Billy Parr' running across the road. He pursued, overtook, and seized him by the arm arm on the road leading down to the cliff near the river. Parr claimed his name was Johnson and refused to go with him. There was a struggle and both men fell to the ground. Edward Upton, a young ferryman, reported seeing the two men against the railway bridge near the cliff, and hearing the officer say he would follow Parr wherever he went. Parr replied that it would be better for him if he did not and added

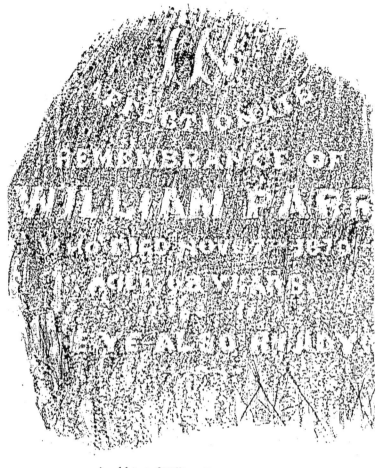

A rubbing of William Parr's gravestone
in Radcliffe cemetery

that he could be home in three minutes if he was let go. The two went into the woodland, and soon afterwards Parr reappeared and ran down the rock side to the bottom of the cliff, pulling off his coat on the way. He went into the water, calling to a fisherman on the other side that he was coming across. When out of his depth he began to swim. By the time the superintendent and Sergeant Allwood were able to ask the fisherman about Parr's whereabouts they were too late. 'He has gone down there,' was the reply. The policemen went in Upton's boat to search and found the body at Stoke Bardolph. At the inquest held at the Black Lion the coroner raised the question of whether the drowning had been deliberate in order to avoid arrest. The jury preferred a verdict of death by misadventure.

William Parr must have been one of Victorian Radcliffe's colourful characters, and his catalogue of petty crime in the incomplete records available makes him memorable to posterity. There may well have been feelings of guilt about his unfortunate death, and unlike many of his humble contemporaries he was given a small, now weathered, headstone in the cemetery. On this he is remembered with affection, along with a warning to the spectator: 'Be ye also ready.'

Civil cases

A number of the Radcliffe cases heard at the monthly county court held in Bingham reflect the agricultural character of the community. A case involving the 'warranty' on a cow in July 1855 was more complicated than most. Mr Foster, a Radcliffe grazier, had bought a cow from a Mrs Pritchett at Granby for £14.10s. The cow had then been sold to a Sneinton man for £15.5s, and had begun to show signs of disease. After giving birth to a calf, the cow was returned to Foster by the Sneinton purchaser and it subsequently died. While it was ill, Mr Foster asked Mrs Pritchett to take back the cow and refund his money on the grounds of a verbal warranty. He also claimed for maintenance, veterinary expenses and for loss of time. When the jury appeared to go against the evidence and find for Foster, Mrs Pritchett demanded a new trial. Despite Foster's claims, it was then proved that the word 'warranty' had never been used. Witnesses testified to the good character of the defendant, a poor cottager, and this time the jury found in her favour. Whether the Foster in this case was the Richard against whom John Marriott successfully claimed £2.4s for the sale of a sheep in July 1855 is not clear. In May 1862, however, Richard Foster, described as a butcher, won his claim for £8.12s - the value of meat sold to a Cotgrave butcher. The debt had to be repaid at 10s a month. The increasing use of farm machinery is indicated in Mr Al[l]cock's claim in September 1861 for

£7.2s.4d for repairing George Benson's 'thrashing' machine. The latter had to pay £1 a month at Allcock's workshops. John Beeson, described as a wheelwright, had to make two claims over unpaid bills for timber. In the first case in September 1861 the claim for £21.4s.2d included £20 lent in money. The debtor, a joiner and carpenter of Lower Broughton, said that he did not know whether he owed or not. Beeson said that he had no wish to be hard on him, but when the joiner offered to pay at 5s a month he said it was too little. The judge settled on 10s a month. In the second case in December 1863 John Beeson had to accept repayment at 5s a month, but this debt was only £4. The largest award found in the local cases was £36.2s in April 1875 - the value of a colt belonging to William Terry and the amount paid by the latter to Thomas Butler for looking after it. The horse had been found in a dying state in snow without hay or fodder. The local vet, Thomas Young, gave evidence as to the horse's condition, and a second confirmed that the animal's stomach was entirely empty. Four of Butler's employees said that straw had been supplied to the field, but William Terry won his case. The vet's bill, however, was not recoverable.

William Upton

In 1862 and 1863 William Upton, a Radcliffe builder, appeared in the courts several times. In March 1862 he was a witness in a case in which Mr Richmond, the owner of some Radcliffe property, claimed back-rent at £6 a year from one of the Bell family. There had been some complicated arrangements involving an old man, Thomas Knight, who expected an inheritance from the will of a 90-year-old Collingham lady. Knight had mortgaged his interest in her will to the tune of £100 in Mr Richmond's favour. When the Bells had wanted to rent property from Richmond, the latter had agreed to waive the rent of £6 per year provided they gave a home to Knight until the old lady's death. Richmond clearly wanted to keep an eye on his human investment. The case was distinguished by interruptions from Thomas Knight and by the irritable evidence of William Upton, protesting that he must be paid his expenses: 'I have been dragged here in this footing several times. I suppose...I must get my expenses as well as I can.' He recollected the signing of the agreement about the rent and looking after Knight. That same evening Richmond had said that if the old lady died soon he would not be particular about the rent provided Knight was looked after. Upton added that they had a bottle of gin before them at the time. The old lady had indeed died soon after the agreement, but, despite his verbal promise, Richmond was now claiming his rent. When Mrs Bell gave evidence she exaggeratedly claimed that Richmond 'had robbed that poor old creature [Knight] out of £400' - his mortgaged inheritance. She admitted that the second part of the agreement had not been put in writing. 'It only ought to have been.' Judgement went against Mrs Bell, whose husband was away in London working as a bricklayer, sending home about 10s a week. She was sure she could not pay at the set rate of 4s a month. A few days earlier, William Upton had lost a case against an absconding apprentice in the petty sessions court as the boy had not been properly indentured. He took the matter further in January 1863 and sued the boy's father in the county court for damages sustained by breach of contract. The boy had been bound to Upton two years earlier as an apprentice bricklayer. The agreement had been made on the usual terms, but there had been no indenture with a seal on it, so the question arose as to how binding it was. It appeared that the lad already knew the trade. In the year in question he had been absent from Shrove Tuesday for two weeks after which he had been brought back by his father. He had again been absent from June 15th to September 1st, and had left on December 20th and not returned. Upton thought the boy was worth about 12s a week to him besides his board.

Defence Counsel:	*Do you know why he went away?*
Upton:	*No I do not.*
Defence Counsel:	*Did you not strike him with a shovel?*
Upton:	*No, I remember batting him with a shovel because he would not work.*
Judge:	*Well, what you would call batting we would call striking.*

Upton said that in the previous July he had ordered the defendant's son to do some haymaking for a friend of his, considering that he had a right to make his servant do whatever work he thought fit. On the grounds that the agreement was without a stamp and was therefore not binding, the judgement went against William Upton in March. Whether or not he was the William Upton against whom on the same day judgement was given for the recovery of £3.9s by a G.N.R. station master for supplying coals is not clear. He must, however, have also attended a coroner's court in Radcliffe in July after his eight-year-old son was drowned in the Trent.

Civil and petty sessions cases heard in Nottingham

A number of Radcliffe civil cases were heard in Nottingham rather than Bingham if any of the individuals involved were connected with the city. Butler Parr, the Radcliffe maltster, lost his case against a bailiff in September 1855 who had failed to collect his debts. In September 1859 Robert Butler was sued for selling a lame mare, but the judgement went in his favour. James Gorse, the hosiery yarn agent of the Manor House, was sued in November 1871 by the purchaser of his pony who said the animal subsequently went 'indifferently'. The judge asked what was to be understood by this term. 'Did it stand upon its head or what?' The plaintiff explained that the pony repeatedly stopped in the road. Four whips were broken in 'coaching' it back to Radcliffe. He was awarded £6.9s.6d, the difference between what he had paid for the pony and what he had managed to sell it for. Mr Gorse was more successful in March 1874 when he was awarded £1.8s, the price of wasted tickets, when a Nottingham cab driver failed to turn up to take him and his friends to the theatre. In May 1880, local magistrate John Taylor's son was sued by a livery stable keeper for £47.1s.6d, the difference in value of a horse when hired out and when it was returned. Taylor's groom, and others in the village, including Richard Daft, gave evidence about finding an old wound on the animal, while two of the owner's former employees stated that the horse had been previously injured by falling into a manure pit. The owner lost his case. In June 1884, under the Employers' Liability Act of 1880, the Radcliffe contractors Foster and Barry were sued for £210 by the widow of a Bulwell man killed in an accident at a culvert in Sneinton. She had been left with seven children. The widow lost her case as no negligence was proved. Foster and Barry offered her £10 'out of compassion' and a subscription was started on her behalf. Financial problems of Radcliffe residents were also regularly aired, not only in the county court in Nottingham, but in special insolvency or debtors' courts.

Petty crimes dealt with in Nottingham show the same range of concerns as those at Bingham. In December 1837 John Richards was sent to the House of Correction at Southwell for six months when he could not pay a fine of £20 for using a gun for killing game without a proper certificate, while George Rockley was sent to Southwell for three months' hard labour in August 1840 for using snares at Radcliffe without a certificate. These seem to be stiffer sentences than those imposed locally at this period. Occasionally, familiar names crop up more than once. Levi Duke was fined 10s.6d at Shire Hall in August 1843 for assaulting Lucy Caunt at Radcliffe. That was his second fine for assault in fourteen months. It is perhaps not surprising that he was replaced as parish clerk in 1844. Although he seems to have become a respected resident, working for the local Oddfellows, at least one other lapse brought him before the Shire Hall magistrates in January 1868. On that occasion he was found by P.C. Walker asleep against a blacksmith's shop at the end of Trent Bridge. He was so tipsy and drowsy that it took him some time to tell the officer his name, and when he set off home he went towards Bridgford instead of Radcliffe. In a while he returned and abused the constable for putting him on the wrong road. He claimed in court that he was not drunk, but merely overpowered with sleep when returning home from his club. He was fined 10s.6d. Charles Chamberlain, a Radcliffe maltster, was found in a similar state in charge of a horse and cart in Willoughby Street in November 1869 and brought before the town magistrates. After an accident in which the horse had fallen down and his cart shaft was broken, a policeman had suggested he 'put up' his horse and trap at the Half Moon. He refused, tried to take the constable by the collar, denied he was drunk and claimed that the horse had got into a habit of lying down in the street. A Nottingham maltster gave evidence that he was perfectly capable of taking care of a horse when he left the Lord Holland Inn. He was discharged on payment of 8s costs.

Domestic squabbles also found their way to the Nottingham petty sessions. In August 1864 Sarah Smith of Radcliffe charged Annie Allen, the wife of a Cropwell

Butler wheelwright, with assault. While on the London Road going home on the previous Saturday night Annie Allen had attacked her and torn her bonnet. Annie Allen claimed provocation because of the victim's association with her husband. Accusations then flew around the court room:

Clerk:	*What were you doing with Mrs Allen's husband?*
Sarah Smith:	*I was going home.*
The Mayor:	*There could be no greater provocation.*
Anne Allen:	*This woman takes my husband home regularly. This is only done to get money out of me,*
Sarah Smith:	*I belong to a family as respectable as any in Ratcliffe.*
Anne Allen:	*The Bingham magistrates did not say so. They said you were a bad woman.*
Sarah Smith:	*Well, and who are the Bingham magistrates. I have never been annoyed so before in my life. Her husband pays her so much a week. I have nothing to do with his money.*

After eliciting what Sarah Smith earned, the Mayor as magistrate ordered the parties to pay the expenses between them and sign the book in token of good behaviour towards each other.

The malt tax case

Probably the most serious case ever heard before the Shire Hall magistrates involved a Radcliffe maltster, John Morley, in 1851. Heavy taxation on malting had caused protests in the 1840s, and John Morley seems to have been in trouble for tax evasion in 1845. On March 21st of that year the *Nottingham Journal* had advertised the imminent sale 'under a seizure for excise duties' of all his 'neat and useful' household furniture, along with livestock, a cart, harness, manure and other farming effects. More significantly, included in the sale were 46 quarters of malt, a 24-gallon copper, and his brewing vessels. This must have been a devastating blow to the livelihood of a married man with three young children. Although the malting premises are not mentioned in the sale, it seems that they did change hands about this time, being bought by Thomas Beeson who was then living in Manchester. John Morley clearly wished to continue as a maltster, but as he was no longer credit-worthy he persuaded his brother-in-law, a John Watson of Market Harborough in Leicestershire, to put his name on the appropriate papers as licensed maltster of the rented premises. Watson subsequently claimed that he had taken no interest in the business, and had only been reminded of its existence when confronted by an excise examiner in the street at Market Harborough in December 1850. He found he was facing charges of collusion and evasion of duty amounting to thousands of pounds. In vain he pleaded ignorance of the whole proceedings. As the story unfolded in court it was clear that there had been consistent and well-organised malt tax evasion for a considerable time in Radcliffe, although the charges were confined to specific dates between November 4th and December 13th 1850. They concerned the use of premises, the steeping of grain and the concealing of large quantities of malt for which an entry should have been made to the excise authorities. So large were the sums involved that at first the Shire Hall magistrates doubted whether they were competent to try the case.

Having received 'some secret information', excise officers from London had searched the Radcliffe malt rooms on December 13th. They had found John Morley there and a surprisingly small amount of malt, although even this turned out to be more than had been entered in the excise book. On going out into the yard they came to a pig sty, and after poking about under the straw discovered seven sacks, each bearing Morley's name, containing steeped grain working into malt. Morley refused to show the officers any more of the premises, so they came back with surveyor-examiners as reinforcements. One of them, Mr Corbett, ordered John Morley to open up or he would break in. Morley then opened a door to reveal a room regularly fitted up for the making of malt, and with grain being processed that had never been entered in the book. Mr Corbett next went round the building and discovered a hen-house fitted up with tubs filled with wetted barley, and a floor of malt in another stage of preparation. All this was seized, but the officers were well aware that they had not got everything - 'some ladies did not like them to go into their bedrooms'. Acting on further information they returned some days later and found more grain in the kiln than had been present on the previous occasion, and noted that there was 'every indication that these private places for malting had been used for a considerable length of time'. Altogether, the officers found about 28 bushels which had been entered, and about six times that amount which had been made illegally. John Watson's claim that he was ignorant about what had been going on was taken into account by the court, and his fine was mitigated to a quarter - £675. John Morley at first pleaded not guilty, but then threw himself on the mercy of the court. He was fined the full £2,700 and forfeited his equipment. How or if he ever managed to pay his colossal fine is not known. While his wife and children continued to live in the Radcliffe house which he owned, the electoral returns for 1850-1 show that he had moved to Manchester. It seems more than coincidence that Thomas Beeson, the owner of the Radcliffe malt rooms, was also living in Manchester. (The Beesons had returned by 1861 when Thomas's 32-year-old son was described as a maltster.)

Although not on so large a scale, another case of malt tax evasion had preceded Morley's. Henry Hickling who lived in Nottingham but owned other malt rooms in Radcliffe was also found guilty of having illegal malt under the supervision of his manager named Butler. His fine, mitigated to a quarter, was £50. For tax evasion on the scale shown by these two cases it was obvious that local officials must have turned a blind eye. In March 1851 Henry Gosden, an excise officer who had been appointed at Radcliffe in 1848 and who lived near Morley, was charged with receiving bribes and neglecting to take account of amounts of malt. Morley gave evidence that Gosden 'knew all that was going on'. He even produced a memorandum book in which he had listed sums for 'Henry' ranging from £2 to £10 between December 1848 and September 1850. He had also supplied the officer with malt and barley. Gosden had subsequently begged Morley to destroy any memoranda about money he had received, and had put a large sum in the hands of Mr Beeson of Manchester to be given to Morley if he did not 'split' on him. It was also claimed that he had met John Watson in Leicester who would not agree to support him. If this evidence is to be believed, it would appear that neither Watson nor Beeson were as ignorant of what had been going on as was originally made out. Morley also claimed that the same situation existed at the time of Gosden's predecessor. Not surprisingly, Gosden was found guilty and fined £500.

Quarter Sessions records

The Quarter Sessions minutes have survived, but although they confirm verdicts given at the petty sessions, neither parish nor sentence is recorded so it is not possible to identify additional cases to those covered in newspaper reports. The minutes, however, do list cases where financial sureties for good behaviour have to be given. Sixteen concern Radcliffe in the fifty years studied. Six require the named person not to enter land at night for the taking of game for one year, and the rest concern the keeping of the peace, usually towards a named individual. William Parr appears twice in this list, the second time for his behaviour to Mary Ann, the wife of William Upton in 1863. In 1886 Mary Upton appears again, with Elizabeth Walker having to keep the peace towards her this time. A year later, William Wright and Edward Wright, Radcliffe's carriers, had to keep the peace towards each other.

Altogether, from 1837 to 1887 twenty-five cases connected with Radcliffe were sent from Bingham to the Quarter Sessions. All involved some kind of theft or fraud. Even so, some caution is needed as a study of the individual cases shows that the court clerk sometimes associated the accused with the parish in which a crime had been committed, rather than with the true place of origin. Even with the help of newspaper reports and census returns it has not been possible to eliminate all uncertainties. On the face of it, a number of cases sent to the Quarter Sessions were as petty as many of those dealt with by the local magistrates. Few theft cases were dealt with at local level, however, and some culprits were given severe treatment at Quarter Sessions. Hugh Hopkins' theft of 2s-worth of lead from William Taylor's roof in 1840, and John Parker's theft of John Brewster's scythe worth 5s in 1844 resulted in their spending a month each in the House of Correction with hard labour - no more than they could have expected from the Bingham magistrates. In January

Indictments at the Quarter Sessions 1837 to 1887

Dates	Charge	Verdict
July 1839	Thomas Meakin, labourer of R-on-T accused of taking goods left with him by Francis Kelly, huckster.	Not guilty
March 1840	Hugh Hopkin, accused of stealing lead from the roof of William Taylor of R-on-T	1 month's hard labour at Southwell
October 1843	Samuel Simpson of Owthorpe, labourer accused of stealing waistcoat worth 1s from George Richmond, labourer, of R-on-T. Pleaded not guilty but admitted taking another man's.	4 months' hard labour at Southwell
October 1843	John Lamb, labourer of R-on-T accused of stealing a coat worth 3s from Thomas Pike, labourer of Holme Pierrepont.	2 months' hard labour at Southwell with 1 week of each month in solitary confinement.
July 1844	John Parker, labourer of R-on-T accused of stealing a scythe worth 5s from John Brewster.	1 month's hard labour at Southwell with 1 week in solitary confinement.
January 1847	John Parker, labourer of R-on-T accused of stealing 3 pecks of potatoes worth 2s from John Beeston of R-on-T.	7 years' transportation.
January 1847	William Bishop, labourer of R-on-T accused of stealing breeches worth 5s from William Bradley of R-on-T servant man.	1 month's hard labour at Southwell with 1 week in solitary confinement.
April 1847	Thomas Meakin, labourer or higgler of R-on-T accused of stealing 78 lbs of Lord Middleton's coal at Trowell.	1 month's hard labour at Southwell with 1 week in solitary confinement.
June 1847	Sarah Streets, single woman of R-on-T accused of stealing trousers worth 5s from William Caunt.	2 months' hard labour at Southwell.
January 1849	John Lee of Old Radford accused of stealing a belly band worth 5s and a pickaxe worth 2s from Joseph Adams, railway contractor at R-on-T.	1 month's hard labour at Southwell with 2 weeks in solitary confinement.
July 1849	Thomas Chapman of East Bridgford accused of stealing iron bars etc. from William Greaves, railway contractor at R-on-T.	3 months' hard labour at Southwell with 3 weeks in solitary confinement.
January 1854	Robert Scrimshaw, farm labourer of R-on-T accused of stealing a pair of gears worth 6s from Elizabeth Johnson, widow of R-on-T.	Not guilty.
January 1855	Peter Smith, framework knitter, accused of stealing a shirt worth 2s from William Judson of R-on-T.	1 month's imprisonment at Southwell and a whipping.
March 1855	John Bacon and Charles Simmons of R-on-T accused of stealing a horse rug worth 1s from Thomas Fisher.	1 month's hard labour each at Southwell, the last week in solitary confinement and a whipping.

Dates	Charge	Verdicts
October 1855	Thomas Brown and John Walker, labourers, accused of issuing counterfeit coin to Francis Hopewell, labourer of R-on-T.	6 months' hard labour at Southwell, with 2 weeks in solitary confinement.
December 1861	William Leverton, Henry Malone, Samuel Goodwin, labourers accused of breaking and entering the shop of William Foster, butcher of R-on-T and stealing 60 lbs of meat.	Leverton, 3 years' penal servitude; Malone, 12 months' hard labour at Southwell; Goodwin, 6 months' hard labour at Southwell.
June 1862	James Slack, labourer of R-on-T accused of stealing 1 watch guard from Thomas Gilmore.	Not guilty.
October 1862	John Barratt, agricultural labourer of R-on-T accused of stealing £1 from Robert Stokes of R-on-T, servant, and clothing from John Sumner.	6 months' hard labour at Southwell with 2 weeks in solitary confinement.
March 1864	William Wright, labourer of R-on-T (given as joiner of Retford at preliminary hearing) accused of stealing a cow from Richard Foster, cattle dealer of R-on-T.	5 years' penal servitude (previously convicted at Bedford).
March 1871	John Starbuck of Cropwell Bishop accused of stealing a leathern strap from Great Northern Railway at R-on-T and a horse belonging to a Nottingham grocer's assistant from outside the Black Lion R-on-T.	Not guilty on both charges.
January 1872	Alexander Good of West Bridgford accused of stealing a silver watch and watch chain from William Nowell, labourer of R-on-T.	4 months' hard labour at Southwell.
October 1874	Thomas Durant, aged 14, labourer of R-on-T and Samuel Howard of Bingham, licensed hawker, accused respectively of stealing and receiving 3 ploughshares worth 2s from Thomas Butler of R-on-T, farmer.	Not guilty.
April 1879	Henry Whyles and Edward Brobson accused of stealing a ploughshare, bought by Mr. Pogson from the premises of Mr. Stone of R-on-T.	Whyles, 2 months' hard labour at Southwell; Brobson, not guilty.
October 1879	Thomas Johnson ('a stranger' at the preliminary hearing) accused of obtaining money by false pretences from the R-on-T branch of the Manchester Unity of Oddfellows at the Manvers Arms.	Not guilty (the requisite evidence not having been obtained from Preston).
June 1880	Charles Beckett Smith, labourer of R-on-T and Charles Boultby accused respectively of stealing and receiving a timepiece worth £1.12s from Frederick Sumners of R-on-T, beerhouse keeper.	No true bill.

1847, however, John Parker was sent to the Quarter Sessions court again, this time for stealing three pecks of potatoes worth 2s from John Beeston. He pleaded guilty, but the fact that he had been indicted before told against him. He was sentenced to seven years' transportation, one of the harshest punishments in the fifty years studied. In the 1841 census he is listed without family.

No case of corporal punishment has been found at petty sessions, but it was sometimes inflicted at Quarter Sessions. Peter Smith, a 16-year-old framework knitter, stole William Judson's shirt worth 2s and was sentenced in January 1855 to a month's hard labour at Southwell, where he was to be once whipped. At the March sessions in the same year two Radcliffe labourers, John Bacon and Charles Simmons, were each given a month's hard labour, of which a week was to be in solitary confinement, as well as a whipping for stealing Thomas Fisher's horse rug worth 1s. Other cases were more serious. Thomas Brown and John Walker, labourers, were imprisoned in October 1855 for six months in Southwell, two weeks in solitary confinement, for 'unlawfully, unjustly and deceitfully uttering' counterfeit coins when buying pigeons from Francis Hopewell in Radcliffe . John Barratt, a 21-year-old agricultural labourer, received a similar sentence in October 1862 for stealing two half sovereigns from Robert Stokes of Radcliffe and a coat worth 15s from John Sumner. Three labourers, unable to give a satisfactory explanation for having 60 lbs of beef and 10 lbs of pork in their possession when challenged by police between Carlton and Nottingham in December 1861, received sentences ranging from 6 months' hard labour to three years' penal servitude for stealing from William Foster, a Radcliffe butcher. The heaviest prison sentence went to William Wright, a Retford joiner, in March 1864 for stealing Richard Foster's cow. Wright had already been convicted at Bedford and was given five years' penal servitude.

In April 1879 two men were tried for stealing an iron plough worth £1 from the sale of Mr Stone's farm stock and agricultural equipment at Radcliffe. Two wooden ploughs had been bought from another purchaser by one of the men named Brobson. All three ploughs had been left overnight for collection, and evidence was given as to how the prisoners went the next morning with a horse and cart and took away the iron plough, leaving one of the wooden ploughs behind. Brobson's defence was that the iron plough had been taken by mistake and he was found not guilty. The second accused, Wyles, who dealt in old iron, was found guilty but recommended to mercy on account of his good character. He also pleaded for leniency on the grounds of having six little children, all unable to work. The deputy chairman of the sessions said he regretted seeing Wyles in that position and his sentence would not be a heavy one. He was sentenced to two calendar months' hard labour.

Assize cases

Only four Radcliffe cases have been found which were sent for trial at the assize courts. The first concerned a fire in 1851 in Thomas Butler's stackyard. Although he lived in the centre of the village he had premises rented from Lord Manvers about a mile and a half away on the Bingham Road. Living on the site were Mary Kirkham and her husband. She gave evidence that after going to bed about 10 p.m. on the night in question, she was called up because of the fire and Butler was summoned. An early report said that fire engines left Nottingham about 11.40 p.m. and reached Radcliffe at six minutes past midnight. Despite all efforts five stacks of wheat, five of barley and one of clover were totally destroyed, as were a number of agricultural implements and a fence round the yard. The farm buildings were only saved with difficulty. Between 4 and 5 in the morning Thomas Butler gave some refreshment to all those present. One man amongst them had been noticed by the sergeant of the fire brigade as particularly anxious to help put out the fire. A Bingham police officer recognised him as 24-year-old John Rockley. The latter subsequently visited an acquaintance in Nottingham whom he had known since the last hay harvest, and admitted that he was responsible for the Radcliffe fire with another man. The other 'chap' who Rockley said had the matches never materialised. He pleaded not guilty at the Assizes in March 1852 and was undefended. He was sentenced to fifteen years' transportation. This was the heaviest sentence of the fifty years studied.

When two Irish labourers were charged with burglariously entering Samuel Parr's dwelling house in 1872 and stealing a quantity of cooked bacon and a brace of mackerel, the evidence against them came from a servant, Hannah Simpson.

Having heard a noise about 11.30 at night, she looked from her bedroom window and saw two men against the pantry window. They went away when she asked what they wanted. When Samuel Parr came home some fifteen minutes later, the pantry window was examined. A coat and waistcoat were lying nearby, the zinc wire was broken off the window, and the bacon and mackerel were missing. He caught one of the men in the garden, and the other was arrested by P.C. Stevenson. They were found guilty, but the judge considered their crime was petty larceny rather than burglary, and as it was their first offence they were imprisoned for only two months with hard labour. The Radcliffe charwoman who had hidden the body of her newly born child under bricks in a closet at Elizabeth Scrimshaw's house where she worked was fortunate in July 1877 to be charged only with concealment of birth. This was a dangerous offence, commented the judge, which often amounted to murder. When tried in July she had already been in prison for over three months, and she was given what the judge called a moderate sentence of two months' further imprisonment with hard labour. The details of the case of Henry Whyld, a former railway employee living at Radcliffe who was charged in 1880 with putting an iron 'chair' on the railway bridge, have already been covered in the chapter on the railway. His action seems to have been the result of resentment at being prevented from crossing the bridge and having to pay ferry fares to get to work. He pleaded guilty and after a rambling and unintelligible petition, delivered in a prayerful attitude, at the end of his trial he was sentenced to five years' penal servitude.

After 1887

The overwhelming impression is that Radcliffe was a law-abiding community, and any experience residents had of the legal system was as likely to be as plaintiff as defendant. Crime during the fifty years studied was petty, although the special circumstances of visitors to the village made for some liveliness around the public houses in the 1870s and 1880s. In general, sentences became more lenient as the century progressed. A look at the period beyond 1887 confirms these impressions. While drunkenness seems to have receded after 1893, traffic offences, particularly failure to show lights at night, poaching, or dog muzzling occupied much of the time at petty sessions. Not until 1901 was there a case of grievous bodily harm with attempt to murder. At the Assize trial, the domestic circumstances of the accused were taken into account and a sentence of only six months' imprisonment with hard labour was imposed. Compared with the sentence of seven years' transportation for the theft of some potatoes in 1847, the judicial system seemed to be showing a more sympathetic attitude to those brought before it, or perhaps it was reflecting society's greater concern for the protection of goods rather than people.

Main sources

Primary

Nottinghamshire Archives Office: Manvers Association records DD 54/1-6; Quarter Sessions minute books QSM 1 44 et seq; Nottinghamshire Constabulary Description Register 12/1.

Radcliffe-on-Trent Parish Council: vestry minute book.

University of Nottingham: Manvers papers Ma 2B 45/16,75.

Secondary

Elwin, Gilbert, *Memories of Radcliffe Hall.* (Typescript in the possession of Radcliffe-on-Trent local history group.)

Newark Advertiser, 7.8.1889, cited in Gedling House topographical card index.

Nottinghamshire County Library (Local Studies Library): Doubleday scrapbook ii, 81; L36.7

Radcliffe-on-Trent local history research group: extracts from Nottingham newspapers 1837-1920.

Radcliffe-on-Trent, Parochial Magazine, 1877.

Reports of Inspectors of Constabulary 1865 and 1886.

Savill, Stanley. *The Police Service of England and Wales.* 1923.

Transactions of the Thoroton Society, Vol. 13, 1909.

POVERTY, CHARITY AND SELF-HELP

I. The working of the poor law

Before 1818 Radcliffe's poor, who could not be maintained by outdoor relief in the village, were sent to a small workhouse in Bingham, holding up to thirty inmates. A rising population and increasing poverty, particularly after the Napoleonic wars, caused parishes to group themselves into more formal unions and to subscribe to larger workhouses. In 1815 Radcliffe was one of twenty parishes which subscribed to a new 'House of Industry' at Basford erected in 1818.

From 1834 the country as a whole adopted a harsher poor law system, based in part on methods applied in the Southwell area and by the Rev Robert Lowe of Bingham, in an effort to reduce the large sums paid out in poor relief. The Poor Law Amendment Act of that year established a central board to control local poor law authorities and under this Radcliffe was transferred from the Basford Incorporation, which was dissolved, to a much larger, newly-formed union of 40 parishes centred on Bingham. The aim of the act was to phase out and finally abolish outdoor relief except to the aged and infirm. The able-bodied who claimed relief would be offered the workhouse where conditions were to be deliberately unpleasant and the standard of living set below the 'situation of the independent labourer of the lowest class'. By this means, it was hoped, applications for relief would be discouraged and real distress would be distinguished from fictitious. Radcliffe was fortunate to have been removed from the Basford Union where violent fluctuations in the staple industry, hosiery, presented problems of unemployment not experienced in a rural union such as Bingham.

It was some time, however, before Radcliffe's involvement with Basford was completely cleared. The parish had made a considerable initial contribution to the Basford Incorporation, borrowing £160 from Edward Barker for this purpose. This money and interest had now to be repaid to his executors, but after many legal negotiations it was discovered that the parish's share of the dissolved workhouse only amounted to £97. By means of levying a rate, £70 was repaid immediately, and whilst awaiting the £97 from the Poor Law Commissioners a further loan of £90, this time from Edward Brewster, was arranged to pay the balance. This was in December 1839 and the parish had to wait until February 1842 before receiving the £97 due to them from Basford and repaying the loan which now, with interest added, amounted to £94. The following September a further cheque for £3.3s.2¾d was sent and set against the parish's proportion of the cost of building the new workhouse at Bingham.

The Board of Guardians of the Bingham Union
Meanwhile the Bingham Union had held the first of its fortnightly meetings at the Chesterfield Arms, which was to be its home until a board room in the new workhouse was ready. At its head sat the chairman, the Rev Lowe, whose success in reducing the cost of poor relief between 1818 and 1822 in Bingham had much influenced the Poor Law Commissioners in drawing up the Act of 1834. It would hardly be surprising if Bingham Union was predisposed to favour the reforms, despite widespread criticism of them from other parts of the country.

The Board was composed of ex officio members (the J.P.s) and the guardians elected annually by each parish, ratepayers' entitlement to vote being fixed on a sliding scale according to the value of the property rated. It was an unpopular post and there was rarely a disputed election. Radcliffe was allowed one guardian until 1883 when, at the parish's own request and in view of the increase in the population of the village and of its ratable value, they were granted two. Richard Butler was the first to be elected, and names familiar among the more respected ranks of Radcliffe society were to recur. Richard Stone was elected in 1839 and another Richard Stone served for eight years in the 1860s when he was replaced by John Green. Thomas Haynes was guardian for seven years in the 1850s; on two occasions he had to be appointed by the Board as apathy in Radcliffe was such that no candidate had been nominated. Another Haynes held the post in the early twentieth century until his death in 1916. Mr James Upton, a nurseryman from the Harlequin, was elected in 1914, and Mr Butler Parr, by then a brewery manager and chairman of the Parish Council, was one of the guardians for the duration of the Great War when no elections were held. For the most part, however, the guardians were small farmers and watchful of the rates which they felt fell with undue heaviness on them.

Contact with the poor law authorities was mainly through one of two salaried relieving officers appointed by the Board; in Radcliffe this was George Upton until 1868. The overseers, appointed by the magistrates, continued to be involved in the recommendation of persons for relief and were able to mitigate the harshness of the law, especially in the early years, but their importance gradually declined. The relieving officer was mainly responsible for regular cases of out-relief, the overseers acting in cases of sudden emergency. From 1847 an official known as the collector was appointed to gather contributions from relations, and finally in 1862 the overseer's responsibility for assessing rates passed to the Board. Such officials were accountable, not just to the parish, but also to the central authorities. In 1889 Radcliffe's guardian caused the resignation of an assistant overseer, Simon Eastwood, over irregularities in his accounts by appealing to the Local Government Board. As the minutes of the Bingham meetings record matters concerning paupers in terms of out-relief (assistance given in the home) or in-maintenance (in the workhouse) it is under these headings they are best described.

1. Out-relief

Central to the aims of the act was the reduction in the number of able-bodied poor applying for relief. It is clear that it failed to take into account the effect of varying local conditions, but the guardians at Bingham were enthusiastic about its benefits. In 1838 and again in 1841 they claimed that

> while on the one hand the helpless and infirm receive every necessary attention and relief, the able bodied are increasingly stimulated to industry and exertion.

Its success, they continued, was demonstrated by the reduction of expenditure to about one half of the former costs of poor relief.

At the very first meeting of the Board the relieving officers were ordered to proceed immediately to obtain accurate returns from the overseers of each parish of the paupers then receiving relief with 'information of the necessities and circumstances of each', and these lists were then revised each year. Except for the years 1847 and 1848 they are not recorded in the minutes. In both these years paupers in Radcliffe were William Walker, Martha Wood, Ann Howard, Dorothy Mellors and Ann Otter. In 1847 they received a total of £18.7s.5½d, William Walker with £7.10s receiving the most during the second half of that year.

The census return of 1851 also notes those who were paupers with their ages and occupations. Two aged 4 and 7 years, receiving 4s. a week between them, were children of a widow, Elizabeth Smalley, who was a lace runner with two older children, a boy of 12 who was a plough driver and a girl of 10. They were not given relief presumably because they were considered capable of earning their own keep. Another two children, aged 6 and 10 years receiving 5s between them, were the children of William Walker, an agricultural labourer aged 59 and himself still receiving assistance, although his wife (also an agricultural labourer) and his older daughter of 23, a lace runner, did not. Six of the paupers, such as Ann Otter, a washerwoman of 80, were over 60 years old receiving 2s to 3s a week. One was a widow of 49, a lace runner living with her son, an agricultural labourer, and her two daughters, also lace runners. Only the mother received relief of 1s.6d a week. Another widow aged 56, a farmer's servant, living with her two unmarried daughters (again lace runners), received 2s.6d. Most of them were thus either old or very young; eight out of the total of fourteen were widows or widowers; one, Elizabeth Scrimshaw aged 24 and unmarried, was a cripple. What is most striking, however, is the number of paupers or members of their families who gave their occupations as being lace runners or agricultural labourers.

Occasional relief

Apart from the lists of 1847 and 1848, paupers from Radcliffe mentioned in the minute books are those receiving occasional relief whose names had to be reported to the Board. They indicate those families on the borderlines of poverty and illustrate the manner in which the system was administered, but they tell us nothing of those whose application for relief may have been turned down or whose fear of being sent to the workhouse deterred them from seeking help in the first place. William Nowell (see page 132) is an example of someone not on permanent out-relief; in 1848 he was twice allowed 11d 'under great necessity'. Perhaps it was the expense of the birth of an illegitimate child to his eldest daughter and the probable temporary loss of her earnings which brought him to this pass. The baby died in March and the Board paid for its funeral.

In 1848 the Holmes family were also granted relief of 3s.4½d 'under great necessity'. John, an agricultural labourer, and his wife Elizabeth had seven children of whom Francis, aged 15, followed his father's calling, two unmarried daughters were lace runners, and a 12-year-old was a sempstress. Three younger children contributed nothing to the family income and although the cause of their temporary distress is not known, it is easy to see that it would take very little to plunge them into difficulties.

The cause of temporary poverty was frequently sickness. Mary Green and Sam Richmond received payments of between 4s and 6s to help them out when they were ill whilst Ann Clarke was only given 8½d. Thomas Smalley, who in the 1841 census was entered as a 35-year-old boatman, received 5s.6d in 1847 during his illness. By 1851 he was dead and two of his children were entered as paupers in the census of that year. It was not just the large family which was vulnerable in times of misfortune. Thomas Green, an agricultural labourer, had only two children who would have been 12 and 8 years old when he fell ill and received relief of 2s.5d in 1847. It was possible that he was the only breadwinner in the household. By 1851 both his wife and his elder daughter were lace runners.

The Poor Law Commissioners encouraged the giving of relief at least partially in kind and in the early years the overseers tried to comply. James Carnell, an agricultural labourer with six children, Joseph Brewster, Thomas and Frances Green and Mary Ann Benson were amongst those who received this form of relief, in value between 10d and 5s.3d. This did not include fuel, however, for in May 1838 the Board resolved that in future no coals would be allowed. Relief in the form of money was in any case soon substituted - William Pepper, a young man in his twenties, was given 2s.6d as early as 1837 and in the 1840s this became the norm.

Money was also allowed for paupers' funerals and for those unable to bear the cost themselves. For an infant such as William Caunt, deserted by his father, for Thomas, son of Maria Richmond, and John, son of Sarah Caunt, the amount given was 10s.3d. Adult funerals cost about £1.3s.6d. Mary Flower was buried at the cost of the parish in 1842, Hannah Richmond, William Hallam and Elizabeth Nowell in 1844 and Ann Thraves in 1845. In 1846 two men were struck by lightning; no doubt the double funeral worked out cheaper for the cost was only 19s.6d each, whereas that of James Jones, an Irishman drowned in the Trent, was £1.7s.6d.

Emigration

Until 1846 a scheme was operated whereby anyone, pauper or not, could have his expenses paid by the parish if he was willing to emigrate. Radcliffe's vestry book contains the names of seven families (fourteen adults and twenty-three children) who were ready to emigrate in 1842. The head of each household was an agricultural labourer, with one having some experience of brickmaking and malting. None was in receipt of poor relief. It is unlikely that any of these families left England, although Thomas Carnell, John Caunt and Thomas Scrimshaw, and their respective wives and children, cannot be identified in the 1851 census. The families of Thomas Clarke and William Judson appear in 1851, and the latter in 1861 too. The two remaining families, headed by James and Harriet Caunt and William and Elizabeth Scothern (or Scoffing), experienced tragedy at home to account for some absences in the census returns.

In March 1846 James Caunt and William Scothern were being employed by Edward Brewster and his son George to cleanse a small drain on the north side of the

Trent, near which was a brick and tile hovel. On the afternoon in question there was a violent thunderstorm and a cow was found to have been killed by lightning. When the two men had not returned home by nine that evening, George Brewster crossed the river with two farm servants carrying lanterns to start a search. On arriving at the hovel they found Scothern

in a sitting posture, with his hand in his pocket, quite dead. Caunt, too, was sitting with both hands in his jacket pockets, at the further end of the hovel, also dead.

Scothern had been wearing a pair of new boots, the soles of which were nearly covered with large bright nails. Three nails had been knocked out, and there were scorch marks on the hair and flannel waistcoats of both men, although the hut was undamaged. It was for these two men that the parish provided funerals at a bargain rate. A fund was opened to help support their widows and seven children, but the bereaved families must have had difficulties in making ends meet. In 1851 Elizabeth Scothern (Scoffing) and her four daughters were all employed at home as lace runners. By the time of the 1861 census Elizabeth and one daughter had died, two daughters were still working as lace runners, and a third as a charwoman. Harriet Caunt fared even less well. By 1849 she was letting rooms in her house on Mount Pleasant to navvies working on the railway when Asiatic cholera struck. She, her five-year old daughter, and her mother-in-law all died in the outbreak.

In general there was not a great response to the idea of emigration. It reminded people too much of transportation, and in Nottinghamshire only eight cases are recorded of people who actually went. One of these was William Pepper who emigrated to America from Radcliffe in 1842 at a cost to the parish of £26.9s.8d. Although he had only once been given any form of relief - in 1837 - the Guardians were no doubt glad to see him go. As an agricultural labourer with a large family (he and his wife were aged 30 in the 1841 census and their five children were all under the age of 10), they probably viewed him as a potential burden on the rates.

The settlement laws

An individual's right to claim relief from a parish was based upon his settlement which was usually his place of birth. The laws, however, were complicated, and some of them proved impracticable when applied. In 1836 a letter from the chairman of Quarter Sessions for Nottinghamshire to the Poor Law Commissioners cited two cases at Radcliffe, among others, demonstrating this. They concerned the rule whereby the settlement of the children of unmarried or widowed mothers was taken to be that of the mother. This could give rise to hardship and sometimes persuaded parish officers into giving illegal relief indirectly. The first case was that of a widow 'with four children and big with child of a fifth, settled at Radcliffe but having a settlement at Kingston-upon-Hull'. It appears that she remarried and soon afterwards her husband applied to Radcliffe, where he resided, for relief, but 'the officer removed him to Hull with his wife and five children'. In the other case, a single woman with two children and a settlement at Radcliffe married a pauper at Bulwell, but she was apparently removed to Radcliffe to receive relief. The writer recommended that in all cases the husband should have to maintain the children as if they were his own. If he was unable to do so, they should all be sent to the workhouse.

Many legal battles took place, even between parishes within the same union, as to their liability and the union was prepared to go to great expense to prove itself not responsible for a pauper. In 1871 Bingham Union paid £19.1s.3d for costs in an appeal against an order which had been given against them. When liability had been accepted, a certificate would be signed and the union seal attached thereto by the chairman, as described in the minutes for 1861 when Hannah Bemrose and her five children were found to have their settlement in Radcliffe.

Once it was established that a pauper belonged to a union he was liable to be removed to his own parish, if he was not already living there, to receive relief. Bingham constantly reiterated that it was not prepared to pay relief to its non-resident paupers 'excepting only such extreme cases of old or infirm persons ....in which it would inflict hardship to have them removed'. Elizabeth Rockley, who was living with her son at Basford in 1840, was allowed to remain there after a surgeon reported that she was 'labouring under paralysis accompanied with other infirmities incidental to old age'. In such a case an arrangement to pay relief would be made with the overseers of the parish where the pauper was residing. In the early years Bingham does not appear to have been very co-operative as regards paying paupers residing locally but belonging elsewhere. In 1838 Joseph Ratten lived in Radcliffe and was allowed 1s.6d and 4 lbs of bread weekly by Radford Union where his settlement was. The Bingham Guardians insisted that this should be received for him in Sneinton, without suggesting how it should be delivered to him. This unreasonable proposal was eventually dropped and they agreed to relieve him themselves, provided Radford repaid them.

The reality of the settlement system as it affected peoples' lives can be seen in the case of Samuel Caunt. In 1846 an act of Parliament made five years in a parish a qualification for non-removal, the parish of residence now having to pay relief. The workings of the act were not entirely clear, especially to the overseers of Radcliffe, on whose behalf the clerk of the Bingham Union sought the advice of the commissioners about Samuel in December 1846. He had lived in Arnold for the past thirty years, apart from three nights about four years previously when he and his wife had been removed to Bingham workhouse because, on claiming relief, his settlement had been found to be Radcliffe. He had then returned to Arnold, which doubtless Bingham Union hoped would now be judged his place of settlement under the new act. They were to be disappointed, for his claim to relief in 1843 had disqualified him from irremovability and once more poor Samuel, now without his wife and probably already in some distress, was shuttled back to spend his last days in Radcliffe. In 1849 he was granted extra out-relief of 3s and was not expected to live for more than a day or two.

After 1866 individual parishes no longer bore the cost of their own poor, this being shared by the whole union, but enquiries as to a pauper's settlement still had to be made. In 1885 Mr Sanday was consulted as to what he knew about a William Robson and his employment in Yorkshire. In the same year Cardiff Union claimed that a William Lamb, aged 69, belonged to Radcliffe. A certificate of his baptism in the parish was found and the clerk then travelled to Cardiff to examine him personally. His hopes that he might find that his settlement was now elsewhere were not to be realised and Lamb was admitted to the workhouse at Bingham, although discharged almost immediately at his own request. He did not trouble the union again - exemplary proof of the deterrent of the workhouse.

Some support for Radcliffe's poor residing in other unions, such as Ann and Thomas Love in Nottingham in 1866 and Hannah Roberts who had gone to live with her daughter in Colwick, had to be continued, but attempts to move a pauper back to his parish of settlement whenever possible were still made. Newark Union claimed repayment for relief given to G. Benson and his family in 1871. An order was immediately given for Bingham workhouse, but he died before it could be put into effect. His wife and children remained in Newark and relief of 2s and 8 lbs of bread a week was continued, as was customary with a new widow, until the end of 1872.

Care of the sick

Although the act of 1834 had ushered in a harsher and more impersonal system of poor relief, with regard to medical care the pauper may well have been better off than his predecessors. Besides seeking out-relief whilst he was unable to work, he could apply for medical attention. Bingham Union was at first divided into two districts consisting of twenty parishes each, and Mr Marriott with a salary of £70 a year was Radcliffe's first medical officer with responsibility for the poor. Then in 1843 at the request of the commissioners, three smaller medical districts were organised. Bingham and Radcliffe were the only two parishes in the union with populations of more than 1,000 and they were grouped with seven other parishes into one district. Mr Rowland was their medical officer and also that of the workhouse. The new arrangements, according to the Board, allowed 'a facility of communication by the best and most convenient Roads' and it was hoped that 'the practice of the Medical Officers of the three districts induces them to visit the parishes within the same frequently'. It did not always prove possible to find a qualified man residing in his own district and professional conduct sometimes left something to be desired. Mr Rowland attended Radcliffe's poor both on out-relief and in the workhouse for nearly thirty years, supplying medicines out of his own pocket, until he was suspended for errors found in his vaccination returns in 1872. Other officers were prone to unpunctuality in their returns, to being neglectful of the paupers under their care or even of making false claims. Their reports and their attendance, however, were monitored by the Poor Law Board, which replaced the commissioners from 1847, and by the Local Government Board from 1871, which then supervised both the poor law and public health, with some inevitable overlap between the concerns of these two areas.

Poor law medical officers were also under the watchful eye of the general public who were paying for them and of other doctors, some of whom had been candidates for the posts they occupied. One such disappointed candidate was Dr Ellam of Radcliffe who in 1882 complained that Dr Wotton, Mr Rowland's successor, had not visited any of the cases of illness in the village for nearly three months. Dr Wotton was required by the Board to make a personal attendance on every one of the cases under his care. He was reprimanded three years later for not visiting William Flower and his excuses were judged unsatisfactory. Dr Ellam was on the offensive again when the extra diet he had ordered for a fever patient who was receiving out-relief was not given immediately. This may imply that some sick paupers were turning to private doctors who perhaps treated them free of charge. Such voluntary care would have gone unrecorded, and Bingham was always anxious to encourage self-reliance. In 1873 the Radcliffe overseer had been requested not to give medical orders when the parties concerned were not destitute, and Dr Wotton had been ordered to discontinue treating two patients, Bemrose and Boyce, as they were considered well able to procure treatment for themselves. A Mrs Foster, whom he attended in 1885, subsequently admitted to possessing £41 and was therefore judged to be able to bear the cost of medical care herself. Complaints against the doctors were relatively few over such a long period, however. Dr Wotton, although medical officer at the workhouse for only two years when his place was taken by Dr Eaton (see p. 203), was poor law doctor for the district from 1872-92. Some years before he retired he was suffering from rheumatism and eventually worked from his surgery at Bingham, with a deputy to visit outpatients, and this may explain why he seemed to be negligent about attendance.

At least a minimum standard of care was offered to the impoverished sick. Mary Benson was attended four times between 1852 and 1858, and others recorded were Mary Barnard, Caroline Caunt and Mary Breedon. Those with special needs also appear in the minutes, such as Sarah Blatherwick who was recommended for removal to hospital in Nottingham in 1890 'if willing to go', and Sam Holmes who needed a truss in 1898. The medical officer had also to pronounce on a patient's fitness to return to work. In 1891, nine months after Dr Wotton had claimed £1 for setting Elizabeth Howard's arm, he reported that she was now able to do light work but Bingham agreed to continue relief at 3s a week for the time being. From 1909, it was agreed that any doctor called in on a confinement should be reimbursed.

Children

The Board of Guardians were empowered to arrange apprenticeships for pauper children and it is clear that some care was taken to investigate the character of those willing to take apprentices. William Walker aged 13, who was probably the son of the William Walker on the parish lists of 1847 and 1848, was bound apprentice to William Javes, cordwainer of New Basford, for seven years in 1857 at a premium of £4. Radcliffe paid his indentures and the consent of Basford Union, where his settlement would eventually be, had to be obtained.

Assistance was given to orphans in care. In 1880 Nottingham Union requested payment of non-resident relief to Mrs Whitehead of The Hill, Radcliffe (probably the lower end of Bingham Road), in respect of a 2½-year-old orphan, Frederick Dale, who was about to reside with her. There seems to have been some pressure on the guardians to act as a safety net for children suffering neglect in these later years of the nineteenth century. In 1880 Police Sergeant Allwood, at the request of the clerk to the justices, reported a case of alleged child neglect by William Howard and his wife. Mr Willey, Radcliffe's guardian, investigated the matter and concluded that the child was basically healthy, his emaciated and neglected appearance being due to an attack of bronchitis, from which he was recovering, and to the drunken habits of his mother. The Board seemed satisfied with this report. Nine years later the Rev Cullen took the initiative and reported a woman called Howard (perhaps the same one) for neglecting two children living with her, one a granddaughter and the other a nurse child. Because the woman was not the parent of either child, Bingham concluded they were not able to prosecute, but they may have been reluctant to intervene in domestic situations. They did not, in any case, appreciate the Rev Cullen's interference. When he requested relief for the father of Stephen Amy, a 15-year-old boy of weak intellect, he was reminded that any application for relief should be made through the relieving officer.

The campaign to eradicate out-relief

After the Poor Law Board had been absorbed into the new Local Government Board in 1871, the drive to eradicate out-relief to the able-bodied was renewed everywhere. The guardians at Bingham had stated in 1875 that the laws of settlement had not caused hardship in their union because of the small number of paupers. Their satisfaction was to be shortlived, for only a year later the inspector was recommending an increase in orders for the workhouse in an attempt to reduce out-relief. Four years later Bingham was commended for having achieved this, but was again urged to give orders for the workhouse whenever there was any doubt as to the deserving nature of the applicant. By 1881 the workhouse was nearly full and the area was clearly feeling the effects of the agricultural depression which afflicted the whole country. Expenditure for that year was £924 on out-relief and £401 on in-maintenance, but according to the *Nottingham Journal* the situation eased the following year when the figures changed to £836 and £305 respectively.

By now the overseers were being accused of giving orders for the workhouse too frequently and reminded that they were only empowered to do so in cases of urgent necessity. In 1881 Matthew Hibbert had been sent to the workhouse by the overseer of Radcliffe at the instigation of Sergeant Allwood. The master had admitted him because he showed signs of illness, but the guardians protested to the police that he was neither lunatic nor destitute, and that the relieving officer should have been consulted first. The next year the overseer was again reprimanded for sending an able-bodied woman called Richmond and her child to the workhouse. The overseers, however, were in an invidious position, because an order for the workhouse was still used as a test of need and as a means of forcing men to maintain their families. In 1881 the guardians resolved to prosecute Tobias Lambert, a sawyer, if his wife, whom he had deserted along with their three children, accepted the order.

Support of deserted wives and their children particularly vexed the guardians. Perhaps Sam Fryer who was a porter at Victoria Station, London, had not truly deserted his wife in 1866. But there was no doubt about William Spencer against whom proceedings were taken the following year, nor about Fanny Bramley's husband who in 1881 deserted her and their three children. Whether these men were successfully brought to book is not revealed, but in 1890 Bingham offered a reward of £1 to any police officer who arrested any man charged with desertion.

The campaign against out-relief appears in the Bingham minute books in a greater determination to follow-up relatives of paupers to extract contributions for their support. Some cases occurred before 1871 and even grandparents were liable to prosecution. In 1850 Mr William Roulstone, a basket-maker, had been threatened with proceedings if he did not continue to pay an agreed sum for his grandchildren's maintenance, and in 1869 Mr John Shelton of Stoke Bardolph was required to pay 1s.6d a week towards the maintenance of his grandchildren at Radcliffe. From the 1870s there was a marked increase in the number of prosecutions and threats to prosecute. The Walker family were among the first to experience the stricter attitude. Frederick, aged 36, a gardener who was married with a young daughter, and John, aged 32, unmarried and living at home in 1871, were required to contribute to the support of their mother, a widow of 72. Frederick's wife, a shopkeeper, and his sister attended the Bingham meeting personally to receive the order. Presumably they agreed for no more is heard of them. Others were not so compliant, but perhaps Philip Richmond, a 28-year-old carter with a wife and child, resented the presence of a stepmother when in 1888 he was asked to contribute 2s.6d a week towards his father George's relief. George, a coal dealer turned labourer, had had six children including Philip, by his first marriage, though only three lived to adulthood. His second wife had brought a son of her own to the marriage and had then produced another five children, all under twelve years of age in 1888. Both families lived in Mount Pleasant and no doubt Philip was able to keep an eye on his stepmother's laundry business, because he claimed that she earned from 15s to £1 a week, and he produced a list of those who employed her to do washing. His father was given an order for the workhouse as a test and Philip's contribution was reduced to 1s.6d, but his liability remained after enquiries revealed that part of his stepmother's earnings belonged to her daughter. Thomas Howard, a boatman aged 74, had also remarried and one of his sons, John an agricultural labourer from Mount Pleasant, had to be summonsed for refusing to contribute 1s a week.

Some families kept up a long-running battle with the authorities. Such were the Carnells (see page 135) and the Blatherwicks. George, who had several sons, first claimed relief in 1879. One of them, Joseph, was summonsed and, even though he had recently been in Lincoln gaol and therefore out of work, the case was not dropped for some time. But problems with the family continued. Sam and Thomas, the other two sons, frequently fell into arrears as they were in and out of work. When they moved to Sheffield, enquiries were made to the clerk of that union about their means. Another branch of the family had a similar history. One son evaded responsibility by disappearing - the clerk's letter to him was returned through the Dead Letter Office. Nor was he the only one to do so. George Parr, probably a 79-year-old bricklayer living on the Green, had three sons, Thomas, George, and Samuel (or John) who were asked to pay 2s, 1s, and 6d respectively for their father's relief in 1887. The usual bargaining and pleas of ill health led to threats of a summons. When Thomas claimed to be supporting his father, Bingham expressed disbelief and resolved to enforce the order which was by then for £7.3s, continuing to press until he complied. Son George, however, disappeared and avoided his share of the burden.

There was some advantage, therefore, in being one of a number of children when parents turned to the parish for relief. In all the cases which occurred in these years, daughters, whether married or not, were never asked to contribute, whereas wives' earnings were clearly taken into account (as in George Richmond's case), and women were held responsible for their own maintenance. Sons, however, were not liable until they were 21 years old. In 1871 the two eldest sons of John Chamberlain aged 31 and 29, both agricultural labourers, were required to pay 1s.6d each whilst the collector made enquiries as to the age of their brothers (who were under 21 at the time). As each brother came of age and depending on the amount of relief given, so the contribution would be redivided among them. Sometimes the guardians were open to persuasion. In 1872 on the evidence of his employer, John Simpson was judged to be unable to pay the 1s a week asked of him. In 1900 John Beet, who was in arrears, was excused as he had gone to the war in South Africa.

The occupations given in the censuses of 1871 and 1881 of families affected by the poor laws were more varied than those of thirty years previously, but the labourer and lace worker or seamstress still predominate, as do the old and widowed. These families only appear in the minutes because their relatives were being sought or pressed by the guardians for payments. Those paupers who had no relatives, or whose relatives paid without complaint, remain unknown (the few marked in the burial register being mainly from the workhouse or asylum).

Twentieth century out-relief

The death of Queen Victoria and the start of a new reign brought no basic changes to the administration of the poor law. The guardians at Bingham viewed their achievements with some satisfaction. In 1903 they were congratulated by the inspector on the low rate in the pound of their poor rate, and two years later they rediscovered with pride the contribution made by the Rev Lowe to the framing of the Poor Law Amendment Act of 1834. There is no doubt, however, that they displayed a certain parsimony throughout their history up to 1920 which, although not approved of by all members, may have assisted in their economies. For example, as far back as 1855 a proposal to raise payments for outdoor relief by 6d during a period of high prices was amended to be left to the discretion of the guardians, and so was never implemented. There had been a week's extra out-relief of 1s for adults and 6d for children for the golden jubilee of 1887 and the coronation of 1902, but throughout the early twentieth century, when neighbouring unions approached them every year to allow extra winter relief to their non-resident poor, Bingham steadfastly refused to give anything extra to their own paupers. Only in 1915 did they match the extra relief granted by Nottingham Union at Christmas for their paupers residing in the city. In 1917 the minutes noted that one union in four was not giving extra winter relief, Bingham being amongst them. At last the severe conditions of the war years persuaded the guardians to increase relief by 1s.6d for adults and 6d for children for four weeks from November 1918.

As before, relief given to the able-bodied sick is noted in the minutes, but the main source of information on out-relief in Radcliffe lies in the demands for repayment made on the victims' families. A number of the younger generation in Radcliffe at this time seem to have moved to Sutton-in-Ashfield and Mansfield. One such family, a casual labourer with a wife and five young children, was judged to be too poor to assist in the support of his mother who remained in Radcliffe. His brother, also still in the village, may well have felt resentful over the fact that he alone was forced to contribute and he fought the order for many years, pointing out that his mother had an adult niece living with her who could well earn her own keep. A summons was brought against him - the last that is known of the case.

In Radcliffe as elsewhere, people increasingly looked to alternative forms of welfare to see them through hard times or to pay for funerals. They must sometimes have wondered if this was worthwhile, for if the guardians had given any form of relief they were obliged to claim compensation from such schemes. On one occasion they paid the funeral expenses amounting to £2.10s of a man whose family received £12 from the Great Central Railway Provident Society. On approaching the Society direct, the guardians were correctly referred to the family for reimbursement.

As the number of official bodies proliferated, especially after the First World War, the guardians' task became more complicated. In 1920, for example, the Civil Liabilities Committee gave a local discharged soldier a sum of money to buy a window cleaner's outfit, but times were hard and he was tempted into committing larceny. While in prison, the money was handed to Mr Haslam, Radcliffe's representative, for safe-keeping. The guardians would almost certainly have liked to make a claim on this as the man's wife and children were now receiving out-relief, but eventually it was decided that the proper thing to do was to return the money to the Civil Liabilities Committee which had already applied for it.

The guardians also found themselves administering new measures brought in by the government. Under the Infant Life Protection Act of 1897 they were required to inspect the homes of people taking in children to nurse. (In 1881 alone there had been two inquests in Radcliffe on nurse children.) At first the relieving officer was made responsible for this, but in 1909 volunteers were appointed in each village. In Radcliffe, Mrs Ward, a district nurse living on Cropwell Road, became the first official visitor. She went into action immediately. As a result of her reports a child was removed from the care of a woman in the village whose house she considered to be dirty and whom she accused of neglect. Mrs Ward was active until her resignation in 1920 when Mrs James Haslam was appointed.

The voluntary work of women in nursing had been growing, but Bingham was slow to recognise its value, while ready to use it. Requests for subscriptions to local nursing associations were turned down until 1920 when East Bridgford pointed out that 'all persons in receipt of parish relief were being attended by the nurse without payment'. The secretary of Radcliffe's association, James Browne, applied in that year and the Bingham guardians agreed to subscribe two guineas annually in future.

2. The workhouse - in-maintenance

In May 1836, a month after the opening meeting of the new Bingham Union, it was resolved to build a new workhouse for 200 persons 'at the top end of town' in Bingham. Two acres of land were to be purchased from Lord Chesterfield at £150 per acre; ultimately the cost proved to be £3,160. 5s.4d, of which Radcliffe's share was £175.16s.3d, and a loan of £2,000 had to be arranged. With added interest it took over twenty years to pay off this debt to the Exchequer Loan Commissioners, the last instalment being paid in October 1858. A year after the tenders were put out the large brick building (on the corner of Nottingham Road, just west of its junction

The workhouse at Bingham opened in 1837

with Stanhope Way) was completed, and paupers residing in workhouses elsewhere but belonging to Bingham Union were moved in. There were to be few structural alterations in the ensuing years, although many internal adjustments were made, but the accommodation was not as large as originally planned. During 1852-3 the Poor Law Board and the Bingham authority disputed the number that the workhouse could accommodate. The latter insisted that it was at least 130, while the former fixed the number to be admitted at ninety-four.

This was symptomatic of the future for, as the Bingham guardians became more concerned with economy, so the London-based Board increased its demands as to the minimum standards of hygiene and comfort acceptable in the workhouse. From the 1850s dissatisfaction was occasionally expressed in the visitors' book and more frequently in inspectors' reports. This culminated in 1867 (a period of national concern over standards in workhouses), when a major indictment was brought by the inspector against the Bingham Board of Guardians which suggested that conditions had actually deteriorated since the workhouse opened. Water closets in the men's and women's yards had been closed for many years. They were, in any case, built over cesspools which were most offensive. Almost all the beds were double ones and the aged and able-bodied occupied the same wards. The guardians agreed to some improvements, but felt that lavatories and a bathroom were unnecessary, as was a receiving ward. They regarded a proposal for the men's day room to have a window in the blank wall next to the garden as 'most objectionable' and maintained that double beds for able-bodied women were better than single ones 'on account of their children'.

Over the next twenty years piecemeal improvements were made, but it was not until 1875 that a receiving ward with a bathroom was provided and in 1881 the medical officer was still pressing for closets in the children's yards. Progress in sanitation followed the same dilatory and penny pinching course as in Radcliffe itself, and the workhouse was only joined to the main Bingham sewerage system in 1914. Fire hazards preoccupied the inspectors in the 1890s and they fought a long and seemingly unsuccessful campaign for alternative exits to sleeping wards. Small improvements to furnishings, such as curtains in the women's wards, suggest that the inmates' surroundings were becoming more pleasant as the century drew to its close, but the essentially punitive aspect of the workhouse could never be forgotten: in 1879 the garden hedge had been raised in height and the walk re-sited to make it more difficult for inmates to communicate with the adjoining allotments.

Inmates and costs

As might be expected, the majority of inmates were elderly (60 years and over) or children (13 years or under), comprising at least half in any one census year. Among those of working age, a few were classed as idiots, as crippled, or (like Harriet Nowell from Radcliffe) as blind. Some were clearly unmarried mothers or widows (and occasionally widowers) with their children. Through the census returns, the minutes and the parish burial registers it is possible to detect paupers from Radcliffe, but not everyone who spent time in the workhouse would have been recorded. For some their stay would only have been temporary, perhaps whilst out of work or ill.

Of long-stay inmates, Joseph Shepperson, an agricultural labourer from Radcliffe, was typical of most adults, who were either unmarried or widowed. His removal from the parish of St Nicholas in Nottingham to Bingham workhouse in 1844 cost Radcliffe 6s, and the parish also had to pay for 2s given to him prior to his removal. He was to spend at least thirty years in the workhouse, last appearing as an old man of 80 in the census returns of 1871. Mary Wiser, who as a 32-year-old spinster was living with her elderly parents in Radcliffe in 1841, spent her last days in the house, dying there in 1877 aged 74. Her father, an agricultural labourer, was unlikely to have been able to leave her anything to maintain her in old age. Joseph Brewster, at the age of 70 in 1842, was the first Radcliffe pauper to die in the workhouse, but there were several others who appear to have entered in extreme old age. William Robson who died at the age of 77 in 1888 was one, and Mary Green in 1882 aged 73 was another. Three years earlier Robert Green aged 42 had also died there, but the relationship between them is obscure. Whatever the infirmity which made these paupers unable to earn their own livelihood in the first place, it was probably the lack of anyone to care for them which first placed them in the workhouse instead of receiving out-relief in the community.

In the early years the guardians were concerned with what they saw as an abuse of the system, whereby some would only stay for a few days, seeking readmission soon after leaving and thus avoiding the full rigours of the law. In other cases, however, the need for temporary in-maintenance was recognised, as when a member of the Durrant family was in the house in 1882. The medical officer judged that he would be well enough to leave in a fortnight's time, so the guardians decided he could do without the daily 2 oz of whisky previously recommended for him. Some Radcliffe children also appear fleetingly - Thomas Walker who died in the house at the age of 8 in 1851, Ruth Nowell who entered in 1868, and Fred Hallam who died there at the age of sixteen months in 1885, having been abandoned by his father.

Until 1847 the number sent from the parish was recorded: between two and nine in any quarter apart from the first two quarters of 1842 (a crisis year for the hosiery trade in Nottinghamshire) when there were thirteen and seventeen respectively. Up until 1865, when the whole union was made liable for all relief, the annual cost to Radcliffe of maintaining its poor in the workhouse ranged from as little as £10.15s.11¼d in 1859 to £41.16s.1d in 1864, although in the main it was below £30. Although the cost per capita of maintenance in the house was inevitably higher than out-relief, it was preferred by the authorities for its deterrent effect. Relatively few of Radcliffe's poor became inmates, but its shadow fell over all. The institutional nature of life in the house, its monotonous regime, the forbidding appearance of the building, the splitting up of families, and above all the stigma attached to it, were to have a powerful influence for many generations.

Conditions and clothes

The early minutes record the intentions of the guardians. The paupers were to be kept clean in mind as well as body. Luxuries, such as smoking or chewing tobacco, were not allowed unless ordered by the surgeon; meals were to be taken in silence; the master was to punish bad language; prayers were to be read every morning. Firmness and decision, together with kindness and humanity, were to be the master's watchwords.

On entering the house the pauper gave up his own clothes and was issued with workhouse dress - 'a suit of clothes for every male person ...and two spare suits to each' with a smock for working in. Women were given coarse straw bonnets, stays, shawls and grey cloaks to wear to church. Improvements in the washhouse in 1880 prompted the guardians to order more economical and more easily laundered clothing. The heavy 'Beaverteen' suits of the men were replaced by grey Melton jackets with cord trousers and vests (waistcoats), lined in checked or striped material. Girls and boys under five were to wear blue serge made up in the house, and a few blue serge garments for women who attended church were kept in stock. The boys were provided with Scotch caps with an anchor on the side, and girls and little children with hats. This was hardly a standard of attire worse than that of the lowest paid workers in the community, but the boots supplied to all, with their heels plated for men and boys, reasserted the workhouse image.

Diet

Bingham adopted the same dietary as at Southwell. This consisted of bread and milk for men and bread and gruel for women for both breakfast and supper. For dinner the inmates had potatoes and meat on three days, peas for men and soup for women on three days, and suet pudding for both on one day. Quantities varied slightly between the sexes and for children, and changes were made from time to time, often in response to local shortages. Towards the end of the nineteenth century, more lenient attitudes allowed visitors to bring gifts of food, and 1 oz of tobacco a week was allowed to those no longer able-bodied. The chief break in the monotonous diet, however, must have been the 'treats' provided to celebrate royal and national occasions, such as the plum pudding and roast beef on Queen Victoria's coronation day in 1838, which also became the regular Christmas day fare.

Recorded complaints were rare, although the inmates were allowed to apply to speak to the Board of Guardians. The request by some paupers in 1845 for a little more bread with their soup, which, they said, was too thin, was rejected by the medical officer. In 1866 the suicide of an inmate in a cesspool caused a resolution to be passed that, in addition to cesspools being kept locked in future, a book for complaints was to be procured and notices about procedure hung up in the workhouse. Several inmates complained about the food in 1877: the bread was very bad, the tea very weak and often with no sugar, and potatoes were not half cooked. The resulting investigation produced some revealing comments. One pauper said he

> *was middling comfortable, but would not say that he got plenty to eat and drink ...The Master scolds us if we complain. Sometimes we have not had any meat in the stew and the men call it 'potato broth'.*

However, another said, 'Generally speaking the Master is kind to me and I liked the mistress.' The committee reported that the complaints were justified, much of the blame being put on one of the servants, but they reprimanded the master for 'scolding' complainers.

John Godfrey and his daughter

The master and matron concerned were John Godfrey and his daughter Alice. They had given many years of faithful service, but she had recently been dismissed after an enquiry into the births of illegitimate children to two inmates. Her habit of taking breakfast in bed, among other things, was construed as negligence. A period of great disharmony followed. Another matron took Alice's place, and two years later John Godfrey was himself asked to resign on a charge of taking away from the workhouse 'both cooked meat and pickle'. He protested that 'whatever little he had taken to his daughter he had back in puddings, tea etc'. But he had to go, although he was allowed to retain his post as collector, and he settled in Cropwell Road, Radcliffe. He was still living there alone at the time of the 1881 census, and his occupation was given as 'Refreshment Housekeeper, Collector to the Guardians and Vaccination Officer.' He died a year later aged 61.

Work

The able-bodied pauper was set to work. It might be in the garden where potatoes, wheat, barley and mangolds were grown and pigs kept, in the kitchen or laundry, or he might be expected to help paint the workhouse or generally assist the master. The performing of some special task might entitle him to a pint of ale. Picking oakum and stone breaking were unpleasant and regular tasks performed by inmates. Rough granite was supplied by the Mountsorrel Granite Co. for 6s a ton in 1882 and sold when broken to the Bingham Highway Board for 8s.6d a ton. An equally monotonous but perhaps more pleasant task was given to Sam Porter of Radcliffe who 'blew' the organ three times on a Sunday. He was already an inmate in 1871 when he was 19. By 1881 he was described as a bricklayer. He may have proved an unsatisfactory organ blower or he may have left the workhouse temporarily, for his place was taken by another inmate within a year. He was to die in the house in 1910 at the age of 60.

The master kept an offence book and a great many of the entries concerned refusal to work. A typical punishment would be twenty-four hours' confinement with boiled potatoes for dinner, but extra work could be given, and at the worst the offender could be taken before the magistrates and finally imprisoned. Occasionally paupers absconded with workhouse clothes or returned late after leave of absence. Tensions within the house erupted from time to time in fighting, bad language or insolence to the officers. Elizabeth Doubleday and Elizabeth Love, both from Radcliffe, were confined for one hour for fighting in 1842. Poor blind Harriet Nowell was the object of an assault by Joseph Shepperson in 1870.

Inmates were allowed out to church and to seek employment, frequently attending the twice-yearly hirings, or statutes, in Bingham to do so. On three occasions in the 1840s Elizabeth Doubleday (aged 13 in 1841 and described as a stocking maker), who was illegitimate, was given money for clothing prior to going into service. In 1843 she and Elizabeth Love received £3.16s.4½d for this purpose. In the previous year William Love had also been given clothing in which to seek work, while John Wright (also from Radcliffe) had been allowed out for three days to look for a job.

Children in the workhouse

Small children were allowed to sleep in the same bed as their mothers, but after they reached the age of seven theoretically they went into their own wards. In 1867 it appears that they had their own dining room. This situation seems to have varied from time to time as the inspectors sometimes complained about the lack of separate accommodation for the children. It was the intention of the Poor Law Act that they should be kept away from possibly harmful influences.

Education was provided and it was almost certainly superior to that enjoyed by most working class families until after the 1870 Education Act. At Bingham, the waiting room was used as a schoolroom and a schoolmaster was employed. He was allowed writing desks for about eight children, along with six testaments, twelve premiers, three dozen cards, one dozen easy lessons, one dozen slates and a box. Later additions included forms with backs for young children and a carpet 'for those children who are tired to lie on'. In 1848 it was resolved that girls as well as boys should be taught arithmetic. The next year a schoolmistress, 'single, steady and active' replaced the master to teach 'knitting, plain sewing, reading, writing and sums', and more text books were provided in arithmetic, grammar and history, as well as maps. Some pupils' interest evidently strayed, for in 1851 the bottom part of the schoolroom window was covered in sheet iron. In 1872 there were no children of school age in the workhouse, so the schoolmistress was dismissed and it was arranged that in future children would attend the Bingham Board School, escorted there by one of the inmates.

The more lenient attitude to children was apparent from the very beginning. There were periodic requests from the guardians that they should be taken out walking, and in 1846 Bingham was allowed to donate a see-saw. This was followed by hoops and skipping ropes and, once they attended the Board School, they also joined the Sunday School which provided regular treats. In 1878 they enjoyed the first of many trips to Skegness. In matters of diet, too, the children may well have fared better than many a family outside. The prevalence of scabies in the early 1880s seems to have been associated with bad weather conditions, making it difficult to obtain potatoes, and a lactometer was brought in to test the quality of the milk. A fresh dietary requested by the medical officer was rejected by the Board of Guardians, but the chairman offered the use of his fields for the children to play in. The only recorded instance of ill treatment within the workhouse occurred in 1879 during the period of tension shortly before John Godfrey's dismissal. He was reprimanded by a committee of enquiry which found several bruises and black patches on the shoulders of one of the boys.

The desirability of removing children from the workhouse environment altogether was becoming more widely recognised and as the number maintained there in the 1880s and 1890s grew, it was decided to follow the example of other unions and have the children boarded out between the ages of eight and thirteen or fourteen. A home in Cotgrave and one in Shelford were selected, and three brothers whose settlement was at Radcliffe were sent to the latter. They were Thomas, William and George Hallam. Thomas had been transferred from Birmingham in 1884 aged 7, and soon after arriving in Bingham had been fitted with boots and leg irons, which had to be replaced three years later at a cost of £5.16s. The master had tried to obtain these at a special price from the supplier, a Mr Hayward, but had failed. Thomas's brothers seem to have been in Bingham when he arrived. Their subsequent history is typical of many workhouse children, and some trouble seems to have been taken over their welfare. The guardians were anxious to have the boys placed in useful employment when they reached the age of thirteen. One went for a month's trial as an apprentice to Mr Millington, a tailor at Langar. Their uncle, Thomas Parr of Arkwright Street in Nottingham, requested that George should go and live with him. The guardians made conscientious enquiries as to the uncle's respectability before letting the boy go. The experiment was short lived and George returned to Shelford three months later. His brother William also stayed with Thomas Parr, but again only for a short while. One brother then absconded with a friend to Nottingham and was brought back and caned. But William was at last successful in being apprenticed, at his own request, to the owner of a Grimsby fishing smack, and was fitted out with clothes costing £5.10s.

In the last years of the nineteenth century overcrowding became a problem and the inspectors were critical of the lack of amusement provided for the children still there. In 1903 an entirely new policy was adopted. A house was purchased in Union Street for eight children with an official known as an 'industrial trainer' to care for them. Later a larger house for eleven children was obtained in Fairfield Street. These were known as the Cottage Homes and toys were donated to them. The Rev Droosten gave a bagatelle board, and a rocking horse and piano were acquired. The minutes record entertainments such as a magic lantern show at Christmas, visits to the homes of the local gentry for tea, an entertainment in the coffee room in Bingham and more trips to Skegness, but they cannot obscure the fact that the children were marked as paupers as long as they remained in the Cottage Homes.

Care of the sick

Sick wards for inmates were provided in the workhouse and the nursing performed by their fellows. One pauper who baulked at this task in 1848 was punished with confinement for twenty-four hours. It was not long before the chronic sick in the community were being sent in when there was no one else to care for them and in the 1880s there were several cases of women using the lying-in room for their confinements. Overcrowding of the wards and constant internal re-arrangements became common.

The need to isolate fever cases became apparent. After the death of two young women from typhus in 1855, the guardians went so far as to have it 'in contemplation to convert an outhouse into an Infectious ward'. They were to contemplate for a long time. National concern over conditions for the sick in workhouses in general was the primary reason behind the searching inspection of 1867, which noted the absence of such a ward in Bingham, as well as the lack of a paid nurse, of water closets and taps for the sick, and of dressing gowns, as well as the fact that the medical officer still had to supply drugs and leeches. The description of the stone floor paints a comfortless picture of the sick ward.

Following the birth of a still-born child in 1872, it was at last resolved to employ a nurse. The first to take up the post at £15 a year was Sarah Walker, a widow from Radcliffe, but she did not stay long. Of all the offices the guardians had to fill, this was to prove the most difficult because of the shortage of trained candidates, even though the salary was soon raised to £25 per year. In nine years there were to be nine nurses. Sarah Walker resigned because of ill health. Others were dismissed for being pregnant, intoxicated, incompetent, negligent, for causing discord and being absent without leave. Similar problems were to recur for many years. From 1900 onwards it became the practice to employ the nurse and the porter as a married couple. Although this may have solved some problems, it made it no easier to find qualified nurses.

At last in 1884 with a smallpox outbreak in the district, a temporary infectious hospital (which became a permanent feature over the next forty years) was opened in the workhouse grounds. Trained staff were hired as the occasion demanded, as when Samuel, John, Martha and Mary Flower from Radcliffe were admitted suffering from smallpox in 1903. Later John and Sophie Headland and a patient from Bingham joined them. The Local Government Board in London were unhappy with the arrangements because of the hospital's proximity to the workhouse. The guardians reassured them that there was no contact between the two and that every endeavour had been made to get the cases, which were mild, admitted elsewhere. The bill for nursing from the Royal Nursing Institute at Derby came to £16.2s.11d and the guardians, through their collector, tried to recoup their loss in Sam Flower's case by applying to the Oddfellows in Radcliffe and to the Great Northern Railway for the amount of sick pay owing to him. The solicitor to the G.N.R.C. denied their right to do this and said the money had been paid to him direct. The guardians allowed the matter to drop.

The hospital was only used intermittently, but as it was on workhouse premises fever patients sent there were classed as paupers. At times the overspill from the workhouse sick ward was placed there, but it was probably unused for much of the time. In July 1914 it was recommended that it should be repaired, cleaned and put in order. Meanwhile, an improvement had been made in the workhouse sick wards. In 1900, after much hesitation, it was decided to provide the wooden floors first requested over forty years before, but it took another two years to have them put in. At this time the medical officer was still supplying medicines (as were the district medical officers), and in 1902 he calculated that for the previous three years the cost averaged £12.15s a year and that savings could be made if they were bought wholesale. Despite the disapproval of the Local Government Board, the guardians decided to leave things as they were and simply to increase the doctor's salary by £10 a year. Another improvement was a hot water supply, which was laid on from 1906.

The mentally ill

A certain number of workhouse inmates were imbeciles or senile. Those needing extra care were sent to the asylum at Sneinton until Saxondale was opened in 1902, and sometimes to asylums in other counties. The cost to the union for their maintenance rose from £135.17s.10d in 1844 to £423.5s.10½d in 1870. Some asylums further afield were particularly expensive as the case of Richard Knight was to show. In 1853 Radcliffe was held liable for £18.4s.6d spent on him at Vernon House in Swansea and further demands for £7 and £8 a year provoked a resolution by the Bingham guardians that all relief paid on his account should be regarded as a loan. Payments ceased after 1856, but no mention occurs of the 'loan' being repaid.

It was up to the relieving officer to give the order for a pauper's removal to the asylum after a medical inspection, his expenses being repaid and charged to the parish of settlement. George Upton claimed £1.10s for the removal of Samuel Howard in 1857 and £1.9s for Hannah Ogle two years later. In 1866 John Hopewell was sent to the asylum, but by this time the expense was borne by the common fund of the whole union. For a short period three years later he moved to the workhouse, indicating the fine line drawn between those considered ill enough for the asylum and those suitable for maintenance in the house. Thomas Durrant was another who, in the 1880s, was first sent to the workhouse and then moved to the asylum.

The total number of paupers from the union in asylums averaged about seventeen a year over a twenty year period from 1869. In 1879 visiting committees were organised to inspect the union's paupers at Sneinton every year, and for ten years their names are given. The largest number to come from Radcliffe was four, two of whom - George Wright and John Haywood - were long-stay patients. Harriet Fletcher, whose labourer husband paid 2s a week for her care, was only there for a few months in 1881, and James Carnell died soon after his arrival in 1882. The visiting committee always reported that the patients were well and in good health.

These were, of course, the certifiable cases; many of a more doubtful nature were sent to the workhouse where maintenance was cheaper. In the 1861 census five inmates were described as 'idiots'. Under the Local Government Act of 1888 unions were to be reimbursed 4s a head per week for every pauper in an asylum, but by 1919 this had become totally inadequate, the cost having increased to 28s a week in some asylums, hence the pressure to keep as many as possible in the workhouse. As in other matters the question of whether the conditions were adequate was raised by the inspectors with increasing persistence as time went by. In 1891 they pointed out that the diet was 'not on so liberal a scale as is now allowed to persons of unsound mind in many workhouses'.

Meanwhile, the new asylum at Saxondale had been opened with the full support of the Board of Guardians. It was soon full and in 1907 they received a letter asking whether the workhouse could accept some patients 'particularly imbeciles and those cases of mental deficiency due to old age'. They replied that they had 'on rare occasions detained in the workhouse an old person who was mentally defective on account of his or her age and ...they would be willing to do so in future if such a case occurred'. Overcrowding in Saxondale continued and the Great War aggravated the situation, but by this time Bingham workhouse no longer had the staff to cope with the mentally ill.

Vagrancy

Bingham Union, lying as it did on several major routes, found vagrancy an intractable problem, and the fluctuations in the number of casuals passing through made it difficult to formulate a consistent and effective policy. The implications for Radcliffe, the last major village before Nottingham, are obvious. Individuals such as Sarah Davies, taken ill in Radcliffe in 1838, and a poor woman with two children travelling through the village at night in 1844, were given relief in kind by the overseers, who then claimed the cost back from the union. Had these women been suspected of begging, their treatment would have been very different. A sentence of one month's hard labour in the House of Correction was imposed on Matthew Martin in December 1841 for begging in Radcliffe. In December 1845 two men who called at Mr Marriott's house asking for poor relief were told that he had no power to help them, but he gave them a penny each out of his own pocket. They obviously considered this inadequate and proceeded to break his windows, for which William Taylor, the local magistrate, sentenced them to a month's imprisonment. The windows of John Green were given the same treatment in April 1847 for similar reasons, one man being sent to Southwell for a month and another for two weeks.

A night's lodging at the workhouse was available for vagrants and, early on, ways of increasing accommodation were sought by converting stables into wards. Efforts to find task work, such as digging by measure, as required by the Poor Law Commissioners, were also made but soon abandoned because of the lack of supervision. From the end of 1845 the number of vagrants coming to the workhouse began to rise, and the problem became acute with the influx of victims of the Irish famine. In the last quarter of 1845 the number recorded was 131; the next year it was 719 in the same period and 1,138 in 1847. A peak was reached with 1,615 for the quarter ending in June 1848, and thereafter numbers fell rapidly away. In 1849 only 38 were relieved in the second half of the year at a total cost of 3s.

The 1860s were to witness another increase, though not on the same scale. A system of issuing tickets by constables to those claiming relief was in operation. The real difficulty was to distinguish between the genuine casual seeking work and the professional able-bodied tramp. At the same time, the inspectors were intervening more in the arrangements made by the union for their reception and were pressing for improvements, especially in sanitation. In 1871 it became obligatory to set a task, provide a bath and to have casuals' clothes disinfected, which necessitated alterations to the workhouse costing £103. The vagrants were set to breaking stones and picking oakum, and in 1874 one dozen stone-breaking hammers were purchased and spikes ominously set along the top of the stone-breaking yard. An inspection made in November 1878 revealed that there were eleven casual paupers at the time, six breaking stones and five picking oakum.

The harsher measures, however, brought no decrease in the numbers and only fresh problems to the guardians. Some tramps scaled the walls before completing their tasks, so the walls were increased in height and nuts and bolts fitted to grates on the roof of the stone-breaking shed. Still the numbers rose - from 519 in 1872 to 3,832 in 1881. The guardians complained that they lacked the powers to deal with the professional tramp, but decided to raise the weight of stone to be broken to 5 cwt for all casuals remaining one night. ('The old tramping vagrant could readily break his 3 cwt in less than three hours', it was said.) Vagrants tore up their clothes and had to be taken before the magistrates, so a canvas suit was designed for them in 1882, with the Bingham Union stamp on the front and back. This was removed two years later on the orders of the inspectors. Their insistence on baths, the disinfecting of clothes and the replacement of wooden by iron bedsteads appeared to be justified in 1892 when one of the tramps, John Hoe, developed a smallpox rash overnight. He was removed to the isolation hospital and no fresh cases were reported, but the danger to the community was clear. Another high figure of 2,158 casuals seeking relief at the workhouse in the half year up to Michaelmas 1895 was explained by the guardians as being the result of new railway work, and the figure did drop dramatically for the same periods in the next two years (to 875 and 294). The guardians did not feel that there was any exceptional distress in the district, but it is probable that the agricultural depression during the last two decades of the nineteenth century had an impact on vagrancy.

In 1913 Bingham Union joined the Nottinghamshire and Derbyshire Vagrancy Committee which operated a way ticket system. This arranged for a more uniform treatment of vagrants within the area, specifying the time they could be detained, their diet and the tasks they had to perform. Those considered to be genuinely seeking work were given a bread ticket, and special stations were set up where they could obtain a midday meal. The clerk was instructed to obtain from the police the names of shopkeepers who would supply food at four places in the union, of which Radcliffe was one. This system was still in operation when the war broke out. The Local Government Board then suggested that with the decrease in the number of casuals, their ward could be closed. The guardians' reply, pointing out the dangers of tramps in winter resorting to outbuildings or to stackyards as sleeping places, revealed the fear the vagrant could induce in a rural community. They did, however, agree to the closure, provided they could reopen the ward at their own discretion.

The public and the workhouse

Beginning with the coronation of Queen Victoria in 1838 when the inmates were allowed to go into the market place 'to witness the festivities in honour of the day', the workhouse had always benefited from events in the life of the royal family. During the 1887 golden jubilee celebrations the old and infirm were even provided with a waggon so that they could join in the procession. There had also been occasional gifts, especially to the children, often from the local clergy. From the 1880s the number proliferated. At first mainly at Christmas - tea, sugar, tobacco, oranges and sweetmeats, mincepies and evergreens, cards, wrapovers and scarves - but then also at other times of the year - fruit and vegetables, plants and jam - gifts were handed in at the workhouse from an ever increasing number of donors. The public conscience over the innocent victims of poverty was clearly aroused. From Radcliffe Mr Upton sent plants, Mr Ramson of Millfield House 'graphics', the Hon Mrs Noel flowers, while others such as the Rev Cullen, Dr Campbell, Mrs Daft, Mrs Foster, Miss Beeson and many more took advantage of the box which was set up to receive periodicals at Bingham railway station and which was cleared daily. Besides gifts, teas and visits to the Bingham Flower Show were regularly arranged, and local amateur performers laid on musical entertainments in the workhouse. Not to be outdone, Radcliffe's Honorary Glee Society offered to give a concert in April 1893, if a piano and platform were provided. The guardians, however, felt that this would entail too much trouble for the small number of inmates who would be able to attend. Evidently enjoyment of these treats was not open to all.

In-maintenance in the twentieth century

Although the overwhelming impression remains that the Bingham guardians had been loth to entertain the possibility of change and slow to implement improvements in the workhouse, on several occasions they had won the approval of the government inspectors. In 1897 they had reported that the workhouse was very clean and that 'the inmates, nearly all of whom are infirm, appear comfortable and well cared for'. In the same year a visiting committee from Shardlow Union had commented that all was 'in perfect order and every credit is due to your Master and Matron'. It is very likely that when there were no exceptional pressures, such as overcrowding, sickness or food shortages, the inmates, especially the old and mentally and physically infirm, were as well cared for as they might have been in the community.

Twentieth century inmates who came from Radcliffe can be detected when something unusual required a note in the minutes. It is not always clear why they were there in the first place. In 1914 the Board agreed to a request from a spinster that her sister should be discharged and return to live with her on out-relief. A mother was allowed to leave her child for many years in the house, contributing at first 2s and then 3s.6d, perhaps because the little girl was crippled in some way. Special boots and a support were provided for her and through one of the guardians she was admitted as an in-patient at Nottingham General Hospital to have her tonsils out.

Just as with out-relief, the proliferation of government bodies involved Bingham in wrangles over the repayment of the costs of in-maintenance, particularly concerning the families of servicemen. In 1918 the question of the care of the two children of a soldier whose wife had to be admitted to the asylum seems to have been settled smoothly between the Board of Guardians and the local War Pensions Committee, but this was not so in July 1920 when the wife of a soldier serving abroad had to go into hospital for an operation. Her five children were admitted to the workhouse at the request of the secretary of this committee, their mother being prepared to pay a little towards the cost of their maintenance. The guardians replied indignantly that they regarded it as the duty of the Ministry of Pensions to provide the full cost for these children. The mother collected her children on 4th August and paid £6.8s, this being the proportion of the separation allowance issuable in respect of the children. The guardians then sent in a claim to the committee for maintenance at the rate of 12s per week per child less £6.8s. The committee, however, maintained that they had no authority to settle the claim of the guardians and that their secretary, in making the arrangements for the children, had been acting in a personal way and not in his official capacity. This the guardians denied and the dispute went first to the Ministry of Pensions and then to the Ministry of Health before they had to admit defeat.

The guardians' sense of duty as keepers of the ratepayers' purse extended to the smallest detail. Was not the charge of 18s for cab hire from Gedling to the asylum excessive, they asked on one occasion, and was the charge of 3s for refreshments really necessary for such a short journey? In 1914 the relieving officer reported that he had taken possession of the bank deposit book of a patient which showed a small balance due to her at Lloyd's Bank in Nottingham, and he noticed that her niece had removed her furniture for storage. The manager of the bank was requested not to pay out the balance or any portion thereof without Bingham's authority, and the niece was not to dispose of the furniture. A claim would probably be made against each, and in the following year an order to withdraw the bank deposit was given.

It is clear that the guardians' obligation to recoup as much of the cost of maintenance of paupers was sometimes contrary to their own sense of humanity. One Radcliffe inmate suffered from a tug-of-war between the authorities as to where her treatment should take place. Classed as an imbecile, she was maintained in the workhouse from 1909 onwards, and in 1913 was one of several inmates mentioned in a report by a commissioner in lunacy, whom he considered suitable for detention under the Lunacy Act. Amongst other things the inspector criticised the arrangements of the workhouse which he found to be of 'a primitive order especially as regards the absence of proper facilities for bathing patients'. The imbecile in question (then aged 38) was removed to the asylum where her father continued to pay 2s a week for her for another two years, until he pleaded that he was ill (he was now 65) and that his employment was precarious. In the meantime the patient had been returned to the workhouse 'on trial' as the asylum was trying to off-load as many patients as possible at the time. The medical officer of the workhouse, however, felt that he could not sign a certificate of recovery and once again she was sent to the asylum, only to be returned to the workhouse the following day. Such a patient could well have been happier in the more familiar surroundings of the workhouse even though the facilities were less suitable that those at the asylum, but the shuttling to and fro between institutions was hardly in her interests.

That the system in itself could be the cause of impoverishment was also recognised by some. Certainly the solicitor acting for two spinster ladies from Radcliffe in the early years of the century believed this to be true. One of these sisters entered the asylum in 1904 and until her death four years later regular payments from rent received from a small property she owned were made by her sister for her maintenance. On her death the balance due was £72.14s.11½d and the guardians made a claim upon her estate. The solicitor explained that the deceased had left her property to her sister for life and after her death to two nieces.

There will be little provision for the sister, however, if the Guardians insist upon payment of their claim. ... She is now in her 64th year, very infirm and in poor circumstances and has every claim to their sympathy and consideration, and the reversioners are two nieces, one a cripple and the other a sufferer from spinal trouble.

The deceased's estate consisted of about £3 in cash and a small freehold house in Back Lane, Radcliffe, let for 2s, against which there was a claim of £30 and interest for money lent, as well as the guardians' claim. To meet these the value of the estate would have to be further reduced.

In the circumstances and advised that the doctor's certificate of death described the deceased a pauper we venture to hope that the Guardians may see their way to leave some little provision for the deceased's sister who is in sore need of it.

The guardians' hands were tied, however, as they themselves pointed out, but following enquiries to the Local Government Board they discovered that they were not obliged to make an order for repayment of that part of the cost born by Parliamentary grant, which amounted in this case to £33.13s.6d. The solicitor was only obliged to forward £39 and the grateful sister thereafter sent regular consignments of periodicals through the railway box to the workhouse. In the end she did not avoid the stigma of pauperism, however, for in 1921 she herself became an inmate, and the collector was claiming £1 a week from her estate.

It is inevitable that the minutes record the more problematical cases which tend to show the board in an unfavourable light. That they were able to use their position in a positive way to assist the poor must also be recognised. For orphaned children, especially, they were a means of help and security that they might otherwise not have known. Why one particular lad whose settlement was Radcliffe was singled out for special treatment is not explained. He was being maintained in the workhouse at South Shields in 1914 and the authorities there asked that they might keep him. The Bingham guardians refused this request and he was removed to the Cottage Home. The Nottingham police court missionary, Mr Lightfoot, took an interest in his case, so perhaps his father was a convicted criminal, his mother having disappeared. He arranged for him to go to Sutcliffe Voluntary Industrial Home at Walcote, near Bath and the guardians agreed to pay the cost of his travel of £1.16s.11d and 5s a week for his keep. After his arrival there the superintendent was soon writing to complain that he was suffering from 'itch' and ought not to have been sent in that condition. Dr Campbell admitted that when he had arrived from South Shields he had been treated for specific ulcers, but that the day before his journey there had been no signs of contagion and none of the other children in the cottage home had scabies. So the boy was allowed to remain at Sutcliffe. Every August he joined other lads who had no parents or friends with whom to spend the summer holidays at a camp by the seaside for three weeks and for this the guardians paid an extra £1. Every year Sutcliffe Home sent a report on his progress. In 1919 the superintendent wrote that he was now over 14 years of age and in ordinary circumstance would already have been placed out, but that he was too 'unreliable' and he therefore suggested some employment should be secured for him where he would be free from temptation. Mr Lightfoot again stepped in and arranged for him to go to a market gardener at Sutton-in-Ashfield with whom the boy had at one time lived and who promised to do his best for him. In gratitude for solving what was likely to prove a thorny problem, the guardians donated £1.1s to the police mission.

Postscript

Times were changing for the workhouse, the guardians and the whole system of poor law administration. Women government inspectors made their appearance in 1913 and the first woman guardian, Mrs Evelyn le Marchant of Colston Bassett, was elected. She proved to be an active and effective member of the board. The billeting of eight officers and 150 men of the 9th Lancashire Fusiliers on 23rd march 1915 (for which £1.6s.4d was received) must have caused a flutter in the workhouse, but in general the records kept during the war years show clearly the strain of staff shortages, food and fuel rationing and an increasing work load for the guardians

Nor did peace bring immediate relief, for the economic situation was critical for some time and it was not until July 1919 that celebrations were discussed. The guardians ended the year 1920 with a resolution that the inmates' evening meal (which was the one most in need of improvement and consisted of 1 pint of tea, 1 pint of porridge and 4 ounces of bread for 6 days), should now be replaced by 8 ounces of bread, 1 pint of tea, half an ounce of margarine or one-and-a-half ounces of jam or treacle on alternate days and that at lunch 8 ounces of rice or sago pudding should be provided.

Their days, however, were numbered. In 1919 control of poor law administration had passed to the Ministry of Health. Ten years later local boards of guardians were abolished, their functions being transferred to town and county councils and the workhouse test was replaced by the means test, although it was not until 1948 that the Poor Law Amendment Act was finally repealed. Bingham workhouse survived as a home for the aged and infirm until 1965 and was demolished in 1967.

II. Charity and self-help

As well as the official poor law provision for the needy, Radcliffe had its own charities, its own benefactors and several schemes encouraging self-help to those in financial difficulties, particularly in the 1840s and at the time of the agricultural depression later in the nineteenth century. Some support was also given to those beyond the village community.

Donations

Collections from both St Mary's and the Wesleyan chapel went annually to Nottingham's hospital fund. St Mary's harvest festival collection in October 1864 went to the Girls' Industrial Training Institution and Orphanage at Lenton, 'into which excellent institution several young persons from the parish of Radcliffe have been admitted'. In 1870 the harvest collection was postponed until Christmas so that it could be 'devoted towards making soup for the most needy of the parishioners through the winter'. Many responded to the Boer War 'shilling fund' in 1899-1900 in aid of wounded soldiers, widows and orphans. Mrs Noel of Lamcote House made two donations of 500s (£25). The pupils of Beaconsfield House school collected 22s. A typical fundraising effort came at a private dinner party at the Manvers Arms in December 1899 'to help the home that Tommy's left behind him'. After a recitation of Kipling's *The Absentminded Beggar* by Mr Will Scanlon, 24s was raised. At the other end of the scale was the shilling collected by 'Gladys, Nellie and Percy at their Grandfather's Christmas Dinner Table, Radcliffe-on-Trent'. There was a similar response to the Indian Famine Fund of 1900: Harry and Bernard Sketchley's 11s, Mr Houldgate's 20s, another 500s from Mrs Noel, and much more.

Benefactors

The gulf between rich and poor may well have been emphasised by the benefaction of the well-to-do. In January 1846 the *Nottingham Journal* reported that the wife and daughters of William Taylor of Radcliffe Hall presented the church Sunday scholars 'that were deserving' with flannel petticoats and books. Any deserving girl who was also a school monitor that Christmas could have ended up with two flannel petticoats, the second from 'the lady of the Rev W. Bury of this village'. Mrs Bury presented boy monitors with shirts. In December 1873 Frederick Wright of Radcliffe Lodge distributed to the widows, aged and infirm of the parish a large trunk of the best Babbington coal. During the 1880s Edwin Green, a lace manufacturer who owned considerable property in the village, made his gift of coal to widows an annual event. There were fifteen recipients in January 1885 and twenty in November of the same year.

Radcliffe's most prolific benefactor was (Anne) Adelaide Burnside, subsequently the Hon Mrs Noel of Lamcote House (see page 151). From her arrival in the 1860s, not only did she contribute generously to all kinds of charitable causes but she expected her household to do so too. When her butler, Thomas Harrison, died in 1874, he left £250 to the General Hospital, a cause close to Miss Burnside's heart. During the period of the Boer War her servants contributed 14s to the 'shilling fund'. In the village, apart from her major contribution to the rebuilding of the church, she regularly provided buns for the children, coal from the Co-operative Society for the poor, and flannel petticoats or shirts for all infant school children (whether deserving or not). She also provided an annual Christmas dinner for 120 or so of the elderly poor and others, which was held either at the Manvers Arms or in the schoolroom. On her death in 1904 she left bequests to a number of charitable and religious causes, including £2,000 each to the Church Missionary Society, Nottingham's General Hospital, the British and Foreign Bible Society and the Pastoral Aid Society. Closer at hand she left more modest sums to all her servants, ranging from £200 to her butler down to £10 each to the lesser ranks who had been in her employment for under five years.

Provident clubs and societies

Thrift and self-help were encouraged locally. The Bingham Provident Society was active by October 1841, providing winter clothing in return for subscriptions of 3d a week. The Nottinghamshire Agricultural Association, among other aims, encouraged independence in agricultural workers. In October 1842 William Barnett, servant to Mr Brewster of Radcliffe, won first prize of £2 'For the labourer in Husbandry, who shall have brought up his Family without parochial relief'. His character, the number of children and the years worked for the same master were all taken into account. In Radcliffe itself, both clothing and coal clubs were flourishing by the 1870s. The parochial magazine of 1877 lists donors to each, including Lady Manvers, the Burnside sisters of Lamcote House, Mrs Wright of Radcliffe Lodge, Mrs Taylor of Radcliffe Hall, Mr Gorse of the Manor House, and Mrs Sanday of Cliff House amongst others. To the coal club sixty-nine members paid in £44.10s.4d, receiving over £64.1s.10d-worth of coal. The clothing club had ninety members who paid in £59.12s.6d, and there were also some contributions from nine widows. As well as the value of their original payments, ordinary members were given a bonus of 2s.6d, and widows a bonus of 4s.3d.

Gardens and allotments

A Gardening Society was established in 1875 'especially to encourage and stimulate the working men to the better management of their gardens and little allotments'. At the annual show held in August or September, labourers entered in class C, paying a subscription of 1s. (Gentlemen or professional gardeners entered in class A at 3s, while tradesmen and cottagers paid 2s in class B. In 1898 these two classes were amalgamated, with 'gentlemen' no longer being mentioned.) The provision of allotments in Radcliffe, however, long preceded the Gardening Society, largely thanks to the work of Mr James Orange of Castle Terrace, Nottingham, secretary and travelling agent to a Northern and Midland Counties Society working to obtain land for labourers and artisans. From evidence that he gave to a parliamentary committee on the labouring poor in 1843 it is clear that his task was not easy. Societies formed in a number of places, including Radcliffe, in the hope of acquiring land had had to be abandoned. Other evidence from Nottinghamshire emphasised that a garden acted as a savings bank for a mechanic or labourer and many at Basford had been saved from the workhouse by having allotments. James Orange's success in eventually persuading landowners to provide land in both

Radcliffe and Cotgrave in the 1840s is made clear in a letter to the *Nottingham Journal* of February 27th 1886. The survey of the Holme Pierrepont Estate in 1861 shows that 6 acres 3 roods 17 perches in Radcliffe's 'Town end Close' had by then been classed as 'allotment gardens', having an annual value of £20.11s.3d. The 1886 letter adds that the earl then allocated over eighty more gardens to labourers in the village, comprising 600 yards each of excellent land let at 5s per annum. It was estimated that there were about 170 allotments in the parish at the time of writing, and provision would be extended to tradesmen and others in the following year. Some of these may have been provided by other landowners, including the church, for a later undated document in the Manvers papers, probably from around 1900, indicates that the estate held only 159 allotments in Radcliffe. Despite some proddings from Whitehall during the First World War, it was not until 1921 that the Parish Council took on any responsibility for allotments.

Penny savings bank

Another institution which encouraged self-help for the poor was a penny savings bank founded about November 1860. Like the coal, clothing and gardening clubs, it seems to have been inspired by the middle classes for the benefit of the less affluent - the vicar was chairman of its management committee in 1864, for example - and there was some reluctance to participate. Deposits by July 1860 totalled £41.14s.5d and withdrawals only £7.5s.2d. The *Nottingham Journal* hoped that this successful start

> ..... will tend to overcome prejudices which may have been entertained with regard to the village bank, and induce many more of the labouring classes to participate in the advantages arising from a connection with such an institution.

Initially no interest was paid to depositors, but in January 1864 a bonus was paid to all those having at least 5s deposited for each of the years 1861-63. Many local savings banks disappeared as the Post Office Savings Bank grew in popularity in the 1860s, but the Radcliffe bank survived this period and was described as being in a 'flourishing condition' in the parochial magazine of October 1877.

Friendly societies

One example of self-help had its roots amongst the artisan classes of the eighteenth century when an inadequate poor law system had caused friendly societies to proliferate. Their general aim was to support the unemployed, the sick and the families of deceased members, while offering conviviality and a regular social outlet through their meetings, normally held in public houses. Eventually, friendly societies themselves became almost elitist, with elaborate initiation ceremonies, secret signs, and high entrance fees as well as regular contributions. The really poor were consequently excluded from their ranks.

As early as 1794 a friendly society was meeting at the Black Lion in Radcliffe. It continued until 1901 when its assets were £917.5s.8d and it had thirty-five members. From 1820 a female friendly society - a much rarer phenomenon - was also meeting there, but was dissolved in 1840. Perhaps the Old Friendly Society for men and women, referred to in the *Parochial Magazine* for 1877, combined the work of both. Across the road by 1832 the Old Oak Lodge (No. 48) of the Nottingham Ancient Imperial Union of Oddfellows (founded in 1812) used to meet. William Barratt was its leading light in the middle of the century and was typical of the kind of member that friendly societies attracted. A cordwainer (shoemaker) with a wife and six children, he or his family at some stage could expect to suffer hardship or bereavement which would be alleviated by the society. On his own death in April 1863 at the age of 63 his work for the Nottingham Oddfellows earned him a brief obituary in the *Nottingham Journal* which concluded with the following tribute:

> His affability and general demeanour had long endeared him to a numerous acquaintance, by whom his memory will be long cherished.

Another typical member was George Richmond, a coal dealer of Mount Pleasant.

Aged 38 in 1864, he would have benefited from the society's funeral fund when his wife died leaving him with six children. In that year the Old Oak lodge had sixteen members, and assets of 18s.1d, most local funds being invested through the Grand Lodge in Nottingham.

In 1844 two new lodges of the Nottingham Oddfellows were established locally - Lamcote Lodge (No. 185) meeting at the Red Lion, and Kingston Lodge (No. 203) meeting at the Manvers Arms. Both the Kingston and the, now Royal, Oak Club are mentioned in the *Parochial Magazine* for 1877, but not the Lamcote Lodge.

Glimpses of the activity of a rival order in the village can be occasionally gleaned from the pages of the *Nottingham Journal*. The Prince of Wales Lodge (3597) of the Independent Order of Oddfellows - Manchester Unity - was established in 1843 and, like the Kingston Lodge, also met at the Manvers Arms. In the mid-1840s it had about thirty-five members, but it flourished as the century progressed, reaching a membership of 138 in 1880 and 178 by 1913. It seceded from the Order in 1922, continuing as an unregistered independent society. (A Kingston Lodge of the Manchester Oddfellows seems to have been formed in 1912, becoming independent in 1938.)

Officials of the Prince of Wales Lodge in 1860 included the names of Duke, Foster and Ledger, the first two being from well-known Radcliffe families. The report of their annual Whitsuntide celebrations in 1872 shows the respect accorded their activities. After processing to the church, preceded by the band of the Sherwood Foresters, the members listened to a 'practical and earnest' sermon from the vicar before enjoying their dinner. The equivalent celebration in 1877 got out of hand when Oddfellow John Howard, having had 'an excess of John Barleycorn' expressed his dissatisfaction at not having had more music from the band by assaulting William Kerchen. The local magistrates fined him 20s. In the previous March the lodge was duped into believing that a shoemaker named Thomas Johnson was a poor oddfellow from a Preston lodge. Levi Duke organised a collection and raised 13s for him. By the time the Prince of Wales Lodge had discovered that the Preston society had never heard of him he was far away. Even when he was foolish enough to try the same trick again in September 1879 and was arrested, Radcliffe failed to get the necessary evidence from Preston and he was acquitted. Such financial trickery, however trivial, was always an embarrassment to a friendly society, and particularly so to the Prince of Wales Lodge. With fifty-eight members and assets of £331 they were of some consequence in the village. At the end of March 1877 they even advertised in the *Nottingham Journal* for a mortgage or other legal security in which to invest £350. Still more embarrassing was the case in January 1883 when William Bramwell, a former secretary, was charged with absconding with £49.8s. The club was so anxious to get the money back that although the case came to court, Bramwell was allowed to repay it in instalments of £10 per year rather than face prosecution. The lodge management was reprimanded for allowing him to have the money in his possession. Despite such aberrations, and the coming of health insurance and pensions which weakened the hold of friendly societies, the Prince of Wales Lodge was still on hand in 1920 to lend £530 to the Parish Council for the purchase of the recreation ground from the Manvers' estate. Friendly societies had come a long way from their humble beginnings in the eighteenth century.

The Jeffrey Dole

The parish's oldest official charity derived from £10 left by the wheelwright Jeffrey Limmer in 1617 to the village poor. Along with some other bequests, a total of £33 was accumulated by December 1714, and in 1718 £31.12s was invested in strips of land in the village's open fields. At enclosure these strips were exchanged for land on the Bingham Road. In addition, in 1763 the parish purchased about half an acre of land at the north end of the Green. Both areas were let, the latter having a 'fishing house' erected on it by 1828, and the proceeds used for the old, sick or poor of the village, half being distributed at Christmas.

Sale of leases 1877

It was not until 1877 that the next major change is recorded. By then Radcliffe was undergoing a transformation as access by rail was encouraging a building boom. The Jeffrey Dole trustees realised that the poor's land could produce more profit by house building than the £24 (according to the Endowed Charities Report of

1871) it could produce by being let for grazing or growing. Consequently on December 3rd 1877, Mr J. M. Pott, a Nottingham auctioneer, offered for sale at the Manvers Arms on behalf of the trustees 'a valuable close of building land' extending to 2 acres 3 roods 6 perches, and fronting the Nottingham - Grantham turnpike road. This was to be sold in ten lots. He was also to sell 'a piece of land' fronting Holme Lane and containing an area of 2,344 square yards as lot 11. Papers held by the present-day solicitors to the trustees enable the plots on the plans of 1877 to be identified with sites and houses still in existence.

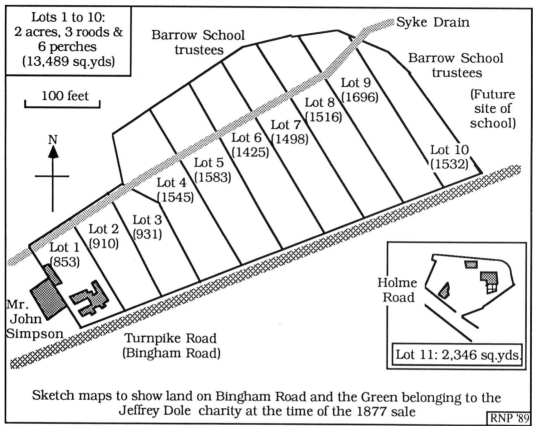

Sketch maps to show land on Bingham Road and the Green belonging to the Jeffrey Dole charity at the time of the 1877 sale

RNP '89

The lots on Bingham Road were sold on 99-year leases and there was a specific requirement that each lessee should erect either one detached house (value £250) or two semi-detached houses (value £400) within a year of the auction. The quality of the houses was also specified: outer walls 9 inches thick, no other timber than sound oak or Russian or Baltic timber, 4½-inch brick-trimmed arches to every fireplace, roofing of slate or Staffordshire tiles, good and sufficient drainage to cisterns or the main sewer. Each lessee was required to build a 4'6" x 4' culvert across his plot 'to take the water and drainage which runs through the same'. This was the Syke Drain running towards the centre of the village from the rising land to the east, the subject of controversy during the 1882 uproar about public health.

Comparison of various sale documents produced over the next twenty years indicates that most of the Bingham Road leases were acquired by Edwin Green, the lace manufacturer of Clyde Villa and later Campbell House on Shelford Road, and George Willey, a retired provisions merchant who lived at Fairfield House on Bingham Road. Indeed, Mr Green seems to have immediately acquired for £5 the rights over lots 2 and 3, which were held by Frederick Shepperson as highest bidder, so that he could then add them to his own lot 1, to form a unified block. He also seems to have acquired lot 8, as in 1894 he notified the Jeffrey Dole trustees of its transfer to Robert Halford for £753.16s.10d for the remainder of the 99 years. George Willey held lots 4, 5, 6, 9 and 10, although the last three at least were not his for long. In 1880 lot 6 was disposed of to a Caractacus Shilton of Sneinton, and lots 9 and 10 to Thomas Butlin of Camden Town. One other lessee can be deduced. In the 1894 revision of the charity a Thomas Murdy is shown as holding land providing £12.12s.8d of its gross annual income. From figures in the parish minutes for 1895 this would imply 1,500 square yards, which looks very much like lot 7.

Papers dated August 1893 indicate that land on the Green went initially to Elizabeth Parr, who constructed a number of greenhouses on it. By 1893 she owed the trustees £41.6s.6d in rent and interest. In lieu of payment she forfeited the greenhouses and the lease of the land was transferred to Henry Walker. By 1907 the lease was adapted to ensure that Mr Walker looked after the greenhouses properly and kept them painted.

Revision of the trust 1880

The revision and updating of the Jeffrey Dole charity was approved by the Charity Commissioners in 1880. The governing body of nine trustees, including a clerk, consisted of the Rev John Cullen, Richard Green and George Parr (the churchwardens), Samuel Barratt and John Simpson (the overseers of the poor), Thomas Haynes and George Morley ('representatives' of owners or occupiers of property rated at not less than £15), and two 'co-optative members' - Richard Daft, the brewer and former cricketer, and George Willey, the holder of a number of the Bingham Road leases. Of the £123 a year in rent and mortgage payments which comprised the charity's income at that time, £57 came from the latter. Some trustees gave very lengthy service to the charity. In particular, Thomas Haynes senior of the Grange was still in evidence in 1902. It was probably this group who organised the public subscription in 1885 for a tablet in the church to commemorate the state of the charity between 1656 and 1687.

From the time of the 1880 revision, once the administrative costs of the charity had been met, the first call on its income was educational. (The provisions were closely in line with the advice of the select committee on the Charitable Trusts Act of 1884.) The first £30 of income was to be set aside to further the education of the poor children of the parish. A maximum of £10 a year was to go towards tuition fees, and £5 was to be available for prizes to a maximum of £1 each. Any balance could be used to provide scholarships not exceeding £5 per year each, tenable for three years either at a public elementary school, or at a place of higher education, or where technical or industrial education was given. Any income over £30 was to be used to provide for the physical needs of 'deserving or necessitous bona fide residents of the Parish'. As the total income at this time exceeded £100 a year, this provision was of more benefit than the educational function. Nevertheless, the implementation of these new guidelines did not at first meet with wholehearted approval. In March 1881 the *Nottingham Journal* reported that at the village vestry meeting there was a large attendance of ratepayers, 'several of whom criticised the manner in which the 'Jeffrey Dole' charity had been distributed by the trustees during the late winter'.

By 1895 the annual income had risen to over £133, with about £100 coming from the Bingham Road site, £27 from Henry Walker's house, land and greenhouses on the Green, and £6.10s from another cottage on that land. As there was also a balance in hand, the trustees had about £150 to spend, out of which £22.10s on administrative costs and repairs to property had first to be found. In that year only £12.10s of the maximum of £30 was spent on education, thus about £100 was available for the poor. (The parish council minute books show the disposable income in some detail only between 1895 and 1898.)

Educational awards

The ways in which the first £30 of income were used soon changed. Prizes which in 1880 could be £1 for children who had attended school for not less than one year (subject always to their receiving a certificate of good conduct, regularity and proficiency) became 10s after two years. Revisions approved by the Charity Commissioners in 1894 and 1899 perhaps indicate that the numbers reaching rewardable
standards were on the increase. Permitted alternative uses of the money included a £5 contribution towards the maintenance of Radcliffe's school, and 10s towards the provision of evening classes or towards prizes for those attending them. The £5 scholarship of the 1880 revision was awarded to Gertrude Barratt in 1894 and 1895. Born in December 1874, the daughter of Samuel Barratt the nurseryman and former

1897	To Payments during the year			
Feb 26	Rent of Room for meetings year 1896		12	0
April 1	Allowed to H Walker for Improvements to property	8 0 0		
" 12	Governors of Barrow School (4 years Rent)	1 3 4		
May 4	H Kirchen A/c for Coal			
	5 tons 10 cwt at 12/6 per ton	3 : 8 : 9		
	Coop. Society do. 5 tons 10 cwt	3 : 8 : 9		
	S Barratt ditto 5 tons 15 cwt	3 : 11 : 10	10 9 4	
	The above 3 lots of Coal were distributed amongst 67 persons at 5 cwt each (Total 16.15 tons cwt)			
May 8	Books A/c for Leather Case		16	0
June 5	Cheque Book		2	0
" 8	Subscription to Radcliffe School	5 0 0		
July 13	Subscription to Nottm General Hospital	3 3 0		
" "	Subscription to Childrens Hospital Nottm	2 2 0		
" "	Subscription to Eye Infirmary Nottm	2 2 0		
Oct 9	J & J Vice A/c for Books		5	0
Novr	Fire Insurance Premium (on property occupied by Walker & Stafford)		6	11
Decr 31	Salary of Clerk (year 1897)	2 0 0		
" "	Receipt & Postage Stamps		7	6
" "	Rates on house occupied by Stafford			
	March 24 Poor Rate	3 " 1		
	" " Lighting Rate	6		
	Sept 24 Poor Rate	3 " 8	7 3	
" "	Amount deducted from Rents for Income Tax during year (Statement 1)	3 6 10		
" "	Doles distributed during the year			
	117 at 10/-	58 : 10 : 0		
	193 at 5/-	48 : 5 : 0		
	3 at 2/6	7 : 6	107 2 6	
	Total Payments		147 5 8	
	Balance in Bank		60 2 6	
			207 8 2	

The Jeffrey Dole accounts for 1897
from the Parish Council minute book (reduced)

trustee of the charity, Gertrude's award must have been for higher education. From 1899, although the overall educational spending was still restricted to £30, scholarships for higher education were increased to £15 a year, while the qualifying period of attendance at a local school rose from three to six years. The trustees were given powers to hold examinations to select suitable candidates, and no award had to be made if candidates were insufficiently qualified. No further reference to scholarship winners has been found until 1909 when Dorothy Tanner and Phoebe Smith were successful. Their ages are not known.

In 1904 the educational side of the charity was hived off to become the Educational Foundation of Jeffrey Limmer and others. The school log books refer regularly to the distribution of prizes by its governors, initially at the end of August but more often in September, throughout the remainder of the period studied.

Provision for the needy

The main beneficiaries of the Jeffrey Dole continued to be those in financial need, as its founder would have wished. Following the 1880 revision, clothing, linen, bedding, food and medical items could be supplied either directly to an individual or to suitable bodies such as hospitals or provident clubs. This aid could extend as far as contributing towards the 'the outfit' needed by a person under 21 entering an occupation or service. Clause 27 of the 1899 revision enabled the trustees to contribute between £13 and £26 towards providing a nurse or nurses for the poor, sick or infirm bona fide residents of the parish. As a result, the accounts show that 15s was paid for cleaning 'poor Wm. Foster's house' and for some nursing. A further £15 was made available to provide him with a nurse.

In general during the mid-1890s, doles of 10s were going to between one hundred and 120 people, and 5s doles to fifty or sixty. Coal was also distributed - 17½ tons of it in 1895 at 12s.6d a ton, including carriage. (It is not clear whether these categories were mutually exclusive.) From 1898 the number receiving 5s doles rose dramatically, reaching 203 in 1900, perhaps suggesting increasing need. Residents in the 1980s still feel the benefit of Jeffrey Limmer's bequest as the Parish Council now administers the income from the sale of the freehold reversions.

The Ann Parr foundation

Another village charity derived from the will of Ann Parr dated August 27th 1834. By this, money was shared between Radcliffe, and Tithby and Cropwell Butler to be spent on prizes for 'proficiency in religious knowledge according to the doctrines of the Christian Faith'. In 1871 the capital stood at £656.12s.9d, producing an income of £19.13s.11d, of which Radcliffe received £9.16s.11d and Cropwell a penny more. Distribution of these prizes seems to have taken place at the same time as the Jeffrey Dole awards. The parish minutes make it clear that in due course, after £2 had been spent on religious prizes, the surplus was used for the same purposes as the Jeffrey Limmer money. Until the 1980s an award was made in Ann Parr's name for religious work at the village junior school.

Arrangements for this charity were contested by the Parish Council in 1905 when none of the co-optative trustees actually lived in the village. It was submitted that John Beeson and Edward Stone should be appointed instead of Henry Smith junior and William Pacey Green, both extensive farmers in Cropwell, the parish which also benefited from Ann Parr's legacy. The Board of Education approved the appointment of Edward Stone, a plumber from Albion Cottage, in place of Henry Smith who expressed his willingness to retire, but Mr Green remained on the grounds that he was one of the largest ratepayers in Radcliffe, irrespective of his living elsewhere. A revised scheme drawn up in August of 1905 shows that Radcliffe was still represented only by Edward Stone, the other trustees being John Parr of Ruddington, Butler Smith of Cropwell and William Green.

The Collier charity

Louis Francois Collier was born in France and first appears in the Radcliffe census of 1871 aged 53, lodging with his wife in the household of George Parr, the cricketer. At that time he would have seemed an unlikely village benefactor since in the previous November he had appeared in the bankruptcy court, having unwisely invested £3,000 in a partnership with a lace manufacturer called Duclos. The latter had already gone bankrupt with a previous partner. Louis Collier, however, claimed he had property in France and a court official was despatched to check on this. Unfortunately the enquiries coincided with the turmoil following the Franco-Prussian war, so a satisfactory report was delayed. In due course, Louis Collier's Nottingham lace business flourished, and he built a stylish house on Shelford Road. After his death in November 1893 the Radcliffe poor benefited through the provision of coal and clothing. His trustees placed £135 in the hands of the Charity Commissioners which was invested in consols. Around the turn of the century this yielded £3.10s in interest which was distributed as one dole of £1, seven or eight of 5s, and the remainder of 2s.6d.

The Hartwell charity

One further scheme dates from June 16th 1911 and was intended to provide stipends for pensioners who were women of irreproachable character, being widows or spinsters of Radcliffe in necessitous circumstances who believed in the apostle's creed, the Lord's prayer and the ten commandments. It was founded by Miss Richmond of Hartwell House in Vicarage Lane, subsequently described by Colet Chamberlain as an eccentric but kindly old lady, generous to the village folk. (On requesting permission children were always allowed to gather violets which grew in profusion in the front of her residence.) Her charity's known annual income ranged between £25 and £50.

In the 1980s there is a tendency for such small charities to be amalgamated and the original benefactors forgotten. In their day, however, they had helped to supplement the incomes of those in need and preserve them at times from the rigours of the workhouse. However socially divisive, along with the encouragement of self-help and donations to good causes, they help to soften the grim picture of poverty in the nineteenth and early twentieth centuries.

Main sources

Primary

Nottinghamshire Archives Office: Bingham Union minute books 1836-1920 PUD 1/1/1-19; Radcliffe parish registers PR 1498-1507; Charity records c. 1965, BL 36.
Nottinghamshire County Library (Local Studies Library): census returns for Radcliffe and Bingham 1841-1881.
Radcliffe-on-Trent Parish Council: parish council minute books; deeds of the Jeffrey Dole trust held by the solicitor to the Parish Council; schedule of Ann Parr charity 1905.

Secondary

British Parliamentary Papers on Agriculture, vol. 9, p. 90. 1843.
Caplan, Maurice. *In the shadow of the workhouse.* 1984.
Chamberlain, Colet. *Memories of the Past.* 1960.
Henstock, Valerie (ed.). *Victorian Bingham.* 1986.
House of Commons report on Endowed Charities, 1871.
Nottingham Oddfellows Headquarters: magazines for 1832 and 1864.
Radcliffe-on-Trent local history research group: extracts from Nottingham newspapers 1837-1920.
Rose, M. *The English Poor Law.*
Webb, S. and B. *English Poor Law history*; vols. I & II.

Additional information on friendly societies has been supplied by Julia O'Neill.

EDUCATION

Little is known about the early provision of education in Radcliffe-on-Trent, although it is clear that in the 1790s some sort of school was being held in the chancel of St Mary's church. The Methodists began a Sunday school between 1812 and 1815 which must also have contributed to general educational standards in the village, while dame schools, such as that run by 'Old Sally Morley' in the early nineteenth century in the area now known as Walker's Yard, would have provided the only opportunity for learning for many children. (Marriage registers show that inability to sign one's name was common in Victorian times.) More regular education for ordinary children was provided from at least the 1820s by a combination of church and estate, the latter represented by the Dowager Countess Manvers who died in 1832. In addition, for middle class children there were a number of privately run day and boarding schools.

Private schools

As early as January 1811 the *Nottingham Journal* carried an advertisement for a Radcliffe day school run by John and Elizabeth Stevenson offering reading, writing and arithmetic, as well as surveying and building if required for boys. Girls would be taught reading and sewing. Between the 1840s and 1860s girls fared better in the school run by the Misses Sarah and Harriet Allsebrooke. In January 1847 the *Journal* reported that the sisters had

> ....*removed to a more commodious and eligible situation, where they will have an opportunity of taking a limited number of young ladies as boarders. Terms - Board and Instruction in reading, writing and arithmetic, English grammar, history, geography, plain and fancy needlework, 16 guineas per annum.*

For 'ladies under 10' the fees were 2 guineas a year less, and day pupils went for 10s per quarter. In the early 1840s the Rev William Bury was running a small boarding school for boys at the vicarage, and throughout the nineteenth century there is evidence of other private schools which came and went, such as those run by Miss Worth and Miss Harrison in Lorne Grove from 1883 and by Miss Jackson in Walnut Grove around 1900. Radcliffe Lodge also became a boys' school from 1923 to 1930, and there were others in the twentieth century.

Two private schools are better documented than these. One with a long history was initially run by Samuel Hemsley. The 1920 reminiscence of an 'old boy' - John Riley - gives an insight into the school in the 1840s. The son of a master slater, his fellow pupils included the sons and daughters of a builder, a plumber and the owner of a lace factory in Nottingham. After breaking ranks from a crocodile on the way to church in pursuit of his parents' trap, which he had spotted passing through the village, the boy spent the day at Bottesford wakes.

> *My father gave me a note for my master, hoping he would not punish me for my boyish escapade. I gave the note to Mrs Hemsley first and she asked her husband not to beat me; but on Monday morning he put me across a double desk and laid on till I was black and blue all over. Mrs Hemsley put me to bed and I did not get up till Wednesday morning.*

With the aid of William Parr, a village rogue, John Riley then escaped home, but was returned to the school after a week on the understanding that he would be removed altogether if he was ever beaten again. He claimed that on his death bed Samuel Hemsley begged forgiveness for the beating.

Mary Hemsley, some ten years her husband's senior, died in 1848 at the age of 56. By the time of the 1851 census the school was run by Samuel and his son, another Samuel aged 21. Samuel senior's death in 1861 left Samuel junior in charge of a 'Commercial Academy' in which venture, according to White's *Directory* of 1864, he was joined by Samuel Cave Tomlinson. Although Samuel Hemsley seems to have retained interest in the property, Samuel Cave Tomlinson (born in Gedling about 1843) was running what was known as either Radcliffe-on-Trent Academy or Vernon House School without him from about 1865. (Vernon Cottage, and neighbouring property near the corner of Walnut Grove and the main street are reminders of its site.)

At the time of the 1871 census only three boarders were listed, all male, but in 1877 an advertisement in the *Journal* stated that '... Samuel Cave Tomlinson has extended his school and has vacancies for several more boarders'. In July 1878 the opening of an associated Vernon House School for Young Ladies was advertised. Nevertheless, in the following December the *Journal's* account of 'a very pleasing entertainment', given in aid of the church restoration fund by the pupils of Mr Tomlinson's school, reveals that only male performers took part, even in female roles:

> .... the programme consisting of vocal and instrumental music interspersed with recitations, was very creditably rendered by the juvenile performers, the pianoforte solos and duets being carefully executed. The vocalists, though unfortunately suffering from colds, gave general satisfaction. Mendelssohn's lovely 'Tis thus decreed' nicely sung by Master Frank White gained an encore, as did Master Savidge's 'Write me a letter from home'. Master Wotton's style of recitation was much admired, and his piece was loudly re-demanded. Mr Barratt with his usual kindness lent his services on the occasion and his songs, which were admirably rendered, elicited great applause. The room was crowded by a highly appreciative audience, who after the conclusion of the programme were invited by Mr Tomlinson to remain and witness the laughable farce 'Done on both sides'. The 'get up' was excellent and the performance, which was gone through in a spirited style kept the audience convulsed with laughter. The cast of characters was as follows:

Mr Whittles	Master Aslin
Mr Brownjohn	Mr Thompson
Phibbs	Master F White
Mrs Whittles	Master Wilkinson
Lydia	Master Savidge

In due course girls did board at the school as four female scholars as well as ten male were listed in the 1881 census. Also in residence on census night were Samuel himself, his wife, sister, a visiting niece, two young governesses, and a female servant. Advertisements during the 1880s suggest an ambitious curriculum. In January 1884 the pupils were not only promised a sound and practical general education, but also that every attention would be paid to their health and comfort, while suitable amusements would be provided for indoors and out. By January 1886 the studies of the upper classes were advertised as based upon the regulations for the Oxford and Cambridge Local Examinations. In that year fees for boarders were from 25 guineas a year. The school may not always have been a paying concern, however. White's *Directory* of 1885-1886 records that in addition to running the school Samuel Cave Tomlinson was also an agent for Royal Insurance and clerk to the Burial Board. In 1899 the school was moved from Vernon House to Beaconsfield House on Bingham Road, where it continued under his direction until at least 1908. According to Wright's *Directory* of 1915 a Miss Ethel Spencer was by then in charge. Samuel Cave Tomlinson died in 1917.

A shorter-lived school was at Cedar House (now the Yew Trees Guest House, 16 Shelford Road). This property had been bought by Edwin Robotham in 1871 for £505. He was a goods manager for the Midland Railway, but he died in 1875 leaving a widow and at least five children. In the 1881 census Hannah Robotham described herself as a Boarding Housekeeper, and had a family of five and a widowed governess living in to help make ends meet. By 1885-6 two of her daughters would have been aged about 22 and 17, and White's *Directory* indicated that the Misses Robotham of Cedar House were now running a boarding and day school. The venture could not have been very profitable. Not only was the property being constantly mortgaged, but the girls advertised that they were also 'fancy dealers'. An inventory of 1898, taken when Hannah Robotham handed over control of the house to her son

Alfred, shows that there were then eight bedrooms and a schoolroom containing a piano, four maps, four desks, a coal box and shelves.

The Dowager Countess Manvers' school

While these private schools came and went, it was the Dowager Countess Manvers who seems to have initiated the one school that was to have a continuous existence, and which was gradually absorbed into a national system. The widow of the first Earl Manvers who died in 1816, the countess survived her husband by sixteen years. According to White's *Directory* for 1832 and Esdaile's *Historical Account of Bingham* for 1851, she founded and subsequently supported a school in Radcliffe in 1825 'for the education of 21 poor boys and girls of the village'. (A legacy to both Radcliffe and Cropwell by Ann Parr in 1834 also provided some money for religious education.) Esdaile claimed that the school was 'the first in these parts, and it has done much good'. The Manvers connection was thus established from the beginning, and the original schoolroom and schoolmaster's house provided by the Manvers estate are now a private dwelling at 46 Main Road. Property advertised in the *Nottingham Journal* in June 1843 and a document of May 1844 in the Manvers papers concern houses and schoolhouses which may have been occupied by both Samuel Hemsley's school and the village school, the plots being adjacent. A list of Radcliffe property and income tax for 1845 shows that £1.14s.6d was due for 'Tenants & School House'.

Among the Manvers papers are to be found two bills paid by the estate for repairs in the early days of the school. One was from John Brice for painting the house and schools in 1850 for £2, and the other from George Bell in October 1851:

Bricklayers and labourers 2½days each	*15s*
Limewashing the outside walls of schools, house, fence walls	
and privys and inside of privys and setting slate pot on.	
Colouring 10/- slate pot 2/6	*12s.6d*

The original schoolmaster's house, now 46 Main Road.
The schoolroom was on the right

297

John Brice's own account books show that in addition to decorating the schools he did regular plumbing work and was frequently called upon to replace broken window panes. In addition to maintenance the Manvers family gave an annual donation to Radcliffe and other estate schools - £10 in two instalments around 1850 - and it was the third earl who provided a new school building in 1870 and who extended it in 1876. (These buildings survive as the Church Hall.) The school never received a government building grant.

The church connection

From the 1840s the school is described as the National School and White's 1864 *Directory* says, 'the school is now taught on the National plan'. It has been verified, however, that the school was not officially linked to the National Society but that the term was used in a general way to mean a Church of England school. The close supervision of the vicar is revealed in surviving records, and a hand-written list of rules in the back of a baptismal register, probably from the 1870s or 1880s confirms the connection. This list lays down the constitution of a management committee, to be chaired by the vicar, with the curate (if any) as secretary, the churchwardens as treasurers, together with three subscribers elected every three years by all subscribers of over 10s per year. (This sum was reduced to 5s in 1886.) The committee was to meet at least once a month but no trace of their minutes or accounts has been found.

The substantial records relating to the school consist mainly of log books kept from 1866, the year that the school first received a government grant and was thus obliged to keep such a record. The grant was mainly for school improvements, the first amounting to £3.16s. In 1868, the average attendance having risen to 50, £40.17s was received. The grant reached the highest sum of £299.13s.11d in 1888 when the average attendance was 277.

Early schoolteachers

Advertisements in the Nottingham papers for schoolmasters around the 1850s show that the usual salary for a village schoolmaster was from £40 to £60 annually, together with a rent free house. A single schoolmaster would earn about half that amount. Before the log books begin in 1866, teachers are little more than mere names recorded in census returns and directories. At the time that John Brice and George Bell were carrying out their painting and repairs the schoolmaster and mistress were Thomas and Mary Ann Foulds. They were born in Sutton-in-Ashfield and Arnold respectively, and at the time of the 1851 census they were aged 49 and 45. White's *Directory* for 1864 gives Thomas and Sarah Parr at the National School. They were a brother and sister recorded as aged about 34 and 39, and living with their widowed mother in 1861. Their father had been a farmer. In charge of the infants was Miss Richmond, almost certainly the Rebecca Richmond aged 36 at the time of the census, living with an elder sister who was a dressmaker. All three had been born in Radcliffe.

John Demment

In October 1866, after being closed for two months, the school re-opened with a new schoolmaster - John Demment, certificated teacher, 3rd class, 3rd division. Born in Whitechapel about 1826, he arrived with a 6-year-old son who had been born in Devon. He may already have been a widower, and was certainly so by 1871 when his household was completed by his elderly mother. He started with twenty-five pupils of whose capabilities in 'catechism, notation and numeration' he held a very low opinion. The roll was up to 66 by Christmas and to 87 by the following March when the first visit of Her Majesty's Inspectorate recorded, '... very creditable work .... considering the short time the Master has been in charge.' New pupils were admitted at any time and were of all ages and levels of attainment which must have added to the problems of organisation. Following the 1867 inspection, another favourable report commented that 'the Master, who works single-handed, deserves great credit for his work'. However, reports for the following two years were not satisfactory and there was some hesitation over paying the full grant.

Throughout the log books the difficulties of keeping order and the disruption caused by poor attendance preoccupied head teachers. Heartfelt complaints over the

Rules

of the Radcliffe-on-Trent Church of England Schools

I. The Schools, house, and garden are the property of the Patron, Earl Manvers, and are placed in the care of the Vicar and Churchwardens for the time being, who shall have three other Subscribers, (elected by the Subscribers every three years, but shall be eligible for re-election) to keep them, as a Committee of management, and three Managers shall also be elected by the Committee so making nine.

N.B. Each Subscriber of 10/- a year and upwards, shall have a vote for every 10/- to the amount of his subscription. This has been reduced to 5/- a vote. 1886.

II. The Committee shall meet on the first Thursday in each month, and at other times when business requires them to do so, for the discharge of business. Three shall form a quorum.

III. The Vicar shall be chairman and correspondent, and the Curate, if any, shall be Secretary, and the Churchwardens shall be Treasurers of the Schools.

IV. All children of the Parish shall be admitted to the Schools for instruction on the payment of the fees which are fixed by the Managers in accordance with the requirements of the Education Department Whitehall, London. The fees must be paid on Monday Morning in each week. The Schools are now free. 1892

The first four rules of the school in the parish register c. 1870s
(Nottinghamshire Archives Office, PR 1507
By permission of the Principal Archivist)

lack of order were particularly frequent during John Demment's headship. With some ninety pupils on the books from 4 to 14 years of age to organise and teach single-handed, the want of perfect order is not surprising. Entries such as 'order still somewhat difficult', 'order somewhat improved, still not what I wish', and 'order improved', are a constant refrain throughout his five years, and he was driven on occasions to feel relieved by lower attendances making it a smaller school which was easier to manage. Without the support of assistant teachers, pupil teachers and monitors, nobody had quite so difficult a task as John Demment. Insolence, lateness, truancy, fighting in school and tampering with the harmonium are all mentioned as offences for which punishment was meted out. In 1871, John Demment left for Bosham, near Chichester. His time in Radcliffe must have had its happier moments, however, for in the following January the *Nottingham Journal* recorded his marriage to Jane Whitehouse of Radcliffe, the daughter of an optician.

James Browne

There followed several years with frequent changes of schoolmaster and a continuing record of discipline problems, until James Browne, who had temporarily taken over immediately after John Demment left, was appointed headmaster in 1875. Born in Cotgrave about 1845, James Browne was to stay beyond the time when the school had been taken over by the County Council and moved to its new building on Bingham Road in 1909. His wife, Sophie, was two years his junior and had been born on the island of Guernsey. She was also a trained teacher, and had charge of the infants' school which had been organised as a separate department since 1874. These key figures in the lives of three generations of Radcliffe villagers, must have been instantly recognisable; he, 6' 3" tall and in later life full-bearded ; she, a diminutive 4' 6" according to Colet Chamberlain. When they took over at the school they had two young children - Mary aged 3 and James aged 2. Christine was born in February 1882 in the midst of the scarlet fever epidemic. In the 1881 census a female servant is recorded as living with them.

Mr and Mrs Browne must have been effective teachers. From their arrival, the HMI reports speak well of the school. That of January 1876 states, 'This school gives promise of making good progress', and the report of August 1876 records that

The National Schools of Radcliffe-on-Trent are in a state of high efficiency. The mixed department is remarkably well taught throughout. Even the dull children have been made to pass a satisfactory examination, while the brighter scholars display much intelligence and accuracy in their answering.

The infant school under Mrs Browne also received a favourable report: '...the Infants are managed with much skill, good method and considerable kindness,' and at this inspection 95.7% of the scholars passed 'as high or higher than any of the Nottingham schools'. Ten years later the report confirmed this high standard of achievement: 'The Elementary Instruction falls but little short of the highest merit.'

Discipline and the pupil-teacher system

At times discipline could be a problem, particularly in the period between John Demment's departure and the permanent appointment of James Browne. Mr William Welling Hart, a master during this intervening period, recorded in the week after his arrival in May 1872, 'Kept all in till 4.30 until silent.' Keeping children in seems to have been the most usual form of punishment for being 'saucy', 'idle', 'neglecting home lessons' and 'latecoming'. Some of the children seem to have been quite spirited in their naughtiness. Complaints about them range from 'talking and playing during sewing' and 'being ill-behaved and boisterous', to being 'wilfully disobedient' and 'insubordinate'. Corporal punishment was sometimes used on the boys for offences such as fighting and throwing stones over the playground wall into the street. Mr Browne recorded the abolition of corporal punishment in 1902, but in March 1905 it was reinstated when the managers resolved that a punishment book be provided, and that chastisement be administered in the form of corporal punishment by the cane, only by the headmaster. Expulsion was a last resort for dealing with older children who persistently misbehaved. Edward Carnell was

Ratcliffe on Trent - National School.
1866

Oct 8th

    John D Emment Certificated teacher 3d Class
3rd dec.r 1859. Entered upon his duties as master.
The School, now assembling after a 2 months vacation
commenced with 25 - proceeded to organize the
School.

9th   Continued organization & examination

10th   Do. Found Religious Knowledge extremely deficient
& vague -

11   The whole school clearly evinces that it has been
closed for a longer period than is general

12th   Attendance for week il

Class	Boys	Girls average	Total	Actual	Total on books
1st	1	1.9	2.9	3	3
2nd	7.9	3	10.9	11	11
3rd	7.9	3	10.9	11	11
	16.8	7.9	24.7	25	25

15th   Several admissions today. Organization continued

16th   New comers shewing great deficiency in writing & Arith.c

17th   Find Ch Catechism very imperfectly known

18   Notation & numeration especially wanting throughout the
school

The first page of the school log book, written by John Demment in 1866
(Nottinghamshire Archives Office, SL 135/1/1
By permission of the Principal Archivist)

expelled for wilful disobedience as his parents had previously objected to other forms of punishment.

One problem to contend with in maintaining efficiency was what one master described as a 'great want of teaching power'. Not until 1871, when the average attendance was ninety-four, was the first paid monitor appointed as a first step to becoming a pupil teacher. An immediate improvement was noted in the log book: 'Work more satisfactory owing to the assistance given by the Monitor who manages his class very fairly.' In 1876, when the average attendance had reached 142, a second pupil teacher was appointed. The HMI report of 1878 remarked on the need for a qualified assistant master.

Monitors and pupil teachers presented their own problems. The first paid monitor, George Clarke, who had made such a promising start, fell ill with typhus fever after six months and was absent for six weeks. Back again, with the status of pupil teacher, Clarke got into difficulties through unpunctuality. The master complained that he was 'slow to profit from instruction', and it must have been with relief that his notice was received. The second appointee, Nathan Clarke, did better. He stayed three years as a pupil teacher but then discovered, as did other pupil teachers, that there were better paid jobs for young men with his level of education. He left to work as a clerk on the Midland Railway. Nathan did not give up his own education or interest in teaching, and ten years later he was back in Radcliffe as an organist and teacher of music. Girls increasingly took advantage of the pupil teacher system to begin a career previously closed to their sex and class. In 1883, two of the three pupil teachers were girls. The role cannot have been easy as they were straight from the classroom themselves, only a little older than their pupils, and were put in charge of a class with only an elementary education behind them. It is surprising that there were not more like Samuel Rushton who was unable to cope. He became a monitor early in 1885 and progressed to become a pupil teacher. In 1888 he was in charge of 'Standard 2' but lacked control to such an extent that James Browne took over, 'to endeavour to restore order'. His apprenticeship was ended a few months later by mutual consent of his guardians and the school managers.

By 1884, with some 350 pupils on the books and the attendance averaging between 150 and 200, Mr Browne had the assistance of one young, recently qualified certificated teacher, Hester Snodin, and three pupil teachers. Miss Snodin, who in 1870 had been one of the seven girls among the twenty-three free scholars in the school, went on to become a pupil teacher and in 1881 won a Queen's scholarship after which she presumably went away to college to return with her teacher's certificate in 1883. Another pupil teacher to win a scholarship was Kate Turner but she appears not to have taken up her place at Lincoln training college as she was away seeking a situation as an assistant mistress a few weeks after receiving notice of her scholarship. One boy who did go on to college was W.J. Pumphrey. He was given a send-off by the master and scholars of his old school with a presentation of a volume of Shakespeare and two Latin dictionaries before he left for Peterborough Training College in 1884.

Absences from school

Poor attendance was also a persistent problem. Some childhood ailments, which have since almost disappeared, were then much more frequent and severe. Pupils fell ill more often than today and poor diet and home conditions contributed to a general state of less than robust health. Epidemics of scarlet fever and measles were frequent. Two pupils died in one week in an epidemic in February 1871. Several cases of scarlet fever 'though situate some distance from the school' were noted in the log book at the end of October 1881, an ominous warning of the outbreak which was to lead to a public health crisis in the village. Attendance fell rapidly and the sanitary authority closed the school for a month. It re-opened on December 5th, with attendance figures fluctuating, and the log book recording constant references to odd cases of scarlet fever until on 13th February 1882 an outbreak of several cases on the Green was recorded. Within the week, one boy from 'Standard 3' was dead. The illness escalated until half the pupils were absent and the managers closed the school until May 8th. In March 1893 an epidemic of the measles spread through the village to be followed in April by an outbreak of scarlet fever and by a longer lasting epidemic of scarlatina which was not completely cleared until July. Not until 1908 was there a routine examination of all pupils by the County Council's medical officer, and from 1909 regular visits were made by a nurse, although she was mainly concerned with weight, eyesight and inspections for lice, rather than with epidemics.

The effect of the weather

The effect of the weather on attendance was also frequently noted. Numbers dropped markedly when it was cold and wet. 1879 was a particularly bad year. On January 3rd the log book records, 'Attendance small through cold and depth of snow.' The wintry weather continued and was 'severe' on January 20th. A month later a quarter of the children were away with colds as it was still cold and snowy. By February 24th only fifty were present as it was so cold and the snow was 'incessant'. Again in mid-March the attendance had fallen off with a conjunction of 'bad weather and bad colds'. May 16th brought 'a very-hot day' but still 'irregular attendance' and then on June 26th the schoolroom was flooded as the back playground was imperfectly drained. The school had to be closed at 3.00 p.m. In the twelve months from December 1885 to December 1886 attendance was again badly affected by the weather. The entry for Friday December 11th 1885 which noted the 'weather very wintry, attendance affected' was followed by similar references until as

James Browne,
headmaster from 1875-1909

late as Monday March 1st 1886, which saw a 'very wintry morning with a heavy fall of snow'. May 14th of that year produced a reference to 'continuous rain since Tuesday, therefore fall off in attendance', and at the end of the year on December 10th children from outside the village were kept at home because of the weather. It is frequently noted that children from Holme Pierrepont, Shelford and Saxondale had to miss school in spells of bad weather. In June 1891 the weather had been very wet the whole week, so 'no children have been from outside the village'. That the weather figured so much more in school life then than now is also apparent from such entries as that of Friday July 10th 1885 which reads, 'Very warm in the afternoon - children listless and inattentive,' and that of Monday December 21st 1892 which says, 'Weather very cold, attendance considerably down, much difficulty in keeping the children warm enough to do their work.'

Absenteeism through child labour

Even more detrimental to the smooth running of the school were the absences caused by child labour. In this rural parish it was mainly agricultural work that took children away from school, particularly in the spring and autumn. The proportion of children involved in the harvest was so large that, school being no longer viable, the summer holiday would then be declared by the schoolmaster. 'Spring work beginning to make itself felt on the attendance,' recorded John Demment in the log book for March 12th 1869. In July of the same year he noted that 'haymaking has taken a large number of children from school this week', whilst on August 4th there were 'but 10 children present and more requiring leave therefore closed for Harvest vacation.' Until 1880 schooling was not compulsory even for the under-tens who could earn pence to supplement the family income from a multitude of tedious tasks in all weathers - from bird scaring to gleaning. The seasonal chart shows the wide variety of land work specified in the first three log books for the period 1866 to 1900. In 1873 it was noted that 'labour being very scarce, more children than ever are employed and at high wages, school as a consequence is very irregular'. April had seen osier peeling and stone gathering, extending into May when there were violets to be gathered. These tasks being done, the wheat fields needed weeding in June, with various forms of harvesting to follow.

Children's agricultural work 1866 to 1900

February   bird tending

March   bean dropping

April   gardening, field operations, stone picking, osier peeling (particularly Shelford children)

May   rod peeling, setting potatoes, gathering violets

June   haymaking, pea pulling, weeding in wheat fields

July   haymaking, pea pulling, weeding, fruit picking, harvesting, gleaning

August   harvesting, gleaning

September   gleaning

October   gleaning, walnut peeling, potato picking

At the end of the busy season the children would return to school and their re-admittance would cause considerable disruption to the timetable, discipline and general organisation. Through the years there are very many comments about the problems caused by these pupils who fell further and further behind those able to put in regular attendances and steady work. The annual inspection, the outcome of which determined the school's grant for the coming year, fell shortly after the autumnal influx of returning pupils - predominately unruly boys. The schoolmaster's Herculean labours can be imagined!

As well as being kept at home to help in domestic crises, girls could be absent to earn money by 'beading', lace work and seaming. The log entry for April 9th 1867, besides noting the re-admittance of George Carter 'who was removed for work', admitted Thomas Rose aged 4 'said to know his letters' in place of Eliza Rose 'who has to be kept from school to nurse'. The factory inspectors who visited the school on occasions from 1873 inquired into the girls' outwork activities and were concerned about boys working in the brick yards. Girls were still being kept at home to do bead work some twenty years later.

Such absenteeism continued into the twentieth century. Near the beginning of the fourth log book on September 7th 1900, headmaster James Browne recorded that the 'upper classes are badly attended'. Boys were seen to be employed as butcher's boys, milk boys and paper boys, and at potato picking. On July 8th 1901 the log book notes that 'the Law now states that no scholar may leave school until he or she has passed the Vth standard', and yet a number of the IVth standard boys were absent at field work. One of the last entries on this subject was made on April 15th 1904:

Mr Thomas Wright has been employing boys at fieldwork on the 'gang system'. The attendance officer being informed he promptly interfered and the boys returned to school this morning.

So by May 9th Mr Browne was able to show 'very few absent except from necessary causes'. On May 11th 1911 seven boys were absent, five being employed as caddies, but after this there were no further references to working absences.

Fees and fines

Before 1892, school fees were collected every Monday morning, but the amount was never noted. The children were frequently sent home to fetch arrears. On December 1st 1879 James Browne noted in the log book: 'Trouble getting in school Fees, sent worst cases home,' and on January 5th 1880, 'Two children sent home, one returned with mother.' The log books make no suggestion that difficulties over payment of fees contributed to absences, but falling attendances in the higher standards were of concern. Comparatively few children stayed on at school beyond Standard III, that is about ten years of age. In 1871 only six of the thirty-nine Radcliffe pupils presented for examination were above Standard III and nineteen were in Standard I. Log book entries in 1891 and 1892 indicate a particularly strong concern felt by Mr Browne over the poor attendances in the upper standards. His analysis of attendance figures showed that of the sixty pupils on the books in classes above Standard IV twenty had attended fewer than five times during the week. From the late 1870s the attendance officer visited the school regularly and with increasing frequency, but his efforts were unavailing.

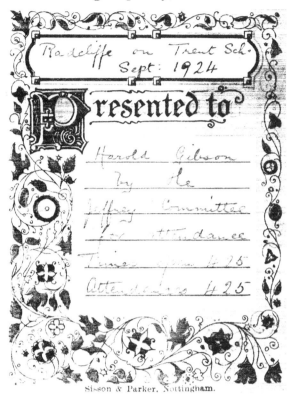

Sisson & Parker, Nottingham.

Book plate from a prize given by the Jeffrey Dole Committee in 1924 to encourage regular attendance

After 1880, when it became compulsory for children to attend school between the ages of 5 and 10 (they could then be exempted to work part-time if they had reached a required educational standard), a number of parents found themselves before the magistrates for neglect. In November 1881 William Nowell's son had made only twelve attendances out of 118. He was fined 5s on that occasion, and at least three more fines followed within the next two years, the last of only 1s. Joseph Hopkinson received the highest fine of 10s in December 1882. As well as trying to improve attendance by enforcing legislation, backed up by attendance officers and magistrates, the school managers used money from the Jeffrey Dole charity to award an annual prize of £5, to be divided amongst the scholars with the most attendances in the past year. There seems to have been little change in the situation when education became free in 1892. According to HMI Mr Green, free education did not improve average attendances although it brought more children onto the register. He could see no improvement arising from the ending of fees, only a 'growing indifference on the part of parents'.

School holidays

Legitimate relief from routine was often provided by some of the school's many visitors. Amongst the most welcome must have been Miss Burnside, later Mrs Noel, who would arrive with oranges or other gifts for the school. Apart from closures in the summer, at Christmas and at Easter, holidays arose in the form of 'fairs, feasts and festivals' to quote HMI Morgan Owen in his *Features of Country Schools*. There were regular absences each October for Goose Fair in Nottingham and a week's holiday in September for the village feast. There were half-day junketings for the Band-of-Hope and all the Sunday School treats. On holy days the children often attended church services in the mornings to be followed sometimes by a half-day holiday. The log for March 5th 1867 has: 'Shrove Tuesday closed at 11.15 in compliance with old usage and gave the afternoon as holiday.'

As the schoolroom was the only large hall in the village there were occasions when it was closed to children and in use for such purposes as a dinner given by Earl Manvers to his principal tenantry on the Holme Pierrepont estate in 1880, Local Government Board inquiries into the sewerage problems of the parish, an annual gathering of the Primrose League in 1888, Band of Hope tea parties, and administrative matters during elections and wartime. After being closed for a day on December 2nd 1885 to be used for polling the pupils gained an extra and unexpected half-day's holiday next day because of demonstrations in the village as soon as the result of the polling was known.

With its central position in the village near the church and at the hub of all activities, the school and its pupils were also often caught up in the excitement of such events as meets of the South Notts Hunt gathering round the steps of the Manvers Arms, the Yeomanry cavalry drilling in the streets, a visiting circus, or a grand funeral procession turning into St Mary's. Children took unauthorised time off, perhaps having lingered too long in their dinner hour among the onlookers. They were given half-day holidays for important cricket matches, athletic sports on the cricket ground and royal occasions. The visit of the Prince of Wales to Nottingham on July 3rd 1873 merited a whole day's holiday, as did a royal wedding on July 6th 1893. The fourth and fifth log books record holidays given across the land to celebrate 'the Relief of Mafeking and the Queen's Birthday' on May 24th 1900, and 'the Relief of Pretoria and the probable end of the War' on May 31st. By instruction of the managers on November 11th 1918 the children were given a half-day holiday the next afternoon in celebration of the armistice being signed at the end of the Great War.

The curriculum

The references to the curriculum in the log books are little more than lists of random topics to be covered in history, geography and nature study; points of grammar to be taught; class readers to be used; and songs and poems to be learned by heart. These latter were often of a patriotic theme or with a severe moral tone.

The first log book opens in 1866 at a time when the curriculum was controlled by the Revised Code of 1862. Under this, a government grant was dependent on the number of pupils passing the annual examination in reading, writing and arithmetic. Apart from religious knowledge, the only other subject offered by the Radcliffe school at this time was sewing for the girls. There are occasional references to a 'sewing mistress', probably an unqualified person who came in just to take sewing. In the earliest days Mr Demment's mother had helped him by taking needlework classes until the employment of a Mrs Parr on January 24th 1870. Other ladies are mentioned in the log books through the years, often as a result of disorder in their classes when girls became noisy and impertinent.

Religious instruction inevitably played a prominent part in the curriculum and was examined annually by a diocesan inspector. The inspector's report of November 12th 1874 advises on the work expected to be undertaken in such a school, suggesting :

> .....the repetition of a few hymns, texts and a prayer for home use together with an elementary acquaintance with the Creation and our Lord's early history might be taught to the little children (first and second standards). An accurate knowledge of the Old and New Testaments is expected of the older children.

The inspectors rarely reported whether the religious standard was satisfactory or not, but on one occasion a diocesan inspector showed an instance of seeing education from a child's viewpoint when he criticised the choice of Psalm 57 for learning by heart on the grounds that he doubted if children could enter into its deep feelings of penitence.

As it was the only school for the parish, apart from the private ones, there were dissenters as well as Anglicans among its pupils. Item V of the Rules of the Radcliffe-on-Trent Church of England School laid down that:

> The Holy Scriptures and Church Catechism and prayer Book and Hymns shall be taught in the school to all scholars at the time of Religious Instruction except to those children whose parents do not wish their children to receive such religious instruction.

There is no indication in the log books of any parents exercising this choice, although in December 1883 John Upton's defence before the Bingham magistrates, when accused of neglecting to send his son and daughter to school, was that 'he objected to his children being instructed in religious matters'. James Browne gave evidence in court that the conscience clause was adhered to and that John Upton had never made any objection to religious teaching in the past. He was fined 5s for each child.

Brave efforts were made to introduce new subjects such as mapping, geometry, drawing, history, drill and the Latin roots of English by a rapidly changing succession of masters working virtually single-handed. William Welling Hart stayed long enough to introduce the children to the joys of singing rounds and tonic solfa, and such stirring musical works as *Rule Britannia, Under the willow she's sleeping* and *Father come home*, accompanying them on the harmonium.

With the introduction of a new code in 1870 extra subjects could earn additional grants. During James Browne's first appointment from May 1871 to May 1872 he introduced geography to the upper, then lower, standards. Lessons were given on such topics as latitude and longitude, islands, lakes and rivers, and the continents. Geography readers were in use from 1881, which was not a forward step according to HMI Mr Green, who reported in 1881 that geography 'is not so good now as it was before the introduction of the Geographical readers'. This suggests that the spontaneous approach of Mr Browne would have been more interesting to the children than the dry style of such school texts. When history was introduced it was also based on readers, this time covering historical myths and legends. Drawing was being taught by 1881 for the examination set by the Science and Art Department.

Such extra subjects created problems in a small school with only one qualified teacher and in the 1878 HMI report on Radcliffe school it was recommended that the number of subjects taught be cut down until a qualified assistant could be procured. From 1884 onwards the log book has annual lists of the reading books to be used in each standard and the pieces of poetry selected for each standard to learn for repetition. Examples are given below:

1884   Reading books

Standard I	1	Jarrold's *Standard I*
	2	Marshall's *Universal*
Standard II	1	Stevens and Holes
	2	Nelson's *Royal series*
Standard III	1	Stevens and Holes
	2	Blackie's *Graded reader*
	3	History reader: *Stories from English History*
Standard IV	1	Blackie's *Comprehensive reader*
	2	Nelson's *Royal series*
	3	History reader: *Simple history of England*
Standard V	1	Blackie's *Graded reader*
	2	Murby's *Excelsior*
	3	History reader: *Pictures from English history*
Standards VI and VII		
	1	*Royal Service*
	2	Murby's *Excelsior*
	3	History reader: *Pictures from English History*

<u>1884</u> <u>Repetition</u>

Standards I and II	*The mother and the babe in the snow*	
	The open window	Longfellow
Standard III	*The village blacksmith*	
	The reaper and the flowers	Longfellow
Standard IV	*The May Queen*	Tennyson
Standards V and VI	*Prisoner of Chillon*	Byron

The curriculum was broadened still further in 1895 with the introduction of gardening lessons. This seems to have been a particular interest of James Browne who was able to expand the horticultural scope when the school moved to its new premises in 1909. There is no indication of what was grown but there are frequent reports of adverse weather conditions preventing gardening 'operations'.

Another innovation in 1895 was the object lesson, an embryonic form of environmental studies much in vogue at the time and covering the main areas of physical geography, natural history, food and clothing. The lists of object lessons from which selections could be made for standards II and III seem a somewhat random collection.

<u>1895 - 1896</u>   <u>Object lessons for Standards II and III</u>

1	Bread	11	The oak	21	The ant		
2	Butter	12	The fir	22	Birds used for food		
3	Cheese	13	Cork	23	Coal		
4	Salt	14	Bricks	24	The building of a house		
5	Tea	15	A plough	25	Coins		
6	Sugar	16	Morton (?)	26	The potato		
7	Coffee	17	Lucifer matches	27	Calico		
8	Wheat	18	The herring	28	Linen		
9	Maize	19	The salmon	29	Snow		
10	Barley	20	The bee	30	Turpentine		

<u>1898</u> <u>Object lessons for Standard III</u>

1	Kettle boiling	12	Wild flowers (2)	23	Lifeboat
2	Steam engine	13	Slate quarry	24	Fruit (1)
3	Feathers	14	Salt mine	25	Fruit (2)
4	Sugar plantation	15	Sponge	26	Pottery
5	Blast furnace	16	Garden flowers	27	Glass making
6	Blacksmith	17	Iceberg	28	Coffee plantation
7	Leaves	18	The diver	29	Poisonous plants
8	The plantation	19	Shipbuilding	30	Bicycle
9	Coal pits	20	Apples and pears	31	Football and cricket
10	Gas works	21	Oranges and lemons	32	Cotton plantation
11	Wild flowers (1)	22	Lighthouse		

Another innovation of the same period was physical education. Military drill for boys was conducted once a week in the playground by Colour-Sergeant Rushton and later by Sergeant Lacey, while the girls had weekly exercises in Swedish drill under the direction of Miss Baxter, an assistant mistress.

Parents seem to have played little active part in the education of their children. The only parents whose names appear in the log books are those causing problems. There is mention of parents of persistent offenders who were visited by the attendance officer and the mother of the Starbuck children who were 'a pest and a plague to the school'. No attempt seems to have been made to involve parents in the school through open days or evenings, or displays of work.

Evening classes

For those who had failed to master the rudiments of education during their official years at school, all was not lost. Continuation or evening classes at the school were very much part of Radcliffe life between 1893 and 1902 when a detailed log book was kept of their progress, but how long they flourished before and after these dates has yet to be determined. During these years they appear to have been efficiently organised, on a sound financial footing and regularly inspected.

Teaching in the early years was by James Browne, master of the day school, and Joseph Wilson of St Luke's school in Nottingham. They were assisted by George Barratt, an assistant overseer, until 1895 when ill health forced him to retire. Then Joseph Wilson was replaced by S.C. Tomlinson, the headmaster of the local boarding school, and from 1898 the staff included J.C. Wood and the Misses Baxter, Barratt and Herod (the last two on an irregular basis). In 1895 and probably other years there were also an unspecified number of pupil teachers. No doubt the standard of teaching varied every year, but the Rev John Cullen made a specific comment in 1895:

> *Arithmetic, mensuration and geography are well taught. The instruction in other subjects is not so successful.*

The classes were administered by a committee of management consisting of all the managers of the day school, the secretary being George Willey, and the chairman the vicar. Members of the committee conscientiously paid regular, often weekly, visits to the school. Her Majesty's Inspectorate also paid an annual visit around Christmas, and there were occasional visits too from the organising secretary of Nottingham City Council, the director of technical instruction for the Nottinghamshire County Council, an inspector from the Science and Art Department and a senior inspector of drawing.

It is not clear from the log books how evening classes were financed. There is no indication at any point that the pupils themselves contributed. Indeed emphasis is on maintaining numbers in the classes rather than any mention of subscriptions. There seems to have been a system of variable government and local grants paid between March and October each year, from which deductions were occasionally made without explanation and which often included extra grants for specific purposes, for example for courses on magnetism and electricity.

The school opened on Monday, Wednesday and Friday evenings, between 7 p.m. and 9 p.m. from October to March. These were regular fixed sessions year after year altered only for inclement weather, political meetings, or when the schoolrooms were used as a polling station or for a jumble sale. The school was divided in the early years into three sections: upper, middle and lower, each group studying two different subjects every evening. In October 1893 there were fifty-four scholars, but the numbers fluctuated considerably over the years, rising to 122 in March 1900 although the average attendance two years later was only twenty-five to thirty. The basic subjects initially were: for the upper group, free hand and geometrical drawing, agriculture, mensuration and the life and duties of a citizen; while the lower groups concentrated on the three Rs together with life and duties of a citizen (covering central government, the judicial system, rates and taxes, public offices, the army and navy) and physiography (geography and geology). As time went by other subjects were added and some disappeared. In 1895 'science of common things' appeared in the lower division; French, shorthand and commercial correspondence in the upper; and life and duties of a citizen disappeared. In 1896 magnetism and electricity was added for the upper division, and history for the lower. In October 1897 girls were mentioned for the first time and needlework and housewifery classes introduced. Hygiene was taught to the lower division in 1898, but after this time no new subjects were added. French for the upper division became quite advanced, and in 1902 included translation of *La Jeune Liberienne* and exercises on irregular verbs. Commercial training at this time included business letters and answering advertisements. Geometry, however, had not advanced beyond first principles. How well the students performed in their subjects, which in some cases were far from elementary, is not known, apart from drawing where successful candidates in the Science and Art examination (freehand and model) are listed fairly regularly. However, in 1893 at least, over 90% of the pupils sat some part of an 'elementary' or 'advanced' examination.

The pupils themselves were of mixed ages from 10 years upwards. Those named were mostly from labouring backgrounds, although the sons of a grocer (Stafford), a farmer (Pike) and a stonemason (Eastwood) are mentioned as well as Christine Browne, the schoolmaster's daughter. Some classes were mixed, but there was a separate girls' school, which in 1898 was 'in good order and doing good work'. As the vicar noted, however, according to the Evening Continuation School Code 'no grant is payable on account of the girls' department'.

Despite the good work, the girls were not entirely enthusiastic. Three weeks after classes began in January 1898 it was reported that 'the attendance at the sewing and housewifery class is gradually falling off', and the class finished for the year a week before the rest. The 1901 class was more successful: 'girls class has been best attended and work done well'. Attendances fluctuated in the boys' classes too. Numbers usually started well, then decreased in bad weather or ceased altogether, as in February 1897 when there were 'no classes this evening: the School not being accessible through the roads being flooded', or on special days such as Plough Monday or bonfire night.

Attendance improved for special events which took place two or three times a year. There was always an entertainment just before Christmas. That for 1893 consisted of 'readings and recitations, interspersed with music'. Occasionally there was one in the spring term as well, as in March 1898, when an 'entertainment was given by scholars and teachers assisted by several gentlemen'. About once a year there were magic lantern shows or lectures given by outside speakers. Travel was a favourite theme and students enjoyed a 'descriptive tour around Great Britain' in 1894, and learnt about the Chicago Exhibition in 1893, the Channel Islands in 1896, South Africa in 1897 and Canada in 1900. A series of scientific lectures in 1895 and 1896 included 'Earth, air and water' by Mr Golding from the University College in Nottingham, 'Food and drink' by W. Finnemore, BA, and three by Mr C. Bryant of the County Council's technical teaching staff on 'Experiments on water and air' and 'How a plant lives and grows'. There were also some electrical experiments. A comment at this time - 'good attendance of scholars but very few others' - suggests that these were open lectures for anyone who cared to come.

Occasionally the *Nottingham Journal* reported the annual Spring prize-giving. In 1893 the prizes, presented by the Rev John Cullen, were mainly for regular attendance, although good conduct and attention to work were taken into consideration. A programme of music followed and tea was provided by Mrs Noel of Lamcote House.

As with the day school, one of the recurring themes in the log book is discipline, particularly in connection with teenage boys. Bruce Wisher is the most frequently mentioned offender - at the age of 11 in 1895 for being 'disorderly and inattentive', in 1897 for being 'a good deal of trouble', and in 1898 when he was suspended for unruly conduct and general bad behaviour. He was by no means unique. The cause of the problem is sometimes made clear. In October 1893 three boys were 'asked to retire for insubordinate behaviour to Mr Wilson'. In 1897 'several boys [were] very rude and noisy and interrupt[ed] work'. In the same year Harold Richmond aged 17 was 'suspended from the art class for throwing walnut shells about the room after being twice cautioned' and William Hale aged 14 was suspended 'for being noisy and unruly after repeated warnings'. In March 1901 the French class was disturbed through the behaviour of Henry Packwood. In his favour, however, Henry Packwood had won first prize for freehand drawing in 1898 and second prize for model drawing in 1899.

Not all behavioral comments in the log book were unfavourable. There are frequent references to order being 'much better'. For example, in 1895 'order and attention to lessons' was 'a great improvement on former years', and in 1898 order had again improved 'though occasionally there is too much talking'. Discipline and motivation did not necessarily go together, however. An entry for March 1901 notes that 'boys, though somewhat unruly at the commencement of the season have gradually settled down quietly, but only half of them have taken proper interest in their work'.

The need for a new school

By the early twentieth century it was clear that the old buildings opposite the church were no longer adequate for the needs of the village. A County Council report of 1903 presents a vivid impression of their condition. The mixed school playground was tar-paved but 'slippery for want of tar-washing', while gravel surrounded the infant school. The brick walls round the playgrounds had loose coping stones, and the steps into the building were so worn that it was suggested they should be turned 'top for bottom'. The infants occupied the part built in 1870, to which additions of 1876 and 1901 were joined. Sanitary arrangements were clearly inadequate. Although there was a dry urinal and three compartments each for boys and girls in a vaulted privy, sewers were not connected to the school. Mains water was still not laid on and water came from a pump. One classroom, divided by a glazed partition, was described as having sound floors, walls with a very dirty distempered dado 5' 6" high, distempered tops becoming dirty, but with clean ceilings. There was a stove but no fireplace, and ventilation was through a Tobin shaft vent in the apex. There were also two broken windows. The room was 23' x 30' and at the time of the inspection held forty-seven children. Average attendance was said to be sixty. The adjoining infant schoolroom boasted a closed-off gallery, and its windows and walls would also have been improved by cleaning. Across the master's yard, and attached to his house was the 'babies room', presumably the original schoolroom of the Countess Manvers' foundation. This had old floors, cracked windows, stained walls, a dirty dado and a bad fireplace. Following this report, repairs and redecoration were carried out, including much washing of woodwork and disinfecting. Work was also carried out at James Browne's house, although it had been 'lately cleaned throughout at the Master's expense'. It had two sitting rooms and four bedrooms, there was no scullery, and the kitchen was 'detached'. It lacked any through ventilation. A note was added to the report: 'If present master left no new master would live here.' At this time James and Sophie Brown's joint salaries came to £245 a year. (The next highest paid teacher was Mrs Adams who earned £60 a year.)

The work needed to bring the school up to the required standard was beyond the means of the school managers. (When the Board of Education wrote to the vicar as chairman of the managers demanding a lavatory and new water closets for the school, he passed the letter to the Parish Council who uncompromisingly said they did 'not feel justified in interfering in this matter in any way'.) The result was that the managers had to hand over responsibility for the school to the County Education Committee. Their report for 1905-1906 made the position clear:

Enlargements and improvements to the Radcliffe-on-Trent voluntary school having become necessary, the Managers, finding that they were not in a position to carry them out decided to transfer the school to the education Committee, and this transfer took effect on the 30th September 1905. The present building is the property of Earl Manvers and the Committee have arranged with him to hire the school at a rent of £50 per annum until arrangements have been made for the erection of a new school. To meet the over-crowding, the Committee has also hired the schoolroom attached to the Primitive Methodist Chapel at a rent of £1 per week; this provides accommodation for 60 children. Negotiations for the purchase of a new site are in progress.

In the meantime, as well as rent the Council paid for any internal repairs. Lord Manvers paid the property tax, tithe rent charge and met the cost of external maintenance. The school furniture (supplied by a grant of £10 from the Diocesan Board in 1873 and supplemented since by Mrs Noel of Lamcote House, the vicar and other churchmen), could be used by the County Council on condition that the buildings would be available for the church Sunday School and for parochial meetings one night a week.

Progress in finding a site for the new school was slow. From correspondence in the Manvers papers it is clear that the County Council quickly ran into objections from villagers. The earl offered land on Cropwell Road, but according to a letter from C.J. Bristowe, the Director of Education, this offended the susceptibilities of

The infant department in 1903. The photograph was taken outside the building
erected by Lord Manvers in the 1870s which is now part of the Church Hall. The
teachers were probably Helen Packwood and Gertrude Barratt

Miss Scrimshaw's class in July 1914 photographed outside the school opened in
1909 on the Bingham Road. The building is still used as an 'annexe'
by the infant and junior schools

the 'Belgravians' who lived on the road. An alternative but more expensive site was offered by Enoch Hind 'on the south side of the main road and up a road which was partly made some time ago about 100 yards east of the Cropwell Road'. As the Director of Education ruefully put it in February 1906: 'It is impossible to get a site that will not offend somebody.' In the end an agreement was entered into with the Trustees of the Perkins School at Barrow-on-Soar for the purchase of about an acre on the Bingham Road. As a result of these lengthy negotiations the new school, designed by Mr L. Maggs, was not occupied until the beginning of 1909. The Education Committee report for 1908-1909 gave the total costs:

Site	£718	5s	4d
Building, fencing boundary, walls, out-offices, tarpaving playgrounds, drainage, etc.	£4,291	1s	3d
Furniture, fittings	£213	0s	11d
Architects' and clerk of the works' charge	£183	10s	11d
Loan charges	£44	4s	7d
	£5,450	3s	0d

The building was formally opened on the evening of Friday January 1st 1909. A contemporary description shows that much survives today:

There is a large central hall, intended to serve both departments, with separate entrances for these, and cloak rooms for boys and girls and infants. A private room is provided for the headmaster and another for the assistant teachers with cloak room and lavatory conveniently arranged. The classrooms are all commodious and well lighted. The floors throughout are of wood block, but the corridors and cloakrooms are done with granolithic paving. The entire building is heated by water and artificially lighted with gas. Considerable attention has been paid to the recreative needs of the children by the provision of a spacious playground which is covered with Val de Travers tar paving. There are also covered playsheds within the precincts of the grounds for the use of the children in inclement weather.

James Haslam, chair-
man of the managers

After village people had had the chance to inspect the new school, there was a ceremony in the hall, presided over by the chairman of the managers, James Haslam. His speech, while emphasising his belief in education and praising the 'solid and substantial' architecture, contained some less than complimentary references to the attitudes of local parents and children:

...it is of very little use the County Council spending money on school buildings and maintaining an efficient staff of school teachers if their efforts were to be thwarted and nullified by the carelessness and indifference of the parents of the children.... It has been said that Radcliffe youths are the most in-corrigible of the whole country [sic!]. I don't think they are worse than other places, but their reputation is bad enough, and we must try now to see whether we cannot, with the assistance of the parents, make the youth of this village more amenable to the rules of sobriety and good behaviour...

Despite these strictures, the speech was greeted with applause, and Mr T.L.K. Edge, a member of the Education Committee responsible for buildings and sites, formally declared the school open.

The children themselves were entertained to tea in the new building two days later, and on January 11th 1909 James Browne and his pupils left the overcrowded old buildings for the last time. (They were temporarily to become the Pierrepont Institute for adult education and have been used since in numerous ways, including as a cinema and for theatrical performances, as well as by the church. The original bell is in the possession of the bellringers.) The new school on Bingham Road to which the pupils and teachers marched still partially serves the educational needs of the village. The accommodation was designed to house 260 in the mixed department and 160 infants. (Children from Holme Pierrepont now went to their own new school.) In the following December James Browne retired, his place taken by George Norton. The changes he had witnessed in his long career reflected in one small place the educational progress of the country as a whole.

Main sources

Primary
Nottinghamshire Archives Office: Radcliffe-on-Trent School Log Books SL 135/1/1-8; DD 345/3; parish registers; CC/ED 6/2/1, 8/6/1, 8/9/1, 12/1/4.
Nottinghamshire County Library (Local Studies Library): census returns.
Nottinghamshire County Council: Annual Reports of the Education Committee 1903-1908.
Radcliffe-on-Trent Parish Council: minute books.
University of Nottingham: Manvers papers Ma B 529/136, Ma B 539/163 and 167, M 3555, Ma 2C 11/2/3/5/17/37/41/42, 12/3/19, 16/94/124, 17/605, 19/137; John Brice's Account Book (photocopy) Acc. 605.

Secondary
Chamberlain, Colet. *Memories of the past.* 1960.
Halse, K.B. *Radcliffe-on-Trent Church of England School in the nineteenth century.* Unpublished dissertation. Summary in the possession of Radcliffe-on-Trent local history research group.
Nottinghamshire *Directories.* 1864-1915.
Radcliffe-on-Trent local history research group: extracts from Nottingham newspapers 1837-1920.
The Trader. January 2nd and 9th, 1909.

As one person's recreation is another's livelihood, it is not easy to define the limits of a study of sports and pastimes. There is inevitably some overlap of interest between, for example, fishing for sport and fishing for food, or between watching cricket as opposed to playing it as either amateur or professional. Similarly, while amateur entertainments abounded in Radcliffe, there were occasional opportunities to hear professional speakers or performers. This study touches briefly on a number of such aspects.

Hunting, shooting and fishing

The traditional sports of the countryside were enjoyed by the well-to-do of the locality. The Manvers estate, for example, retained fishing rights in the Trent at Adbolton, Bassingfield, Holme Pierrepont and Radcliffe, poachers being frequently punished in the magistrates' court at Bingham.

Up to 1859 the names of those holding game certificates appeared annually in the Nottingham newspapers. Initially these cost £4 (later £4.0s.10d) and entitled the holder to shoot locally. In 1841 there were five holders in Radcliffe: Samuel Parr of the Manor House, Thomas Butler and Edward Brewster who were affluent farmers, and William and John Taylor from Radcliffe Hall. By 1859 John Taylor still had this right, as had Henry Wright and Ichabod Charles Wright (the latter currently occupying Lamcote House), and Edward Smith, a farmer with connections at Cropwell Butler. Lord Newark, then in residence at Holme Pierrepont Hall, also held a certificate in that year and employed a gamekeeper, George Whatton (licensed for £1.17s.6d) to cover Cotgrave, Clipston, Gamston, Bassingfield, Hickling, Holme Pierrepont and Radcliffe. As third Earl Manvers in the 1860s, he regularly brought parties in September or October to shoot on the Holme Pierrepont estate, and the Hall was described as his 'shooting box' in 1878. Newspaper reports suggest that while hares and rabbits were plentiful, birds were often scarce. This may account for the heavy fine of 5s per egg imposed on Henry Parr who was found guilty in 1865 of taking a partridge and seventeen eggs on land up Cropwell Road. It is significant that not only was the Manvers estate gamekeeper involved in the case, but a game watcher was being employed to keep an eye on the nest. By the early 1900s the fourth Earl Manvers found it profitable to let the shooting rights on 7,000 acres of the Holme Pierrepont estate to Colonel Leslie Birkin of Basford for £400 a year.

While hare coursing was regularly organised over the Bingham border by Lord Caernarvon's gamekeeper, Radcliffe's elite were more interested in fox hunting. In July 1837 a newspaper advertisement for the sale of Radcliffe Lodge gave as one of its attractions that it was 'in the midst of the very popular hunt of Mr Musters and within reach of several others'. Notices of hunting appointments in newspapers throughout the century show that Saxondale guidepost was a regular venue. In the 1850s Sir Richard Sutton's hounds occasionally met in the village, and for some 40 years afterwards the South Notts Hunt organised the local sport. Although a fox would often lead its pursuers through Radcliffe, an actual meet in the village was sufficiently rare for the schoolmaster to record it in his log book. Occasionally incidents were reported in the local papers. In October 1892, for example, the hounds got on to the railway line near Radcliffe and were run into by an excursion train. Five or six were killed outright and several others were so badly injured that they had to be shot. Much fuller newspaper reports were produced about Lord Harrington's hounds which met locally from around 1900. A typical meet in December 1902 at Lamcote House was attended by Earl and Countess Harrington and their friends, as well as by local riders and drivers including Major Noel, Mrs Butler Parr, Mr J. Fryer, Miss S. Fryer and Isaac Kirchen. Radcliffe's days as a centre for fox hunting are still recalled by the site of today's Covert Crescent, while the area known as the Harlequin, formerly Mile End, was reputedly named after a favourite hound.

The Volunteers

Shooting of a military kind was encouraged through groups of amateur soldiers which flourished locally. One of the most prestigious was the South Notts Yeomanry

Cavalry (later the South Notts Hussars) which had been founded in 1794 during troubled times. By 1799 there was a Holme troop drawing on support from both Radcliffe and Bingham, and often headed by a member of the Pierrepont family. Between 1868 and 1879 Lord Manvers was Lieutenant-Colonel in charge of all troops, regularly attending the annual reviews on the Forest. Those involved from Radcliffe are not always easy to identify, although the muster roll of the Holme troop for 1828 shows that out of eight-six enrolled, seventeen came from the village. The names of Butler, Brewster, Bell, Buxton, Foster, Green, Knight, Morley, Parr, Richmond and Stone featured prominently. Richard Daft, the cricketer, was a member in 1856, although perhaps with a Nottingham troop. James Upton was particularly long serving. He was certainly in the Holme troop in 1864 when he is recorded as having an accident on the turnpike road, caused by a broken stirrup. He became the troop quartermaster and retired in 1889, the year before his death at the age of 55. Two years earlier, 24-year-old Private Edwin Upton of the 4th Notts Rifle Volunteers had been buried at Radcliffe with full military honours, three volleys being fired over his coffin which bore his helmet and bayonet.

It was the Rifle Volunteers who provided improved shooting facilities in Radcliffe. In December 1884 a concert was held to raise money for the construction of rifle butts on land rented from Lord Manvers, the site of the present Golf Road. The targets were on the hillside to the south. The range was open by August 1885 when it was used by the South Notts Cavalry Carbine Club, but more local groups were to use it for regular shooting competitions. A keenly contested match took place in August 1888 when eight men of the Radcliffe half-company of the 4th Notts Rifle Volunteers met a company from the Robin Hood Rifles. Each man fired seven shots at 200 and 500 yards. The Radcliffe team won, their top scorer being Private Rushton, followed by Corporal Bell. On a more regular basis Radcliffe and Bingham riflemen contested for the Burnside challenge cup over five monthly competitions, the four highest aggregate scores to count for prizes. Sergeant Allwood, a local policeman, was presented with the cup in 1889 at a dinner at the Manvers Arms. He crowned his achievement by contributing a piano solo during the after-dinner entertainment. By 1891 the ability already shown by Private A.J. Rushton (from a Radcliffe family of painters and decorators) made him the outstanding local marksman. As the winner in two consecutive years, he won the Burnside challenge cup outright - it was valued at 5 guineas - as well as £1.10s. Amongst the list of prizewinners were four other members of the Rushton family. Presumably Miss Burnside provided another cup, for in February 1892 Private Rushton was presented with the cup again. He was then beaten by his brother, Bugler W. Rushton, who was also to win the cup outright and make the highest ever score of 237 points. Yet another cup must have been produced, only to be won outright by Corporal Dyson in 1900.

Pedestrianism

More energetic was the vogue for 'pedestrianism' (foot racing) in the 1840s and 1850s, although Radcliffe residents tended to be spectators and gamblers rather than participants. So enthusiastic did the crowds become that police intervention was often needed to clear the highway and control ensuing violence. An account of one such colourful occasion appeared in the *Nottingham Journal* in April 1849:

On Monday a race came off between a Ruddington 'Don' and a Nottingham one. We have never before seen such a large number of velveteen coats and short pipes at Radcliffe as met on this occasion. The Nottingham hero was at Mr Bell's, the Manvers Arms, the other at Mr Clarke's Fox and Crown.

There was some heavy laying of bets with unfortunate consequences:

It appears some of the 'swell mob' paid great attention to the Nottingham hero previous to the race, whilst he was at the Manvers Arms and wishing to back their man to the uttermost they continued to ease Mr Bell of the money taken in his house that day. No doubt they intended to refund the cash, if their man had won, but happening to be the other way, of course Mr Bell cannot expect it. There never was seen a more disgraceful sight than at the

316

race. The Ruddington man was 3 or 4 yards first; but when 20 or 30 yards from the goal he was knocked down and the other man fell over him. Kicking and fighting was the result; the greatest wonder was no lives were lost.

Both men were subsequently charged at the Shire Hall with causing a breach of the peace by running a race on the turnpike at Radcliffe-on-Trent, about 1,000 people having been present. Despite their indignation they had to find sureties of £10 each and pay costs of 14s.6d. Similar incidents were reported in 1852. In January, John Marriott was fined 18s for taking part in a race along the Nottingham to Grantham road on the previous Christmas day, and in the following November two men were fined 30s including costs for obstructing the highway when some 1,000 spectators had attended another race.

Participation in athletic events must have been in more modest ways for most villagers. William Sanday of Cliff House used to organise Easter sports for the neighbourhood on his land at Holme Pierrepont. An account of this event in April 1866 shows the names of G.H. Sanday, George Parr and W. Tidy amongst the most frequent winners, but the mile race was won by J. Kitchen in 5 minutes 48 seconds, with J. Hind and R. Wright second and third. A large-scale event which foreshadowed the 'fun runs' of the 1980s occurred about 1905, when judging from a contemporary photograph a large number of the male population gathered at the Red Lion to run a mile to Saxondale.

Participants in a mile-run to Saxondale outside the Red Lion
in Water Lane c. 1905

Cricket

Radcliffe's real fame in recreational events was through cricket, played at first on a Wharf Lane ground, and from the mid-nineteenth century on a picturesque ground on Holme Pierrepont Lane. While some villagers participated, many were entertained by the exploits of county and England cricketers who lived in their midst. The detailed careers of such players as Butler Parr, George Parr and Richard Daft are fully covered in cricketing histories, but their links with the village reveal a close-knit sporting community, moving easily between professional and amateur status, while taking a full share in business and local activities.

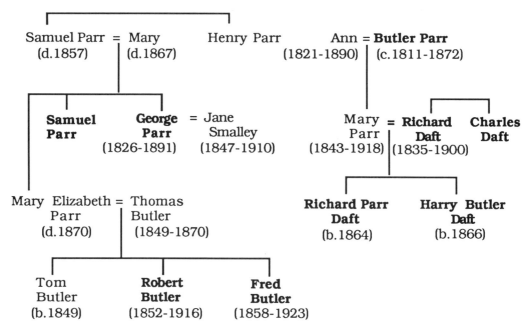

Family links between some nineteenth century Radcliffe cricketers
(County players appear in bold type)

Butler Parr

Some confusion arises because there were two separate cricketing Parr families. Butler Parr was a comparative outsider. He was born at Martin in Lincolnshire about 1811 but came to Radcliffe before he was two years old. As a brewer and maltster his business commitments prevented him from playing on a regular basis, but he was considered a sufficiently good batsman and wicket keeper to play for Nottinghamshire from 1835, three years before William Clarke began to make Trent Bridge the home of county cricket. One of his best performances there was of 61 not out against a Nottingham Eleven in 1842, while for Radcliffe he is reported to have scored 147 in a match against Grantham. His great knowledge made him a walking encyclopaedia of cricket, and he served on the county committee for a number of years. Within Radcliffe he was a well-respected figure, taking part in parish government, and occupying The Poplars on the main street for the last twenty years of his life. He died in March 1872 aged 61.

Samuel Parr senior and junior

The village to which Butler Parr was brought as a child was already a thriving centre for cricket. The Brewsters and the Richmonds were known for their cricketing interests around 1800, but the focal point was the Manor House occupied by local farmer Samuel Parr. Born about 1781, the latter's cricketing exploits included a score of 58 against Nottingham bowling in 1800, while in a match against Cropwell in 1814 he carried his bat for 32 out of a total of 63. His brother Henry was a noted bowler of the time. A diminutive man, Samuel Parr enjoyed recalling past incidents in his later years which doubtless grew with the telling. In particular he would describe a tremendous leg hit which went out of sight of all the fielders, and nearly killed a farm labourer cutting a hedge several fields away from the cricket ground. Samuel and his wife Mary produced nine children. The boys were encouraged to play cricket and two were soon known beyond village circles. Samuel junior came to the fore locally at the age of 18 in 1838. A noted leg hitter and brilliant fielder, he first played for Nottinghamshire in 1840, brought Trent Bridge to its feet with his 40 not out for the county against England in 1845, and scored 53 for England against Kent and Sussex in 1853. A somewhat insensitive practical joker, he is reputed to have misled a barber into cutting the hair of a fellow cricketer so short that the latter felt obliged to wear his hat at meals, and to have put a gooseberry branch into the bed of another player who suffered from gout.

George Parr

It was his younger brother George, a far more reserved character, who was to earn national fame while still remaining a part of the village. Born in 1826, his talent was spotted when he was only 14 by one of the Foster family (three played for Radcliffe in 1841), who suggested that he should displace his brother William in a village match against Bingham. He carried his bat and Radcliffe won by ten wickets. At the age of 18 he made his first appearance at Clarke's Trent Bridge ground in September 1844 when he scored 20 and 5 for the Players of Nottinghamshire against the Gentlemen of the County. His first real county match was in the following June, the prelude to a career in which he was to captain both Nottinghamshire and England, lead undefeated touring teams to America in 1859 and Australia and New Zealand in 1863-4, be acknowledged the world's greatest batsman, and amply justify his nickname of the *Lion of the North.*

As things turned out, George Parr needed to be a professional cricketer as his father allegedly got into financial difficulties before dying in February 1857 at the age of 78. The family then left the Manor House which they rented from Earl Manvers. Bonuses, such as the presentation by players at Lord's in 1857 of a gold watch in appreciation of his not-out scores, a benefit match at Lord's in 1858, or the 'extremely liberal' terms offered for the tour of Australia in 1863 would have been particularly welcome. According to the *Nottingham Journal* each man was to enjoy a 1st class passage, receive £50 to help keep wife and family (George was unmarried), and was expected to realise between £400 and £600. In the October before setting sail, he was entertained at a complimentary dinner at the Manvers Arms, presided over by Butler Parr, and attended by his brother Samuel as vice-chairman and by Richard Daft, a rising young cricketer who had lodged with George's mother in 1861. In reply to the toasts praising his exploits, George stressed how much he appreciated being treated in this way by the residents of his own village.

Twice at least his skills were recorded in doggerel verse. The Australian tour was the occasion of the first effort:

> Then comes the captain of the North, a star
> From Nottingham, well known as old George Parr;
> Tis not through bowling he is known by name,
> His bat to him has been the source of fame;
> Well may he use it o'er the distant sea,
> And if that is your wish, 'tis shared by me.
> Long be that day from us, and far off yet,
> When he to play again is no more fit.

A more contentious occasion was after the 1865 cricket season when George quarrelled with the Surrey county club and refused to allow any players over whom he had control to play at the Oval. Surrey accused him of cowardice, and in the following February a Nottingham pantomime took advantage of the publicity surrounding the quarrel. A twelve-man team of northern cricketers was put on stage, including both George Parr and Richard Daft, while Miss Clara Denvill (Jack in the pantomime) delivered a rhyming address about each in turn, ending with George:

> Though last not least, I turn me now to Parr.
> From chicken-heartedness, he's very far;
> ... Best in defence as yet, and hitter hard,
> To sing his praises puzzles much our bard;
> I might say more about him; only, hush!
> I'm fearful if I did that George might blush....

While his great feats were entered into county and national records, George Parr continued to entertain Radcliffe in celebrity matches alongside his younger colleague Richard Daft. His last match for the county was in 1871 when he scored 32 not out and 53 against Fourteen Gentlemen of Nottinghamshire at Trent Bridge. From then on he took little interest in cricket, but for the last twenty years of his life was a familiar figure in the village, enjoying fishing and snipe-shooting on the Trent. One resident later recalled that he kept a tortoise. Richard Daft left an account of him in retirement:

> *He was a martyr to gout, and always walked very lame. In hot weather he generally wore an old hat with a kind of curtain at the back of it, which he had brought with him from Australia. Besides this he often used an umbrella as a protection from the sun, and also assisted himself along by a thick walking-stick. Besides having the umbrella opened in one hand and the stick in the other, he often, too, had one or a couple of fox-terrier dogs chained and tugging at him.*

Of above middle height and powerfully built, George Parr had always stooped and walked with a slight limp. He aged rapidly, becoming very bowed and weak and was confined to a Bath chair at the end of his life. Eight months after marrying his housekeeper, Jane Smalley, he died at his house on Shelford Road on 23rd June 1891 at the age of 64. Play was suspended at Trent Bridge to coincide with his funeral, which was noted for its cricketing as well as village associates. A sprig from the elm tree at Trent Bridge (known as 'George Parr's tree' because of the frequency with which he sent the ball hard against it) was placed in his grave in the cemetery. Always a taciturn man, he nevertheless could be credited with a sense of humour if a story recalled by Ashley-Cooper is to be believed. His advice to young cricketers was as follows:

> *When you play in a match, be sure not to forget to pay a little attention to the umpire. First of all enquire after his health, then say what a fine player his father was, and, finally present him with a brace of birds or rabbits. This will give you confidence, and you will probably do well.*

Richard Daft

As George Parr was at the height of his fame, he was joined as a player by Richard Daft who had once lodged in the Parr household, and subsequently made Radcliffe his home. Born in Nottingham in 1835, he was the youngest of five brothers, another of whom - Charles - was also to play for the county. Richard's first county appearance was as an amateur in 1858, playing against Surrey at the Oval, when he scored 13 and 44 not out. From the following year until about 1881 he played as a professional. Noted for his wristy, graceful play, he became county captain in succession to George Parr in 1870, played for England, was in controversy with W.G. Grace in 1874 as the latter continued to receive the social distinctions of a 'gentleman' while being paid, led a Nottinghamshire and Yorkshire tour to America in 1879, and was elected to the county committee in 1886. In that year, playing as an amateur again and at the age of 50 he made the highest innings of his career, 222 for Mr William Wright's Nottinghamshire Eleven against the North Riding at Scarborough. Such stamina was the result of a rigorous programme of

Richard Daft (left) and George Parr
at the height of their fame c. 1865-70

320

physical training. Every morning he used 7 lb. dumb-bells, had a cold bath and took a long walk. His athletic skills were also used for football in the 1860s, tennis at which he won prizes in three tournaments when over 50, lacrosse and golf.

The advantage of having two outstanding players in their midst was brought home to Radcliffe residents in June 1869 when a three-day Grand Cricket Match was arranged between an Eleven of England (for whom both Richard Daft and George Parr were to play) and Twenty-Two of Radcliffe and District. According to the *Nottingham Journal* the turf of the picturesque Radcliffe ground was as level as a billiard table for this special occasion. Admission cost 1s on the pavilion side and 6d to the rest of the ground, and excursion trains were advertised to bring spectators from Nottingham.The local team included George Parr's two young nephews, Tom and Robert Butler, and other village players were H.J. Levi and T. Stone, with Samuel Brittle as wicket-keeper. (The Parr influence was at work here too, for the 1851 census shows that the latter had been a 'boarder' at the Manor House at the age of 3.) The team was supplemented by amateurs from further afield, as well as by two professional bowlers.

The England Eleven won the toss and play should have started at 11 a.m. but two Cambridge men (Hayward and Carpenter) had not arrived, so there was a delay until 1 o'clock when it was decided to put the Twenty-two in first. The scoring was slow, with Jalland of Shelford making the only 4 of the day, and the home side being all out for 147. The spectators were again deprived of cricket when it was decided to draw stumps half an hour early. In fact, the attendance had been disappointingly small on this first day, perhaps because the match coincided with an election in Nottingham.

On the second day the English weather did its worst. A showery morning caused another delayed start, and when the England team came out to bat there was great disappointment when Richard Daft scored only 1 run. At 85 for 5 the dinner bell rang, but before the diners could be seated a strong gust of wind blew up the canvas, upsetting the catering arrangements laid on by Mr Bell of the Manvers Arms. The players helped to peg down the canvas and dinner continued as comfortably as possible in the circumstances. The high winds of the afternoon were to leave players and spectators alike shivering with cold, and tents and 'telegraphing board' blown over. After dinner George Parr was cheered to the wicket and was soon at the centre of controversy. The ball rolled from his bat to the stumps with just enough force to knock a bail out of its groove, from where it was blown off by the wind - or so the umpire said. He refused to give Parr out, to the annoyance of some of the Twenty-two. Parr then got 'well set', scored 37, and was cheered again on his return to the pavilion. His side was all out for 153.

On the Wednesday, the local team were all out for 84 in their second innings, protesting at the position of the umpire in a mis-sighting of the ball. At 4.45 p.m. England had scored 41 for 4, still needing 38 to win, when Oscroft who was not out 30 'retired' to catch a train from Nottingham with most of his colleagues in time to be in Ireland for a game to be played the next day. It was decided that the match was a draw, but Richard Daft and George Parr continued batting to entertain their local supporters

Despite the star attractions, the event was a financial disaster. The election and bad weather had kept the crowds away, and it was thought likely that any profits taken at the refreshment booths would have to be spent on repairs to storm damage. Nevertheless, a similar match was staged in the following year when both Richard Daft and Parr played again for an England team which made 504. The local team this time fielded eighteen and scored 123. The match was nevertheless again drawn.

Although serious cricket was to dominate Richard Daft's life for another eleven years, Radcliffe had already provided him with a wife and the start of a second career. In 1862 he had married Mary Parr, the daughter of Butler Parr the maltster and former cricketer, ultimately taking over the latter's business near the Royal Oak and living at The Rosary, the house now used as the Scout Headquarters in Walker's Yard. Unfortunately, after the death of his father-in-law in 1872 he extended the range of his business interests with disastrous consequences. By 1874 he had established a sports equipment shop in Lister Gate, from where the manager disappeared to New York with between £150 and £200. In 1879 he was commissioned to find players for leading cricket clubs in America. He ran refreshment booths at

Trent Bridge cricket ground for some years, and leased the Cliffe Inn in Radcliffe and the Chesterfield Arms in Bingham during the 1880s. He gave up his main sports business when the lease ran out in 1893, his two sons opened a new establishment at Carrington Street bridge which failed after four years. In 1896, already in debt, he borrowed £1,400 from his three daughters so he and his son, Harry, could take over the Trent Bridge Inn. The enterprise lasted only twenty months. Generosity to customers and losses at racecourses contributed to the appearance of father and son in the bankruptcy court at the end of 1897.

Despite these failures, Richard Daft remained a highly respected and popular figure locally. At a public dinner at the George Hotel in Nottingham in January 1877 he was presented with a silver tea and coffee service, together with £500, and other gifts including clocks, a silver tankard, a hunting flask and luncheon case, bronzes and candlesticks instead of money from his benefit match. In Radcliffe he was on the committee which organised the rebuilding of the church,

Richard Daft in later life

served as churchwarden, was well known for his Tory views, took the chair at the village cricket club dinner in 1894, and wrote his cricketing memoirs - *Kings of Cricket* and *A Cricketer's Yarns*. He died in July 1900 at the age of 64 after suffering from heart trouble. As in the case of George Parr, play was suspended at Trent Bridge during the time of his funeral when hundreds turned out in the village. He was buried in the cemetery a short distance from his county colleague and close to his father-in-law, Butler Parr.

Richard Daft's sons

Apart from being associated with their father's business concerns, Richard Daft's sons were themselves well-known in sporting circles. Richard Parr Daft played cricket for the county in 1886 and 1887, and although his name does not appear amongst the regular players in the village cricket team he had the second best batting average in 1889, beaten only by another former county player, Robert Butler. His average of less than 24 for six innings could not have included the 242 not out for Radcliffe against Nottingham St Luke's, recorded for the same season by Ashley-Cooper.

Harry Butler Daft, his younger brother, was born in 1866, played for Trent College at the age of 12, made over 1,200 runs in local matches in 1884, and played for the county from the following year. His strong defensive play led to his being sent in to bat in difficult conditions, perhaps adversely affecting his average. His highest county score was 103 not out against Northamptonshire. At first playing as an amateur, from 1890 he became a professional cricketer, his county career ending in 1899. His reputation as a cricketer was almost surpassed by his excellence as a footballer, and both brothers were involved in the introduction of lacrosse to Radcliffe.

The Butler brothers

George Parr's eldest sister Mary Elizabeth had married Thomas Butler, a substantial local farmer, and produced at least nine children. (Mary and Thomas were both to die during the cemetery controversy in 1870. See page 189.) Three of

CRICKET, FOOTBALL, LAWN TENNIS,
AND
BRITISH SPORTS WAREHOUSE,
1, LISTER GATE, NOTTINGHAM.

RICHARD DAFT,
(MEMBER OF ALL ENGLAND ELEVEN,)

Has the largest and best assorted Stock of all articles required in the above Games, of any House in the Trade.

LAWN TENNIS.—The Game complete in boxes from £2.

LAWN TENNIS RACQUETS, with wooden handles, from 6/6 each; NETS, complete with Poles, &c., each 15/6, 18/6, 21/-, 25/-; Ladies' and Gent's SHOES, with all the latest improvements; PRESSES, to hold four or more Racquets, from 12/6 each; BALLS, exact in size and weight according to Revised Rules. Any article required in the game may be had separately.

SELECTED PRESENTATION BATS,
With Silver Shields engraved, 25/-, 27/6, and 30/-

R. D. CALLS SPECIAL ATTENTION TO HIS
NEW PATENT FOOTBALL,

Waterproof lined, which will wear twice as long as the ordinary Ball. Match size, Rugby or Association, 12/6 each.

Illustrated Price Lists, containing Laws of Cricket & Football (Rugby & Association), Post Free.

ADDRESS :—
RICHARD DAFT, 1, Lister Gate, Nottingham.

THE BREWERY, RADCLIFFE-ON-TRENT.

RICHARD DAFT

Having purchased the above OLD-ESTABLISHED BREWERY, with which he has been connected for upwards of twenty years, from the Executors of his late Father-in-law, Mr. Butler Parr, thanks his Friends for past favours, and begs to inform them that in future the Business will be carried on solely by himself.

PALE, MILD, AND STRONG ALES

In splendid condition, in 9, 12, 18, and 36 Gallon Casks, at 1/-, 1/2, 1/4, 1/6, 1/8 and 1/10 per Gallon, delivered free of charge.

All orders addressed to the Brewery, or to the Nottingham Office, 1, LISTER GATE, will receive prompt and careful attention.

13

Some of Richard Daft's business interests advertised
in Wright's *Directory* of 1881

their sons continued the Radcliffe cricketing tradition. Tom Butler was born about 1849 and took over the farming of 420 acres on his father's death. He played only locally, usually in his everyday clothes, was full-bearded and not unlike W.G. Grace in appearance. Richard Daft recalled once seeing him practising before a match. 'Why, Tom, I really thought you were W.G. Grace,' he exclaimed. 'You will have cause to think so before the day is over!' was the reply. It was Tom Butler's slow lob bowling that removed two England century-makers in the 1870 match between an England Eleven and Eighteen of Radcliffe. His brother Robert was three years younger, a batsman of considerable ability, who played for the county for the first time in that summer of 1870, scoring 60 against Kent at the Crystal Palace. His auction business in Radcliffe and the Black Boy Yard, Nottingham, prevented a full-time commitment to the game, but in club cricket in 1873 he had a batting average of 98, and was offered a place in the Middlesex team. For many years he continued to live in Radcliffe and was the centre of a long and ultimately unsuccessful divorce case. He died in Nottingham in 1916 but was buried in the village. Fred Butler was born in 1858 and played for the county from 1881, but without always living up to his promise. His score of 171 against Sussex at Brighton was probably his best. He then left Nottinghamshire, played for Durham County, and was professional to the Sunderland Cricket Club for fifteen years. He died at Staten Island, U.S.A., in 1923.

The local club

With players of such calibre in the community it is not surprising that village cricket thrived at a humbler level. Matches between Radcliffe and other local teams were recorded in Nottingham newspapers from the beginning of the nineteenth century, and as early as July 1838 a Radcliffe team was playing at William Clarke's new ground at Trent Bridge, opened two months earlier. The team for a 2-day match with Bingham in September 1841 reveals typical Radcliffe names: Samuel Parr as top scorer and wicket taker, William Parr (George's brother), three Fosters, as well as Richmond, Jerram, Roulston, Morley, Brewster and Widdowson. Radcliffe won by 31 runs. By the 1870s Radcliffe was playing teams such as Nottingham Amateurs, Gitanus, Park Wanderers, as well as Bingham. In this last match, Bingham scored 200 and beat Radcliffe by 77 runs. The names of Henry Parr, Foster and Butler indicate that long-standing families still contributed to the local teams, but newer names such as Keeley, Bright, Lamb, Parnham, Levi, Forman, Miles, Pare and Burgin also appear. John B. Taylor from Radcliffe Hall and Charles Martin, the son of a former village doctor, sometimes played too. By 1889, the local club seems to have been organised on a more formal basis. In that year about fifty members and friends attended the annual dinner at the Red Lion Inn, the proceedings being under the chairmanship of the sporting Dr Campbell. Judging by newspaper coverage of the event the club was in a thriving condition:

> In the hands of the new secretary, Mr H. Redgate, the club this season has been placed in a much more flourishing position, both as to membership and funds, and considerable care has also been devoted towards improving the state of the club's ground.

Twenty matches had been played: seven won, five lost and eight drawn. From this time the names of Redgate, Barratt, Hallam, Hassall, Bishop, Swales, Fryer and Whitlock tended to be most prominent, although occasionally a Parr, Daft or Butler still appeared. From 1898 Lord Newark was president of the club, retaining his interest after becoming fourth Earl Manvers in 1900, and for a while annual cricket club concerts were added to the village calendar. A respectable success rate was maintained in matches, typified by the results for 1901. In that year eleven Thursday matches were played, of which four were won, three lost and four drawn. The Saturday and all day matches were less successful: out of seventeen games, only three were won, six being lost and eight drawn. There was a sensational success in the 1904 season when Radcliffe dismissed the Notts Waverley team - a strong batting side - for 9 runs after totalling 280 for two wickets (declared). J. Fryer scored 101 not out, and went on to make 1,000 runs for the season. Charlie Parr took nine wickets for 1 run, eight of which were clean bowled and the other l.b.w.

The Radcliffe tradition in cricket continued into the 20th century with strong local players such as Samuel Dyson Parr and Thomas Leonard Richmond. The latter, born in the village in 1892, was to play for the county particularly after the First World War. Principally a bowler, he could also score freely, making 70 against Derbyshire in 1922. J.F. Bishop was yet another local player who from 1923 played at county level. In 1965 the club was forced to leave its Holme Pierrepont Lane ground, but play continues on the outskirts of the village beside the main road to Nottingham.

Football

Although organised football does not have such a long history in Radcliffe as cricket, the current Olympic football club traces its beginnings to 1876, and newspaper reports during the 1880s show that not only was there a main Radcliffe team which played for the Nottinghamshire Junior cup in 1888 and for the Newark cup in 1889, but also a Radcliffe West End team. Games were played on a Holme Lane ground at this time, but a match report for September 1892 mentions a new ground on Bingham Road. There were some spectacular successes in these early days - such as a victory by 8 goals to 3 against Bohemians in October 1889 - and some disastrous failures. An away match in the Nottinghamshire League against Forest Reserves in December 1890 was particularly controversial. Because of thick fog the Radcliffe team arrived late, and by the end the spectators were unable to see the play. The Forest team won by 9 goals to 1, and Radcliffe threatened to protest against the game being counted as a league match because of the fog. The winners were then prepared to make a counter-protest because of the late arrival of the Radcliffe team. The outcome of this acrimony is not recorded. The Radcliffe team on this occasion was as follows: J. Wright in goal; backs Fryer and Rolleston; half-backs Carnell, H. Howard and S. Bell; Hassall and Spencer on the left wing, and G. Howard and J. Upton on the right; the centre forward was W. Whitlock.

It was Harry Butler Daft, Richard's son, who was to play football at a far more competitive level about this time. His father had been a founder member of Notts County Football Club, and Harry became the club's left winger as well as playing at international level. He was in the County team which was beaten in the cup final in 1891, and was in the victorious team of 1894.

By this date Radcliffe was struggling in its amateur league, regularly lying ninth out of twelve teams, although in that same season they beat Collingham in the Newark Charity Cup by 6 goals to 1, and reached the final. Nevertheless, at the A.G.M. held at the Royal Oak in June 1894 the secretary's report showed that out of thirty-two matches played only nine had been won and four drawn. Fifty-two goals had been scored for, and ninety-seven against. It was pointed out that the team had had to compete against a better class of club than ever before, and for an amateur club con-

Harry Butler Daft in 1891

ducted on such small expenses the results were regarded as satisfactory. Club assets were 10s.9d after an unusually expensive season when expenditure had reached £31.4s.6d. Gates were down, but income had totalled £31.15s.6d from a combination of increased subscriptions, a guarantee match and the proceeds of a concert. The club's officers were re-elected. Mr J. Russell was president, T. Bell the treasurer, J.H. Scriven the secretary who was given a 'handsome present' for his services, and Mr A. Burgess the captain. There were ambitious plans to enter for the Notts Senior Cup and the Mansfield Charity Cup, but little Radcliffe footballing activity is found in the newspapers for the following season. At the beginning of September the team played a match against Kimberley in the Notts League and was beaten 9 - 0. By the end of September Radcliffe was no longer listed in the league's table. Nevertheless, amateur football has clearly continued in the village up to the present day. In 1902, for example, a team was in the Junior Cup competition in Division II of the Notts Football Association, while numerous photographs show football teams of various organisations, the names of the players now largely forgotten.

Lacrosse

Lacrosse was introduced into England in 1876, and in the autumn of 1883 a club was formed in Radcliffe with thirty members. Viscount Newark was the president, George Willey the vice-president, and the captain was Richard Daft, then aged 48. Practice matches took place on Thursday and Saturday afternoons on the cricket ground, and for two seasons reports appeared in the Nottingham newspapers of the team's successful exploits. The mainstays of the team were clearly Richard Daft and his two sons, but they were ably supported by Butler Parr (Richard's brother-in-law), Dr Campbell in goal, and various members of the Butler, Beddard, Caporn, Bishop, Green, Bell, Rushton and Barratt families. The standard of play must have been high, for in March 1884 the Radcliffe team beat Derbyshire 15-0, and the three Dafts, Butler, Butler Parr and Dr Campbell played for Nottinghamshire against Cambridge University, winning by 9 goals to 4. The village team was beaten by South Manchester in April 1884, but drew with Cambridge University in March 1885. By then the first annual ball had been successfully held in the schoolroom with the promise of more to come. However, reports of the club's activities no longer appeared in the newspapers, and it is now difficult to know when it ceased to function.

Tennis

From the 1880s a number of the larger houses, including the Manor House, Oakfield House and Bailey House (now Brick House) had their own tennis lawns. A Radcliffe club was formed about 1886, but little is known about its activities. A report of the fourth annual ball held in the schoolroom in February 1890 suggests that it had considerable support since it was attended by nearly 100 guests. Those officiating included Messrs J.H. Richards, J.R. Haslam, S. Garrett, Edward Green, L. Rockley and the indefatigable Dr Campbell. The club was still in being in June 1900 when the Radcliffe team won a mixed doubles match against Lenton. Colet Chamberlain recalled that the tennis club was eventually incorporated with the cricket club, the courts occupying the full length of the viaduct side of the Holme Lane ground. (A hockey club was also to share this ground in season.)

Golf

Although Richard Daft had contributed to the founding of the Nottingham golf club in 1887, a club was not formed in Radcliffe until 1909. In that year an agreement was reached with Lord Manvers for the lease of some 23 acres of land for twenty-one years at the modest annual rent of £100. His terms included the retention of all hedges, the preservation of any game, and no buildings except for a club house with outbuildings and stables necessary for members and their servants. There was also a clause indemnifying him should any member be injured by firing

The original golf club house, demolished in 1986

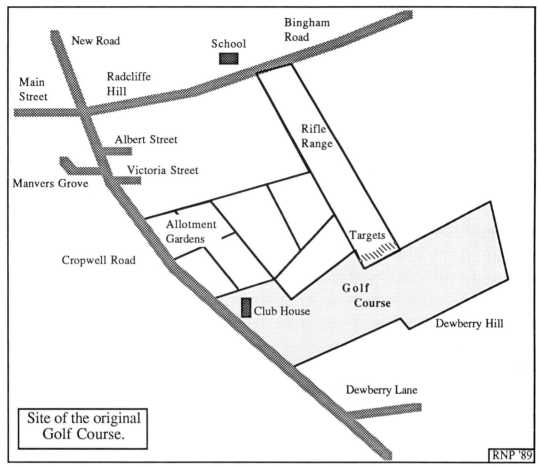

New Road

Bingham Road

School

Main Street

Radcliffe Hill

Albert Street

Victoria Street

Manvers Grove

Rifle Range

Allotment Gardens

Cropwell Road

Targets

Golf Course

Club House

Dewberry Hill

Dewberry Lane

Site of the original Golf Course.

RNP '89

from the adjacent rifle range, which he also owned, and no play was to be allowed on Sundays! These terms were signed by J.F. Bishop and Henry Elsom, the club's directors, and by Charles Pike, the secretary.

The club was formed as a limited liability company with a share capital of £250 in shares of £1 each to act as security to those who subscribed funds for the laying out of a 9-hole course by Tom Williamson and the erection of a club house. Tom Williamson and Harry Vardon played in the opening exhibition match on 9th October 1909 when some 200 people were present. When the Manvers estate was sold in 1920, the club bought the land, and a further purchase of 50 acres four years later allowed the course to be extended to 18 holes from 1925. It was in this era that the Prince of Wales played on the course when visiting Lamcote House, and was made an honorary member of the club. A further purchase of land alongside Dewberry Lane was made in 1966, while a proposed new road scheme meant that the original club house had to be abandoned in 1972 along with a large part of the original course. In an exchange of land a further 30 acres was gained, and the present course laid out by Frank Pennick. The old club house survived in a decayed state until the end of 1986.

Cycling

As has already been seen (page 10) the impact of the bicycle on ease of travel and road hazards was considerable, and as a leisure time activity it contributed to the irritation of villagers who were disturbed at weekends. When members of the Nottingham Castle cycle club visited Radcliffe one Sunday in April 1890, they were warned in the vicar's sermon of 'the need to lead quiet, sober and steady lives if they desired to follow this recreation to the advantage of body and soul'.

There was, however, already a class of wheeled rider who took these leisure pursuits very seriously. One such was Thomas Marriott, a resident of the village in 1885, when he was also captain of the Nottingham and Nottinghamshire tricycle club. From 1882 his name was associated with tricycling achievements: 180 miles from Derby to Holyhead in 23¾ hours, including stoppages, in July 1882; a record

218³/₄ miles in one day in August 1883; and a record ride from Land's End to John o' Groats in 1885. In the hotel register at John o' Groats on September 28th of that year he recorded his name, gave his address as Ratcliffe-on-Trent, and claimed to have accomplished the ride in 6 days, 15 hours, 22 minutes 'at a time of year highly impropitious for a performance of this description and under a succession of adverse circumstances....' His ride eclipsed 'the best known performance upon a bicycle by 48 minutes and the tricycle record by 1 day 13 hours and 58 minutes'.

Reading rooms

There were also far less energetic ways in which villagers could spend their free time. From the late 1860s attempts were made to provide reading rooms, initially under church patronage, but they could not have survived long. At least the fourth was in existence in February 1892, but judging by some correspondence in the *Nottingham Daily Guardian* not all residents were aware of the fact. A *Working Man* wanted to know why Radcliffe was so destitute of places of recreation:

> We have a population of upwards 2,000 inhabitants, a fair portion of whom are in a fair social position and yet we have not a single institution where a working man may go after his work is done to read a newspaper or enjoy his pipe. With the young folks the case is even worse, for having nowhere to go they stand at street corners, and become an annoyance to the more grave inhabitants.... [He proposed] a reading room for the benefit of the working men, who are going to the public [houses] and spending as much money in one night as would furnish them with a week's recreation and amusement if suitable provision were made for them.

A reply was soon forthcoming from George Willey who had recently resigned as treasurer of just such an institution already in existence:

> There has been a reading room centrally situated in the village open for six winters, which has mainly been supported by subscriptions from non-members, the cost to the members being only 1s per season for years and 1s.6d for the last two seasons. For this there was a warm, comfortable room provided, five or six daily papers, several weekly papers including the 'Graphic' and athletic papers. Games of chess, draughts, and other games (except cards) have been provided and smoking was allowed. For the last two seasons it has been open to every parishioner who wished to become a member. The members were principally young men, but the bona fide working man did not avail himself of it very much....

Fundamentally, subscriptions had not covered costs, which accounted for his resignation as treasurer.*Working Man* replied that the room was popularly regarded as having political links, and anyway was of insufficient size. Mr Willey admitted that it had been started by the Conservative party, but it was now open to all, and at least four members were sons of the most prominent radicals in the village. As far as accommodation was concerned, the room contained tables and seats for thirty or more, but there were rarely twenty present at the same time. At this point the editor cut short the correspondence, and the subsequent history of the reading room is unknown.

Lectures and concerts

Throughout Victorian times visiting speakers drew audiences to the schoolrooms. Three examples recorded in the newspapers show that not all subjects were well received. In April 1843 a Mr Briggs of Nottingham lectured in Radcliffe and other villages on the science of *Phreno-magnetism*, but with singular lack of success. By the time he got to East Bridgford some members of the public were demanding their money back and Mr Briggs required a police escort. More welcome was the 'special treat' of a lecture by the Rev Hale, vicar of Caunton near Newark, on *The Vulgar Tongue* in November 1874. Wisely dividing his talk into two parts with a musical interval, the speaker's dry humour, and sparkling vivacity delighted an appreciative audience.

Totally disastrous was the lecture given by the Rev Fred Bell in December 1881 on *Midnight scenes in New York*. This turned out to be less a study in topography than an account of the lecturer's experiences amongst the fallen women and low drink shops of America. The audience was considerably boosted by a party of the speaker's admirers who had come by special train from Nottingham, but local attenders were not impressed. When the reverend gentleman claimed that he did not stay in Nottingham to make money, since he could make a sovereign in New York for every shilling made locally, one villager asked why he did not stay there and demanded to know why he had left Brooklyn. A scene of disorder ensued, only quelled when the speaker sent a dozen supporters to the point of the disturbance ready to give the culprit 'plenty of air' should he give the order. Fortunately Mrs Bell was on hand to bring a temporary calm to the proceedings with a pianoforte selection, but the evening closed in further disorder, attributed in part to the Rev Bell's appearance which had been 'much talked about in the village'. Most talks were on far more conventional subjects and by much less colourful speakers, but proceedings were enlivened towards the end of the century with the arrival of 'dissolving limelight views' shown by Mr E. Green on behalf of the football club in January 1890. Magic lantern entertainments became almost routine around the turn of the century.

A popular form of entertainment or fund-raising was a concert. Brass bands came and went. Local amateurs sang with distinction, notably Samuel Barratt and George Bell in the 1880s, while visiting performers ranged from choristers from St George's Chapel, Windsor, in November 1888 to the Nottingham minstrels with their banjo band in May 1894. Many causes and societies benefited from and participated in such activities: the church restoration fund, the organ fund, the cricket club, the rifle butts, the Wesleyan Band of Hope, the Oddfellows, a commemoration of the vicar's thirty-eight years in the parish, the Nursing Association and many more. There were some unfortunate clashes. The *Nottingham Daily Express* reported on March 1st 1889 that the annual church choir concert was well attended 'considering a similar entertainment was also taking place at Radcliffe Lodge.' Down Wharf Lane Mrs Lambert had lent the Lodge

Radcliffe brass band in the vicarage garden in 1902
Back row: A. Hopkins, A. Howard, W.Hames, Hopkins jnr, W. Price, Jim Upton
Front row: A. Howard, E. Howard, R. Rose, J. Kennedy, C. Barnard, Jack Richmond

dining room for a concert to raise money for Holme Pierrepont's church organ fund, and the 'large and fashionable audience' included 'the elite of Radcliffe and neighbourhood.'

A development from the straight concert came from the 1890s when the Band of Hope added tableaux to their songs, chorus and recitations. The entertainment for February 1891 involved a large number of eminent villagers. The musical part of the programme was conducted by Thomas Barratt, with Mr A. Barratt as his accompanist. Mr William Rushton appeared as a clown, and a maypole dance was performed by twelve little girls. But the tableaux were the high spot of the occasion with Miss L. Barratt as Mary Queen of Scots, Galatea etc., Miss A. Eastwood as Queen Elizabeth, Mr T. Barratt as Henry VIII, Mr T. Scrimshaw as Bluebeard, Mr William Rose as Robinson Crusoe, Mr R. Reast as Man Friday, Mr H. Dougall as Pygmalion and Sir Walter Raleigh, Mr T. Howard as Macbeth and the last bachelor in the village, and Mr J. Dann as Barnum.

Many other activities abounded, some on an organised scale, such as the gardening society which was partially intended to encourage self-sufficiency rather than provide recreation. Similarly, the formation of groups such as the Band of Hope (in 1871) and the Boys' Brigade (in 1902 under the captaincy of James Haslam) had more than a recreational purpose. Occasionally glimpses occur in the records of less well-documented activities: hoops in the street in the 1840s; a bowling alley in 1872 in the rear of Bateman's bakehouse near the Wesleyan chapel; a secret prize fight in July 1886 near Radcliffe railway bridge when Rawson severely punished Harrison for stakes amounting to £1 a side; piano playing revealed by the numbers of instruments in furniture sales from the 1880s; billiards in the grander houses of the same period; feast fairs on a field near the station each September. Of the everyday fireside entertainments which must have made up the routine of life, however, Radcliffe's records tell us little.

Main sources

Primary

Nottinghamshire Archives Office: Radcliffe-on-Trent parish registers.
Nottinghamshire County Library (Local Studies Library): census returns; DD 121/149, *Memories of a villager.* C. Hurd. 1960.
Radcliffe-on-Trent Parish Council: cemetery records.
University of Nottingham: Manvers papers 3 Ma 2D 14; 3Ma 2D 16.

Secondary

Ashley-Cooper, F.S. *Nottinghamshire Cricket and Cricketers.* 1923.
Chamberlain, Colet. *Memories of the Past.* 1960.
Fellows, George. *History of South Notts Yeomanry Cavalry.* 1895.
John o' Groats House Hotel. Information from Mr Keith Muir.
National Cycle Museum, Brayford Wharf North, Lincoln. Information from the curator, Mr A. West.
Nottingham Evening Post. 28.6.1935.
Radcliffe-on-Trent local history research group: extracts from Nottingham newspapers, 1837-1920.
Radcliffe-on-Trent *Parish Guides,* 1979, 1983, 1987.

THE FIRST WORLD WAR

Even before the outbreak of war in August 1914 the old order in Radcliffe was beginning to change. The hold of the Manvers estate was still felt through the person of the fourth earl, but other more local families had gone - the Taylors of Radcliffe Hall after more than a century, the Burnsides at Lamcote House after more than forty years, and the Sandays at Cliff House. Other familiar figures, too, had been replaced. James Browne, the village's long-serving schoolmaster, had retired in 1909, having first taught in Radcliffe in 1871. Another patriarchal figure, the Reverend John Cullen, after almost forty years' service in the parish died in the January of 1914. On June 24th and 25th in the hot summer of that year the King and Queen visited Nottinghamshire. The village children were given the previous day off school, presumably to see the rehearsals and decorations in Nottingham. By the following Sunday the festive atmosphere was destroyed as the crown prince of Austria and his wife lay dead in Sarajevo, and the train of events was set in motion which led to Britain's declaration of war on Germany on August 4th 1914.

Recruitment

At first the British army was swelled by volunteers, but as the casualty toll mounted, men between 18 and 41 were conscripted from 1916. Some in essential occupations were exempted from military service, such as James Bird, Radcliffe's cemetery keeper. Volunteers outside the call-up ages were given permission by the Parish Council in January 1917 to use the playground for drill practice. It has not been possible to assess how many men altogether from Radcliffe were involved in war service, but a look at the school log books shows how one aspect of village life was affected.

Early in 1916 one of the junior masters, Thomas Alfred Peck, was 'called to the colours'. He served with 143 Siege Battery, was killed in action probably in 1917, and was buried at Feuchy near Arras. Headmaster George Norton was called up later in the same year, his place taken by two temporary headmasters until his safe return in January 1919. Nor were the women teachers immune to the impact of the war. Miss Scrimshaw became Mrs Hall in June 1916 and was absent from school on September 17th as her husband was going out to France. She was absent again in November 1918 when he unexpectedly arrived home from hospital. Others were less fortunate. Miss Packwood from the infants' department was absent in October 1918 suffering from shock on hearing the news of her brother's death. Mrs Pike of the junior department had become a widow in October 1917 when her husband Charles had been mortally wounded at Ypres. (She placed a memorial to him in the parish church.) In November 1918 she was absent from school, seeing her brother off to France in the last days of the war. On December 28th she herself was dead.

The home front

As the war tightened its grip the effect was felt by the whole community. In October 1915 the threat of Zeppelin raids caused the Parish Council to order the shading of streetlights, and from 1917 they were not used again until after the war. It was on Sunday night, March 5th 1916, that Zeppelins reached Nottinghamshire, having dropped a trail of bombs from the coast westwards, killing up to eighteen people and injuring fifty-two. There was damage in Nottingham itself, particularly in Newthorpe Street, off Arkwright Street, near the station. An elderly Radcliffe resident remembers looking up at about half past six that Sunday evening and seeing the shape of an airship across the moon. A stark entry in the churchwardens' book confirms the event: 'No collection - Zeppelin Raid.' An equally laconic entry in the Parish Council minutes for June 12th 1916 hints at a further dramatic incident. The clerk was ordered 'to get the Playground Fence damaged by the Aeroplane repaired and to charge the cost to the Military Authorities'.

Fundraising became a major contribution to the war effort. When only a short-term conflict was envisaged, a modest £5.8s.7½d was raised by the church for the 'War Fund' in October 1914. In contrast, the collection for the 'Prisoners of War Fund' in June 1918 came to a substantial £30. A War Savings Association was operating in the village by July 1916, and at the beginning of 1917 the schoolchildren were collecting money for the relief of Belgium, only to have the envelopes containing the money stolen when someone broke into the infants' room. At Whitsuntide 1917 a huge Patriotic Fair was organised in Nottingham's Market Square. Lord Manvers was on the overall general committee, and Radcliffe was allocated stall 31, selling miscellaneous goods under the heading *You Buy It*. Mrs Roberts was the village organiser, assisted by the vicar's wife (Mrs Cecil Smith), three doctors' wives (Mrs Allaway, Mrs Lloyd Jones and Mrs Campbell), Mrs Dowson of the Manor House, as well as Mesdames Greenwood, Johnson, Jones and Walker. Other community efforts included Red Cross training at Lamcote house, and the collection of funds for Christmas presents for Radcliffe men in the forces in 1918. Numerous ministry instructions were received by the Parish Council about food supplies throughout the war. In the later stages rationing had to be imposed, at first on bread, and on meat and butter from February 1918. The Parish Council distributed 500 ration leaflets, and the school had to be closed for two days as 'the teachers were assisting in the Food Registration of the district'.

Servants at Lamcote House as VADs. Elizabeth Pratt (left) from Tibshelf, cook/housekeeper, who married Arthur Buxton of Radcliffe in 1921

The wounded and the dead

In 1916 Radcliffe Hall became a convalescent home for wounded officers. One patient, Captain Lloyd Dexter who had lost an arm, subsequently married the owner, Helena Smith, the widow of a lace manufacturer. (After the war the couple continued to live at the Hall until 1939.) Another temporary change came in May 1918 when the War Office turned the Asylum at Saxondale into a military hospital. The parish agreed that soldiers who died while receiving treatment should be buried in a special part of the cemetery set aside at the southern end. Six deaths at the hospital are recorded in the cemetery register between November 1918 and August 1919, and, unlike asylum victims, a separate grave was provided for each. A public memorial in the cemetery, requested by the hospital visitors, was never erected, but the graves are routinely visited as part of the Remembrance Day services. (The dramatic drop in deaths once the hospital came under military supervision may be a reflection of a reduction in the number of inmates rather than just improved care.) The hospital returned to being a lunatic asylum in December 1919.

Influenza

Across Europe an influenza outbreak turned into a bigger killer than the war itself. In Radcliffe there were undoubtedly many sufferers. Colet Chamberlain recalled that his sister, a schoolteacher, died from it the day before the armistice. The junior department at the village school had to close for a fortnight in mid-November 1918 because of the prevalence of influenza locally and the number of absentees. When at attempt was made to re-open on December 2nd an attendance of less than 50% caused the school to close again. Another attempt to re-open a week later had also to be abandoned. Not until January 2nd did school restart, and even then Miss Frear in the infants' department was still suffering from the disease.

As the burial register does not give the cause of death, it has not been possible to assess the number of deaths due to influenza, but the overall death rate for 1918 was abnormally high. For example, in 1917 the parish register records sixty-seven burials (non-C. of E. burials are recorded elsewhere). Of these, fifty-six were from the lunatic asylum. In 1918 there were only twenty-three asylum deaths and five when it became a war hospital, and yet the number of burials recorded in the parish register was still as high as sixty. In the following year burials were down to twenty-six, including hospital deaths. The indications are, therefore, that the death toll during the influenza epidemic was heavy.

Celebration and mourning

Against this background the relief at the ending of hostilities on November 11th 1918 must have been somewhat muted. Nevertheless, the Parish Council interrupted its activities on that day to record a grateful tribute in its minute book:

> *The Chairman [Butler Parr] in opening the meeting said we could not let this great day pass, a day on which such great issues had been settled, without offering our grateful thanks to the army and navy for their great work and especially our devout thanks to those who in such great numbers had gone from this village as from everywhere else and had died fighting for the protection of this and future generations.*

There was a service of thanksgiving on the 11th itself and those schoolchildren still in attendance were given an instant half-holiday, and another on the following day.

Not until the summer of 1919 was victory celebrated with a parade through the village, but all was tempered by respect for the dead. The bell ringers' minutes show that by the beginning of 1919 half-muffled bells had been rung for almost forty Radcliffe men who had been killed or died of complaints as a result of the war, and on Saturday May 24th the ringers celebrated with a date touch of 1919 changes of Bob Minor lasting one hour and twenty minutes 'as a welcome and save [sic] return home of S. Loach ringer of the 4th bell after serving 2 years & half with the forces in France'. In 1919 also, a public meeting was called to consider the provision of a war memorial to all the dead. The church vestry agreed in the following year that it should be sited at the east end of the churchyard. Costing about £660, it was unveiled by Colonel Birkin of Lamcote House, himself an officer who had served in France, in April 1921. On that Sunday afternoon practically the whole village assembled outside the churchyard. There was a sudden hush as the local brass band, heading about 250 ex-servicemen, approached playing the *Dead March* from *Saul.* All stood to attention for the sounding of the *Last Post, Reveille* and the National Anthem. A service was led by the vicar, the Rev R. Cecil Smith, after which the relatives of the deceased men placed wreaths on the memorial plinth. As Colonel Birkin described the day as one 'of great pride, of great hope, and of intense sorrow and sympathy', the tall cross with its bronze figure of St George with head bowed in silent grief, was unveiled to reveal the names of fifty-two Radcliffe men who had been killed, and nine who had died as a result of illness on active service. From a population of some 2,800, the sacrifice had indeed been great.

Colonel Charles Birkin of Lamcote House who unveiled the war memorial in 1921

The memorial park

One other memorial was eventually provided by a generous benefactor. Lisle Rockley, the son of a joiner, had been born in Radcliffe in December 1859. As a young man he worked as a 'bill discounter', prospered, and eventually lived in Mapperley Park, Nottingham. His son, Lieutenant William Lisle Rockley MC of the 10th Yorkshire and Lancashire Regiment had, like Charles Pike, been killed at Ypres in 1917. In 1926 Lisle Rockley wrote to the Parish Council, offering to buy land along the cliffs which he would present to the parish as a public memorial park:

> *As a native of the parish I have felt that it is an anomaly that with regard to the River Trent and the Cliffs, which together account for the name of the Village that no inhabitant of Radcliffe-on-Trent is entitled as such or has any legal right to enjoy the possession of any portion of either the Cliffs or any land having access to the River and I feel that I should like to secure for*

The main street during the victory celebrations in 1919.
The tall gentleman in the centre wearing a Panama hat is James Browne, the retired
headmaster. In a row, bottom left are Mrs Speed (with pram), ?, ?, Annie Foster (in
white), Nancy Rowe, George Howard, Martha Howard (George's wife and Nancy's
sister). In the foreground left are Violet Barratt and Marguerite Barratt

The scene near the churchyard at the unveiling of the war memorial in April 1921

the inhabitants of Radcliffe-on-Trent, my native village, the enjoyment of their Cliffs and access to their River Trent for ever.

The object of my proposal is intended to provide a permanent, pleasant and useful memorial to the men of Radcliffe-on-Trent who gave up their lives in the Great War, where, as some of you are no doubt aware, my only son made the supreme sacrifice, and I should like with your permission that his name be in some way associated with the memorial.

Lisle Rockley realised that without legal right future building developments could prohibit public access to the cliffs. Lord Manvers had previously owned most of the land, but since the sale in 1920 some twenty-five small owners had to be approached and some six acres purchased. As a result, the Rockley Memorial Park and the whole of the Cliff Walk, including the area above Slack Hollow used as a children's playground, were presented to the parish. The work of clearing and planting with flowering trees was carried out as far as possible by ex-servicemen. The opening ceremony was performed in October 1927 by Viscount Galway, chairman of the County Council, and a service supported by the combined church choirs ended with the buglers of the Robin Hood Rifles sounding the *Last Post*.

The end of an era

The war left its effect on the village in other ways too. The compulsory purchase of land by the County Council to provide smallholdings for returning soldiers had encouraged Lord Manvers to sell off most of his estate in Radcliffe, so breaking the hold of the Pierrepont family as Lords of the Manor after some two hundred years. The end was symbolised by the quiet demise of the already obsolete court leet which had its roots in medieval times. Although the book of suit rolls of tenants had been made out as usual from 1910 to 1919, the jury did not meet after the outbreak of war in 1914. Manorial courts had no place in the modern world where at local level the Parish, District and County Councils were now all-powerful. Radcliffe escaped Nottingham's attempt in 1920 to include the village within its boundaries, but the village was to become ever more dependent on the city as the future was shaped by the motor car, a forthcoming by-pass, and by the commuter.

Main sources

Chamberlain, Colet. *Memories of the Past.* 1960.
Nottinghamshire Archives Office: Churchwardens' book PR 2885, school log books SL 135/1/5 and 8.
Nottingham Guardian, October 11th 1927.
Nottingham Weekly Express, 4th January 1921.
Radcliffe-on-Trent bellringers: minute books.
Radcliffe-on-Trent Parish Council: minute books, cemetery records.
University of Nottingham: Manvers papers Ma 244; *Notts. Patriotic Fair* in East Midlands Collection Not 3 D34.

A chronology from 1837 to 1920

Year	National and international	Nottingham and Nottinghamshire	Radcliffe-on-Trent
1837	Accession of Queen Victoria	New workhouse in Bingham	Rev Wm. Bury's *Pastoral Letter*
1838	Steamship crosses Atlantic		
1839	Opium War with China First Grand National	Midland Railway in Nottingham Formation of county police	New Wesleyan chapel opened
1840	Queen Victoria marries Prince Albert Penny post established		
1841	New Zealand becomes colony Sir Robert Peel prime minister	St Barnabas Roman Catholic cathedral	
1842	Queen Victoria's first railway journey		
1843	Wordsworth poet laureate	Queen Victoria visits Nottingham	Independent Primitive Methodist chapel opened
1844	YMCA founded		Church clock bought

1845	Engels publishes 'The condition of
	  the working class in England'
		Nottingham Enclosure Act
		George Parr plays for Notts
			Rev William Bury succeeded by
			  Rev Robert Burgess

1846	Famine in Ireland Mendelssohn *Elijah* at Birmingham	Newark Castle railway station	Storm damage to windmill
1847	Californian gold rush *Jane Eyre* & *Wuthering Heights* Factory Act; Poor Law Board	Newark Corn Exchange built	
1848	Communist manifesto published First Public Health Act Revolutions across Europe	First horse omnibus	Railway bridge over Wharf Lane
1849	Disraeli leads Tory party	Public baths opened; cholera Corn Exchange, Thurland Street	Cholera epidemic Methodist controversies
1850	Public Libraries Act Stephenson's High-level bridge at Newcastle-on-Tyne	Jesse Boot born	Opening of railway Rebuilding of cottages on the Green
1851	King's Cross station built Religious census taken		New pews and church furniture American claimant to Holme Pierrepont estate

1852	Dickens' *Bleak House*
	  Harriet Beecher Stowe's
	  Uncle Tom's Cabin
		Arboretum opened
		Great Northern Railway in
		  Nottingham	

1853	Smallpox vaccination compulsory Queen Victoria's 7th child born with chloroform as anaesthetic		
1854	Crimean war begins Charge of the Light Brigade	Synagogue in Shakespeare Street (built as Wesleyan chapel)	
1855	Livingstone at Victoria Falls Steamship crosses Atlantic in less than 10 days	Broadway in Lace Market	
1856	'Big Ben' cast for Houses of Parliament Bessemer converter for steel making		PC William Eason appointed
1857	Start of Indian Mutiny First transatlantic cable laid	Great Northern (London Road) & Bingham stations built	
1858	Lord Derby becomes prime minister Suez Canal Co. formed		New chancel built Samuel Morley wins VC
1859	Lord Palmerston prime minister Blondin walks Niagara on tightrope	County Cricket Club formed Richard Daft's first professional appearance	Smallpox outbreak

Year	National and international	Nottingham and Nottinghamshire	Radcliffe-on-Trent
1860	Abraham Lincoln is US president First Open golf championship	First Chief Constable appointed	Death of 2nd Earl Manvers Penny savings bank
1861	American Civil War begins Prince Albert dies	Bingham butter-cross built	Survey of Holme Pierrepont estate
1862	First cricket tour to Australia	Notts County Football club	Cliff House and first new villas built
1863	First London underground railway		PC John Stevenson appointed
1864	Louis Pasteur invents pasteurisation		
1865	American Civil War ends Abraham Lincoln assassinated Transatlantic cable completed	William Booth starts Salvation Army Nottingham Forest Football Club New Thoresby Hall begun	Primitive Methodist chapel opened on Knight's Hill
1866	Dr Barnado's Home in Stepney	Nottingham High School in Arboretum Street	School applies for Government grant
1867	Canada granted Dominion status Russia sells Alaska to USA Extension of vote to town householders		Gas reaches Radcliffe
1868	Disraeli becomes Prime Minister and is succeeded by Gladstone	John Player enters tobacco trade & opens shop in Radford Southwell House of Correction extended	First sanitary inspector appointed
1869	Suez canal opened Girton College, Cambridge		Removal of Lamcote Leys windmill England cricket XI v. R-o-T XXII
1870	Education Act Franco-Prussian war begins	Wilford toll bridge opened Clifton colliery opened	New school buildings Opening of cemetery Death of Dr Martin
1871	Local Government board replaces Board of Health & Poor Law board Bank holidays introduced	New Trent Bridge opened	
1872	Secret ballot introduced in Britain		
1873	County cricket championships begin Severn tunnel begun		Death of Rev Robert Burgess
1874	Disraeli becomes Prime Minister Winston Churchill born	Parliament Street Methodist church	Rev John Cullen becomes vicar
1875	Captain Webb swims English Channel	New Thoresby Hall completed	Gardening society established James Browne becomes headmaster Police station built
1876	Telephone invented	High Pavement chapel Grantham turnpike trust replaced by Bingham District Highways Board	School enlarged Gas lighting in centre of village Football club formed
1877	Queen Victoria Empress of India All England Lawn Tennis championships at Wimbledon	University College opened Bulwell, Basford, Radford, Lenton, Sneinton, Mapperley & Wilford taken into city.	Sale of Poor's land by Jeffrey Dole trustees
1878	Electric street lighting in London Benz builds motorised tricycle	Horse 'tram route organised Midland Counties Art Museum opened by Prince of Wales Smith's Bank, Market Square	Sergeant George Allwood appointed Police campaign against illegal drinking begins
1879	Zulu war in South Africa Collapse of Tay Bridge in Scotland	Closure of Southwell House of Correction	St Mary's church opened after rebuilding

Year	National and international	Nottingham and Nottinghamshire	Radcliffe-on-Trent
1880	Gladstone is Prime Minister Boers declare Transvaal republic First test match England v. Australia in England	'Bendigo', the bare knuckle fighter, dies aged 68 Newark General Hospital Mapperley Hospital	First government inquiry into sanitary matters Revision of Jeffrey Dole charity
1881	First Anglo-Boer war Disraeli (Lord Beaconsfield) dies	Horse 'tram routes reach longest route distance (7 miles & 40 ch.)	Start of scarlet fever epidemic
1882	Phoenix Park murders Daimler's petrol engine	National Westminster Bank in Thurland Street Ossington Coffee Palace, Newark	*Nottingham Journal* wages campaign against village's sanitary state
1883	Kruger proclaimed president in S.Africa Orient Express (Paris - Istanbul)		Second government inquiry into sanitary matters Lacrosse club formed
1884	First London underground railway Gold discovered in Transvaal Extension of vote in counties	Present Pavilion at Trent Bridge cricket ground	Third government inquiry into sanitary matters
1885	Gordon killed at Khartoum Electric 'tram at Blackpool	Papplewick pumping station	Thomas Marriott's record tricycle ride: Lands End to John o' Groats Riotous opposition to Liberals
1886	Gladstone introduces Home Rule Bill Severn railway tunnel opened		Lawn tennis club formed
1887	Queen Victoria's golden jubilee	Players *Navy Cut* cigarettes produced	
1888	Jack the Ripper murders	Nottingham Guildhall completed	
1889	County Councils formed	Nottinghamshire County Council City Hospital begun	
1890	First power station at Deptford Forth railway bridge opened	Nottingham Corporation resolve to supply electricity	Parish room built
1891	Trans-Siberian railway begun		
1892	Keir Hardie Labour Prime Minister		
1893	Independent Labour Party formed Benz constructs four wheel motor car Manchester Ship Canal opened		Collier charity founded Evening classes started New Primitive Methodist chapel on Shelford Road
1894	Death duties introduced	Chief Constable reports drunkenness is most common offence	Parish Council established & Viscount Newark is first chairman
1895	Gillette safety razor Keil canal opened in Germany	Worksop College built	
1896	Kitchener's Sudan campaign begins Nobel prizes instituted First modern Olympic games		
1897	Q.Victoria's diamond jubilee	Borough of Nottingham becomes City of Nottingham First 'horseless carriage' in city Great Central Railway: Victoria station	Wharf Lane recreation ground
1898	Kitchener occupies Omdurman Gladstone dies Vaccination no longer compulsory	Theatre Royal lit by electricity Lilley & Stone school Newark	Hon Henry Noel chairman of PC Death of Hon Henry Noel Approval given for piped water
1899	Second Anglo-Boer war London borough councils established		
1900	Commonwealth of Australia created Cadbury founds Bourneville village trust		Death of 3rd Earl Manvers
1901	Queen Victoria dies K.Edward VII succeeds	Electric 'trams introduced	Building of Saxondale Hospital (County Lunatic asylum)

Year	National and international	Nottingham and Nottinghamshire	Radcliffe-on-Trent
1902	Boer war ends		Sewage farm opened
			Horse trough & drinking fountain
			Boys' Brigade branch formed
1903	Entente Cordiale established		
	Motor car speed limit set at 20 mph		
1904	Russo-Japanese war	New Midland Railway station	Butler Parr chairman of
		Boots Chemists in High Street	Parish Council
1905	Russo-Japanese war ends	Nottinghamshire Automobile Club	First 'motor car shed'
	Mutiny on *Potemkin*		New Co-op store and meeting room
	Soviet set up in St Petersburg		at Shelford Road corner
	Motor 'buses in London		
1906	HMS *Dreadnought* launched	First motor 'bus route opens	
	San Francisco earthquake	Meadows suspension bridge	
1907	New Zealand becomes a Dominion	Albert Hall built	
	Boy Scout movement		
1908	Union of South Africa established		Consecration of cemetery extension
	Olympic Games in London		
	'Model T' Ford motor car		
1909	Old age pensions introduced		New school on Bingham Road opens
	King Edward VII visits Berlin		Golf club formed
1910	King Edward VII dies	Aeroplane forced to land at Colwick	New railway viaduct completed
	King George V succeeds		
	More than 120,000 telephones in GB		
1911	National Health Insurance		Hartwell charity founded
	Official Secrets Act		
	Shade temperatures of 100°F in London		
1912	GPO takes over telephone system		
	SS *Titanic* strikes iceberg & sinks		
1913	Suffragette demonstrations		District Council representation
	Zip fasteners become popular		increased to 4
1914	First World War		Death of Rev John Cullen succeeded
	Panama Canal opened		by Rev R. Cecil Smith
1915	SS *Lusitania* sunk by German navy		
	Zeppelin attacks on London		
	Landings at Gallipoli		
1916	Conscription introduced GB	Zeppelin drops bombs in January	Zeppelin seen over Radcliffe
	Easter rebellion in Ireland	and September	Radcliffe Hall becomes convalescent
	Battle of the Somme		home for wounded officers
1917	October revolution in Russia	Patriotic fair in Nottingham	
	USA declares war on Germany		
	Battle of Paschendaele		
	Trans-Siberian railway completed		
1918	Armistice signed in November	Explosion at Chilwell Ordnance	Saxondale becomes temporary
	Women over 30 given the vote	Factory kills 130 people	military hospital
	Worldwide influenza epidemic starts		Influenza epidemic
1919	Peace of Versailles ends World War		Meeting about War memorial
	German fleet scuttled at Scarpa Flow		(unveiled 1921)
	Alcock & Brown fly the Atlantic		Victory celebrations
1920	League of Nations formed	Failure of Nottingham's extension	Main sale of
	Prohibition of alcohol in USA	scheme to absorb Radcliffe and	Manvers estate properties
		a number of other parishes	

MEASUREMENTS

Square measures of land

square mile	640 acres		2.59 square kilometres
acre (a)	4 roods	4,840 square yards	0.405 hectares
rood (r)	40 perches		
perch (p)	30.25 square yards		

Measures of length

mile	8 furlongs	1,760 yards	1.61 kilometres
furlong	220 yards		
chain (ch)	22 yards		
yard (yd)	3 feet		0.914 metres
foot (')	12 inches		30.5 centimetres
inch (")			2.54 centimetres

Measures of weight

ton	20 hundredweight	1,016 kilograms
hundredweight (cwt)	112 pounds	
pound (lb)	16 ounces	0.453 kilograms
ounce (oz)		28.35 grams

Measurement of volume

gallon	4 quarts	4.545 litres
quart	2 pints	
pint		0.568 litres

Money

No attempt has been made to modernise monetary values in the text. The following explains currency terms prior to 1971 when the coinage was decimalised:

4	farthings	= 1 penny (1d)		
2	halfpence	= 1 penny (1d)		
12	pence	= 1 shilling (1s)		(= modern 5p)
24	pence	= 1 florin	= 2 shillings (2s)	(= modern 10p)
30	pence	= half a crown (2/6)		(= modern 12Xp)
120	pence	= 10 shillings (10s)		(= modern 50p)
20	shillings	= 1 pound (£1)		(= modern £1)